# CHILD WELFARE
# A SOURCE BOOK OF KNOWLEDGE AND PRACTICE

EDITOR
FRANK MAIDMAN

ASSOCIATE EDITORS
SHARON KIRSH
GREG CONCHELOS

WITH CHAPTER CONTRIBUTIONS BY
SHIRLEY FISH
JOSEPH PIPITONE

AND GENERAL ASSISTANCE OF
CAROLYN BAXTER

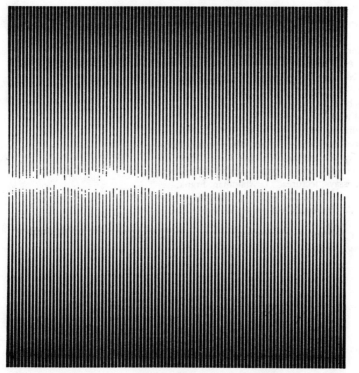

PRODUCED UNDER THE AUSPICES OF THE CHILDREN'S AID SOCIETY OF METROPOLITAN TORONTO

PUBLISHED BY
CHILD WELFARE LEAGUE OF AMERICA, INC.
NEW YORK, NEW YORK

Child Welfare League of America
67 Irving Place, New York, NY 10003

Copyright © 1984 by the Child Welfare League of America, Inc.

Current printing (last digit)
10  9  8  7  6  5  4  3  2

*Cover and title page design by Paul Agule*
*Book design by Rose Jacobowitz*

Printed in the United States of America

*Library of Congress Cataloging in Publication Data*
Main entry under title:

Child welfare.

   "Produced under the auspices of the Children's
Aid Society of Metropolitan Toronto."
   Includes bibliographies and index.
   1. Child welfare—Ontario—Toronto Metropolitan
Area—Addresses, essays, lectures.  2. Social work
with children—Ontario—Toronto Metropolitan Area—
Addresses, essays, lectures.  3. Social case work
with children—Ontario—Toronto Metropolitan Area—
Addresses, essays, lectures.  I. Maidman, Frank,
1940-    .  II. Fish, Shirley.  III. Pipitone,
Joseph.  IV. Children's Aid Society of Metropolitan
Toronto.
HV746.T6C45   1984        362.7        84-12650
ISBN 0-87868-236-8

# Contents

Foreword                                                                    v

Preface                                                                   vii

Acknowledgements                                                          xi

Contributors                                                            xiii

1  Child Welfare Problems and Practice: An Ecological Approach            1

    SHARON KIRSH, FRANK MAIDMAN

2  Child Protection: Issues and Practice                                 15

    FRANK MAIDMAN

3  A Theoretical View of Community Work                                  65

    GREG CONCHELOS

4  Working with Neglecting Families: Dynamics and Practice               89

    FRANK MAIDMAN

5  Physical Child Abuse: Dynamics and Practice                          135

    FRANK MAIDMAN

6  Sexual Abuse in the Family: Dynamics and Treatment                   183

    FRANK MAIDMAN

7  Social Work Practice and Foster Care: Pre-Placement Activities       213

    SHIRLEY FISH

8   Casework to Foster Parents and Children                     235

        SHIRLEY FISH

9   Residental Child Care                                        263

        JOSEPH PIPITONE, FRANK MAIDMAN

10  Adolescent Problems: Dynamics and Practice                  289

        SHARON KIRSH

11  Adoption: Problems and Related Practices                    323

        GREG CONCHELOS

12  Working with Unmarried Parents                              357

        SHARON KIRSH

    Appendices                                                  389

A   A Problem-Solving Approach to Child Welfare, Practice       391

        FRANK MAIDMAN

B   Assessment Frameworks                                       423

        FRANK MAIDMAN

C   Staff Practice Statements:

    Group Work with Unmarried Parents                           437

        PAT CONVERY

    Do We Serve the Best Interests of the Infant? An Unmarried Parents
    Worker's Dilemma                                            441

        LYN FERGUSON

    Working with West Indian Adolescent Mothers                 445

        BETTY KASHIMA, DEBRA FELDMAN, CHRISTINE LOWRY

    Index                                                       451

# Foreword

Dear Reader:

It is well known that the crisis nature of much of child welfare makes it difficult for the practitioner to take time to stop his or her activities, consult the literature, and reflect on how current research and programme development can better inform practice. In addition, reports of new initiatives and treatment approaches are scattered through many journals, and this fragmentation creates yet another barrier to the upgrading of a worker's job skills.

Believing that continuing education in child welfare suffers more from a lack of time and energy than from any lack of motivation, the Children's Aid Society of Metropolitan Toronto has developed *Child Welfare: A Source Book of Knowledge and Practice*. It is a "one-stop", "hands-on" volume to which workers at all levels of experience can turn for the practice wisdom they seek or for references regarding more detailed information, if needed.

The *Source Book* has been put together in a unique manner. Several full-time researchers under the direction of a steering committee composed of academics, supervisors, and front-line workers have produced material that has been vetted by over 100 staff members from one of the largest child welfare agencies on the continent. Their efforts have resulted in a document that can be used as a personal reference manual for practitioners, a resource tool for supervisors, and a basic text for in-service training.

Although not a substitute for professional education, regular supervision, and up-to-date agency procedures, we recommend the *Source Book* to you, believing that it can provide concrete assistance to child welfare practitioners in carrying out their everyday work.

Douglas H. Barr
*Executive Director*
*Children's Aid Society of*
*Metropolitan Toronto*

Edwin F. Watson
*Executive Director*
*Child Welfare League of America, Inc.*

v

# Preface

The reader who begins to use this volume might well pose the six fundamental questions that frame any experience: what, why, how, where, who, and when.

WHAT does the book aim to do? It aims to meet a professional need in child welfare practice for a general source book of up-to-date knowledge relevant to the understanding of client problems and of the main practice issues and options for helping clients. This material is potentially useful for new workers, and can serve as a comprehensive reference and guide for front-line workers, supervisors, managers, and agency policy planners.

The content of the *Source Book* is varied, and includes such diverse topics as the dynamics and contexts of child neglect and maltreatment, adolescent runaways, principles for engaging resistive clients, conceptual frameworks for understanding client problems, the use of residence as a therapeutic milieu, recent issues in foster care and adoption, and many more.

Since an important assumption guiding the development of a source book is that knowledge, however imperfect, must underlie practice, knowledge is offered in the following areas:

> *theoretical approaches* to child welfare practice and child welfare problems
>
> specific *research findings*
>
> *practice* roles, phases, principles, and types of intervention, in relation to helping clients in need
>
> *practice issues* (e.g., working with authority, preparing for court, working in a bureaucracy, stress in residential work) related to the *organizational contexts* of child welfare work
>
> *assessment frameworks*
>
> *further readings*

Naturally, this knowledge is based on the cumulative generalized wisdom of countless practitioners and researchers, and cannot be directly applied to the solving of specific problems. Between professional knowledge and actual practice lies the domain of a child welfare worker's creativity, sometimes called artistry. The skilled child welfare worker must learn to combine this book's general knowledge with his or her knowledge of specific client problems and needs.

WHY is there a need for a source book of child welfare knowledge? The need can be traced to (1) the work demands on child welfare workers, (2) the current nature of the professional literature, (3) the organization of child welfare agencies, and (4) the dilemma of integrating knowledge and practice. Like most professional practitioners, child welfare workers find it difficult to keep abreast of current practical, theoretical, and research knowledge. The crisis nature of the work, plus heavy caseloads, limits the reading and reflection necessary for integrating new knowledge with practice.

Child welfare literature is not organized for easy access. It is dispersed over a multiplicity of journals and books, and is not integrated for practice needs. In addition, the current organization of child welfare agencies, with their diversification of specialized staff members, means that many workers are not conversant with the knowledge and practice issues of their colleagues. Caseworkers and community workers, for example, may be unfamiliar with each other's work. A source book, then, can be a fount of mutual enrichment in a large, professionally and functionally diversified child welfare agency.

Finally, a source book in child welfare should help reduce the long-standing gap between knowledge and practice. No one has solved the problem of how practitioners can use general theoretical and practice principles to guide the specific activities of their work. Everyone is familiar with the frustration of reading a journal article or attending a workshop in which the material is interesting and perhaps innovative, but somehow unconnected with one's daily work.

HOW can this book aid a child welfare worker's practice? It is a useful adjunct to problem solving, the assumed common element in everyone's work. Specifically, the information should:

> introduce new perspectives on problems, including broad theoretical approaches or ideas about specific elements in the dynamics of client problems and practice dilemmas
>
> suggest a broader variety of problem-solving interventions or solutions
>
> help the practitioner choose among different approaches to understanding and intervention (e.g., Has a particular approach worked before? With what kinds of clients?)
>
> help plan the implementation of a particular intervention (e.g., What staff members and how much time are needed?)
>
> aid the process of evaluating one's intervention solutions (e.g., What objectives were being pursued? Were they accomplished?)

For a discussion of a problem-solving approach to child welfare practice, see Appendix A.

WHERE does the content of the book come from? It was drawn from published literature in the child welfare field. Two bodies of literature were reviewed: (1) material on the causes and consequences of child welfare problems was abstracted from original research monographs or extensive literature reviews; and (2) practice information was drawn from published practice literature written by practitioners or by research and development specialists. Useful practice material also was found in government policy guidelines. In a few instances, staff members of the Children's Aid Society of Metropolitan Toronto volunteered to discuss or write about their own practices (see Appendix C).

WHO participated in the book's development? Three specific groups participated—a steering committee of fourteen people who represent child welfare consultants, agency staff, academics, and management of other service agencies; a team of consultants hired on contract through the Children's Aid Society of Metropolitan Toronto Foundation; and several staff members from the Children's Aid Society of Metropolitan Toronto.

This volume is the product of a complex resource development process, and participation in content formulation also had an especially broad base. An important part of the project's methodology was the extensive participation of front-line staff members who assisted the project team in five ways. First, they were interviewed individually or in groups to identify their information needs. Content ideas were also solicited through a project newsletter. Second, the staff reviewed and criticized drafts of chapters. Third, they attended meetings with the project staff and Steering Committee to discuss drafts and propose revisions. Fourth, a sample group of staff members participated in an evaluation of one of the final drafts. Finally, as mentioned above, several workers wrote about their own practices.

WHEN was the book written? Although there was a definite starting date (August 1981), there is no date of completion because the book is designed as, it is hoped, a dynamic resource, that is, one which will be revised in the future.

One final question: HOW is the book organized? It is divided into twelve chapters, three appendices, and an index. All chapters are organized around a series of relatively independent sections or modules. These are cross-referenced to other chapters where topically relevant material is discussed.

Certain chapters and appendices, (e.g., Chapter 1, Appendices A and B) present general frameworks for thinking about child welfare problem dynamics and practice, and are germane to all professionals in the child welfare field. All three reflect an *ecological* approach to child welfare practice. The remaining chapters are more appropriate for the various specializations: child protection, community work, foster family care, residential child care, youth work, and service to unmarried parents. Despite the specialized nature of many chapters, subject matter necessarily overlaps, and the cross-referencing provides connections. A chapter-by-chapter overview follows.

Chapter 1 presents a brief introduction to an ecological approach to child welfare problems and practice. Some important elements of child protection work are examined in Chapter 2, with special attention given to the investigation process, preparing for court, the therapeutic use of authority, and using volunteers. Community work in child welfare, the subject matter of Chapter 3, is one kind of prevention-oriented practice. The latter part of the chapter introduces daycare as a service in which community workers are particularly interested. Chapters 4 through 6 outline the dynamics of child neglect, physical abuse, and sexual abuse, respectively. Each of these culminates in reviews of practice options. Chapter 7 reviews the range of pre-placement services and practice issues pertinent to social work with foster parents. Chapter 8 attends to casework service after placement, with special consideration of the separation process, fostering adolescents, and the interaction between the foster and biological families. Chapter 9, an introduction to child care in residential settings, sees the residence as a therapeutic milieu within which several traditional treatment options are possible. Because they are important actors in the total milieu, child care workers are urged to reflect on their own place in the system and make efforts to minimize stress. Chapter 10 deals with those adolescent problems most prevalent in child welfare agencies: running away, delinquency, and self-injurious behaviour. The latter part of Chapter 10 offers treatment options in youth work. Chapter 11 reviews six major phases of adoption work, along with practice principles and selective issues at each phase. The last module in Chapter 11 identifies several trends in adoption work that are likely to have an impact for years to come. Chapter 12 is a general review of the causes and consequences of teenage pregnancy. Practice approaches for unmarried parent workers are summarized in the concluding module.

The three appendices provide several different, though equally important, aids to child welfare practice. The *problem-solving* practice framework in Appendix A is a generalized scheme which can be used to give rationality and order to child welfare work processes. Both Appendices A and B contain recently developed *assessment frameworks* derived from an ecological perspective to social work practice.

Appendix C provides three different *practice statements*, written especially for this book by staff members of The Children's Aid Society of Metropolitan Toronto. The publication of this material is an encouragement to child welfare workers across North America to share their practice experience in a similar way.

We hope that this *Source Book* will be used when workers are thrust into case situations which call for a brief refresher course on the theory and practice of the problem at hand, or when workers have the opportunity to read, mull over, and discuss their ideas with colleagues.

# Acknowledgements

The completion of this book would not have been possible without the able assistance of many people. Thanks are due first and foremost to the members of the project Steering Committee, whose commitment, patience, and assistance were a constant source of support to the project team.

The members of the Steering Committee were:

Connie Barbour (Chairperson), *Children's Aid Society of Metropolitan Toronto*

Dr. Kirk Bradford, *Child Welfare League of America*

Professor Joyce Cohen, *School of Social Work, University of Toronto*

Ron Coupland, *Children's Aid Society of the Regional Municipality of Halton*

Robert Fulton, *Children's Aid Society of Metropolitan Toronto*

Britt-Inger James, *Ontario Ministry of Community and Social Services*

Mary McConville, *Children's Aid Society of Metropolitan Toronto*

Lois Murray, *Children's Aid Society of Metropolitan Toronto*

Dr. Naomi Rae-Grant, *Ontario Ministry of Community and Social Services, Chedoke Child and Family Centre*

Steven Raiken, *Children's Aid Society of Metropolitan Toronto*

Susan Silva, *Children's Aid Society of Metropolitan Toronto*

Dr. Michael Thompson, *West End Creche Child and Family Clinic*

Jessie Watters, *Province of Ontario Family Court*

Molly Wildfong, *George Brown College of Applied Arts and Technology*

I wish to extend particular thanks to two members of the Steering Committee. As Chairperson, Connie Barbour should receive much credit for giving valuable time and effort to the administrative functions of the Committee. Steven Raiken, too, was a constant source of support and many contributions from the outset.

The process of developing this book depended significantly on the participation of over one hundred staff members of the Children's Aid Society of Metropolitan Toronto. Their ideas, suggestions for improving draft chapters, and participation in a final evaluation, gave the project a dynamism and validity which similar resource development exercises rarely have. Special thanks to the following agency staff members who wrote practice statements for Appendix C: Pat Convery, Lyn Ferguson, Betty Kashima, Debra Feldman, and Christine Lowry.

To the regular project staff, I extend my deepest personal gratitude. My friend and colleague, Sharon Kirsh, lent her considerable talents to planning, research, writing, and staff consultation. Greg Conchelos, in addition to his chapter contributions, was instrumental in planning and conducting consultations with agency staff. Shirley Fish and Joseph Pipitone interrupted their busy lives to make useful chapter contributions, and generally provided important practitioner perspectives. Carolyn Baxter, our Administrative Assistant, showed exceptional administrative and editorial skills throughout the project. Cathy Patterson and Godfrey Glasgow also made useful research contributions at various stages. Thanks are due as well to Louise Kelly, Patricia Himmelman, Rob Howarth, Monique Ladanyi, and Nicole Ladanyi, for their secretarial, library, and clerical assistance.

Douglas Barr, Executive Director of the Children's Aid Society of Metropolitan Toronto, had the initial idea for a child welfare practice manual. He, along with Steven Raiken, should be commended for their early and continuing efforts in obtaining agency support.

I extend my thanks to the Province of Ontario's Ministry of Community and Social Services for making library, word processing, and many other resources available to the project, especially the services of Julie Walsh and her word processing staff.

Special thanks are due to Sue Bochner and The Children's Aid Society of Metropolitan Toronto Foundation for securing funding for the project. Contributions were made by:

Children's Aid Society of Metropolitan Toronto Foundation

Children's Aid Society of Metropolitan Toronto

J. W. McConnell Foundation, Inc.

Province of Ontario, Ministry of Community and Social Services

Gannett Foundation/Mediacom Industries, Inc.

Suncor, Inc.

Without their assistance, this professional effort in behalf of children and the child welfare field would not have been possible.

Last, I wish to thank the publications and editorial staff of the Child Welfare League of America for their able assistance. Alice Misiewicz, Carl Schoenberg, and Arlene Stern were most helpful during the final stages of publication of this volume.

Frank Maidman, Ph.D.
*Editor*

# Contributors

CHAPTER CONTRIBUTIONS
Frank Maidman, B.A., M.A., Ph.D.
Private Consultant
Frank Maidman Associates
Toronto

Sharon Kirsh, B.A., M.A., Ph.D.
Project Co-ordinator
Canadian Mental Health Association National Office
Toronto

Greg Conchelos, B.A., M.Ed., Ph.D.
Project Co-ordinator
Canadian Mental Health Association National Office
Toronto

Shirley Fish, M.Ed., M.A.
Child and Family Clinic
Mississauga Hospital
Mississauga

Joseph Pipitone, Child Care Worker Diploma
Child Care Worker-in-Chief
Clarke Institute of Psychiatry
Toronto


STAFF PRACTICE STATEMENTS
Pat Convery, B.S.W.
Children's Resource in Consultation Centre
Toronto

Lyn Ferguson, M.S.W.
Family Services Worker
Children's Aid Society of Metropolitan Toronto
Toronto

Betty Kashima, M.S.W.
Family Services Supervisor
Children's Aid Society of Metropolitan Toronto (North Branch)
Toronto

Debra Feldman, M.S.W.
Family Service Intake Worker
Children's Aid Society of Metropolitan Toronto (North Branch)
Toronto

Christine Lowry, B.S.W.
Family Services Worker
Children's Aid Society of Metropolitan Toronto (North Branch)
Toronto

# 1

# Child Welfare Problems and Practice: An Ecological Approach

## SHARON KIRSH, FRANK MAIDMAN

| | |
|---|---|
| I. THE ECOLOGICAL PERSPECTIVE | 2 |
|   A. Introduction | 2 |
|   B. What Are the Practice Implications of an Ecological Perspective? | 3 |
| II. THE ECOLOGY OF CHILD WELFARE PROBLEMS | 4 |
|   A. Ideological/Cultural Factors | 5 |
|   B. Economic Factors | 7 |
|   C. Political Factors | 7 |
|   D. Community Factors | 8 |
|   E. Family Factors | 9 |
|   F. Individual Factors | 10 |
|   G. A Developmental Perspective | 11 |
| III. THE WORKER'S ECOLOGY | 11 |
| IV. SUMMARY | 13 |
|   REFERENCES | 14 |

## I.  THE ECOLOGICAL PERSPECTIVE

### A.  Introduction

This Source Book is written from an ecological perspective. Human ecology has arrived at the forefront of individual and social analysis, and most recently has influenced professional practice writing in social work [1, 2].

What is the ecological approach? It is a framework for understanding and aiding the individual's or group's adaptation to the environment. As such, it reinforces social work's long-standing commitment to help individuals *and* change their environments.

The ecological approach is a type of "general systems" thinking in that it:

assumes relationships of interdependence between events and patterns

assumes circular or multidirectional causality

looks for the mutual impacts of systems and their component subsystems

assumes that cause-effect relations are characterized by probability rather than certainty

Closer to the human level, ecological analysis examines how human development, human behaviour, and human problems are affected, and in turn affect biological, interactional, group, societal, and cultural factors. In particular, ecology is concerned with how individual needs are met, and takes the position that the success or failure of this process is affected by individual characteristics (e.g., a lack of knowledge about opportunities) and those of the environment (e.g., limited opportunities).

The concept of adaptation is central to ecological thinking. Humans are regarded as having both passive and active relations with their environments as they strive to achieve their goals and meet their needs. As culture-bearing and symbol-using beings their efforts are not determined by biological, psychic, or environmental factors. However, the choices and decisions may be *limited* by such factors, as when certain types of people are limited by previous socialization experiences and/or current socially structured opportunities (e.g., job opportunities, housing policy).

What individual characteristics affect adaptation? This, of course, is a wide-open question subject to much discussion, research, and speculation. Germain, for example, suggests that human adaptive achievements are affected by the individual's autonomy, competence, relatedness to others, and sense of identity [1]. The contributions of ego psychologists, such as Erik Erikson, have also provided useful information on individual adaptation. With the benefit of such research, this Source Book reviews updated theories about individual factors, including levels of parenting skills and knowledge, low self-esteem, ignorance of birth-control information, a sense of futility, and psychological alienation. The environment limits or opens up opportunities for human need fulfillment in endless ways. Access to human and material resources occurs largely through social interaction. This in turn is affected by the physical environment, the character of communities, social perceptions and attitudes, beliefs, and a host of institutional characteristics.

The interplay of individuals with environments determines whether and how needs are met; whether "needs" refers to health, safety, food, care, or esteem. The global concept of "stress," discussed here, refers to an upset in the adaptive balance between the person and the environment. We now turn to a discussion of the general implications of the ecological approach for practice.

## B.     What Are the Practice Implications of an Ecological Perspective?

Germain discusses the practice implications of the ecological perspective within the following categories: professional objectives, knowledge base, values, problem definitions, structure of worker-client relationships, the nature of professional action, and agency arrangements. This discussion is presented in a highly summarized form, thus inviting the reader to consult the original sources for a fuller discussion [1, 2].

### 1.     Professional Objectives

Practice is directed towards improving the transactions between people in order to enhance their adaptive capacities and improve their environments.

General professional objectives involve releasing, developing, and strengthening people's innate capacity for growth and creative adaptation; removing environmental blocks to growth and adaptation; and positively increasing the nutrient properties of the environment.

### 2.     Knowledge Base

Professional knowledge is based on psychology, sociology, evolutionary biology, environmental psychology, ethnology, and organizational theory.

### 3.     Value Base

The importance of people's ability to adapt to the environment; environmental responsiveness to diverse human characteristics and change; and the value of a society made up of diverse individual, social, and cultural characteristics

### 4.     Definitions of Problems

"Problems in living" are defined as arising from life transitions (developmental and social), interpersonal processes, and environmental issues.

Problems and needs result from person-environment transaction processes.

Emphasis is placed on progressive rather than regressive forces, on health rather than sickness, and on potential for growth.

*5        Client-Worker Relationships*

The worker is interested in enhancing the client's identity, autonomy, competence, and relatedness.

The worker promotes a relationship of mutuality and reciprocity manifested in openness, authenticity, honesty, naturalness, and human caring.

*6.        The Nature of Professional Action*

Professional action is directed to the person, the environment, and interaction of the two.

Person-focused action includes procedures to increase self-esteem, reduce psychic discomfort, strengthen adaptive patterns, teach coping skills, and provide information.

Environment-focused action includes providing opportunities for action; decision-making; mastery and restructuring situations for better adaptive fit; procedures to mobilize and support social networks; efforts to influence organizations; the creative use of available resources; taking action on the physical environment; and modifying interpersonal processes.

*7.        Agency Arrangements*

Organizational flexibility for responsiveness to client needs

Service programs in the client's life space where and when stress is experienced

Service structured for compatibility with client life styles, interests, and tempos

Differential entry at individual, group, family, and organizational levels

Service before stress becomes insurmountable

Agency creativity for the deployment of unique staff skills, qualities, training, and experiences.

This section has provided a brief introduction to broad principles of an ecological perspective. The next section illustrates many of these principles with reference to the field of child welfare. The practical intent is to create or reinforce a certain holistic perspective on child welfare problems, one which provides the basis for later chapters.

## II.        THE ECOLOGY OF CHILD WELFARE PROBLEMS

Which factors create the necessary and sufficient conditions to bring about the potential for child abuse and neglect and for adolescent problems? Workers who adopt the ecological approach perceive child welfare issues in systems terms, and are sensitive to societal conditions that can indirectly affect the individual.

A systematic view can be useful to workers in the child welfare field because: (1) it takes them beyond the realm of the individual by connecting the client to structural conditions and social issues; (2) it enables workers to expand their approaches to practice by examining connections between behaviour and structural factors (e.g., a possible link between parental isolation and maltreatment can be explained in various ways, one or more of which can be pursued in developing a treatment plan; (3) it affects both the interpretation of the child welfare agency's mandate and agency policy planning (e.g., if lack of emotional support from extended kin and neighbours is found to be the basis of a wide range of child welfare problems, then the agency must begin to consider interventions beyond individual treatment to alter this state).

Workers hold varying implicit assumptions about the factors affecting child welfare problems. Such diversity is to be encouraged and shared through group discussion because, in fact, there is not a unitary explanation or cluster of factors which can tie together the bits and pieces of theory and put them into one package.

For purposes of clarity, in this chapter, factors affecting child welfare problems have been divided into six clusters: ideological/cultural, economic, political, community, family, and individual.

While reading through each section, the reader might benefit by drawing upon recollections from her or his caseload, especially as these relate to child abuse, neglect, sexual abuse, and problems associated with adolescent clients. Patterns of factors may begin to emerge. These will either lend credence to, or refute, the material presented in this chapter, most of which has been drawn from academic studies in the child welfare area. While contributing factors have been presented as six discrete units, it should be noted that they function as melding layers, each interacting with the others. No one factor can be seen as the culprit; for example, being poor does not cause child neglect—most poor people do not neglect their children and some rich people do. What is critical is the combination of stressors that impinge upon the individual, creating more (or less) vulnerability to child neglect.

## A.    Ideological/Cultural Factors

In every society there exists a system of beliefs, concepts, and goals about human life and culture which is held by the majority of people within that society. Such a system (an ideology) legitimizes certain behaviours for those who accept its basic tenets. In turn, these behaviours can sometimes be misconstrued in such a way that they lead to unintended and negative consequences. For example, physical abuse of children may be associated with a child rearing ideology which maintains that physical discipline is good and appropriate, that children are the possessions of their parents who are at liberty to handle them as they wish. On the other hand, children may be neglected by a parent who simply does not know how to provide the necessities. Lack of knowledge may be grounded in a widespread belief that parenting is instinctual (a "maternal instinct"), and therefore does not require learning.

Who can say what constitutes a child welfare problem? In fact, what we define as problems today may be given no attention in another historical era or in another culture. The very concept of child maltreatment is socially and historically produced, varying in its definition according to the ethnicity, sex, class, race, and age of those who use the concept. We can assume that its shape and content will continue to evolve as the surrounding society continues to change. Sometimes social behaviours are defined by certain groups as problematic simply because this definition serves the group's interest and not because the behaviours are inherently problematic. These self-interests may reflect varying value positions on a number of different issues, such as appropriate child-rearing practices. It is thus in the best interests of workers in the field of child welfare to question assumptions that underlie definitions of certain behaviours/dynamics such as: deviant, inappropriate, resistive, and disorganized, in order to clarify in whose terms they have been made and to what end and to whose benefit this behaviour has been defined in such a way.

Mainstream society's ideas about the nuclear family (mother, father, children) can affect inter- and intra-familial dynamics. For example, the belief that the nuclear family is superior to the single-parent family or to extended family-and-community configurations renders single-parenting and shared-parenting as less acceptable and respectable to those who hold the dominant ideology. Another example is the ideology of autonomy/privacy, which discourages people from seeking help outside the nuclear family even when resources within it are inadequate to meet the situation.

The connection between women's position within the family and within the marketplace can have an impact on parenting: to the extent that women in our society are shuffled in and out of the labour market as the economy dictates, women remain perceived as primarily houseworkers, and secondarily, as wage labourers. Thus, women who cannot find paid labour or afford daycare facilities, whose mates will not permit them to seek employment, or who themselves believe that a mother's place is in the home, are potentially isolated within the home. The loneliness, frustration, and stress associated with such isolation may increase the chances of child abuse.

Men in our society are economically more powerful than women and children and therefore hold the prerogative of power within a family. This partially stems from the family's reliance on the husband's income (the very word "family" comes from the Latin *famulus* meaning "servant"). In many societies husbands have not been punished by law for raping their wives because their wives are deemed possessions and therefore at the mercy of their owners. Children, too, are at the mercy of their owners, and just as society tends to close its eyes to violence perpetrated against women, so too does it tend to ignore the psychological violence and physical or sexual abuse perpetrated by parents against their children.

One factor which feeds into the symptoms manifested by many adolescent clients is their societal position of relative powerlessness and disenfranchisement. While North American adolescents are expected to participate in a school system designed to produce at least semi-skilled workers for a future labour market, they remain in a state of suspended animation throughout adolescence, a state in which they do not have access to jobs and are thus dependent on family. Teenagers who are not in school and who are not employed are left with few options in a society which tends to dislike and mistrust its youth. Even within the family, as adolescents walk the precarious line between autonomy and dependence, they may be devalued, receiving neither the privileges of childhood nor the rights of adulthood. Perhaps delinquency, running, and self-injury are manifestations of a need to be acknowledged, loved, and granted esteem by the adult world.

The dominant North American ideology of individualism and the autonomy of the family is a complex weave. Each belief within the system represents a tension, a push-and-pull which, over time, may lead to subtle changes in people's behaviours. In this section we have looked at some ideological concepts that affect, even if indirectly, the behaviour of individuals within families.

## B.     Economic Factors

Although it cannot be claimed that economic factors create child abuse and neglect, it can be argued that one's access to material resources affects one's range of possible responses in any given situation. For example, lack of money makes it difficult to provide even the necessities of food, clothing, and adequate housing for one's self and family. Lack of money means not being able to buy formal daycare or to hire babysitters, and children may have to be left alone for long periods of time. The need to work outside the home in order to put food on the table may mean a lack of time to spend with children, especially for single-parents who carry the full burden of breadwinning, housekeeping, and childrearing.

During harsh economic times when there are relatively few employment opportunities and when financial stability is a luxury of few, geographic mobility is common—people must go to where they can find work. Being transient inhibits the growth of community roots which in a cohesive community can provide the individual with several resources. These include critical feedback about her or his behaviour (e.g., child rearing practices), and the exchange of emotional and material supports (e.g., free babysitting), thereby making the exchange of assistance part of the rhythm of everyday living. In some cases, geographic mobility can exaggerate individual and family isolation and, in turn, increase the probability of unmet needs.

In summary, lack of material resources (including jobs, money, and various forms of help provided by others which, if bought in the market, would be too costly) can create forms of stress which may translate into child maltreatment. This is not to imply that people who have riches do not maltreat their children; rather, people who do not have riches must deal with a set of stressors not experienced by those with wealth.

## C.     Political Factors

Connections between child welfare problems and politics in the narrow sense (i.e., legislation) are not always obvious and yet are powerful. For example, teen mothers and other single parents often have trouble obtaining government-subsidized housing because they do not fulfill the criteria established by housing policy makers (e.g., minimum age of parent must be 18); new legislation in parts of Canada is pushing women off Family Benefit Allowances and onto Welfare, which they can continue to receive only if they actively seek employment. Without accompanying daycare facilities, this means that more and more children will be left alone; minimum wage is barely a livable wage, which means that sole support families often lack even the necessities; teenagers are sometimes forced into unemployment because they have not reached the minimum age for gainful employment; abortion on demand is not a legal reality in Canada, which means that many young women are forced to show just cause; men who sexually abuse their daughters tend not to be severely dealt with by the judiciary, thereby allowing room for continuation of this behaviour. Every worker could add to this list of legislative frustrations and impediments examples from their own child welfare experience. The fact is that much legislation in our society either directly or indirectly limits access to basic needs satisfaction and to support systems, without which many people cannot provide adequate parenting.

## D.     Community Factors

The past has seen a proliferation of writings on the human need for "a sense of community". Many studies have investigated the mental health consequences of varying social network configurations. Social networks usually include one's nuclear kin, extended kin, friends, neighbours, co-workers, organizational ties (e.g., fellow team members), and institutional ties (e.g., teacher, social worker, bank manager, clergy, physician). Human connectedness is seen as important both as a source of support and as a source of social control.

Support systems may be at a broader level (e.g., public daycare facilities, accessible housing, adequate income) or at a local level (e.g., neighbourhood babysitting exchanges). Resources, in order to be useful to parents, must be affordable, easily available, adequate to meet basic needs, and adequate to meet particular preferences of parents. These resources, which are exchanged within the social network, manifest themselves in several forms: as emotional support (lessening stress), material support, practical services, as brokerage (e.g., a friend introduces you to her employer who happens to need someone with your skills), and as a system of attitudes, beliefs, and norms (e.g., regarding the value of seeking professional help). Generally, people who are members of tight-knit networks are carefully observed and therefore pressured to perform according to group standards. Where child maltreatment is not acceptable, the individual is unlikely to indulge in such behaviour, in part perhaps because privacy and isolation are not acceptable either.

Although many contemporary social networks are not bound by geography and may in fact not incorporate any neighbours, the concept of neighbourhood as it relates to child welfare remains a relevant one. For example, it has been speculated that neighbourhoods with relatively higher rates of child maltreatment encompass a higher rate of families who are struggling economically, are in crisis states, place low value on having good neighbours, are dissatisfied with the neighbourhood and housing, and have fewer available support people for child care (most adults are employed and residential mobility is high). Thus, because social control is loose, cases of maltreatment are likely to be undetected/unreported and supportive resources are not likely to be forthcoming.

Extended families continue to play an important role in providing support/companionship even when members are not geographically close. An unmarried teen mother is much more likely to return to school after the birth of the baby if her family is willing to provide child care and especially if they are willing to provide room and board at home.

While a cohesive social network and a tight-knit neighbourhood do not ensure protection against child welfare problems, they do enhance the likelihood that people will have access to much-needed resources (e.g., emotional support, information about how to contact an agency, babysitting exchanges), as well as access to appropriate role models, thereby reducing risks that are higher when individuals are forced to cope with stress entirely on their own. For more detailed discussions of community, network support, and child maltreatment see Chapters 3–6, Chapter 10, and Appendix B.

## E.      Family Factors

The family itself is a system, often portrayed as a microcosm of the grander social system. Much of child welfare practice is based on a family systems approach to problem-solving. The following dimensions of family life are considered important for understanding and helping families who come to the attention of child welfare agencies:

### 1.      Family Resources (Material and Human)

These are income; adequacy and safety of housing; access to needed material possessions; management of available resources (how time and money are apportioned); access to health care and other institutional resources; access to a support network; awareness of services; and previous experience with agencies.

### 2.      Family Composition and Structure

These comprise size; number of parents; birth spacing; stage in family life-cycle; and ages of family members.

### 3.      Family Interaction

To be considered are parent-parent, parent-children, and sibling interactions; types of responses exchanged among family members (e.g., physical, verbal, and emotional); distributions of exchanges; and patterns of control and compliance

As we have noted in other sections, a family which lacks economic resources and adequate material resources (e.g., safe housing) and which is emotionally isolated from kin and neighbours is likely to be more at risk of stress than is a more connected and materially wealthy family. In addition, a family, or even a network of families with underdeveloped problem-solving abilities may be more at risk. This stress can get translated into various forms of maltreatment of family members.

Much discussion has centred on the importance of role modelling within the family. It has been suggested that parents who abuse were themselves abused; that adolescents who are delinquent have parents who are/were delinquents; that teen moms are the products of mothers who were themselves teen moms; that self-destructive adolescents have family members who are/were self-destructive (either overtly through suicide or covertly through alcoholism, for example). However, an argument has been made that it is not the modelling per se which creates a new generation in the image of its elders, but rather that there tends to be an intergenerational transmission of social isolation (and particularly emotional isolation) which is at the root of all child welfare problems. The issues of intra-familial and inter-familial dynamics are complex; suffice it to say at this point that most people are created and re-created through the family and social network and to ignore these contexts in understanding clients' behaviour is to see only a tiny part of a large picture. For additional information on family characteristics see Chapters 2, IV; 4, III, IV; 5, III–V; 6, III–VI; 10, II, IV, V; 11, III; and Appendix B.

## F.    Individual Factors

Thus far we have focused on large-scale systemic factors which can influence the likelihood of child maltreatment and adolescent problems. Another system, the interaction between an individual's psychological and biological workings, cannot be overlooked as an integral factor in understanding human behaviour. It is fascinating to ponder that two individuals can be exposed to parallel events and levels of stress and yet may respond in two extraordinarily different ways. Their responses are in part shaped by environmental influences and yet not entirely . . . there is a component of behaviour which captures the uniqueness of each human being.

Psychobiological explanations for this uniqueness have been put forward. It is widely held that much of our behaviour is profoundly influenced by our biochemistry, by our hormonal balances and imbalances, and by our physical make-up (including shape and size). Even our state of physical well-being at any given moment may affect our responses (e.g., a parent suffering from a migraine headache may be considerably less patient than otherwise with her or his child).

On the other hand, one psychodynamic model of behaviour posits that human personality involves three levels of functioning: (1) the id (source of powerful instinctual tendencies which are primarily sexual and aggressive); (2) the ego (reality-based aspect of personality); (3) the superego (social and cultural beliefs about morality and immorality). Our instinctual urges (id) are continually thwarted by our immediate circumstances (ego) and by the fact that society does not permit (superego) unbridled expression of urges. This conflict results in anxiety, which, if severe enough, may manifest itself in mental disorder; anxiety may be reduced in a number of ways, including defense mechanisms.

Psychodynamic models include descriptions of normal development through psychosexual stages, as well as abnormal development manifested in fixation at an early stage, or regression to a previous stage. It has been suggested that parents' developmental histories may predispose them to abuse or neglect their children if they were abused or neglected when they were young—however, being predisposed is not sufficient to cause maltreatment.

Child welfare clients, especially adolescents and abusing/neglecting parents, are often described as having low self-esteem, feelings of alienation and depression, poor interpersonal communication styles, and as lacking in impulse control. Many of these characteristics are attributed to clients as personality traits, as though they are innate and immutable qualities. In fact, it seems highly unlikely that anyone is born with low self-esteem or with any of the other traits associated with child welfare clients; rather, the individual, unique in biochemical make-up, responds to and interacts with other people in ways which shape her or his development. For further details on psychological and biological influences on child maltreatment, see Chapters 4, III, V; 5, III, 6, IV, 10, III–IV. Individual characteristics and teenage pregnancies are discussed in Chapter 12, II, III.

## G.      A Developmental Perspective

To all things there is a season, a time of unfolding. Just as individuals pass through developmental stages, so too do the family, the neighbourhood and community, and the broader societal structures. Each layer of life evolves at its own pace, in its own way, and yet none is unmoved by the rhythm of others.

The individual resonates to the hourly, daily, monthly cycles of the body; she or he interacts within a family which itself resonates to the cycles of an aggregate of individuals and to those of each member. The family is responding to the forces which impinge upon and support it, and which, in turn, it affects—the social support network, the neighbourhood and community, and the economic, cultural, political, and ideological structures. All systems are in motion, changing, developing, and profoundly affecting one another.

As an example, we might consider the ecology of a family in the following situation: a young couple has a 3-year-old child who is developmentally behind her peers. Both parents, as individuals, have strong unmet needs for recognition and love, and have not yet developed a sense of mutuality and exchange within their relationship. Due to an economic recession, employment is difficult to find, which results in frequent moves. As jobs, even low-paying temporary ones, come available in various communities, the family shifts locations and consequently has not become connected with support systems in their present neighbourhood and community.

Even this brief sketch can highlight the critical points at which the individual(s), the family unit, and the broader structures converge and diverge. Developmentally the child is behind her peers; developmentally the couple's relationship is not yet capable of providing each other with much needed support; developmentally the economy is in a state of recession which creates conditions of high unemployment. It is obvious that stress can arise from any one aspect of this family's ecology; in combination, the stresses might be so overwhelming and the support network so inadequate, that the child becomes the obvious target of her parents' frustrations, anger, and unmet needs.

By intersecting developmental stages with layers of factors associated with child welfare programs, the worker can create a picture which will lead her (him) down many possible avenues of intervention.

## III.     THE WORKER'S ECOLOGY

Just as one might take an ecological approach in analyzing child welfare problems and applying solutions, so might one take a similar approach in reflecting upon workers and their milieu within a child welfare agency.

The worker operates within an ecological system of push-and-pull force. As in previous sections, we can conceive of multiple layers interacting, one with the other, to create the ever-changing work conditions of child welfare workers. The layers include: individual/intrapsychic, agency (i.e., "family") systems, community, political, economic, and ideological.

As an individual with her (his) own physical and psychological makeup, the worker brings to her (his) practice a particular temperament, personality, and motivation. Her (his) experience, knowledge, political orientation, interests, self-image, and level of self-confidence will affect her (his) choice of clients (e.g., adolescents vs. children), her (his) area of specialization (e.g., adoption vs. community work), and the types of intervention she (he) is likely to select (e.g., individual Reality Therapy versus facilitating community organizing meetings). The success of her (his) practice will depend in part on her (his) personal qualities and her (his) expectations of others.

Analogous to family systems are agency systems with their specific composition and structure, interactions, and resources (material and human):

1. *Agency resources (material and human):* budget; physical plant; access to needed material resources; management of available resources (how are money and time used/apportioned;) awareness of an access to other institutions/agencies' resources; knowledge technology (e.g., training sessions; manuals)

2. *Agency composition and structure:* number of employees (proportion of managers, supervisors, workers, support staff); workers' experience levels (on average); stage in agency's life cycle; hierarchical structure

3. *Agency interaction:* director-manager, supervisor-worker, worker-worker, and so on; types of resources and responses exchanged between/among agency members; distributions of exchanges; patterns of control and compliance

This book is one piece in a large selection of knowledge technology available to workers. Regardless of how useful such resources may be, this technology cannot stand alone in helping workers to enhance their practice. Conditions are needed which support good practice; examples of such conditions include manageable caseloads which do not leave workers drained and exhausted; team work approaches which allow the sharing of information, group problem solving, and the exchange of emotional support; workshop training sessions which are highly relevant to the specific needs of child welfare workers; a system of sabbaticals and study leaves which reduce burnout and allow time for formal educational experiences; a case report information retrieval system which gives workers easy access to client information; and a system of protection for workers so that they need not be ever-fearful of legal problems.

Another layer of the worker's ecology is the community in which she (he) works. This might include the "extended family" of inter-agency exchanges, in addition to the specific neighbourhoods and communities in which she (he) practices. While some communities are rich with resources/supports for clients, others are not.

The degree to which such resources are available affects the nature of the worker's practice (e.g., if an Unmarried Parent Worker's Community does not have pre-natal classes designed for teen moms, she (he) may spend time persuading a fearful client to travel far from home in order to take classes, or the worker may have to accompany her, which is also time consuming). Furthermore, communities with relatively few resources are more likely than well-supported areas to have child welfare problems. This means that caseloads may be particularly heavy and that workers are especially frustrated by the cycle of *lack of resources–high incidence of problems–lack of resources* to eradicate the problems. In addition, the image of the agency in the community may affect the degree to which people are responsive to its services.

Political considerations, especially legislation, help to shape the worker's experience. A worker may be hesitant to make certain recommendations pertaining to a client if she (he) is legally responsible for any error in judgement. Legislation which directly affects clients' lives (e.g., Young Offenders Act; age at which Family Allowance Benefits are available) also dictates the limits of the worker's practice.

The economic climate of society is a vital aspect of the ecological system. When economic times are hard, the incidence of stress-related problems (e.g., abuse) rises, thereby increasing people's needs for resources/supports. At the same time, publicly funded agencies may also be hard hit financially, prohibiting appropriate increases in salaries, expenditures for new programs, and so forth, while being asked to work with increasingly needy populations.

As previously mentioned, the issue of whose ideology and knowledge are "legitimate" is a thorny one. The worker whose ideology pertaining to child welfare is congruent with that of the agency will likely experience fewer internal contradictions and work-related interpersonal conflicts than the one whose system of beliefs flies in the face of agency premises. For example, one who maintains that the State has no right to interfere in child-rearing practices of individuals would suffer tremendous cognitive-dissonance in a child welfare agency. Again, a worker whose political orientation supports the notion of community action-as-practice might feel uncomfortable with interventions focused on the individual only. Any worker who insists on dealing with root causes rather than symptoms is likely to eventually become frustrated since the eradication of root causes is generally not the mandate of a child welfare agency.

At present, mainstream society supports the premises and assumptions which form the foundation of child welfare work. Without this implicit (ideological) and explicit (financial) support, such agencies would not exist.


## IV.    SUMMARY


This chapter has presented an introduction to the ecological perspective. The latter was described as a type of systems thinking, with emphasis on the adaptive transactions between individuals and environments. A range of practical implications were summarized. Finally, the application of ecological thinking to the understanding of child welfare problems and the worker's situation was illustrated. This introductory chapter provides a broad perspective for the remainder of the manual. For additional information on the ecological perspective and social work, see Chapters 3,

III, IV; 4, III, IV; and 5, IV, VI. Assessment frameworks consistent with the ecological approach are presented in Appendices A, II and B, II. For additional reading on the implications for practice, see Germain [1], Germain and Gitterman [2], and Mayer and Timms [3]. A review of research literature within an ecological framework is provided by Belsky [4].

## REFERENCES

1. Germain, C. (ed.). *Social Work Practice: People and Environment*. New York: Columbia University Press, 1979.
2. Germain, C., and Gitterman, A. *The Life Model of Social Work Practice*. New York: Columbia University Press, 1980.
3. Mayer, J., and Timms, N. "Clash in Perspective Between Worker and Client", Social Casework, Vol. 50, January 1969, pp. 32–40.
4. Belsky, J. "Child Maltreatment: An Ecological Integration", American Psychologist, Vol. 35, April 1980, pp. 320–335.

# 2
# Child Protection: Issues and Practice

FRANK MAIDMAN

I. INTRODUCTION                                                          16
II. CHILD WELFARE WORK                                                   16
    A.  Activities and Roles                                           16
    B.  The Child Welfare Worker as a Change Agent                     17
III. INVESTIGATING REPORTS                                               19
    A.  The Report                                                     19
    B.  The Investigation                                              20
    C.  Assessment                                                    23
    D.  Methods of Gathering Information                               30
    E.  Critical Decisions in an Investigation                        31
IV. THE FAMILY PERSPECTIVE AND PRACTICE
PRINCIPLES                                                               32
    A.  Introduction                                                  32
    B.  A Family Perspective                                          32
    C.  Problem Families                                              33
    D.  Family Practice Guidelines                                    34
    E.  Family Assessment Protocols                                   35
V. WORKING WITH CHILD WELFARE CLIENTS                                    36
    A.  The Involuntary Client                                        36
    B.  Communication                                                 45
    C.  The Emotional Aspects of Client Relationships                 46
    D.  Contracting                                                   48
VI. PREPARING FOR COURT                                                  51
    A.  Introduction                                                  51
    B.  Preparing the Child for Court                                 53
    C.  General Preparation and Participation in Court                54
VII. THE THERAPEUTIC USE OF AUTHORITY                                    56
VIII. WORKING IN A BUREAUCRACY                                           58
IX. USING VOLUNTEERS                                                     60
X. SUMMARY                                                               62
    REFERENCES                                                       62

## I.     INTRODUCTION

This chapter reviews the core practice issues in child welfare, beginning with the major roles of child welfare workers (Section II). The process of investigation marks a crucial point of contact between the agency and the potential client. Section III reviews the difficult emotional aspects of investigations, and provides guidelines for information-gathering and assessment.

Child welfare problems are frequently manifestations of general disturbances in family functioning. For this reason, an important practice perspective for child welfare workers is one which allows the worker to think about the multiproblem family in its totality. Section IV provides this perspective, along with general family practice guidelines.

Among the helping professionals, child welfare workers face special challenges in establishing relationships with their clients. Many of these challenges derive from the non-voluntary character of the relationship, and the workers' mandate to represent society's interest in child protection (Section V). Because of the legal aspects of their position, child welfare practitioners need to develop ways of using their authority in a therapeutically useful way (Section VII). As well, an important part of practice is their preparation and participation in the court process (Section VI).

Child welfare agencies, particularly those in urban centres, are large bureaucracies. Another challenge for the practitioner is the reconciliation of administrative demands and the helping process. Section VIII addresses this issue.

Finally, professional principles for the use of volunteers, although usually omitted in graduate school training, are an important part of practice guidelines. As suggested in Section IX, volunteers may enact special functions in child welfare work.

## II.    CHILD WELFARE WORK

### A.    Activities and Roles

Child protection workers have the mandate of society to help maintain minimal standards of child care. In the course of fulfilling this mandate they receive reports of child maltreatment (physical abuse, sexual abuse, and neglect), investigate these reports, determine their validity and decide whether intervention is necessary for ending the maltreatment. These activities are aided by workers' use of legal authority, professional expertise, and personal influence. In addition to the leverage of the court, they strive to help clients by means of skillful use of relationship-building techniques, brief crisis-oriented or reality intervention, and referrals to community resources. In the course of implementing the mandate, workers ally themselves closely with other professionals, including the police, lawyers, doctors, nurses, and educators.

As workers carry out these activities, a number of specialized roles are enacted; these may be summarized as:

| | |
|---|---|
| information-gathering | human relations intervention |
| liaison tasks | monitoring |
| supporting | problem-solving |
| contracting | resource brokerage |
| change agent activities | team facilitating |

Child welfare work is a specialization which differs from general social work in the following ways [1]:

Expertise is often learned on the job rather than in school.

Clients are often involuntary, and may react to worker involvement with extreme resistance, hostility, and problem denial.

In fulfilling a legal mandate, strong use is made of legal authority along with other types of influence; society's delegation of power must be accepted.

Some child protection actions may *seem* to contradict sacred societal and social work professional values (e.g., family intactness; the right to self-determination; confidentiality).

Long-term clinical treatment approaches are rarely employed.

These differences, and others, comprise the facts of life in child protection work; successful practice in many ways entails mastering the dilemmas associated with each.

## B.    The Child Welfare Worker as a Change Agent

Many clients of child welfare agencies are involuntary; they (especially parents) have behaved in ways which are illegal according to child welfare laws. When parents are "found out" they tend to be thrown into a crisis state; the very act of having been caught and described as criminal can lead to feelings of anger, frustration, and despair. It then becomes the task of the agency to help the client (or client's parents) to work through the crisis in the hope that new and more productive ways of behaving will emerge. However, there are many impediments to change, not the least of which is the client's attitude towards a public agency which has interfered with her or his private behaviour.

Aware of impediments to change, child welfare workers perform several tasks which are potentially change-enhancing. These include setting the conditions under which changes may occur; perhaps the most fundamental is the material condition of clients (i.e., income; housing situations, childcare arrangements). Since impoverished material conditions are often at the base of stress which can lead to child maltreatment or dysfunctional family dynamics, it may be impossible to bring about lasting changes in client's behaviour without first bringing about lasting improvements in their living conditions. Unfortunately, this is a mammoth task which cannot be dealt with single-handedly by caseworkers; thus most workers are forced to do what they can, with the knowledge that more could be done, if they received assistance with improving clients' material conditions.

Child welfare workers *do* enhance change, however, through several activities: they role-model appropriate communications, life skills, and problem-solving techniques which clients can learn and apply independently to their particular situations; they provide nurturance and a sense that they genuinely care about their clients' well-being; clients can simultaneously learn nurturance-giving behaviours. Workers create linkages with outside resources in the capacity of resource brokers on behalf of clients. They also act as agents of social control to the extent that they educate clients as to what is morally and legally acceptable child-rearing behaviour, according to community standards; they then enforce these standards by acting as agents of the child welfare laws. It is also the task of workers to engender in clients a belief that change is possible; sometimes simply by re-labelling an act workers can help clients to reinterpret their behaviour and thereby render it less self-demeaning and hopeless.

Some workers tend *not* to perceive their practice as therapeutic. It might be argued, however, that even those acts which are not labelled or organized for planned change can still be change-enhancing and therefore therapeutic. Nonetheless, the reality is that such support-behaviour provides clients with role models and gives clients a sense that someone cares about their well-being. Thus, what appears to be a simple maintenance task is really a complex interaction with educational and support components, both of which might catalyze changes in clients' attitudes and behaviours (e.g., increases self-esteem; increases ability to seek employment independently). Thus, any interaction between two people is potentially therapeutic, in the sense of being change-enhancing in a positive direction.

Child welfare workers perform a wide range of functions. For example, workers educate parents, role-model for adolescents, orchestrate group dynamics, provide companionship and custodial control, assess and make recommendations, act as community liaisons, and so on. Community workers play advocacy roles, do needs assessments, make practical arrangements for support activities, talk with community and government groups, and bring resources into the community. Family service workers investigate reports of abuse/neglect; make decisions based on investigations; supervise homes, recruit foster and adoptive parents; help unmarried parents with decision-making; act as resource brokers; consult with lawyers, police, and psychiatrists; supervise volunteers, perform administrative tasks, and much more.

It is not our intention to list every aspect of child welfare work; however, even a partial accounting provides an impressive array of functions. Most of these can be categorized into one of five broad types: (1) assessment, (2) resource brokerage, (3) education/socialization, (4) emotional support, and (5) social control.

These practices are geared towards a range of units of intervention, for example, the individual, the family unit, the community, and any other point along the continuum (e.g., a residential group; the extended family).

Referring to the table below, the left-hand column lists five broad categories of tasks performed by workers, while the horizontal column presents the three most predominant units of intervention handled by child welfare workers.

|  | Units of Intervention | | |
|---|---|---|---|
|  | Individual | Interactive (e.g., family; small group) | Societal (e.g., neighbourhood community) |
| Assessment<br>Education<br>Emotional support<br>Resource brokerage<br>Social control |  |  |  |

It is interesting to note that while there is considerable structural specialization within child welfare agencies (e.g., adoption, Unmarried Parents work; foster care specialists), in reality many workers perform similar types of tasks, with differences in the unit of intervention rather than in the nature of the tasks.

Assessment is performed by a variety of workers at various levels; for example, an Unmarried Parent Worker might assess the needs and psychological level-of-development of a unitary client; a youth worker might do an assessment of a delinquent teen and her (his) family; a community worker might assess the needs of a particular neighbourhood. At the same time, the youth worker might also be acting as a liaison between her (his) clients and certain resources in the community, while the Unmarried Parent Worker performs a comparable liaison task between a teen mom and her family and/or neighbourhood, and the community worker shifts direction to deal with an individual crisis situation. Thus, while workers tend to view themselves as performing generically distinct tasks, they are, in fact, often carrying out parallel functions at different points along the ecological scale.

It is probably safe to assume that one's theoretical/philosophical perspective affects one's choice of practice interventions. Presented in Chapter 1 are those factors which are thought to increase the likelihood of child welfare problems (e.g., lack of emotional support, lack of community supports, inadequate legislation). Upon examining the ecological scale, a worker who determines that the roots of child welfare problems lie primarily in social structures, and secondarily in individuals or in family systems, is more predisposed to select intervention geared towards advocacy within the community. Similarly, a worker with a holistic perspective, yet slightly oriented towards dysfunctional family dynamics as the basis of problems, is more predisposed to interactive intervention involving the nuclear family or perhaps even the most significant members of the family's social network.

## III.    INVESTIGATING REPORTS

### A.    The Report

Reports of child abuse or neglect come from three possible sources: self-referral, other agencies, and other members of the community (e.g., client's neighbour, relative). Reports are not always valid. In addition to valid reports, three types of questionable reports have been identified [2]:

*Summer complaints:* those made in summer when open doors and windows make it easier to overhear events in neighbour's homes

*Spite complaints:* reports by relatives, neighbours, or spouses as ways of seeking revenge

*Crisis complaints:* sudden increase in reports subsequent to a newspaper report of a child's injury or death due to maltreatment

Although it is difficult to assure validity, the following cues are suggestive of questionable reports [3]:

The caller is unable to provide specific descriptions of vague observations.

The caller communicates in inconsistent and incoherent speech patterns.

Full information about the alleged maltreatment should be obtained as best as possible in the first call or contact, since the reporter may change her or his mind or forget details. Finally, all reports should be approached with an open mind. The investigation, not the report, establishes the existence of maltreatment.


## B.    The Investigation

The general purpose of an investigation is to determine the existence of abuse or neglect. More importantly, workers must assess the child's physical and emotional safety. If actual or potential harm is evident, a number of interventions are possible which temporarily remove the child from the home until the investigation is complete. Temporary removal is a delicate matter, but should be considered under the following conditions:

The present or potential maltreatment could cause permanent damage to the child's body or mind.

The child is in immediate need of medical and/or psychiatric care which the parents refuse to obtain.

The child is already physically and/or emotionally damaged by the home environment and requires an extremely supportive environment in which to recuperate.

The child's sex, age, or physical or mental condition renders her or him incapable of self-protection—or for some reason constitutes a characteristic the parents find completely intolerable.

Even if the report is valid, it is useful to ascertain the reporter's motives, particularly if she or he is closely involved with the family. Any doubts should lead to direct contact with the person and possibly a check on the existence of previous reports by the same person [4].

Workers can enhance the accuracy and validity of a report by:

not asking lay persons to make judgements or draw conclusions [3]

attending to the emotional needs of the reporter by supporting the decision to report, eliciting fears of possible retaliation, conveying the agency's policy about anonymity, and encouraging reporters who are professionally involved with the family (e.g., family doctor) to acknowledge their actions to the family [4]

The most salient report activity is obtaining useful and accurate information. Although agencies may have differing policies, minimally the information should include:

data about the child (age, birthdate, address)

data about the parents (name, address)

where parents can be reached

the incident precipitating the report

present condition of the child

siblings in the home

witnesses to the occurrence or the child's condition

other individuals or agencies that know the family

evidence that parents are torturing the child, or are systematically resorting to physical force which bears no relation to reasonable discipline

physical environment of home posing an immediate threat to the child

In addition, if the child shows signs of injury or physical neglect, the following indicators also suggest immediate interventions:

evidence that the investigation may provoke retaliation by the parents against the child

evidence that parent(s) are out of touch with reality and cannot provide for the child's basic needs

a family history of hiding the child from outsiders

parents who are completely unwilling to cooperate with the investigation or to maintain contact with any social agency [4]

Every effort must be made to obtain parents' co-operation before legal action is enlisted to remove the child. Whether or not immediate intervention is needed, a child maltreatment investigation is difficult for all concerned. Workers, like all helping professionals, are advised to approach the subject(s) of the report with understanding, compassion, and kindness. At the same time, clients must be approached with firmness and sometimes confrontation. Striking a balance between these two orientations is one of the challenges in child protection work.

To achieve compassion in an investigation, the following ideas may be kept in mind:

> Parents are usually not deliberately or perversely willful in their behaviour; child maltreatment is a response to social and personal difficulties.
>
> The cause of maltreatment, if discovered, can be alleviated; people can, and do, change with the help of an agency.
>
> The parents are unhappy about the situation; despite their negative responses to agency contact, they want changes.
>
> For the good of everyone, particularly the child, first efforts should be directed at changes in the family while keeping the child at home; for example, the family **may** be willing to contract for immediate services.

The attitude and tone, of understanding and compassion, must be accompanied by the firmness and authority that reflect the seriousness of the situation. Parents are informed about the report and the agency's legal mandate. If necessary, consequences of non-cooperation in the investigation should be conveyed. Also, parents should be informed of their rights.

Above all, a message should be given that the agency and worker are there to help change conditions so that future problems can be avoided. Such a message should be delivered in a nonaccusatory and nonjudgemental manner [3].

The investigation as with later initial interviews, should be child-centered. This can be accomplished by:

> showing concern over the child's condition and the desire to help change whatever brought on the condition
>
> inquiring about the behaviour that made the child difficult to handle and brought on discipline.
>
> beginning to suggest and model alternative approaches to childrearing

This child-centered approach, while showing the worker's interest, immediately relieves pressure and shifts focus from the parents. Also, the worker begins to set the stage for later helpful involvement. Since the child may be present, it is important to avoid creating a situation of competition between parent(s) and worker.

Despite concerted efforts, the investigation may not proceed smoothly. Parents may be hostile, denying, and generally uncooperative. For these reasons, workers must be prepared to confront. Although all investigations have their unique characteristics, confrontation will be aided by:

> firmness and coolness of manner
>
> persistence in obtaining information from parents
>
> emphasizing the facts of the child's condition and alluding to others' perceptions of the problem
>
> returning to the focus of the interview, despite denials and sidetracking efforts by parents
>
> reminding parents that, by law, the investigation must be completed

To summarize, workers implement an investigation in such a way that the facts can be obtained and a potential treatment-relationship established. This can be aided by:

> understanding rather than judging
>
> respecting people without condoning their behaviour
>
> remaining firmly child-focussed
>
> confronting, if necessary

Conditions of an investigation call forth all worker skills in dealing with a resistive client. For more information on this, see Section V in this chapter.

## C.    Assessment

### *1.    Definition*

Assessment is generally regarded as one of the most important phases of the helping process, yet one which frequently presents problems. Although it is key in making decisions about clients (e.g., what is the problem? what can be done?), it should also be considered a process of interaction which may set the conditions for client change.

In broad terms, the assessment process combines the following phases: problem identification, information-gathering, integration of information, ranking of possible solutions, and planning for assistance [31].

### *2.    General Assessment Standards*

Professional assessment has the following distinctive characteristics [31], which can be taken as a set of general practice standards:

> It is the result of disciplined, thoughtful response, and not intuition alone.
>
> It involves a creative balance between intuition and factual knowledge.
>
> It requires personal reflection on the information gathered against professional knowledge and experience, and on the assessment process itself.
>
> It is coherent; there is a clear relationship between the collection of facts, observations, and hypotheses and plans for assistance.

An additional general standard for the development of professional assessment comes from the recognition that assessments have different purposes. For example, assessments are made to facilitate court decisions, collect further opinions, and determine whether change has occurred. Depending on the purpose, there may be selective attention to, or omission of, certain information. For this reason, every professional assessment should include a clear statement of the purpose, identified for: (a) the clients, (b) referring persons or agency, and (c) potential service providers [31].

Hood has identified a number of typical problems associated with assessment [31]. These can be avoided if the following guidelines are kept in mind:

Avoid unnecessary repetition of assessments.

Assume a broad focus: include individual, family, medical, and educational information; information that could help unravel causes and situations; and information on available services.

Link information to service solution: integrate multifaceted information so that connections are shown between elements of the problem and the situation.

Avoid problem-focussed assessments which risk missing important areas of functioning.

Ensure that assessments are not directed to obtaining specific services; information should be sufficiently broad to enable a service choice.

Include the family and the school (if applicable) in the assessment process, in order to enhance the scope and depth of the assessment.

Share deliberations and findings with children and families.

A more detailed elaboration of these guidelines is presented in Appendix A, where assessment is discussed within a problem-solving framework.

### 3.    Assessment and Problem-Solving

The assessment process, as traditionally conceived, is equivalent to the problem-solving phases of "understanding the problem" and "selecting a solution". If this point is kept in mind, workers will avoid the trap of giving inappropriate attention to assessment protocols, techniques of information-gathering, the written assessment, and the like. These are important, of course, but should not become ends in themselves.

### 4.    Assessment Frameworks

Assessments are difficult to complete without some guiding framework, for example, a set of interrelated categories which guide the assessor's information-gathering and ultimate understanding of the problem. All frameworks, however, are limited to the theoretical approach of its professional discipline. This means that "understanding" is also limited. As one solution to this limitation, social work has recently incorporated an "ecological perspective" into its practice [32]; this perspective increases the worker's sensitivity to the broadest range of factors (e.g., personality, relationship, cultural, developmental) in a client's situation. Hence this Source Book provides samples of assessment protocols (Appendix B) which are informed by the ecological perspective. Workers are urged to adopt the "spirit", rather than the letter, of these tools, and to shape them for appropriate use.

In addition to its effect on the scope of information gathered, an ecological perspective also requires the worker's sensitivity to the context in which assessment information is obtained. The type of information, its quality, scope, and accuracy are all affected by a number of situational factors, including persons present, relationships, physical setting, situational norms, circumstances of the assessment, and so on. For this reason, workers are advised to:

> Identify salient aspects of the assessment context.
>
> View behaviour in different situations.
>
> Use multiple assessment data-gathering methods, if possible.
>
> Consider gathering data in changed circumstances, in cases where assessment information, however obtained, may have been influenced by the situation.

For more discussion of assessments and the ecological approach, see Appendix A, II.

### 5.    Assessing High Risk

When investigating child maltreatment reports, workers are advised *not* to treat information as definitive "proof" of abuse or neglect. On the other hand, such information can alert workers to a family situation of high risk for child maltreatment. Beyond this, a number of principles will aid the assessment process.

First, child abuse does not occur as an isolated event or pattern. As implied in previous chapters, it is inter-related with a complex web of psychological, interactional, family, situational, and crisis factors. These constitute a "breeding ground" for abuse, and are detrimental to the child's opportunity for development.

Secondly, workers are advised to apply three criteria in drawing conclusions from reported information: pervasiveness, duration, and consistency.

> *Pervasiveness* refers to the scope of high-risk factors in the lives of a family. Is there one factor known to be associated with abuse and neglect, or is there a set of factors related to individual makeup, parental interaction, social isolation, stress, and so forth?
>
> *Duration:* Is there evidence that observed events are long-standing patterns in the lives of the family, or are they related to recent crises or changes?
>
> *Consistency:* Do different sources of information about the family lead to the same conclusions? For example, is a teacher's comment about a child's behaviour or appearance supported by worker observations and home interview? Is there an expected connection between patterns (e.g., marital problems and blaming the child)?

Thirdly, medical practitioners should be involved in the assessment process. Although agency policies may differ, it is advisable not to undress the child to look for visible signs of injury.

### 6.    High-risk Indication

With these general principles as background, the following are indicators of high-risk abuse or neglect situations. For the evaluation of each case, workers are advised to use these in conjunction with their own service experience and knowledge of the literature [5].

(a) The child

Children may exhibit some or any of the following indicators:

>           unusually fearful or withdrawn
>           overly compliant or aggressive
>           irritable, listless, detached
>           affectionless or indiscriminately seeking affection
>           poor physical care, i.e., pale, bruised
>           attempts self-care
>           attempts to please parents are met with adverse parental reactions
>           upon going to school, child becomes emotionally distressed
>           separated from parents for a prolonged period
>           premature child
>           unplanned or unwanted child
>           child labelled as wrong sex
>           school-age child having academic difficulties or behaviour problems
>           role reversal: child attempts to "parent" (care for) the parent

When seen in conjunction with other indicators, the following may add additional assessment clues:

> *Habit disorders:* sucking, biting, enuresis, headbanging
> *Conduct disorders:* defiance, rebellion, tantrums, lying, stealing, withdrawal, deviant sexual activities
> *Chronic neurotic traits:* hysterias, phobias, compulsions, hypochondriasis

(b) Parents

The following high-risk indicators are considered common to both physically abusive and neglecting parents:

>           abused or neglected as children
>           disorganized and disordered or compulsively organized
>           rigid, i.e., unable to learn from experience without help
>           impulsive
>           low self-esteem
>           self-centered, competitive with children

> impaired judgement
> crisis-ridden
> action-oriented: strike first, talk later
> immature
> socially isolated
> suspicious, distrustful, hostile (e.g., will not allow helping agencies in)
> give harsh or unusual punishments, too severe for the act
> follow ritualistic practices jeopardizing the child's health

### Physically Abusive Parents

In addition to the aforementioned, physically abusive parents are likely to demonstrate the following:

> insufficient parenting skills (precludes satisfaction in parenting)
> ignorance of basic child development with unrealistic expectations of child's behaviour
> excessive control of child's behaviour through punishment
> lack of emotional bond
> possessiveness towards children
> self-righteousness to point of viewing child as "monster", "crazy"

### Neglectful Parents

Several behaviours and attitudes are specific to the neglecting parent. Some are essentially extreme versions of the general indicators; such parents are:

> very disorganized
> very impulsive
> very infantile
> very restless and rebellious

They also crave excitement, constant activity, and change.

### (c) Sources of stress

In previous and later chapters, the link between child maltreatment and stress is noted. The following characteristics, common to both neglectful and abusive parents, are probable sources or indications of stress:

> marital problems
> physical abuse of spouse (e.g., wife-beating)

permanent or temporary absence of mother or father (e.g., single-parent; parent in jail)

unrelieved child care responsibility

new baby

pregnancy

mentally retarded child or parent

emotional handicap of child or parent

current treatment in, or recent discharge from, mental health facility

physical illness, handicap, or injury

alcohol abuse or addiction

drug abuse or addiction

The following socio-economic factors might be evident:

*Income:* insufficient; misuse; debt

*Employment:* unemployment; poor work stability; work-related stress

*Environmental:* insufficient accommodation; recent relocation; social isolation

For fuller discussion of these and other factors accompanying child maltreatment, see Chapters 4, 5, 6 and 10.

(d)  Sexual abuse

Assessment of either actual or potential sex abuse is difficult. Family dynamics surrounding sexual abuse are such that abused children are under pressure to withdraw their accusation. Also, other family members may deny the report (see Chapter 6). A medical doctor is the best qualified person to examine a child for the physical indicators of sexual abuse. However, there are certain superficial indicators in children about which other professionals should be aware; and child protection workers are best advised to treat the following as tentative indicators of sexual abuse and risk.

The experience of pain or itching in the genital area

Venereal disease (young children)

Stained or bloody underclothing, which the child attempts to hide

Unexplained pregnancy

For more detailed recommendations regarding medical assessments see Sgroi [6].

Similarly, a number of child behaviours may alert workers to sexual abuse or risk:

One child is especially favoured by one parent.

Child behaves inappropriately in a sexual way towards an adult.

Extreme reaction to males (i.e., preoccupation with, or avoidance).

Depression or low self-esteem.

Hysterical incidents (e.g., uncontrolled crying and screaming at school), particularly in otherwise "model" children.

Runaways girls/boys, or expressed wish to live away from home.

Sudden regression, especially in young children.

Poor peer relations.

Sudden involvement in delinquent behaviour.

Unwillingness to participate in physical activity (e.g., school gym).

Drug use or abuse.

A tentative picture of sexually abusive parents and family life is beginning to emerge from clinical practice and research (Chapter 6). Important indicators may be summarized as follows.

The father is:

controlling

egocentric

strict in the family's relations with the outside world

timid and passive with the outside world

jealous of daughter

withdrawn from family life (e.g., has own private room)

shows hopelessness and anxiety

manipulative with other family members

As reviewed in Chapter 6, the mother in sexually abusive families is caught in circumstances of dependency on an authoritarian and manipulative husband, in a society which, for many women, offers few independence opportunities. For these and other background-related reasons she may show indications of being:

passive, dependent, and infantile

poor in self-image

hostile towards husband, but jealous if he shows an interest in other women

cold

worthless-feeling as a mother, wife, and woman

The family might present the following indications:

absence of marital discord, even though parents have problems

"model children", i.e, absence of "acting out" outside of home presence of sibling rivalry due to parental favours

social isolation

## D.    Methods of Gathering Information

There are three methods for gathering information during an investigation: interview, observation, and documentary records.

### 1.    Interview

Minimally, interviews should be held with the reporter, the family, and the family doctor. Although the focal child and other children in the home may be interviewed, the decision about this should be made with great care, taking into account the following considerations:

Is the child old enough to talk?

Might the interview have a bad effect on the child, and on parent-child relationships?

Does the child have the capacity to deal with information?

If a decision is made to interview the child, and appropriate arrangements are made with parents [4], the following guidelines may help the interview process:

The worker should alleviate the child's anxiety by raising such issues as confidentiality; the difficulty of talking with a stranger; and parents' permission.

The worker should avoid taking sides against the parent.

The worker should use language understandable to the child.

The worker should permit the child to talk about the situation in her or his own way; open-ended questions are preferable.

Without over-informing the child, the worker should include a discussion of what will happen next, and how the child's information will be used.

Given the circumstances, interviews with other family members may be tense and subject to resistance; thus, information should be gathered in a supportive, nonaccusing manner. Guidelines for establishing good relationships with difficult clients are presented in Section V of this chapter.

### 2.    Observation

Observations of the family's activities, during the interviews or otherwise, are useful sources of supplementary data. To build a strong case and to achieve impartiality, full documentation of observations should begin with initial contacts. Observations can be gathered about the physical situation of the home (e.g., cleanliness, safety) as well as behavioural and emotional aspects of family life. Special attention can be given to:

the congruence between what people say about relationships and emotions, and what is observed

non-verbal messages (such as eye contact, facial expressions, and voice tone) and how these support or contradict verbal messages

cultural background and life style as a contributing factor to abuse or neglect

Observations may be done either as a discrete part of the interview, or as an explicitly introduced part of the investigation [4]. Other approaches include observing the child outside the home (e.g., play groups; babysitting), observing parents outside the home (e.g., shopping), and joint interviews [4].

### 3. Use of Documentary Evidence

A third source of information is documentary evidence. Such documentation may involve primary information gathered by the interviewer, or secondary information (e.g., medical reports, photographs) provided by others.

One final comment about gathering information: a poor prognosis for change may become quickly evident. Workers should prepare for a possible court case by starting careful documentation early in the involvement.

## E. Critical Decisions in an Investigation

The worker who has completed an investigation of abuse or neglect is faced with immediate critical decisions concerning the continuance and nature of agency involvement. Or, as Kadushin says, the focus of the decision is on what should be done for the optimum benefit of the child [2]. Workers have four options:

to withdraw from the case

to offer help to the family

to make arrangements for taking the family to court

to apprehend the child immediately

In arriving at the most appropriate decision, workers are advised to consider the following kinds of information: the nature, duration, pervasiveness, and consistency of the abuse or neglect; the responses of the parents to the investigation; and the nature of the family support system. Parents who admit responsibility for having abused or neglected their children, and are willing to work for change, are good candidates for a voluntary service arrangement with the agency. Those who have seriously maltreated their children, however, and deny or otherwise resist suggestions for help, probably will respond only to court intervention.

The decision to apprehend a child is taken when the child is in imminent danger. Although such an extreme level of risk is difficult to assess, some efforts have been made to establish criteria. For example, the Children's Aid Society of Metropolitan Toronto specifies the following high-risk indicators for immediate apprehension:

> There is little or no co-operation from parents or caretakers with agency or hospital.

> There is a current crisis, i.e., parent is highly intoxicated from alcohol or drugs; parent is psychotic.

> A new baby is born to a parent who has previously battered a child (i.e., Battered Baby Syndrome).

> Parent or guardian expresses a wish to kill or injure the child.

> Apprehension is requested by the child in cases of incest.

In all instances of potential apprehension, workers are advised to discuss the case with a supervisor.


## IV.   THE FAMILY PERSPECTIVE AND PRACTICE PRINCIPLES

### A.   Introduction

When child protection workers approach families for purposes of investigating child maltreatment or assessing risk, they seemingly talk to and observe people as individuals. However, this is only true from a physical viewpoint, that is, the perceived behaviour is associated with a body that can be easily identified in space. Genuine family assessment requires a "family perspective," one which views family members functioning as units in a larger entity, even though all members may not be present. This section first presents principles of a family perspective, ideas which form the basis of many family assessment approaches. Following these, several important qualities of family life are identified, qualities which have emerged as core in the analysis of problem families. Finally, a number of general practice guidelines are presented. These are particularly oriented to the process of gathering information.


### B.   A Family Perspective

A number of assumptions about families as units constitute the base of most family assessments:

> Families are *systems*, i.e., the behaviours of family members are mutually influencing, and there is relative stability (patterning) of behaviours over time.

> Families have their own sub-cultures, i.e., shared meanings which are cognitive (knowing, understanding, sense-making) and evaluative (values, goals), concerning themselves, outsiders, and the world in general.

Families organize themselves to perform various functions, such as providing necessities, distributing roles and responsibilities, meeting emotional needs, facilitating growth and development.

Families have internal boundaries, i.e., limitations (or strictures) concerning who interacts with whom about what issues, tasks, or functions; boundaries also exist on family members' experience of self, others, and the world of the family.

Families have external boundaries, i.e., patterned limitations as to which family members interact with which outsiders, and about what things.

Families have rules; these may be either patterns (or redundancies) in their behaviours; *or* implicit or explicit dos and don'ts concerning certain ways of thinking, behaving, and feeling.

Family members label one another's behaviours, thoughts, and feelings; such labels either constantly change to reflect growth, or they become rigid.

The individual belongs to different sub-systems within the family (e.g., spouse, parent, sibling, extended family) in which she or he has a variety of power-and-skill-development opportunities; such participation can enable each member to grow and contribute to family development, but can also be a source of conflict, stress, and dysfunction.

Families are often organized around special functions or activities such as secrets (incest), family myths, celebrations; these are frequently important in inhibiting or enhancing a family's growth.

## C.    Problem Families

Research on problem families is still in its infancy, yet a number of dimensions of family life are emerging as important ways to discriminate problem from nonproblem families. Eull [38] cites the following dimensions:

*Individuation versus enmeshment:* Individuated families encourage or support "a sense of autonomy in their members, responsibility for self and clear recognition of where self leaves off and other begins" [7]. In enmeshed families, individuals have unclear ideas about who they are, and are heavily dependent on others for their sense of self.

*Mutuality versus isolation:* In mutual relations, individuals share intimacy and closeness without a loss of identity; disengaged families contain isolated individuals with little capacity for relating.

*Flexibility versus rigidity:* Rigid families tend to maintain their patterns of relationships, despite pressures for change from individual growth, external circumstances, or crises. Flexible families maintain a balance of stability and adaptive change.

*Stability versus disorganization:* Stable families retain consistent patterns of interaction, with clear definitions of responsibility and member security.

Members of disorganized families are unsure of mutual responsibility and are unable to predict one another's responses.

*Clear versus unclear perceptions:* Members of families with clear perceptions either share, or are able to negotiate, shared perceptions of themselves, their relationships, and their environment. This propensity for developing common perceptions and understanding is important for problem-solving.

*Clear versus unclear communication:* Clarity of family communication involves clarity of meaning, and permission to verify whether messages have been understood. This aids in developing common understanding of expectations, instructions, thoughts, feelings, and external information.

*Clear versus breached generational boundaries:* Clear generational boundaries require the maintenance of clear differences between marital, parent-child, and sibling relationships. A breach occurs when one member of these subsystems plays a regular role in another subsystem, as in a father's reliance on his daughter for sexual satisfaction.

To these eight properties of family functioning a ninth may be added:

*Externally open versus closed families:* open families are more likely to be involved with non-family members, are responsive to other ideas (e.g., child-rearing ideas) and utilize environmental resources when necessary and appropriate. Closed families are limited in their interactions with and responsiveness to the outside world.

When implementing these ideas and concepts, workers should avoid directly associating one or more family characteristics with pathology, since some seemingly negative family qualities may be neutralized by strengths. Also, the cultural backgrounds of families are important to consider. Native Canadian Indians, for example, involve non-nuclear family members in parenting. Despite these cautions, the preceding dimensions of family life cited are emerging as important generic factors associated with a host of family and individual problems.

## D.    Family Practice Guidelines

The family system perspective has fostered a number of family therapy modalities and a large body of literature. To review the variety of family therapy techniques is beyond the scope of this manual. However, interested readers may wish to consult overview materials on the subject [39, 40], and/or the work of Minuchin [41, 42]. Minuchin's approach is particularly recommended for its applicability to low-income multi-problem families, and its compatibility with ecological thinking.

Child welfare practice—assessment interviews in particular—can benefit from a number of general practice guidelines drawn from the family perspective [38]:

Presenting problems are interrelated with other family patterns and may contribute to certain aspects of stability. The emotionally disturbed child as the family scapegoat is a classic example [4]. Presenting problems may be regarded as "symptoms" of problems in family functioning, and will change only when the latter are alleviated.

Every family member regards his or her viewpoint as accurate and truthful; for example, each member may perceive a different "cause" of problems or events. Workers are advised to assume equally valid multiple truths.

Every person's behaviour is partly a product of the family's shared patterns of thinking, believing, and acting, and is an expression of their "solution" to assigning functions, responding to crises, meeting individual needs to grow, and so forth.

Every person is, at the same time, a family member and an individual in her or his own right; individual behaviour sometimes reflects tensions and ambivalences of this duality.

Hearing and showing sympathy for each family member's viewpoint demonstrates concern for the whole family and each individual.

If possible, the family as a whole, and the various subsystems (e.g., marital pair, siblings, mother-son), should be interviewed in addition to interviews with individual members.

The family should be seen at least once in the home in order to observe how it functions in its own environment.

Workers should respect the "risk" taken by family members in talking about their family; the extent of such risks should be gauged (e.g., noting non-verbal reactions) before probing deeply for additional information.

Observing interactions, rather than interviewing, may be a more sensitive way (in an emotional and an accuracy sense) to gather certain information (e.g., disciplinary practices; handling disagreements).

Individual and subsystem secrets and privacy should be respected when this is deemed desirable and appropriate; some family secrets are dysfunctional, however, and should be aired.

As a final point, workers should view themselves as an important part of the family's environment during the assessment process, both influencing and influenced by family behaviour. How, and by whom, workers are listened to, involved in coalitions, interrupted, and so on, are all sensitive indicators of family functioning. How a worker thinks and feels about family interaction when in its presence are useful pieces of assessment information for a general understanding of the family's effects on others, and for service prognosis.

## E.    Family Assessment Protocols

The literature contains numerous tools or protocols for assessing family systems, although specific indications of *what to observe* or *what to ask* are often missing. Appendix B contains several samples of system-oriented frameworks for assessment.

## V.     WORKING WITH CHILD WELFARE CLIENTS

This section examines factors affecting client-worker relations, and provides guidelines for working with difficult clients. Brief reviews of communicational and emotional issues are provided, culminating in a lengthier module on contracting.

### A.     The Involuntary Client

The need to establish and maintain good client relationships is a particularly challenging aspect of child welfare work. Research on the efficacy of helping relationships attests to the importance of trust, empathy, respect, and other relationship qualities.

Difficulties between worker and client are manifested in a number of ways. These difficulties are often described as client behaviours, such as denial, hostility, violent and threatening behaviour, unwillingness, non-acceptance of therapeutic interpretations, sabotaging treatment, non-cooperation in contracting, passivity, and so on. "Client resistance" is a term applied to the *client* in efforts to make sense of problems in helping relationships.

Recent efforts to understand difficulties between worker and client have supplemented a client-centered explanation of problems with an analysis of two-person interaction, situations, and societal forces. This parallels, of course, the changing understanding of client problems reflected in the holistic or ecological viewpoint (see Chapter 1).

What are the most important elements affecting a child protection worker's relationship with a client? The ultimate objective in developing good relationships with clients is to create an appropriate context in which to establish the existence and nature of a problem, what to do about it, how to make changes, and how, eventually, to dissolve the relationship. Intermediate goals and strategies depend on one's usual ways of thinking about relationships, and the nature of specific clients and client situations. As one thinks about this, the following factors and strategies may be useful to keep in mind.

### 1.     Worker-Client Differences

Different social and cultural backgrounds, physical dissimilarities, interpersonal style variations, and variations in ways of meeting needs—all have enormous implication for relationships. Such differences may lead to misunderstandings, discrepant values, stress, and mistrust. These relationship problems may be overcome by:

> contemplating client characteristics before the encounter, and thinking through potential differences and their implications for the relationship

> emphasizing and acknowledging the other's viewpoint as important; listening carefully to the client's ideas and having them firmly in mind before proceeding

avoiding a conclusion that the client is intentionally acting differently, or that she/he is uncooperative

Such efforts encourage clients to perceive workers as wanting to be helpful and understanding.

People vary in their methods of realizing their goals or meeting their needs. Some are able to get what they want through purchase, others use status to gain respect; still others rely on force and intimidation. Often when one strategy is blocked, other less socially appropriate ones, such as threats, are used. If clients threaten a worker with violence and anger, the following ideas may help:

Consider the meaning of this behaviour in terms of the situation, the problem, client's needs and objectives.

Establish in a cool, firm tone that you respect the client and expect to be respected in turn.

Establish the rules of your encounters firmly and politely, using "I" rather than "you" statements:

I realize you are angry. I'd probably be too. It is very important to you that I work with you on this problem. But, obviously, if you threaten me, I cannot continue in this conference with you. . . . I hope you will let me work with you on this problem [8].

Some clients, because of their interpersonal style, are understandably irksome to workers. Workers want to help, but some responses make it difficult to do so. Examples of bothersome styles include certain non-verbal behaviours, withdrawal, clinging, "yes, but" statements, self-centredness, and the abusive behaviour caused by drugs or alcohol. If a particularly bothersome client appears in a caseload, a worker should make good use of peer consultation. Failing that, transferring the case should be considered.

Other potential worker-client differences relate to age, sex, and race. Noting an awareness of such differences should communicate a sensitivity without creating an issue. Much has been written on matching workers and clients on various characteristics (e.g., race, ethnicity), and still the appropriate strategies are unknown. In some cases, emotions relating to ethnic differences may be entrenched in complex social and political factors. On the whole, Ontario urban Native people, for example: (a) are very critical of child welfare rules and practices, (b) prefer to receive social services from Native agencies, or at least, (c) wish to be serviced by their own people in non-Native agencies [9]. In such complex instances, it may be useful to:

know something of the cultural differences in family life and child rearing

know the social and economic situations of the ethnically and/or racially different client

consult with an ethnically similar worker or one knowledgeable about ethnic differences

2.      *Client Guilt and Fear*

Workers and clients are engaging each other in a tense situation, possibly characterized by guilt and fear. In the initial contact, the worker's presence may symbolize for the client that he or she is deviant, unworthy, or inadequate. Clients may think this even though workers do not want to be perceived as social control agents, and may do everything in their power to communicate another image. The very context of agency-client contact creates this client self-image. Guilt and fear are inevitable, and workers must accept this fact and develop ways of dealing with it in order to promote change. Also workers must strive to prevent, in clients, the development of a deviant self-image, such as one which suggests a totally bad person rather than one having difficulties in providing appropriate child care. Although specific communications should evolve for each case, some useful guidelines follow:

> Clients' communications, however abusive and hostile, may reflect guilt and fear as well as (perhaps clumsy) efforts to thwart a deviant public and private self-image.

> Workers can assist by acknowledging that child care is difficult and that various life and personal circumstances often prevent parents from doing what is truly best for their children.

> Workers can help clients realize that the reported problem is only one part of child care and total functioning, and that there are probably many ways in which clients are good parents, family members, and citizens; it is useful if "evidence" of these strengths can be cited for the client.

> Since child welfare agencies are often publicly viewed as sources of punishment, efforts must be taken to clarify the image of the agency; emphasis might be given to its helping functions and specific services; in this way workers educate clients and help remove the social control threat and accompanying deviant self-image.

Despite the preceding comments, it is important to convey the inappropriateness of clients' parenting. This is addressed below.

3.      *Child Care Standards*

Clients may be unaware of, or disagree with, the agency's child care standards. Part of the difficulty in early worker-client relations may stem from client's unawareness of society's interest and investment in assuring good child care. Children's Aid Societies have a mandate to act on behalf of society's expectations, as these are reflected in the Child Welfare Act. Some clients disagree with society's intrusion into people's lives and with the so-called consensual child care standards. Consequently, they do not accept the inference that the child is neglected if he or she comes to school hungry; is left alone; or is constantly being chastised in a negative way. In other words, they do not accept the standards, the intervention process, or the definition of the problem. Sometimes these stances are not individual, "defensive" reactions, but rather, are supported by indentifiable anti-child welfare groups and anti-social interventionists. Thus, in some cases, the tensions, hostilities, and resistance of worker and client represent a clash of social belief systems.

With this complexity, what do workers do to establish a good relationship with clients? This professional dilemma is not easily translatable into concrete solutions; however, the following guidelines reinforce workers as educators and caseworkers:

> If the client's protestations do, in fact, reflect a set of beliefs, these should be actively listened to and understood; this should enhance a feeling of being respected as an individual.

> The worker should neither argue with correctness of the client's beliefs, nor attempt to change them.

> Rather, the worker should clarify how the client's beliefs differ from those affecting community child welfare attitudes as reflected in the child welfare legislation and the agency's mandate.

If these guidelines are followed in a cool, factual manner, then workers can educate clients in ways that respect differences and build trust. Moreover, clients become aware that regardless of viewpoint, there is a legal situation within which problem-solving must be done. Both worker and client are accountable to a set of child care norms. For additional material on differences in child care standards, see Chapter 4, V.

### 4. Bases of Worker Influence

Clients will not automatically accept workers' attempts to help. During early and subsequent contacts, workers strive to influence the client. This is true whether or not the worker tries to convince the client that there is a problem; that certain actions can be considered and chosen to alleviate the problem; that without cooperation, negative consequences for both child and parents may ensue. In preparing for, or analyzing engagement with a client, workers should consider the various ways in which helping professionals can influence persons with problems. What are the potential bases of influence?

> Influence can be exerted because of a person's official position; in this case, the authority of office gives certain people the right to exert control over others.

> Influence frequently emanates from the moral authority of the person attempting to influence; acts of influence are accepted as legitimate because the situation to be changed is considered morally reprehensible.

> Those with influence may be in a position to gain access to punishments or rewards in order to bring about compliance.

> Some people may successfully exert influence because their knowledge and skills are respected; their expertise is evident and valued.

> Other attempts to influence are affected by psychological and/or interpersonal factors, such as:

   • difficulties with those in positions of authority or with those who act authoritatively, because of earlier bad experiences with parents, school authorities, or community (i.e., the problem of clinical transference)

   • factors inhibiting or enhancing trust

   • factors which affect liking, admiration, wanting to emulate, and other sentiments of bonding or identification

Influence attempts by workers are often resisted by clients. Clients may be unaware of, or disagree with, workers' right to intervene. Moreover, workers *themselves* may be ambivalent about their official sanctioning powers. The value of worker skills and knowledge is not recognized in situations where clients do not acknowledge a problem or a parenting need. Also, the investigatory legal aspects of initial contacts, coupled with previous negative experiences with community representatives, and a general pattern of social isolation, all make trust and linking difficult to achieve in early contacts.

The following guidelines may aid workers in their early efforts to establish sound bases of influence with clients:

Workers' attempts to influence are affected by clients' experience of the larger socio-legal situation, by workers' behaviour, and by clients' needs.

At some point in the relationship, particularly if there are problems, clients must be clear about the purpose, mandate, and moral implications of agency contact.

Although clients may not experience needs directly related to parenting, there may be other needs which, when addressed by workers (e.g., housing, employment), enhance an image of expertise.

Previous experiences with community agencies may have embittered clients, thus leaving the current worker with a poor foundation for trust, respect, and cooperation; such experiences should be checked out with the intention of making a clear distinction, to the client, between previous experiences and current possibilities.

Based on clients' history or initial contacts, workers should form quick impressions of the most appropriate way(s) to influence them; modifications can be made as this impression is confirmed or negated.

5.     *Initial Expectations*

Workers and clients bring different expectations to initial encounters. For most of the reasons stated—previous experiences, stereotypes and community images, personal beliefs, characteristics, experiences with authority—both parties bring separate expectations concerning each other's behaviour, the process, and possible outcomes. Such expectations may colour interpretations of behaviours and communications, and/or lead to a mutual testing of assumptions about the other and the situation. Assuming that one objective in worker-client relations is the establishment of clarification and mutuality, workers can take the following steps:

Prior to meeting with clients, think through the elements of the situation in terms of client-worker characteristics, the problem, and other aspects of the situation; what are the typical expectations and images that may prevail in the early encounter?

Assess whether early communications indicate an incongruent set of assumptions between the principal parties in the relationship.

Create conditions for moving toward a shared understanding (e.g., equalizing contributions to the conversation, listening actively and with interest, checking out ambiguous statements, clarifying false assumptions).

If relationship difficulties persist, it may be necessary to "step back" from the issues in the conversation, and assess the process; such metacommunication is difficult and requires special capacities which may not exist in all worker-client relationships.

The last two activities have the added consequence of communicating respect, a message which is quite important to socially isolated clients with low self-esteem. This exemplifies ways in which the process goal of "establishing a relationship" has potential therapeutic effects.

6.    *Establishing Rules*

Early encounters with clients establish ground rules or norms for later relations. Thus, most of the these guidelines have an immediate purpose, such as clarifying communication, communicating the gravity of the problem, or ascertaining clients' previous agency involvements. Some are quite specific and practical (e.g., is the child left alone at night while parents work?); others are relational and reflect goals of a professional helping process (e.g., building trust).

All communications contribute to the development of interpersonal standards which will affect future client-worker and client-agency relationships. Relationship standards created between client and worker have three possible outcomes:

> the enhancement of problem-solving
>
> the development of a foundation for a good working relationship
>
> the encouragement of client and worker growth

To illustrate with a simple and well-used example: encouraging clients to express opinions and perceptions about an alleged incident or pattern of neglect begins to set standards of personal respect and openness. Such standards encourage full sharing of information about a problem, thus promoting understanding and selection of solutions (problem-solving). As well, these standards promote behaviours which communicate respect for the individual. All things being equal, this builds a foundation of trust and liking, both of which are conducive to mutual influence (i.e., elements of a good working relationship). Finally, these norms promote opportunities for talking, expressing uniqueness, and negotiating one's fate with an outsider. Such skills, along with heightened self-esteem, are essential for socially isolated, low-esteemed persons. As well, standards—if they evolve in worker-client relations—aid workers' knowledge of, and empathy for, the social and personal circumstances of child neglect.

This discussion suggests three questions for workers interested in assessing their style of initially engaging a client:

> What standards or normative climate do I wish to establish in my relations with this client?

> What behaviours, from myself and my client, are likely to build such norms?

> In what ways will such standards promote the growth of our relationship, and our individual skills, sentiments, and values?

## 7.    Resistance

Resistance may reflect a basic lack of client capacities. For workers using brief task-centered methods, client resistance is made apparent through unattempted, partially completed, or poorly done tasks [10]. These results are particularly frustrating for workers who have fully involved clients in assessing the problem, establishing goals, and identifying tasks for problem-resolution. Analysis of such problems suggests that the following factors inhibit task completion:

> Clients may view tasks as imposed by the worker, thus activating personal difficulties with authority.

> Clients may fear and misperceive task demands and their own capabilities.

> Clients may lack the knowledge and interpersonal skills necessary for successful task enactment.

> Clients may not be fully committed to the change.

Recent research and development in task-centered casework suggest the following guidelines for these difficulties:

> Identify the psychological and situational obstacles to undertaking the task; this process is enhanced by direct questioning, problem-posing by workers, observation of non-verbal cues, and supporting clients' potential success.

> Remove barriers; usually this involves working on the commitment level (e.g., return to the problem), enhancing knowledge and skills (e.g., role-playing and interview situations), working with negative transference, and reducing misconceptions and irrational fears.

> Reinforce success.

## 8.    Mutual Influence

Clients and workers may be engaged in a relationship of mutual influence. The guidelines above emphasize the ideal of consensus in establishing relationships with clients. Ideally, workers attempt to stabilize relationships by establishing common definitions of the problem, building client acceptance or recognition of workers' basis of influence, and clarifying expectations. In the course of establishing such relationships, traditional helping skills are used: showing empathy, building relationships, and acceptance.

In recent years, a new understanding of resistive, non-voluntary clients has been suggested. This approach assumes and accepts *conflict* in the client-helper relationship, and attempts to develop guidelines based on an understanding of adversary tactics [11]. More specifically, the following elements of the worker and non-voluntary client relationship are assumed:

> The chief characteristic of the relationship is not cooperation, but conflict.

> Helpers and clients are not viewed as partners, but as partisans, each with a different definition of the problem, different loyalties, commitments, and investments in outcome; both engage in a process of mutual influence in order to maximize benefits for themselves.

> Required interventions are those designed to redress power imbalances rather than relieve individual suffering; negotiation processes of bargaining and pursuasion are cited as desirable strategies for containing or resolving conflict.

What practitioner skills and recommended strategies are associated with this approach? Four main skill categories are suggested: keen powers of observation, the capacity for detachment in tense circumstances, the ability to bargain convincingly, and tactics of persuasion.

Bargaining is divided into four components:

> 1. *Discovering the bargainable:* That is, identify goals, changes, or intervention arrangements which can or cannot be bargained for. (Leaving a child alone at night may not be negotiable, whereas the type of babysitting arrangements may be.)

> 2. *Finding areas of agreement:* What changes, intervention modalities, etc., represent common areas of agreement between practitioner and client?

> 3. *Critical bargaining:* Offer proposals and counter-proposals.

> 4. *Public presentation of results:* Publicly display an understanding (e.g., contract).

Throughout these phases of bargaining, interpersonal persuasion is important. Some important elements of persuasion are as follows:

> In cases of conflict between worker and client, review steps leading to the impasse, examine various definitions of the problem causing the conflict, and the consequences of each party's position.

> Worker and client may attempt mutual influence through an exchange of promises, rewards, and favours.

> Worker and client may invoke their respective formal statuses and positions in order to gain compliance from the other; for example, workers

may invoke their agency's Child Welfare Act mandate, whereas clients may invoke the rights and privileges of being an agency client.

Both parties may use social pressures to exert influence through third-party alliances with, for example, family members, community authorities, and so on.

Behaviours implying "client resistance" may reflect the normal activities of persons trying to realize their own interests. Seen in this light, a comprehension of practical problems in client relationships may benefit from an understanding of normal processes of strategic interaction [12]. On the other hand, the image of a child welfare worker as an expert in "tactics and counter-tactics" may not conform to the general "helping" image. Furthermore, outcomes of strategies implied in the previous discussion are affected by power inequalities between workers and clients. Persuasion tactics are enhanced by legal support, knowledge, agency support; some workers may resist a conscious capitalization on such differences.

9.      *Family Influence*

Client behaviours such as ignoring appointments, peripheral involvement in groups, withholding information, and denying problems are frustrating for helping professionals. Although personality traits may be involved, this behaviour may also reflect client membership in a family system. Family members may be under specific pressures to conceal certain information; their specialized family roles perhaps do not involve contact with the "outside world". Collusions and alliances with other members may support dysfunctional parenting. Thus, client role demands can activate a disruption in long-standing family arrangements.

The implication is captured in the following quotation:

> Resistance to therapy may be viewed, then, as the family unit's reluctance to change. The family's initial lack of involvement in treatment must be understood in light of the underlying resistance to change and interpreted as a normal reaction of families entering the treatment process. Instead of terminating or delaying treatment because of resistance, the therapist must concentrate on the family unit as the identified patient, working to reduce the family's resistance before focusing on the dynamics of any individual family member [13].

10.     *Clients' Attitudes Towards Help*

Many clients believe that receiving help is a sign of weakness or extreme incompetence. Some groups have strong independence values, reflected in desires to "look after their own problems". In such cases, expressions of hostility, anger, or general non-cooperation may signify a rejection of a helping relationship.

The solution to difficulties embedded in cultural differences is not readily apparent, since child welfare institutions are based on a belief in society's right to intervene in the best interest of the child. At the very least, workers' external authority should be played down in favour of helping the family take charge of its own life. This can be accomplished by involving clients as true partners in the change process with an opportunity to influence goals, tasks, and service conditions. This should be done in a manner that does not weaken the basic message to clients: that their parenting approach is unacceptable.


## B.    Communication

The art and science of communication are core resources for child welfare practice. Skillful communication helps workers to: (1) exchange information, (2) establish a relationship with clients, and (3) promote change. The complexity of worker-client relations in child welfare work, with its social control *and* helping roles, makes careful communication particularly important.

Literature on communication in the helping process has grown in the last several years, particularly in its theoretical aspects. However, Satir's *Conjoint Family Therapy* remains a good source of general theoretical and practice principles, and a useful starting point for reviewing communication for practitioners [5].

Recent communication guidelines urge practitioners to consider how the broader situation (e.g., physical setting, rules and roles, participants) affects interpersonal communication. For *theoretical* perspectives on communication which are suitable for helping professionals, readers are directed to the works of Ruesch et al. [53], Satir [55], Watzlawick et al. [59], Bandler et al. [56], and Grinder et al. [57].

At the core of communication is *language* itself, and language differences between individuals and groups have been analyzed in recent years [44]. Of considerable importance for helping professionals is the work by Bandler et al. [56] and Grinder et al. [57]. Recognizing the subtle relationships among the structure of one's language, one's experience of the world, and one's choice-making, these authors set about to increase client choices by modifying the way in which they talk about themselves and their world. The theoretical basis of their practice and their specific communicational strategies are deemed appropriate for various helping professionals and treatment modalities.

Communicational difficulties in child welfare work have been attributed to the "verbal inaccessibility" of some clients. As with other psychological approaches to communication, this characteristic has been traced to clients' developmental backgrounds and aspects of character structure [61]. One recent practice article treats verbal accessibility as an element of family group process [62]. Both articles present numerous practice guidelines for working therapeutically with verbally inaccessible child welfare clients. These are reviewed in Chapter 4, Part 1, "Practice Guidelines", II.

As indicated above, communication occurs on a number of different "levels", in addition to *what* people say to one another. *Non-verbal* aspects of communicating, particularly "body language", have been given extensive professional [50] and popular treatment. In a recent practice article, child welfare practitioners are given detailed guidelines on how to use non-verbal communication to "break the communication barrier" during initial interviews with abusive parents [60]. These guidelines, referring to body positioning, chair angles, voice pitch, and voice volume, are designed to communicate positive feelings and enhance client comfort.

Other than body language, communication is affected by the structural and interpersonal context in which it occurs, including the physical setting, the numbers, types, and other aspects of process, such as interruptions. The cultural dimension of communication is also important, given the existence of cultural and family sub-cultural norms governing who speaks to whom about what. For excellent discussions of social and cultural contexts of communication, see the monographs by Ruesch [49], Ruesch and Bateson [53], Satir [55], and Watzlawick [59].

Much of the literature cited forms the foundation of practice guidelines for helping professionals in general and are written on a theoretical plane. For social workers and child care workers, most standard texts address communication in a concrete way [64]. Also, one recent book is totally devoted to communications in social work practice [46]. Finally, a needed addition to practice literature is a volume on the helping process and communicating with children [45].

## C.      The Emotional Aspects of Client Relationships

Helping professionals must be prepared to understand and minimize the negative emotions in their relationships with clients. Clients are most receptive to change efforts if they:

> trust and like the helper
>
> feel a minimum of guilt, anger, hostility, and anxiety
>
> feel reasonably comfortable towards themselves

Workers are best able to help if they, themselves, feel and convey empathic understanding, and are able to contain feelings of condemnation and judgement. Finally, the change process is most promising if clients feel some degree of identification, similarity, or "oneness" with the worker. Although these emotional states are easily given in theory, the special conditions of child maltreatment and child welfare interventions make them difficult to achieve in practice. One needs to return to casework basics for establishing adequate emotional relationships.

### 1.      Anxiety

Anxiety is experienced by child-maltreating parents because of their guilt and fear of unknown reprisals, their contact with external authorities, and their reaction to the pressure for changes. Also, anxiety may exist because of a particular stressful living situation (e.g., unemployment, inadequate housing, family discord) and their sense of hopelessness concerning solutions. To help alleviate such anxiety, workers are advised to:

> Be very clear about the client's situation and future investigative or intervention steps.
>
> Take reasonably quick action to reduce situational stress.
>
> Quickly define the situation as one of concern and help, rather than punishment.
>
> Show interested, sympathetic listening.
>
> Become aware of a client's behavioural manifestations of anxiety (e.g.,

missed appointments, topic changing, withdrawal), and avoid responses which may further increase anxiety (e.g., forcing discussion of an issue).

Take the focus away from any member of the client family system who may be taking the blame from other family members.

## 2.   Guilt

Guilt feelings are probable emotional responses in parents who have abused their children. Although workers will not condone such actions, an excessively condemning approach will do nothing to build relationships and create conditions for change. For these reasons, workers are advised to:

Show acceptance and continuing good will, while acknowledging the error and hurtfulness of the actions [31].

Reassure the client through acknowledgement of guilt feelings and their source; such reassurance should not be excessive, however, lest the client's motivation to understand and solve the problem is hampered [31].

## 3.   Inadequacy

Feelings of inadequacy are strong in maltreating parents, and these may be reflected in resistance to helping relationships and difficulties in implementing task-oriented contracts. Traditional casework principles suggest that workers:

Express confidence in the client's abilities, recognize achievements, and demonstrate pleasure in successes [31].

Convey a sense that client's inappropriate behaviours (e.g., parenting) are a small part of the total person.

## 4.   Anger

Considerable client *anger* often prevails in child welfare work, particularly during the investigation period. To avoid possible displacement of anger on children subsequent to the worker's departure, common methods for promoting *ventilation* are urged. One approach is to obtain descriptions of events, interactions, or situations about which the client is angry, and encourage the expression of feeling; attend to non-verbal communications as these may be quite helpful in freeing up contained anger.

## 5.   Transference and Countertransference

The emotions in helping relationships may be affected by transference and countertransference phenomena. Transference refers to the subconscious tendency to relate to others in terms of relationships with previous significant people, usually a parent. For example, a client's relationship with a worker may evoke feelings associated with dependency or authority in the family. Countertransference refers to similar feelings experienced by the worker towards the client. In intense psychotherapeutic relationships, transference phenomena are used as important tools for therapeutic insight. However, since transference and countertransference may be inevitable in any helping relationship, the following ideas should be kept in mind:

>   Transference phenomena mean that unusual or intense emotions may be expressed by the client towards the worker; these should not be taken as personal, but should be the basis for greater understanding.

>   The institutionalized authority aspect of child welfare roles probably means that such transference responses will relate to the client's difficulty in authority relations.

>   Transference phenomena related to the need for dependency may be a useful leverage for creating a helping bond, but efforts to create independence should eventually be introduced into the relationship.

>   Transference phenomena should not be used to "explain away" legitimate grievances or other negative feelings held towards the worker, the agency, or those currently controlling the client's existence; transference is only one of many sources of positive and negative feelings brought to, or developed in, a helping relationship.

## D.      Contracting

Contracting is a highly formalized technique for establishing helping relationships with clients, although with some clients the same objectives could be realized through informal understandings. Contracting provides an opportunity for workers and clients to be specific about *what* they would like to accomplish, *how*, and *when*. In addition to this instrumental use of contracting, a therapeutic opportunity for client change is also present.

Contract difficulties are a normal part of practice, however, and workers are advised to show particular sensitivity to the stresses of implementing contractual relationships. Although it is tempting to infer a willful or otherwise psychological process of "client resistance", the modules on "working with the difficult client" and "contracting" urge a broader perspective and practical implications—ones compatible with the ecological perspective.

What is contracting? It is a particular kind of relationship between workers and clients. This should be kept in mind, because the term "contracting" is also used to refer to a treatment modality component (usually behaviour modification), the technicalities (e.g., writing up lists of things to change), or the product (i.e., a written contract between worker and client). Important aspects of a contractual relationship are characteristics of the relationship between worker and client, and not the ways and means of accomplishing these. The latter may vary according to the situation, client characteristics, and worker skills.

Contractual relationships between workers and clients aim to establish agreement about target problems, goals, methods and techniques, and the reciprocal roles and tasks for worker and client. Ideally, the plan should be acceptable to all parties, with each one participating in problem-solving.

Although often difficult to implement, the following relationship norms are considered essential to a contractual arrangement between worker and client [18]:

*Mutual agreement between worker and client concerning goals, roles, and tasks.* Are usually established at the outset, and maintained throughout the relationship.

*Differential participation of worker and client in understanding the problem and making changes:* One of the worker's major responsibilities is to maintain a clear understanding of the unique aspects of all contributions to the process.

*Reciprocal accountability of all parties:* "The client and worker are accountable to each other in various ways, each having an on-going responsibility to fulfill agreed upon tasks and goals" [18].

*Explicitness:* An open and clear specification of conditions, expectations, and responsibilities is inherent in the relationship; it is the worker's role to clarify expectations and obligations.

*Flexibility:* Unlike a legal contract, new information, crisis conditions, failed efforts, problem solutions, and so on, may necessitate a review and revision of understandings.

Efforts to implement a contractual relationship may be hampered by a number of factors. Some of these relate to the nature of the desired changes; others are inherent in the contractual process. Still others pertain to elements in the worker-client relationship. The following section reviews these difficulties, and suggests guidelines.

*1. The pre-contractual relationship between worker and client may be unsuitable.* A contractual relationship does not occur in a vacuum. Establishing mutuality, differential participation, and other problem-solving ideals may be affected by previous contacts with the agency, worker-client personal characteristics, and so on. For example, it may be difficult to implement a contractual relationship when early contacts between worker and client were characterized by extreme conflict. For general guidelines on improving early relationships, Section V, A of this chapter should be consulted.

*2. Certain client characteristics may work against a successful contractual relationship.* A client's attitudes and skills may contraindicate contractual relationships. Some important impediments are as follows:

Clients may not want to change.

Clients may not be accustomed to relationships of mutuality; they may "expect" to be told what to do.

Clients may not possess the interpersonal skills (e.g., verbal ability, negotiation skills) and analytical abilities for contractual relationships; nor may they have skills for accomplishing certain tasks.

Clients may lack the self-esteem for co-participation and task accomplishment.

Clients may simply not understand the contractual arrangements.

If these, or other client characteristics, seem problematic, the following steps may help:

Review the problem, and draw attention to the client's "pain", including potential legal implications.

Review benefits of co-participation, particularly in relation to early problem-solving, possible acquisition of life skills, and termination.

Identify skills necessary for contracting and carrying out agreed-upon tasks and, if necessary, provide role-playing and other skill-building exercises; assure that client has a concrete awareness of what is required.

Use appropriate casework skills to enhance self-esteem and alleviate task-related anxiety.

*3. There may be difficulties in deciding, and agreeing upon, change goals and tasks.* An essential part of a contractual relationship is the mutual identification of suitable target goals and tasks. This can be particularly difficult if the problem is complex, thus necessitating many change goals and sub-goals. The following guidelines may expedite this process:

Establish goals that clients can associate with the target problem.

Establish the easiest goals first.

Clearly identify goals that cannot be pursued, whether for reasons of ethics or loyalties, limited resources, or unrelatedness to the problem.

Express goals in clear, behavioural terms for easy monitoring and recognition of goal-attainment.

Express goals in positive terms (e.g. "apply for five jobs next week", rather than "don't be lazy about getting a job").

*4. The client may not complete the agreed-upon goal-related tasks.* Some reasons why a client fails to carry out the negotiated tasks are that:

Clients may not understand what needs to be done.

Clients may lack skills and knowledge needed for the task.

Clients may not truly believe that the task is all that important in relation to the problem or in relation to their values.

Clients may not experience any intrinsic or extrinsic rewards in relation to the task; in fact, there may have been expected or actual punishments (most contracting technologies reviewed emphasize the reward element of client task behaviour).

Clients may have lacked the resources necessary to do the task (e.g., money, time, facilities).

Clients' personal networks (e.g., family, friends, kin, neighbours) may have directly or unwittingly inhibited successful completion of the task.

These factors should be used as a checklist for thinking through potential trouble spots in task completion. This can be done beforehand when helping clients prepare for tasks, or in a contractual problem-solving process.

Approaches to identify appropriate rewards or reinforcers for task behaviour include [19]:

*The reinforcement "menu":* Client is asked what she or he wants.

*Application of the "Probability of Behaviour Rule":* The worker learns clients' behaviour choices in unlimited situations; behaviour choices are taken as potential reinforcers.

*Reinforcement sampling:* Client is encouraged and given the opportunity to become involved in what are thought to be enjoyable activities; the seemingly most enjoyable activities are used as reinforcers.

*Valued incentives:* Use objects or events valued by the client for desired rewards.

*5. Workers may have their own hidden agenda of change goals and strategies.* As indicated above, contracting is a process where worker and client agree on the purposes, roles, and tasks of intervention. One problem in implementation occurs when workers develop other ideas about service needs, ones which are not explicitly shared with the client. Although this may be a gradual, unwitting process, such developments become confusing to the client. If clients are passive, and they view the worker as an authority, they may not share these confusions. A gradual psychological withdrawal from the service process may occur. For these reasons, the following guidelines are important:

Workers should be fully open about their perceptions of service needs; initially resisted services (e.g., both parents attending parent education groups) may be more acceptable at a later stage in the process; by proposing them at an early stage, clients have an opportunity to consider service options, while less threatening services are delivered, and relationships are solidified.

Workers and clients should constantly monitor the service process to assure that no confusion has risen concerning the relationship between the actual process and earlier understandings.

*6. The contract and contracting process become ends in themselves.*

Although the process of contracting is potentially useful as a direct source of client growth, it should not be allowed to dominate the interaction between worker and client. If this happens, the real change objectives within the contract may not be fulfilled. For further readings on contracting, see Douds [64], Jayaratne [63], Maluccio [18], Sanson-Fischer [19], Saxon [65] and Pincus [66].

## VI.    PREPARING FOR COURT

### A.    Introduction

Much of a child protection worker's time is spent preparing for, and contributing to, the court process. A case may proceed to court in different ways, depending on provincial or state law, and the specific circumstances of the case. In Ontario, child welfare cases usually go to court through an "order to produce" or within five days of apprehending the child. Other options are also available upon apprehension (e.g., care by agreement; returning the child home).

Whatever the routes to court, involvement in legal proceedings has been a constant source of frustration for some child welfare workers, and a source of satisfaction for others. What factors have contributed to frustration? There is wide debate concerning the value of legal authority as a source of change in family and child problems. This debate has frequently been described in terms of role conflict ("therapist versus watchdog"). Workers' helping or therapeutic roles are undermined by their social control functions as mandated by provincial or state legislation. The use of legal force is said to conflict with certain professional values, such as clients' right to self-determination. Another perspective views many child welfare problems as "problems of the poor", which, in turn, are symptomatic of a faulty society. Involving the client in legal proceedings is tantamount to "punishing the victim". Why is court involvement counterproductive to workers' helping efforts? Reasons for this may be summarized as:

destruction of trust

interference with open communication between worker and client

destruction of workers' efforts to convey empathy

undermining of workers' attempts to influence through their expertise and personal attractiveness

introduction of strain, fear, and anger into the relationship

time taken away from the helping process

On the other hand, many caseworkers believe that legal authority is itself therapeutic, or at least conducive to therapeutic changes. Reasons for this are that:

Legal intervention dramatizes the seriousness of the problem, particularly in terms of its moral inappropriateness.

Legal apparatus provides a firm structure of expectations and sanctions in the lives of people who lack organization and stability.

The court forces an opportunity for change through other therapeutic processes.

Kadushin [2], quoting Thomson and Paget [69], offers the following simple principle:

In taking (court) action . . . "use of the court should be constructive— as a resource, not as a last resort!" The court process needs to be seen as a "means of protecting the child rather than prosecuting the parents" . . . the caseworker attempts to exercise his [sic] authority in a positive, supportive manner.

The remainder of this section presents material which will assist workers in their court functioning. The following text provides information and guidelines for preparing a child for court. Next, general guidelines for preparing evidence and participating in the court process are presented.

## B.      Preparing the Child for Court

In cases of child neglect or abuse, termination of parental rights, child custody, or adoption, children are potential sources of testimony in court. The actual use
of children in court varies across North America. In Ontario, for example, young
children are rarely used. Nevertheless, some background knowledge may be useful.
Decisions about a child's contribution to the court process are based on legal considerations and on psychological/developmental matters [21]. In making a decision
about the former, lawyers will consider the following questions:

> Can the child be spared the ordeal of testifying?
>
> Will the child be an adequate witness?
>
> Is the child believable?
>
> Can the child's testimony be supported by other evidence?
>
> Is there evidence that will contradict the child?
>
> Can the child be prepared to be a good witness?
>
> Will the child provide reliable evidence, given possible self-interest or
> immaturity?

Success of a child's contributions will also depend somewhat on her or his
psychological readiness, attitudes, and awareness of what to expect. If a child is being
considered as a witness, the child welfare worker and lawyer may consider the
following questions:

> How stressful will the court situation be for an individual child? Does
> the child's evidence justify the stress?
>
> Does the child understand the process and know what to expect?
>
> How does the child perceive the outcome?
>
> How will the child testify when others are watching?
>
> Will the child be capable of coping with examination and cross-
> examination in the adversary process?
>
> Will the child testify privately in the judge's chambers?

In addition, attention must be given to the possible effect of the court experience and records on the child's future. Decisions about using children in court should
take into account some of the possible qualities of neglected or abused children. Many
of these same questions may be considered in non-court interview situations.

Normal developmental psychology suggests that children between the ages
of six and twelve years are developmentally capable of serving as court witnesses [21,
22, 23]. This is assumed because healthy children at this age:

> can take another person's point of view and communicate about a par-
> ticular subject
>
> can compare what they hear and see with what they know, and there-
> fore can make judgements of truths and falsehood, reality and appearance
>
> can reason from premise to conclusion, from general to particular

have the personality strength (e.g., autonomy, trust, initiative capabilities) to appear as witnesses, given support and legal coaching

There are certain characteristics of this age group, though, that may make the child an inappropriate witness. First, when trying to explain things, six-to-twelve-year-olds typically settle on one fact rather than many, and hold on to that fact quite rigidly. Adolescents, on the other hand, are likely to consider many facts and possible explanations [2].

Another argument against the use of young children in court processes is that they may be reluctant to report negative facts about their parents. Such children believe that adults are benevolent and well-intentioned. As well, young children may be torn by loyalty conflicts and fear of loss of love [21].

Children who have suffered neglect or abuse have a variety of feelings, emotional states, and behaviour styles, some of which may present difficulties for the child as a witness or indeed as a source of information in general. As well, these may interact with the court experience to produce further difficulties. These characteristics include:

> a sense of loss and heightened sense of vulnerability and mistrust
>
> loneliness, anger, and conflicting loyalties
>
> withdrawal and passivity in the case of severely abused children, and aggressiveness in the case of mildly abused or neglected children
>
> verbal developmental lags and other speech disorders

For these reasons, the protection worker and lawyer must give careful and systematic consideration to the question of involving the child. In summary, this involves the assessment of [21]:

> the child's understanding of her/his family situation
>
> the child's emotional reactions: defensive and adaptive responses to the situation
>
> the child's ability to speak clearly and the capacity to be consistent, truthful, and to deal with a conflict of loyalty
>
> the child's willingness to testify and ability to understand why testifying is necessary

In those rare cases where the child is being prepared to serve as witness, attention should be given to cross-examination, and to the way the child behaves in pre-trial activities.

## C.    General Preparation and Participation in Court

Social workers and child care workers rarely receive adequate professional training in court preparation although orientation and legal consultation are available within most agencies. Nor is there much published literature on the topic in professional journals [24]. For these reasons the following guidelines are presented:

*1. A worker has contacts with a client well before court action is considered.* All significant contacts should be recorded as an aid in court. Such notes should be clear, comprehensive, and detailed, since notes referred to in court may be examined by counsel.

*2. When a worker has a case coming to court she/he is advised to make contact with the agency lawyer as soon as possible.* In this way evidence can be reviewed, evidentiary matters canvassed, witnesses lined up and possibly interviewed, and other counsel contacted [25].

*3. Judgements in neglect and abuse cases* are based on legally admissible evidence in the form of descriptive material which clarifies the abuse or neglect patterns.

*4. The descriptive evidence presented should be both accurate and conducive to emotional impact;* consider the following two answers to the same question in a testimony on emotional neglect:

Q. Did she discuss her son?

A. Yes, Sir. She said he was a typical bad boy who misbehaved frequently.

A. Yes, Sir. I heard Mrs. Jones tell her daughters that they were very sweet and nice, a constant help around the house, and that they always made her happy. She then turned her head toward Johnny and looked him straight in the eye. She said, Johnny, you are a bad boy and mean just like your father. She kept on with this tone of conversation for several minutes. I observed the daughters giggling, pointing fingers at Johnny and laughing. I could see tears well up in Johnny's eyes. His face turned from a frown and his head bowed down. He then picked up a broom and began to chase his sisters. Mrs. Jones caught him and spanked him on the buttocks with her right hand until he began to cry. She then led him to his room by holding his wrist. The door closed, and as Mrs. Jones returned to the living room, there was silence except for Johnny's quiet sobbing [24].

Although such a lengthy response may not be permitted, the example illustrates the presentation of facts in a more detailed and picturesque way. The seriousness of the situation is conveyed in a way that has emotional impact. Also, note that there is nothing inferential about what is going on in anyone's mind, nor is there a prediction about the consequences of this exchange. The facts are outlined accurately and in detail:

*5. The words chosen to describe observations are important in a testimony.* The use of such words and expressions as "it seems", "it appears", "it feels", may give an impression of uncertainty.

*6. Workers in Ontario are allowed to give theoretically-based opinion evidence in court.* However, opinions should not be boldly stated without hard observations. Observations are best stated first, followed by conclusions. Phrases like "In my professional opinion . . ." should accompany remarks which suggest uncertainty, speculation, or ambiguity.

7. *Hearsay evidence is not admissible in a court of law.* For example, written material on teachers', neighbours', and professionals' perceptions of a case is considered hearsay evidence, and is not admissible. However, statements made to the witness by parties in the case (e.g., parent, child) are admissible.

8. *Workers must be prepared for direct and cross-examination in court.* Role-playing with a lawyer may be valuable preparation for this [24].

9. *Testimony can be improved if workers review every word of their testimony.* The lawyer can alert workers to possible objections, and can assist so that evidence will emerge in a proper fashion in court. Finally, the lawyer can "prepare the worker for cross-examination by suggesting areas where the worker is vulnerable" (e.g., improperly formed recommendations, inadequate consideration of other dispositions, inaccurate observations) [25].

10. *Case record material should be reviewed and organized before the worker enters the court.* Attempting to review notes in court is less efficient and may lead to an examination of notes during the court proceedings [24].

11. *Workers can assist the lawyer in case preparation* by preparing a sequence of exhibits and a list of supportive witnesses along with a brief statement of their testimony [24].

12. *Finally "the worker completes trial preparation by a full review* of the case file, a rereading of all correspondence, letters, memoranda, interrogatories, dispositions and an examination of pictures, photographs, tests, diagrams and all other items to be introduced into evidence" [24].


## VII.   THE THERAPEUTIC USE OF AUTHORITY

How to help a client while holding positions of legal authority remains a problem for helping professionals. Some workers recognize that without court enforcement many families would never change their neglectful or abusive behaviour. Thus, official authority is necessary in the best interests of the child. The dilemma has received extensive treatment in the professional literature [29], although often in an analytical rather than practical way. The legal context of child welfare help is inevitable, suggesting that practice guidelines for working with authority are useful additions to practice.

This discussion starts with the assumption that any interpersonal experience with a client, whatever the context, can be helpful or therapeutic. A starting point for assuring this is to understand the types of influence that a worker has at her or his disposal. Also, workers should understand and be comfortable with their authority vis-á-vis clients, since ambiguities and discomfort may undermine influence attempts. Beyond these, the following principles may help:

1. *Be very clear about those areas in which clients do and do not have choices.* Despite the inevitability of restrictions on freedom, it is still possible for clients to reaffirm choice-making options. For example, clients can be shown how certain consequences

(e.g., court involvement) flow from choices and actions taken by them (e.g., not assuring that the child attends school). However, in cases where no choice is available to clients, it should be clearly and honestly conveyed. This assumes that clients will feel worthwhile and mature when they know their options [30]. To convey a false sense of choice is harmful for the helping relationship and possibly reflects discomfort with authority. However, in those areas where client choice is still possible, the choices should be clear.

*2. Avoid finding a scapegoat for authority.* Dealing honestly with the rationale behind the law and agency rules is better than depicting authority as something beyond the control of the caseworker. A comment like "those are the rules, that's the law" in itself does not convey the morality of the law and thereby the seriousness of child neglect. Also the worker's position is left ambiguous.

*3. Allow clients to experience authority in a more positive way.* Workers have more than the authority of office with which to influence clients. While official or legal authority may prevail at the beginning, these can be supplemented with personal influence. Although provincial legislation gives child welfare agencies and their workers clear legal authority in child welfare matters, it is best to use legal intervention with caution and knowledge, since many clients have had a history of negative experiences with authority figures; that is, authority has been used in a punishing way:

> For so many of these people whose socialization has produced an innate, blanket hostility toward, or fear of authority, the fundamental treatment need is that of an opportunity to experience and learn from the relationship with positive and caring authority [4].

How can clients experience the positive aspects of authority?

Parents should be allowed to work out their anger and confusion towards authority.

Authority is used by the worker to help parents meet their basic needs (e.g., housing, job-hunting, daycare).

Authority is enacted with interest and care, and respect for clients as individuals.

Workers use such traditional casework sustaining techniques as concerned listening, reassurance, and encouragement; such sustaining techniques are particularly useful with clients experiencing low self-esteem and anxiety.

Workers recognize that clients' expressions of hostility do not indicate personal rejection; by refraining from a negative reciprocal response, workers avoid feeding clients' negative images of authority.

Finally, workers are advised to exercise great care in the use of authority as a dependency-creating tool. On the one hand, some clients have a tradition of dependency on service institutions. Such people may capitalize on the unwary worker's excessive use of authority in making most decisions. On the other hand, some clients need an initial dependency relationship in order to move towards independent functioning. Official authority provides the leverage for creating this initial dependency; however, steps must be taken to foster independence at later stages. This can be aided by clear messages to clients concerning their choice-making opportunities as time progresses and change occurs.

*4. Use the legal procedures and institutional experiences as opportunities for supporting treatment goals.* The legal position of protection workers requires participation with clients in a number of institutional processes (e.g., court). Although learning opportunities in court preparation are limited by clients' hostility and anxiety, it may be useful to think about how such institutional experiences can promote therapeutic goals. Work with families around court actions can involve the following activities [4]:

> explaining the court process as the worker understands it
>
> explaining the reasons for going to court
>
> interpreting the roles of social worker, parents, lawyers, etc.
>
> advising clients about their preparation for court (e.g., obtaining a lawyer)
>
> reviewing the proceedings in court during the follow-up
>
> clarifying meanings, perceptions, and feelings
>
> reviewing the findings and the disposition
>
> setting goals for further work

In carrying out these activities, workers have an opportunity to:

> reduce clients' alienation from social institutions
>
> enhance clients' self-esteem
>
> support life-skill development
>
> allay clients' anxiety
>
> role-model institutional activities

## VIII. WORKING IN A BUREAUCRACY

Child welfare workers often work in large bureaucratic organizations. Because of their accountability to society, child welfare agencies have numerous rules and regulations which structure staff activities [1]. Those rules, and other bureaucratic practices, often conflict with the preferred professional style associated with helping clients. Briefly, these areas of conflict are:

> Administrative efficiency requires the categorization of people, whereas clients have unique qualities suggesting special treatment or consideration.

The neutrality of feelings often conveyed during administrative processing conflicts with the personal, nurturing needs of child welfare clients.

Child welfare administration often requires the worker to respond to a *part* of the client's existence (e.g., inappropriate parenting), thus ignoring the client's *wholeness*.

Administrative requirements take time away from direct service to clients.

The child protection worker's task is frequently one of establishing a compromise among bureaucratic/legal requirements, client needs, and professional convictions. Pruger [7] offers some tips for managing this tension:

1. *Recognize that negotiating for client needs within bureaucratic limits is a skill.*

2. *Recognize that change is slow in bureaucracies;* be persistent in the face of an organization's tendency to be stable.

3. *Maintain a vitality and independence of thought;* document your efforts and identify alternatives.

There are other ways of resolving tension between administrative requirements and humanistic change goals. These require an adaptation of helping principles to the administrative process. To illustrate, consider the following steps to obtain information during a self-referral.

The main objective of the self-referral interview is to obtain information for judging whether the client's problem is a suitable one for agency services. In the course of asking questions, the client can be prepared for possible service in a number of ways:

Clients can develop a sense of self-respect through questioning which encourages description of the problem in their own words; the articulation of clients' perspectives develops a feeling of being understood.

Clients can help the agency determine what eventually might have to be changed; for agency personnel to accomplish this, descriptions of the problem must be developed in concrete, behavioural terms; such descriptions should happen as quickly as possible in the relationship.

Problem-solving occurs when clients begin to view their life situations in new ways, for instance, to think about new contributory factors in their problems. Early questions about various interactions and involvements of other people in the problem will aid this process. Questions about the timing, parallel events, and other aspects of the context may also help. For example, through careful questioning clients may make the association between abusive incidents and family crises.

Initial contacts with clients can help to change pervading feelings of hopelessness. Initial interviews should probe the positives and strengths of the client's life. Re-labelling negative perceptions will help; for example, a client's expressed guilt at abusing her or his child may be taken as a sign of recognition that help is needed.

Developing an overall profile for the problem is a useful way to assemble and organize information [3]. By showing this profile to clients, workers demonstrate that information is shareable, that clients will have the opportunity to correct misunderstandings, and that they are participants in the problem-solving process.

In addition, workers can show respect for, and interest in clients by providing information about the agency, asking for a clarification of ideas, paying careful attention, and being non-judgemental in verbal and non-verbal behaviour.

In conclusion, child welfare workers are advised to experiment with ways to reduce the alienating effects of the administration process on clients. This can often be done through an incorporation of helping principles into administrative activities.

## IX.    USING VOLUNTEERS

Difficulties in serving abusive parents cannot be minimized; because of these, numerous adaptations of professional treatment are used in child welfare work. To supplement the use of professional intervention, agencies across North America and Britain are successfully using volunteers in child abuse cases. In the Children's Aid Society of Metropolitan Toronto, for example, volunteers are used to working closely with preschool and early school-aged children (Home Care, Caring and Sharing), to nurture abusive parents and to help them in their use of community resources (Parent Aid). (See Appendix C)

The use of volunteers is encouraged by the special characteristics of abusive parents and the unique nature of the child welfare system. Abusive parents are often isolated, immature, unskilled parents, lacking in internal controls against child-directed rage, unable to trust official community representatives, strong in their need for nurturance, and struggling with different types of environmental stress.

The provision of help in these matters is affected by the legal aspects of child protection work and the difficulties of maintaining extensive contacts with abusive clients. Child protection workers in their investigations often meet with hostility, ambivalence, and mistrust. Administrative work and heavy caseloads limit the amount of client contact time so necessary for developing a solid client relationship. In this context, volunteers can:

Be available when needed, and perhaps for longer periods of time.

Concentrate on establishing a relationship.

Make suggestions rather than demands.

Encourage openness about client problems in an otherwise guarded situation.

Encourage constructive ventilation of hostility against the agency; this should be handled cautiously lest the volunteer get caught in the middle, or be seen as forming a coalition against the agency.

Rely on personal rather than authoritative means of influencing the client.

Volunteers are able to supplement workers' accomplishments through the flexibility of their roles and personal influence, rather than through professional knowledge and skills.

Given the needs and characteristics of abusive parents, the following roles for volunteers can be considered:

*Reparenting:* Creating a trusting relationship, one with unconditional acceptance and a good parent model [6].

*Befriending:* "The relationship can develop so they can go out for lunch, coffee, visit with each other, etc. . . . . The trust the parent finds in this relationship can be transferred to other people. Our parents may never have had a relationship with a friend in which they have felt special and that someone really cared" [27].

*Teaching:* Child rearing, household management, gaining access to resources, the responsibility of adulthood [28].

*Sponsoring:* Directly helping clients to obtain community resources; advocacy [28].

*Guiding and counselling:* Giving moral support at the time of crisis and stress [28].

*Modelling:* Demonstrating problem solving and the general enhancement of quality of life [28].

*Driving*

*Job searching*

When making decisions about the use of volunteers, it is important to remember that volunteers *supplement* professional workers' roles. Also, the successful use of volunteers in abuse cases requires a contract, adequate training (e.g., in characteristics of abusive families and in problem-solving with supervision), a clear division of roles between the volunteer and the worker, and self-actualization opportunities for the volunteer.

Within the parameters of agency policy, workers are advised to brief volunteers on the client's circumstances and on other services being delivered.

In anticipation of possible problems with clients, volunteers should be told of situations to avoid and of matters which should be referred to workers. For example, they should be cautioned against becoming embroiled in the client's problems and warned of the latter's possible excessive personal and material demands.

Regular meetings between workers and volunteers can be useful not only for progress with the case, but also for worker and volunteer growth. Workers will have an opportunity to note volunteers' emotional reactions to involvement with clients. Treating volunteers as colleagues is a useful approach, in that it capitalizes on the insights and recommendations coming from extensive and informal contacts.

Finally, volunteers often have high expectations for quick and noticeable results from their contacts with clients. Workers should be alert to signs of disappointment or frustration, and be prepared to make volunteers aware of difficulties in working with abusive, neglecting parents. The value of seemingly small gains should be emphasized. For additional information on using volunteers, see Chapter 5, XIII, E, 5.

## X.    SUMMARY

Child welfare practice presents special challenges to trained social workers and child care workers. It is often said that, of all helping professions, the largest gap is the one which separates social work education from application in child welfare. This chapter has reviewed some of the core practices and practice dilemmas.

Beginning with the challenges of the initial child protection investigation, special attention is given to establishing relationships with involuntary clients. Part of this difficulty is the struggle to offer help while at the same time acting as one of society's legal agents in child protection. Guidelines for the therapeutic use of authority and for court preparation address this issue.

Offering help to clients while fulfilling administrative functions is often regarded as a contradiction. In Section VIII, workers are advised to incorporate social work principles into the bureaucratic aspects of their work.

Finally, using volunteers may seem an unattractive possibility to workers facing the particularly troubled families in their child welfare caseloads. Yet, clients' needs for community involvement, plus the relationship difficulties associated with child protection work, make lay involvement a viable option.

## REFERENCES

1. Falconer, N. "The Special Role of the Child Welfare Worker and the Constructive Use of Authority", Unpublished paper, Children's Aid Society of Metropolitan Toronto, 1979.

2. Kadushin, A. *Child Welfare Services* (3rd Ed.). New York: The Macmillan Company, 1980.

3. Stein, T. *Social Work Practice in Child Welfare.* Englewood Cliffs, New Jersey: Prentice-Hall, 1981.

4. Ministry of Community and Social Services, Children's Services Divisions, Front Line Protection Staff. Training Program for Children's Aid Societies, Vol. 2, 1980.

5. Children's Aid Society of Metropolitan Toronto. "Definitions and Indicators for High Risk Parenting", Unpublished document, 1979.

6. Sgroi, S. "Child Sexual Assault: Some Guidelines for Investigation and Assessment". In Community Council of Greater New York, *Sexual Abuse of Children: Implications from the Sexual Trauma Treatment Program of Connecticut.* New York: Community Council of Greater New York, 1979.

7. Pruger, R. "The Good Bureaucrat", Social Work, Vol. 18, July 1973, pp. 26–32.

8. Pippin, J. "Developing Casework Skills", Sage Human Services Guide, 15; London: Sage Publications, 1980.

9. Maidman, F. "Native People in Urban Settings: Problems, Needs and Services". A Report Submitted to the Ontario Task Force on Native People in the Urban Setting, 1981.

10. Hepworth, D. "Early Removal of Resistance in Task-Centered Casework," Social Work, Vol. 24, July 1979, pp. 317–323.

11. Murdach, A. D. "Bargaining and Persuasion with Non-Voluntary Clients", Social Work, Vol. 25, November 1980, pp. 458–463.

12. Goffman, E. *Strategic Interaction*. New York: Ballantine Books, 1969.

13. Larson, C. and Talley, L. "Family Resistance to Therapy: A Model for Services and Therapists' Roles", Child Welfare, Vol. LVI, February 1977, pp. 121–126.

14. Mayer, J. and Timms, N. "Clash in Perspective Between Worker and Client", Social Casework, Vol. 50, January 1969, pp. 32–40.

15. Silverman, P. R. "A Re-examination of the Intake Procedure", Social Casework, Vol. 51, December 1979, pp. 625–634.

16. Garvin, C. "Complementary of Role Expectations in Groups: The Member-Worker Contract", *Social Work Practice, 1969*, New York: Columbia University Press, 1969, pp. 127–145.

17. Raven, B. H. and Rietsema, J. "The Effects of Varied Clarity of Group Goal and Group Path upon the Individual and his Relation to his Group", in Cartwright, D. and Zander, A. (eds.), *Group Dynamics: Research and Theory*. Evanston, Ill.: Row, Peterson and Company, 1960, pp. 395–413.

18. Maluccio, A. and Marlow, W. "The Case for the Contract", Social Work, Vol. 19, January 1974, pp. 28–36.

19. Sanson-Fisher, R. and Stotter, K. "Essential Steps in Designing a Successful Contract", Child Welfare, Vol. LVI, April 1977, pp. 239–248.

20. Marmor, J. "The Nature of the Psychotherapeutic Process Revisited", Canadian Psychiatric Journal, Vol. 20, December 1975, pp. 557–565.

21. Bernstein, B., Claman, L., Harris, J., and Samson, J. "The Child Witness: A Model for Evaluation and Trial Preparation", Child Welfare, Vol. LXI, February 1982, pp. 95–104.

22. Elkind, D. "Cognitive Structure in Latency," in J. D. Westman (ed.), *Individual Differences in Children*. New York: John Wiley and Sons, 1973.

23. Erikson, E. H. *Childhood and Society*. New York: W. W. Norton, 1950.

24. Harris, J. C. and Bernstein, B. "Lawyer and Social Worker as a Team: Preparing for a Trial in Neglect Cases", Child Welfare, Vol. LIX, September/October 1980, pp. 469–477.

25. Cohen, R. Personal Communication, 1982.

26. Tweraser, G. et al. "Every Parent's Birthright: Bonding as the Key to Effective Lay Therapy", Unpublished Paper, S.C.A.N. Services of Arkansas, n.d.

27. Parents Assistance Center, "Program Design Brochure", Oklahoma City, n.d.

28. Withey, V., Anderson, R., and Lauderdale, M. "Volunteers as Mentors for Abusing Parents: A Natural Helping Relationship", Child Welfare, Vol. LIX, December 1971, 637–644.

29. Yelaja, S. A. *Authority and Social Work: Concept and Use*. Toronto: University of Toronto Press, 1971.

30. Handman, D. "Authority in Casework—A Bread and Butter Theory", in Yelaja, 1971.

31. Hood, E., and Anglin, J. "Clinical Assessment in Children's Services", Toronto: Ministry of Community and Social Services, Children's Services Division, April 1979.

32. Germain, C. (ed.). *Social Work Practice: People and Environments*. New York: Columbia University Press, 1979.

33. Moss, S. Z., "Integration of the Family into the Child Placement Process", Children, Vol. 15, November–December 1968, pp. 219–224.

34. Roth, F., "A Practice Regimen for Diagnosis and Treatment of Child Abuse", Child Welfare, Vol. LIV, April 1975, pp. 219–224.

35. Shah, C. P. "Health Services in Child Welfare Agencies: An Integrated Approach", Canadian Journal of Public Health, Vol. 65, 1974.

36. Shah, C. P., "Assessing Needs and Board Rates for Handicapped Children in Foster Family Care", Child Welfare, Vol. L, December 1971., pp. 588–592.

37. Shah, C. P. "Assessing Needs and Board Rates for Handicapped Children in Foster Family Care: Progress Report", Child Welfare, Vol. LIII, January 1974, pp. 31–38.

38. Eull, W., "Working With the Family", Training Program for Children's Aid Societies, Vol. 6, Ministry of Community and Social Services, Children's Services Division, January 1982.

39. Erickson, G. O. and Hogan, T. *Family Therapy: An Introduction to Theory and Technique*. Monterey, California: Brooks/Cole Publishing Co., 1972.

40. Haley, J. (ed.), *Changing Families: A Family Therapy Reader*. New York and London: Grune & Stratton, 1971.

41. Minuchin, S. *Families and Family Therapy*. Cambridge, Massachusetts: Harvard University Press, 1974.

42. Minuchin, S., et al. *Families of the Slums: An Exploration of Their Structure and Treatment*. New York: Basic Books, 1967.

43. Vogel, E. and Bell, N. "The Emotionally Disturbed Child as the Family Scapegoat", in Bell and Vogel (eds.), *A Modern Introduction to the Family*. Glencoe, Ill.: The Free Press of Glencoe, 1960.

44. Cormican, J. D. "Linguistics Issues in Interviewing", Social Casework, Vol. 59, No. 3, March 1978.

45. Crompton, N. *Respecting Children: Social Work with Young People*. London: Edward Arnold, 1980.

46. Day, P. R. *Communication in Social Work*. Oxford: Pergamon, 1972.

47. Hugman, B. *Act Natural: New Sensibility for the Professional Helper*. London: Bedford Square Press, 1977.

48. Lesly, P. *How We Discommunicate*. New York: AMACON, 1979.

49. Ruesch, J. *Therapeutic Communication*. New York: W. W. Norton, 1973.

50. Speer, D. C. (ed.). *Nonverbal Communication*. Beverly Hills, California: Sage Publications, 1972.

51. Steinfatt, T. M. *Human Communication: An Interpersonal Introduction*. Indianapolis: Bobbs-Merrill Educational Publications, 1977.

52. Aponte, H. "Diagnosis in Family Therapy", in Germain, C. (ed.), *Social Work Practice: People and Environments*. New York, Columbia University Press, 1979.

53. Ruesch, J. and Bateson, G. *Communication: The Social Matrix of Psychiatry*. New York: W. W. Norton, 1968.

54. Curnock, K. and Hardiker, P. *Towards Practice Theory*. London, Boston, and Henley: Routledge and Kegan Paul, 1979.

55. Satir, V. *Conjoint Family Therapy*, Palo Alto, California: Science and Behaviour Books, 1967.

56. Bandler, R. and Grinder, J. *The Structure of Magic, Part I*. Palo Alto, California: Science and Behaviour Books, 1975.

57. Grinder, J. and Bandler, R. *The Structure of Magic, Part II*. Palo Alto, California: Science and Behavior Books, 1975.

58. Raush, H., Barri, W., Hertal, R., and Swain, M. *Communication, Conflict and Marriage*. San Francisco, Washington, London: Jossey-Bass Publishers, 1974.

59. Watzlawick, P., Beavin, J., and Jackson, D. *Pragmatics of Human Communication*. New York: W. W. Norton, 1976.

60. Goldberg, G. "Breaking the Communication Barrier: The Initial Interview with an Abusing Parent", Child Welfare, Vol. LIV, April 1975, pp. 274–282.

61. Polansky, N., Borgman, R., De Saix, C., and Sharlin, S. "Verbal Accessibility and the Treatment of Child Neglect", Child Welfare, Vol. L., June 1971, pp. 348–356.

62. Wells, S. J. "A Model of Therapy with Abusive and Neglectful Families", Social Work, Vol. 26, March 1981, pp. 113–118.

63. Jayaratne, S. "Behavioral Intervention and Family Decision-Making", Social Work, Vol. 23, January 1978, pp. 20–25.

64. Douds, A., Engelsgjerd, M., and Collingwood, T. "Behavior Contracting With Youthful Offenders and Their Parents", Child Welfare Vol. LVI, June 1977, pp. 409–417.

65. Saxon, William. "Behavioral Contracting: Theory and Design", Child Welfare, Vol. LVIII, September/October 1979, pp. 523–529.

66. Pincus, A. and Minahan, A. *Social Work Practice: Model and Method*. Itasca, Ill.: F. E. Peacock Publishers, Inc., 1973.

67. Hollis, F. and Woods, M. *Casework: A Psychosocial Therapy*. New York: Random House, 1981.

68. Lidz, T. *The Person*. New York: Basic Books, 1976.

69. Thomson, E. M. and Paget, N. *Child Abuse—A Community Challenge*. Buffalo, N.Y.: Henry Stewart, 1971.

# 3

# A Theoretical View
# of Community Work

GREG CONCHELOS

I. INTRODUCTION                                          66
II. THE EVOLVING ROLE OF COMMUNITY WORK                  66
  A.  A Brief History                           66
  B.  Prevention: Policy, Goals, and Objectives  67
  C.  Three Possible Approaches in Community Work 68
III. AN ECOLOGICAL APPROACH TO COMMUNITY
WORK                                                     69
  A.  Rationale                                  69
  B.  Links Between Community Work and Casework   69
IV. PRACTICAL WAYS TO DEFINE COMMUNITY WORK
PROBLEMS                                                 70
  A.  Isolation                                  71
  B.  Feedback                                   71
  C.  Networks                                   72
  D.  Neighbourhoods                             73
V. DAYCARE AS A COMMUNITY WORK ISSUE                     78
  A.  Definitions of Daycare                     78
  B.  Historical Forces                          79
  C.  Obstructions                               81
  D.  Daycare Debates                            81
  E.  Community Work Practices                   83
VI. SUMMARY                                              84
  REFERENCES AND BIBLIOGRAPHY                    85

## I.    INTRODUCTION

Community work in the field of child welfare has a unique role. Its mandate is to address those conditions contributing to child maltreatment which transcend the scope of casework. Its function is to treat societal, rather than individual, "aspects" of the environment. This has meant that its structure, which emphasizes intensive consultation with the community, has developed unique operating methods directed towards child welfare. Overall emphasis is upon prevention and upon nurturing the strengths found in the community, rather than upon simply redressing its weaknesses.

What is child welfare community work? It is the enhancement of a community's strengths in order to create pro-child, nurturing communities. It involves addressing issues of children's welfare as they apply to specific geographic communities or to a broader context. Of critical importance is the community's input in defining the pertinent issues.

What does one do in community work? The worker uses various activities for community consultations and outreach. These should demonstrate:

1. a primary prevention function in the context of child welfare with low-income people

2. accessibility to the service by the low-income community as a whole, and not limited to agency clientele

3. a clear link between community work and the child welfare mandate of the agency and of child welfare legislation

The complexity of community work theory and practice is given dimension in the following sections.

## II.    THE EVOLVING ROLE OF COMMUNITY WORK

### A.    A Brief History

In some agencies community work has moved away from its support role of agency functions towards direct development of capacities within communities. An important dimension of this change has been the inclusion of work with groups and communities which are not formally agency clientele. Gradually, the evolution can be characterized as a move to a more preventive posture.

In many Canadian child welfare agencies during the 1960s and early 1970s, community work led to improved casework service delivery by first clarifying community expectations and preferences. The result was a greater role for clients and community residents in the delivery of the agency's services.

Throughout the remainder of the 1970s, there was a shift from facilitating community consumption of *agency* resources towards developing resources within the community. There was also emphasis upon needs assessment by a community rather than by the agency, and upon entirely new alternative child welfare services.

During the past few years community work objectives have expanded to include not only local resource development, but also the linking of communities across their boundaries. This has promoted self-sufficiency and control on new levels and has placed greater emphasis upon social planning, and particularly, social action.

## B.      Prevention: Policy, Goals, and Objectives

These historical developments mean that community work has a largely preventive focus, its goal being the prevention of circumstances requiring the protection of children. This is a somewhat broader undertaking than the protection of children who have been maltreated:

> Primary prevention, the goal of community work, is defined as an attempt to reduce the incidence of new cases of child maltreatment by changing the environment and by strengthening the individuals involved; primary prevention does not rule out casework, but its environmental emphasis makes demands beyond casework resources.

> While community workers focus on primary prevention, other staff are more likely to focus on secondary and tertiary prevention; these latter two forms correspond to treatment and rehabilitation—activities which occur in casework services.

Community work, as primary prevention work, concerns itself with the larger structural conditions that determine whether incidence of new cases of child maltreatment are reduced. Focus upon prevention has resulted in two general goals:

> 1. to enable both interest-based and geographically-defined communities to define their own needs and to develop community-based approaches to meeting those needs

> 2. to assist communities in identification of large issues, and to establish networks with other interested groups to facilitate needed change

Efforts to achieve these goals, both of which entail cultivating local control of resources necessary for child welfare, involve the following:

> assessment of local community needs, the appropriateness of agency involvement, and the specific methods to be used

> development of mutually satisfactory objectives in working with community residents, and provision of assistance with community program-planning, implementation, and evaluation

> liaison with other community groups regarding problem identification and strategy planning towards solutions

> liaison with self-help community-based groups and assistance with implementation of community projects

The distinct characteristic of community work is the development of a community's capacity to solve problems beyond the level of individual cases. Community work creates conditions by which individuals and groups can gain greater access to, and control over, resources which both remedy and prevent child maltreatment. These programs are carried out by non-community work staff after community workers help to organize boards, liaise between agencies, and carry out other organizational preparations.

Preparation is accomplished by meeting with members of the community and generating a comprehensive description of ways in which they perceive the problem (e.g., feeling of isolation; lack of networks; recognition of high prevalence of abuse or neglect). Ultimately, the community must either accept and value the resources which community workers can offer, or the worker has no place there. Hence, a "user-choice" focus leaves both initiative on the problem and involvement of workers within the control of the community, rather than within the agency's mandate alone. This means that community work may involve persons beyond the agency's clientele.

It also means that the community may not have local, geographically-based boundaries. For instance, all persons living in scattered assisted-housing may face the same city management policies in their buildings. Community work could involve social action by this interest-based community, especially with a view to preventing problems in new areas. Throughout the process the workers use a supportive style, avoiding leadership roles as a rule.

## C.     Three Possible Approaches in Community Work

Community work can be done in three different ways, depending upon the nature of the problem and the practice possibilities involved. Rothman's three models of community work practice [27] summarize these approaches:

> 1. *Locality development* is intended to increase a geographically-based community's capacity for self-help and may focus upon local situations as a basis for this. A key strategy is involvement of a broad cross section of people directly affected, with emphasis upon fostering agreement among various parties. In this situation, a community worker can play several roles which give direct support: enabler-catalyst, coordinator, and teacher of problem-solving skills. Working with a tenants' organization is an example.

> 2. *Social planning* is an approach which may be once removed from a concern of a given locality. The objective is to solve a specific problem rather than to promote general development of local capacity. The problem may affect several localities, such as the uneven distribution of assisted-housing. The professional can play a role as expert, bringing technical skills central to the process. Strategies may include fact-gathering (e.g., geographical dispersion of single-parent families) and developing of consensus among experts (such as developing new policies on how the city and province should share housing responsibilities). In social planning, community workers may take more active, up-front, yet more structured roles, such as fact-gatherer, analyst, and program implementer.

3. *Social action* mixes the activism of locality development with social planning's breadth of focus. Objectives may include basic institutional changes or major shifts in power relationships among institutions. For instance, the amount of daycare allocations from government sources may be questioned, or guaranteed annual income programs might be promoted. Two chief strategies here are: clarifying the issues (making them concrete in public arenas), and organizing pressure groups. The community worker's roles have been characterized as activist, advocate, agitator, and broker.

## III. AN ECOLOGICAL APPROACH TO COMMUNITY WORK

### A. Rationale

Evidence is growing that it is both possible and desirable to promote the welfare of children by dealing with both large-scale structural conditions (community and societal characteristics) and local, individual characteristics of parent and child [11]. Such an approach pays close attention to the dynamic processes which link institutional factors (such as economic and educational systems) in the child via the immediate parenting setting [10].

Social support systems (such as income, housing, and daycare) comprise the human ecology. Various aspects of this ecology can either help or hinder effective parenting practices. Together these factors form a scale or pyramid of resources which, if inadequately developed, could contribute to child maltreatment. Five dimensions have been noted:

> home, physical space, and belongings of parent and child
>
> relationships and roles of people in relation to the child
>
> child's daily activities which bring her or him into contact with others
>
> institutional systems (e.g., school, social agencies, hospitals)
>
> ideological systems (e.g., religion, government)

At the centre is the child, living with the parents, and possibly other relatives. Next is the local network; tied to this is the neighbourhood and the greater community; finally there are social or economic class influences, ideologies, and so on [10]. For a review of the research literature on ecological factors and child maltreatment, see Chapters 4, 5, and 6.

### B. Links Between Community Work and Casework

It is the nature of social services to be negatively self-defining. They are brought into existence to deal with less-than-satisfactory conditions. When they institute units such as community work, their new primary preventive agenda moves them into a positive role. The essentially positive purpose of community work is the creation and promotion of community strengths in order to foster healthy child development. As such, child development is inextricably linked to community development [12].

Community work tends to involve large-scale factors such as neighbourhoods or government economic policies and other social structures which carry cultural attitudes and expectations. Casework focusses upon smaller units where the child maltreatment is most visible and the needs most immediate. Together, they form a comprehensive approach to child welfare.

The ecological focus defines and inter-relates factors which may help in understanding community-related child welfare problems, and their corresponding solutions in practice.

The task of the community worker is to trace the societal-environmental sources of child maltreatment (which can be done in many ways, including across communities) in order to identify those community characteristics which breed conditions leading to healthy or weak childrearing practices.

No single factor is the source of child maltreatment. For instance, while parents may have poor child rearing skills, emotional problems, or other contributing factors, abuse by such parents may be prevented through the influence of strong social networks, tightly-knit neighbourhoods, or government programs.

Garbarino identifies five principal causes of child maltreatment: (1) psychopathology of parents; (2) temperamental incompatibility between parent and child; (3) perverse family dynamics; (4) interpersonal deficiencies of parents; and (5) culturally-based inappropriate attitudes and expectations about child rearing and development [12].

Garbarino argued that the first four factors are merely secondary, disposing conditions which rest upon more fundamental necessary conditions (e.g., the culturally normalized use of force in child rearing [12]. This argument explains the existence of abusing communities as well as abusing individuals. The primary preventive nature of community work rests upon undercutting the fundamental, necessary conditions contributing to child maltreatment. Indeed, the implied significance of this is expressed by Garbarino: "I suggest that in primary prevention we attempt to prevent the arbitrary use of power in ways that damage others or reduce their opportunities" [12].

## IV.    PRACTICAL WAYS TO DEFINE COMMUNITY WORK PROBLEMS

Child maltreatment may stem from poor allocation of various resources (such as economic, social, emotional ones). These resources are exchanged within systems (e.g., in the neighbourhood) and between systems (e.g., between the family and the State). Four concepts associated with resource exchange are: isolation, feedback, social networks, and neighbourhoods. (A more complete explanation would include broader factors such as economics, politics, culture, and ideology, in addition to the more local ones discussed below.) The four concepts are closely related, at times appearing to be two sides of the same coin (isolation and feedback are two examples). It is important, however, to maintain some distinctions for the sake of clarity. Their essential unity is demonstrated and acknowledged in the day-to-day tasks of community work.

## A. Isolation

Child maltreatment is more likely to occur when families are socially isolated [11]. While this isolation may be physical, it is "loneliness" and "vulnerability" (i.e., emotional isolation) which appear to be the most crucial aspects.

Such isolated families act in particular ways:

They prefer to solve problems on their own, but may not be adept at doing so.

They have few relationships outside of their home, and generally non-supportive ties within the home.

They are likely to discourage their children from having involvement outside of the home.

They tend to be transient, with few enduring social roots.

They have long-held habits of avoiding activities which foster social contacts [13]. (For additional material on social isolation and child maltreatment, see Chapter 1, II; Chapter 4, IV, and Chapter 5, IV.)

These characteristics of individuals or families, while more related to casework approaches, may result from broader community characteristics. Viewing the family at the social network level helps to explain why maltreatment occurs and suggests possible community work intervention. For instance, isolation can be described as the relative lack of resources for family support. Helping individuals to learn practical ways to seek support of others in child rearing, may be a casework, rather than a community work, concern; however, promotion of a community's healthy networks must go hand in hand with a worker's personal help. Where one or more parents have "isolating personalities", practice would involve intensive personal attention, perhaps using volunteers on a one-to-one basis; group-based programs with non-individualized content are likely to be ineffective. A community work approach would be inappropriate without casework helping people to connect with the community's healthy aspects [24].

The concept of interacting conditions allows the worker to think in terms of isolated families, self-isolating individuals, and isolating communities, neighbourhoods, or networks, since each may be a factor contributing to child maltreatment.

## B. Feedback

Feedback is letting a person know one's opinion of the nature and consequences of that person's actions. The availability of feedback depends partly upon the extent and nature of a community's interaction. It is an information or communication resource which combats isolation. The quality of feedback to parents about how well they are doing their job can be determined by certain aspects of a community's strength, such as the availability of neighbours as informal advisors and the degree to which parents allow or encourage such interventions. Feedback is an informational resource which is also transmitted through cultural values, institutions, and prevailing ideologies.

## C.     Networks

A community work approach to child welfare problems increases the potential number of ways in which those in need of assistance can be supported. It has been found that, to date, people use either social networks or a mix of these and professional services more than they use formal agency services alone [11].

A social network has been defined as "those people outside the household who engage in activities and exchanges of an affective and/or material nature with members of the immediate family." Network characteristics influence the child's welfare [8].

One essential characteristic of networks is the way in which they put an individual in contact with others [2]; another is the way in which they serve as reference systems through which one can learn more about one's way of coping.

Networks vary according to size, degree of openness, density, degree of reciprocity, purpose, intensity, frequency of contact, geographical structure, and so on. They need not be entirely local in nature, but rather, based on shared interests and geographically dispersed. Given these variations, it is possible to study the individual's networks along each dimension and to determine whether inadequacies exist which might be related to child maltreatment. Community workers can then determine which modifications are needed in order to promote child welfare.

Networks support child development particularly well by supporting parents. For example:

> Parents get support about general child-rearing worries.
>
> They are helped with unhappy emotions.
>
> Both family members and friends help in life-crises.

Four general functions of networks are:

> lessening the experience of stress
>
> providing support and services in a practical way
>
> transmitting attitudes, values, and norms about seeking help [16, 17]
>
> screening and referring users to professional help

Networks can influence the child not only indirectly through the parents, but directly as well. They can do this in several ways. Direct support can be given, such as in the case of aunts or uncles substituting for sick parents. A child can observe network members as models supplementing the more direct moral education which she or he receives from parents. Networks can also enhance cognitive development and social development (in the areas of attachment, independent behaviour, experiences with social roles) [8].

There are several ways in which networks, aided by community work, can augment a community's capacity to provide support. For example, women on one floor of a high-rise building gather informally over coffee and begin to share common concerns about the need for a drop-in centre. A community worker helps in exploring the municipal landlords' policies on space-use, liabilities, and so forth. Eventually, a basement apartment is freed. The worker holds evening meetings on basic organization skills needed (e.g., who will negotiate with management).

The centre attracts women from the community. Children are brought along a good deal of the time. This leads to ad hoc daycare arrangements among small groups of the centre's "regulars". Management raises questions about the zoning for this. The worker trains one person to do a simple survey of the building while the centre staff writes a brief to management asking for expansion of space for a daycare centre. The worker puts residents in touch with a government liaison who helps write capital grant and child care training proposals. The new daycare staff also finds time to join a municipal coalition on daycare.

In this case, the role of the community worker is one of social animator. Working largely in the background, she or he arranges access to skills. Not directly involved in programming, the worker enhances the network's capacity to provide itself with services, focussing upon the preventive involvement of other agencies.

The degree to which network resources influence child welfare is affected by the following factors:

> *Cultural and ideological:* particularly attitudes towards the relationship of the family and the child, towards the distribution of economic resources, and towards self-sufficiency and the interdependence of individuals
>
> *Community and neighbourhood:* particularly demographic characteristics of the neighbourhood, and agency characteristics (functions, accessibility, methods of service delivery)
>
> *Family characteristics:* particularly those which determine family need for support (e.g., number of adults present, level of income), and family ability to seek and get support (e.g., awareness of services; previous experience with agencies)

Network analysis is a useful tool by which community workers can come to understand the nature of the community in which they work; learn ways in which community characteristics are associated with child maltreatment; and get directions for community work solutions to such problems.

## D.    Neighbourhoods

Neighbourhoods, particularly urban ones, seldom have clear boundaries and simplicity in their composition. However, they are not merely accidental contexts in which cases of child maltreatment are found; rather, they are environments in which people live and interact, and in which resources are made available or withheld.

Neighbourhoods can be described in terms of residents' sense of identity (they may or may not express a sense of belonging); interactions (people encounter each other with some noticeable frequency and intensity); and linkages (locally or in the larger community)[31]. Certain aspects of identity, interaction, and linkages form the basis of problem-solving capabilities of neighbourhoods.

The four stages of problem-solving are:

*Problem definition:* A community defines a problem in a certain way (e.g., coming home from school to an empty house may be a problem for some children, but not for others).

*Mobilization:* This has been defined as the ability of a local community to interact quickly, to contact agencies, to obtain information and fulfill communication needs, and so forth.

*Saturation:* Somewhat related to mobilization, saturation is the extent to which messages from the media reverberate throughout local informal networks and cliques.

*Maintenance:* This is "the ability of a community to sustain its newly generated response to a problem" [31].

These stages can be seen as four somewhat intertwined steps by which a community attains greater or lesser success in resolving a problem. Oftentimes, the victories are partial—perhaps an issue gets public airing and little else. On an historical level, the process is cyclic—solving one problem may elicit another more fundamental one. Furthermore, these stages can occur at different levels and at different times. There may be movement through locality development, social planning, and social action before solutions are found.

The final stage is not the attainment of a solution, but rather the successful maintenance of it through increased community health or capacity for self-reliance. Learning, defined as self-imposed permanent change, is a basic process which community workers facilitate, so that maintenance of child development is a permanent state, a result of problem-solving.

An example taken from an actual case illustrates stages of problem-solving:

A group of tenants in a 400-unit apartment complex face a 40% rent increase. In addition, there are serious substandard conditions. Clarification of the problem involves creating shared awareness that all tenants face the *same* problem. Other factors contribute to problem definition (e.g., the rate increase is beyond the government-controlled rental limit; the increase will have an impact on other money-related needs). The community worker might help set up informal meetings through which neighbours exchange impressions and compare needs. She or he might call in a housing authority representative to explain technical aspects of rental policies or housing standards. While individuals might focus on one aspect of the problem, the definition of it involves helping the community to organize the various perceptions into a popular, public definition which they truly own. This may be an irregular and long-term process lasting several months.

Mobilization somewhat overlaps the first stage. Legal aid clinics may be consulted. Meetings increase. Persons originally peripheral to the issues, such as new tenants or alderpersons, may be drawn in. Strategic targets for change, such as the Rent Review Commission, are identified. The community worker might work on both the locality development and social action levels in this stage.

Mobilization involves saturation of the community with the issue. Television coverage may result. There are greater opportunities for the community to see itself as a unit. Workers might provide advice about which media to pursue. (In the present true example, the Rent Review Commission, under pressure from the tenants, lowered the rent increase from 40% to 16%. It could do nothing about substandard housing, which had to be pursued elsewhere.)

Preserving victories is the final challenge. The tenant group may not remain a transient, issue-based group, because as soon as such militancy is relaxed new problems may arise. The now-permanent organization may realize that there are other buildings with problems. Their learning becomes a resource for others. Community workers can link such groups on the trans-community social action level.

Building organizations which have had experience in getting by-laws enforced might be connected by social action measures and eventually organize themselves into a coalition. This becomes a social structure which finds and maintains solutions at the level of housing policy.

In such cases, problem solving and self-change may evolve from a reactive to a pro-active process. The coalition might get funding from the province to purchase their own building, do renovations, and develop a cooperative. While apparently successful, these problem-solving processes and resources are likely to be quite fragile.

While the foregoing example represented locality development, it is also possible to begin with non-geographical communities. For example, sole-support mothers live in various parts of a city, but because they share problems of limited income or unemployment they are potentially a community, based upon common interests rather than geography. Cross-branch work may aid them in defining a common problem.

For instance, women's groups in certain Metropolitan Toronto community centres became the forum through which to diffuse information. Such interaction led to the formation of a city-level sole-support group. Interaction and maintenance of policy initiatives are common ongoing processes in community problem-solving.

Neighbourhoods vary in their capacity to handle problems, and methods have been developed to explain links between community capacity and the incidence of child maltreatment. There appear to be six types of neighbourhoods, each with varying problem-solving capacity.

While there are no pure cases, the typology is useful in that it provides a working definition of a given community for practice purposes. It is important to get the community's assessment of these dimensions, and not the agency's assessment only. For example, one study showed that parents' assessment of the riskiness of their neighbourhood was quite accurate: ". . . it suggests that parents are sensitive to the way neighbourhood factors establish a particular climate for families and parent-child relations" [12].

The six neighbourhood types are described below [3]:

1. *Integral neighbourhoods* are strong in all three areas of identity, interaction, and linkages. They will quickly "own" the problem of, for instance, young children on the street late at night, arrange ways to discuss it, and call in a child welfare agency if appropriate. Quite simply, integral neighbourhoods usually are not in need of community work assistance. Their

general "health" is intact. (What is assumed here, of course, is that all critical needs are met. They may not have a tennis court, but they do have parks.)

2. *Parochial neighbourhoods* may react in the same way, but since they have fewer ties to outside agencies, interventions may not occur, or may be carried out by local organizations. "First generation" ethnic communities are examples of this. In such areas, resource persons such as priests, doctors, and lawyers may act as brokers or go betweens for the community. Hence links to, for instance, municipal councils may be more indirect than in other cases. (This case illustrates how these characteristics occur in degrees or grades). Community work can play a role in helping a parochial community strengthen its links to the outside. For instance, an ethnic group may have its own parent-school association. Because few members speak English, they discover that they have not been receiving information about daycare opportunities. A worker may pick up this need and help the group establish a liaison with the daycare centre involved. As a result, the centre's newsletters become multilingual. Such linkage development is dynamic and evolving. Perhaps the ethnic group decides to write letters of endorsement in support of the daycare centre to the municipality in return for the centre's responsiveness.

3. *Diffuse neighbourhoods* are strong in only one area—their identity. Consequently, if there were, for example, an increase of teenage pregnancies, there may be little more than intense awareness of this and little discussion. An example of a diffuse community is a newly-developed, high-rise subdivision. Here, residents may see themselves as members of a district, but are largely anonymous to each other. Furthermore, they may have no tenants' associations, local schools, or other links to the outside. There are several such developments in Toronto which serve as "gates" to new immigrants. Population turnover (as high as 90% in five years) may be a major obstruction to the community worker's efforts to help the community strengthen interaction and linkages. A special note: peculiar to the Canadian experience is the "cultural mosaic" ideology, through which a community could be strengthened by the ethnic cohesion of immigrant sub-communities in such diffuse neighbourhoods.

4. *"Stepping-stone" neighbourhoods* tend to be strong in interaction and linkages, but weak in identity. Socially mobile, middle-class neighbourhoods are of this type. Problems of teenage "running" might get quick reaction, but the neighbourhood would tend to farm out the problem and its solution to outside agencies. Families involved would be averse to, say, community-based teen discussion groups, and would try to deal with running individually, on a non-public basis, with a public or private agency. Within Metropolitan Toronto, there are boroughs composed mainly of this type of neighbourhood. If there is frequent population turnover, the community may never establish a sound identity and, in effect, may not want to. A community worker's job may be limited. Since such an area is quite healthy in interaction and linkages, it may ask for help only in functional, or technical matters. Once a daycare centre or legal aid clinic is established, residents are satisfied. In short, there may be little locality development which can be

done in stepping-stone communities; rather, the worker uses such occasions to augment cross-community social action, noting this as an example of a more widespread need already evidenced in other communities.

5. *Transitory neighbourhoods* are strong only in their links to the larger community. For instance, in "bedroom suburbs", children going to school alone or without breakfast might be noticed only by the schools. Since both parents work and commute to do so, no local public awareness or deliberation may result. Population turnover is high, and family and neighbour interaction is low. There is little interest in community identity, in "owning" the area psychologically, although the Chamber of Commerce may struggle with this. In such a case, locality development might be limited. Community work might dwell mainly on social action; for instance, getting legislation for around-the-clock daycare centres.

6. *Anomic neighbourhoods* are the weakest. A rooming house area, locked in by industrial districts, may put children at great physical risks. Child abuse, accidents, or truancy may go unchecked because there is neither local nor municipal awareness of resources at hand [31]. Anomic neighbourhoods may appear to be very similar to diffuse ones, but lack even superficially-shared notions of identity among residents. Several areas spread out along the lake shore near Toronto are examples. Since they are in the least healthy condition, anomic or "normless" districts present challenges to all styles of community work. They can benefit from straightforward social planning (rezoning; improving park space; having its own meeting hall) in order to change basic, structural conditions. Locality development and social action might be slow to develop until these are in place. Only after there are identifiable local groups formed could such an area begin to define and to solve its problems.

Possible causes of child maltreatment can be linked, as in the foregoing examples, to the ways in which a neighbourhood does or does not solve problems.

Types or models of neighbourhoods have been based upon urban information and urban needs. However, it is important to consider suburban and rural factors in describing the capacity of communities to care for their children.

While it has not been treated in this chapter, there is a clear need to organize knowledge about rural community work in child welfare. One reason for this is that rural and (in Canada) remote areas (Indian reservations) are highly sensitive to economic and social pressures. In recessive times, as mines close or tourism declines, such communities have much smaller resource margins and fewer services to augment drops in a family's economic, social, and moral capacities. In short, the ecological fragility of rural and remote areas dictates that community workers define locality development, social planning, and social action in entirely new ways. The fewer absolute numbers of children at risk in such situations (compared to cities) cannot be accepted as an argument against this need.

The actual "social cement" which comprises identity, interaction, and linkages is important to community workers:

> Informal, day-to-day, back-fence or street-corner activity provides a chance for ad hoc, non-threatening encounters; this atmosphere of approachability may allow a parent to accept advice on a child.

On a longer-term basis, neighbors cultivate mutual personal influence, which makes such things as a Block Parent program more easily acceptable.

People give each other mutual practical aid, such as a floating daycare group.

Values and standards of behaviour are informally maintained or negotiated within neighbourhood groups on such subjects as child management.

Finally, organizational capacity is developed, particularly for linkages outside the neighbourhood (a residents' association may join a city-wide coalition on increasing park space) [32].

Information about ways in which neighbourhoods provide resources for parenting may suggest approaches for defining and solving problems through community work. Additional information on the impact of neighbourhoods on child maltreatment is contained in Chapters 4, IV and 5, IV.

## V.    DAYCARE AS A COMMUNITY WORK ISSUE

There are numerous crucial issues (e.g., housing, employment, health services) which vie for the attention of community workers. In contemporary society one of the most immediate needs is affordable, accessible daycare; it remains for community workers and caseworkers to understand the daycare issue as one which influences child welfare.

### A.    Definitions of Daycare

The term daycare refers to a resource in which the care normally given by parents is either replaced or supplemented by another's care. Several types of daycare have been defined; they are as follows:

*Family daycare:* "A program involving the selection and supervision by a government or authorized private agency of private families who give care to children during the day" [16]. (Family daycare is distinguished from care in the child's own home by relatives, friends, or other persons, paid or unpaid, live-in or not.)

Family daycare is usually provided by women who care for several children in their home for a fee. Family daycare is distinguished from formal daycare by its location in a home (not an institution) in a neighbourhood; its informal, personal, unbureaucratic atmosphere (hours and days are flexible); its environment (sometimes a mom-and-pop operation); its small group compositions of usually three or four children per adult; and the close attachments which develop between the children and their teachers [23].

*Private or casual daycare arrangements:* ". . . the use of babysitters, or other similar types of arrangements, which are made between the parent and provider and not under the supervision of a licensing authority or daycare agency" [16]. This can include either family daycare or in-home daycare. Both regulated and unregulated forms may be considered together under the term "family day care" because it is the more common term and because there are many similarities.

*Commercial centres* (private, profit-making centres): "A licensed daycare centre set up as a proprietory operation. It includes the larger franchise operations, as well as the small, singularly-owned centre" [16].

*Public daycare:* "A licensed daycare centre owned and operated by a municipal or provincial government" [16].

*Community board centre:* "A licensed daycare centre that is established as a non-profit organization and is governed by a community board of directors" [16].

*Cooperative daycare:* "A licensed daycare centre set up as a non-profit association and governed by a board of directors of which at least 50% are parents of children in the centre" [16].

*Infant daycare:* "Care provided by a daycare centre or a family daycare home for children under the age of two" [16].

## B.    Historical Forces

Over the past century, and particularly in the last few decades, important social and economic changes have re-arranged child care resources available to parents.

With the fluctuation in immigration, and the social formation brought about by industrialization, families have moved from an "extended" to a "nuclear" form. Since aunts, uncles, and grandparents are less likely to live with parents, parents finding themselves to be the primary, or even sole, managers of their children is something of a new development.

A more recent social force has been the decline in birth rates. Even within nuclear families, there are now fewer brothers and sisters for a child. Such siblings once were key child care resources, and, like relatives in extended families, were both accessible and affordable to parents [16, 26].

It should be noted, however, that in urban Canada there has been a recent and large-scale immigration from countries in Asia and Southern Europe. These new arrivals have brought with them, and continue to maintain, extended families. In addition, they are likely to have more than one or two children. Thus, in such cases, two "naturally occurring" elements of child care resources (i.e., extended family and children) remain available.

In a 1977 Canadian study [18] of reasons why parents use daycare, the sample surveyed presented the following reasons:

preference or need to be employed (52%)

attending full-time educational courses (7%)

health condition which necessitates help in caring for children (7%)

freed-up time for volunteer work (2%)

Of these reasons, employment is the central one. Closely related to this is society's traditional view that child rearing is solely the woman's responsibility. In addition to the change in family structure and drop in population noted above, the increased entry of women into the labour market has been a third historical force behind the development of daycare.

In Canada, in 1977, 52% of all mothers with children age 7 (or less) were employed. While the hours worked per week were as low as 10 in some cases, over three-quarters were working full-time, from 30 to 49 hours per week [18].

There are not enough daycare spaces available to meet the need, and where parents have been able to arrange child care, often there are too few hours of supervision to meet the parents' needs, or there is supervision, but inadequate quality-control. One source argues that 68,000 children in Canada are "at risk" due to such conditions [18].

There is a high demand for daycare, but scant resources by which to meet it. Presently in Canada, 600,000 daycare spaces are needed as compared with the 27,000 now available [17]. Other figures indicate an even greater need: 335,000 spaces are needed for children ages 1 to 3, and another 800,000 for ages 4 and 5 [8].

The historical trend has been an increase in the need for both more, and new forms of, daycare in order to supplement what has been seen as women's work role. The effect of the creation of small, nuclear families in which both parents are employed, or in which there is a single parent, has been the erosion of parental capacity for child care.

Questions have been raised about the impact of chronic recession upon the demand for daycare. One argument is that during recessions, the simple unavailability of work would undercut demands for daycare, given its intimate link with employment. However, women have been traditionally confined to the tertiary sector of the labour market, that is, to the services section (e.g., food-delivery systems, telephone systems, secretarial work), whereas recessions tend to have a greater impact upon the primary or extraction sectors (e.g., nickel mining) and upon the secondary or manufacturing sectors (e.g., automobile production). With services becoming an even greater segment of the employment market, the need for daycare in all its forms could become expanded and more stabilized, regardless of economic downturns [17].

It is evident that employed women, particularly those who are low paid or single-parents, need daycare as a critical support system for their child care.

The family daycare council model, used in Calgary, has these advantages: It can involve other community services, and it has been found to be more economical than satellites.

Edmonton has combined the satellite and council models (see page 83). The key advantage is that the council aspect identifies and attracts parents who would be missed by a given satellite, yet the satellite aspects appeal to the locally-based, family-oriented style of the lower-income users [9].

Flexible response to the peculiarities of a given user group is crucial. Reflecting the emergency capacity of child welfare agencies, groups in Edmonton and North Vancouver started two emergency floating daycare homes. Children are placed there when parents' work patterns, availability of other family daycare, and other factors suddenly change.

There can also be cross-over to the education system. Groups in Winnipeg have designed a program by which children in family daycare homes use a group pre-school program for a few hours per week [9].

Other centres have used other aspects of school systems such as involvement of older students as volunteers. (Curricula such as "family life education" are one such source of volunteers) [12]. Generally speaking, the use of volunteers in any kind of daycare setting has been minimal, and could be further developed [18].

## C.     Obstructions

Explanations have been offered for the link between the kind and quality of daycare resources which a community can offer, and the potential for child maltreatment within that group. Important characteristics of daycare are its affordability, accessibility, sufficiency, and appropriateness.

A number of obstructions to good daycare have been identified. Among one group of employed mothers [6]:

58% desired institutional daycare, but were not able to arrange it.

60% had arranged daycare outside of their home.

57% found any sort of daycare hard to obtain.

39% had made two or more arrangements in one year.

25% indicated some sort of dissatisfaction with their present arrangement [6]; (another source [5] indicated 69% for this last item).

Stress from such factors may lead to maternal unhappiness which, in turn, may lead to emotional problems in the children [5].

For many, daycare represents a struggle to ensure both income security and minimal child welfare. This struggle has both subjective, personal aspects as well as objective aspects (e.g., affordability, availability). There are personal factors which may determine the amount and type of daycare which a mother uses. Two such factors have been identified among low-income women who are *not* employed: (1) they generally know less about daycare as an option, and (2) they tend to hold stronger positive views about mothers as primary care-givers.

Such a value position demonstrates that links between resources and child welfare go beyond issues of affordability, access, sufficiency, and adequacy. Information flow and personal values are important factors, as are structural conditions such as the availability and distribution of daycare spaces.

## D.     Daycare Debates

There is no evidence to show that good quality daycare adversely affects the attachment, intelligence, or social development of the child [8, 11, 18, 25].

Studies of child development have strongly emphasized the interaction between mother and child. This has resulted in the position by some social scientists that replacements or supplements to this relationship (such as daycare) should be minimized [23, 24]. Known as the "maternal deprivation" view of child welfare, it has proposed that daycare and other supplements to the "mother as chief resource" should be allowed only in "hardship" cases [13, 14, 18].

On a policy level, this perspective takes several forms. One is a bias against infant daycare (up to age two or three) because of the imputed emotional damage to the child by prolonged separation from the mother [5].

These deprivation studies, done in the 1940s and 1950s, have been questioned both in focus and method. Deprivation proponents extrapolated from *clinical* studies of maternally deprived infants and children and concluded that *any* separation would lead to damage. However, there is no clear link between institutional daycare and adverse effects. That is, separation in itself may only be a necessary, but not a sufficient condition for damage [12, 14, 18, 23].

Evidence shows that cognitive and intellectual development of children is not influenced by the fact of their mother's employment [24]. Nor is the status of the single employed parent itself a detriment to child development [12].

In Sweden, where daycare centres are widely used, critics have raised three points:

Parents can easily come to rely on leaving the child for 10 or more hours at a time, to the point where the child feels that she is "visiting" her home.

Parents tend to lose parental expertise due to such long separations; emotional development between parent and child can become episodic.

Finally, as in North America, extensive exposure to daycare may mean that the child is exposed to **few** male models [16].

Critics of this position counter-argue that, above and beyond economic necessity as a rationale for daycare, as a resource it makes positive contributions to child welfare. It can introduce resources which the family itself does not provide. Influences before the age of five account for about 50% of all the factors related to intellectual development; stimulation through daycare can enhance this stage of development [14].

Supporters argue for readily available daycare for purposes well beyond prevention of maltreatment. Daycare is viewed as a positive social intervention. In Sweden, it is not seen as a supplemental resource to child welfare, whose desirability and necessity can be debated. Rather, it is part of a broader social policy. The presence of daycare is universal and "normalized" as much as banks, hospitals, or fire departments. It becomes a social force, not just a service, and contributes to minimizing class differences [26].

This position has also been voiced in Canada. Supporters argue that daycare must be seen as part of a social service system which is as ". . . inescapable for a healthy society as is spending on police and fire protection . . ." [17]. A shift towards viewing daycare as a right and as a public responsibility may be possible.

## E.     Community Work Practices

Daycare services have tended to develop separately from, rather than in tandem with, child welfare services [7]. This point raises questions about what constitutes a need. Child welfare agencies base their mandates upon the idea of "risk". Historical separation of agency and daycare has been grounded in the idea that daycare does not help to avoid risk, but rather, is a "luxury" service to parents and children.

Daycare services are not the result of community work. Rather, community work changes or creates broader structural conditions by which specific daycare programming is possible. For example:

> Community planning might incorporate an educational component designed to change attitudes about daycare.

> Social action efforts might lead to increased government funding for daycare.

> Locality development might help a neighbourhood voice its preference about standards for licensed family daycare.

Below are descriptions of some practices that have been tried. They represent a limited sample of community-oriented approaches.

There have been attempts to bridge institutional and family daycare by bolstering the weakness of the latter through various supervision and training programs.

One model is the "satellite approach," in which a daycare centre supervises several family daycare homes in a neighbourhood. There are advantages to this:

> A family's children can be placed in several locations, depending upon age or other factors.

> Staff become familiar with all children, thereby improving continuity of service.

> The centre is a regular base for in-service training.

> Supervision of family daycare homes is facilitated [9].

Supervision with this approach is somewhat limited because the supervisor is not always there. Her or his role is more than supervisory; it includes recruiting, interviewing, and other non-program responsibilities [9].

Another variation, the "council model", has less of a geographical focus than the "satellite model". In Toronto an agency recruits, screens, and trains mothers interested in running a family daycare setting. The agency itself is not a daycare centre, and the family daycare centres can be located anywhere. The system supplies operators with on-going advice, equipment, and guaranteed pay in the event of absenteeism or withdrawal of children [22].

Daycare tends to be associated with the child's home territory. Depending upon daily routines, this need not be the case. For instance, it can be based near or in the workplace [9, 28].

A recent study in Toronto recommends that:

"Housing developers be encouraged to provide daycare space in new and renovated buildings".

Municipal zoning laws should not impede the implementation of daycare centres in industrial or commercial areas [7].

Some drawbacks to daycare at the work-place have been indicated as well:

Parents may share taking children to daycare, so that proximity to home may be preferred.

Parents do not like taking children on the transit system during rush hours or poor weather.

It takes the child out of the community, something particularly relevant to *older* children [28].

This brief review indicates both the technical complexity and potential for community-based child welfare practice in the area of daycare resources. Most of the practice interventions described represent network, neighbourhood, or municipal layers of child welfare ecology.

## VI.    SUMMARY

This chapter has presented some practical theory about the nature of communities and their capacity for child protection and development.

An ecological view was proposed which describes child maltreatment as a product of interacting environmental factors ranging from individual to cultural, economic, and ideological ones. The nature of available resources contributes to, or prevents, child maltreatment. Current theory about the affordability, accessibility, sufficiency, and appropriateness of such resources provides explanations as to why certain community characteristics make possible child maltreatment. Community work attempts to change the more fundamental "necessary" conditions related to maltreatment, drawing on a community's strengths rather than its weaknesses.

Because daycare has a decidedly preventive, health-promoting side, it is amenable to community work approaches. By working with the close-to-home issues it allows people to develop their own social power. What were largely local, practical, short-term concerns or needs may lead to a politicizing process. A parent's growing awareness of the "politics" of her or his daycare experiences is a step towards broader societal concerns. With this there is the discovery of more fundamental solutions to the provision of child development resources.

## REFERENCES AND BIBLIOGRAPHY

### General

1.  Albee, G. "Politics, Power, Prevention, and Social Change", Presented at the Vermont Conference on the Primary Prevention of Psychopathology, June 1979.

2.  Bott, E. *Family and Social Network: Roles, Norms, and External Relationships in Ordinary Families.* London: Tavistock Publications, 1957.

3.  Brim, O., Jr. "Macro-Structural Influences on Child Development and The Need for Childhood Social Indicators." American Journal of Orthopsychiatry, Vol 45. July 1975, pp. 516–524.

4.  Canadian Council on Social Development. "The One-Parent Family", 1981 (Summary in Canadian Welfare, June 1982).

5.  Caplan, G. *Support Systems and Community Mental Health.* New York: Behavioral Publications, 1974.

6.  Caplan, C. and Grunebaum, H. "Perspective on Primary Prevention: A Review", Archives of General Psychiatry, Vol. 17, 1967.

7.  Carota, M. *The Citizen Group Movement Among the Low Income Citizens of Urban Canada.* Canadian Association of Neighborhood Services, February 1970.

8.  Cochran, M. and Brassard, I. "Child Development and Personal Social Networks", Child Development, Vol. 50. Sept./Dec., 1979, pp. 601–616.

9.  Croog, S. et al. "Help Patterns in Severe Illness: The Roles of Kin Network, Non-Family Resources, and Institutions," Journal of Marriage and the Family, Vol. 34, February 1972, pp. 32–41.

10. Garbarino, J. "A Preliminary Study of Some Ecological Correlates of Child Abuse: The Impact of Socioeconomic Stress on Mothers", Child Development, Vol. 47, March 1976, pp. 178–185.

11. ——— and Crouter, A. "Defining the Community Context For Parent Child Relations: The Correlates of Child Maltreatment", Child Development, Vol. 49, September 1978, pp. 604–616.

12. ———. "Preventing Child Maltreatment", in Price, Richard H., Ketterer, Richard F., Bader, Barbara C., and Monahan, John (eds.), *Prevention in Mental Health—Research, Policy, and Practice*, Sage Annual Reviews of Community Mental Health, Vol. 1. Beverly Hills, California: Sage Publications, 1980, pp. 63–79.

13. ——— and Stocking, S. H. (eds.). *Protecting Children from Abuse and Neglect.* San Francisco: Jossey-Bass Publishers, 1981.

14. ——— and Sherman, D. "Identifying High Risk Neighborhoods", in Garbarino, J. and Stocking, S. H. (eds.), 1981.

15. Garber, M. "Neighborhood-Based Child Welfare", Child Welfare, Vol. LIV, February 1975, pp. 73–81.

16. Gottlieb, B. "The Role of Individual and Social Support in Preventing Child Maltreatment", in Garbarino, J. and Stocking, S. H. (eds.), 1981.

17. Gourash, N. "Help-seeking: A Review of the Literature", American Journal of Community Psychology, Vol. 6, October 1978, pp. 413–423.

18. Greenberg, M. "A Concept of Community", Social Work, Vol. 19, January 1974, pp. 64–72.

19. Holland, T. "The Community: Organism or Arena?" Social Work, Vol. 19, January 1974, pp. 73–80.

20. Jonassen, C. "Community Typology", in Sussman, Marvin B. (ed.), *Community Structure and Analysis.* New York: Thomas Y. Crowell Co., 1959.

21. Leitenberger, M. et al. "Community Worker and Agency Involvement in Neighbourhood Services— The Future (A Model for Discussion)", Community Work Unit, Children's Aid Society of Metropolitan Toronto, August 1981, Unpublished.

22. Meenaghan, T. "Clues to Community Power Structures", Social Work, Vol. 21, March 1976, pp. 126–132.

23. Mitchell, J. C. "The Concept and Use of Social Networks", in Mitchell, J. C. (ed.), *Social Networks in Urban Situations.* Manchester, England: Manchester University Press, 1969.

24. Polansky, N. et al. "Isolation of The Neglectful Family", American Journal of Orthopsychiatry, Vol. 49, January 1979, pp. 149–152.

25. Quarentelli, E. L. "A Note on The Protective Function of Families in Disasters", Journal of Marriage and Family Living, Vol. 22, 1960, pp. 263–264.

26. Rosenblatt, A. and Mayer, J. E. "Help Seeking For Family Problems: A Survey of Utilization and Satisfaction." American Journal of Psychiatry, Vol. 128, March 1972, pp. 126–130.

27. Rothman, J. "An Analysis of Goals and Roles in Community Organization Practice", Social Work, Vol. 9, April 1964, pp. 24–31.

28. Sanders, E. *The Community: An Introduction to a Social System* (2nd ed.), New York: Ronald Press, 1966.

29. Teitjen, A. "Integrating Formal and Informal Support Systems: The Swedish Experience", in Garbarino, J. and Stocking, S. H. (eds.), 1981.

30. Wagenfeld, M. O. "The Primary Prevention of Mental Illness: A Sociological Perspective", Journal of Health and Social Behaviour, Vol. 13, June 1972, pp. 195–203.

31. Warren, D. "Support Systems in Different Types of Neighbourhoods", In Garbarino, James, and Stocking, S. H. (eds.), 1981.

32. Warren R. *The Community in America*. Chicago: Rand McNally and Co., 1963.

33. ———. *Types of Purposive Social Change at the Community Level*, Brandeis University Papers in Social Welfare, No. 11. Waltham, Mass.: Brandeis University Press, 1965.

34. Wharf, B. "CAS—Community Action or Community Planning?" Ontario Association of Children's Aid Societies Journal, Vol. 15, September 1972, pp. 1–6.

35. Wharf, B. (ed.) *Community Work in Canada*, Toronto: McClelland and Stewart, 1979.

36. Wirth, L. "Urbanism as a Way of Life", American Journal of Sociology, Vol. XLIV, July 1938, pp. 1–24.

## Day Care

1. Action Day Care Organization. "Day Care Crisis—Fight for the Direct Grant and More Spaces Now!", pamphlet, Toronto: undated.

2. ———. "Action Day Care Newsletter," April 1982.

3. ———. "Action Day Care Newsletter," June 1982.

4. ———. "Day Care in Canada: Towards a Universally-Accessible System," Policy paper prepared for discussion at the National Day Care Conference, September 23–25, 1982, Winnipeg, Manitoba.

5. Adams, D. "Among Society's Neglected–the Working Mother." Canadian Welfare, Vol. 46, July/August 1970, pp. 18–19.

6. Brillinger, B. and Adams, D. "Day Care: Guidelines for Action". Kitchener-Waterloo Social Planning Council, December 1968 (unpublished).

7. City of Toronto. "A Strategy for the Promotion of Work-Related Daycare in Metropolitan Toronto". City of Toronto-Community Services Department, June 1982 (unpublished).

8. Clifford, H. *Let's Talk Day Care*. Edmonton—Canadian Mental Health Association, 1972.

9. ———"Family Day Care: A fast growing resource". Canadian Welfare, Vol. 5, September/October, 1974, pp. 7–9.

10. Department of Health, Education, and Welfare. "Basic Tabulation", Office of Child Development, National Child Care Consumer Study, Washington, D.C., 1975.

11. Epstein, J. "Day Care: A Research Report to the Community Day Care Study Commission". Institute of Urban Studies. University of Winnipeg, 1979.

12. Fowler, W. and Khan, N., "Day Care and Its Effects on Early Development—A Study of Group and Home Care in Multi-Ethnic, Working-Class Families". Toronto: The Ontario Institute for Studies in Education. Research in Education Series, No. 8, 1978.

13. Greenblatt, B. *Responsibility for Child Care*. San Francisco: Jossey-Bass, Inc., 1977.

14. Health and Welfare Canada, National Day Care Information Centre, Canada Assistance Plan Directorate. "Canadian Day Care Survey: A Review of the Major Findings". Ottawa: 1972.

15. Health and Welfare Canada, National Day Care Information Centre, Social Service Programmes Branch. "Status of Day Care in Canada—A Review of Major Findings of the National Day Care Study". Ottawa: 1979.

16. Health and Welfare Canada, National Day Care Information Centre, Social Services Programmes Branch "Status of Day Care in Canada—A Review of Major Findings of the National Day Care Study". 1979.

17. Hepworth, P. "600,000 Children: Report of a Survey of Day Care Needs in Canada". Canadian Welfare, November/December, 1974.

18. Lightman, E. and Johnson, L. "Child Care Patterns in Metropolitan Toronto", "Project Child Care Working Paper No. 2". Toronto: Social Planning Council of Toronto, July 1977.

19. Oettinger, K. "A Spectrum of Services for Children". Spotlight on Day Care. Washington, D.C.: U.S. Department of Health, Education, and Welfare, Children's Bureau, 1965.

20. Ontario Coalition for Better Day Care Newletter. Toronto: May 1982.

21. ———. "Day Care: Deadline 1990, Brief to the Government of the Province of Ontario", no date.

22. The Toronto Globe and Mail, "Parents Prefer Day Care in a Home", June 24, 1982.

23. Rhodes, S. "Trends in Child Development Research Important to Day-Care Policy". Social Service Review, Vol. 53, June 1979, pp. 285–294.

24. Siegel, A. and Haas, M. "The Working Mother: A Review of Research". Child Development., Vol. 34., 1963, pp. 513–542.

25. Silverstein, L. "A Critical Review of Current Research on Infant Daycare". November 1977 (unpublished, no source).

26. Wahab, Z. "Infant and Early Childhood Education and Socialization." Sweden. ERIC reports. Report number E D 128 093, PS 008 786. U.S. Department of Health, Education, and Welfare, National Institute for Education, Educational Resources Information Center. Washington, D.C., 1976.

27. The Toronto Globe and Mail, "What Things to Ask Before Putting Child in Day Care Setting", June 28, 1982.

28. "Workplace daycare conflict simmers". Now—News and Entertainment Newspaper. Toronto. Vol. 1, No. 39, June 10–16, 1982.

29. Johnson, L. and Dineen, I. *The Kin Trader: The Day Care Crisis in Canada*. Toronto: McGraw-Hill Ryerson Ltd., 1981.

30. Ross, K. (ed). *Good Daycare: Fighting for It, Getting It, Keeping It*. Toronto: The Women's Press, 1978.

# 4

# Working with Neglecting Families: Dynamics and Practice

**FRANK MAIDMAN**

THE CAUSES AND CONSEQUENCES OF CHILD NEGLECT 90
I. INTRODUCTION 90
II. THE MEANING OF CHILD NEGLECT 91
  A. An Operational Definition of Neglect 92
  B. Characteristics of Neglected Children 94
III. WHY PARENTS NEGLECT: GENERAL THEORETICAL APPROACHES 94
  A. Socio-Economic and Cultural Approach 95
  B. Family System Approach 95
  C. Interactional Approach 95
  D. Individual Psychological Approach 96
  E. Ecological Approach 96
IV. DYNAMICS OF CHILD NEGLECT 96
  A. Socio-Economic and Cultural Factors 97
  B. Neighbourhood Characteristics and Neglect 98
  C. Family Characteristics and Child Neglect 98
  D. Family Interaction and Child Neglect 102
V. THE BACKGROUNDS AND PERSONALITIES OF NEGLECTFUL PARENTS 104
  A. Personality and Inadequacy 104
  B. Parental Identity Needs and Neglect 105
  C. Background Factors 107
VI. CONSEQUENCES OF CHILD NEGLECT 108
  A. Neurological and Physical Consequences 108
  B. Emotional Consequences 109
  C. Cognitive Consequences 109
  D. Behavioural Consequences 110
  E. Summary 110
PRACTICE GUIDELINES 111
I. INTRODUCTION 111

II. INTERVIEWING THE NON-VERBAL CLIENT ................................ 112
   A. Assessing Verbal Accessibility ................................ 112
   B. Enhancing Verbal Accessibility ................................ 113
   C. Improving Family Problem-Solving ................................ 113
III. TEACHING PARENTING SKILLS IN THE HOME ................................ 114
   A. Establishing a Relationship with Parents ................................ 115
   B. Worker as Consultant ................................ 116
   C. Placing Children's Behaviour in Context ................................ 117
   D. Worker Behaviour with the Child ................................ 118
   E. Limit-Setting by Parents ................................ 118
   F. Alternative Parent Resources ................................ 119
IV. DESIGNING PARENT EDUCATION GROUPS ................................ 119
   A. Goals ................................ 120
   B. Settings ................................ 120
   C. Content ................................ 121
   D. Roles ................................ 121
   E. Methods and Materials ................................ 122
   F. Packaged Courses ................................ 122
V. TEACHING SKILLS FOR COPING AND INDEPENDENCE ................................ 123
VI. WORKING WITH HIGH-RISK PARENTS ................................ 125
   A. Premises and Goals ................................ 125
   B. Assessment of High-Risk Situations ................................ 126
   C. Parent Education Groups for High-Risk Parents ................................ 127
   D. Family Advocacy: The Use of Non-professional Aides ................................ 128
   E. Mother-Child Groups ................................ 128
   F. Individual Counselling ................................ 130
VII. WORKING WITH UNMODIFIABLE FAMILIES ................................ 130
VIII. SUMMARY ................................ 131
   A. The Causes and Consequences of Child Neglect ................................ 131
   B. Practice Guidelines ................................ 132
   REFERENCES ................................ 133

**Part 1    The Causes and Consequences of Child Neglect**

## I.    INTRODUCTION

Many child welfare cases involve child neglect as a core component of the family's problem. This chapter examines child neglect as a socially unacceptable form of parent-child relations. First, the meaning and types of neglect are reviewed, along with the societal, family, and individual factors associated with the phenomenon. Next, the chapter follows with an examination of known or suspected consequences of neglect. Finally, treatment approaches are reviewed.

## II.    THE MEANING OF CHILD NEGLECT

Child neglect refers to inappropriate parent-child relations or family conditions affecting the child's health, safety, and development of competence. Such relationships, whether planned or unplanned, controllable or not, are viewed scientifically and morally as unacceptable.

An ideal definition of child neglect should be sufficiently detailed and linked to observable events that child neglect is easily recognizable. For many reasons, existing knowledge of neglect does not permit this [7, 14]. Polansky offers the following working definition (14):

> Child neglect may be defined as a condition in which a caretaker responsible for the child either deliberately or by extraordinary inattentiveness permits the child to experience avoidable present suffering and/or fails to provide the ingredients generally deemed essential for developing a person's physical, intellectual and emotional capacities [14].

The State's involvement in child protection has produced numerous attempts at legally sound definitions. For example, the Province of Ontario's statute identifies the following neglectful conditions [1]:

desertion

inability to care for child for whatever reason, or absence of suitable person to care for child

child living in unfit or improper place

child found associating with unfit or improper person

child begging or receiving charity in public place

those in charge are unable to control child

child habitually absent from school

neglect or refusal to provide or obtain proper medical care or treatment for child's health or well-being

emotional rejection or deprivation of affection leading to the endangerment of the child's emotional or mental development

conduct of care-giver that endangers the child's health, life, or morals

Most available definitions of child neglect are somewhat vague. Because of the current state of knowledge, operational procedures are undeveloped. However, Polansky's research in Appalachia and Philadelphia has produced a tool in "The Childhood Level of Living Scale" for assessing the quality of child care, one which has increasingly been used in research and assessment [13]. An examination of the information gathered using this tool provides one example of how general definitions of child neglect have been operationalized.

## A.    An Operational Definition of Neglect

Child neglect refers to a set of family conditions which are assumed to be detrimental to the child's health, safety, physical, and psycho-social development. Rightly or wrongly, it is usually assumed that parents or care-givers have some control over these conditions. They are usually described in terms of their effect on the physical and cognitive/emotional care of the child.

### 1.    Physical Care

*Abandonment:* Children are abandoned totally or for long periods of time.

*Lack of supervision:* Children are inadequately supervised for long periods of time or are engaged in dangerous activities; children are left in the care of other children too young to protect them.

*Lack of adequate clothing and good hygiene:* Children are dressed inadequately for the weather or suffer persistent illnesses (pneumonia, frostbite, or sunburn) associated with excessive exposure; children have severe diaper rash or other persistent skin disorders resulting from improper hygiene; children are chronically dirty or unbathed.

*Lack of medical or dental care:* Children's needs for medical or dental care or medication and health aids are unmet.

*Lack of adequate education:* Children are chronically absent from school.

*Lack of adequate nutrition:* Children are lacking sufficient quantity or quality of food; children consistently complain of hunger or rummage for food; children suffer severe developmental lags.

*Lack of adequate shelter:* structurally unsafe housing or exposed wiring; inadequate heating; unsatisfactory housing conditions.

In all of the above elements of neglect, it is important to be sensitive to

issues of poverty versus neglect

differing cultural expectations and values

differing child-rearing practices

### 2.    Emotional/Cognitive Care

These dimensions of child care pertain to family conditions which are assumed to affect the child's cognitive and emotional development. One concept which cuts across cognitive and emotional dimensions, and suggests criteria for all cultural groups, is the development of competence. It is defined as the ability to interact in a variety of social contexts. In the case of children, a low level of age-appropriate behaviour hampers development of competence. In a recent book on maltreatment, competence is analyzed in terms of the following abilities [7]:

*Communication skills:* the ability to receive and transmit messages verbally and with gestures; empathy

*Patience:* being able to delay one's response in a socially effective way

*Moderate goal setting:* being able to recognize and commit oneself to realistic challenges

*Ego development* (self-esteem): feeling basically confident and secure about one's ability to handle day-to-day challenges

These abilities seem somewhat limited, and should be taken as a tentative framework only. For example, future work may incorporate notions of moral development.

The following categories of activities are currently being studied by researchers:

the scope of experiences provided for the child

exposure to different events

T.V. watching

the existence and nature of parent educational roles vis-à-vis the child

the provision of materials necessary for child development

parental empathy for child's physical and emotional needs

the provision of opportunities for moral development (e.g., religion)

parent modelling of appropriate and inappropriate behaviour

sanctions of the child's behaviour—rewards and punishment:

consistency

types of rewards and punishments

immediacy

nature of children's family roles:

compatibility with child's development

sex role appropriateness

family norms (rules)

parent-child attachment:

bonding

responsiveness

receiving and giving affection

encouragement of questions and choice-making (independence)

teaching respect for:

adults

others' and own property

## B.    Characteristics of Neglected Children

Because of inadequate income conditions, neglected children are likely to show several of the following [5]:

*Evidence of inadequate home management:* unclean; unkempt; dirty and torn clothes; often unbathed; obvious need of medical attention for such correctable conditions as poor eyesight, dental care, and immunization

*Hunger:* have neither food nor money for lunch; some taking of lunch money or food of other children and hoarding whatever they obtain

*Signs of malnutrition:* pallor; low weight relative to height; lack of body tone; fatigue, inability to participate in physical activities; lack of normal strength and endurance

*Irregular school attendance:* absence from school without reason or parental consent

*Irritability:* unusual annoyance, impatience, or anger

*General repressed personality:* inattentiveness and withdrawal

*Wild acting-out behaviour:* particularly when inadequately supervised at home

*Troublesome or unusual behaviour:* hyper-aggressive, disruptive, and demanding, or withdrawn and passive

For another sample of an instrument for assessing child neglect and abuse, see Appendix B.

## III.    WHY PARENTS NEGLECT: GENERAL THEORETICAL APPROACHES

In this section, a selective summary of factors believed to be associated with child neglect is presented. Unfortunately, most studies of neglect have not pinpointed the specific elements which were identified here. We cannot say, therefore, that "x types of parents or families do *not* expose their children to a wide variety of experiences".

Five broad theoretical approaches have been used to explain child neglect: socio-economic and cultural, family systems, interactional, psychological (individual), and ecological. A brief definition of each approach follows.

### A. Socio-Economic and Cultural Approach

This approach to child neglect examines those conditions in society, or parts of society (e.g., the neighbourhood), which may be conducive to neglect. Examples include socio-economic inequalities, unemployment, inadequate housing, lack of dissemination of information, lack of neighbourhood cohesion, and so on. Also included are culturally-based beliefs and values possibly affecting childrearing, family life, and support-seeking (e.g., the norm of family privacy). The reasons why such conditions bring about child neglect are reviewed below.

Social, economic, and cultural characteristics of whole societies or sections of societies cannot explain individual cases of neglect, since not all people exposed to such conditions actually neglect their children. They are public issues which explain different rates of neglect. Explanations of individual cases require an examination of characteristics of families and individuals.

### B. Family System Approach

A family system perspective examines the relationships between family characteristics and parental maltreatment. Such an approach might concentrate on the family's relationship and its environment (e.g., limited income, isolation from neighbours, kin) or internal characteristics, such as family size, lack of learning materials, strained marital relations, and so on. Another focus on this approach concerns individuals' memberships in non-family roles (e.g., work, school) and how changes (e.g., unemployment) or demands in these roles might impinge on child rearing (e.g., stress). Although a number of different assumptions prevail in family systems models, one important principle stands out: family patterns, such as child maltreatment, should be viewed in their interdependence with a multiplicity of other family patterns (e.g., marital instability, sibling rivalry, strained kinship relations). Consequently, efforts to change undesirable patterns typically meet the resistance of other enduring conditions. Also, changes may have reverberating effects on other areas of family life. For other concepts for understanding family systems and problems, see Chapter 2, IV.

### C. Interactional Approach

Like proponents of the family systems approach, interactionists view child neglect as a type of relationship, typically a parent-child relationship. However, unlike the family systems approach, the family context of this interaction (e.g., sibling relationships, stage of family life-cycle) is usually ignored in favour of dyad analysis only (i.e., two persons). The neglecting parenting interaction (e.g., rejection of child) is usually explained in terms of individual characteristics (e.g., maternal infantilism) rather than as a manifestation of certain qualities of interaction.

## D.      Individual Psychological Approach

This approach, like others, generally assumes that child neglect occurs because of inadequate functioning in the parent role. The explanation is typically cast in terms of the parents' (usually the mother's) psychological makeup (e.g., low self-esteem), developmental failures (e.g., infantilism), skills and knowledge (childrearing), or energy level. These, in turn, are frequently associated with previous experiences in the parents' own families (e.g., rejection). Polansky explains the "intergenerational cycle of neglect" (i.e., repeated patterns of child neglect over subsequent generations) as a recurring developmental pattern of "infantilism" passed on from generation to generation [13].

## E.      Ecological Approach

A frequent problem in the foregoing approaches is that personality or family characteristics thought to be true of neglecting parents are also true of many non-neglecting parents. For example, many people who have been abused or neglected as children do not, in fact, maltreat their own children. The "ecological approach" seeks to avoid this limitation by specifying how different factors combine to increase the possibility of neglect. A typical question from this tradition might be: "Under what marital, community, and economic conditions does a person who has been neglected, neglect his or her own children?" Such an approach recognizes that negative background experiences may be neutralized by positive forces or strengths in one's current situation. Other than identifying multiple interacting factors affecting child maltreatment, the ecological approach also has a developmental perspective. The needs of children vary over the life cycle, as do the needs of families. Parents who have been unable to give and receive support, from within or outside their marriage, are not as likely to meet an infant's needs. For other discussions of the ecological approach, see Chapters 1 and 3, III.

## IV.     DYNAMICS OF CHILD NEGLECT

This section presents factors associated with neglect and the possible explanations of these observations. A mid-1970s review of the research on child neglect suggested that existing knowledge be taken as hypotheses rather than as confirmed findings. This comment holds true in the early 1980s.

It is unlikely that a given set of factors causes child neglect in a simple linear dynamic, as in the statements "unemployment causes child neglect" or "mothers who felt unwanted as children neglect their children". Rather, it is our best guess that the following principles of dynamics will eventually be accepted:

Patterns of child neglect will occur because of combined effects of many factors.

The same pattern of neglect may develop from different combinations of psychological, interactional, family group, and socio-cultural conditions.

Some factors may emerge as necessary conditions for the occurrence of neglect (e.g., inadequate knowledge and skills concerning child care); others will operate to increase the probability that neglect will happen. As these occur in the life of the parent they will have a certain funnelling effect, (i.e., as additional factors are "added" to the family's life—perhaps over their life-cycles—the risk of child neglect increases).

This perspective looks beyond the deficiencies in the parents and individuals. Increasingly, interaction with the family, which itself functions within broader social contexts, is the unit of concern. Analysis of the impact of individual characteristics (e.g., depression) should continue; however, these should be examined along with other factors, some of which neutralize or accelerate the net risk factor. Depression, when accompanied by an unsupportive marital relationship, an absence of community supports, and a lack of child care knowledge, may, in their combination, create high-risk conditions.

## A. Socio-Economic and Cultural Factors

It is assumed that child neglect is a more frequent occurrence among members of lower socio-economic strata. Socio-economic status, of course, is a global term summarizing a host of life events, including less access to income, formal schooling, life opportunities, power, and prestige. Sorting out which specific factors affect parenting, and through what processes, is difficult. To date, the following factors have been cited to explain the assumed relationship between socio-economic status and child neglect:

*Stress:* Conditions of low income generate unusual stress; this in turn, hampers adequate child care.

*Material deprivation:* Limited income and accompanying material conditions, such as housing inadequacy, make it objectively difficult to meet the community's standards for adequate parenting, and to take stress-alleviating actions.

*Cultural values, beliefs, and attitudes:* Poverty and social conditions faced by low socio-economic groups can create a set of subjective conditions (e.g., fatalism, alienation, hopelessness) which affect parenting and growth.

These points of view suggest that conditions in the social structure promote different child-neglect rates among social groups. Another viewpoint maintains that child-neglect differences among socio-economic strata *do not* in fact exist, but that they are identified and reported differently in various types of neighbourhoods. Economic inequalities in society also affect child care and maltreatment indirectly through the quality of neighbourhoods. (For information on how social class factors affect physical child abuse, see Chapter 5, IV.)

**B.        Neighbourhood Characteristics and Neglect**

The effects of neighbourhood characteristics on child neglect are receiving more and more attention. Generally, neighbourhoods are viewed as "ecological niches" which, through their level of support to families, either impede or enhance adaptation and growth. The assumption is that neighbourhood qualities may even counteract the personal deficiencies of parents. We are just beginning to learn about neighbourhood characteristics seemingly associated with child neglect [7, 8]. Also, the explanations of various observations are in an early stage of development. Thus far, neighbourhoods with higher rates of child maltreatment (child neglect and abuse) have:

more families who are struggling economically

fewer available support people for child care (as indicated by high residential mobility, a higher percentage of female-headed households, and a higher percentage of families with children over 18 and both parents working)

lower neighbourhood morale as reflected in higher percentages of people wanting to move, who are dissatisfied with the neighbourhood and housing, and who rate the neighbourhood as poor

higher proportion of families in crisis states

low value on having good neighbours and neighbourliness

It is assumed that these characteristics affect three major social processes relevant to child care and neglect:

*Social control:* Cases of maltreatment go undetected and unreported.

*Network support:* Those who are generally absent or who are themselves needy are unavailable for child care support (e.g., taking care of children; providing child care feedback, emotional support, and support during stressful times).

*Role modelling:* For child care.

See Chapter 3, IV for a more detailed discussion of the impact of neighbourhoods and other community characteristics on child maltreatment.

**C.        Family Characteristics and Child Neglect**

Research is slowly developing an image of family characteristics conducive to neglect. Most of these are known by experienced child welfare workers and have been the target of many interventions. Unfortunately, many explanations for the association between family patterns and child maltreatment are speculative. The following review categorizes family characteristics into three broad areas: family resources (material and human), family composition, and family interaction.

*1.     Family Resources*

The material conditions of the home seem clearly associated with child neglect, although it should be emphasized again that the vast majority of families in inadequate material circumstances do *not* neglect their children. Nevertheless, studies indicate that, compared with non-neglecting families, neglectful families have lower incomes, inadequate housing and crowded conditions, and fewer material possessions [9, 13, 21].

These conditions are assumed to promote child neglect through the creation of parental stress and feelings of futility, opportunities for hazards and unhealthy conditions, and insufficient income and materials for child care. However, consideration must be given to the human element which mediates the limited resource conditions and child caring. What, for example, affects decisions to use limited income for one thing or another? For this reason, assessment of material conditions must incorporate a concern for human interactions, skills, attitudes, and experiences.

A family's limited income has been frequently associated with child neglect. Studies concentrating on poor families have found that finer graduations in income correlate with neglect, leading to the speculation that child neglect seems to exist in the "poorest of poor" families [14].

*2.     Family Composition and Structure*

American studies searching for the cause of child neglect have made observations on family size, number of parents, and birth-spacing [9, 21]. On the basis of research and clinical wisdom, neglecting families, when compared with non-neglecting, are more likely to be fatherless, larger (i.e., more children), and closely birth-spaced. Such conditions are believed to increase the chance of neglect by increasing the mother's stress.

Father absence from neglecting families has been documented in only a few American studies. Rather mixed results have also been produced on its effects. For example, no studies have clearly documented that fatherless families experience more psychological problems than those with fathers.

A recent study of low-income Philadelphia families has advanced the thinking and has reduced stereotypes about the possible impact of fatherlessness on child neglect [13]. Here are the main findings:

> Families labelled neglecting were more likely to be fatherless.
>
> Although in general, father-present families have larger incomes, such differences were not associated with labelled child neglect.
>
> Fatherlessness was associated with less adequate physical child care (feeding, safety, health) in both labelled neglecting and non-neglecting families, but this was not due to income level.
>
> Fatherlessness had no effect on the level of psychological or emotional care in either neglecting or non-neglecting families; this is true on all dimensions of psychological care (e.g., discipline, empathy, attachment).
>
> Having a father present had a positive effect on household maintenance

in non-neglecting families only; a father's presence in the labelled neglecting families did not enhance the quality of house maintenance.

Some evidence suggested that a father's presence in neglecting families actually lowered the quality of health care provided.

Women in fatherless neglecting families were more active socially than those with fathers in the home; married women in non-neglecting families were most active socially.

Single mothers in non-neglecting families were more likely to be receiving child support.

Some negative results of this research are also worth noting:

Father presence did not enhance the overall level of family support, i.e., communication and help received from kin, friends, or professionals; this was true both for neglecting and non-neglecting families.

In both neglecting and non-neglecting families, father absence was associated with a heightened state of maternal feeling of personal alienation.

Father absence did not make a difference in such child-rearing attitudes as the importance of communication, closeness, and discipline (see next section for a further discussion of child-rearing attitudes and neglect).

### 3.    Isolation and Support

Researchers and child welfare practitioners speak with a common voice in identifying isolation from friends, family, and neighbourhood as a distinguishing characteristic of neglecting families. This observation is generally indicative of a weak support system for the family, specifically for parental functioning. What is a family support system?

The concepts of "support" and "support system" are both widely used by child welfare practitioners (see Garbarino and Stocking, 1980 [8] for an up-to-date review of important concepts and international research on support systems and child maltreatment). Support systems, whether individual or family, are usually defined in terms of links between a person/family and one or more people. Persons in the support system or network may be relatives, friends, or members of community organizations. The assessment of support systems may be useful in understanding the behaviour of people involved, including whole families. Most important for understanding their potential impact on child maltreatment are the following functions of support systems:

provision of information

provision of material support

provision of emotional support and aid in controlling impulses

enforcement of social norms, through observation of caregiving patterns, and instructive feedback upon violation of community norms provision of opportunities for stress-release through social recreation

      role-modelling for parents for appropriate parenting

It is not necessarily the existence of a support system in a person's or family's life that ensures these functions, but rather, the nature of the relationships among members.

Child welfare practitoners are well advised to assume that neglecting parents are socially isolated. However, there may be qualifications to this assumption; support systems function differently for different people. Consider the following findings:

      Generally, lower-income child-neglecting individuals and families when compared with non-neglectors, are more isolated from friends, relatives, and neighbours as sources of help [21, 13, 11, 4].

      Estrangement from kin may be the most negative factor, across all ethnic groups, in the breakdown of social support systems [9].

      Despite the foregoing generalization, there are noteworthy variations among ethnic groups. For example, among white and black low-income Americans, daily contact with kin differentiated neglecting and non-neglecting families; yet, this was not a significant factor among families with Latin backgrounds [9].

      Among black families, child care adequacy was more strongly affected by the exchange of mutual aid with kin, whereas among white families, recreational and other affective ties were more important [9].

Apart from support gained from relations with neighbours, friends, and kin, participation in formal community organizations also seems to distinguish neglecting and non-neglecting parents. Research has shown that [9, 13]:

      Non-neglecting parents are more likely to be involved with church and other community organizations.

      Neglecting mothers without partners are more likely to be involved only with the community.

      Finally, neglecting mothers and fathers are less likely to engage in informal socializing (i.e., "going out", going to bars), as is true, but not quite as pronounced, for neglecting fathers with partners. However, neglecting mothers and fathers without partners are more likely to socialize informally.

Why are neglecting parents socially isolated? Several speculations have been offered, most of which have been supported by research [13]. Such explanations touch upon the residential mobility patterns and personality characteristics of neglecting parents. In sum, neglecting parents:

      rarely live in the neighbourhoods of their childhood

      show high residential mobility

have strong attitudes of alienation

lack interpersonal skills for socializing

Neglecting parents, then, have not had the opportunities to develop community roots. Because of their generalized mistrust of others, plus their limited social skills, few social contacts have been developed.

One final comment on the subject of social isolation. In some cases, the actual number of contacts with others may not be as important as the experience of isolation in the dynamics of neglect. For this reason, it is important that the assessment process take into account clients' experiences and feelings about the quality of their relationships with others. For additional information on isolation, networks, and supports, see Chapters 1, II; 3, IV, and 5, IV.


## D.    Family Interaction and Child Neglect

Factors affecting child neglect may be found within the patterned interaction among family members, including parent-parent, parent-children, and sibling interaction. Interactional analysis includes an examination of the neglected child's contribution to the interaction. Close observation (as a supplement to clinical assessment, ratings, and questionnaires) has increased over the last decade, particularly in studies of family etiology of mental illness and deviant behaviour. Observation studies of child neglect and abuse are now emerging [3, 16].

Thus far, the following characteristics of family interaction have been studied:

1. *Types of responses exchanged between family members:* Physical (touching), verbal

2. *Emotional affect:* Neutral (content and expression are matter-of-fact); positive (verbal or physical liking, approval, or support of the recipient's actions, characteristics, or possessions); negative (statement or physical demonstration of dislike, disapproval, or lack of support of the recipient's actions, characteristics, or possessions)

3. *Distributions of these interactions among family members:* Who interacts, in what ways, with which family members?

patterns of control and compliance

prescriptive commands

proscriptive commands

compliance with prescriptive and proscriptive commands

refusal

no response

Preliminary, exploratory comparisons of neglecting, abusive, and normal families reveal that:

In terms of numbers of behaviours directed towards others in the family (regardless of type of interaction), parents in normal families interact most, abusive parents interact least, and neglecting parents are near the middle.

Neglecting parents are more negative in their interactions, i.e., they make more verbal or physical demonstrations of dislike, disapproval, or lack of support for others' actions, characteristics, or possessions.

Neglectful and abusive parents show the same low rates of compliance (i.e., adhering to others' expectations or demands) as compared with other parents.

Neglecting parents, as compared with non-neglecting families, demonstrate fewer positive or compliant behaviours towards their children.

Neglecting parents, compared with non-neglecting families, issue more commands to others in the family, and are twice as likely to behave in a negative fashion towards all others in the family; neglectful parents, of all three groups, are the least positive and most negative in their interactions.

Neglecting parents make more requests of their children, and are the least compliant with them.

Neglecting mothers, when their behaviour is analyzed separately, show the most extreme negative behaviour and are the least compliant.

Neglecting fathers have the lowest rates of positive and compliant behaviours towards others.

Children in neglecting families speak to their fathers less often, interact less positively with them, and initiate fewer physical contacts than do children in non-neglecting families.

If those observations of family interactions are replicated in later research, the following implications for practice should be considered:

Neglecting families, because of their high levels of negative interactions towards others in the family, create a more destructive climate for self-esteem and family problem-solving than do abusive families.

The limited, negative, and non-compliant interaction between fathers and children in neglecting families, argues strongly against a "mother only" intervention strategy.

For many interactions, the negativism usually associated with child emotional neglect is, in fact, an "interactional style" common to all relationships within the family.

Because these findings are based on family experiments in other than child-rearing tasks, it is likely that the negativism is an all-pervading quality of neglecting families; negativism in word and deed, accompanied by apparent non-compliance with others' requests, has serious psychological repercussions for self-esteem throughout the family; as well, family group problem-solving is hampered. Consequently, there may be serious limitations in focussing on childrearing interactions only, and/or individual personalities.

An adequate understanding of the distinctions among "normal", neglecting, and abusive family environments may benefit from collaborating individual, developmental, and environmental approaches. For example, individual and family characteristics may combine in different ways to form a continuum of caretaking causality [19]. At one extreme, very needy children (e.g., critically ill) may be born to highly adaptable families, the net result of which can be adequate development. Some families, on the other hand, have normal children but are so disorganized and chaotic themselves, that the risk to the child increases. Thus, no one factor predicts child neglect, but several in combination at different stages of individual and family life-cycles may be implicated.

For additional information on family interaction and child maltreatment, see Chapters 5, V; 6, IV; and 10, III, V.


## V.     THE BACKGROUNDS AND PERSONALITIES OF NEGLECTFUL PARENTS

Most researchers agree that parents who maltreat their children have themselves experienced a childhood history of abuse and neglect [2]. However, despite consensus, this research has been soundly criticized on methodological grounds. Self-reports of childhood experiences have been invalidated in both child maltreatment and general parenting studies. As well, caution must be taken in assuming that all previously neglected or abused persons themselves abuse their children. The ecological approach to child maltreatment offers perhaps the best approach to incorporating background experiences and parent personality characteristics in developing an understanding of child neglect. Quoting Belsky,

> . . . It is doubtful that a parent's experience as a child is sufficient, by itself, to account for the occurrence of abusive or neglectful behaviour as an adult. Most probably, parents' developmental histories play a role in the abuse and neglect process by predisposing them, as adults, to respond to certain situations . . . in aggressive (abusive) and insensitive (neglectful) ways. [2]

One positive explanation linking a multiplicity of personality, genetic, and situational factors with neglect is the stress accumulated with each factor [12, 17].

A second caveat about personality-oriented causal studies of maltreatment is that parent behaviour may have its root in current interactions, as well as or instead of, in psychological forces. A recent comparative study of normal, abusive, and neglectful families shows how parent behaviour is responsive to broad patterns and sequences of negative and withdrawing interactions [2].

After two cautionary notes about background experience and personality studies, inventories of current knowledge are presented in the following sections.


### A.     Personality and Inadequacy

Why do some parents not fulfill their parental role obligations? A frequent answer is that, due to their own developmental experiences, such parents do not have the requisite personality characteristics, (e.g., self-esteem and independence). To date, most research on this topic has focused on the mother, although recent research presents father characteristics [13].

Do neglecting parents have different child rearing attitudes and values? One explanation for apparent class variances in neglect rates is that values and attitudes differ, but American research on class differences in child rearing has provided very mixed results. On the issue of attitudes towards child neglect, recent American research on group differences tells us that:

Lay members of the community, when compared with professionals, do not make fine distinctions in the seriousness of certain child maltreatment behaviours.

Members of low-income groups generally view mistreatment as more serious than do those of high-income groups.

Better educated people give lower seriousness ratings to a variety of child mistreatment acts.

White members of society may be less critical of child neglect than Black or Hispanic groups [9].

Mothers of all classes show the same attitudes towards child care as do social work professionals.

Middle-class women place greater emphasis on psychological/emotional child care, whereas working-class mothers place more value on physical care [13].

There is no evidence to date that persons from low-income backgrounds hold child-rearing attitudes disposing them to neglect.

## B.      Parental Identity Needs and Neglect

A range of traits (e.g., low maternal self-esteem; poor sexual identity) may be associated with inadequate child care, and this is because of the child's meaning to the mother. Mothers with low self-esteem, for example, may view their children as critical judges of their caring abilities. Those with poor sexual identity seek validation of their identity through giving birth, but basically do not want the child as a person in her or his own right. Another perspective sees the child as symbolizing certain undesirable traits in the spouse. Finally, maternal loneliness may contribute to child neglect. In this instance, the young, dependent baby serves hypothetically as an "adult pacifier". With growth, however, the child ceases to have such meaning. In all such explanations, the birth of the child or the child itself serves to identify needs of the parent; the child's physical and emotional needs go unrecognized and unmet.

Other similarly psychodynamic approaches view mothers as conflict-ridden about their maternal role because as children they were forced to take care of their parents' children.

In a recently-completed research monograph [13], considerable information on parent personality and child neglect is provided. The following descriptions, conceptualized as ego functions, were found to significantly characterize neglecting low-income parents when compared with non-neglectors:

1. Apathy-futility, a global term, defines the following feelings and behaviours:

> pervasive conviction that nothing is worth doing
>
> emotional numbness
>
> interpersonal relationship typified by desperate clinging; superficiality, lack of pleasure; intense loneliness
>
> lack of competence in many areas of living, partially caused by unwillingness to risk failure in acquiring skills
>
> anger expressed passive-aggressively, and with hostile compliance
>
> non-commitment to positive stands
>
> interpersonal style which brings about the same feelings of futility in others

2. Verbal inaccessibility is a communication style characterized by:

> brief responses to questions
>
> non-verbalization of embarrassment
>
> lack of warmth when talking about or to children
>
> indirect statements of opinion

3. Impulsivity, defined as a failure to develop normal internal control systems, is typified by such characteristics as:

> inability to delay gratifications
>
> low tolerance for frustration or delay
>
> frequent absence of planning
>
> shortened time perspective
>
> poor judgement about consequences of action

4. Lack of workmanship connotes inability, and lack of desire, to become engrossed in tasks if steps involved are neither intrinsically nor immediately rewarding (e.g., child care, housekeeping, home chores, job).

5. Lack of capacity for object relations defines parents' inability to relate warmly and to give to a younger generation. It is indicated by:

> inability to offer supportive, nurturing relationships with reasonable consistency
>
> the breakdown of such a capacity under internal and external stress
>
> inability to separate others' needs from own needs

6. Personal alienation is manifested in not knowing whom to count on, and a belief that the average person's lot is worsening.

In Polansky's studies of low-income families the aforementioned character traits [13] distinguished between identified child neglecting parents (both mothers and fathers), and those identified as non-neglecting; and are associated with the quality of physical child care. Although mothers' character traits, in comparison with fathers', are more strongly associated with child care quality, fathers' capacity for object relations, social participation, and workmanship also affected child care quality.

In the previous section, several parental behaviours, feelings, and attitudes were listed—characteristics currently thought to distinguish parents who adequately care for their children from those who do not. Future research must ask the extent to which behaviours, feelings, and attitudes ultimately affect the parent-child interaction normally described under the rubric of child care or child neglect. No studies have been done which systematically make such connections. For additional information on this subject, see Chapters 5, III and 6, IV.

## C.    Background Factors

Characteristics of neglecting parents are believed to develop from either (1) their current socio-economic and family situations, and/or (2) their previous experiences, particularly events in their childhood families. In terms of background factors, neglecting parents often come from:

families where parents used excessive physical force in discipline

families which were broken, particularly when the current maternal parent was still very young; otherwise, a broken home is not a distinguishing background characteristic of neglecting parents

families in which the child felt unwanted

situations necessitating placement in homes or institutions other than natural families

families in which the mother was physically abused by the father

families in which the father was seen to use alcohol excessively

families which had other problems

Such background experiences may be assumed to affect current parenting by:

hampering the early acquisition of knowledge and skills necessary for adequate child rearing

weakening commitment to the parental role

impeding the maturity and identity formation of the parent

See also Chapter 5, III.

## VI.   CONSEQUENCES OF CHILD NEGLECT

Scientifically-based knowledge concerning the effects of child neglect is at an early stage. The challenge of obtaining definitive knowledge is great, since neglect takes so many forms and exists in such troubled family situations. Nevertheless, it is possible to summarize currently-presumed outcomes, even though findings are tentative. Information is presented for the following categories: neurological and physical consequences, emotional consequences, cognitive consequences, and behavioural consequences.

### A.   Neurological and Physical Consequences

Failure to provide adequate nourishment is one of the most serious forms of child neglect. Although malnutrition studies, case reports, and research all support an hypothesis concerning the links between neglect and neurological/physical deficiencies, no definite conclusions should be drawn.

From animal studies, it's known that:

Inadequate feeding of rats during pregnancy produces smaller pups with small brain size and deficiency in the number of brain cells; such deficiencies are difficult to overcome after birth.

The earlier the nutritional deficiency and the longer the duration, the greater the severity and permanency of consequences for the brain and the central nervous system [14].

From human studies, it is known that:

Malnutrition can cause up to 60% deficit in brain cells, abnormal head circumferences, and smaller intracranial volumes [14].

To what extent is child neglect associated with physical deficits in children? Generally, research has provided rather contradictory answers to this question, although methodological inconsistencies across studies may account for the confusion. Somewhat better designed studies yield interesting results:

British "disadvantaged" children, when compared with the "advantaged," suffered hearing loss, school absence due to physical and emotional reasons, and were below average in height.

Mothers of "failure to thrive" children, when compared with others, showed less verbal interaction and physical affection towards their children; such differences could not be explained by aspects of the mother's mental health, marital relationships, or childhood experiences [15].

Other studies have duplicated this rather interesting link between the emotional and cognitive aspects of child care and the child's nutritional status and physical growth. The "failure to thrive syndrome "(i.e., stunted growth, developmental retardation, and other evidences of malnutrition) has been identified as having no apparent organic basis. Baltimore studies of child care revealed that malnutrition is affected by emotional child care, quite independently of income, family expenditures for food, and caloric intake [10].

Just as nutritional status and physical development may be affected by emotional and cognitive care, the provision or deprivation of food is highly interrelated with the affective elements of parent-child interaction. Deprivation of food, for example, similarly deprives the child of closeness, sensitivity to needs, and empathic stimulation.

## B.       Emotional Consequences

Little is known about the emotional consequences of neglect. However, some indirect evidence comes from studies of children in institutions who had been deprived of maternal care and human stimulation. Such children were apathetic, listless, and displayed infantile depression and withdrawal. Studies in the home suggest an association between cuddling by whim, rather than baby's needs, and apathy, flatness, and withdrawal. Although suggestive, these studies have been criticized for not clearly ruling out other elements of care in the home, and for over-emphasizing maternal involvement at the expense of the father's contacts.

Supporting evidence for the possible effects of child neglect on the child's emotional functioning can be drawn from the many studies of family dysfunctioning and emotional disturbance [18]. For example, the association between marital disharmony and children's psychiatric disorders has been attributed to the displacement of anger and aggression onto the child, the child's assumption of adult responsibilities, and maladaptive role-modelling.

## C.       Cognitive Consequences

An enormous literature exists on child care, other home factors, and their relation to the child's intellectual development. Once again, the main challenge is to identify specific home and parenting factors: cultural deprivation, cognitive stimulation, nutrition, poverty, family interactional differences.

Differences in I.Q. scores between "normal" and maltreated children as reported by Polansky [13] show that:

> Although within the normal I.Q. range, neglected children score significantly lower than non-neglected.

> No I.Q. differences existed between abused and neglected children.

Quite apart from the labelled "neglect" and "normal" distinction, Polansky's Philadelphia study of low-income families drew interesting conclusions about the impact of child care quality on the child:

> Child I.Q. seemed affected by the quality of child care, particularly the cognitive/emotional aspects of care; I.Q. was also affected by income level,

maternal maturity, and maternal I.Q., but not general socio-economic position or paternal I.Q.

Maternal I.Q. and child care quality were shown independently to affect child's I.Q.; this supported other studies [13].

The question of whether the association between maternal and children's I.Q. reflects genetic or interactional/situational processes is a complicated one.

The child's "verbal accessibility" (see section entitled "Personality and Inadequacy" for definition) may also reflect cognitive development. These findings from Polansky's study are worth noting:

Neglected children had lower verbal accessibility than other children.

Whether or not children were labelled neglected, those experiencing lower-quality child care were more verbally inaccessible.

Verbal inaccessibility in children is affected more by the mother's verbal inaccessibility and apathy-futility than by the father's [13].

## D.      Behavioural Consequences

Evidence in both the U.S.A. and Europe suggests that neglected children may be more likely than non-neglected children to engage in behaviours socially defined as unacceptable or "anti-social". Other outcomes of early neglect point to delinquency and later alcoholism and psychiatric symptoms. An American longitudinal study of neglected children noted that at approximately 12–13 years of age, behaviour shifted from passive odd behaviour to aggressiveness and trouble with the law. Rutter's review of delinquency research shows that when family disharmony leads to troublesome behaviour in pre-adolescent children, later delinquency is more likely to occur. When troublesome children's behaviour did not occur, neither did delinquency [18]. This suggests that the dynamics linking family neglect factors and later delinquency are complex, and may require knowledge of community reactions to earlier behaviour.

## E.      Summary

Knowledge concerning later outcomes of child neglect is at a primitive stage. Longitudinal studies which isolate the parent-child relationship from other socializing influences are needed. In broad terms, evidence to date suggests that however abhorrent child neglect may seem, other situational or personal factors may either soften or increase the negative developmental implications of deviant child rearing. Empirical results from neglect and I.Q. studies are the best sources for this position.

For discussions of the consequences of physical and sexual abuse, see Chapters 5, VII and 6, VI, respectively.

**Part 2.   Practice Guidelines**


# I      INTRODUCTION


The relationship between a worker and a client is a potential source of client growth and problem reduction. This statement is supported by the following definition of "treatment" for child neglect:

> . . . Actions taken with the intention of bringing about a change in the caliber of child care, so it is no longer regarded as neglectful [14]

According to this definition, steps to establish a good client relationship, including the use of contact principles, would qualify as treatment. These topics are covered in Chapter 2.

Apart from good working relationships, a number of planned treatment approaches have been described in the child care and social work literature [14]. These are:

> social casework
>
> group work
>
> parent-child community programs
>
> daycare
>
> engineered communities

To these remedial approaches we may add the emerging preventive work with high-risk parents and children [22, 23, 24, 25, 26] and services to unmarried parents (see Chapter 12). This chapter concentrates on social casework and group work efforts; for critical summaries of other approaches, see Polansky [14].

Treatment goals may be summarized as addressing the following needs of neglecting parents:

> social contact
>
> child development knowledge and childrearing skills
>
> basic nurturance
>
> life-skills training
>
> problem-solving and crisis-resolution skills
>
> a sense of mastery over the environment
>
> validation as a worthwhile human being
>
> basic interpersonal skills
>
> basic material needs, such as housing and income

It bears repeating throughout this chapter that treatment goals can be achieved through a combination of *what* the worker provides and *how* the resource is provided.

## II.   INTERVIEWING THE NON-VERBAL CLIENT

Ideally, investigation or counselling relations proceed best when there is open communication between workers and clients. However, many neglecting parents seem either unable or unwilling to discuss problems. This means that child welfare work may proceed with workers doing much of the talking. In recent years an appropriate conversational style has been termed "verbal accessibility," defined specifically as

> . . . the readiness of the client to talk directly about . . . important attitudes
> and feelings, and to discuss them with the worker [27]

The worker's effort to enhance a client's verbal accessibility has been described as a strategy for engaging, as well as an actual treatment approach [27]. Improving verbal accessibility is usually considered a one-to-one approach, but has recently been described as a potential family treatment goal for neglectful and abusive families [28].

Although behaviours associated with verbal inaccessibility have been attributed to many causes, most attention has been directed to the client's psychological characteristics, particularly immaturity, neurosis, and low intelligence [27, 28]. In recent years, the effects of cultural imperatives and family group norms have been considered.

Improving client verbal accessibility is believed to promote positive effects:

> It helps the worker engage the client in problem-solving by facilitating diagnosis and promoting tension release and clarification.

> It promotes such psychological processes as anxiety discharge and conceptual thinking.

> It enhances family group problem-solving by opening up communications towards better understanding of problems and possible alternative solutions.

> It provides basic interpersonal skills which help to combat loneliness.

### A.   Assessing Verbal Accessibility

Assessment of verbal accessibility requires some measure of clients' willingness to talk meaningfully about feelings. A worker-applied protocol can use the following scale categories [27]:

spontaneous verbalization (6)

spontaneous with caseworker's explicit encouragement (5)

responsive; equal give-and-take with the caseworker (4)

receptive; little give, lots of take (3)

unresponsive; complete lack of response despite explicit encouragement (2)

avoidance or evasion of verbal expression (1)

As the client communicates in a style closer to the lower end of the scale, she or he is regarded by Polansky as less verbally accessible.

## B.    Enhancing Verbal Accessibility

To change the client's verbal style towards a more open expression of feelings and attitudes, Polansky recommends the following eight-step guideline [27]:

At the outset, encourage conversation on any topic, at any pace.

First topics should be concrete, external, and superficial.

Provide ego support to the client through improving her or his self-image.

Help the client to name her or his feelings.

Find any opportunity to have a conversation (e.g., while in the car).

Help client to deal with possible guilt from speaking out about problems, or against family members.

Encourage an atmosphere of open communication.

Be verbally accessible through active listening and modelling behaviour.

A non-verbal communicational style may be strongly entrenched in many clients' family life [4]. For this reason workers should be advised of the extensive period required for change in a counselling relationship, let alone in brief contacts. In some service programmes verbal stimuli and learning opportunities have been provided during "natural" situations, such as hair-dressing (see Chapter 5, XIII).

## C.    Improving Family Problem-Solving

Many neglectful families display problems other than dysfunctional parenting, and their internal crisis state and disorganization make them inadequate problem-solvers. Intervention methods designed to enhance group problem-solving processes are useful tools in child welfare work. Although basic research on family problem solving is relatively new [30], some recent service developments associated with verbal accessibility may prove useful.

A lack of openness about feelings, attitudes, and problems may reflect family group norms rather than individual personality functioning. The proponents of a family approach recognize the difficulty of changing long-standing family norms and interactional dynamics (possibly requiring a minimum of one year). However, assuming that such intervention will enhance group problem-solving, the following guidelines are recommended [28]:

The eight-step procedure outlined above constitutes the core of this approach; in addition:

Whole families should be encouraged to participate in concrete activities which increasingly give opportunities for talk (e.g., arts, crafts, games, household tasks, negotiating community services).

Talk is gradually encouraged as the major method for solving problems related to these activities.

Early imposition of limits and control may be necessary, with gradual relaxation of structure as problem-solving is improved.

Note experiences of success.

Avoid open competition and limit expectations of performance.

Consistently label actions verbally, and help family members do the same.

If deemed useful, audio recorders may be used to provide feedback on communications.

Activities may start out parallel, i.e., family members are in the same place, but are not doing things requiring co-operation and co-ordination; this is gradually changed.

With increasing openness, activities relying on more verbal skills may be introduced, including such learning activities as role-playing and family sculpting; talking as a problem-solving process is emphasized and supported by rules for communication and teaching multiple-level messages, formulation of alternatives, and partializing problems.

Home visits and a team orientation may improve the usefulness of this approach.

## III.   TEACHING PARENTING SKILLS IN THE HOME

Many neglectful parents are believed lacking in the skills and knowledge required for socially acceptable child rearing and social involvement. A successful contractual relationship could itself be an opportunity for developing interpersonal and analytical life skills. This section considers strategies for teaching parenting skills in the home.

Parenting skills have always been a function of learning. Each generation ensures human survival by transmitting past coping skills to meet the future. These may be inadequate in a dynamic and changing society and may need adaptations or major alterations.

The mental health movement has generated a great deal of divergent thinking on what constitutes effective parenting and how it can be achieved. Regardless of orientation, professionals share some common ideas concerning the best ways to transmit their ideas to parents. This section assumes that professionals will offer their knowledge to parents in the context of support, and parents are in the best position to influence their children.

## A.      Establishing a Relationship with Parents

It is assumed that parents experiencing a crisis want to reduce stress and are looking for ways of doing it. This creates a favourable climate in which the worker can offer alternate problem-solving approaches. She or he should not be surprised to find that once stabilization of the crisis state occurs, additional services may be resisted. What is important is the establishment of a responsive pattern in parents, so that when a crisis recurs they will call upon appropriate external resources. Once this pattern is established and tested they may be open to explore more pervasive areas that impair their functioning. The worker must approach parents according to parents' perceptions of need [40]. Often they cannot identify with their children's needs unless those are seen within the context of their own needs. It is necessary to respond to parents first as individuals and as adults in society. This has particular relevance to the worker who represents a child welfare agency, who by implication may be perceived by parents as concerned only with the child's interests. This is particularly important in cases that involve:

protection with respect to neglect and physical and sexual abuse

foster care or adoption supervision where threat of removal of the child is possible

multi-problem families who are involved with several specialized agencies at a time

a single-parent who assumes major responsibility and guilt for parental failure

parents whose child's anti-social conduct in the community has forced them to seek professional help

Parents in these circumstances may experience feelings of anger, depression, resentment, helplessness, and a general sense of frustration and failure. It is understandable that parents, while seeking help, may at the same time feel defensive and hyper-sensitive to the worker who perhaps is not completely responsive to their needs. Some clients may feel so inadequate as to abandon their parenting responsibilities to the worker, whom they view as more capable in managing their child than they can ever become. Consequently, the worker may find that she (he) has temporarily alleviated the crisis and has created a surrogate parental role for herself (himself), with the entire family dependent on her (him) for daily coping. Some parents may feel so inadequate when they compare themselves to a young, competent, energetic worker that they completely abandon their parental role.

Building a strong alliance with parents is important because:

Parents have been trying their best to help their children.

Parents will continue being with their children after the worker leaves.

Children view their parents as more important and significant than professionals.

Parents are more likely to implement suggestions from someone who is genuinely sensitive to them and is trying to help them rather than replace them.

Parents are their child's best therapists.

A number of techniques and principles developed in adult education may assist in strengthening parent-worker relationships [41]. They include reinforcing the following:

*Self-identity:* As individuals grow they develop needs to be perceived by others as self-directed; this reinforces self-esteem and self-identity. Parents should be approached as independent rather than dependent adults. The independent relationship between parent and worker can foster the alliance necessary for building good relationships.

*Parents' experience:* It is important to incorporate parents' wealth of experience into any intervention plan. Accepting their experience is accepting them as important.

*Parents' needs:* Any successful intervention plan addresses the needs of the user. Responding to these through a careful needs assessment can promote a readiness to learn and strengthen parent-worker relationships.

Additional guidelines for establishing relationships with particularly resistant families can be found in Chapter 2.

## B.     Worker as Consultant

Effective consultants learn to understand and use their clients' language, thinking, experience, and immediate needs. They frame their recommendations or suggestions in ways that allow parents to relate to them and understand how to implement them. Important considerations for evolving recommendations include exploring the following areas:

parental values about child care

areas of strength and success at managing their children

level of effective communication

expectations and needs of parents

needs of the child

Two examples of workers' comments illustrate typical problems confronting the worker, with suggested strategies for dealing with them:

1. overanxious, overprotective parents:
   "It's clear that you have exercised great care and concern for your child's welfare and have lost many a night's sleep worrying about him. This is a sign of parents who are working hard at taking their job seriously. Now that your son is entering school you will have to work a bit harder to prepare him to be more independent. At first he may resist doing things on his own and it will be difficult for everyone for awhile. We can work together to continue giving your child the best parenting you can offer."

2. physically abusive parents:
   "I am impressed by your level of concern, involvement, and sense of frustration in managing your child's behaviour, even to the point of losing control of yourselves. I'm sure you end up feeling depressed and punish yourself sometimes for not getting your child under control before you lash out. I would like to help you learn to discipline your child more effectively—that is, to work with you to find ways of disciplining your child to change his behaviour without you both feeling helpless and frustrated and having the school or police on your back. Let's look at things that are really seen as punitive by your child. How does he feel about losing T.V. privileges?"

Basic strategies employed in these examples use the parents' frame of reference. The worker fosters an alliance with them, meets their immediate need to gain control over their child, promotes the feeling that they are being supported, and suggests that they simply require additional resources to improve their parenting skills.

Parents are more likely to accept the worker's suggestions if they are presented in a non-judgemental, supportive way, that respects and fits their existing role perceptions. Once an alliance is formed and change occurs, parents may be more willing to explore sensitive assumptions about parenting.

## C.    Placing Children's Behaviour in Context

Most parents begin to learn about child development through observation of their first child or from other parents' wisdom. Stage-specific behaviours often do not have a context for first-time parents; children's sometimes atypical behaviours may lead parents to believe that they are incompetent. To counter this it may be necessary for the worker to act as follows:

Support parents for feeling concerned.

Explain appropriate levels of previous, present, and future developmental stages of their child and what parents can expect.

Place specific behaviours in their proper context (e.g., adolescents' need for autonomy, or acting-out behaviours in response to feelings).

Help parents learn to explore their child's feelings and behaviours.

Devise plans of action for future behaviours by preparing parents and others in the child's life with appropriate management strategies and responsibilities.

### D.    Worker Behaviour with the Child

The worker's involvement should help all family members function more effectively. Both the child and worker may harbor rescue fantasies which need to be carefully handled so as not to undermine the parental role. This problem can be minimized by utilizing the following suggestions:

Support parents openly in front of the child, and minimize the amount of direct involvement with the child particularly during observation, information-gathering, and modelling periods. If possible, have parents present at all times.

Be firm in the presence of the child and even exaggerate (prudently) instructions to parents on managing negative behaviours, so that the child will prefer to deal with parents instead of worker.

Suggest rewards for the child privately to parents, so as not to take credit for rewards that parents will deliver.

### E.    Limit-Setting by Parents

A common problem is effective limit-setting. Causes of ineffectiveness range from feelings of guilt, uncertainty, fear of loss of control, to parental lack of adequate exposure to limits as a child. The worker can support parental limit-setting by placing her or his own limits on the parents. Appropriate limit-setting provides parents with the same security, certainty, and structure as it does children. The worker must learn to feel comfortable in setting limits if she or he hopes to have them generalized to the child. Opportunities for limit-setting include:

meeting and ending at designated times

completing "homework" assignments

maintaining reasonable phone contacts during office hours

meeting only when both parents are available (in two-parent families).

contracting and recontracting for specific periods of time

## F.      Alternative Parent Resources

From the beginning, the worker should strive to minimize parental dependency by explicitly conveying the temporary nature of the worker-client relationship. Parents should be encouraged to participate in community activities; the broader and perhaps more relevant support system in the community will have a normalizing and more permanent impact on the family. Useful support systems include:

> parent education groups
> recreational clubs or interest groups
> community action/political groups
> community religious institutions
> family and extended family members
> volunteer groups
> parent-teacher association
> community library activities

## IV.      DESIGNING PARENT EDUCATION GROUPS

Parent education may be defined as a type of purposive learning activity by parents who are attempting to change their methods of interacting with their children, for the purpose of encouraging positive behaviour [32]. This is accomplished in a number of ways: the use of mass media, one-to-one counselling, parent groups, and home intervention. This section concentrates on parent education groups.

Parent education groups, whatever their content and format, usually are premised on some notion of the ideal parent. When designing parent education groups, workers should make their assumptions explicit. Examples of images of the ideal parent are [32]:

The parent is a rule follower with expert knowledge and opinions about child rearing, and training to follow it.

The loving and accepting parent follows expert advice, and unconditionally accepts the child.

The parent has knowledge of child development and is able to understand and interpret the child's behaviour in a way that leads to better parenting practices.

The parent understands the effect of parental behaviour on children and changes her or his behaviour to achieve the desired effect.

The problem-solving parent who analyzes a child rearing problem obtains necessary information, and then uses judgement and creativity in applying that information to the problem.

The home manager has the techniques and skills to make the home environment as pleasant and problem-free as possible.

The natural, confident parent is secure, comfortable, and relaxed about her or his own self, and has the ability to sense and do what is best for the child.

General guidelines are presented in the following categories: goals, settings, roles, content, and methods.

## A.     Goals

In formulating general goals of the parent group, it is useful to distinguish between *content goals* (i.e., which parenting knowledge and skills should be learned from the materials and experiences in the group?) and *process goals* (i.e., what personal changes can be achieved through the organization and processes of the group?).

Content goals for parent groups have been determined in many ways: large-scale surveys of parent educational needs, needs analysis of specific groups [36], clinical expertise, and research knowledge. If the neglectful parent group itself is specifying its own needs, then a group discussion may be more appropriate than self-administered questionnaires.

Because neglectful parents typically have needs other than learning parenting skills, the determination of process goals is also important. For example, research and clinical experience suggest that such parents are socially isolated, lack self-esteem, have poor verbal skills, and are alienated from society. The challenge in designing parent groups is to provide appropriate structure and growth-inducing opportunities. Examples of relevant goals, then, are:

> to provide opportunities for socializing
>
> to enhance group members' self-esteem
>
> to develop trust in agents of institutions
>
> to improve general life skills

Since there is a multiplicity of possible content and process goals, good planning requires identification of both primary and secondary goals.

## B.     Settings

Parent education groups have been held in numerous locations: public schools, agencies, daycare centres, homes, hospitals, and the like. In selecting appropriate settings it is important to remember that group members may have:

> limited resources for travel
>
> limited or negative experiences with community institutions
>
> needs for free and easy socializing

In general, both the task-related structure of the setting and its symbolic meaning for the participants, should be kept in mind.

## C.    Content

Depending on client needs, the content of parent education groups varies considerably. Although child growth, guidance, and discipline tend to dominate, other topics can be covered:

> how to provide for physical growth and health
>
> how to manage home and family life (food purchases and preparation, clothing care, organization of time)
>
> how to meet the child's social and emotional needs
>
> how to stimulate intellectual growth
>
> how to foster moral and cultural development, and socialization
>
> how to use community resources when additional help is needed

In planning for groups, consideration should be given to the following aspects of different family situations:

> atypical family forms (e.g., single-parent families; reconstituted families; communal living)
>
> child and family developmental stages
>
> family changes (e.g., mother employed full-time)
>
> family crisis

In general, parent education has been rather weak in considering the wider context of parenting. One way to redress this is through "back-home" preparation built into group content and methods. This can assume a problem-solving focus, as follows:

> Parents are asked to identify possible difficulties in putting into practice their new skills and knowledge (e.g., other parent won't cooperate); these are shared with the group, and the leader develops categories of possible problems as discussion is facilitated.
>
> Brain-storming occurs to develop ways and means of overcoming such problems.
>
> Feasible solutions are converted to specific behaviours, which are practised and discussed in a role-play format.

## D.    Roles

In parent training groups, parents play traditional student roles: discussing,

volunteering information, questioning, receiving information, and preparing assignments. To some extent, and with skilled guidance, the parent can act as a teacher of
others, by providing accounts of successful parenting. This is particularly important
for persons who have a general self-concept of worthlessness.

The worker as a teacher has a variety of roles. As an information provider,
she or he assures that the appropriate information is transmitted through the appropriate medium: modelling, encouraging discussion, showing films, giving short lectures. Group facilitation is important for drawing-out parents who have been socially
isolated, are not confident in their social skills, and feel guilty about their parenting.
At the same time, workers may retain other elements of their casework role: listening
for opportunities for individual assessment and referral. In general, workers should
provide rewarding experiences, both in terms of learning opportunities and social
participation. Given the passivity and alienation of many participants, opportunities
for influencing their own learning should be introduced. Finally, with appropriate
training and practice, volunteers may be useful resource persons in a number of
different ways.

### E.    Methods and Materials

Four basic types of group interaction methods can be identified: discussion
groups, study and discussion groups, workshops, and informal support groups [34].
In discussion groups, parents share knowledge, experiences, and problems in child-
rearing. The group leader helps the exploration of topics by adding information and
guiding discussion. Parents are expected to work through resolutions to problems and
to try out new solutions at home. One important consequence of such groups is that
parents learn that their feelings and problems related to parenting are commonly
experienced by others.

In study and discussion groups, another element is introduced. Each parent
studies a particular topic before the meeting and comes prepared for discussion. In
some cases, a list of study questions may be provided. Study material may be a T.V.
programme, cassette tape, book, pamphlet, or one's own child. This approach has a
"school-like" character, and may not appeal to those with previous negative experiences in school.

In workshops, there is a heavy emphasis on learning-by-doing. Creativity is
the order of the day, with opportunities for role-playing, community theatre, and
other special projects. Considerable spontaneous socializing is possible—a learning
atmosphere perhaps more appealing to tired people who are reluctant to talk.

Finally, informal support groups generally take the place of the extended
family, friends, and neighbours. The top requirement is a place to gather, perhaps
some simple refreshments, an informal class for new parents, or parent councils.
Ideally, through sharing frustrations, joys, and problems, parents can gain perspective on child rearing and receive a boost in confidence.

### F.    Packaged Courses

In recent years a number of packaged courses for developing parent skills and
knowledge have become available. Although these have been inventoried in the jour-

nal *Child Welfare* [35], the direct suitability for special-needs parents is not clear. Nevertheless, examples of such packaged programmes are:

> Systematic Training for Effective Parenting (S.T.E.P.)
>
> Communication and Parenting Skills (C.A.P.S.)
>
> Parent Effectiveness Training (P.E.T.)

These particular courses address such topics as promoting self-esteem, understanding, mutual respect, the use of reflective listening, encouragement, "I" messages, and family meetings to facilitate family interaction and communication. Other courses are:

> Practical Parenting
>
> Parent Growth Groups

For a brief synopsis of these packaged courses, and other resources for help in parenting, the *Child Welfare* article should be consulted.

## V.    TEACHING SKILLS FOR COPING AND INDEPENDENCE

One of the great dilemmas for child welfare workers is how to remove immediate environmental pressures from clients' lives without fostering dependency on the worker. Many neglectful parents live in situations of poverty, unemployment, inadequate housing, crisis, and general disorganization. Such factors are believed to promote child neglect by creating stress in clients' lives. Worker assistance in such cases is often described as environmental modification.

Environmental modification is a major approach used by social workers. Although definitions and emphases differ, three common elements have been identified [36]:

> reducing environmental pressure on clients by providing for such concrete needs as income, housing, food, and protection from violence
>
> modifying attitudes of significant people in clients' lives
>
> providing positive experiences for clients (e.g., friendship groups)

Through these intervention activities, work is accomplished on behalf of the client.

Although a given worker can implement environmental modification techniques in creative ways, client dependency may still be fostered. This happens because:

> Clients have learned to ask for or receive help from another party.
>
> Clients are passive recipients in the process.
>
> Clients have not developed certain necessary skills.

A supplementary approach to traditional environmental modification is one which reduces external pressures, but involves clients in working out problems to the full extent of their abilities. Because clients differ in their skills, knowledge, problem-solving ability, and psychological state, such an approach requires differing types and degrees of worker involvement. These are conveyed in the following discussion of worker strategies for four client types [36]:

1.      *Clients in emergency situations with low resources and/or disorganized thinking*

Clients in this category (e.g., a poverty-stricken mother whose husband has left her) are probably *least* able to fully involve themselves in problem-solving. The worker should be most active, but allow maximum opportunity for client learning. Specifically, the worker:

> works with the client to define immediate problems
>
> identifies possible avenues of action
>
> selects a strategy with as much help from the client as possible
>
> carries out the selected strategy
>
> later describes the action taken and how it relates to other problems in the client's life

The practitioner must be patient with a client's problem-solving attempts, and allow full expression of thoughts on how the problem should be handled.

2.      *Clients with limited information, problem-solving and social skills, but without a serious crisis*

In this case, the client is able to assume *more active* involvement. The worker should still be heavily involved in all phases of problem solving, but tries to encourage a more collaborative approach with the client. Specifically, the practitioner:

> works with the client to define needs and to develop possible courses of action
>
> develops with the client a joint decision concerning an action to be taken
>
> discusses with the client discrepancies in viewpoints, in order to insure a true consensus
>
> helps the client to develop a series of tasks and to determine mutual responsibility and completion; no task is done by the practitioner in cases where the client can take on the task with help
>
> encourages extensive discussion during development of strategy, thus incorporating the client's other experiences and problem-solving efforts

3       *Clients with adequate basic skills, but who are uncertain of their problem analysis and are hesitant to implement a plan of action*

Although the practitioner may do a better intervention job than the client, for learning purposes the latter assumes most of the responsibility. The worker should be primarily a consultant who:

gives information and direction in analyzing alternatives

gives reassurance and support while the client completes the tasks

*4.    Competent clients who lack information*

This type of client assumes maximum responsibility for changing her or his own environmental conditions. The practitioner:

supplies information

encourages the client to decide upon a reasonable course of action and implementation plan

The foregoing categories of client resourcefulness and practitioner response represent points along a continuum. The worker should choose where to begin with particular clients and help them to move along the continuum towards greater problem-solving abilities and independence.

## VI.    WORKING WITH HIGH-RISK PARENTS

In the realm of prevention, interventions are being developed to head off the possibility of child neglect or abuse. High-risk casework has the general goal of improving parental functioning, but change efforts differ in their premises about high-risk behaviour. Also, treatment programmes differ in their approaches and staff resources.

### A.    Premises and Goals

Despite variation in emphasis, the basic premise of high-risk service is that, given certain negative social, psychological, and health conditions in the lives of parents and children, there is a high likelihood of later neglect or abuse. If these conditions, known through research and clinical observations, are identified and changed early in the parenting process, then risks of neglect, abuse, handicap, and child removal are reduced.

High-risk factors include:

1. Child health and development

low birth weight

congenital defects or complicating medical problems

feeding problems or diagnosis of "failure-to-thrive"

multiple developmental delays

2. Mother's characteristics and behaviour

age: early teens

suspicion of drug or alcohol abuse

mental retardation

lack of child-rearing skills

inconsistent parental care

lack of education

refusal to return to nursery or pediatric unit for instructions on infant or child feeding, care, or contact

3. Parents' experience and situation

stress related to basic life necessities (money, housing, etc.)

stress related to child's characteristics, behaviour, or development

home crisis (marital, illness, death, sudden unemployment)

negative delivery experience

inadequate facilities in the home

lack of personal and family supports

poor marital relationship

household disorganization and mismanagement

past history of abuse, neglect, or of children with poor growth

parents' negative perception or assessment of the newborn

4. Parent-child interaction

infant-mother bonding problems during neonatal nurturing, as manifested by mother being reluctant to hold the baby; little or no eye contact; indifference to feeding [13]

disregard for child's physical and emotional needs (children up to 3 years old)

no limits for child (up to 3)

over-involvement with child, at expense of adult contacts

constant criticism

## B.   Assessment of High-Risk Situations

Assessments of high-risk situations focus on the aforementioned factors. Implicit in the discussion of risk factors is the notion of degree of risk, rather than risk versus no risk.

Depending on the developmental stage and circumstances, high-risk assessment may be done in a number of different situations—hospital, groups, the home. Assessment protocols, particularly those measuring mother-child interactions, should take into account the immediate social and physical context. For example, a mother's early contacts with the child in the audience of hospital professionals may differ from contacts when they are alone.

Methods of assessment also vary. Interviews and unsystematic and systematic observations are the most frequently used techniques, although the use of audio and video technology has been reported [6]. The "Instrument for Systematic Assessment of Parent Attachment Behaviours" is a highly structured approach to assess high-risk cases shortly after birth [24]. Based on theory and research on the early bonding process, the instrument allows classification of mother-child interaction along four dimensions: body contact (e.g., holding); eye contact (e.g., looks at infant during feeding); tempo (e.g., child is allowed to feed at own pace); and communication (e.g., smiles at infant). A quantitative scoring system is used which allows the development of four risk levels. Parents exhibiting certain behaviours after the first few months are recommended for serious family intervention.

The ultimate objective of intervention in high-risk cases is to change the quality and quantity of parent-child interactions towards more suitable child bonding (e.g., try to increase bodily and eye contact, establish a more appropriate tempo, and enhance the quality of communication towards the child). The primary goal involves expansion of knowledge and skills relevant to the parenting process.

Secondary goals may be directed towards changing other high-risk factors such as low self-esteem, social isolation, inadequate use of community resources, and poor problem-solving [6].

Four methods of working with high-risk parents have been identified in the literature: parent education groups, one-to-one counselling, mother-child groups, and family advocacy. Each of these is briefly reviewed.


## C.    Parent Education Groups for High-Risk Parents

General principles of parent education were presented in a previous section. In this section, one application of this approach with high-risk mothers, the Parent Education Program (P.E.P.), is described [23].

The Parent Education Program aims to improve parenting skills of high-risk mothers, while assisting them to cope with current stress situations. As parenting skills and knowledge are improved, clients develop a sense of personal efficacy and control. They begin to see themselves as active agents rather than as passive victims, and are better able to control their physical and psychological environments.

Two aspects of successful parenting receive emphasis in this programme. First, parents are helped to avoid unrealistic expectations for children through exposure to information about child growth and development. Second, parents are taught how to organize their general household activities and child care in ways that prevent their mutual interference. For example, methods for keeping children entertained during housework are taught.

In addition to direct assistance with child care, parents receive information about community resources, job training, and the formulation of career goals. A number of practical skills are developed, including budgeting, time-planning, and goal-setting.

The important feature of this type of programme is the recognition that potential child neglect may be affected by broad situational factors. Parents are given direct child care help, but they are also provided with life skills to assist in their own crisis situations. The P.E.P. program, described here, was available to mothers on a volunteer basis. A group leader met with approximately 8 to 12 mothers in two-hour sessions once a week for 12 to 14 weeks. Child care was provided at the centre.

## D.    Family Advocacy: The Use of Non-Professional Aides

In a recent review of programmes for abusive and neglectful parents, the use of lay services was identified as an important factor in successful programmes. Well-trained lay assistants can also be used in high-risk programmes. In one such programme [23] local residents were given extensive supervision and job-training. Families who had requested assistance with specific problems (e.g., housing, welfare, daycare, and employment) received problem-solving assistance by advocates and were helped to use community resources. Work with such cases typically requires several weeks of intensive contact. Lay helpers work as members of multi-professional teams.

The three main features of this programme are:

Its uses of multiple techniques, depending on the particular problem.

Advocacy supplements rather than replaces traditional forms of intervention in order to maximize the family's access to and use of services.

Emphasis is given to the promotion of skill-learning, and the gradual independence of the client from the lay resource person.

For further information on the use of volunteers, see Chapter 2, IX.

## E.    Mother-Child Groups

A third type of approach with high-risk families requires group participation of parents and children. In this context, workers have an opportunity to observe and correct the interaction within the family, as well as promote help-seeking contacts with outsiders. Also, workers are able to see how children relate to their peers. Positive interactions can be reinforced in a natural way, and otherwise isolated families have an opportunity to form natural supportive networks. Such groups are particularly useful for clients who are nervous about individual casework interviews or who are fearful of problem-focussed groups.

One example of this type of group is the Mother-Child Interaction Group [26]. The key assumption of this programme is that the mother-child bond is crucial in determining later development. Meetings are led by social worker and teacher-therapist (in this case, a nursery school teacher trained in psychodynamics and group treatment of preschool children, and in parent counselling). Four or five mother-child pairs are deemed an optimal size for the group, thus allowing individual attention where necessary.

In forming the group, co-leaders introduce the idea of a group as a way of aiding mutual understanding (e.g., reading non-verbal cues from children), or providing opportunities for play, and as an opportunity for mothers with similar concerns to meet. Group members are encouraged to bring family members and friends. Workers should realize that irregular group attendance can be attributed to:

> fear of criticism
>
> avoidance of anxiety-producing discussions
>
> difficulties in structuring time

For these reasons the development of an appropriate group atmosphere is important. Some guidelines are:

> Recognize and respect client difficulties in talking in a group and need to maintain privacy about lives.
>
> Build trust by not responding immediately to inappropriate behaviour.
>
> Establish structure by identifying regular meeting times, places, leadership, routines, and resources.

In this particular programme, six intervention techniques have been used to correct disturbances in mother-child interactions:

> *Providing nurturance:* Provision of lunch is an opportunity for broad discussion of nutrition, preparation, and problems pertaining to eating.
>
> *Supporting mothers and children:* Sensitive responses and use of video-feedback encourage discussions of difficult problems.
>
> *Modelling behaviour:* Leader demonstrates constructive interactions and play.
>
> *Teaching alternative behaviour:* The leader explains anticipation and avoidance of unpleasant incidents with children.
>
> *Helping mothers identify problems:* Group work aids clients' ability to evaluate situations objectively.
>
> *Encouraging mothers and children to request help:* Mothers and children are helped to seek out resources within the group to meet their needs.

Although no formal evaluation is reported, a number of impressions concerning the success of this programme have been noted. Mothers learned new ways of disciplining, feeding, and responding to their children. Socializing occurred outside of the group, even among isolated clients. Children developed more appropriate ways of behaving towards others.

Two important elements are key in this programme's success. First, co-leaders should try to foster change by encouraging member participation rather than through a direct expertise approach.

Second, successful group outcomes seem to be enhanced by the pre-existence of friendship among group members.

Finally, many parent-child groups for high-risk parents have involved only the mother. To some extent, this reflects the reality of the abundance of single-mother families in child welfare agency caseloads. However, future programming for high-risk families should involve the father and members of the extended family. Not only does this respect the changing reality of modern family structures (e.g., shared parenting of infants), but it builds broader supports for parenting activities.

## F.    Individual Counselling

Depending on the age of the child and perhaps the comfort of the parents, group approaches may not be appropriate. In cases of infants with developmental problems, including "failure-to-thrive", direct infant-care teaching may be provided either in the hospital or in the home. This intervention is usually supplied by health care personnel, such as nurses or social workers with medical or nursing backgrounds. In some cases, at-risk teams are used [22].

Although physical and medical concerns are central to many high-risk interventions of this nature, some programmes delve into the situational and attitudinal aspects of the potential neglect situation. For example, in a programme for screening suspected child abuse and neglect cases (S.C.A.N.), interviews with parents address such issues as mutual feelings, feelings towards the baby and other children in the home, whether the pregnancy was planned, and so forth.

The following programme exemplifies an individual approach with high-risk parents currently being developed at the Children's Aid Society of Metropolitan Toronto. The central person is a Nurse Practitioner, and the five components of the programme are assessment, education, support, supervision, and monitoring [38].

Assessment focusses on the nutritional and developmental status of the infant, and the adequacy of medical care. In the educational phase, the nurse "would teach and demonstrate handling and caring techniques, sharing knowledge with the parent, to improve responses to the infant's changing developmental needs" [38]. Support is provided to the parent during the growth of the child. This support is deemed particularly helpful during illness and other stressful events. The nurse also acts as a liaison with other sources of community care. Through intensive supervision and monitoring she is in a good position to identify early signs of inadequate care and to make specific observations of parenting.

Although this intervention requires the special expertise of a medical professional, the family worker is also an important part of the process.

## VII.    WORKING WITH UNMODIFIABLE FAMILIES

It is the case in child welfare work that some families are seemingly unmodifiable, yet do not provide sufficiently bad experiences to warrant a court-ordered removal of the child. Resistances of the family to change may result from many factors, including parents' attitudes, the complexity and dynamics of the problem, or the non-changeable situational elements, such as housing or job availability. Limitations in professional change techniques may also be a contributing factor.

Given the difficulties in such situations, workers should evaluate the possibilities, and avoid feeling guilty from a sense of professional failure. Four options are possible:

> Persist in trying to change the family.
>
> Try to establish community-based opportunities for the child.
>
> Refer.
>
> Close the case.

In evaluating these options it may be useful to keep in mind:

> that continued involvement with parents who do not want help may aggravate the problem for the child
>
> that families, although extremely important, are not the only sources of socialization opportunities for the child; efforts to find daycare, improve school experiences, and enhance peer opportunities within the community may prove extremely beneficial to the child's growth

The decision to refer clients is aided by consideration of alternative resources within one's own agency, one's own feelings (e.g., frustrations, hopelessness) about the case, clients' needs and characteristics, and availability of community resources. Referring clients is a useful step, but one which should be thought through carefully because of the instability introduced into the clients' lives. When considering referring, the following questions can be raised:

> Is the problem due to personal difficulties with the client, or limitations of resources? Could another person within the agency be useful?
>
> Does the image of the agency interfere with the successful provision of help?
>
> Will the relationship between this agency and the new agency be sufficiently cooperative to assure an easy transition?
>
> Will the change in resources introduce chaos into the client's current life situation? Is this an appropriate time to refer?
>
> How will the client perceive referral: failure? punishment? hopelessness?

## VIII.   SUMMARY

### A.   The Causes and Consequences of Child Neglect

This chapter began with comments on the difficulty of determining child neglect, and reviewed several elements of care which usually enter research and treatment discussion. A distinction between physical and cognitive/emotional neglect was noted.

Five broad theoretical approaches to understanding neglect were delineated: socio-economic and cultural, family systems, interactional, individual psychological, and ecological. The ecological approach, with its dual emphasis on individual and family development, and interdependent system of causality, was highlighted as possibly the most useful for future understanding and intervention.

The review of causal dynamics began with the observation that few studies analyze factors associated with different types of neglect. Polansky's recent research with low-income families found that physical and cognitive/emotional neglect were likely to occur together. It was predicted that child neglect will eventually be associated with many interacting factors, not necessarily in the same combinations.

Socio-economic inequalities probably play a decisive role in the child neglect process. As children, neglecting parents likely grew up in family conditions which negatively affected their capacity as future parents (e.g., they developed identity needs that their own children are expected to fulfill; early child care involvement with siblings undermined their commitment to parenting). All of this suggests a deficiency in personal resources brought to parenting. However, there is no evidence that child care values and attitudes differentiate neglecting and non-neglecting parents.

The immediate socio-economic situation of neglectful parents probably reinforces these resource deficiencies in several ways. Neighbourhoods' composition and organization tend to reflect political and economic realities. Urban neighbourhoods with high neglect rates tend to have few support systems, little neighbourliness, and low morale. Such conditions negate the learning of appropriate parenting through role modelling, feedback concerning inappropriate and appropriate parenting, stress and anxiety reduction, and general personal acceptance. Apart from adult learning opportunities, such neighbourhoods may not provide the parental role supports (e.g., babysitting, material exchange, crisis support) which are periodically needed.

Neighbourhood analysis must be supplemented with family and individual analysis, since not all people living in such environments neglect their children. Early evidence suggests that as individuals and as family members there may be a reinforcement of personal deficiencies and neighbourhood resource gaps. Apathetic, alienated, and low-verbal individuals are unlikely to reflect on their own needs or to seek out limited resources which are within the community. Similarly, their own limited personal and family networks of kin, friends, and neighbours do little to take up the resource slack from the neighbourhood-at-large. Finally, what little is known about interaction within neglecting families suggests a limited, negative quality which undermines members' self-esteem, family group problem-solving, and crisis management.

## B.    Practice Guidelines

The "Practice" section selectively reviewed relationship and treatment guidelines for work with neglecting parents. Considerable attention was given to "establishing a relationship with the client". A number of potential difficulties in this phase were highlighted, along with suggestions for aiding the process. A review of treatment approaches included individual work to enhance verbal accessibility, family problem-solving, group work, and working with high-risk families.

A common thread in this chapter is the enormous difficulty in working with child-neglecting parents. In some cases, the personal and social characteristics of clients both inhibit good parenting and undermine efforts to help. Engaging the client in a good relationship may be the most powerful leverage for change.

Dysfunctional parenting often occurs within a stressful context of unemployment, inadequate housing, marital estrangement, and social isolation. Treatment approaches increasingly recognize the need to address these situational factors. Also, the ultimate independence of the client can be enhanced by the provision of generalizable problem-solving and life skills.

To date, most studies have focussed on mothers, to the neglect of fathers. Recent research points to "father bonding" processes, and to the important direct and indirect effects of father behaviour on mother-child attachments. These developments must continue to be addressed, and their implications for practice acknowledged by both researcher and practitioner.

## REFERENCES

1. Province of Ontario, Bill 114. An Act to Revise the Child Welfare Act, 1978.

2. Belsky, J. "Child Maltreatment: An Ecological Integration", American Psychologist, Vol. 35, April 1980, pp. 320–335.

3. Burgess, R. L. and Conger, R. D. "Family Interaction in Abusive, Neglectful and Normal Families", Child Development, Vol. 49, 1978, pp. 1163–1173.

4. Elmer, E. Children in Jeopardy. Pittsburgh, Pa.: University of Pittsburgh Press, 1967.

5. Eskin, M. "Child Abuse and Neglect", Washington, D.C.: U.S. Department of Justice, 1980.

6. Evans, S. L., Reinhart, J. B., and Succop, R. A. "Failure to Thrive—a study of 45 children and their families", Journal of the American Academy of Child Psychiatry, Vol. 11, 1972, 440–457.

7. Garbarino, J. and Gilliam, G. Understanding Abusive Families. Lexington, Mass.: Lexington Books, 1980.

8. Garbarino, J. and Stocking, S. Protecting Children from Abuse and Neglect. San Francisco: Jossey-Bass Publishers, 1981.

9. Giovannoni, J. and Billingsley A., "Child Neglect Among the Poor: A Study of Parental Adequacy in Families of Three Ethnic Groups", Child Welfare, Vol. XLIX, April 1970, pp. 196–204.

10. Hepner, R. and Maiden, N. "Growth Rate, Nutrient Intake and 'Mothering' as Determinants of Malnutrition in Disadvantaged Children", Nutrition Reviews, Vol. 29, 1971.

11. Martin, H. P. The Abused Child, Cambridge, Mass.: Ballinger, 1976.

12. Ministry of Community and Social Services, Children's Services Division. "The State of the Art: A Background Paper on Prevention, 1979.

13. Polansky, N., Chalmers, M., Buttenweiser, E., and Williams, D. Damaged Parents: An Anatomy of Child Neglect, Chicago: University of Chicago Press, 1981.

14. ———, Hally, C., and Polansky, N. "Profile of Neglect", U.S. Department of Health, Education, and Welfare, Social and Rehabilitation Service, 1973.

15. Pollitt, E., Eichler, A., and Chan, C. "Psychosocial Development and Behavior of Mothers of Failure-to-Thrive Children." American Journal of Orthopsychiatry, Vol. 45, July 1975, pp. 525–537.

16. Reid, J. B. and Taplin, P. S. "A Social Interactional Approach to the Treatment of Abusive Children," Unpublished Manuscript, Eugene: Oregon Social Learning Centre, 1977.

17. Pelton, L. (ed.). The Social Context of Child Abuse and Neglect. New York and London: Human Sciences Press, 1981.

18. Rutter, M. Changing Youth in a Changing Society: Patterns of Adolescent Development and Disorders. Cambridge, Mass., Harvard University Press, 1980.

19. Smith, S. The Maltreatment of Children. Ottawa: M.T.P. Press, Ltd., 1978.

20. Smith, S. M. and Henson, R. "Failure to Thrive and Anorexia Nervosa", Postgraduate Medical Journal, Vol. 48, 1972.

21. Wolock, I. and Horowitz, B. "Child Maltreatment and Material Deprivation Among AFDC-Recipient Families". Social Service Review, Vol. 53, 1979, pp. 175–194. Summarized notes from Polansky.

22. Ayoub, C. and Pfeifer, D. "An Approach to Primary Prevention: The 'At-Risk' Program", Children Today, Vol. 6, May–June 1977, pp. 14–17.

23. Daniel, J. H. and Hyde, J. N., Jr. "Working with High Risk Families: Family Advocacy and the Parent Education Program", Children Today, Vol. 4, November–December 1975, pp. 23–25, 36.

24. Floyd, L. "A Model for Assisting High-Risk Families in Neonatal Nurturing", Child Welfare, Vol. LX, November 1981, pp. 637–643.

25. Jones, J. and McNealy, R. L. "Reaching Children at Risk: A Model for Training Child Welfare Specialists", Child Welfare, Vol. LX, March 1981, pp. 148–160.

26. Phillips, N., Gorman, K. H., and Bodenheimer, M. "High Risk Infants and Mothers in Groups", Social Work, Vol. 26, March 1981, pp. 157–161.

27. Polansky, N., Borgman, R., De Saix, C., and Sharlin, S. "Verbal Accessibility and the Treatment of Child Neglect", Child Welfare, Vol. L, June 1971, pp. 349–356.

28. Wells, S. J. "A Model of Therapy with Abusive and Neglectful Families", Social Work, Vol. 26, March 1981, pp. 113–116.

29. Cook-Gumperz, J. Social Control and Socialization. London: Routledge and Kegan Paul, 1973.

30. Aldous, J., Condon, T., Hill, R., Straus, M., and Tallman, I. Family Problem Solving. Hinsdale, Ill.: The Dryden Press, 1971.

31. Marmor, J. "The Nature of the Psychotherapeutic Process Revisited", Canadian Psychiatric Journal, Vol. 20, December 1975, pp. 557–565.

32. Croake, J. W. and Glover K. E. "A History and Evaluation of Parent Education", The Family Coordinator, Vol. 26, April 1977, pp. 151–158.

33. Brim, O. Education for Child Rearing. New York: Russell Sage, 1965.

34. Nedler, S. and McAfree, O. Working with Parents. Belmont, Calif.: Wadsworth Publishing Co., 1979.

35. Turner, C. "Resources for Help in Parenting", Child Welfare, Vol. LIX, No. 3 March 1980, pp. 179–188.

36. Hashimi, J. "Environmental Modification: Teaching Social Coping Skills", Social Work, Vol. 26, July 1981, pp. 323–326.

37. Cohn, A. "Effective Treatment of Child Abuse and Neglect", Social Work, Vol. 24, November 1979, pp. 513–520.

38. Pearson, M. Infant High Risk Program. A proposal submitted to the C.A.S., Toronto, 1982.

39. Caplan, Gerald. Principles of Preventive Psychiatry. New York: Basic Books Inc., 1964.

40. Scheinfield, D. R. "On developing developmental families", Paper presented at Head Start Research Services #5 (Jan. 1969), Washington, D.C.

41. Shearer, D. and Shearer M. "A Home-Based Parent Training Model", in Lillie, D. and Trohanis, P. (eds.) Teaching Parents to Teach. New York: Walker and Co., 1976.

42. Hill, R. "Social Stresses on the Family", Social Casework, Vol. 39, 1958, pp. 139–150.

# 5
# Physical Child Abuse: Dynamics and Practice

FRANK MAIDMAN

I. INTRODUCTION 136
II. PHYSICAL CHILD ABUSE: DEFINITIONS,
BEHAVIOURAL INDICATORS, AND DESCRIPTIONS 137
  A. Definition of Child Abuse 137
  B. Number of Children Abused in Canada and the
    U.S.A. 138
  C. The Victims 138
  D. Behavioural Indications 139
  E. Those Who Abuse 139
III. DYNAMICS: CHARACTERISTICS OF ABUSING
PARENTS 140
  A. Theoretical Approaches 140
  B. Parents' Family Backgrounds 141
  C. Psychiatric Abnormalities, Alcohol, and Drug Abuse 142
  D. Parenting Behaviour 142
  E. Birth Experience 142
  F. Motivational Patterns 143
  G. Intelligence 144
  H. Life Changes and Stress 144
IV. DYNAMICS: SOCIETAL CONDITIONS, FAMILY
SITUATIONS, AND ABUSE 144
  A. Societal and Cultural Conditions 144
  B. Class 145
  C. Unemployment and Job Dissatisfaction 146
  D. Housing 146
  E. Marital Situation 147
  F. Family Composition and Structure 147
  G. Social Isolation 148
V. DYNAMICS: FAMILY INTERACTION AND ABUSE 149
  A. Introduction 149
  B. Parent-Child Interaction 149

    C.  The Child's Role                                        150

    D.  Maintaining an Abuse Pattern                      151

VI.  CHILD ABUSE HAS MULTIPLE CAUSES        152

    A.  The Ecological Approach                           152

VII. CONSEQUENCES OF PHYSICAL CHILD ABUSE   152

VIII. PRACTICE GUIDELINES: AN INTRODUCTION   154

    A.  General Guidelines for Engaging Child Abusers  155

    B.  Crisis Intervention                             157

IX.  RESOCIALIZATION                             161

X.  WORKING WITH RECONSTITUTED FAMILIES    164

XI.  ADDITIONAL TREATMENTS FOR CHANGING

ABUSIVE PARENTS                               166

    A.  Introduction                                 166

    B.  Individual Psychotherapy                    167

    C.  Group Psychotherapy                      167

    D.  Group Transactional Analysis             168

    E.  Behaviour Therapy                       169

    F.  Humanistic Behavioural-Group Therapy     169

XII.  TREATMENT OPTIONS FOR ABUSED CHILDREN   170

    A.  Individual Therapy                       170

    B.  Behaviour Therapy                       171

    C.  Foster Care                          171

XIII. TREATMENT OPTIONS FOR CHANGING MARITAL

AND FAMILY INTERACTIONS                 172

    A.  Marital Therapy                       172

    B.  Parent Guidance Therapy               172

    C.  Family Therapy                     173

    D.  Multiple Family Therapy             173

    E.  Multiple Method Programmes         174

XIV. SUMMARY                               177

    REFERENCES                              177

# I.    INTRODUCTION

In this chapter the subject of physical child abuse is addressed. Recently, this problem has drawn nation-wide concern in both Canada and the U.S.A., thus evoking considerable writings on dynamics and practice.

Sections II to VII review factors associated with physical child abuse. The information should help child welfare workers' general understanding of abuse, and should expand their thinking about causal dynamics. For specific practice, the information will be most useful for the assessment process, insofar as it identifies "high-risk" situations. Also, by presenting the various explanations of abuse, this part of the chapter should aid the practitioner's decision-making about goals and service solutions.

Sections VIII to XII review practice guidelines, treatment modality options, and treatment programmes for child abuse intervention. The general aims of these sections are:

> to suggest a general crisis intervention perspective to guide practice

> to establish some general principles for ongoing child abuse clients

> to present optional treatment approaches for consideration in establishing service plans

## II.    PHYSICAL CHILD ABUSE: DEFINITION, BEHAVIOURAL INDICATORS, AND DESCRIPTIONS

### A.    Definition of Child Abuse

Physical child abuse is an inappropriate use of force against a child. Although the acts themselves may not do long-standing damage to the child's health, the family environment in which they occur is likely to place the child at developmental risk.

Most definitions of physical abuse have focussed on the physical behaviour without taking into account the family context, and have struggled with making a distinction between abusive and non-abusive behaviours. The difficulty with this is that the "abusiveness" of the acts is affected by the environment, including:

> the *meaning* of the *physical force* to parents and child (e.g., does the parent view the physical act as corrective action? does the child see the punishment as a sign that she or he is hated)?

> other *events* and *behaviours* going on at the same time, prior or subsequent to the abusive acts (e.g., is there a situation of stressful marital discord or other out-of-control behaviours, culminating in physically striking out against the child?)

Attempts to define physical child abuse are complicated by the variant standards of appropriate parenting held by different ethnic, social, and professional groups in society. For example, an American study found wide disagreement in judgement of child maltreatment in different parental behaviours [9]. Some members of society believe that physical punishment is an appropriate form of child discipline; others do not. Also, there may be disagreements over which particular behaviours are inappropriate acts of physical punishment. Extreme cases, such as burning the child or inflicting physical injury with other material objects, are clear-cut. Other acts of punishment, such as spanking with a belt, are ambiguous and may not be judged abusive by some parents and professionals. In other words, there is no consensus over what constitutes "excessive" and "inappropriate" physical punishment.

Some writers believe that professional standards should contribute to the definition of physical child abuse, particularly those based on scientific knowledge of child rearing [6]. Unfortunately, some areas of knowledge, such as the effects of physical punishment, are either inconclusive or in opposition to community standards.

For many reasons, then, it is difficult to offer a precise and operational definition of physical child abuse. Even state and provincial definitions are quite general and vague. The child protection worker is best advised to view abuse within the context of a configuration of high-risk family characteristics, and to use the best professional judgement. To aid this judgement, the following general working definition is offered:

Physical abuse consists of any non-accidental form of injury or harm inflicted on a child (under 16) by a caretaker. This includes, but is not necessarily restricted to: physical beating, wounding, burning, poisoning, and related assaults causing visible or non-visible physical harm (20).

### B.    Number of Children Abused in Canada and the U.S.A.

In Canada and the U.S.A., the exact scope of child abuse is unknown, although it is generally agreed that reported cases are only the "tip of the iceberg" [2]. Depending on the methods for gathering information, the most recent American estimates range from 41,104 to 167,000 cases in 1972, and 1.4 to 1.9 million in 1975 [2]. The most recent Canadian estimate is 1,085 in a 1973–74 period [12]. These statistics do not warrant comparative conclusions, since they are absolute numbers taken at different points in time.

### C.    The Victims

In this section, demographic descriptions of child abuse victims are presented. The question of why certain children are abused, and not others, is raised in a later section.

Current knowledge of the *age* at which children are more likely to be abused is quite inconsistent. Speculation is that abused children are more likely to be younger than six [16], and that the very young may receive the most serious injuries [10].

Concerning *sex differences*, it may be that more males are abused, although this pattern changes as children grow older. Females tend to outnumber male abuse victims during adolescence, a fact supported by Ontario statistics [10], and explained by culturally specific sex-role differences in childrearing practices. In the early years females are socialized into passive behaviour. However, they may be more susceptible to abuse as they become more independent and involved in heterosexual relationships.

Other facts and speculations concerning sex differences among victims are that:

Female abuse victims are more likely to suffer fatal physical abuse.
Females are more likely to be *confirmed* abuse victims [16].

These observations lead to the important speculation that female physical abuse may be very severe before it is finally reported [16].

## D.    Behavioural Indications

Abused children tend to display different behaviours. These represent survival styles learned primarily in the disturbed family environment.

In summary, the victims of child abuse may show behaviour that is:

> overly compliant, passive, or undemanding; low profile; avoidance of confrontation with parents

> extremely aggressive; demanding and rageful (more common in the mildly or inconsistently abused child)

> overly adaptive: either inappropriately adult and responsible, or clinging and babyish

> behind the norm in toilet training, motor skills, and socializing—generally indicative of developmental lag

The behavioral differences in abused children are likely affected by age.

Differences between mildly and severely abused children have been noted but research is inconclusive on this matter. Mildly abused children may show hyperactivity, temper tantrums, short attention spans, and aggression. Severely abused children, on the other hand, are more likely to display:

> inhibited verbal or crying responses
>
> shyness
>
> immobility
>
> dependence
>
> lack of curiosity
>
> wariness of physical contact
>
> excessive concern for parents' needs
>
> excessive self-control

## E.    Those Who Abuse

The best sources of data on the demographic characteristics of abusive parents are American studies; Canadian studies are presented when available.

The largest majority of child abusers are natural parents or their substitutes. Interestingly enough, abuse reports are more often confirmed when the victim is living with a stepparent [16].

It is not clear whether fathers or mothers are more likely to abuse their children. On the one hand, mothers have been identified in the literature as more frequent abusers of their children, particularly younger ones. However, when fathers are unemployed, they are just as likely to be abusive. As well, where the mother is the initial perpetrator, both parents may become involved later in the process. Yet, Ontario statistics show the *father* to be the most frequent abuser [10]. Despite statistical differences, analysis of abusive dynamics leads most authors to agree that parents share in the abuse pattern [16].

Although abusive parents are thought to be young, this may be an artifact of the victim's age. In most clinical studies, victims are more likely to be young, having been more readily identified.

The question of the racial characteristics of abusive parents is a delicate and inconclusive matter. Although a number of major American surveys have found a disproportionate number of non-whites as abusers, many of these studies have sampling biases. Also, clinical studies have found no over-representation of non-whites in their abuse sample [16].

Additional descriptions of abusive families are provided later when the question of why child abuse occurs is raised.


## III.   DYNAMICS: CHARACTERISTICS OF ABUSING PARENTS


### A.   Theoretical Approaches

Physical child abuse is considered symptomatic of a dysfunctional family environment, one in which the child's development is at risk. At this stage of knowledge there is no indication of a clear set of family, parent, or child characteristics which are *always* associated with abuse. It is better to assume that a number of different factors may combine to create and sustain physical child abuse. For this reason, the worker faced with the task of assessing high-risk family situations should have broad exposure to the possible dynamics of abuse.

There are basically five different theoretical approaches to understanding child abuse: (1) psychological, (2) intrapsychic, (3) family situational, (4) sociocultural, and (5) ecological.

Analysis from the viewpoint of *individual psychology* assumes that child abuse occurs because of some personality characteristic of the parent (e.g., aggressiveness) and/or individual deficiency in childrearing skills and knowledge (e.g., inadequate knowledge of child development). Such characteristics are usually traced to development and socialization experiences in the parents' own backgrounds.

An *intrapsychic* analysis of abuse attempts to identify pathologies in the parent, traditionally categorized as psychosis, character disorder, and the like. Descriptions of alcohol and/or drug abuse may fall within this category, as would parent criminality.

Those concerned with understanding abuse in terms of *the family situation* look at many possible aspects, including class, social isolation, unemployment, and other dimensions of the family's external social functioning. Internal family characteristics also come under scrutiny, including child-rearing or disciplinary interaction, and marital relations. Analysis of interaction may include the victim's characteristics, (such as her or his interactional responses to parents), family composition, and family structure. The recurring family explanations of child abuse emphasize stress, the isolation from stress-reducing resources, the breakdown of mother-infant bonding, the escalation of aggression, and scapegoating.

The *socio-cultural* approach to child abuse sees it as symptomatic of broad social and cultural conditions. Such conditions do not explain why specific individuals or families abuse their children. Instead, these conditions are thought to predispose certain individuals to commit abuse, given other life conditions. For example, societies condoning physical punishment as a method of child rearing are more likely to have higher rates of child abuse. Other socio-cultural conditions which have received attention include the society's concept of childhood and the rights of children, the economic situation as a source of stress, and the availability of supportive resources within communities. The socio-cultural perspective is particularly useful for prevention work.

A final approach to understanding child abuse, the *ecological perspective*, assumes that no one factor in isolation explains the occurrence of abuse. The best analysis will combine variables from all approaches. For example, ecological analysis might require knowledge of legitimizing belief systems; socially-structured stresses; opportunities for help; the quality of family life as a source of individual satisfaction, support, and control; and individual personality dispositions to commit physical aggression. An ecological analysis, unlike most others, would assume a two-way process of causality. For example, behavioural outcomes of abuse would create further stress and scapegoating in the family, thereby promoting further abuse.

For theoretical perspectives on child neglect and sexual abuse, see Chapters 4, III and 6, III–VI, respectively.

Do the personalities of abusive parents differ in any significant way from those who do not abuse their children? Many years of research have been devoted to this question; unfortunately, results are inconclusive. Efforts to answer the question have concentrated on:

> previous experiences of abusive parents, including family backgrounds and the birth experience
>
> psychiatric abnormalities
>
> motivational characteristics
>
> parenting attitudes and abilities

Each of these is reviewed in turn.

## B.    Parents' Family Backgrounds

Abusive parents' childhood family experiences have been the subject of considerable conjecture. Although few studies have actually compared the backgrounds of abusive and non-abusive parents, many researchers and clinicians believe that abusive parents were either physically or emotionally abused or neglected as children [26]. Essential aspects of this background may be summarized as an absence of basic emotional nurturance and the sense of being cared for, rejection, indifference, and hostility. One author says that:

The capacity to love is not inherent; it must be taught to the child. Character development depends on love, tolerance and example. Many abusing parents were raised without this love or tolerance [26].

### C.     Psychiatric Abnormalities, Alcohol, and Drug Abuse

Early thinking on the etiology of child abuse assumed that abusive parents were either psychotic or severely neurotic [26]. Recently, a consensus is emerging that only the most violent and abusive parents are psychotic. However, interest in parental psychopathology may arise again because two recent controlled studies show evidence of psychopathology in fathers and less severe mental illness among abusive mothers [16].

Although an association between alcoholism or drug abuse and child abuse was once considered, the consensus is that abusive and nonabusive parents show similar rates. In truth, alcoholism may be a *precipitating* factor in abuse [16,8].

### D.     Parenting Behaviour

Physical abuse of children is inappropriate parenting, and numerous intervention efforts aim to correct parenting knowledge and skills. Many child abusing parents have general inadequacies in their parenting skills and knowledge. For example, they:

> have common misunderstandings with regard to the nature of child-rearing and child development

> expect high levels of age-appropriate emotional and performance responses

> are unable to empathize with their children's needs

> emphasize physical punishment strongly, and believe in the parental right to exert such punishment

Those taking individually-oriented approaches to explaining dysfunctional parenting emphasize either that parents have unmet dependency needs or that inadequate parenting (including abuse) was learned in their own childhood.

Critics of these assertions argue that no empirical evidence, based on methodologically-sound comparative analysis of abusive and non-abusive parents, exists to substantiate the ideas [11].

### E.     Birth Experience

Abused children are more likely to be lighter at birth and to be born in an abnormal pregnancy. One study found that abused children were twice as likely to have been born prematurely and were more likely to have been delivered by Caesarian section [14]. Another study found that abusive parents experienced more abnormal pregnancies and deliveries, neonatal separation, and postnatal illnesses [15].

Why are children with a lower birth weight more likely to be abused? Their physical susceptibility to injury has been ruled out, but a number of other speculations have been developed [23, 26], some of which are supported by research. Low birth weight may lead to later abuse for the following reasons:

Parents are disappointed with the child's physically abnormal appearance, and form weak attachments to the child.

Parents are frustrated when the child does not meet their lofty expectations: low birth weight children show slower development in social responsiveness, walking, talking, reading, math, and spelling.

Parents are frustrated by the particularly demanding care required: low birth weight children show more feeding disturbances, crying, irritability, and medical problems.

The initial mother-infant post-partum separation in the case of low birth weight children hampers the development of bonding, suitable child care techniques (e.g., feeding), and confidence in the instrumental (e.g., bathing) and social (e.g., calming) tasks of infant parenting.

## F.    Motivational Patterns

Another explanation of physical child abuse seeks to identify a configuration of personality characteristics which predispose the parent to abuse. Although the specific configuration has yet to be established, a number of separate personality traits are discussed in the literature. Thus, abusive parents have been variously described as having:

unmet dependency needs

a lack of identity, or unresolved identity conflict; low self-esteem

rigid or inadequate defenses

oral dependency

underlying depression

difficulties in managing responsibilities of life

high group conformity

Despite much personality research, few definitive conclusions can be drawn. There is little or no agreement among various personality researchers, except that "there is a defect in the abusing parent's personality that allows aggressive impulses to be expressed too freely" [26]. There is also considerable disagreement over the *source* of aggressive impulses; four possibilities have been considered: (1) a final outburst after a long period of tension, (2) inability to face life's daily stresses, (3) deep feelings of inadequacy and/or inability to fulfill parental role expectations, and (4) immaturity, self-centredness, and impulsiveness.

Finally, some efforts have been made to recognize that child abuse may be committed by people with distinct *combinations* of personality characteristics. The most frequently quoted scheme identifies four personality composites [18], one of which applies to abusive fathers only. Abusive mothers may be:

continually and pervasively hostile and aggressive, either focussed or general

rigid, compulsive; lacking warmth, reasonableness, and flexibility in thinking and belief, defending their right to abuse; self-concerned and rejecting of children, feeling that the latter were primarily responsible for troubles

strongly passive and dependent; often competing with children for spouse's attention; depressed, moody, unresponsive, unhappy, and immature

The fourth category describes young fathers who are intelligent and skilled, but for some reason (e.g., physical disability), are unable to work and support their families. Frustrated, they frequently and severely abuse their children.

In summary, knowledge of the personalities of child abusers is incomplete. Further work on validating and refining typologies needs to be done before practitioners can use such knowledge systematically. Considerably more work on father characteristics is needed.

### G.    Intelligence

There is no clear evidence that child abuse is related to subnormal intelligence [16]. Studies are inconsistent in their findings, probably attributable to inadequate methodologies. As with other studies, many have not incorporated a comparison group of non-abusive parents.

### H.    Life Changes and Stress

Recent research reports that physical child abuse is more likely to occur when parents are experiencing life changes (e.g. job change, separation). Life changes produce stress and exhaustion which cause lower-class parents to lose control, and raise the possibility of striking out against the child. Further, life changes are even more likely to promote child abuse risk when the parents were themselves abused as children [2]. Child abusers learned to cope with stress *inappropriately* in their own childhood.

For comparative information on the personality and background characteristics of neglecting parents, see Chapter 4, III. Fathers who sexually abuse their children are described in Chapter 6, IV.

### IV.    DYNAMICS: SOCIETAL CONDITIONS, FAMILY SITUATIONS, AND ABUSE

### A.    Societal and Cultural Conditions

Another approach to understanding child abuse argues that certain cultural or institutional factors affect child abuse rates. This, however, does not allow an understanding of specific instances of abuse. Rather, it isolates factors which may constitute a "breeding ground" making abuse more likely to happen. Since not all persons in such cultures commit abuse, further psychological or interactional information is needed. However, cultural and societal approaches are useful for prevention purposes.

What kinds of socio-cultural factors affect child abuse rates? First, some societies condone corporal punishment as a legitimate method of disciplining children. Several cross-cultural studies (in U.S.A., China, Taiwan, Japan, and Tahiti), suggest an association between the legitimation of physical punishment and child abuse [23].

Child abuse seems more prevalent in societies where physical force is deemed an appropriate way of resolving conflict. In one study using criminal aggressive activity as an indicator of violence, the author found that lower rates in Canada compared with the U.S.A. were reflected in lower rates of violent physical acts within the family [27].

For a long time, corporal punishment was described as a lower-class phenomenon in the U.S.A. Research has not substantiated this claim [16]; furthermore, there is no apparent class connection with attitudes towards child mistreatment.

Another socio-cultural factor is the dissemination of child development knowledge. Child abusers in the U.S.A. are frequently described as holding inappropriate expectatons for their children, such as the belief that infants should know right from wrong. These observations promote speculation that social isolation and the decline of extended kin interaction possibly limit the circulation of child development knowledge [22].

Ecological researchers see community and neighbourhood factors as key. Limited access to support resources, such as daycare centres, self-help groups, job counselling, and integrating mechanisms have been associated with high rates of child abuse [6].

## B.    Class

Most authors report that child abuse is more likely to occur among low-income groups who have relatively less access to money, schooling, and employment opportunities [23]. This observation is supported by one of the few existing Canadian studies [25]. The explanation is that life conditions typically associated with low-income family life create stress, frustration, aggressiveness, and ultimately, child abuse.

Despite considerable data supporting the association between class and abuse, one author cautions against such a conclusion [23]. The following reasons provide insight into ways in which child abuse becomes socially visible:

Studies drawing samples from hospitals, police records, and social agencies are biased towards low-income people; middle-class people are likely to use private practitioners who may not reveal the abuse.

Middle-class families are more likely to live in private detached homes where abuse is less detectable.

Community agencies are probably less likely to intervene in middle-class homes.

Better educated people are better able to hide their abusive behaviour.

These reasons may eventually discredit studies of social class and abuse. Nevertheless, the stress-frustration-aggression chain may still hold true. Those in different social classes may experience different objective conditions, but react with the same aggressive and abusive behaviours.

## C.    Unemployment and Job Dissatisfaction

Under some conditions, child abuse may be affected by the unemployment of the father or mother [23]. Moreover, studies of family violence show that sudden unemployment stimulates physical aggression among all family members [28].

For purposes of planned intervention, it is important to be aware of the possible reasons for child abuse at times of unemployment. In summary:

The unemployed parent is home more, thus increasing the chances of conflict.

The unemployed father may assume a greater role as disciplinarian.

As a consequence of unemployment and loss of status, the father's abuse of children is a way of restoring his authority and self-esteem.

Unemployment may be associated with other frustrating circumstances within the home; reduced income, for example, may complicate household and child care [23].

Presumed effects of unemployment on physical child abuse are indirectly supported by other bodies of research [23]. In one American study, those with low job satisfaction were more likely to use physical punishment with their children, regardless of social class. Also, another large-scale American survey argues that child abuse may be symptomatic of the work alienation of many segments of society.

## D.    Housing

In addition to income, education, and employment, the quality of housing often reflects one's class position. Unfortunately, the specific effects of housing on child abuse are little understood. Child abusers are more likely to live in rental housing, are less likely to be satisfied with it, and are less likely to share their quarters. Yet most studies suggest that abusers' housing and living conditions do not differ from their immediate neighbours' conditions [23].

Although little is known about the impact of physical housing space on child rearing and family interaction, a few observations are noteworthy [23]:

In dwellings with fewer rooms, fathers but not mothers are likely to support power-assertive disciplinary approaches.

In a British study, the punishment of low-income children was more frequent in unimproved and densely populated housing.

In a Hong Kong study, more family hostility prevailed in upper-floor apartments.

One fruitful line of inquiry identifies the effects of housing on interaction with neighbours and friends, as potential sources of support. Research on child abuse and neglect reveals that child maltreaters are socially isolated. Our knowledge suggests that those living in high-density housing have limited involvements with friends and neighbours. This observation holds true for people in all classes [21].

## E.    Marital Situation

Those investigating or working with child abuse cases frequently report family problems other than abuse. One approach to understanding the dynamics of either physical or emotional punishment of children is to regard the victim as a scapegoat for other family problems. In classic discussions of scapegoating, marital partners are usually unable to deal with their own problems directly. Yet in abusive families, there appears to be a general atmosphere of interpersonal violence among *all* family members [27], suggesting that the scapegoat theory may not be appropriate.

Despite consistent reports of marital discord, separation, divorce, and father absence among abusive families, it is not known whether these differ significantly from the non-abusing population of the same class [16, 22].

## F.    Family Composition and Structure

Another aspect of family life that should be considered in developing an understanding of child abuse is the family composition and structure. For example, does abuse typically occur within large or small families? Are reconstituted families more likely to be abusive? Are abused children usually the first-, second-, or third-born?

Considerable evidence supports the view that child abuse more likely occurs in larger families than in the general population. More important, this observation is true for different countries (U.S.A., New Zealand, England), in different ethnic groups, and in families with varying paternal educational and income levels [23, 16, 22].

Concerning family composition, a large-scale American study offers the following findings [3]:

Father-only households have the highest risk of both abuse and neglect, particularly in the case of young children (i.e., 2 years of age and younger).

Mother-only households are also at risk, but somewhat less than father-only households.

Stepparent households have high abuse and neglect risk when compared with the general population but less than mother-only and father-only households.

The explanations for these family-composition effects are speculative only: fathers are ill-prepared to fulfill the emotional and task aspects of child care. American studies generally show that fathers are not the prime care takers, and are not fully involved in the bathing, clothing, and feeding of children. Canadian studies would probably confirm this, although this may be less true in modern two-career families.

The explanation for the high-risk factor in stepparent households emphasizes the attachment process between parent and child. Stepparents, it is proposed, have not had the opportunity to develop the strong "parental feeling" that comes from involvement with newborn children. This explanation is supported by studies documenting weaker parental feelings towards stepchildren [3].

Birth order of the abused child, considered alone, does not enhance our understanding of why child abuse occurs. However, when taken together with other family characteristics, the child's birth order seems more significant. This issue will be pursued in the ecological approach section in which the interdependence of many situational factors is examined.

## G.    Social Isolation

Clinical observation and research consistently portray abusive parents as isolated from friends, neighbours, and extended kin. Generally, they are highly mobile people, possibly explained by their lack of community roots. When problem solving, their preference is to handle crises within the family rather than tapping community resources. Other community members minimally accept abusive parents at best and strongly rebuff them at worst [23].

Parental social isolation extends to the lives of their children. They are often prevented from participating in the usual extracurricular activities at school, and from forming normal peer attachments [23].

How does the social isolation of abusive parents contribute to abuse? The usual explanation is that such isolation closes off opportunities for natural stress- or crisis-reduction interactions. These families, as a consequence of other conditions in their lives (e.g., economic difficulties, mobility, marital difficulties, childrearing stress) do not find the emotional or marital help-giving often available from friends, relatives, and neighbours. The continuation of problems and build-up of psychological stress at some point manifests itself in striking out at the child.

In addition to stress-reduction through emotional and material aid, a family's friends, relatives, and neighbours are potential agents of social control against unacceptable parenting, as well as sources of learning appropriate skills and roles. Also, the child abuse may itself "cause" social isolation, in a typical vicious cycle.

The emotional aspect of the abusive family's relationship with outsiders is vividly experienced by the child welfare worker. As with other problem families, a depressive element is often conveyed. Workers should realize that this is a manifestation of the family's quality of life, and a "pulling back" from outside contacts. It is a message that helping the family to change will not be an easy task.

For the societal conditions affecting child neglect, see Chapter 4, IV. The social context of sexual abuse is reviewed in Chapter 6, III.

## V.    DYNAMICS: FAMILY INTERACTION AND ABUSE

### A.    Introduction

Conditions of family life, as reviewed above, do not go far in explaining why or how child abuse actually occurs in the family. In fact, most of the conditions are also associated with child neglect. How then can we explain the fact that some parents, under conditions of stress and social isolation, brutally strike out at their children? Answers will probably come from a close analysis of interactions between parents and their children. Although such interactions have been analyzed in myriad ways, three simple principles will help the worker to think about the content of interactions within abuse families:

Parent-child interaction is partially affected by socialized attitudes and behavioural responses that adults bring to their family and parenting roles.

Parental behaviour towards the child is affected by the child's behaviour towards the parent in a circular kind of pattern.

Parental behaviour towards the child is affected by the nature of interaction between the spouses.

### B.    Parent-Child Interaction

Parents who abuse their children were likely abused themselves as children, or they grew up in a family where physical aggression was used to resolve conflict. Hence, abusive parents are *socialized* to be physically punitive towards their children. From this social learning perspective, it follows that:

Physical abuse is an impulsive, automatic reaction against their children when parents are angry.

Physical abuse is the result of a limited repertoire of child disciplining responses, learned during the parent's own childhood.

Physical abuse is believed to be a legitimate part of childrearing, and is seen as necessary to instill appropriate conduct in the child.

The important point is that child abuse may be a pattern transmitted from generation to generation through the continuity of a family sub-culture.

Another interaction perspective suggests that abuse is the culmination of unsuccessful attempts to control the child's behaviour. What are these attempts and why are they unsuccessful? Recent research points to several characteristics of control attempts [23]:

Parents are inconsistent in disciplining their children.

This inconsistency means that the child's inappropriate behaviour does not change.

Parents intensify their disciplining attempts as a result of disobedient behaviour.

Parents finally find success in controlling the child's increasingly intense responses through the use of very intense disciplinary measures; they come to believe that these are the only responses that work.

Note that this sequence of interactions involves an *escalation* of intense reciprocal responses between parents and children. This escalation culminates in the parent's learning a certain type of disciplinary tactic.

In understanding why or how child abuse occurs, one must remember that behaviour of other family members may be etiologically important in starting and maintaining a pattern of abuse. According to one study, one parent in abusive families was more controlling than the other; the hunch is that the passive parent, unable to direct aggressive behaviour towards the other, is likely to direct the aggression towards the child [23].

## C.    The Child's Role

A fully interactional understanding of abusive dynamics must include the child. This in no way suggests that children should be "blamed" for "inviting" abuse or that difficulties associated with rearing some children make abuse inevitable. It simply acknowledges that interaction, by definition, is a two-way process. By excluding the child's behaviour, one "sees" only parental behaviour, thereby constructing inappropriate explanations.

There is a disproportionately large number of the following kinds of children among the abused: mentally retarded, premature and low birth weight, physically handicapped, emotionally handicapped (schizophrenia), congenital physical abnormalities, and those with high rates of illness during the first years of life.

Why is there an unusually high number of atypical children who are abused? Answering this question requires caution because in some cases (e.g., mental retardation, schizophrenia, and some physical defects) these characteristics may be a *result* of abuse. Nevertheless, there are a number of speculations [23, 4]:

Physically or mentally different children may be scapegoated within the family.

Physically different infants may be particularly difficult to care for; for example, premature infants are known to be hypersensitive to all stimuli, restless, distractible, prone to anoxia and colic, and disorganized sleepers.

Parents may emphasize the abnormality of their children.

Hospital policies and procedures may require lengthy separation between the parents and infants.

In addition to genetically-based physical or mental abnormalities, simple genetic differences contribute to the infant's behaviour. For example, some babies are irritable, difficult to soothe, and engage in less eye contact. Depending on the parent's knowledge, child care flexibility, and emotional response, such behaviours may lead to tension and weakening of the initial attachment process.

This discussion of infant and children differences suggests the following interactional dynamics surrounding child abuse:

Physical characteristics or infant behavioural style may impede the development of the parent-child bonding or attachment process. An important element is the parental response, as affected by knowledge, skills, and emotional needs. Child differences may later promote a scapegoating process. Finally, the discussion hints at the importance of the wider context, at least in some cases: troubled families may promote scapegoating; hospital policies may hamper parent-child bonding.

One final point: as a result of physical abuse or possibly other family interactions, the child may behave in ways that elicit further abuse. Such behaviour may occur inside the home or outside. For example, abused children whose academic work suffers or who behave inappropriately in school or in the community, may develop a bad reputation, thus fuelling a family scapegoating process.

The older child's reaction to discipline may in turn evoke harsher discipline, possibly culminating in abuse. This escalation was discussed in Section V, B, "Parent-Child Interaction". Studies have shown that, of the various responses to discipline (e.g., ignoring, seeking reparation, pleading, defiance), defiance is likely to lead to harsher discipline [23].

## D.      Maintaining an Abuse Pattern

Most of the explanations reviewed thus far have concentrated on factors leading up to child abuse. A complementary approach, one particularly valuable for treatment, involves an analysis of parental and family factors which maintain the abuse occurs in single-parent households (see Section IV, F on family composition), engage in a series of tactics to minimize, justify, or shift responsibility for the abuse [23]. Four parental tactics have been identified:

*Justification of abuse:* condoning the abuse in the name of a higher principle, such as the importance of using harsh discipline to assure appropriate social and moral conduct

*Minimization of abuse:* minimizing the incident and/or selectively forgetting the consequences

*Shifting of responsibility:* blaming the child, shifting responsibility to other family members, or not sharing the responsibility

*Derogation of the victim:* attributing negative characteristics to the child, and using verbal aggression such as name calling, insulting, and mocking

In addition to these normalizing tactics, the parental partner's reactions to abusive incidents may either curtail or maintain abuse as a pattern. Since so much abuse occurs in single-parent households (see Section IVF on family composition), partners are unavailable as potential agents of control. Although research is lacking on this dynamic, it is probably the case that abuse is indirectly supported by a partner's indifference or nonreaction [23].

Abusive patterns may endure in families because parents do not react to the child's pain. Low-empathy parents may not realize the extent of the child's suffering. Observed signs of pain do not stimulate one marital partner's control over the other's behaviour. The child's crying or resistance stimulates, rather than curbs, further abuse.

As a final point, the family's social isolation may be a structural characteristic which helps maintain the abuse pattern. For a discussion of how this might happen, see Chapter 7. Also, interactional dynamics of *child neglect* and *sexual abuse* are reviewed in Chapters 4, III and 6, IV–VI, respectively.

## VI.    CHILD ABUSE HAS MULTIPLE CAUSES

One of the most encouraging trends is the recognition that no single factor, such as class, parental emotional needs, or children's physical differences, stands alone to explain abuse. The ecological approach suggests that maltreatment should be viewed as an outcome of interdependent individual, interactional, family system, family environmental, and broad socio-cultural conditions (see Chapter 1 for a fuller discussion of the ecological perspective).

### A.    The Ecological Approach

What do we now know about how conditions combine to produce child abuse? Some preliminary observations slightly advance our understanding of how social stress and resource availabilities are associated with abuse.

First, we noted above that unemployment might be a factor in child abuse, possibly because of the resulting stress. However, not all unemployed parents will abuse their children. It is more likely to happen when the families of unemployed parents live in apartments. Also, abuse is more likely when families of unemployed or less educated parents do not share their quarters. Abusing families with an unemployed parent tend to have more children, as do abusive families with less educated parents. Finally, in cases where the parent is unemployed, the victim is more likely to be the youngest child. These observations, based on American studies, point to the possible importance of increasing stress in abuse, particularly when combined with opportunity to abuse.

In addition to the influence of situational stress in the etiology of abuse, isolation from stress-reducing resources is a contributing factor. Parents may bring about this isolation themselves in a variety of ways. However, one should not discount the fact that some communities do not objectively provide such resources. This, in fact, was supported by another American study which demonstrated that rates of abuse and neglect were lower in communities with better support systems and human resources [6].

## VII.    CONSEQUENCES OF PHYSICAL CHILD ABUSE

Discussion of the consequences of child abuse must proceed very cautiously because of the known methodological problems with existing research. Briefly, these research limitations are [22]:

Observed differences in the functioning of the abused child may have preceded rather than followed the abuse; the inference of causality requires a complex longitudinal study.

Differences may be due to the family environment and/or environmental conditions of the abusive acts; studies have not examined the effects of abuse within different family situations.

Studies have not consistently used control groups, therefore making it difficult to rule out the possibility of observed effects happening in cases of non-abuse.

Most studies of abuse have not examined physical abuse separately from neglect.

In addition, no study has examined the impact of the "institutional reaction" (e.g., court process, multiple placement, separation) on the child. The handling of child abuse cases may increase the negative effects on the child.

Despite these research limitations, the psychological and behavioural long-term effects on the abused victim are summarized here. Historically, the seriousness of this problem was first noted when Kempe observed that in 302 cases of U.S.A. child abuse 11% of the children had died and 28% had received permanent injury. Subsequent to this initial observation, the following characteristics of abused children have been noted [17]:

mental retardation

temper tantrums; hostility

delayed speech development and other language deficits

self-mutilation among abused schizophrenics

failure-to-thrive

deficiency in hemoglobin

infant withdrawal, indifference to mother, and psychomotor retardation

shallow relationships with parents and other adults, particularly among older children

lower intelligence

neurological damage

less overt and fantasy-aggressive behaviour

Summarizing descriptions of abused children from follow-up studies, the children may be characterized as stubborn, unresponsive, negativistic, apathetic, and unappealing; somber, docile, and placating [22].

Despite some reports of hostile and aggressive behaviour, one of the few well-controlled studies of behavioural and personality characteristics concluded that ". . . in general, abused children do not seem to indicate problems by acting out but rather through docile and passive behaviour" [22].

Apparently, violent behaviours of juvenile delinquents who were abused as children emerged at a later stage in their development.

As indicated above, observed developmental differences in abused children may have been the result of the family environment rather than, or perhaps in conjunction with, the actual abuse. A number of negative family and socialization patterns accompany most cases of abuse; physical aggression, parental psychiatric disturbance, and other elements of what has been referred to as "parental deprivation" [17].

The abusive family's lower socio-economic situation, particularly when accompanied by stress, may also affect the abused child's development. An isolated family's efforts to control the child's extra-familial school and peer activities result in low self-esteem and limited interpersonal skills (e.g., empathic capacities, verbal abilities).

Characteristics of the victim's siblings provide added evidence that the context of child abuse may be as malevolent as the physical abuse itself. It has been found that [22]:

> The favoured sibling was more openly damaged in personality than the abused.

> The abused child's siblings were less able to establish emotional ties with foster parents.

> A large portion of siblings showed language-learning delay.

Recent sociological work raises the question of the degree to which societal intervention itself brings negative consequences to deviants and to the victims of deviance. This line of thinking might argue that child welfare agencies' responses contribute to the developmental problems of child abuse victims. Although no data are available to pursue this speculation, the possible developmental implications of U.S.A. findings should be kept in mind. In 1977, The National Center on Child Abuse and Neglect made the following comments [22]:

> The process of handling abuse cases has been described as filled with "confusion, delays, poorly coordinated efforts and failure of the agency and individuals to assume responsibility for action".

> In intake, more than one-third of those expressing a need for service are not accepted by the agency.

> Court reviews of cases have been described as haphazard and without permanency planning.

Institutional conditions like these may not exist across North America. Any organization, however, has the potential to break down in these ways, and place the child at added risk.

Since physical abuse likely occurs within conditions of child neglect, the reader will benefit from reading the consequences of child neglect, Chapter 4, VI.


## VIII.    PRACTICE GUIDELINES: AN INTRODUCTION


The remaining sections review a number of treatment guidelines for those working with abusive parents. Practice literature is voluminous, although generally it is more appropriate for clinically-oriented practitioners [36, 37, 40, 47, 49, 50]. Child welfare workers, in their investigative, assessment, monitoring, and other roles possess limited opportunities for long-term therapeutic involvement. Nevertheless, their interaction with clients presents some critical moments for introducing change. The perspective in this chapter is that such change efforts are best viewed within the broad perspective of crisis intervention.

## A.    General Guidelines for Engaging Child Abusers

Regardless of how involved the child welfare worker becomes in direct extensive treatment to abusive families, a number of general principles will aid the change process:

### 1.    *Keep the focus of treatment on the family as a whole.*

The immediate concern is the protection of the child; nevertheless, when investigating, considering treatment options, or case monitoring, the needs of other family members should not be forgotten. Because of the atrocious nature of child abuse there is a desire to "save the child", a phenomenon referred to as the "rescue fantasy" [63]. However, it is becoming clear that: (a) personal needs of parents, (b) the interactional context of the abuse, and (c) the family's relationship with its environment are dynamically related to abuse (see previous sections). Furthermore, siblings may be negatively affected by the environment [39] and may become later targets of abuse.

### 2.    *Keep attention on the abuse pattern.*

As part of a general child protection focus, child welfare workers must strive to create conditions for changing abusive patterns within the family. One possible impediment lies in parents' efforts to direct the worker's attention to themselves and other problems. This is because:

Parents are uneasy about the abuse.

Abusive parents may never have been nurtured themselves and have strong psychological needs.

Abusive families are often multi-problem families with a host of basic needs (e.g., housing, employment).

Workers are advised to keep their attention focussed on the abuse, while tending to other family needs. The importance of nurturing and addressing material needs is reviewed next. While keeping abuse in the forefront of their service goals, workers should not allow this aspect of parents' identity to dominate their contacts. A proper balance is a worthwhile ideal, since from a change agent perspective:

There is constant reinforcement of what *must* be changed.

The changing person's *total self* is never in question, thus avoiding the anxiety of total rejection.

A *bond* with the worker is created and maintained.

3.    *Attend to the "meaning" of precipitating factors in the abuse.*

Physical child abuse is either an act of punishment or angry striking out which is inappropriate to the child's precipitating behaviour. The parent's *experience* of the child and the child's behaviour (and the accompanying *self* experience of the parent), are undoubtedly important factors in understanding *why* inappropriate responses occur. For example:

> A mother believed that her 1-year old infant's habit of dropping toys from her high chair was a sign that the child was out to get her to show her who's boss.

> Another mother, when questioned about beating her 6-year-old daughter for not eating properly, replied, "You know, it's not Betty's eating. There is nothing she could do to please me. I feel that she has trapped me by her very existence."

Such experiential information, as illustrated above, provides valuable insights into the wider psychological and situational dynamics of child abuse.

4.    *Help parents to distinguish between anger and rage.*

Many abusing parents displace stress and anger onto the child, or allow anger to escalate into rage and physical abuse. Workers have an opportunity to help parents understand the difference between anger and rage, and to express anger in socially appropriate ways:

> Anger is the emotional reaction to the present situation in which an individual perceives himself as hurt or mistreated. . . . The person is easily able to identify the reason for his anger and his angry reaction is proportional to the severity of the perceived injury. . . . Rage . . . is suppressed anger and fear that has been stored up, often from early childhood, so that its cause can no longer be easily remembered nor [sic] identified [41].

The worker can help the client sort out anger and rage in the following ways:

> She (he) can help the client recognize rage, and possibly its sources; in some cases, here-and-now problem-solving may alleviate the rage.

> The client, in interaction with the worker, can be encouraged to experiment with new ways of expressing anger without fear of losing control or destroying the relationship.

> She (he) can help the client to appreciate how angry feelings can coexist with positive feelings in close loving relationships [41]. Client expression of anger and rage may be inevitable in child welfare work; workers are advised to capitalize on these opportunities for change.

5.      *Be persistent.*

A dogged persistence is essential with abusive clients; they do not want agencies in their lives, and in many ways (e.g., through missed opportunities) complicate workers' efforts. One manifestation is a superficial adoption of worker recommendations which, on the outside, presents a significant change. A continuing presence in clients' lives allows workers to check the durability of changes, and offer on-going proof of the community's concern.

6.      *Strive for modest changes.*

The probability is not high for immediate, extensive changes with abusive families. Dysfunctional patterns have long histories in problem families, often inappropriately serving subtle individual needs and family functions. Workers must be satisfied with such gains as: keeping a child in the home, correcting obvious inadequacies of child care, alleviating the consequences of former maltreatment, reducing the social isolation of parents—all of these are important attainable goals for child protection workers.

7.      *Help break down the barrier of isolation.*

As with many problem families, physical abusers tend to be socially isolated. This isolation, as discussed in Chapters 4 and 6, sustains maltreatment by depriving parents of positive and negative feedback on their behaviour, information and models for learning new behaviours, resources for handling stress, and alternative life satisfactions. To help reduce the isolation, workers can integrate clients into the community and/or can themselves serve the above functions. Workers are urged when selecting service options to consider reducing social isolation as an essential selection criterion. As community representatives in abusive parents' lives, workers can:

> convey appropriate childrearing standards
>
> give feedback on appropriate and inappropriate behaviour
>
> provide information on child development, childrearing, community resources, and so forth
>
> model appropriate behaviours relating to childrearing, problem-solving, using community resources, communication, and so on
>
> listen empathetically to a client's troubles, frustrations, and setbacks
>
> provide new interpersonal experiences, and help parents to expand their life satisfactions

General guidelines, such as those described, should be kept in mind when carrying out a variety of child welfare functions with abusive parents.

## B.      Crisis Intervention

Descriptions of crisis intervention may differ in detail; yet several core ideas are essential to all approaches. Although child welfare practitioners may not consciously apply crisis intervention methods, their general orientation likely contains the following assumptions:

> Crises in people's lives are sufficiently disorganizing and unpleasant that potential for change exists.

> Intervention in crises is present-oriented; the main goal is to remove the crisis (e.g., child abusive pattern) through understanding and dealing with forces in the "here and now", and to help the client return to a pre-crisis level of functioning.

> Workers take an active, direct stance to induce change, relying more on authority (legal and professional) than on relationship building through attachment and transference; in particular, workers are apt to act as advice-givers, educators, and resource brokers.

> Workers become involved in environmental modification in their treatment roles, helping clients change the stressful conditions of their immediate interpersonal or material milieu; the immediacy of such intervention is essential for building a base for further change.

> Efforts are made to link the client with a natural support system of friends, relatives, and community resources; the aim is to leave the client with resources for further problem-solving and crisis resolution.

> Both the client and the worker structure the process; during assessment there is mutual definition of the problem, of the specific goals to be reached, and of the period of time to be used for this work—the contracting process.

What causes a crisis? It develops as follows:

> An "emotionally hazardous situation" occurs when a shift in one's psychosocial environment alters relationships with others (or expectations of the self), in ways perceived to be negative.

> The resulting rise in stress motivates one to use coping mechanisms or problem-solving behaviours that help to reestablish a balance (homeostasis) and to reduce or to eliminate feelings of discomfort.

> Coping can be a process of mastering a problematic situation, or it can be a process of protecting a vulnerable sense of self without mastery of the situation.

> When one experiences an emotionally hazardous situation and cannot effectively use previously learned coping behaviours, or cannot reduce stress by using new problem-solving behaviours, then an emotional crisis may occur; an emotionally hazardous situation becomes an emotional crisis when there is failure to cope effectively.

Throughout the years, various theorists have created classification systems in order to categorize types of crises. Presented next is Baldwin's System (1978). With movement from Class 1 to Class 6, crises becomes more serious; the locus of stress shifts from external stressors to internal conflicts.

## TYPES OF CRISES

| Class Definition of Crisis | Intervention Strategy |
| --- | --- |
| 1. *Dispositional:* Results from a problematic situation. | Clarify client's problematic situation. |
| | Intervention is not primarily directed to an emotional resolution. |
| | Intervention may involve referral, information dissemination, administrative action, or psychological/medical education. |
| 2. *Anticipated Life Transition:* Results from life transitions over which the client may or may not have control (e.g., becoming a parent). | Develop with client an in-depth understanding of the changes that have or will take place, and explore the psychological implications of these changes. |
| | Help client to plan adaptive coping responses to problems that result from life transition. |
| | Trend is towards group approach. |
| 3. *Sudden Traumatic Stress:* Results from strong externally imposed stresses or traumatic situations that are unexpected and uncontrolled and emotionally overwhelming to the client (e.g., sudden death of someone close); usual coping behaviours are ineffective due to sudden nature of the stress; client may be emotionally paralyzed for a period, during which coping behaviour cannot be mobilized. | During client's period of emotional paralysis, the worker provides or mobilizes support. |
| | Client is helped, later, to emotionally acknowledge the situation. |
| | Client is helped to acknowledge and express negative emotions that result from the stressful situation. |
| | Worker aids client in planning for and coping with changes that result from the traumatic experience. |
| 4. *Maturational/Developmental:* Results from attempts to deal with interpersonal situations and usually involves developmental issues such as dependency, value conflicts, emotional intimacy, power issues or attaining self-discipline. | Help client to identify and conceptualize underlying and unresolved developmental issue. |
| | Emphasis is on helping client to respond to the present problematic situation more adaptively while resolving the developmental conflict. |
| 5. *Psychopathological:* Results from a pre-existing psychopathology rather than from external stressors per se. | Respond in terms of the present problem with emphasis on problem-solving skills and environmental manipulation. |
| | Acknowledge client's deeper problems, but do not try to resolve problems representing deep emotional conflicts. |
| | Stabilize client and prepare client for longer-term therapy or other services. |
| 6. *Psychiatric emergency:* Results from situations in which general functioning has been severely impaired; client is incapable of assuming responsibility; medical interventions may be required; may involve intoxications. "impulse control" (e.g., suicidal impulses) or acute psychoses. | Assess psychological and/or medical condition as rapidly and accurately as possible. |
| | Clarify situation that led to client's condition. |
| | Mobilize mental health and/or medical resources necessary. |
| | Arrange for follow-up or coordination of services to ensure continuity of treatment. |

## BALDWIN'S STAGES FOR CRISES INTERVENTION

| *Stage* | *Therapist's Tasks* |
|---|---|
| 1. Catharsis/Assessment | 1. Encourage client to acknowledge and express feelings generated by the crisis situation. |
| | 2. help client explore and define the emotional meaning of the precipitating event that produced the crisis. |
| | 3. Help client to mobilize appropriate support. |
| | 4. Help client restore a realistic perspective of the situation and define options available. |
| | 5. Help client conceptualize the precipitant or psychodynamic meaning of the crisis situation that links present to past (when this component of a crisis is present). |
| | 6. Obtain *relevant* background information in order to more fully understand the crisis situation. |
| 2. *Focussing/Contracting* | 1. Help client develop awareness of feelings that impair or prevent use of adaptive coping behaviours in response to the crisis. |
| | 2. Develop therapeutic alliance with client, emphasizing client responsibility for adaptive change and eventual crisis resolution. |
| | 3. Obtain from client an agreement on a concise statement of the core conflict or problem that has produced the crisis. |
| | 4. Define with client a time and goal contract for the crisis resolution process. |
| | 5. Agree with client on a tentative therapeutic strategy or plan to attain the goals necessary for crisis resolution. |
| 3. *Intervention/Resolution* | 1. Define and directly support client strengths and adaptive responses to the crisis resolution. |
| | 2. Help client work through feelings that support maladaptive coping responses (i.e., resistance) directly and appropriately to the situation in terms of issues and feelings (i.e., direct communication with significant others involved is encouraged). |
| | 4. Help client to develop new or more adaptive coping responses or problem-solving skills. |
| | 5. Help client define progress in working towards defined goals and crisis resolution. |
| | 6. Prevent diffusion away from the focal problem and the goals defined. |

## BALDWIN'S STAGES FOR CRISES INTERVENTION—*Continued*

| Stage | Therapist's Tasks |
|---|---|
| 4. *Termination/Integration* | 1. Elicit and respond to client termination issues, but do not prolong resolution of the situation. |
| | 2. Reinforce changes in client coping behaviours and affective functioning; relate these changes to the resolution of the situation. |
| | 3. Evaluate with the client goal attainment or non-attainment during the intervention process. |
| | 4. Help integrate adaptive changes and help prepare client to meet future similar situations more adequately. |
| | 5. Provide client with information about additional services or community resources needed, or make a direct referral for continuing therapy as appropriate. |

What is the process of crisis intervention? Baldwin's model for crisis intervention has four basic stages [5], and most crisis interventions occurs in 1 to 8 therapy hours; the time required to move through each phase varies.

Some subgoals of crisis resolution are as follows:

The individual in crisis is prevented from using or learning maladaptive coping responses and/or regressing, thereby avoiding maladaptive crisis resolution.

The individual is helped to learn new and more adaptive coping responses that will result in reintegration at a more stable level of functioning post-crisis.

The individual is helped to use the crisis experience to become aware of and to resolve underlying conflicts and/or ambivalence that determine the crisis.

The individual is helped to integrate changes resulting from adaptive crisis resolution.

The information presented in this section on crisis intervention is merely the "tip of the iceberg". References [76] and [86] are books pertaining to crisis intervention which might prove useful to the worker.


## IX.    RESOCIALIZATION

Many child abusers have experienced an emotionally deprived childhood.

Whether abused or neglected, they have been left with low self-esteem, a limited sense of social competence, an inability to trust, and deficient parenting abilities. With this background, one of the frequently cited treatment activities is described as "reparenting" or "resocialization". Resocialization requires learning basic skills and attitudes which, in normal development, have their basis in childhood socialization. It involves both nurturing and teaching processes [34].

Nurturing helps to meet the following serious emotional needs [35]:

Parents need help to feel good about themselves, to make up for devastating belittling.

Parents need to be comforted when they are hurt, supported when they feel weak, and liked for their likable qualities.

Parents need someone they can trust and lean on, and someone who will put up with their crankiness and complaining. They also need someone who will not be tricked into accepting their low sense of self-worth.

Parents need someone who will not be exhausted with them when they find no pleasure in life and defeat all attempts to help them seek it.

Parents need someone who will be there in times of crisis and who can help them with their practical needs, by leading them to resources that they can use or by giving them more direct help.

Parents need someone who understands how hard it is to have dependents when they have never been allowed to be dependent themselves.

Parents need someone who will not criticize them, even when they ask for it, and who will not tell them what to do or how to manage their lives; they also need someone who does not need to use them in any way.

Parents need someone who will help them understand their children without making them feel either imposed upon by having to understand what they cannot, or stupid for not having understood in the first place.

Parents need someone who can give to them without making them feel of lesser value because of their needs. Parents need to feel valuable, and eventually they need to be able to help themselves and to have some role in helping others.

Workers who have experienced the frustration and emotional drain of the nurturing role should remember that people with tension and unmet basic needs do not learn new behaviour quickly.

Of considerable importance are opportunities for modelling child care behaviours, and sharing information on child development. Although it is beyond the scope of this chapter to review all known problems in parent-child interaction, special consideration should be given to:

providing attention to and verbal praise for co-operative behaviour

ignoring aggressive behaviour

distracting the child from aggressiveness by attending to behavioural cues possibly leading to conflict and aggression self-time-outs (physical withdrawal) upon feelings of possible loss of control

limit-setting

For more information on teaching appropriate child care methods, see Section XIII in this chapter, and Section III in Chapter 4.

One cautionary note: A worker's positive interaction with the child may increase the alienation between parent and child, and/or strain the worker-parent bond. Parents' nurturing needs place them in potential competition with their child for the worker's attention. Also, demonstrations of appropriate parenting may be threatening to those rendered highly sensitive by an abuse investigation. Workers are advised to build a base of trust by nurturing parents before risking those developments. Nurturing creates a bond of liking and trust with workers—a leverage for further change. Thus, through *being* nurtured, parents learn to nurture *others*.

The steps in the nurturing process aid parents (1) to meet their immediate needs, (2) to cope with stressful situations, and (3) to deal with their lack of motivation and feelings of helplessness.

1.      *Help parents to meet their immediate needs.*

When beginning treatment, rather than dwelling on the details of child abuse, workers should help meet immediate needs and problems as defined by parents. Although possibly frustrating for workers, concrete tasks such as providing transportation, organizing the house, and finding accommodation, help to build a nurturing relationship. In addition to alleviating stressful conditions, such acts convey a message of care and concern. A dependency relationship is created which serves as leverage for further changes.

2.      *Teach parents to deal with stressful situations.*

One of the important stress-reducing needs of abusive parents is to learn how to master their environment; that is, to control events rather than to be controlled by them [34]. Such skills are the core of competence. Workers can aid this process by contributing to the solution of small, concrete, easily-solved problems as identified by parents. Care must be taken to involve parents in establishing and setting priorities for goals, in addition to providing support for their decisions. Dependency in problem-solving can gradually be reduced as parents increase their skill and confidence.

3.      *Respond to parental lack of motivation.*

A serious barrier in the resocialization process is parents' lack of motivation to change, and their sense and expression of hopelessness. Recognized as depression by workers, these feelings are inevitable products of resocialization with such clients. Although it can be emotionally draining for workers, empathy with this depression has been described as a key element in the treatment process [34]. In addition, hopelessness will be reduced through continual efforts to meet basic needs, and a constant challenging of parents to develop their sense of competence through mastery of small tasks. Involving them in the identification of goals should also reduce apathy and resistance [34].

Nurturing, however, is a means towards learning new knowledge and skills and should not be considered a treatment objective in itself. In a way, learning is a parallel process because the worker models the nurturing process in her or his interaction with the client. Also, in the process of assisting with material needs, several opportunities will develop for modelling life skills in socially competent ways.

In summary, this section has reviewed the main elements of socializing treatment with abusive parents. An important phase is establishing a nurturing relationship, one which satisfies fundamental emotional needs, builds trust, and establishes hope and motivation. Nurturing is seen as a means towards the end of creating parent change, particularly in childrearing knowledge and skills.

## X.    WORKING WITH RECONSTITUTED FAMILIES

Although there is no direct causal link between reconstituted families and child maltreatment, child welfare workers frequently must face the special challenges of working with troubled reconstituted families.

As the divorce rate escalates, so does the rate of remarriage; in fact, approximately 85% of divorced men and 75% of divorced women remarry within three years following a divorce: 60% of remarriages involve stepparenting; (and 40% of second marriages end in divorce within four years).

Given the endless combinations and permutations that have replaced the nuclear family, it is essential that child welfare workers become acquainted with those special aspects of reconstituted families which affect workers' assessments and intervention approaches.

Reconstituted families (otherwise known as "stepfamilies", "blended", etc.) come in three basic forms:

1. Families with a stepfather (married or common-law) who brings no children of his own to a relationship with a woman who has children

2. Families with a stepmother who is in a situation parallel to the stepfather mentioned above

3. Families in which both partners have children of their own from a previous union and now have established a family in which each partner is both a biological and a stepparent (the "combination family")

Reconstituted-family members have likely been exposed to two strong, culturally fostered myths: (1) the wicked stepmother myth, and (2) the instant love between stepchild and stepparent myth.

A child who has already lost her or his nuclear family is vulnerable to the fantasies of the perfect parent or the wicked parent.

Visher's guidelines [88] which workers might keep in mind when dealing with reconstituted families are as follows:

A primary couple relationship is crucial for the healthy functioning of a reconstituted family in that a strong adult bond can provide a sense of security to children, in addition to providing a positive relational model; adults need time alone to devote to their relationship (in spite of feelings that they are "betraying" the parent-child bond)

It is important that natural parents and children have some time together in order to preserve their original tie and to help the child experience less loss at sharing a parent.

Stepfamily relationships should be allowed to develop at their own pace rather than be pushed to expand.

It is important that family members acknowledge that stepfamilies are emotionally and structurally different from nuclear families, and that this difference does not obviate the possibility for harmonious relationships.

Children who suffer from a sense of divided loyalties between their natural parents and their stepparent can learn that children can rightly care for more than two parental adults—this information may alleviate their guilt.

When possible, courteous relations between ex-spouses should be maintained in order to remove the child's felt need to take sides or to be a message carrier.

Stepparents should try to carve out a unique role for themselves that does not compete with that of the biological parent.

The stepfamily unit should develop new family traditions and patterns and ways of accommodating individual needs and preferences.

In a stepfamily, jealousy, rejection, anger, and guilt may be more pronounced than in a biological family and therefore fairy-tale expectations are highly unrealistic; when reconstituted families understand and accept their negative feelings, they are likely to be less disappointed and frustrated. The worker's job is to help the family to separate myth from reality.

With regard to integrating *adolescents* into a stepfamily: This can be particularly challenging because adolescence is the developmental stage during which teenagers move away from their families and tend to want relatively little to do with them; teens who have been "young adults" in single-parent families may resent becoming a "child" when the parent remarries. Withdrawal is one way of dealing with the demotion, along with an "I don't care" attitude.

The most difficult step-relationship tends to be between a stepmother and adolescent stepdaughter. The teenage girl identifies strongly with her mother and tends to resent any woman who replaces that mother in her father's affection; the adolescent girl herself may compete with her stepmother for her father's affection.

Teenage boys living with their mother may displace their anger with their mother (for betraying the father) onto the stepfather.

Often new reconstituted families are more aware of sexuality than are biological families because the new couple may be in the honeymoon phase of their relationship; furthermore, in reconstituted families the incest taboo is not as entrenched as in biological families; stepchildren's attraction to step-relatives (and vice versa) may lead to hostility and withdrawal as a way of dealing with unacceptable feelings; furthermore, adolescents are often disturbed by their biological parents' sexuality and they may deal with this by becoming sexually competitive (e.g., a girl may get pregnant simultaneously with her remarried mother).

The worker's task is to help the couple help their adolescents to understand, accept, and to control their sexual attractions to stepsiblings and to stepparents.

The worker's task is to help older adolescents attain an independent identity apart from their family—in this way they can participate with parents, stepparents, and siblings as self-sufficient, maturing individuals.

The worker might point out to adolescents (depending upon the circumstances) that certain stepfamily characteristics can be used to their advantage:

A stepfamily can be like an extended family, containing a new set of people who can potentially meet unmet needs, provide information, act as role models, and so on.

Sometimes it is possible to relate even better to a stepparent than to a biological parent.

For additional readings on reconstituted families, see Pill [87] and Visher [88].


## XI.    ADDITIONAL TREATMENTS FOR CHANGING ABUSIVE PARENTS


### A.    Introduction

Crisis-oriented and nurturing interventions are prevalent in child welfare practice; not all workers provide long-term clinical treatment. There are many reasons for this, not the least of which is that child welfare administration, investigations, court preparation and participation, and agency liaison work are time-consuming. Also, some workers do not place clinical treatment within the mandate of child protection work.

Despite these realities, this section assumes that knowledge of alternative treatment modalities is valuable because:

Treatment alternatives need to be explained to clients when treatment is recommended by the court.

Workers do carry treatment caseloads.

Appropriate referral requires the ability to match service options with client needs.

Monitoring treatment progress requires some working knowledge of treatment.

In the review of treatment options, material will be organized in the following categories:

the unit of intervention—parents as individuals, parental or parent-child dyads, family systems, larger social units

the change objectives

techniques

evaluation (where available)

Child abuse is sometimes attributed to the individual characteristics of parents. Treatment approaches based on this broad perspective try to change personality characteristics, and teach child development and childrearing and social skills.

## B.    Individual Psychotherapy [55, 65, 66]

Individual psychotherapy approaches typically assume that symptoms of an underlying personality disorder are: low tolerance for frustration, hostility, rigidity, depression, low self-esteem, and anxiety. Treatment strives to overcome emotional disturbances and promote such changes in ego functions as impulse control, improved object relations, and problem-solving. Depending on the therapist's theoretical bent, the therapeutic process utilizes unconscious material, experiences of the past, or information relating to here-and-now problems. Therapeutic techniques include support, catharsis, ventilation, anxiety reduction, uncovering, insight facilitation, interpretation, clarification, use of the transference relationship, and reassurance.

Estimates of the success of various psychotherapeutic interventions in child abuse cases vary from 50% to 80%. Limitations of individual psychotherapeutic approaches work are as follows:

There is a lack of focus on parent-child interactions.

Changes in parents' behaviour may be too slow to protect the child's psychic development.

Abusive parents are too mistrustful and erratic in their behaviour to come to an office punctually for a 50-minute hour.

Psychotherapeutic interventions are expensive.

## C.    Group Psychotherapy [60, 61, 64]

Changes in personality functioning of abusive parents have been attempted through group psychotherapy methods. Group methods are deemed useful for abusive parents because:

They are a means of decreasing parent isolation and of developing mutual support systems.

There is an increased confrontation of denial and problems among group members; this takes place earlier and more intensely than in individual approaches.

Parents feel they can be helpful to others.

Opportunities exist for sharing childrearing and child development information.

Although scant information is available on the psychotherapeutic use of groups, one author claims that this approach provides a positive reparenting experience for those who were deprived during infancy and childhood [64]. The group encourages resolution of early developmental problems through regression, reliving early experiences, and insights. Male and female therapists facilitate a surrogate parent identification process. Psychotherapeutic techniques include reassurance, abreaction, catharsis, confrontation, and group facilitation. Although no statistical evaluation results are available, one study reported success with 54 abusing parents after three years of work [64].

Limitations of group psychotherapeutic work are:

length of time needed for success

only for parents who are not threatened by exposing their feelings to others

not useful for those in severe crisis situations in which one-to-one support is needed

not useful for extremely disturbed parents who may be destructive in groups and thereby experience further rejection

## D.    Group Transactional Analysis

Transactional analysis has been used with groups of abusing parents [43, 44]. The causal assumption underlying T.A. with abusers is that parent and child, and the two parents, are locked in symbiotic relationships. The parent demand for caring and nurturing from the child is frustrated, causing anger, resentment, and abuse. The other parent passively abuses the child by allowing this to happen.

The major treatment goal is the elimination of symbiotic relationships within the family through (1) strengthening the separateness of parental ego states, and (2) confronting parents' efforts to deny the existence of the problem, its significance, and its solvability.

Transactional analysis techniques with abusing parents have been accompanied by contracting arrangements, script questionnaires, and teaching correct information about parenting. Couples meet in groups of four or five, for 1½ hours a week, during approximately five to six months.

One evaluation report indicates that 22 of 30 couples successfully completed treatment [45]. Many of the same limitations of group psychotherapy apply to transactional analysis in groups.

## E.     Behaviour Therapy

Abusive parents are believed to behave in ways (e.g., using physical force in problem-solving) which precede or set the context for child abuse. Also, they are known to lack information, or be misinformed about child development and child-rearing. Based on social learning theory, these problems are attributed causally to (1) parents' own socialization experience (e.g., lack of exposure to knowledge, inadequate parental role-modelling, and lack of closeness with their own parents), and (2) their current social isolation (e.g., lack of adult learning and feedback for inappropriate behaviour). Behavioural therapeutic treatment methods aim to increase knowledge and skills for effective parenting, to correct information, and to reduce the frequency of undesirable behaviour [64]. Such techniques work directly on the knowledge and behaviour problems, without inferring or treating underlying personality disorders. Techniques used include social reinforcement, extinction, response shaping, behavioural rehearsal, modelling, discrimination training, relaxation training, desensitization, correct feedback, cognitive restructuring, homework assignments, and instructions. Environmentally-oriented support services may accompany these approaches [64]. Behavioural methods can be used in an office, clinic, or home setting, and treatment can vary anywhere from one month to one year.

Many of the behaviourally-oriented programmes available for child abusers attempt to enhance parenting skills, particularly those related to disciplining and child management [27, 43, 23]. Some of these are highly specialized interventions focusing on discrete aspects of parenting, such as improving positive reinforcement practices [62].

Other behavioural approaches are directed not so much at parenting knowledge and skills, but towards the development of more appropriate techniques for controlling anger [55]. It is assumed that physical abuse emanates from an escalation of anger, consequential to frustrating stimuli within the family (e.g., a child's disruptive behaviour). Recommended techniques include "(a) the reinforcement of non-angry responses; (b) role playing and modelling of non-angry reactions, and (c) desensitization in the presence of the anger-evoking stimuli" [55]. No evaluation results of such techniques are available.

The social isolation of abusive parents, whether actual or psychological, has been described as one of the most recurrent and prevailing qualities of child maltreatment. (For a discussion of social isolation dynamics in abuse and neglect, and in communities, see Chapters 4 and 3). This belief has prompted an incorporation of isolation-reduction components in many group-oriented and multi-service approaches. In addition, recent writings have urged the development of social skill-building programs for abusing parents. Such programs could utilize modelling and behaviour rehearsal techniques to overcome shyness and increase social assertiveness [55].

## F.     Humanistic Behavioural-Group Therapy

This approach uses both humanistic and behavioural methods [40, 64]. One illustrative program incorporates self-reflective methods and learning opportunities in a therapeutic camp setting [40]. Group discussions of self-esteem, self-gratification, mutual sharing, and responsibility for one's own life are promoted. As well, family life education sessions are held, with emphasis on behaviour management for children. Patterson's book *Living with Children* [59] is used as a guide. Early results of the programme are described as positive, with reports of a decrease in shouting, screaming, or hitting, and a complete absence of reported abuse [40].

## XII.   TREATMENT OPTIONS FOR ABUSED CHILDREN

### A.   Individual Therapy

Abused children may suffer from short-term or long-standing emotional or developmental problems (see Section VII). For this reason a number of individual treatments (including therapeutic playschools, individual play therapy, and group therapy) have involved children.

Therapeutic playschools [30, 53, 38] are typically staffed by early childhood education teachers and paraprofessionals, and aim to provide therapeutic experiences through interaction with peers and adults. The general objective is the promotion of developmental and emotional growth, without the use of structured cognitive learning experiences.

The playschool approach may be particularly useful for the following clients:

> 2 to 5-year-olds who have not had other pre-school experiences, and who are isolated from peers

> parents who are unable to tolerate daily separation and personality changes in their children

> parents who will make themselves available for parent conferences or parent groups

Therapeutic playschools may not be appropriate for children who are severely emotionally disturbed or retarded [54].

Individual play therapy [30] is particularly useful for those abused children who have severe conflicts and fears, and who could benefit from play materials and a safe setting. It may be particularly useful for children with low self-esteem, depression, aggressive behaviour, and severe behaviour management problems [32]. Parent conferences are necessary for parents to deal with their ambivalences concerning having a child in treatment, and to help them grow with their child's personality changes. One cautionary note is that child therapy may reinforce a parent's notion that the child is "sick". This is particularly inappropriate when parents need to change scapegoating behaviour and/or to examine their own problems.

Finally, group therapy for abused children and their siblings may be particularly appropriate for latency-age children who need to develop peer interaction skills [32]. Male and female co-therapists act as parent models. Parent conferences or parent groups may be necessary to keep their children in therapy and to grow with positive changes [32.]

## B.  Behaviour Therapy

A child's behaviour in interaction with parents is part of the dynamic which leads to child abuse. A number of treatment approaches have focussed on changing this behaviour. The assumption is that by changing one element in the negative parent-child interaction, other elements will also change.

Those using behaviour modification techniques based on the application of appropriate punishments should be aware of the following [55]:

> The effectiveness of punishment depends on a number of factors: timing, intensity, consistency, and the nature of the relationship between the punishing agent and the child.

> Teaching parents the use of more effective punishment techniques as a way of controlling their children may have the following effects: the child develops aggressive behaviour through role-modelling and the inflicted pain; the child avoids the parent, thus undermining all influence attempts; the child becomes passive and withdrawn.

However, in situations where child care agents reward and encourage much of the child's behaviour and selectively punish some behaviour, negative side effects may not occur [55].

Behavioural techniques for changing undesirable behaviour include [55]:

> *Extinction:* the non-reinforcement of undesirable response

> *Reinforcement* of incompatible responses (e.g., ignoring aggressive responses while rewarding cooperative behaviour)

> *Time-out:* removal of the child from the situation for a brief time period

> *Verbal rationales:* provided as needed

## C.  Foster Care

Foster care can be seen as a treatment strategy, particularly when accompanied by post-placement services to foster parents and children. In the case of emotional disturbance and behavioural problems, foster placement is a particularly challenging intervention approach. The premise that many abused children need to be removed totally from their environment for treatment (as well as for safety) purposes has been supported by research. An American study showed that "removal to foster care improved the physical, emotional, and cognitive functioning of abused children—they improved in nearly all problem behaviours, especially emotional withdrawal" [48].

The effectiveness of foster placement as a treatment strategy is related to foster parents' abilities, availability of supportive agency resources, and the involvement of the legal parents. Separation from natural parents may, however, further weaken the parent-child bonds. For further information on fostering and separation, see Chapter 8, III.

## XIII.  TREATMENT OPTIONS FOR CHANGING MARITAL AND FAMILY INTERACTIONS

One of the criticisms of efforts to change individuals is that child abuse is an interactional phenomenon. Thus treatment efforts must (1) advise parents on how to bring their attitudes and behaviour into line with their child's characteristics; and/or (2) involve parents and children as the unit of assessment and treatment; and/or (3) involve the marital partners in treatment.

### A.      Marital Therapy

Although parents and children together have been used as the unit of observation in treatment, and in post-treatment evaluation, most programs work directly with the parent only. On the other hand, marital therapy has its value [32]. Assuming that marital problems are being displaced onto the child in a scapegoating fashion, marital therapy focusses directly on these problems with the goals of improving communication and enhancing need gratification within the marriage.

Group methods have been used for therapy with couples [53]. Groups are invited to focus on marital problems (e.g., financial management, sexual incompatibility) as the root causes of abusive behaviour. As well, groups are used as arenas for learning more appropriate childrearing methods. With co-therapists as role models, couples also learn appropriate decision-making methods and techniques for support-giving. Success with this approach has been reported.

Marital treatment may not be suitable when:

Individual parents are dependent and eager for attention from the therapist.

One parent is psychotic or schizophrenic.

### B.      Parent Guidance Therapy

Parent guidance therapy assumes that the child victim's characteristics and/or behaviour contribute to the interaction leading to abuse. Central to this process is the parental *response* to the child. For example, easy to-care-for infants may assure a parent that she or he is adequate as a parent. On the other hand, difficult infants may promote three different parental responses [44]:

anxiety and threat as a consequence of feeling inadequate as caretakers

blame and resentment for the extra burden presented by the child

intimidation by the infant's difficult nature

These responses to the child are, in turn, affected by parents' psychological state (e.g., low self-esteem or low sense of competence), by their beliefs about child development (e.g. development is affected wholly by parental response), or by their child-rearing goals (e.g., parents wanting to curb aggressiveness in the child's person-ality may respond harshly to what they see as aggressive behaviour).

This line of thinking has promoted a parent-guidance therapy which focusses on the transaction between child and environment. The objectives are to improve the fit between the child's temperament and parental response. Briefly, parent guidance requires two essential elements [73]: (1) identification of parental behaviours and overtly expressed attitudes that are deleterious to the child's development, and (2) a programme of changed reciprocal behaviour between parent and child; this pro-gramme utilizes specific incidents in the child's life.

The major limitation of this, or any dyadic approach, is that persons outside of the parent-child dyad are omitted from the field of assessment and intervention. It assumes, for example, that the other parent or perhaps siblings have no impact on the feelings and behaviours within the dyadic interaction.


## C.      Family Therapy

The use of family therapy as a treatment option in child abuse cases assumes that each family member has played some part in the abuse process. These may be direct (e.g., the actual application of excessive physical punishment) or indirect (e.g., one parent passively supporting the abuse). Unfortunately, research on family system dynamics is just beginning, so that a full inventory of family patterns leading to abuse is not yet available. However, the family systems-oriented worker may keep in mind patterns identified in the literature on family dysfunctioning, including scapegoating, the failure of intergenerational boundaries, communicational pathologies, and role rigidity. Family workers may also keep in mind the importance of family life-cycle developmental stages, with child abuse as a possible symptom of the failure to meet family developmental tasks (see Chapter 2).

Family therapy relies heavily on communicational analysis and group inter-vention techniques. For this reason it is more suitable for children who are old enough to express their feelings, and for adults with verbal skills. Family therapy would be contraindicated where members compete for the therapist's attention or in the case of intense anger [32].


## D.      Multiple Family Therapy

Multiple family therapy in child abuse treatment requires the participation of four to six families in large treatment groups [64, 53]. Two assumptions from the causal basis of the approach are:

> that social isolation, disorganization, mobility, and loss of extended family are important contributing factors

> that child abuse by one family member is a symptom of dysfunctional family patterns

The focus in one known multiple family therapy programme is family problem-solving, particularly around interactional problems. Also, a mutual support system is encouraged among families [52].

Treatment resources include three or more therapists working with a group, using techniques such as listening, support, interpretation, and problem-solving facilitation. Group processes include problem specification, bargaining, conflict resolution, and contracting. Initial observations indicate that multiple family therapy may be a useful approach [52].

## E.    Multiple Method Programmes

Many of the programmes developed for child abuse treatment are comprehensive in their scope; that is, rather than having a singular focus (e.g., enhancing child-rearing knowledge), such programmes combine a number of components directed at several changes in the family's life. The rationale for comprehensive programmes is that abusive parents face many social and psychological difficulties. In any one case of child abuse, parents may have personality and interpersonal problems, lack adequate child care knowledge and skills, and experience a number of situational crises. Brief summaries of selected programmes follow:

*1.      The Child Abuse Project at the University Medical Center at the University of Pennsylvania, Philadelphia [67, 68]*

This programme aims to (a) teach parents skills to help them function as adults, (b) give them knowledge related to healthy child development, (c) teach alternative child care management methods, and (d) help them obtain needed social services. Seven staff members provide assistance through teaching, demonstration, and monitoring. As well, they act as role models for obtaining needed social services. Families participate for one year. A success rate of 84% in achieving treatment goals is reported.

*2.      Intensive Crisis Intervention: Catholic Children's Service Program, Tacoma, Washington [48]*

This programme is unique in its intensity and the short-term duration of therapeutic input. The main objective is to avoid out-of-home placement of children in highly troubled families. To be successful, workers must have small caseloads and be capable of offering a wide range of services. Close liaison with other community agencies is a requisite. Clients receive intensive therapeutic input during a six-week period, receiving as much contact as is needed. If problems are not resolved after six weeks, the child is removed. Intervention goals are crisis resolution and improving relations and child rearing, using a mixture of group and individual modalities. Techniques include operant and respondent conditioning, parent effectiveness training, values clarification, fair-fighting techniques, and crisis intervention. The staff estimated that, during the first few years of the program, placement of the child was avoided in 87% of cases.

3.     *Intensive Training in Child Care and Management: FACT: Families and Children
       Together [40]*

This programme is also designed to provide intensive intervention to abusive
and high-risk families who otherwise might have their children removed.

Clients, including parents and children, are brought together away from the
home for three days a week. A child care teacher works closely with her or his
assigned clients, and provides a series of therapeutic experiences involving formal and
informal teaching, modelling, and practice in appropriate child rearing and family
management activities.

The programme is goal-oriented and individualized: parents set goals for
themselves and their children, plan methods for achieving goals, and keep records.
Individualized training is supplemented with group discussions and child rearing or
family life workshops.

This programme was designed for adjudicated parents. After a six-month
period, a progress report is given to the court, with three possible outcomes: (a)
release from the programme with no further comment, (b) continued participation for
another six months, or (c) the removal of the child from the home. No evaluation
results are available other than qualitatively reported positive change in all participants.

4.     *Multiple-Level Skill Development Programme [72]*

This programme is designed to improve several aspects of the abusing parents' child-rearing techniques, family life, and life conditions. It is based on five
general research findings concerning child abuse:

> Abusive parents lack consistency in child rearing and, consequently,
> are ineffective in managing their children's behaviour.

> Abusive parents have unrealistic expectations concerning appropriate
> behaviour at each developmental stage.

> Abusive parents, including unmarried adult partners, experience a high
> degree of interpersonal strain.

> Abusive parents are dissatisfied with their jobs and their interpersonal
> relationships with others.

For these reasons, the programme has components in (1) child management,
(2) marital relations, (3) vocational skills, and (4) interpersonal skills. Each of these is
briefly summarized.

### 1. The Child Management Programme

Drawing on Patterson's [56, 58], Patterson and Fleischman's [75], and
Jensen's [42] work, this programme module provides:

> an introduction to age-appropriate behaviour
>
> instructions on the use of consequences

guidelines on the isolation of behaviour to be changed

instructions on the use of stimulus control techniques to influence rates and types of behaviour

guidelines on graphs and tables to chart change

### 2. The Marital Enrichment Programme

Based on Wodarski's work [72], the marital enrichment element offers:

training in communication: active and non-judgemental listening, openness, etc.

ways to analyze elements of conflict in relationships

training in marital contracting

### 3. The Vocational Enrichment Programme

This programme develops interpersonal skills and assertive behaviour, and includes training in introductions, conversation initiation, making and refusing requests, and appropriate use of nonverbal behaviour.

Each programme segment, with vocational and social enrichment combined, is presented for eight weeks. A number of assessment instruments are utilized, including the Parental Attitude Towards Child Scale, Marital Satisfaction Scale, Social Satisfaction and Family Relations Scale.

### 5.       *Facilitating Nurturing and Problem-Solving in Groups [33]*

This is a community-based programme for abusive or high-risk mothers. The structure of activities is based on a number of research observations concerning abusive parents:

They lack abilities to nurture.

They lack verbal communication skills and rely on physical contact.

They are socially isolated.

They lack problem-solving skills.

They lack knowledge of child development, as well as child management knowledge and skills.

The programme was designed to reverse deficits in all of the foregoing areas, and primarily to provide resocializing opportunities in nurturing and problem-solving. Nurturing is provided by program staff, and is manifested through hairdressing, lunch preparation, and social conversations. The main assumption is that abuse-prone parents were never nurtured themselves, and therefore benefit from exposure to nurturing models.

Problem-solving opportunities arise from naturally-occurring difficulties within groups. These stressors allow participants the chance to take risks, solve problems, and make decisions, thereby enhancing their skills in these areas. It is recommended that nurturing and problem-solving activities proceed concurrently.

Staff members include social workers, mental health workers, volunteers (lunch preparation), and a hairdresser. Social worker roles involve teaching, nurturing, group dynamics, and problem-solving activities. Group work consultants are instrumental in helping workers integrate the nurturing and problem-solving aspects of the programme, as well as deal with the frustrations of working with depressed clients who feel hopeless.

The evaluation of the programme was inconclusive, with groups differing in their levels of success in changing social isolation, self-esteem, and behaviour. However, staff felt that mothers gained social skills and outside interests.


## XIV. SUMMARY


The first sections of this chapter reviewed the personality, family situational, and societal conditions affecting child abuse. To expand the worker's understanding, attention was given to (a) theoretical approaches and (b) an inventory of factors associated with abuse. Despite the wealth of research, only recently has the search for single-factor explanations been abandoned. An ecological approach, with its emphasis on how the many aspects of personalities and situations combine to affect needs attainment, may be an important development. The implication for assessment is that high-risk family environments represent a wide spectrum of personal, interactional, and situational characteristics. Some highly negative factors, however abhorrent, may be neutralized by others.

The last several sections described a range of practice guidelines and treatment options for working with physically abusive parents. Recognizing that child welfare workers have limited opportunities for lengthy clinical treatment, the chapter began by suggesting that realistic interventions should incorporate crisis intervention and nurturing principles. Several general principles were outlined, many of which would guide workers' interaction with clients and facilitate treatment outcomes. Nurturing aspects of the role were described. The chapter concluded with a review of various treatment modalities, ones which workers might keep in mind when considering referral or longer-term programs.

### REFERENCES

1. Bender, B. "Self-Chosen Victims: Scapegoating Behavior Sequential to Battering", Child Welfare, Vol. LV, June 1976, pp. 417–422.

2. Conger, R. D., Burgess, R. L., and Barrett, C. "Child Abuse Related to Life Change and Perceptions of Illness: Some Preliminary Findings", The Family Coordinator, Vol. 28, January 1979, pp. 73–78.

3. Duberman, L. The Reconstituted Family. Chicago: Nelson-Hall, 1975.

4. Friedrich, W. N. and Boriskin, A. "The Role of the Child in Abuse: A Review of the Literature", American Journal of Orthopsychiatry, Vol. 46, October 1976, pp. 580–590.

5. Baldwin, B. A. "A Paradigm for the Classification of Emotional Crisis: Implications for Crisis Intervention". American Journal of Orthopsychiatry, Vol. 48, 1978, pp. 538–551.

6. Garbarino, J. and Gilliam, G. Understanding Abusive Families. Lexington, Mass.: Lexington Books, 1980.

7. Gelles, R. "Violence Toward Children in the United States", American Journal of Orthopsychiatry, Vol. 48, October 1978, pp. 580–592.

8. Gil, D. G. *Violence Against Children: Physical Abuse in the United States.* Cambridge, Mass.: Harvard University Press, 1970.

9. Giovannoni, J. M. and Becerra, R. M. *Defining Child Abuse.* New York: The Free Press, 1979.

10. Greenland, C. *Child Abuse in Ontario.* Toronto: Ministry of Community and Social Services, 1973.

11. Jayaratne, S. "Child Abusers as Parents and Children: A Review", Social Work, Vol. 22, January 1977, pp. 5–9.

12. Justice, B. and Duncan, D. F. "Life Crisis as a Presursor to Child Abuse", Public Health Reports, Vol. 91, 1976.

13. Kadushin, A. *Child Welfare Services* (3rd ed.). New York: Macmillan Publishing Co., Inc., 1980.

14. Lenoski, E. F. "Translating Injury Data into Preventive and Health Care Services", Draft, University of Southern California School of Medicine, Los Angeles, 1974.

15. Lynch, M. "Risk Factors in the Child: A Study of Abused Children and Their Siblings", in Martin, H. et al. (ed.) *The Abused Child: A Multidisciplinary Approach to Developmental Issues and Treatment.* Cambridge, Mass.: Ballinger Publishing Co., 1976, pp. 43–56.

16. Maden, M. and Wrench, D. "Significant Findings in Child Abuse Research", Victimology: An International Journal, Vol. 11, No. 2, Summer 1977.

17. Martin, H. P., Beezley, P., Conway, E. F., and Kempe, C. H. "The Development of Abused Children", in Shulman, I. (ed.) *Advances in Pediatrics*, Vol. 21, Chicago: Year Book Medical Publishers, Inc., 1974, pp. 25–73.

18. Merrill, E. J. "Physical Abuse of Children: An Agency Study", in De Francis, V. (ed.) *Protecting the Battered Child.* Denver, Colo.: American Humane Society, 1973.

19. Province of Ontario Ministry of Community and Social Services, Children's Services Division, "Report of the Task Force on Child Abuse," June 1978.

20. Province of Ontario Ministry of Community and Social Services, Children's Division, "Standards and Guidelines for the Management of Child Abuse Cases," April 1979.

21. Mitchell, R. E. "Some Social Implications of High Density Housing", American Sociological Review, Vol. 36, February 1971, pp. 18–29.

22. National Center on Child Abuse and Neglect. "1977 Analysis of Child Abuse and Neglect Research", January 1978.

23. Parke, R. and Collmer, C. "Child Abuse: An Interdisciplinary Analysis", in *Review of Child Development Research*, Vol. V., Chicago: University of Chicago Press, 1975.

24. Polier, J. W. "Professional Abuse of Children: Responsibility for the Delivery of Services", American Journal of Orthopsychiatry, Vol. 45, April 1975, pp. 357–362.

25. Schlesinger, B. "Child Abuse in Canada", Guidance Centre, Faculty of Education, University of Toronto, 1977.

26. Spinetta, J. and Rigler, D. "The Child Abusing Parent: A Psychological Review", Psychological Bulletin, Vol. 77, April 1972, pp. 296–304.

27. Steinmetz, S. K. "Intra-familial Patterns of Conflict Resolution: United States and Canadian Comparisons", Paper presented at the Annual Meeting for the Society for the Study of Social Problems, 1974.

28. _____ and Strauss, M. (eds.) *Violence in the Family.* New York: Dodd, Mead, 1974.

29. Van Stolk, M. *The Battered Child in Canada.* Toronto: McClelland and Stewart Ltd., 1978.

30. Bean, S. L. "The Use of Specialized Day Care in Preventing Child Abuse", in Eberling, N. B. and Hill, D. A. (eds.) *Child Abuse—Intervention and Treatment.* Acton, Mass.: Publishing Science Group, Inc., 1975.

31. Beezley, P., Martin, H. P., and Kempe, R., "Psychotherapy", in Martin, H. P. *The Abused Child: A Multidisciplinary Approach to Developmental Issues and Treatment.* Cambridge, Mass.: Ballinger Publishing Co., 1976, pp. 201–214.

32. ———. "Modern Treatment Options", in Schmitt, B. (ed.) *The Child Protection Team Handbook*. New York and London: Garland STPM Press, 1978, pp. 267–277.

33. Breton, M., Welbourn, A., and Watters, J. "A Nurturing and Problem Solving Approach for Abuse-Prone Mothers", Child Abuse and Neglect, Vol. 5, 1981.

34. Breton, M. "Resocialization of Abusive Parents", Social Work, Vol. 26, March 1981, pp. 119–123.

35. Davoren, E. "Working with Abusive Parents: A Social Worker's View", Children Today, Vol. 4, May–June, 1975, pp. 2, 38–43.

36. Eberling, N. B. and Hill, D. A. *Child Abuse: Intervention and Treatment*. Acton, Mass.: Publishing Science Group, Inc., 1975.

37. Franklin, A. W. (ed.). *Concerning Child Abuse*. New York: Churchill Livingston, Medical Division of Longman Group Ltd., 1975.

38. Gardener, L. "The Gilday Center: A Method of Intervention for Child Abuse" in Eberling, N. B. et al. (eds.), *Child Abuse: Intervention and Treatment*. Acton, Mass.: Publishing Science Group, Inc., 1975.

39. Halperin, S. L. "Abused and Non-Abused Children's Perceptions of their Mothers, Fathers and Siblings: Implications for a Comprehensive Family Treatment Plan", Family Relations, Vol. 30, January 1981, pp. 89–96.

40. Helfer, R. E. and Kempe, C. H. *Child Abuse and Neglect: The Family and the Community*. Cambridge, Mass.: Ballinger Publishing Co., 1976.

41. Holmes, S., Barnhart, C., Cantoni, L., and Reymer, E. "Working with the Parent in Child Abuse Cases", Social Casework, Vol. 56, January 1975, pp. 3–12.

42. Jensen, R. E. "A Behaviour Modification Program to Remediate Child Abuse", Journal of Clinical Child Psychology, 1976.

43. Justice, R. and Justice B. "TA Work with Child Abuse", Transactional Analysis Journal, January 1975.

44. Justice, B. and Justice R. *The Abusing Family*. New York: Human Sciences Press, 1976.

45. ——— and ———. "Evaluating Outcome of Group Therapy for Abusing Parents", Corrective and Social Psychiatry, January 1978.

46. Kadushin, A. "Protection Services", Chapter 5 in Kadushin, A. (ed.) *Child Welfare Services* (3rd ed.), New York: Macmillan Publishing Co. Inc., 1980.

47. Kempe, C. H. and Helfer, R. E., *Helping the Battered Child and His Family*. Philadelphia and Toronto: J. B. Lippincott Co., 1972.

48. Kinney, J. "Homebuilders: An In-Home Crisis Intervention Program", Children Today, Vol. 7, Jan.–Feb., 1978, pp. 15–17, 35.

49. Lee, C. M. (ed.) *Child Abuse: A Reader and Sourcebook*. New York: The Open University Press, 1978.

50. Martin, H. P. and Kempe, C. H. *The Abused Child: A Multidisciplinary Approach to Developmental Issues and Treatment*. Cambridge, Mass.: Ballinger Publishing Co., 1976.

51. Mastria, E., Mastria, M., and Harkins, J. "Treatment of Child Abuse by Behavioural Intervention: A Case Report", Child Welfare, Vol. LVIII, April 1979, pp. 253–261.

52. McKamy, L. R. "Multiple Family Therapy: A Treatment Modality for Child Abuse Cases", International Journal of Child Abuse and Neglect, 1977, pp. 339–345.

53. McNeil, J. S. and McBride, M. L. "Group Therapy with Abusive Parents", Social Casework, Vol. 60, January 1979, pp. 36–42.

54. Oppenheimer, A. "Triumph over Trauma in the Treatment of Child Abuse", Social Casework, 59, June 1978.

55. Parke, R. D. and Collman, C. W. "Child Abuse: An Interdisciplinary Analysis", in E. M. Heatherington (ed.) *Review of Child Development Research*, Vol. 5. Chicago: University of Chicago Press, 1975.

56. Patterson, G. R. *Families: Application of Social Learning to Family Life*. Champaign, Ill.: Research Press, 1971.

57. ———. "Interventions for Boys with Conduct Problems: Multiple Settings, Treatments and Criteria", Journal of Consulting and Clinical Psychology, 1974.

58. ———. Families. Eugene, Ore.: Castalia, 1975.

59. ———. Living with Children: New Methods for Parents and Teachers. Champaign, Ill.: Research Press, 1976.

60. Paulson, M. J. and Anne Cheleff. "Parent Surrogate Roles: A Dynamic Concept in Understanding and Treating Abusive Parents", Journal of Clinical Child Psychology, Fall 1973.

61. ——— et al. "Parents of the Abrasive Child: A Multidisciplinary Group Therapy Approach to Life-Threatening Behaviour", Life-Threatening Behavior, Vol. 4, Spring 1974, pp. 18–31.

62. Sandler, J., Van Dercar, S., and Milhoan, M. "Training Child Abusers in the Use of Positive Reinforcement Practices", Behavioral Research and Therapy, Vol. 16, 1978.

63. Sharer, K. M. "Rescue Fantasies: Professional Impediments in Working with Abused Families", American Journal of Nursing, Vol. 78, September 1978, pp. 1483–1484.

64. Shorkey, C. T. "A Review of Methods Used in the Treatment of Abusing Parent", Social Casework: The Journal of Contemporary Social Work, Vol. 60, 1979, pp. 360–367.

65. Steele, B. F. and Pollock, D. A. "A Psychiatric Study of Parents Who Abuse Infants and Small Children", in Helfer, R. E. and Kempe, C. H. (eds.) The Battered Child. Chicago: Chicago University Press, 1974, pp. 89–133.

66. ———. "Working With Abusive Parents From a Psychiatric Point of View", Washington D.C.: U.S. Department of Health, Education, and Welfare, 1975.

67 Tracy, J. and Clark, E. "Treatment for Child Abusers", Social Work, Vol. 19, May 1974, pp. 338–342.

68 ———, Ballard, C., and Clark, E. "Child Abuse Project: A Follow Up", Social Work, Vol. 20, September 1975, pp. 398–399.

69 Walters, D. R. Physical and Sexual Abuse of Children: Causes and Treatment. Bloomington and London: Indiana University Press, 1975.

70 Williams, G. J. and Money, J. Traumatic Abuse and Neglect of Children at Home". Baltimore and London: The John Hopkins University Press, 1980.

71 Wodarski, J. S. and Bagarozzi, D. Behavioural Social Work. New York: Human Sciences Press, 1979.

72 ———. "Treatment of Parents Who Abuse Their Children: A Literature Review and Implications For Professionals", Child Abuse and Neglect, Vol. 5, 1981.

73 Roberts, M. "Reciprocal Nature of Parent-Infant Interaction: Implications for Child Maltreatment", Child Welfare, Vol. LVIII, June 1979, pp. 383–392.

74 McRae, K. N., Ferguson, C., and Lederman, R. "The Battered Child Syndrome", Canadian Medical Association Journal, Vol. 108, April 7, 1973, pp. 859–866.

75 Patterson, G. R. and Fleischman, M. J. "Maintenance of Treatment Effects: Some Considerations Concerning Family Systems and Follow-Up Data", Behaviour Therapy, Vol. 10, 1979, pp. 168–185.

76 Aquilera, D. and Messick, J. Crisis Intervention: Theory and Methodology. (3rd ed.), St. Louis, Mo.: The C. V. Mosby Company, 1978.

77 Butcher, J. N. and Maudel, G. R. "Crisis Intervention" in Weinder, I. (ed.) Clinical Methods in Psychology. New York: John Wiley & Sons, Inc., 1976.

78. Calhoun, L. C., Selby, J. W., and King, M. F. Dealing With Crisis. Englewood Cliffs, N.J.: Prentice-Hall, Inc., 1976.

79 Dixon, S. L. Working with People in Crisis: Theory and Practice. St. Louis, Mo.: The C. V. Mosby Company, 1979.

80. Golan, N. Treatment in Crisis Situations. New York: The Free Press, 1978.

81. Hoff, L. People in Crisis: Understanding and Helping. Menlo Park, Calif.: Addison-Wesley Publishing Company, Inc., 1978.

82. McKee, R. K. Crisis Intervention in the Community. Baltimore, Md.: University Park Press, 1974.

83. Parad, H. (ed.). Crisis Intervention: Selected Readings. New York: Family Service Association of America, 1965.

84. Puryear, D. *Helping People in Crisis*. San Francisco: Jossey-Bass, Inc., Publishers, 1979.

85. Reid, W. and Epstein, L. *Task-Centered Casework*. New York: Columbia University Press, 1971.

86. Smith, L. L. "Crisis Intervention Theory and Practice: A Source Book", Washington, D.C.: University Press of Washington, 1975.

87. Pill, C. "A Family Life Education Group for Working with Stepparents", Social Casework, Vol. 62, March 1981, pp. 159–166.

88. Visher, E. and Visher, J. *Step-Families: A Guide to Working with Step-parents and Stepchildren*. New York: Brunner/Mazel, 1979.

# 6
# Sexual Abuse in the Family: Dynamics and Treatment

FRANK MAIDMAN

I. INTRODUCTION 184
II. SEXUAL ABUSE: MEANING AND OCCURRENCE 184
   A. Definition 184
   B. Prevalence and Incidence 185
   C. Social Background 186
III. THE CONTEXT OF SEXUAL ABUSE 186
   A. The Societal Context of Sexual Abuse 188
   B. The Sexually Abusing Family's External Context 189
IV. DYNAMICS: INDUCTION 189
   A. Motivation to Seek Sex from Child 189
   B. Weakening of the Incest Taboo 190
   C. Social Control 191
   D. Access to the Child 192
   E. Fear of Abandonment 193
   F. The Victim's Understanding of Appropriate Sexual
      Behaviour 194
V. DYNAMICS: MAINTENANCE OF SEXUAL ABUSE 194
   A. Forestalled Awareness of the Incest Taboo 195
   B. Family Control 196
   C. External Responses 196
   D. Denial and the Family Secret 196
   E. Sexual Abuse as a Symptom of Family Problems 197
   F. The Victim 197
VI. DYNAMICS: DISSOLUTION OF THE PATTERN 198
   A. Attempts at Revelation 198
   B. Family Response to Crisis 198
   C. The Effects of Sexual Abuse on the Victim 199
VII. WORKING WITH CASES OF SEXUAL ABUSE 200
   A. Introduction 200
   B. Guidelines for Investigating Sexual Abuse 201
   C. Referring the Family for Treatment 204
VIII. SUMMARY 209
   REFERENCES 209

## I.    INTRODUCTION

Current knowledge of intra-familial sexual abuse is in a primitive state. Not only are its true rates unknown, but those cases that are known are imperfectly understood. Most of the information comes from American clinical studies which draw from certain sectors of society and which do not make adequate comparisons to non-sexually abusing groups. Because of these and other technical inadequacies of the research, the present state of knowledge must be described as exploratory [28].

The current state of sexual abuse treatment is also underdeveloped. Family therapy, the emerging treatment of choice, has clear difficulties which weaken this modality. Significantly, only two instances of treatment evaluation have been reported in the literature [15, 24, 6].

This chapter aims to assist the assessment process by providing a review of sexual abuse dynamics and consequences. Also, some guidelines are presented for the investigation process, including ideas on interviewing various family members. Finally, a brief review of treatment options is presented to assist workers' referrals to community resources.

## II.    SEXUAL ABUSE: MEANING AND OCCURRENCE

### A.    Definition

In the literature, sexual abuse has been used synonymously with such terms as "sexual assault", "incest", and "sexual victimization". Sexual abuse may be regarded as a type of incest involving a child as one of the participants. Incest, although subject to different legal definitions, is typically regarded as sexual relations between people who are so closely related by blood that they are forbidden to marry. Presented below is a definition of intra-familial sex abuse:

> Sexual abuse . . . is perpetrated on a child by a member of that child's family group (and) includes not only sexual intercourse, but also any act designed to stimulate a child sexually, or to use the child for the sexual stimulation, either of the perpetrator or of another person. "Family" . . . who includes parents and parent surrogates . . . people who, by sexually abusing a child, are exploiting some kind of non-sexual parent relationship, no matter how indirect or temporary, with that child [29].

Sexual acts between adults and children which come to the attention of social agencies and courts include fondling, exposure, genital intercourse, oral-genital contacts, and sexual kissing. Genital intercourse is most likely to occur with teenage children.

For child protection purposes then, sexual abuse is viewed as a type of child abuse. Both sexual abuse and physical abuse are likely to be inter-related with other family problems, and both involve an enduring family pattern sustained by complex forces (see Chapter 5). However, they are dissimilar in the following ways:

Physical abuse is rarely used as a punishment to induce sexual abuse.

Lasting trauma from sexual abuse is more likely to be psychological than physical.

Different motivations are involved.

Different societal reactions are evoked, with society being less tolerant of sex with children.

Unlike physical abuse, the social visibility of sexual abuse occurs mostly at adolescence.

One characterization of sex abuse uses the phrase "sexual victimization" to call attention to participants' age-inequalities in terms of knowledge and power [11].

## B.    Prevalence and Incidence

The rate of occurrence of sexual abuse in North America is unknown. Knowledge of it is based primarily on cases which come to the attention of courts and social service agencies, although a few surveys of non-clinical populations have been conducted.

Highlights from American studies estimate that:

From 2% to 4% of the general population have experienced incest [28, 42].

These figures are much higher in clinical populations (e.g., 15% of training school women, 10% of social agency female clients, 4% of female psychiatric patients, 25% of women with three or more illegitimate pregnancies, and 9% of imprisoned male rapists) [28].

28% of women and 23% of men in a non-clinical, university student survey reported experiences of incest within the family [42].

Reports of sexual abuse within the family are on the increase [43] (possibly due to improved reporting procedures and openness in society rather than changes in occurrence rates).

70% to 80% of child sexual abuse occurs in the family [42].

Brother-sister incest occurs most often [11], possibly five times as often as that between father and daughter.

Father-daughter and stepfather-stepdaughter sexual abuse, however, is reported most.

Mother-son incest is rare, and father-son incest is rarest [39].

Since child sexual abuse is under-reported, prevailing estimates are conservative. Under-reporting may be attributed to fear of family disruption and/or loss of breadwinner, fear of court proceedings, threats within the family, and disbelief or recognition difficulties by professionals.

Although officially reported sexual abuse cases may differ from those unreported, no large-scale studies have identified these differences. An American non-clinical survey of child sexual victimization both inside and outside of the family suggests that among reported cases, there are more girls, more younger children, more parents and known offenders, fewer young offenders, and fewer reports of coercion. At this writing comparable Canadian statistics were unavailable.

## C.    Social Background

Most studies of incest and familial sexual abuse suggest that the phenomena are more prevalent among lower-income families. However, critics of such studies argue that (1) these deviances are probably as prevalent in upper classes, but that they are better able to conceal them, and (2) clinical samples which form the basis of many studies tend to over-represent lower-income families. Notwithstanding these considerations, the most recent survey available of a non-clinical population shows a clear relationship between class and the experience of incest and extra-familial sexual victimization, particularly among females.

There is an emerging belief that incest often occurs in rural areas. This hypothesis has been confirmed in studies conducted in four countries, as well as one survey in which rural and urban rates were compared.

## III.    THE CONTEXT OF SEXUAL ABUSE

An inventory of conditions thought to be related to sexual abuse, although far from conclusive, suggests that:

No one explanation is sufficient to account for the occurrence of different types of intra-familial sexual abuse.

Intra-familial sexual abuse occurs when a number of social, individual, biological, and family conditions are present, and it likely occurs when a number of different combinations of conditions are present.

In considering the dynamics of intra-familial sexual abuse, three types of information are presented:

1. *The contexts of sexual abuse:* Societal conditions, individual characteristics, and family situations which have been typically associated with sexual abuse are explained.

2. *The process of sexual abuse:* Given that it involves certain types of individuals and occurs within certain families, which behaviours or interactions start and maintain a pattern of sexual abuse? Part of this "maintenance"

process is the family's reaction or presentation to the outside world upon discovery. These presentations are particularly important for officials and staff of social and legal agencies, since efforts to change must also address these discovery and maintenance issues.

3. *The consequences of sexual abuse:* This addresses the consequences to individual victims and provides information on those aspects of abusive relationships which seem most traumatic.

Clinical and survey research have associated a host of individual and family factors with sexual abuse. However, these findings are inconsistent and difficult to compare because research samples are from vastly different sectors of the population (e.g., prison/court populations, social agencies, university student populations). For a tentative picture of sexually abusive parents and indicators, see Chapter 2, Section III, "Assessing High Risk".

A second problem is that most research has investigated families in which sexual abuse has occurred, and comparisons have not been made with non-abusing families. Thus, we do not know whether the correct causal factors have been identified; in fact, many are similar to causal factors identified in the development of other deviances (e.g., parental emotional deprivation, marital conflict, passive or over-controlling fathers, inappropriate family roles, and the like).

A further consideration is that clinical research observations may reflect simply the individual or family responses to the *identification* of sexual abuse and the initial stages of society's intervention.

Finally, any family phenomenon takes place in a web of interacting factors; no one factor can cause sexual abuse. Despite this awareness, there is always the temptation to isolate one family or individual characteristic as more "pathological" than others.

In considering the context and dynamics of sexual abuse, one should keep in mind that those individual and family factors now assumed to be instrumental to the development of sex abuse may, upon further inquiry, prove to be less "pathogenic" when combined with other forces. The search must continue for "family strengths" which may nullify negative family characteristics. For a fuller discussion of family factors, see Chapters 1, II E and 2, IV.

Despite these research limitations, it is possible to establish some order to our knowledge. Most of the observations on the context of sexual abuse (whether societal, familial, or individual), are premised on certain fundamental processes, both interactional and psychological, which are assumed to operate within the family and to govern the family's relationships with the outside world.

These processes are presented within three general categories which conceptually isolate three phases of sexual abuse:

1. The induction of the victim into the role of sex partner

2. The family's maintenance of this pattern over time

3. The dissolution of the sexual abuse pattern

Before discussing these three processes, some observations on the societal context of sexual abuse are presented.

## A.    The Societal Context of Sexual Abuse

Although the incest taboo is considered a universal norm, rates of sexual abuse are higher in certain societies and in certain subgroups. Three broad social and cultural conditions have been cited to explain a high rate in North America: a patriarchal system, lack of children's rights, and social fragmentation.

### 1.    *The Ideology of Male Supremacy*

Sexual abuse of children and women is believed to be more prevalent where men are the dominant group. In patriarchal families the incest taboo is more likely to be broken by men than by women. With unrestricted rights of physical control and sexual access, men have better opportunities to extend their prerogatives to sexual contact with children, should they so desire. The absence of maternal protection against the abuse is explained by the mother's powerlessness in the family and extreme dependency on her husband.

Men are rarely involved in child rearing. According to recent psychoanalytical thinking [15], in a situation where mother is the prime love object in childrearing and is generally a low-status person, men's and women's development may provide the psychological conditions for father-daughter incest. For example, men learn to suppress the capacity for nurturance and affectionate identification with women. Thus, a contemptuous attitude towards women becomes part of normal masculine identity.

The partriarchal family structure and the sex-role division of labour are, of course, supported by the society-at-large. In addition to an ideology of male supremacy, socio-economic factors which limit women's opportunities to gain independence are most important. Limited job and daycare opportunities, for example, keep women economically dependent on their husbands and reinforce their child-rearing functions within the family.

### 2.    *Children's Rights*

Certain features of children's power positions in society may indirectly contribute to sexual abuse. Without adequate sex education, for example, many young victims are unaware of the inappropriateness of their abuser's actions. Also, society grants inordinate adult rights over the bodies and minds of young children. Children's rights advocates argue that no one should have sanctioned powers to make children uncomfortable in mind or body. If this happens, children should be made aware of their right to take action [15].

### 3.    *Social Fragmentation*

This refers to social isolation of individuals and families. Social isolation develops from increased mobility, the disintegration of neighbourhoods and communities, and a weakening of extended kin ties. Such factors promote a reduction in social supervision and control, and deprive family members of social support and intimacy. This is likely to increase the prevalence and decrease the visibility of socially unacceptable behaviour. Although social fragmentation is cited as an explanation of differences in rates of deviance, it does not explain the choice of one deviant behaviour over another. (For further discussion of social isolation, see Chapters 1(D) and 3, IV, A, D.)

## B.    The Sexually Abusing Family's External Context

A family's relationship to the outside world (i.e., its class position, degree of social isolation, and subcultural membership) is often cited as a factor conducive to the perpetration of sexual abuse. These external social factors may promote sexual abuse in various ways.

Many sexually abusive families are described as socially isolated, whether living in secluded rural communities or isolated from their urban communities. This isolation weakens external social controls and removes the opportunity to satisfy sexual needs outside the family. In general, there is a high degree of intra-familial dependency for needs-satisfaction in socially isolated situations. The father is usually depicted as instrumental in controlling family members' outside interests and contacts, particularly those of the early adolescent female victim. Such limited experience tends to forestall not only her awareness of the incest taboo but also forestalls the dissolution of the sexually abusive behaviour. (See Section VI: "Dynamics: Dissolution of the Pattern".)

## IV.    DYNAMICS: INDUCTION

We now turn to the first of three processes of sexual abuse: induction of the victim, maintenance of the abuse pattern, and dissolution of the abuse pattern.

The methods and explanations for how a socially and psychologically inappropriate person is chosen and influenced to be a sex partner have been given piecemeal treatment in the literature. These processes and the factors influencing them are either individual or social/interactional phenomena. These distinctions will be retained in the following discussion.

## A.    Motivation to Seek Sex from Child

Why does an adult seek sexual gratification from a child in the family? As a starting point for this discussion, it must be assumed that the sex drive differs among men. Beyond this, one very consistent clinical observation is that marital sexuality has broken down; in addition, many perpetrators of sexual abuse are unwilling to seek sexual gratification in extramarital liaisons. Decline in sexual activity between spouses is usually cited as an antecedent factor; although this may be true initially, the decline in the marital relationships conceivably has a circular relationship to sexual abuse. Once started, sex abuse further contributes to marital estrangement.

Although pedophilia has been ruled out in the psychological explanations of parent-child sex, consideration is nonetheless given to some husbands' inability to enjoy sexual relations with adults. The so-called "introversive" father, for example, has experienced an emotionally deprived childhood and has developed hostility towards his own mother. Psychodynamically, the search for mother, coupled with hostility and fear of abandonment by his wife and the identification of the daughter with his mother, promotes a psychological situation where the daughter is a more desirable source of sexual gratification. This psychodynamic explanation should be compared with the focus on current family roles in a later description of the "little mother" syndrome. (See Section IV D: "Access to the Child".)

## B.    Weakening of the Incest Taboo

Although the family is regarded as an appropriate and desirable context in which to have sexual relations, the incest taboo is a universal norm prohibiting sex between *certain* members of the nuclear and extended family. Parental use of children sexually is a violation of the incest taboo and one which invokes particular horror. One of the explanations of sexual abuse is that the incest taboo is either unknown or weak. The following observations support this explanation:

Sexual abuse often occurs between a stepfather, father-substitute, or mother's boyfriend and a female child within the family; not being natural father and daughter, the incest taboo is a weaker source of inner control on sexual behaviour. This explanation has been invoked for both the adult males and the daughters, particularly when the latter are near or in adolescence.

The perpetrator of sexual abuse, regardless of social class, is himself often from a poor parent-child situation, in which there was conflict and emotional deprivation; this background is believed to be unconducive to learning norms of morality and, in particular, the incest taboo.

In some cases, perpetrators and their spouses are themselves known to come from families where incestuous relationships occurred; this weakens the awareness of, and later commitment to, the incest taboo.

The young victim of sexual abuse has not yet learned and experienced social reinforcement of the incest taboo; under certain conditions, the incest taboo is a weak source of inner control.

Many, although clearly not all, sexual abuse perpetrators are observed to use and/or abuse alcohol; although the role of alcohol in sexual abuse is a complicated matter, one explanation is that, under the influence of alcohol the moral inhibitions governing sex in the family are inhibited.

Some sexual abuse cases have begun under conditions of situational stress (e.g., unemployment, divorce, death, accident); it is assumed that stress weakens the strength of the incest taboo.

Other family conditions can influence the incest taboo:

A number of studies indicate that some cases of sexual abuse occur in small isolated rural communities with distinctive subcultures; those in such communities do not look upon incest with the same negative attitude as does the larger society.

Many sexually abusive families are socially isolated; this pattern creates a moral vacuum whereby the incest taboo lacks symbolic reinforcement, either through the cues from normal involvement with others or comparable reinforcements from the mass media and other institutions.

Sexual abuse frequently occurs in multiproblem families where incest is one component of a subculture of "loose" sex. The manifestations include parental extramarital promiscuity, general incest, a lack of privacy, generally diluted sexual taboos, and the like.

In summary, nine different findings are consistent with the notion of a weak or non-existent incest taboo, based on either (1) individual consciousness or (2) subcultures created through family or community isolation.

Early thinking claimed that sexual abuse was committed by degenerate personalities (e.g., those with psychopathology, sociopathy, and low intelligence). All of these characteristics were assumed to affect or subsume a weak or non-existent taboo. However, recent research results are not consistent with such personality types.


## C.    Social Control

Whereas the incest taboo is an inner source of control, the external sanctions against unacceptable behaviour are referred to as social controls. Although the external control process is complex, it may break down in simple ways. The very structure of the nuclear family, with its limited visibility to the outside world, together with the accepted norm of family privacy, are impediments to the visibility necessary for social control. As well, we noted how societal fragmentation is believed to lessen social controls by weakening kin, neighbourhood, and community ties. The acute social isolation of sexually abusive families is thought to limit incest's visibility, the potential for disclosure to social control agents within the community, and the activation of social sanctions.

Within the family, external control breaks down in the following ways:

In most sexually abusive families, the non-participating members are thought to know about the abuse, and not take any action. Although the mother is usually singled out in this family pattern of collusion, there is considerable clinical evidence that other family members are aware of the abuse. Personality characteristics of the mother (weakness, passivity, dependency) are usually cited as instrumental in her weak efforts to stop the abuse. Also important is the ideology of male supremacy, i.e., the dominance of men over women and children.

In many sexually abusive families, the father perpetrator is depicted as a particularly domineering figure—authoritarian, controlling, and cruel. This behaviour should be seen as reciprocal to the wife's passivity, and probably undermines actual or potential efforts to stop the sexual abuse, if it is in fact known.

The control against sexual abuse can also come from the victim, and several factors may be cited which mitigate the victim's control of the perpetrator:

Victims are usually passive recipients, particularly during the early phases, either feigning sleep or accepting the father's explanation as to the meaning of the sexual overtures (e.g., it's a game).

All children hold positions of powerlessness, but most are able to exert influence by mobilizing the help of other family members.

In many cases where victims tried to enlist the aid of others to control sexual advances or to end a long-standing sexually abusive relationship, they failed.

There are clinical reports of mothers being angry, disbelieving, or simply not reacting to revelations by their children. In addition to this, children have been described as lacking in interpersonal skills to control the perpetrator's advances. Passive mothers in sexually abusive families provide inadequate role models. With adolescence, the victim's interpersonal skills may improve as a result of peer group involvements and sexual awareness.

Marital conflict, typical of many abusive families, also works against the child seeking assistance to control the abuse; the key dynamic here is that the child is not sure who can be counted on for protection.

What tactics do perpetrators use to induce children into sexually abusive relationships? Tactics fall into three classifications: (1) punishment or the threat of punishment, (2) reward, and (3) normalizing the relationship. All three tactics accrue from the position of power held by the perpetrator over the victim:

> 1. The degree of coercion in sexual abuse is important to know, since this seems to affect the degree of emotional trauma. Other than the sexual acts themselves, there is no strong evidence that sexual abuse is controlled by actual physical punishment or physical pain. However, as a survey of sexual victimization among college students suggests, force and coercion (physical constraint, threat) are important factors, although not necessarily in a majority of cases. The considerable clinical descriptions of authoritarian, tyrannical fathers reinforce this viewpoint.

> 2. Rewards frequently take the form of money, presents, better food, clothes, and privileges; such rewards are reportedly the cause of sibling envy, further family pathology [41], and the victim's own low self-esteem.

> 3. The perpetrator attempts to normalize the sexual abuse in the young child's mind by explaining sex: as a new game; the child's "duty" to replace an unwilling or incapacitated mother; as sex education, and the like. With adolescence these tactics cease to have much power.

Thus far, the breakdown in external and intrafamilial controls against abuse have been discussed. Other aspects of the family context addressed in the literature are those promoting access to the child as a sex partner.


## D.     Access to the Child

It was once thought that sexual abuse was more likely to occur in large families with close living and sleeping arrangements. However, there are no data to support this. A lack of supervision of the child may be a contributory factor, particu-larly in those instances where the mother has abdicated the parental role or is absent from the home (e.g., death).

A confusion of family roles is a frequently described feature of family struc-ture which indirectly increases access to the child as sexual object. Daughters are viewed as "little mothers" in the following scenario:

> Long before the incest occurs, the mother develops a special, conflict-laden relationship with the daughter.
>
> The daughter is initially treated well, is over-indulged in relationship to her siblings, and is given the responsibilities of an adult woman (e.g., child care, household tasks).
>
> Gradually, the role assumes a special wife-like relationship with the father, particularly when the marital sexual relationship is disturbed.
>
> The wife gradually becomes dependent on her daughter in a child-like fashion, displacing her feelings for her own mother onto her, a dependence which later is accompanied by hostility [28].

The family role pattern has several outcomes: the mother's inability to pro-tect her daughter, a growing and "adult-like" bond between father and daughter, and the extension of the "little mother" role into a sexual relationship. Although this pattern is frequently reported in the clinical literature, no studies have documented its *absence* in non-sexually abusive families. Nonetheless, the analytical approach is useful in order to examine the various roles and role relationships within the family. For example, one can ask:

> Who interacts with whom in regard to specific family and personal functions?
>
> How do these roles and interactions set the stage for inappropriate types of interactions?

Such role relationship patterns should be regarded as facilitating factors which, *given other conditions in the family*, help funnel relationships towards sexual abuse.

## E.     Fear of Abandonment

Normal families promote a strong sense of continuity and durability among their members; families in which sexual abuse occurs, however, harbour fears of abandonment. Such fears are attributed psychodynamically to the emotionally de-prived backgrounds of parents, or to the reality-based changes (e.g., conflict, divorce, parental absence, people coming and going) in the current family. Regardless of the etiology, the fear of abandonment may constitute a family theme, that is:

> "A pattern of feelings, motives, fantasies and conventionalized understand-ings grouped around some . . . concern which has a particular form in the personalities of the individual members" [15].

This abandonment fear affects the dynamics of sexual abuse in two ways. First, the child passively engages in the sexual relationship as a way of connecting to another family member in order to "keep the family together". This dynamic not only contributes to the induction of the child into a sexual relationship, but serves to maintain an ongoing pattern. Secondly, the discovery of sexual abuse within the family, along with the involvement of the law, social agencies, and the threat of breaking up the family, reinforce the fear of abandonment. Such a dynamic represents a particular challenge to practitioners looking for the appropriate leverage to bring about change.

### F.      The Victim's Understanding of Appropriate Sexual Behaviour

The very young child does not understand sexual behaviour and, accordingly, has not learned the incest taboo. As well, the special quality of the perpetrator's relationship to the victim, one of emotional closeness, trust, power, and authority, allows the former to label sexual advances as appropriate and even desirable. This labelling process by powerful people is particularly potent when the non-participating family members are either prevented, or refrain from, offering challenging viewpoints.

Additionally, the sexually abusive family, particularly if characterized by an atmosphere of multiple problems, sexual "looseness", and conflict, may generate very unclear messages about appropriate behaviour.

### V.      DYNAMICS: MAINTENANCE OF SEX ABUSE

Sexual abuse is frequently an ongoing family pattern rather than an isolated event. One recent survey estimates that 40% of sexual victimization has a lasting duration, and that experiences happening more than once will likely endure for an extensive period. This suggests an important diagnostic question: Why and how does sexual abuse last for so long within a family?

In many ways, the family dynamics sustaining sexual abuse are the same as those attributed to its beginnings, such that the distinction between initiating and sustaining factors may seem unnecessary. Only a longitudinal study would justify such a distinction. However, it is assumed that the configuration of causal factors will change over time. Also, family patterns which were important in the early development of sexual abuse continue to sustain the abuse, but through different processes.

This section identifies core processes presented in the literature and indicates individual or family characteristics affecting these processes. They are complex and are controlled by the operation of personality, family, societal and helping profession factors.

The maintenance of the sexual abuse within families is affected by:

a forestalled awareness of the incest taboo

the non-revelation of sexual abuse within the family

the non-revelation of sexual abuse to non-family members

personal and family accounts of what is going on

family responses to the victim's efforts to reveal the abuse

power processes within the family in which the perpetrator is able to maintain compliance with his wishes

the dynamic interdependence between the sexual abuse relationship and other disturbed family patterns

Although the current state of knowledge is rather sparse on the nature of these processes, there are sufficient clinical observations to help further research as well as identify important diagnostic questions.


## A.    Forestalled Awareness of the Incest Taboo

One of the key operating factors contributing to the maintenance of a sexual abuse relationship is the young child's lack of knowledge of the inappropriateness of such behaviour. The key question here is: How do family members, or general family characteristics, prevent the child from learning the inappropriateness of the relationship?

Case descriptions reveal that even the very young child has a *notion* that something is wrong. Charlotte Vale Allen's memory of her early conversations with her father is illustrative:

> "Daddy, are we bad?"
> "Bad, shmad. What's that, for chrissake?"
> "I don't know, but we are, aren't we?"
> "Course not."
> "And you really mean it, this is what all little girls and their daddies
> do?"
> "Didn't I tell you, eh?"
> "I know, but if everyone does it, then how come I can't tell?" [38]

The key point is that the child's notion of morality is not a fixed state, and it must be controlled in order for the abusive relationship to endure. The social isolation of the family and the initiation of sex abuse at a preadolescent age serve to limit the child's interactions with others, thereby preventing the development of moral ideas from shattering the status quo.

The perpetrator's power to control the child's moral judgements exists in the face-to-face manipulation of experience and in the control of extra-familial relations. Power to induce deviance stems from a misuse of the specific authority that parents have over their children. Clinical descriptions, however, cite other deviant-inducing relationships between the perpetrator and the victim, for instance, the "little wife/ mother" and "favorite child" syndromes. An unusual closeness, trust, and dependency for affection as a result of these roles give the perpetrator strong leverage in controlling the child's moral experience.

## B.      Family Control

At some point in the sexually abusive relationship, victims want the relationship to stop, yet, as one survey shows, most victims of sexual abuse do not tell anyone
about it.

Although evidence is sparse, it appears that the greatest pressure to change
the relationship occurs at adolescence, the family life-cycle stage when most families
are under pressure to change their parent-child relationships. The strength of family
control against this pressure to reveal the sexual abuse is apparent in the kinds of
reasons given by victims for their reluctance to reveal the abuse: the anticipation of
anger, hysteria, blame, non-belief, and/or punishment. (For an understanding of the
changes inherent to adolescent development, see Chapter 10, IA)

The balance of power in many sexually abusing families (i.e., an authoritarian father and a passive mother and victim) serves to maintain the status quo, and
often extends the abuse over many years.

## C      External Responses

Other than the occasional case history or autobiographical account, little
systematic knowledge is available concerning the victim's efforts to break the pattern
through seeking help outside the family. Vale Allen's account, however, suggests that
friends, teachers, and other trusted people are viewed by the victims as potential
"saviors" [38]. Often the sexual abuse becomes visible through the intervention of
society in other personal or family problems. Many clinical articles discuss the concern of helping professionals with the incest hoax, in which the victim claims sexual
abuse in order to punish the alleged perpetrator for other family problems. The
emphasis on incest fantasy in psychodynamic theory, the general horror concerning
incestual relations, and limited intervention skills are usually cited by concerned
critics to explain the frequent non-response by professionals to sexual abuse reports.

## D.      Denial and the Family Secret

Personal defense mechanisms, guilt, and "the family secret" are frequently
cited social/psychological mechanisms which serve to contain the knowledge of the
sex abuse. Also, the victim's retraction of accusations to authorities is common. A
host of justifications by the perpetrator are mentioned in the clinical literature:
benefits to the family, the wife's "frigidity", the daughter's inevitable promiscuity,
contributions to the victim's sexual education, and the victim's seductiveness.

Part of the family pathology in sexual abuse is that often the abuse is known,
but unrevealed, by non-participating family members. The persistence of the abuse
hints at enormous individual pay-offs (e.g., mother's avoidance of sex), and the collu-
sive family processes in maintaining the secret. While fear of punishment is one
dynamic, revealing the secret outside the family may also be controlled by a general
family rule prohibiting the discussion of family affairs with outsiders. (Vale Allen's
autobiographical account [38] provides excellent material concerning the victim's psychology and the secret.)

## E.     Sexual Abuse as a Symptom of Family Problems

Recent literature identifies sexual abuse as symptomatic of family pathology. Sexual estrangement within the marital relationship, the confusion of family roles, the extreme imbalance of family powers, and the lack of protection of the victim, promote the initial development of sexual abuse and serve to keep the pattern intact over time.


## F.     The Victim

Clinical observations of victim behaviour, the persistence of sexual abuse, and the victim's passivity, have raised several questions with respect to the role of the victim in actively promoting sexual abuse. Such questions have led to speculation about seductiveness and the actual enjoyment of sex. These issues have been discounted for the following reasons [11]:

> To infer sexual enjoyment from passivity ignores the victim's experiences of: obedience to the perpetrator, anticipation of punishment, confusion, love of perpetrator as parent, fear of betrayal, and a host of accompanying rewards (material, favoured child, pre-genital physical cuddling, and so forth).

> Inferences of "seductiveness" have often been made from the perpetrator's rationalization in court, or on the basis of victim behaviour in therapy many years later.

> Labelling a child's behaviour and motives as seductive (e.g., sitting on one's lap) infers adult motives; the naive attention-seeking of the child lacks the willfulness and awareness of consequences, particularly in the case of the very young. Children do not share adult meaning of sexual gestures and to imply otherwise is to exercise the power of adults over children.

> Even where the victim's behaviour and intent are sexual (e.g., teenage children and foster fathers), the perpetrator's behaviour is affected by his own decision-making.

> Recent large-scale research on the victim's reactions to the sexual abuse leads us to suspect that the victim experiences physical pleasure in less than 10% of the cases. Even in these cases, the experiences were part of a confusing flood of feelings and sensations, and suggest more of a general longing for physical affection than adult passion.

Charlotte Vale Allen's account of her reactions to sexual abuse during adolescence illustrates the confusion:

> What I hadn't anticipated, though, was the sudden, quite violent awakening of my sexual responses. The caresses I had received so passively for eight years now created sensations, reactions I had to struggle to conceal. Mindlessly, I'd find myself enjoying the stimulation of his attentions. And then, appalled, my self-hatred assuming newer and bigger proportions, I began a

concerted effort to stifle my responses, bury them; rejecting them one by one until nothing he could do, made me feel anything at all. I was wood. I was concrete. I could effectively segregate sensation out of my body, controlling it and my feelings with deadly determination. I would allow nothing to move me from the stiffly inflexible posture I maintained throughout our sessions [38].


## VI.    DYNAMICS: DISSOLUTION OF THE PATTERN


### A.    Attempts at Revelation

It is said that only one in four mothers takes steps to end sexual abuse in the family. In most cases, mothers continued the denial, believed the daughter but did nothing, or punished the daughter. Clinical reports also describe mothers who actually discouraged siblings' efforts to stop the abuse. Siblings who had been previously victimized are reportedly more supportive. The daughter's revelation of the secret typically occurs during adolescence, and in cases where no action is taken, a gradual alienation between mother and daughter ensues.

Weinberg [40] provides the most detailed account of how the revelation of incest affects family life. The revelation does not automatically lead to action. Family efforts to change the relationship happen only when there is dissatisfaction with the marriage, where the father is tyrannical, or where the family is not dependent on the father for economic support.

The daughter's eventual refusal to participate, sometimes with the help of her mother, or a pregnancy and scandal in the community can assist in the dissolution of the relationship. However, the most common method is for the daughter to leave home, typically before the age of eighteen.

It is estimated that only one-quarter of sex abuse cases are reported to legal authorities.

From data on an American psychotherapy sample [28], four types of father responses to sex abuse revelation have been identified:

> broken-hearted rejection
>
> guilt
>
> denial
>
> displacement of sex to a younger daughter (an estimated 20–30% of cases)


### B.    Family Response to Crisis

For intervention purposes, family crisis theory provides perhaps the most useful approach to the family's response to the identification of sex abuse. To date, this has not been done in the most sophisticated way, but Holder [44] has identified the following family crisis and adjustment stages:

    1. denial

    2. regrouping

    3. reaching out

    4. fall-out

    5. reaching towards something better

    6. adjustment

The useful aspect of Holder's framework is its focus on family rather than individual responses to crises (e.g., family problem-solving techniques) and its formulation from family-clinic observations, which easily lead to implications for interventions. (For additional information on the family perspective, see Chapter 2, IV)

## C.    The Effects of Sexual Abuse on the Victim

Sexual activities between adults and children are not abhorrent to all writers. Divergent views concerning consequences to victims may be summarized as follows:

    1. Some believe that most sexual offences are innocuous and are best treated as a minor and transient hazard of childhood. The innocence of childhood protects against long-term effects. Children do not have the same sense of sexuality as adults, and do not react with the horror assumed by adults.

    2. Others take the opinion that child sexual abuse is widespread and has permanently scarring effects. This latter position is supported by clinical case reports, the child's frequent failure to report the abuse, and the frequency of abuse in reported studies of such deviant groups as female drug addicts, prostitutes, and adolescent runaways.

    3. Still others think that sexual abuse per se is not the traumatic aspect; the real difficulty lies either in the reactions of parents, police and/or agencies, and/or in the guilt induced by reporting a family member, followed by family condemnation.

Sexual abuse is believed more traumatic

    the closer the relationship (as a result of trust violation, the complication of family dynamics, and taboo violation)

    the longer the experience

    the more elaborate the sexual activity (e.g., fondling versus penetration)

    the more aggressive the sexual abuse

On the other hand, the more the child participates and enjoys the relationship, the less the guilt and negative feelings, and the less the trauma.

It should be noted, however, that the foregoing propositions are based on adult inferences about child experience and may not stand the test of research.

An additional methodological problem, particularly with respect to the identification of trauma, is the necessity of separating the impact of sex abuse from other family factors (e.g., financial, social, and emotional problems; limited capacities for handling stress; and minimal environmental support). The impact of adult-child sexuality must also be distinguished from the psychological consequences of those kinds of structures which induce and maintain sexual abuse. It was noted earlier that perpetrators label the acts as "good", "dutiful", and "in the child's best interest" while, at the same time, they maintain a state of secrecy and threat. These tactics, coupled with the child's vague notions of inappropriateness, create a social-psychological environment much like the "double binds" and "mystifying" communications in the families of schizophrenics.

A number of early psychological symptoms have been associated with sexual abuse: depression, anxiety, confused sexual identity, fear of sexuality, oral deprivation, oral sadism, behaviour problems, and school problems.

It is assumed that sexual abuse during adolescence creates the most severe psychological problems because the adolescent is more aware than the child of extrafamilial standards. However, one of the most recent surveys of a non-clinical university sample showed that the degree of trauma was found unaffected by the victim's age, homosexuality, particular kinds of sex acts, and the duration of the experience. According to this study, the degree of trauma increased with

a greater age difference between the victim and the perpetrator

the degree of closeness in the relationship (e.g., the greatest trauma came from father-daughter incest)

the sex of the partner (e.g., sexual experiences with males were more traumatic for both male and female victims)

the degree of force. The use of force is strongly associated with trauma. The interpretation is that force signals something negative to the child, symptomatic of a whole negative relationship, characterized by the child's reluctance, use of pressure, and differences in power and control. That sex is involved may be less important than the presence of aggression [11].

## VII.    WORKING WITH CASES OF SEXUAL ABUSE

Readers are encouraged to review in conjunction with this section the discussion on problem-solving in child welfare contained in Appendix A.

## A.    Introduction

Many factors contribute to the difficulty of working with cases of sexual abuse. The repulsiveness of such acts reflects the strength of the incest taboo in society. Training in sex abuse intervention still does not receive adequate attention in professional schools of social work. Sexual abuse reports are frequently accompanied by family denial and sometimes a victim's withdrawal of the complaint. An accusation of sexual abuse constitutes a personal and family crisis of the severest kind. The resulting emotions and strained relationships present a considerable challenge to the child protection worker.

Another problem for those working on sexual abuse cases is the absence, in some communities, of a clear division of responsibilities between the police and child welfare workers in the investigation process. In communities where integration has not been fully developed, workers are advised to familiarize themselves with the customary practices of investigation as these may be elaborated in local procedures manuals (e.g., *Children's Aid Society of Metropolitan Toronto Service Manual*).

Child welfare workers are more likely to be preoccupied with the initial contact and investigation processes, and less with the delivery of treatment. Thus, this section gives more attention to guidelines for interviewing during the investigation phase. The discussion of treatment addresses the general goals rather than specific treatment modalities. For a more general review of investigating reports, see Chapter 2, III "Investigating Reports" and VI, "Preparing for Court".

## B.    Guidelines for Investigating Sexual Abuse

The atmosphere surrounding a sexual abuse report and investigation has been described as a "crisis of disclosure" [17]. Although there is probably a broad continuum of reactions, some of the possible reactions to this crisis are:

> the child's fear, anxiety, and possible guilt over taking action to end a possibly long-standing family pattern, and thereby perhaps invoking a retaliation

> the mother's possible disbelief, shock, or pressure to deny the accusation

> the father's anticipation of losing his wife, family, job, liberty, and a source of sexual gratification

> a general disruption of a fragile family equilibrium

> the fear, in everyone's mind, of an unknown future

Workers should realize that many of these anticipated repercussions actually do occur. Retaliation, suicide attempts, and family break-up are often reported.

For these reasons the information-gathering activities of the investigation must be accompanied by a therapeutic interviewing approach. Sensitive initial interviewing will increase the chances of a family's seeking treatment. Many protection workers describe their approach as one of focussed, rapid crisis intervention.

Sgroi suggests three general guidelines for conducting an investigation [35]:

> 1. Keep an open mind. Workers may be under pressure from the family and their previous training to question the truthfulness of the report. A better assumption is that the child is indeed telling the truth.

> 2. Keep cool. Objectivity in cases of sexual abuse requires effort and self-discipline.

3. Keep alert to possible reactions from *all* family members. Because of the crisis of disclosure, volatile reactions are possible.

In addition, a number of specific guidelines will help the interviewing process with family members.

## 1. Interviewing the Victim

The investigation process will be facilitated if the worker takes steps to reassure the victim. Victims need to be told that:

Their stories are believed.

They are not to blame.

They are to be praised for their courage [17].

Other guidelines for interviewing are good casework principles known by most child protection workers. Questioning the child about the facts of the abuse should proceed slowly; a good relationship should be established before details are pursued. The child's level of understanding of human anatomy should be ascertained, along with the terms used to describe bodily organs and functions. Communication will be aided by the use of diagrams, pictures, or dolls. Also, the interview will move better if children are allowed to proceed at their own pace, and are given the freedom to describe events in their own way. Rather than interruption, clarifications are best sought later in the interview.

It is tempting to assume that victims experience negative feelings towards the perpetrator, or that they feel guilt or shame. However, it might be that the non-sexual aspects of the relationship have left the victim ambivalent at worst. In many cases, they may have a "special status" with their fathers and receive considerable attention and care.

For these reasons, no outward judgement should be voiced about the information provided or the child's state of mind.

The interview with the victim should be conducted alone or in the company of a person with whom the victim feels comfortable. It should be remembered that other family members may place the victim under pressure to change the details or even to withdraw the complaint. The victim should not be expected to confront the perpetrator or other family members.

## 2.    Interviewing the Mother

Most treatment approaches in sexual abuse cases aim to develop the mother-daughter bond. This should be kept in mind during initial interviews, since there are several things that can be done towards that end. In addition to gathering facts, the worker is in a position to help the mother believe the child. Also, the mother may need assurance that her own life will not fall to pieces because of the revealed abuse.

The mother should not be interviewed in the company of the victim. It is difficult for her to express her true feelings in such circumstances, and also it may be difficult for the daughter to hear ambivalences about the report, or possible denials. The worker can help the mother deal with feelings related to her own involvement or non-involvement in the family problem. For example, if she is angry or hurt at not being approached by the daughter for protection, she can be helped to understand the possible reasons. If the mother had ignored the daughter's efforts to reveal the abuse, she should not be condemned. Efforts should concentrate on the present situation, particularly whether she believes and supports the daughter's story.

In cases of teenage sexual abuse, mothers may actually blame the daughter, citing seductiveness, provocative dress, and sexual immorality. Rather than supporting such claims, workers should help the mother see her daughter as a victim.

Anger towards their husbands may lead some mothers to immediately seek worker support for the idea of a separation or divorce. Such a decision is not appropriate during the early stages of crises, and workers are best advised to promote longer-term thinking on the matter. In general, a message of hope should be communicated as much as possible.

In some cases specific advice can be extended to the mother on how to enhance her relationship with the daughter. For example, an apology may be in order, either for not protecting the daughter or for not believing her accusation. Assurance should be given that in the future the daughter will be protected against sexual abuse.

Finally, mothers of victims should be advised of the various treatment options available for families in which sexual abuse has occurred, and that the agency is available to assist the family in obtaining help. She should be prepared for the possibility of criminal charges being laid against her husband, and should know why these are important in bringing about change.

### 3. Interviewing the Perpetrator

For some workers, interviewing the perpetrator may be the most difficult part of an investigation. Ideally, the purpose is to obtain an admission of the incest, and a willingness to take responsibility for it. However, such admissions are not always readily obtained; this, plus the repulsiveness of sexual abuse, create difficult investigation conditions. Many workers believe that during the initial phases of the investigation, the victim and the perpetrator should be separated. Ideally the father, rather than the victim, should leave the home because:

> As an adult he will find it easier to obtain accommodation.
>
> Temporary arrangements for girls are often inadequate.
>
> The victim will feel punished if asked to leave.
>
> Staying home gives the mother and daughter an opportunity to build their relationship [17].

Unfortunately, it is often the case that the victim is taken out of the home, and this should be regarded as a weakness of the child welfare system.

Despite the enormous difficulties in working with perpetrators of sexual abuse, future legal and treatment processes will be improved if the abuser is treated with dignity, although a confrontative attitude is necessary at the outset. This is accomplished by:

presenting a strong, factual, and clear description of the sexual abuse report

indicating a belief in the victim's report and that children usually do not lie about such matters

not accepting the abuser's denials or excuses, such as daughter provocations, being under the influence of alcohol, and so on

relating the effects on victims of sexual abuse [17]

In addition, the perpetrator should be given hope and encouragement, and told that the damage done can be helped considerably by an admission of responsibility and an apology to the victim. If the police are not already involved, he should be made aware of their imminent involvement. Finally, the perpetrator should be advised to find separate living arrangements until after the court process and participation in treatment [17].

Because of possible serious physical and emotional effects, and the family's denial and resistance to change, placement of the child is an option. The risk of seeming to blame an already victimized child makes this an unpleasant alternative for many workers. Nevertheless, depending on the legal guidelines in the worker's province or state, placement should be considered when the situation is serious.

## C.    Referring the Family for Treatment

A sensitive approach to the investigation process is an important first step towards treatment of sexual abuse. However, in most cases, the severity and complexity of sexual abuse dynamics requires long-term intervention, best obtained through referral to community resources. This section will aid the worker with the referral process by reviewing the general goals of treatment and presenting samples of treatment modalities. The reader is also encouraged to read Herman's description of "restoring families" [17].

Individual psychotherapeutic approaches used with perpetrators of sexual abuse have been criticized as inappropriate for such cases. Such methods usually assume that the patient suffers from inner stress, voluntarily seeks treatment, and is willing to be open with the therapist. In the case of abusive fathers, these assumptions rarely hold true. In fact, they are likely to be highly manipulative, often seeking to involve the therapist as an ally in an effort to deny the incest or to avoid blame. Individual psychotherapy has been used with the victim of incest, particularly in later years when she/he is coping with the ill effects of the abuse. A review of therapeutic work with victims is provided by Herman [17].

In recent years, the usual approaches with sexual abuse cases are crisis intervention, family therapy, group work, and multiple-intervention programmes.

### 1.    Crisis Intervention

As indicated above, the principles of investigatory work in sexual abuse reports should be based on an assumption that the family is in a crisis state. Longer-term intervention with the family can also draw upon family crisis intervention work. Holder [44], for example, bases his work on the premise that, upon detection, sexually abusive families are likely to pass through six stages: denial, regrouping, reaching out for help, fall-out or disorganization, movement towards something better, and a new adjustment. Workers are urged to recognize the possible indicators of each stage and to adopt appropriate strategies. In the denial phase, for example, the typical family responses are: an expression of disbelief or shock; change of stories; expectation that workers will criticize, judge, or condemn; and efforts to maintain the status quo. During this phase, workers are urged to

> be realistic about potential accomplishments
>
> gather and sort information
>
> identify distortion and defense
>
> reduce authority and critical judgement
>
> show acceptance of the family while not condoning the acts

This approach is particularly useful in the early stages of intervention where a family seems willing and able to problem-solve as a unit. For a detailed summary of the indicators of each phase, relevant treatment goals and strategies, the reader can consult Holder's article [44]. Many of the guidelines can be usefully incorporated into the investigation process.

## 2. *Family Therapy*

Like a family-oriented crisis intervention approach, family therapy modalities generally assume that the entire family is implicated in the sexual abuse. Disturbed family relationships serve either to bring about the occurrence of incest or to deny its existence. Examples of such disturbed family dynamics are:

> husband-wife sexual estrangement
>
> unwilling family members' support of incest
>
> age- and generationally-inappropriate role assignments to the incest victim
>
> over-controlling father and passive mother
>
> lack of mutual trust within the family, and a lack of trust towards outsiders
>
> lack of respect for the physical and intellectual integrity of others in the family [9, 27]

Some family therapies focus entirely on the underlying family dynamics assumed to bring about the incest. Eist and Mandel [9] describe ways to provide families with positive growth-producing experiences with outsiders, and to help family members increase their mutual respect for others and their rights. Therapeutic methods in this approach include:

> role-modelling for handling differences
>
> teaching alternative techniques for handling problems
>
> encouraging factual reporting and open sharing of affect

active limit-setting on shaming, scapegoating, indulgence of negative behaviour, and disrespect for personal integrity

encouraging appropriate family responses to unacceptable behaviour, mutual listening, and understanding [9]

Other family approaches assume that denial dynamics are the key to understanding family pathology, and that useful intervention should focus on the here-and-now interactions supporting denial. As outlined by Machotka and his colleagues [27], this approach generally aims to distribute responsibility for the incest throughout the family, and assumes that change will occur through:

promoting insight into denial and collusion

sharing the guilt

inducing pain in the family by reinforcing the negative consequences of denial

Although family therapy is grounded in a useful premise, namely that incest is symptomatic of dysfunctional family dynamics, there are some difficulties in implementing this approach:

The crisis nature of incest revelation may not be conducive to the collaboration needed for family therapy.

The victim may find it psychologically difficult to be exposed to the blatant denials and ambivalences expressed by other family members.

Some family therapies give insufficient attention to the weak power position of the mother in the family [17].

The broader social structure (e.g., sex-role inequalities) reinforces the power inequities in sexually abusive families (e.g., authoritarian, controlling fathers, and ineffectual mothers).

Sexual abuse perpetrators may be unwilling to attend family therapy sessions.

## 3.    Group Methods

Group work approaches strive to meet the specific needs of each family member.

For the daughter as abuse victim, group involvement helps to remove shame, and offers a safe place to share feelings about the abuse and about various family members. Well-run groups have the potential of moving quickly from the sexual issues to some of the basic emotional needs related to the family situation. For example, where appropriate, female victims can be encouraged to express their desires for their mother's care, affection, and consolation. In addition, problem-solving teaching can be provided. The useful functions of groups for sexual abuse victims are:

relief of guilt

increase of self-esteem

reduction of the child's isolation

development of autonomy

development of the idea that the victim has a right to defend herself [17]

One limitation of group work with sexual abuse families, particularly those emphasizing assertiveness training, is that the change in the victim's interpersonal style may promote friction in the family and school [17].

Group participation has proven useful for the mothers in abusive families. Self-help groups, for example, give mothers the opportunity to:

express their feelings

develop contact with peers

obtain practical help (e.g., finding a job)

build self-esteem through the alleviation of shame and the opportunity to help others in similar situations

develop interpersonal and life skills

Self-help groups are particularly valuable for those mothers whose inaction in the incest situation resulted from oppression in an extremely authoritarian patriarchal family. With the development of self-confidence and a sense of well-being, they are less willing to tolerate a repressive marriage. As well, when total dependency on husbands is reduced, the context for mother-daughter rivalry for the husband/father's attention is changed [17]. The important bond between the mother and daughter is strengthened.

Group-oriented treatment programmes have also been designed for the sexual abuse offender. So far, the more successful programmes have had a strong relationship with the court system, since treatment participation by offenders usually requires legal coercion [17].

Treatment programmes for offenders are frequently patterned after addiction programmes. These programmes assume that the internal motivation to change is absent, as is the capacity for self-control. Tangible rewards and motivation to change are provided within the structure of the group. Generalizing from an analysis of several group treatment programmes, Herman identifies the following typical characteristics [17]:

All rely on peer confrontation and pressure within an atmosphere offering support, community, and self-esteem.

Non-exploitative and non-sexual behavior is demonstrated.

Strong encouragement for adult sexual relationships is provided.

An awareness of the effects of the sexual abuse on others is emphasized in order to change the offender's selfishness.

As with addiction programmes, many group approaches have a graded series of steps towards change. In some, the ultimate goal is a confrontation between the father and daughter in which the abuser:

assumes full responsibility for the sexual abuse

admits that he has failed as a parent

apologizes for the harm done

promises never to make sexual overtures again

Herman's review of group approaches for the offender provides useful advice for implementing and evaluating such programmes. Good group leaders are usually authoritative and charismatic people. Group leadership should never be extended to the perpetrator, since anti-social cliques may be allowed to support each other's evasions and excuses. Treatment success should be indicated by the well-being of wives and daughters in the family, and not by the comments and attitudes of the father, or by recidivism rates. Quoting the author, success can be assured:

> . . . when no one feels bullied, pressured or intimidated by the father, when
> the daughter feels comfortable in his presence, and when the mother finds it
> possible to relate to the father as a mate rather than an overlord. . . . [17]

Outpatient group treatments are not useful for all sexual abuse offenders. The best prognosis is likely when the offender is non-violent, has no other history of sexual abuse, admits to his actions, expresses remorse and the desire to change, has a strong work history, and is not abusing alcohol [17].

### 4.    Multiple Intervention Programmes

Many treatment programmes for sexual abuse have a number of components and include several treatment modalities. There is a recognition that complex family dynamics are at the root of incest, and that the discovery process has created a difficult situation for all members. Family-orientated and couple therapy approaches are combined with individual counselling and/or group modalities, so that all individuals and relationships within the family receive attention.

Giarretto's humanistic approach to treating father-daughter incest has possibly received the most attention in the professional literature [15], and has been subjected to extensive evaluation [24]. The programme requires participation of all family members, including the abuser, whose attendance is assured by the court. Theoretically, the programme is informed by a combination of humanistic and existentialist psychology, and family-systems thinking. The key assumption is that incest is a symptom of other disturbances within the family, particularly a troubled marital relationship, and low self-concepts. Programme treatment modalities include family therapy, dyad counselling, individual counselling, and group work. Considerable emphasis is given to the self-help process in programmes known as Parents United and Daughters United. General programme goals are:

> to provide immediate counselling and practical assistance to sexually
> abused children and their families in order to hasten the reconstruction of
> the family and the marriage, since it is assumed that children prosper best in
> normally functioning families headed by natural parents

> to foster self-managed growth of individuals capable of positive con-

tributions to society; in particular to promote self-assessment and confrontation, to achieve self-identification by all family members, and to achieve self-management

Programme staff carry out a number of activities and roles, including: educator/trainer, communication analyst, and gestalt therapist. The positive evaluation of Giarretto's programme is based primarily on an absence of sexual abuse recidivism, the saving of marriages, an accelerated rehabilitation of offenders, and the restoration of normal relationships between father and daughter. Critics of the evaluation point to an absence of verification interviews with the victims, the admission by several parents that further incest might be kept a secret, and the limitation of recidivism rates as a programme success measure [17].

## VIII. SUMMARY

This chapter has reviewed the dynamics of sexual abuse and practice guidelines. The review began with an analysis of broad societal factors which have been linked to sexual abuse rates, including the ideology and practice of male supremacy, children's rights, and social fragmentation. Family processes of sexual abuse were summarized within a social psychological framework of induction, maintenance of the sexual abuse pattern, and dissolution. The section on working with sexual abuse emphasized the investigation process, and ended with a review of clinically-oriented interventions.

### REFERENCES

1. American Humane Association, Children's Division. "Protecting the Child Victim of Sex Crimes", Denver, Colo. (no date).

2. Bagley, C. "Incest Behavior and Incest Taboo", Social Problems, Vol. 16, Spring 1969, pp. 505–519.

3. Bender, L. and Blau, A. "The Reaction of Children to Sexual Relations with Adults", American Journal of Orthopsychiatry, Vol. XII, July 1937, pp. 500–518.

4. Browing, D. and Boatman, B. "Incest: Children at Risk", American Journal of Psychiatry, 137, 1977.

5. Burgess, A. W. et al. Sexual Assault of Children and Adolescents. Lexington, Mass.: Lexington Books, 1978.

6. Community Council of Greater New York. Sexual Abuse of Children: Implications from the Sexual Trauma Treatment Program of Connecticut. Special Report of Two Research Utilization Workshops, New York, 1979.

7. Ontario Ministry of Community and Social Services. "Interviewing the Child Sex Victim", Training Key 224 (no date).

8. Cormier, B. M., Kennedy, M., and Sangowicz, J. "Psychodynamics of Father-Daughter Incest", Canadian Psychiatric Association Journal, Vol. 7, October 1962, pp. 203–217.

9. Eist, H. and Mandel, A. "Family Treatment of Ongoing Incest Behaviour", Family Process, Vol. 6, No. 1, 1967.

10. Elwell, Mary E., "Sexually Assaulted Children and Their Families", Social Casework, Vol. 60, April 1979, pp. 227–235.

11. Finkelhor, David. *Sexually Victimized Children*. New York: The Free Press, 1979.

12. Froelich, J. E. "Family Crises Intervention", Juvenile and Family Court Journal, November 1978.

13. Garbarino, J. and Gillian, G. "Sexual Abuse: A Special Case?" in *Understanding Abusive Families*. Lexington, Mass.: Lexington Books, 1980, pp. 151–165.

14. Geiser, R. L. *Hidden Victims: The Sexual Abuse of Children*. Boston: Beacon Press, 1979.

15. Giaretto, Henry. "Humanistic Treatment of Father-Daughter Incest", Journal of Humanistic Psychology, Vol. 18, Fall 1978, pp. 59–76.

16. Henderson, D. J. "Incest: A Synthesis of Data", Canadian Psychiatric Association Journal, Vol. 17, No. 229, 1972.

17. Herman, J. *Father-Daughter Incest*. Cambridge, Mass.: Harvard University Press, 1981.

18. Inglis, R. *Sins of the Fathers*. New York: St. Martin's Press, 1978.

19. Johnson, Clara. "Child Sexual Abuse Case Handling in Mississippi", Georgia Regional Institute of Social Welfare Research, Inc. (no date).

20. ———. "Child Sex Abuse Case Handling Through Public Social Agencies in the Southeast", Georgia Regional Institute of Social Research, Inc. (no date).

21. Justice, Blair. *The Broken Taboo: Sex and the Family*. New York: Human Sciences Press, 1979.

22. Kaufman, I., Peck, A., and Tagiuri, C. "The Family Constellation and Overt Incestuous Relations Between Father and Daughter", American Journal of Orthopsychiatry, Vol. 24, 1954, pp. 266–277.

23. Kempe, C. H. "Incest and Other Forms of Sexual Abuse", in Kempe, C. (ed.), *The Battered Child* (3rd ed.), Chicago: The University of Chicago Press, 1980.

24. Kroth, J. A. *Child Sexual Abuse: Analysis of a Family Therapy Approach*. Springfield, Ill.: Charles C Thomas, 1979.

25. Krywulak, W. and Elias, J. C. "The Physically Abused Child", Manitoba Medical Review, Vol. 47, April 1967.

26. Lustig, N., et al. "Incest: A Family Group Survival Pattern", Archives of General Psychiatry, Vol. 14, January 1966, pp. 31–40.

27. Machotka, P., Pittman, F., and Florenhaft, K. "Incest as a Family Affair", Family Process, Vol. 6, No. 1, 1967.

28. Meiselman, K. C. *Incest: A Psychological Study of Causes and Effects with Treatment Recommendations*. San Francisco: Jossey-Bass Publishers, 1978.

29. Ministry of Community and Social Services. "Child Abuse: Interdisciplinary Resource Materials," Toronto (no date).

30. Pincus, L. and Dare, C. *Secrets in the Family*. New York: Pantheon Books, 1978.

31. Rist, K. "Incest: Theoretical and Clinical Views", American Journal of Orthopsychiatry, Vol. 49, Oct. 1979.

32. Rush, F. *The Best Kept Secret: Sexual Abuse of Children*. Englewood Cliffs, N.J. Prentice-Hall, 1980.

33. Schlesinger, B. (ed.). *Sexual Abuse of Children: A Book of Readings*. Toronto: University of Toronto Press, 1981.

34. Schultz, L. E. (ed.). *The Sexual Victimology of Youth*. Springfield, Ill.: Charles C Thomas, 1980.

35. Sgroi, S. "Child Sexual Assault: Some Guidelines for Investigation and Treatment", Appendix A, in Community Council of Greater New York. *Sexual Abuse of Children*, New York, 1979.

36. Tilelli, J. A. "Sexual Abuse in Children: Clinical Findings and Implications for Management", New England Journal of Medicine, Vol. 302, Feb. 1980.

37. U.S. National Center on Child Abuse and Neglect, Children's Bureau. "Child Sexual Abuse: Incest Assault and Sexual Exploitation", Washington D.C., 1978.

38. Vale Allen, C. *Daddy's Girl: A Memoir*. New York: Simon and Schuster, 1980.

39. Walters, D. K. *Physical and Sexual Abuse of Children: Causes and Treatment*. Bloomington: Indiana University Press, 1935.

40. Weinberg, S. K. *Incest Behaviour*. New York: Citadel Press, 1955.

41. de Young, M. "Siblings of Oedipus: Brothers and Sisters of Incest Victims", Child Welfare, Vol LX, September/October 1981, pp. 521–568.

42. Luther, S. and Price, J. "Child Sexual Abuse: A Review", The Journal of School Health, March 1980, pp. 161–165.

43. Nakashima, I. and Zakus, G. "Incest: Review and Clinical Experience", Pediatrics, November 1977, pp. 34–40.

44. Holder, W. *Sexual Abuse of Children*. Englewood, Colo.: The American Humane Association, Child Protection Division, 1980.

# 7

# Social Work Practice and Foster Care: Pre-Placement Activities

**SHIRLEY FISH**

I. INTRODUCTION                                                     214
II. WHEN FOSTER FAMILY PLACEMENT IS
APPROPRIATE                                                         214
III. POTENTIAL STRESSORS                                           215
IV. RECRUITMENT OF FOSTER HOMES                                    217
V. SELECTION                                                       218
  A. Motivation to Foster                                218
  B. Expectations of the Role                            219
  C. Personal Qualities of Potential Foster Parents      219
  D. Assessment of Healthy Family Functioning            220
  E. Parenting Styles and Skills                         221
  F. Ability to Relate to Agency Staff                   221
  G. Ability to Accept the Role of Substitute, Short-Term
     Parent                                221
  H. Ability to Accept Child's Family                     222
  I. Approaches to the Selection Process                  222
VI. FOSTER PARENT PRE-SERVICE EDUCATION AND
TRAINING                                                           223
  A. General Overview                                     223
  B. Pre-Service Foster Parent Training: Theory and
     Practice                              224
  C. Matching Foster Parents and Child                    227
  D. Learning to Foster the Abused Child                  227
VII. PLANNING FOR PLACEMENT                                        230
  A. Short-Term Planning                                  230
  B. Permanency Planning                                  230
VIII. SUMMARY                                                      232
  REFERENCES                                              232

## I.    INTRODUCTION

The realities and necessary practices associated with foster care are highly complex. Practices related to finding appropriate people to look after someone else's children, preparing them to do so, and helping them during the process, make tough demands on human and organizational resources. The next two chapters aim to identify professional dilemmas in foster family care, and to provide guidelines to aid practice.

This chapter presents information that is pertinent to pre-placement service, including recruitment, selection, training, and placement planning. As a starting point, the topics of foster placement appropriateness and the general stress of fostering are addressed.

The next chapter provides selected material for the post-placement process. Considerable attention is given to conflict resolution as a strategy for dealing with those stressors introduced in the present chapter. Working with parents in the fostering process receives emphasis as one dimension of permanency-planning work. As used here, the term "parents" refers to legal parents, who may or may not be the child's biological parents. Foster parents are referred to as such.

## II.    WHEN FOSTER FAMILY PLACEMENT IS APPROPRIATE

This is one of the most difficult practice issues in child welfare work, and one for which no definitive answer is available. Some attempts have been made to develop specific guidelines, drawing upon practitioner wisdom, and upon research pertaining to practitioner decision-making [1, 2]. The complexity of the decision is reflected in the disagreement among experienced practitioners as to the criteria for foster family placement.

Despite gaps in our knowledge the following general guidelines may be useful.

Foster family placement is a potentially significant resource for the child who has the capacity to participate in and contribute to normal family living [1]. On the other hand, such placement may not be appropriate if:

The child's behaviour problems would not be tolerated in a community.

The child's behaviour would prevent living in a family group (e.g., severe and unpredictable aggressive behaviour).

The child has severe problems with the transference process, such that she or he is unable to cope with the intensity of an intimate parent-child relationship.

The child who has personality disorders or emotional disturbances that require therapeutic attention is likely to be placed in a specialized foster home.

## III.    POTENTIAL STRESSORS

There is much concern regarding provision of service to foster families. Unless there is awareness of the stresses of fostering on foster parents and their children, it will be difficult to meet the needs of the foster family and thereby the foster child [20].

It is not easy to be a foster parent. Pressures are enormous, and in many ways fostering is more complex than raising one's own children. Nonetheless, there can be abundant emotional rewards that grow out of fostering and these are what attract people to it. Some people want children as part of their lives; fostering provides that opportunity. Other foster parents may perceive fostering almost as a career, one which involves caring for children and perhaps teaching them new skills or exposing them to new interests.

Stresses on the foster family can come from expectations of themselves, which are often lofty, and perhaps unrealistic. New foster parents, for example, may want to succeed quickly or to be perfect parents. When difficulties occur, as they always do, they feel guilty.

Other sources of foster parent stress are the expectations and stereotypes held by others. The notion that foster children are "nobody's children" is unfortunate, but real. Difficult practical situations may develop from these attitudes.

Foster children may create stressful situations for their foster parents. The history (e.g., neglect, abuse) of many children can lead to behaviours that challenge parenting. Also, developmental stages, particularly adolescence, may introduce strong pressures within the foster family.

One fundamental source of stress for foster parents is the expectation of relating in a warm, open, loving way, coupled with the realization that the relationship will some day end. This is particularly difficult if the length of the placement is vague, or if a deep relationship is broken on short notice. Fear of losing the foster child, often with no possibility of future contacts, is pervasive. Furthermore, sometimes children *cannot* respond in a loving way through no fault of either party; however, the foster parents may need a warm, grateful response in order to define the fostering experience as successful.

The addition of a foster child is an inevitable disruption to family equilibrium. For example, the addition of one child to a three-person family considerably increases the number of new relationships. The transactional and power implications of this structural change are enormous.

Considerable stress for foster parents could result from the continuing involvement of the parents in the child's life. Such pressures could result from:

> emotional problems, defensiveness, and guilt on the part of parents and/or child
>
> sabotage of foster parents' work
>
> temporary worsening of the child's behaviour after visits
>
> the child's playing off the two sets of parents against each other
>
> difficulty in being friendly to people who have inadequately parented

the child—to parents who are more needy than their child and also need parenting

Pressures on foster parents may also result from the complex relationship with the agency. Some of these are by-products of agency processes; others relate to agency short-comings. For example, foster parents are under scrutiny and assessment; this they may experience as an intrusion. Moreover, they may be unsure of their opportunities and rights. Other potential agency-based sources of stress include:

> non-participation in decision-making
>
> inexperienced workers and high turnover
>
> inadequate information about the child's background and potential behaviour
>
> reluctance to tell the agency of the child's difficulty for fear of criticism

It should be noted that agency standards and practice are changing in this area, thereby lessening the likelihood of stress arising from the foregoing sources.

For further discussion of the agency's and worker's ecology, see Chapter 1, III.

Lack of privacy sometimes presents special problems for foster parents. Fostering "special needs" children, for example, is quite demanding and can leave little time for foster parents to strengthen their own relationship. Apart from the demands of special placements, foster care is clearly a full-time job (i.e., 24 hours, 7 days a week). Spontaneous activities and normal social life may be curtailed.

Foster parents' own children also are confronted with potentially stressful situations when a foster child comes to live in their home. They may be confronted with:

> potential lack of privacy (e.g., may be expected to share room and possessions)
>
> potential peer strains
>
> upset relations with parents and siblings (e.g., rivalry)
>
> altered role in the family (e.g., no longer the oldest or youngest)
>
> necessity to share special relationship (e.g., with grandparents, special friends)
>
> the stress of seeing foster child receive different privileges, attention, and responses from foster parents

Where crises and mild problems require foster parent attention, natural children are indirectly affected.

In summary, the introduction of a foster child into a family has numerous ramifications. Although debilitating stress is not inevitable, it is useful to anticipate possible sources in order that understanding and help can be offered. The fostering process is a challenge to the foster parents' self-identity as good parents. Moreover, it is a tremendous challenge to their adaptive capacities as individuals and as whole families. The introduction of new people into anyone's life presents a growth challenge. New people with problems, unusual behavior, hostilities, different values, and special needs are particularly challenging.

Chapter 8, II details interventions for coping with such stress.


## IV.     RECRUITMENT OF FOSTER HOMES


Recruitment involves a program of interpretation to the public of the need for foster homes for children and the satisfactions to be derived from fostering a child.

Recruitment methods have been based on: (1) conceptualization of the sociocultural characteristics of the population presenting to foster (e.g., rural, working class, black); (2) current views of the roles of foster parents; (3) the numbers of families available to foster; and (4) the kinds of children coming into foster care.

General recruitment methods include all of the mass media, speaking engagements (e.g., church groups, service clubs) and "prospecting", that is, utilizing preferred leads. Mass media campaigns, especially important for recruiting *new* foster parents, are most effective when continuous, rather than sporadic. Speaking engagements keep the issue of fostering in the public eye, yet provide a low yield in terms of applicants.

Prospecting is a relatively recent method, utilized to recruit foster parents with particular skills for specific children. Contacts in professional organizations are approached for preferred leads. For example, when recruiting for a child needing special medical care, a nurse may be approached and asked whether she knows of anyone who may be interested.

Community workers may be useful as resource persons in the recruitment process. For an elaboration of their role, see Chapter 3, II–IV.

An extremely important factor in the decision to foster is knowing a foster family. These interpersonal contacts provide first-hand information and help with the decision.

The following factors appear to have some association with the decision to foster:

> pre-schoolers in the home
>
> comfortable economic level
>
> desire to help children

Studies of fostering "normal" children and those with special needs have tended to conclude that:

> Foster parents should be encouraged to recruit.
>
> Foster parents should be encouraged to increase their visibility in the community.
>
> All staff should be encouraged to recruit by word of mouth.
>
> Mass media should continue to be utilized for recruiting.

There is a high attrition rate among families who show initial interest in fostering. Studies estimate that between 10% and 30% of initial applicants eventually accept placements; further attrition frequently follows the first placement. This is an important issue, as there is a cost of several hundred dollars in recruiting and selecting one foster home.

## V.    SELECTION

Selection of suitable foster parents is a difficult task as there is no single characteristic or time-honoured method that guarantees success. Thus, a number of characteristics must be considered in any attempt to select. At the same time, there is a need to maximize the potential success of a foster home through contact and support with the agency, and through foster parent training.

The selection process is aimed at assessing the following characteristics, each of which will be dealt with in turn:

> motivation to foster
>
> expectations of the role
>
> personal qualities of each of the potential foster parents
>
> family dynamics of potential foster family
>
> parenting styles and skills
>
> ability to relate to agency staff
>
> ability to accept the role of substitute, short-term parent
>
> ability to relate to situation of the foster child and her or his family

### A.    Motivation to Foster

Motivation to foster stems from various needs and desires. These may include:

> a desire to express one's capacity to give love to a child
>
> a desire to express one's own maturity through parenting
>
> a desire to watch a baby or young child grow
>
> a commitment to the task of caring for those who are needy
>
> a commitment to being useful to one's community

At times, motivation to help children can mask underlying attitudes (sometimes pathological) towards child rearing; unconscious motivations may surface later, once a child is placed in the home. These motives may relate to ways in which foster parents were parented, or to current met or unmet needs. Assessment methods provide some means of determining these motives. It is important for the homefinder to draw out and to examine applicants' motives, to understand that some of these may present problems under certain circumstances. For example, a worker may be wary of potential foster parents who have poor relationships with their own children. In some cases, when potential foster parents express negative attitudes (e.g., a dislike for working with older children), this may help the worker in deciding upon appropriate matching.

Further examination of the rejected applicant, possible reasons for rejection, and the handling of rejection are discussed in Chapter 11, "Adoption: Problems and Related Practices".

## B.    Expectations of the Role

Another important factor in the selection process is the potential foster parents' understanding of the foster parent role. It is essential to clarify applicants' conceptions of:

> what the foster parent does
>
> whom the foster parent must relate to
>
> ways in which the foster parent must relate to others, particularly agency representatives

Thus, the homefinding process is an educative one in which the aforementioned issues are thoroughly covered. It is desirable that applicants with gross misconceptions opt out at this point.

Descriptions of the foster parent role are covered in the first interview. This can take a number of forms:

> one or several group interviews
>
> a first interview with the applicant couple
>
> contact at this point with an experienced foster family

## C.    Personal Qualities of Potential Foster Parents

The homefinder makes an assessment of each foster parent in terms of:

> personal maturity
>
> self-esteem
>
> general level of mental health
>
> relatedness to the community and friends (sociability)
>
> intelligence
>
> flexibility (ability to "share" the child with her or his family)
>
> capacity to tolerate differences

From this list, *personal flexibility* is a characteristic that is relative for each person. It depends on both the issue involved and its relative importance (cognitive) and the amount of stress the person is under, since one is less flexible when under stress (emotional). In parenting relationships, flexibility can be developed over time. Standards can change and personal discipline can help handle stress. The level of flexibility for each person can be determined by:

> assessing his or her personal standards (e.g., which are most important, which are least, whether there is room for change)

> asking whether the person has ever changed a standard: how did it feel, was it a good idea, would he or she do it again, in what circumstances?; answers to these questions can help establish the relative flexibility of a person

The individual's level of sociability can be determined by answering questions regarding:

> patterns of socializing, past and present

> values regarding friends, neighbours, and families

> values and attitudes regarding socializing of children

Finally, a sense of humour is an ally for coping with stress. During the assessment it is important that the homefinder ascertain when and how foster parent applicants call upon it as a coping mechanism.

## D.    Assessment of Healthy Family Functioning

An assessment of family dynamics, both material and family system level, is critical. The foster child, in being "difficult", can become a focus or catalyst for stimulating weaknesses in the foster family system. One scheme which classifies family dynamics is the "McMaster Model of Family Functioning" (see Appendix B). It defines family processes within the following categories [3]:

> *Problem-solving:* "family's ability to resolve problems to a level that maintains effective family functioning"

> *Communication:* "how the family exchanges information"; focusses only on verbal exchanges

> *Roles:* "the repetitive patterns of behavior by which individuals fulfill family functions"; five necessary functions are: provision of resources, nurturance and support, sexual gratification of marital partners, personal development functions (e.g., helping a child to get through school), and management and maintenance of the family system

> *Affective responsiveness:* "the ability to respond to a range of stimuli with appropriate quality and quantity of feelings"

> *Affective involvement:* "the degree to which the family shows interest in and values activities and interests of family members"

*Behaviour control:* "the pattern the family adopts for handling behaviour in three specific situations—physically dangerous situations, situations involving the meeting and expressing of psychobiological needs and drives, and situations involving specializing behaviour both inside and outside the family"

## E. Parenting Styles and Skills

Parenting styles and skills are important considerations in selecting a foster home; collecting information about these enhances the matching of foster parents to the child's needs.

Parenting styles vary from person to person (e.g., authoritarian versus permissive; use of psychological versus physical punishment; explanation of rules versus non-explanation), and within each culture there is a range of acceptable styles and legitimate differences. The healthy family in one culture may look very different from its counterparts in another culture. In acknowledging this phenomenon, the worker does not rule out selections on the basis of personal value systems or biases.

Parenting skills refer to an adult's ability to communicate with a child and to structure a child's life through support, caring, and discipline.

Parental attitudes and skills can be at least partially determined through discussion, using examples of childrearing situations, and observation of adjustment of foster family's children.

## F. Ability to Relate to Agency Staff

Foster parents must feel good about themselves in order to willingly accept and to co-operate in the agency's ongoing assessment of their relationship with the foster child. The family must be a somewhat open system which will allow the agency in, and not perceive it as an intrusion or as a menacing authority figure. This issue must be discussed with potential foster parents in light of agency expectations.

## G. Ability to Accept the Role of Substitute, Short-Term Parent

Applicants for fostering can select from a range of responsibilities, which generally include:

> short-term fostering
>
> permanent long-term fostering
>
> subsidized adoption

Foster parents must be able to accept that their role may be as short-term parents even if they wish the relationship to continue beyond the pre-set limit. On the other hand, it is beneficial if foster parents are flexible enough to switch from the short-term path to that of long-term fostering or possibly subsidized adoption, when called upon to do so.

**H.     Ability to Accept Child's Family**

Compassion results in an acceptance of the child's family's situation. In addition, this family can be viewed as a source of input both in helping foster parents to understand the child and in providing some love and support for the child when possible.

At the same time, acceptable standards of parenting must be adhered to by the child's family. Foster parents, regardless of their capacity for compassion, must understand that there are indeed non-negotiable aspects of parenting which must be accepted by the child's parents if the child is to return to them. For example, feeding a child is non-negotiable, as are housing, clothing, and emotionally supporting a child.

**I.     Approaches to the Selection Process**

The selection process begins with the initial phone call: About 25% of applicants are screened out at this point for reasons which include gross unsuitability and gross misunderstanding of the role.

The application may be a disguised request for help from a social agency. This may be evident at the time of the phone call or may become evident later. These requests must be referred to an appropriate agency.

All methods of selection include:

a general orientation interview to describe the agency and its work; this may be in a group

a number of other interviews to determine suitability

Experienced foster parents have been requested at this stage to speak to prospective foster parents. While a study which investigated the process did not uncover higher approval rates or significant efficiency, new foster parents nonetheless found it helpful.

The number of interviews to determine suitability varies from four to six. The following procedures are mandatory:

a home visit (e.g., to assess the physical environment)

an interview with all members of the applicant family present (e.g., to ascertain dynamic issues such as styles of communication, coalitions within the family, and level of differentiation)

individual interviews with the prospective foster mother and foster father

conjoint interviews with the prospective foster parents

a medical examination of applicants

a police check on applicant parents

references, in written form or by telephone or through in-person interview

Procedures which are not mandatory, but which have been found useful in the selection process include:

> questionnaires
>
> an ecomap
>
> a genogram

There are several tools for developing an understanding of family dynamics. For example, a genogram is very helpful in facilitating the gathering of family history. It is basically a family tree, but offers an opportunity to discover family history (e.g., who are the parents of the children in the prospective foster family?—have there been divorces or remarriages?). Sometimes people omit information due to embarrassment or not considering it important. The genogram structures the kind of information that is needed and sets a tone of openness for future dealings with agency personnel.

An ecomap is essentially a network map; it captures the interactive character of family members, noting how and with whom individuals interact both within the family and within larger social circles.

## VI.     FOSTER PARENT PRE-SERVICE EDUCATION AND TRAINING

### A.     General Overview

As a response to increasing demands for accountability by funding agencies, community groups, and foster parents, there has been a widespread agency effort to provide pre-service training to foster parents. Unlike traditional orientation sessions which tended to focus on the requirements of licensure, contemporary approaches provide educational materials and training pertaining to salient fostering issues (e.g., special needs of children in care; supportive resources for foster parents). Sometimes experienced foster parents are drafted to assist with training novices.

Pre-service training is generally regarded as advantageous to the extent that [4]:

> It may reduce re-placements of children.
>
> It may reduce foster parent turnover.
>
> It better qualifies foster parents for their job.
>
> It facilitates and promotes worker–foster parent partnerships.
>
> It allows for a more efficient use of staff time.
>
> It emphasizes the high value placed on foster parenting by both the agency and the community.
>
> It increases foster parents' identification with agency goals, and with the child's parents' tasks.

Stone and Hunzeker [4] note several conditions that must be created in order to facilitate the initiation and implementation of agency pre-service training, as follows:

> Agency administration must recognize the need for a review of their foster family care services.
>
> All staff involved, plus foster parents, should form a committee to plan sessions for prospective foster parents.
>
> There must be total agency support.
>
> Staff must be given time to carry out committee work, to write letters to applicants, to set up and publicize meetings, and so on.
>
> It is best if one staff member is made responsible for coordinating pre-service training, thereby facilitating committee work, continuity, and evaluative feedback.

Roadblocks to progress include: an agency suspicion of group work techniques and of non-client roles for foster parents; a fear of imposing education or training on applicants and therefore losing them before sessions are fully planned or training is implemented. Staff inexperience in training or group work is another impediment. Despite these potential impediments, the notion of pre-service training is rapidly gaining ground.

### B.      Pre-Service Foster Parent Training: Theory and Practice

Adult learning theory underlines foster parent education. Accordingly, such programmes should:

> Build on and reinforce the knowledge and the psychological health of participants.
>
> Remain cognizant of participants' attitudes and feelings.
>
> Use emotional mobilization as well as intellectual stimulation.
>
> Recognize that adults (and children) have a deep psychological need not to be talked down to, embarrassed, punished, or judged.
>
> Realize that adults expect to be relatively autonomous in their daily functioning, and that:
>
> > Adults have life experience and knowledge upon which to draw.
> >
> > Adults are ready to learn that they need to carry out certain life tasks and responsibilities.

There is a range of possible sites for foster parent education and training programmes. These include:

> child welfare agencies
> placement agencies
> community colleges

university extension departments

committees or combinations of the foregoing groups

One school of thought on agency-based education and training suggests that these programs are best conducted by the agency that has contracted with the foster parents. This orients foster parents to the work style of the agency and facilitates problem-solving.

The other major school of thought maintains that the location of education and training programmes must be neutral, such as the community college or the university. This is based on the notion that the authority of the hiring agency interferes with and severely inhibits the education process.

The following is an abbreviated course outline for pre-service education for foster parents [4]:

*Pre-Service Education for Foster Parents*

A. Description of Population: prospective foster parents in the licensing or screening process, or those newly licensed or approved

B. Objectives of Course: to help foster parent applicants to:
   Understand foster care
   Aid agency in making decisions regarding selection and licensing
   Understand agency structure and their rights and obligations
   Begin to develop self-awareness and use of self
   Recognize foster care as a community investment

C. Content Areas for Foster Parents
   Legal base for foster care (define legal status of children, parents, foster parents, and agency)
   Understanding the agency and the social service system (purpose, philosophy, goals; agency structure; agency procedures regarding selection, placement, and payment; division of responsibilities for programme among agency, staff, and foster parents)
   The foster child's growth, development, handling of separation, and continuing relationships
   Placement preparation of child, parents, siblings, foster family, their relatives, and the community
   Available community resources
   Fostering as a career

D. Methods
   Factors affecting methodology (purpose for providing this information to the group; length of course and number of hours of each session; season of year, time of day, geographic location, setting; availability of specialized speakers and panelists)
   Possible methods (lecture, group discussion, panel presentations, field trips, demonstrations)

E. Implementation Guides
   When to initiate (during screening/licensing, after licensing but prior to placement, as a community education program about foster care)
   How to initiate (administrative support, foster parent involvement, coordination via advisory committee)

F.  Resources
    Films, filmstrips, film loops, videotapes
    Handouts (e.g., manuals, reading materials, charts)
    Slides, transparencies
    Tapes
    Case vignettes
    Professional publications

One example of a pre-service training programme is that developed by the Children's Aid Society of Metropolitan Toronto in 1979. It comprised five sessions:

Two sessions dealt with the foster child, emphasizing the importance of understanding and nurturing in fostering; stimulating a problem-solving approach to fostering; and presenting a realistic picture of what the children are like, where they came from, and how this influences their development.

Two sessions dealt with the foster family, explaining fostering as a life style and the effects of fostering on a family.

One session dealt with the agency, giving foster parents an understanding of the agency departments and services with which they would have contact and clarifying responsibility of agency and of foster parents.

This programme was implemented during a probation period for new foster parents, and attendance was compulsory. For foster parents who have already begun fostering, the agency presents programmes covering the following areas of concern:

fostering an adolescent (8 sessions)

separation (5 sessions)

foster fathers (1 session)

fostering West Indian children (1 session)

parents in placement—moving toward adoption (1 session)

assertiveness for better communication (all day workshop)

grief—terminally ill foster child; death of a foster child (2 sessions)

incest (1 session)

fostering a retarded child (8 sessions)

community college certificate course for foster parents, (one evening per week consisting of four 10-week courses, two of which are taken during each of 2 years)

## FOSTER PARENT TRAINING PROGRAM

| | |
|---|---|
| Year I | Human Growth and Development |
| | Child Management I |
| Year II | The Foster Parent and the Community |
| | Child Management II |
| Conclusion: | Evaluation of Fostering Skills |

In-service foster parent training can take several forms:

1. behaviour modification approach to child management (Penn [5]; Hampson and Tavormina [6])

2. reflective group training approach, which alters parental awareness and facilitates understanding and acceptance of child's feelings [6]

3. training in child development using one-way mirrors, an approach designed to increase foster parents' knowledge of normal growth and development; to provide guidance on child rearing; to encourage child's intellectual, emotional, and social growth (Gross, Shuman, and Magid [7])

4. skills training group, which increases foster parents' ability to respond to child in ways that reflect sensitivity while providing appropriate controls (Guerney [8])

5. skills enrichment and empowerment group model, which is based on the assumption of powerlessness and isolation experienced by foster parents, and therefore emphasizes foster parents' self-esteem and assertiveness (Jacobs [9])

## C.    Matching Foster Parents and Child

Readers are encouraged to review the discussion of problem-solving contained in Appendix A, particularly those sections dealing with the search for solutions and assessment.

There is a paucity of literature that addresses the process of matching children with appropriate foster parents and foster siblings. However, agencies generally do attempt to determine foster family strengths and to facilitate placement of children whose needs mesh with these qualities. This is a delicate process, and care must be taken to match with sensitivity (e.g., a child needing to develop peer group skills may be best placed in a large family).

A discussion of the factors crucial to successful matching in adoption is provided in Chapter 11, IV.

## D.    Learning to Foster the Abused Child

At this point, it may be useful to review the discussions in Chapter 5, particularly Sections VII, "Consequences of Physical Child Abuse", and XII, "Treatment Options for Abused Children".

Fostering an abused child may call to attention a number of philosophical, moral, and behavioral issues for prospective foster parents. They must think through a number of issues *before* accepting an abused child; for example:

Do they believe in physical discipline in some circumstances? (If so, then they will be inappropriate for fostering abused children, or any other foster children.)

Do they feel at least some compassion for abusive parents? (If not, then there may be mutual discomfort between the two families.)

Do they feel comfortable about the parenting they received? Do they feel comfortable about their ability to handle frustrations? (If not, then fostering less "difficult" children may be more appropriate.)

Ryan, Warren, and McFadden [10] have articulated a number of points about abused children and abusive parents which should be highlighted for prospective foster parents. Some of these are presented below.

1.    *Physical Needs*

Foster parents should enquire about the child's medical condition, making certain that any internal injuries or healing fractures have been detected.

Because severely battered children may have to spend time in the hospital or visit doctors often or wear orthopedic devices, and so on, foster parents should be made aware of the time commitment required to adequately handle such contingencies (e.g., transportating to doctor's appointments; visiting the child in the hospital).

Foster parents must help the child learn to feel "safe" in her or his own skin; young children can be massaged, held, bathed gently, while older children may recoil from physical contact—also, they may overreact or underreact to pain; foster parents can tell a child who apparently feels no pain: "I see that you hurt yourself, that must hurt"; "It's okay to cry if it hurts; I can help you feel better".

2.    *Emotional Needs*

Foster parents must realize that trust takes *time* to build; at first, physically abused children may hide from physical proximity and this should not be construed as a personal rebuff.

Foster parents must learn to acknowledge children's feelings about separation from parents and siblings and learn to reassure children that they are *not* being punished.

Abused children must be reassured by foster parents that they are valuable human beings; e.g., "You are terrific, and I love you very much, it was not your fault that your dad hurt you—he had problems of his own, and you just happened to be around".

Foster parents should not speak ill of children's parents; such attacks will merely compound mixed feelings of love and hurt children already have for their parents.

Abused children are likely to harbour fairly strong fears; foster parents must assess behaviour in this context and ask themselves *Is there anything she or he is afraid of?*

*3.       Cognitive Development*

Abused children may have suffered some damage to the central nervous system; in combination with emotional trauma the results may be learning difficulties, speech problems, perceptual or memory problems, poor motor control, and so forth; foster parents must ensure that special school personnel evaluate and assist the child, and that the school *not* subject the child to physical discipline.

*4.       Social Development*

Abused children may suffer developmental lags because of their fears, lack of trust, and low self-esteem; foster parents must learn to assess the child's level of emotional development to reinforce incremental steps forward.

Foster parents may recognize some of the behavior patterns of abused children:

(a) *Caretaker:* wards off abuse by being overly compliant and pleasing; must learn that it is safe to be a child and to have her or his own needs met.

(b) *Hider:* carefully monitors parents' behavior, and hides when parental anger is imminent; must learn that it is safe to be near foster parents when they are angry or tense.

(c) *Scapegoat:* offers herself or himself as the target for others' problems; must learn that punishment is not forthcoming when someone else misbehaves or has a problem.

(d) *Provocatuer:* gets no attention and soon discovers that bad behaviour evokes attention, even if it is negative attention; parents' guilt over abuse may be manipulated by the child during the aftermath; must learn that attention is forthcoming through good, not bad, behaviour.

*5.       Moral Development*

Abused children must *not* be handled with physical force by foster parents; rather, they should be handled with very firm consistent limits.

Foster parents must learn to model empathic and nonviolent behaviour for children, and to develop in them a sense of trust, security, and safety.

Foster children who have been *sexually* abused may recoil from physical affection; also, they may have learned sexually inappropriate interaction patterns with adults which could shock or upset foster parents. Thus, prospective foster parents must learn the causes of sexual abuse and how to teach children appropriate behaviours while showing warmth and caring through non-threatening, non-sexual interactions. It may be necessary to open up communications between foster mother and foster father in order to encourage later discussion of their foster child's sexuality.

For additional information on sexual abuse, refer to Chapter 6.

## VII.   PLANNING FOR PLACEMENT

### A.   Short-Term Planning

Planning for a child entails much more than deciding where and with whom
she or he will be living in the future; rather, it is a process to be engaged in by
workers, community resource people, foster parents, and parents which delineates
specific tasks required to help move the child developmentally and to compensate for
past or present difficulties.

Just as "natural" children are guided by parents' plans for them, so too should
foster children know what is planned for them in order to develop a sense of security
about the future.

Foster parents should be taught how to assess the child's needs, how to
establish priorities and target behaviours to be modified, how to set small and attainable goals, how to implement plans, and to record results. The value of specific
planning is as follows [10]:

It can ease the initial adjustment of both child and foster family.

It establishes priorities for the child.

It specifies tasks of all involved parties (the child, foster family, parent,
worker).

It can involve the child's parent(s), and perhaps encourage them to
acknowledge that positive change is possible in the present and future.

It helps foster parents to evaluate a child's progress realistically—to see
specific gains.

It can assist workers (and the court) with long-term planning.

Such planning is here subsumed under "Permanency Planning".

### B.   Permanency Planning

Permanency planning describes the planning that occurs from the pre-
admission period until the child returns home, or until an alternative permanent plan
is secured. Synonymous with "life planning", this process is thought to represent
sound child welfare practice. The worker's job is to ensure that the child is in care for
only the time allotted by the court and agency.

While permanency planning is considered an ideal model by most agencies,
there are large variations in the degree to which it has so far been implemented.
Where such planning does not occur, it is usually the result of inadequate resources
and a paucity of workers. Planning on a crisis basis is a last resort and should be
strongly avoided.

Several sources [11, 12, 13, 14, 15] link parental visiting with placement
stability and an eventual return home. Such a process requires that the worker
facilitate an optimal developmental experience for the child, maintain links with
parent(s), and help the child's family to rectify problematic aspects of their living

situation in such a way as to enable them to accept the child back into the home or to facilitate relinquishment of parental rights.

Where permanency planning has *not* occurred, problems have arisen:

It is far easier for a child to enter the foster care system than to exit from it.

Little effort has gone into either keeping families together or reuniting the child with the family after placement has occurred.

If a child remains in the foster care system, the likelihood of restoration to family is seriously diminished.

These problems exist for a number of reasons. One factor is the pressure on child welfare workers, who necessarily focus on children who remain at home under sometimes less-than-ideal circumstances. Another factor is the child's family's depression over the loss of family; this may result in a lack of motivation to do the work required to solve the problem that led to placement [12].

The adversarial system represented by the court exacerbates both the dual roles played by child welfare workers (authoritarian law enforcer and helper) and the resistance of the family to authority and .change. The law itself and the agency hierarchy militate against crown wards returning home. Families of crown wards are sometimes encouraged to leave agency treatment when their problems require long-term solutions.

Finally, in the worst possible instances, children's placements continue from year to year without ongoing evaluation. Changes in placements sometimes occur without reference to a plan for stable, continuous care.

However, these kinds of problems can be solved. Solutions require intensive work with parents who have tended to receive too little attention from workers, and who have received inappropriate pressure that does not acknowledge their needs.

Solutions have been offered and are based on decision-making models and case management approaches.

Commonalities in these programmes include early planning, focus on the goal of facilitating a permanent plan, and recognition of a longitudinal view (longer than 2 years) of family rehabilitation. The goal of permanency planning is a commitment to continuity in child care and to placements designed to last indefinitely.

There are a number of groups whose best interests are served by permanency planning. These include the children, families, community groups, and social agencies. Many programmes have been initiated to meet these goals. For example, a California programme described by Stein et al. [16] attempted to provide continuity of care by having the child's parent(s) participate in decision-making regarding the child's future. Two other approaches to permanency planning are those described by Pike [17] and Sisto [18].

Some authors (e.g., Rooney [19]) urge caution in viewing permanency planning as a panacea for problems related to foster care. While these programmes offer both reduction of foster care drift and cost effectiveness, they must be adapted to local conditions, and be well planned, carefully implemented, and monitored.

Permanency planning is a relevant concept for every child. It should be noted that the time for concentrated services to parents is at the point of entry into care and during the time soon thereafter. In addition, the population of children who drift in foster care must be identified, described, and commonalities noted. Child welfare workers can then begin to ascertain appropriate resources to prevent such drift.

Workers manage to return a sizable proportion of children to their own homes and to make permanent plans for others. These workers need continuing agency support and resources in order to make permanency planning possible for all children.

For a discussion of adoption as a permanency planning option, see Chapter 11.

## VIII.  SUMMARY

This chapter has explored the more salient issues related to pre-placement in foster care. While prospective foster parents must look with clear vision at their motivation, capacities, abilities, and so on, the worker must also be capable of recruiting and selecting women and men who will provide foster children with what they need. Fostering is potentially a stressful process for all individuals but also potentially an experience that enriches foster families, foster children and their parents, and workers alike.

Pre-service educational and training sessions for prospective foster parents have been recognized as significantly worthwhile exercises which ultimately benefit the entire fostering process. Likewise, efforts at permanency planning have reaped abundant rewards.

## REFERENCES

1. Flint, B. M. *New Hope for Deprived Children.* Toronto: University of Toronto Press, 1978.
2. Bernstein, B., Snider, D. A., and Meezan, W. *Foster Care Needs and Alternatives to Placement.* New York: New York State Bureau of Social Welfare, 1975.
3. Epstein, N. B., Bishop, D. S., and Levin, S. "McMaster Model of Family Functioning", unpublished paper, December 1977.
4. Stone, H. and Hunzeker, J. *Education for Foster Family Care: Models and Methods for Foster Parents and Social Workers.* New York: Child Welfare League of America, 1974.
5. Penn, J. "A Model for Training Foster Parents in Behaviour Modification Techniques", Child Welfare, Vol. LVII, March 1978, pp. 175–180.
6. Hampson, R. and Tavormina, J. "Feedback from Experts: A Study of Foster Mothers", Social Work, Vol. 25, March 1980, pp. 108–113.
7. Gross, B., Shuman, B., and Magid, D. "Using the One-Way Mirror to Train Foster Parents in Child Development", Child Welfare, Vol. LVII, December 1978, pp. 685–688.
8. Guerney, L. "A Description and Evaluation of a Skills Training Program for Foster Parents", American Journal of Community Psychology, 1977.
9. Jacobs, Marc. "Foster Parent Training: An Opportunity for Skills Enrichment and Empowerment", Child Welfare, Vol. LIX, December 1980, pp. 615–624.
10. Ryan, P., Warren, B., and McFadden, E. *Course Outline: Foster Parent Training Project.* Ypsilanti, Mich.: Eastern Michigan University, April 1977.
11. Fanshel, D. *Foster Parenthood.* Minneapolis: University of Minnesota Press, 1966.

12. Hubbell, R. *Foster Care and Families: Confronting Values Policies.* Philadelphia: Temple University Press, 1981.

13. Palmer, S. *Children in Long-Term Care.* London: National Health and Welfare, 1976.

14. Northup, E. "A Study of Success and Failure in Long-Term Foster Care", University of British Columbia, M.S.W. Thesis, 1969.

15. Hepworth, H.P. *Foster Care and Adoption in Canada,* Ottawa: Canadian Council on Social Development, 1980.

16. Stein, T., Gambrill, E., and Wiltse, K. E. *Children in Foster Homes: Achieving Continuity of Care.* New York: Praeger, 1978.

17. Pike, L. *Permanent Planning for Children in Foster Care: A Handbook for Social Workers.* DHEW Portland State University, Washington D.C.: 1977.

18. Sisto, G. "An Agency Design for Permanency Planning in Foster Care", Child Welfare, Vol. LIX, February 1980, pp. 103–111.

19. Rooney, R. "Permanency Planning: Boon for All Children?", Social Work, Vol. 27, March 1982, pp. 152–158.

20. Wilkes, James. "The Stresses of Fostering: Part 1: On the Fostering Parents; Part II: On the Fostering Children", Ontario Association of Children's Aid Societies Journal, Vol. 22, November and December 1979, pp. 1–5, 8; 7–12.

# 8

# Casework to Foster Parents and Children

SHIRLEY FISH

I. INTRODUCTION                                                    236
II. CASEWORK SERVICES TO FOSTER PARENTS AND
CHILDREN                                                           236
   A.  Introduction                                        236
   B.  Foster Fatherhood                                   237
   C.  Foster Effectiveness                                238
   D.  Placement Difficulties                              239
   E.  Coping with Stress                                  240
   F.  Conflict Resolution                                 242
III. THE SEPARATION PROCESS                                        243
   A.  Introduction                                        243
   B.  The Mourning Process                                244
   C.  Working with the Separated Child                    245
   D.  Separation Intervention Techniques                  247
   E.  Foster Parent Grief                                 248
   F.  Helping Foster Parents Grieve                       249
   G.  Case Description of Separation and Grieving         250
IV. FOSTERING ADOLESCENTS                                          251
   A.  Introduction                                        252
   B.  Approaches to Practice                              252
V. INTERACTION BETWEEN FAMILIES                                    253
   A.  Introduction                                        253
   B.  Effects of Interaction                              254
   C.  Traditional Foster Care Roles                       255
   D.  The Developing Role of Fostering                    255
   E.  Alternate Roles                                     256
   F.  Developmental Stages in Role Modelling               257
VI. SUMMARY                                                        259
   REFERENCES                                                   259

## I.    INTRODUCTION

At a time when the foster care system is being examined and revised, it is difficult to select post-placement practice guidelines which have relevance for *both* current and future conditions. The solution lies in giving emphasis to traditional problems in service, and to some associated with modern trends in fostering practice.

Section II presents strategies for helping foster parents cope with stresses in the fostering process, and guidelines for conflict resolution. An examination of the separation process, and a discussion of ways in which it can be facilitated by social worker intervention are dealt with in Section III.

Fostering adolescents is challenging for foster parents. Service guidelines are suggested in Section IV.

Finally, the discussion of permanency planning (Chapter 7) noted the importance of involving parents in the fostering process. Section V examines reasons for this, as well as service roles and strategies. (The term "parents" is used here to mean legal parents as opposed to foster parents. Legal parents may, or may not, be biological parents.)

## II.    CASEWORK SERVICES TO FOSTER PARENTS AND CHILDREN

### A.    Introduction

Difficulties in providing services to foster families cannot be underestimated; for example, placement of a troubled child requires adjustment, and adaptations must be made to a complicated relationship among the foster family, the agency, and the legal family. Normal casework services occur within a potentially stressful situation. That these difficulties are real is reflected in a recent government suggestion that weighting caseloads would provide a way of protecting foster care caseloads and of assigning a higher priority to these support systems. It would also acknowledge that the foster child and foster parents are separate entities who have different needs and thus make different demands on the worker [8].

To describe various roles and activities organized for foster parents is itself a tremendous challenge. However, a recent literature review [1] suggests that, generally, social workers:

act as advisor-teachers, counsellors, and sources of psychological support

help foster parents to understand the child's behaviour through briefing and real life discussions

provide assistance in restructuring relationships within the foster family upon arrival of the foster child

help the foster family deal with the child's feelings and behaviour in response to separation from, and return to, the parents help to put problems and failure in a broader fostering context, beyond the individual case

work to assure that occasional negative feelings towards foster children are understandable, acceptable, and normal

act as agency and community representatives to ensure that foster parents are doing a good job, and that they *know* they are doing a good job

The remainder of this section looks at two characteristics of the fostering process which have a strong impact on the service process—foster fatherhood, and foster parents' perceptions of help. Placement difficulties are examined, followed by guidelines for working with stress, conflict, and separation. These, of course, do not represent the gamut of issues confronting workers who provide foster care services; however, they are topical both in the literature and in workers' discussions of professional dilemmas.

## B.    Foster Fatherhood

Foster fathers generally receive scant attention from agencies, even though their involvement has been related to overall placement success [25].

There has also been a long history of neglect by researchers—something which foster fathers share with natural fathers. However, those few studies which have compared foster father with natural father roles concluded that foster fathers may need help in coming to terms with their role [10]. Traditional fatherhood usually connotes ideas of provider, transmitter of faith or values, involvement in child-rearing decisions, authority, and of being aware of their contributions to child development. However, foster fathers can take little pride in any of these usual sources. They are not the providers, as the agency is financially responsible for the foster child. They do not transmit their faith, but rather are expected to maintain the child's previous ideological status. The agency has final authority and makes all major decisions concerning the child. They are less aware of their contributions to the child's development [13] because of the many problems the child often brings with her or him. Davids [9] found that foster fathers were somewhat less active in rearing boys than other fathers, but were involved for specific activities such as trips, buying furniture or toys, or settling quarrels. Foster fathers who had their own sons conversed with foster sons more concerning life (i.e., sex, future goals, religion, politics, and guidance) than did foster-only fathers. Also, the more self-assured the foster fathers, the more likely they were to have a negative attitude to caseworkers [10].

In order that foster-father care become more than a custodial arrangement, caseworkers must be trained and reminded to work with foster fathers rather than ignore them. Evening group activities with other foster fathers would reinforce their sense of worth and give them recognition, help them to see ways in which they do make significant contributions and do influence their foster child's value system. Foster fathers need to be reassured of the importance of their role and of the great responsibilities for the child which have been delegated to them. Meeting agency personnel in a sociable rather than investigatory setting may "unfreeze" communication and decrease social distance from caseworkers. Possible contributions of foster fathers should become essential criteria of the home-finding process.

**C.    Foster Effectiveness**

Aldridge and Cautley [1] found placement success in a new foster home to be largely related to:

> characteristics of the worker
>
> amount and kind of placement preparation given to new foster parents
>
> availability of the worker during placement
>
> preparation of the child

Number of years of worker experience was found to be positively related to the success of new foster parents. A discussion paper on foster care [8] states that: "it has long been recognized that the combination of being young, single, and inexperienced results in workers who are frequently of little help to foster parents", particularly when foster parents need practical suggestions. Frank, open, collegial relationships between workers and foster parents were preferred by the latter. When information was not fully forthcoming it was interpreted as a lack of confidence in them as foster parents [25]. The helpfulness of workers' advice was positively related to success.

Adequate foster parent preparation is a good investment of workers' time and energy because inadequate preparation cannot readily be compensated for later. In only 50% of cases reviewed [8] was there any evidence of foster father preparation, but where foster fathers were included they were more likely to be involved with and to enjoy the foster child early in the placement. This was related to overall success [25].

Workers' willingness to be available, to make quick responses to phone calls, and to provide clear answers to questions was significantly related to attitudes of both foster mothers and foster fathers regarding workers, general satisfaction with their new roles, and to their morale in general. These attitudes affected the overall performance of foster parents. Workers' involvement in the placement during the early months, particularly when requested by foster parents, was more likely to produce positive results than were later efforts when workers perceived that things were not going well.

Placements of children who had been prepared were slightly more successful even though the better-prepared children had the more disrupted pasts [25].

The effectiveness of fostering can be further enhanced by other placement supports. These can help to provide maximum continuity for the child. For example, other foster parents can be used for support or relief of child care, thereby relieving the primary foster family. The "extended family" model has been used to enable foster parents to receive mutual support similar to that of a natural extended family group [46]. They may also serve as alternate placements in case of a crisis in the original foster home, thus allowing a child to be placed with people whom she or he knows [50].

Resident child care worker services may be helpful in supporting foster parents dealing with a disturbed child or a child going through a particularly difficult time. Babysitter or homemaker services may help support a placement when the foster home has been overloaded, when a foster parent is ill, when a crisis situation has arisen, or when the foster child's needs warrant it.

As Ontario's Foster Care Proposed Guidelines [39] state: 'Relief services such as babysitting, child care or homemaker assistance, day care and holiday relief are thought to be essential to foster parents. Regular "breaks" and relief from the responsibility of 24-hour-care may help to avoid foster parent "burn outs" and re-placements of children'.

Community workers may be useful resource persons in arranging these support services. For a further discussion of community work and casework, see Chapter 3, III and IV.

Research on foster parent satisfaction shows that foster parents' perceptions of social workers and the nature of their consultation are important factors. Foster parents reported more positive views of the agency when:

> they believed that workers showed a good understanding of the child and of her or his problems

> they were treated with respect as adults and not as clients

Therapeutic attempts, such as family counselling, are frequently viewed as intrusive rather than helpful.

Whether intended or not, workers are sometimes viewed as critics of foster parents' parental adequacy. Workers' intention of providing guidance may be seen otherwise.

In summary, workers can enhance the fostering process by providing adequate preparation to both foster parents and the child on a case-by-case basis. Detailed knowledge of the foster child is welcomed, as is good practical advice. The sheer amount of contact with the foster family may not be as crucial as responding to their expressed needs. As open "colleague-like" partnership is valued, more so than a worker-client relationship [25]. Finally, foster parents' perceptions of the relationship are as important as actual events, particularly where worker feedback is required.


## D.    Placement Difficulties

Despite careful planning and preparation for placement, things may go wrong. An important component of the casework function is a sensitivity to placement difficulties and timely intervention.

Aldrige and Cautley [1] articulate three warning signals that indicate placement trouble:

> 1. Expressions of dissatisfaction with being a foster parent, or with the placement generally

> 2. A report by either foster parent that the child's condition is not improving

> 3. A report by the foster father that the child's presence is having a negative effect on him, his wife, or his children

It is important for workers to respond to questions and requests from new foster parents at the time they are presented. The most effective learning takes place when one's desire for information is expressed. It also leads to foster parent satisfaction. Foster parents may need specific help with the child or with coming to terms with their new role [1].

If the foster child is perceived as not improving or as getting worse, foster parents may need repeated explanations that progress is a slow and irregular process and that regressions, setbacks, and plateaus are normal and to be expected. Foster parents need support and encouragement and may need specific help for a disturbed child.

In another study, Cautley and Aldridge [5] isolated high-risk characteristics of foster children. These were children who had a period of institutional care, a history of poor physical care and social neglect, an inability to relate, legal status as agency wards, and who had experienced rejection in their longest previous foster placement.

If children and their foster siblings are not getting along, then specific help is desirable. Foster parents will need reassurance that rivalry and disagreement represent normal behaviour and are common in foster homes. Suggestions should be made concerning ways in which to give each child individual attention and to help each establish her or his own niche in the family.

Negative reports by foster fathers about the effect of the foster child may be a sign of noninvolvement in the care of the child. Providing information about the child's background and needs, and the ways in which the child might be helped, could encourage greater involvement.

### E.    Coping With Stress

The preceding chapter noted various stresses on foster families. One way to aid the fostering process is through stress-reduction interventions.

Fostering puts stress on the foster family's relationships. The way they adapt to this will determine whether it strengthens or weakens their relationships. Together the couple must work out and regularly review their reasons for fostering, their expectations of fostering, and their expectation of the effect fostering will have on their marriage and family relationships. They should undertake a team work approach so that one partner does not foster to the exclusion of the other. Activities should be planned for themselves alone so that they experience some areas of privacy [60].

To facilitate stress reduction, a number of specific activities can be encouraged. A climate of open discussion and acceptance of all feelings should be created. This encourages the acknowledgement of feelings about problems, so that they can be dealt with in a positive manner.

Meetings with other foster parents can be encouraged. Informal or formal opportunities promote sharing of mutual experiences, feelings, and difficulties. The supportive function of these meetings is enhanced when specific practical ideas are shared.

A specific understanding of problem behaviour may also aid stress reduction. Training can be provided to aid understanding of the dynamics of foster child and legal parent behaviour. Of particular importance is the notion that such behaviours do not reflect badly on them as foster parents. This awareness can be strengthened by helpful suggestions from the worker on handling difficult situations.

It is essential that the relationship among the agency, workers, and foster parents encourage mutual sharing of information and direct communication. In particular, clear information should be provided concerning:

> agency expectations
>
> the length of a child's placement or the time when this will be decided
>
> foster parent and worker roles
>
> previous and possible future behaviours of the foster child

Stress reduction can be facilitated by worker accessibility (particularly to new foster homes), foster parent involvement in some decisions, team work, and a home study which carefully examines the needs of the foster family as well as those of the agency. Finally, stress may be avoided through the provision of time for planning in anticipation of the foster child's arrival.

Since foster parents' children may also be touched by stressful situations, they must be involved in the planning process. For example, they may be involved in discussions at the time decisions to foster are being made. Discussion of concrete situations and encouragement of questions promote the exchange of practical advice and the expression of feelings.

Exploration of concrete expectations and role changes will help children adjust to a foster child. Specific expectations rather than generalities are most useful: "We will expect you to babysit once a week", rather than "We will expect you to help". Pointed discussions of possible impediments to necessary family changes, and a removal or negotiation of these impediments, will also help.

Once the fostering process has begun, other stress reduction procedures may be put into place. Children and foster parents should have the opportunity to express their views, and to review progress and expectations in an on-going way. Parents should be alerted to changes in their own children's behaviour or moods. The latter should be involved in problem-solving, and generally respected for their own unique feelings and reactions. Private time and space should be respected.

A good general principle to follow is that stress avoidance will be aided if the collective identity of the foster family and the unique identities of individual members are respected. Minimal disruption to children's friendships and social relationships should occur. Family members should have time alone as a family group; children should have time alone with their parents just as temporary foster children need time alone with their parents.

Stress and the successful coping with stress can have very positive results:

> It can increase openness and awareness among family members.
>
> Children may develop greater awareness of their own strengths and of their family's strengths.
>
> Family members may broaden their understanding of the world and empathy for others.
>
> In dealing with the experiences of children in transition, the foster family may find strength in dealing with their own separations.
>
> Family members may confront issues and develop a deeper sense of respect for each other and a deeper sense of confidence in the family.

The foster family may learn to achieve empathy for and understanding of foster children and help them to grow and develop their potential.

In summary, workers help foster families to change and grow in response to the fostering process. Certain strategies help prepare for specific family change around the introduction of a new member. Processes which promote stress reduction include open discussion of problems, sharing ideas within and outside the family, maintaining individual and collective identities, problem-solving and planning.

## F.    Conflict Resolution

Casework service to foster families has always been considered one of the major support services which an agency can provide. Ironically, it is also often a major source of conflict, annoyance, and dissatisfaction for foster parents. In the foster care area, social work practice contains much potential for conflict and there appears to be a need for conflict resolution training. This might best be realized by training both workers and foster parents in constructive strategies.

Roles and relationships created by placement give foster parents and workers different and often incompatible perspectives. Other areas of potential conflict include relationships between parents and foster parents, foster parent acceptance or non-acceptance of worker involvement, conflict regarding perceived motivations of foster parents, and professional expertise versus parenting knowledge. Each feels that she or he knows the child best and what is best for the child.

The foster child's ambivalence towards and testing of all adults involved may contribute to disharmony.

Further conflict can arise from destructive conflict resolution. It is possible to resolve conflict so that participants retain their commitment to the relationship and find the resolution a mutually rewarding process, minimizing negative results of the encounter and maximizing the strengthening tendencies of a conflict.

Destructive conflict resolution occurs under the following conditions [59]:

when comments about the other's viewpoint are evaluative

through reliance on a strategy of power—threat, coercion, and minimized communication

by highlighting issues of who will *win* or *lose*

when conflict occurs over broad issues (principles and precedents), rather than over specifics

when precedents are cited

by noting who is watching the outcome

through a claim of inherent superiority, legitimacy, morality, authority, ability, knowledge and/or relevance

through a focus on issues that threaten the self-esteem of those involved, thus putting them on the defensive so that the real issues can never be considered

A more productive and constructive mode of interaction over conflict issues relies on positive strategies:

recognizing the legitimacy of each person's interests and that the solution sought must be responsive to the needs of each party

building on common interests, similarities, and on the convergence of beliefs and values

minimizing differences and enhancing mutual understanding and good will

breaking down conflict into separate issues so that it is not an "all or nothing" matter

highlighting mutual interests, mutual power, and the mutual problem

showing a readiness to respond helpfully to the other's needs and requests and showing a positive interest in the other's welfare

focussing on diminishing perceived opposition in values and interests, decreasing perceived opposition to achieving common interests, and shrinking perceived importance of what is at risk

emphasizing commonality and the belief that more can be gained by continuing relationships in the context of shared facilities and procedures

## III.  THE SEPARATION PROCESS

## A.  Introduction

Separation is a complex issue [5]. The significance to the child of separation from her or his family depends on many variables:

*Age at time of separation:* Reaction to separation seems to be less severe in the very early infancy before the establishment of a significant relationship with the mother figure. A very sensitive time may be when the child is establishing stable, affectional relationships, approximately between six months and two years of age. However, each developmental stage has its own sensitivities and vulnerability to separation.

*Quality of the relationship with the mother prior to separation:* Children showing the most severe reaction to separation are those with the closest relationship with their mother [23]. However, older children who have experienced close relationships with parents may be better able to tolerate separation and to establish meaningful relationships with substitute parents than children who have never bonded.

*Quality of maternal care during the foster care experience.* Provision of adequate mothering after separation may prevent the development of serious disturbance, while the traumatic impact of separation is likely to be exacerbated by unsatisfactory foster care relationships.

*Character of the relationship with the own parents during separation:* If the child is unable to maintain a relationship with the parents, the impact of separation is likely to be more severe.

*Duration of separation:* Repeated long-term separations imply continuous family crisis. They may involve serious emotional deprivation, since the original sense of loss and abandonment is reinforced and reactivated by each re-placement.

It may be useful to review the discussions of child neglect (Chapter 4) and child abuse (Chapter 5) in order to acquire a fuller understanding of the dynamics of neglected and abused children.

## B.      The Mourning Process

When children are separated from and have no contact with their families, they begin to go through the painful process of mourning. By virtue of being separated from parents or foster parents (even when some contact is maintained), the child and her or his family will experience anxiety.

For the child, separation may mean feelings of abandonment, rejection, worthlessness, anger at the person who deserted (whether it is actual or perceived), feelings of responsibility for the desertion, with concomitant shame or guilt, and expectation of one's own death or other's death. The child may fantasize about and idealize the parents or exaggerate their problems and their treatment of her or him. The child may exhibit many anxieties or regressive behaviour such as enuresis, speech problems, and "acting out" behaviours [36, 37].

Steinhauer, drawing on Bowlby's work [32], outlines the stages in the mourning process. He states that the purpose of mourning is to help the mourners accept that someone they love is lost to them, to help them withdraw their love, interest and investment and to reinvest these feelings in an available substitute. Mourning will inevitably occur in any child separated from those with whom she or he has formed an affectional bond. A highly ambivalent relationship to the lost person will make the mourning process more difficult in terms of successful completion.

There are typically three stages in the mourning process [32]:

1. *State of protest:* This lasts as long as there is hope of reunion, and consists of crying, kicking, screaming, threatening, pleading, or any behaviour which the child thinks may bring about the return.

2. *State of despair:* This lasts as long as there is hope of reunion but affections have not been transferred. The child is listless, apathetic, lethargic, depressed, and withdrawn.

3. *Mourning successfully completed or mourning never successfully completed:* either external or internal factors may interfere with a child's successful completion of the mourning process. These include the lack of an adequate available mother substitute due to delay, interim placement, or anything that blocks the child from being free to form a bond with an adequate available substitute. Examples include repeated separations, failure to receive ade-

quate preparation for placement, or failure to receive help in dealing with reactions to the separation.

What are the long-term effects of aborted or pathological mourning?

*Permanent detachment:* The child relates in a shallow, superficial, and manipulative manner; there is an inability to become emotionally involved with other people or, alternatively, the child combines demands for closeness with an inability to tolerate closeness.

*Persistent, diffuse rage:* The child demonstrates intense, violent, and persistent hatred of the parent figure.

*Chronic depressions:* These may present as sadness, loneliness, helplessness, self-destructive behaviour, or suicidal thoughts or attempts.

*Chronic dependency on others:* This is an inability to make independent decisions.

*Asocial and antisocial behaviour:* Seen as failure to form stable relationships or to allow solid identification to occur; as a result there is lack of appropriate guilt, diffuse feelings of shame and worthlessness, and lack of inner defences to keep behaviour within appropriate and socially acceptable limits. Later parenting abilities may also be affected.

*Low self-concept:* The child is setting up herself (himself) for repeated rejections, thus proving again that there is nothing good or lovable about herself (himself).

For a discussion of adolescence and loss, see Chapter 10, VI "Self-Injurious Behaviours".

## C.    Working with the Separated Child (here designated as "she")

Though physically separated from the family, the child is still a member of that family and continues to feel emotionally connected. She will need help in dealing with a number of issues. It is important to understand and to respect the child's feelings and to provide opportunities to work them through and in accordance with her readiness and capacities. The tendency to "protect" a child from facing and expressing what may be painful feelings about separation and placement is unrealistic and psychologically unsound.

Cull [40] outlines practice guidelines for helping the separated child:

A. Helping the child understand her role in the family:

Frequently, the separated child leaves behind a significant role. She may have been needed as a scapegoat, or as one who defuses inter-parent anger by focussing attention on herself. She may have been encouraged to "act out" as a way of expressing parents' unconscious rage. In any case, the child may have had an important role to play; withdrawing her from the family may leave her hurt, confused, angry, and feeling betrayed.

The child needs help to explore previous roles so that fantasies, distortions and self-blame can give way to a realistic understanding of the family's situation. She needs reassurance that she is an important member of her family, and that separation is not a punishment.

B.  Reassuring the child that her parents care:

The child may behave as if she is relieved or furious and the parents may wash their hands of the child. Both are going through a very emotional time and immediate reactions should not be taken at face value. The worker's initial role at this time may be one of active listening and eventually one of helping the child maintain a balanced picture of the family.

C.  Helping the child recognize the realistic limits of her parents:

If the child was separated because the family could not contain her (for whatever reason), then the child needs help to understand that that was a function of their limitations and not of hers alone. When the child is ready, she can be helped to understand her parents as people with their own weaknesses and problems just like other people. She needs help to talk about and to understand who she is, who her parents are, and how she is like them and different from them. She needs help in disputing the irrational, negative beliefs that she holds about herself and her parents so that she can see herself and her life in a positive and realistic way.

D.  Helping the child recognize her "unacceptable" behaviour in the context of the family:

The assessment of the family will bring to light the importance of the child's "unacceptable" behaviour to the overall functioning of the family. She was not "bad" just because she behaved "badly". This kind of reframing is crucial for some children who experience the rejection as a sign of their basic unacceptability and worthlessness.

E.  Helping the child to sort out the inconsistencies:

The process leading up to the separation may have been filled with confusing events. She may try to interpret these events and may need help sorting out faulty facts and ambivalent feelings.

F.  Supporting the child through the mourning process:

The child separated from her family, community, routines, structures, and relationships will experience loss. The worker needs to be familiar with the process of mourning and to be prepared to support the child and to alleviate the pain when possible through family or community contact. When the child must go through the process it is important that the worker be sensitive to the child's needs. Hancock [43] describes her experience in caring for her 3-year-old grandchild while his mother went to the store:

> I suggested we close the inner door and play elevator. "No." he said firmly, "you leave the door open while I cry." I was to pay attention to his sorrow. I was not to offer superficial comforts and diversions which would not meet his need because indeed they were totally unrelated to it. I was not to pretend that my presence made up for his mother's leaving him. But he did not want to be alone in his grief and,

at a distance he, himself, indicated as acceptable, I sat down to be
with him while he cried.

G. Supporting the child through the process of change:

Placing the child in a new environment, no matter how safe and caring,
is disruptive to her sense of continuity and stability. She may revert to
regressive behaviour. The child will require help and compassionate guidance through this period of adjustment.

H. Helping the child adjust to new relationships:

Just as she will replay old comfortable roles she may try to get others to
respond to her in familiar ways. The child can be expected to try to reor-
ganize the foster home to match her former home. She may provoke and
manipulate and test; she has had experience in trying to control the situation
for her own preservation and may be very astute in finding just the right spot
of vulnerability in the foster family. She will need guidance, support, and an
understanding of her behaviour as she finds her way in these new relationships. She may also need some interpretation as to why people react to her in
certain ways; she needs to know that her foster family is also adjusting to a
change in their family and getting to know her. The worker may sometimes
need to interpret and discuss these interactions with the child.

I. Supporting the child in her concern for her siblings:

The child may have had complicated ambivalent relationships with her
siblings. She may now focus attention on them as symbolic of her loss. She
may obsessively worry about the younger siblings left at home, or feel guilty
about leaving them, or be jealous of them. She will need reassurance and
information about them; contact when possible is a very important means of
helping a child maintain her identity and be reassured of her siblings' welfare.

J. Preparing the child for her return home:

The child and her family will need a great deal of support when she
returns home. Separation from the foster family will need to be dealt with
and the role that the foster family will play after placement should be
defined. As parents and child learn to live together again, they will need
encouragement to use skills in communication and in seeking help. The
worker will need to be very supportive and to help them deal with issues in a
practical and resolute way.

## D.    Separation Intervention Techniques

Should separation be unavoidable, the damage done can be minimized:

If at all feasible or possible, the child should be actively involved
throughout the intake, pre-placement visits, and placement process. She
needs to be aware of what is going on so she can feel assured that there are no
realistic alternatives and that at least temporarily her parents cannot care for
her. Joint interviews with parents and/or close relatives may facilitate the

process so that distortions, misgivings, fears, anger, and guilt may be aired, thereby avoiding denial and suppression of feelings.

Basic standards concerning preparation for separation are outlined in the *Manual on Foster Care: Proposed Standards and Guidelines* [39].

In addition to, or in lieu of visiting, the child can sort out common feelings and reactions to separation through the use of the Life Story Book [37, 38]. Through the use of pictures, scrap books, family history, mementos, documents, and drawings, children can sort out the confusion about their identities, their families, and their pasts. It can be a therapeutic tool if used by the worker and/or families in a sensitive informed manner. This close look at their families, separations, histories, and feelings will often be painful and anxiety-provoking. They may set up resistances to this intimate process in a variety of ways, from "forgetting" pictures to self-destructive or aggressive behaviours. Consultation needs to be available to workers during this sensitive work and caretakers must be prepared for and supported through an often difficult period.

The Life Story Book and the worker's individual counselling are valuable tools to help the placed child understand and differentiate from dysfunctional family patterns; to connect her or him with strengths and sources of pride; to help her develop a more positive self-concept, and to develop a more realistic accepting view of her parents, self, and environment; to have a better understanding of her past and future; to improve interpersonal relationships and increase her tolerance of separation and change [37, 38].

Whenever there is a likelihood that a child will eventually return to her family, a continuous relationship between foster parents and the parents should be encouraged. The conditions and manner in which this might take place will be discussed later; however, if the child is to have the least disruptive, and most growth-enhancing experience, it is important that her connectedness to the family be fostered. Lack of family participation can have serious repercussions; the more the child is emotionally and physically distanced, the more the family system forms a new homeostatic balance without her presence. When the child returns, she may find that the family has adapted to her absence in a variety of ways which may be experienced as further rejection and isolation. Or, she may be quickly recast in her traditional role of scapegoat, delinquent, and so forth.

Skilled and committed work with foster families, despite resistances and difficulties, will be crucial if the child's needs are to be met and re-placements and further separations minimized.

## E.      Foster Parent Grief

Foster parents are not immune to the range of emotions generated by separation. Furthermore, child care personnel and social workers are vulnerable to separation anxiety when a child leaves their caseloads.

We will focus on the foster family's experience when a child is returned home, or moves on to adoption or to another foster home. Edelstein [41], in looking at how foster families are affected by separation, states that they are expected to invest emotionally and physically in the foster child, nurture her, cope with and help her through behavioural difficulties. Then they are expected to separate gracefully in a way helpful to the child and not disruptive to the parents, adoptive parents, or the placement agency. Little attention is given to the foster parents' or their children's grief over the loss of a foster child.

As for the foster child, there is no set timetable for the duration of grief and no standard approach to helping the bereaved. There are many variables that affect reactions to loss and grief. There are no shortcuts because recovery occurs through the painful process of grief itself. Procedures to speed up, avoid, delay, or dam up grief can then cause future physical, emotional, or mental problems. Only after absorption of the pain can the bereaved begin to let go and reinvest in the present and future.

Time alone does not heal; rather, it is the way in which time is used and the willingness of the worker to be of help which heals.

There are situations which may create a barrier to the healthy expression of grief. These include an ambivalent relationship with the child, rule and reality demands, social expectations, community lack of understanding, and personality facto.

If relationships have been strained, there is relief when the child leaves, or there may be relief in no longer having to contact a difficult parent. This allows a defense against the pain of grief and the foster parents may disparage the value of what was lost. Another defence against facing pain may be the demand for early replacement, thereby aborting the separation process and trying to avoid the pain.

Semas [42] notes that foster parents' grieving may be impeded by the demands of other children (biological and foster), demands of child care and homemaking, and by the foster parent role. She also warns against making important decisions immediately after the separation because of the danger of creating secondary losses at such a vulnerable time.

Working against the healthy expression of grief are a lack of social supports for grieving, the warning that foster parents should not get "too attached", and the feeling that deep sorrow and grief are remote. It is even more difficult if there has been disagreement between foster parents and agency regarding such issues as the foster parents' desire to adopt.

Foster parents who want to avoid feelings of loss and dependency or who inhibit grief because of their need to appear independent and competent, may have a difficult time with grief. Those who find it hard to be vulnerable and dependent, when they are accustomed to being nurturers and strong, will not easily resolve the separation grief.

Colón [7] suggests that persons who experience unresolved emotional cut-offs from significant others are at higher risk psychologically than those who have resolved such separations.

## F.    Helping Foster Parents Grieve

Workers must be willing to listen and not cut off expressions of pain and loss. Grief must be shared with another to be most effectively resolved. Workers must therefore be supportive and understanding to deal with the other's sense of help-lessness, loss of self-esteem, and fears of abandonment. To do this, they need to be caring, warm, respectful, empathic, hopeful, and desirous to understand. They must be strong and not join in the sense of helplessness, yet be able to cope with the other's vulnerability, dependency, and anger. The bereaved needs to hear that tears and confusion are normal and do not indicate weakness.

Noting the growth process the child has gone through may aid foster parents in handling their grief. People tend to see only fixed outcomes, and therefore it is helpful to remind foster parents that the nurturing given to the child will have made a difference and will always be a part of her or him.

Workers' direct and honest communication regarding duration of placement will make it easier for foster parents to accept separation when the time comes. The foster parents' relationship with the child requires that they participate in the deci-sion-making process; without such participation they cannot emotionally accept the decision and help the child to understand and accept it.

The relationship with the worker is important to grieving foster parents. The worker's energies almost always go towards helping the child and her family (or adopted family) adjust to one another. This loss of the relationship with the worker adds further pain for foster parents. It could be helpful in this situation to have follow-up contact and to not leave the foster family when the child leaves.

Social and educational programs can also help. Relationships can be very beneficial during periods of extreme strain. Training is needed to help foster parents understand their own as well as children's reaction to loss. They also need training or permission to say no to new placements when they are not ready for them.

Workers, too, need to be sensitive to the timing of a new placement.

Self-help groups provide the support and empathy needed by grieving foster parents. Those who have been through it can offer ths support.

Legislation designed to implement quick permanent planning and definite time limits for temporary placements must be more conscientiously enforced than it has been to date.

Contact after the child has been moved is a great consolation and reassurance to both the child and foster family. The child is reassured that she or he has not been rejected, that the others still love and care, and that nothing terrible has happened to them. The foster family is reassured that the child is fine and finding her (his) place in the family, beginning to adjust and feel secure, and that the child also remembers and cares. Under these conditions it is much easier for each to let go and to re-invest in new relationships.

## G.    Case Description of Separation and Grieving

One foster mother describes her experience regarding separation when her foster daughter moved on to adoption:

> I had fostered Tracy for two years—from her sixth to eighth birthday.
> When she first came to me the workers had serious concerns about whether
> she had the ability to bond. She had experienced much neglect, had not
> been close to her mother and no relationship had developed between her and
> her previous foster home. Even her relationship with her brother, with
> whom she had previously been placed, had negative overtones.

Tracy needed a great deal of attention and mothering, but over the months it became clear that she could relate deeply with people. Also, through frequent contact with her brother, she developed a warm relationship with him. Because of this, the adoption process was begun with a priority of placement being that she be placed with her brother—something they both wanted. I had considered adopting Tracy; however, I knew that as a single parent, I would not be an appropriate adoptive parent for both children, particularly considering her brother's needs.

Even though the agency undertook the adoption process with much sensitivity and a great deal of understanding about the separation issues, it was still a very difficult and painful experience for both Tracy and myself. When the adoptive family was found and introductions made, Tracy was very positive towards them, while still being able to express her sadness around leaving me.

Probably the most difficult part of the process for myself in terms of the agency was their seeming reluctance to just let me be angry. I seemed to go through a stage, much like what is experienced in handling death, of being angry and needing someone to accept my anger. The only reasonable person to project this onto seemed to me to be my worker; however, I felt that she was uncomfortable with my anger and tried pushing me on to the 'sad stage' before I was ready to let go of my anger. It was probably as disconcerting for her as for me because there was no logical reason for feeling angry. The adoptive home could not have been more appropriate. They were loving, committed people, able to meet both children's needs. The children liked them instinctively and I liked them. There were pre-placement visits even though they were many hundreds of miles away. I participated closely in these visits, even accompanying the children when they visited their new home for the first time. The process was closely geared to the children's and my level of readiness and, despite the distances and cost, plans were arranged for the children to return months later after the placement to spend a weekend with me. The best process for myself and for the children was undertaken. There was no logical reason to be angry. Still I needed to go through that stage. Luckily, I also had the support of another foster mother who had gone through a similar separation.

I often had and still have the feeling that I gave birth to Tracy, even in a biological sense. And now, a year later, despite my knowing that Tracy has adjusted well, that I have gone on to other things in my life and that I can have occasional contact with her, I sometimes experience deep sadness and a strong sense of loss. But there is a basic peacefulness.

What must it be like for those who have not had the sensitive intervention of the agency that Tracy and I have experienced?"

## IV.    FOSTERING ADOLESCENTS

At this point, it may be useful to review Chapter 10, "Adolescent Problems: Dynamics and Practice".

A.      **Introduction**

Foster care is the intervention choice for some adolescents being placed—
adolescents who have no extreme behavioural or emotional difficulties.

Successful foster home placements for teens are possible. Rosenblum [27]
notes that adolescents in foster homes tend to be:

> conventional people
>
> eager to be with and to be accepted by others
>
> mostly positive about foster parents

In most cases, the foster family's own situation has the strongest impact on
the decision to start or to stop fostering. However, for those who have thought about
stopping and those who have stopped, the relationship with their particular foster
child is also cited as crucial (e.g., lack of response to their efforts; the adolescent's
development of symptomatic behaviour). The relationship of the foster parents and
the adolescent is central to many different aspects of foster care. Thus, a strong
mutual liking or a show of motivation from the adolescent can contribute to the
weathering of storms. Also, termination is less likely if problems are handled with the
guidance of a worker.

B.      **Approaches to Practice**

Rosenblum's approach to foster care for adolescents emphasizes the central
nature of the relationship between the teen and foster parent [27]. Because relationships have the following dynamic components [62], these serve as motivators for the
teen-foster parent dyad:

> *Affectional behaviour:* seek to maintain satisfactory relationship with peo-
> ple, to exchange affection and love.
>
> *Control behaviour:* seek to maintain satisfactory relationship in the con-
> text of control and love.
>
> *Inclusion behaviour:* seek to maintain satisfactory relationship so as to
> fulfill the need to be with people.

Crucial to facilitating these behaviours is the problem-solving role of the
worker. This approach can facilitate successful long-term placements.

(For a detailed discussion on a problem-solving approach to child welfare
practice, see Appendix A).

Reistroffer utilizes a problem/solution focus based solely on case vignettes.
Its goals are to facilitate understanding, problem-solving, and overall development for
the teen. Techniques include modelling and discussion. Each vignette illustrates
appropriate handling of issues [25].

Jurick's approach [63] aims to help the adolescent achieve a functioning set of
moral values which are to some degree compatible with society's values. Again, a
developmental perspective is utilized. This involves facilitating the convergence of
cognitive development (abstract thinking) with moral development.

Techniques advocated are derived from a metaphor for the teen's consideration of any moral problem. They include:

> opening the discussion
>
> keeping your cool
>
> seeing the adolescent's world through her or his eyes
>
> accepting the adolescent's point of view
>
> sharing your own views
>
> discussing alternative views
>
> discussing consequences
>
> compromising
>
> dealing with your own feelings
>
> letting the adolescent decide

The use of alcohol and other drugs is something to which most teens are exposed. Each teen needs to decide whether to partake and to what extent. Foster teens may be particularly vulnerable to easing their pain through such means.

Group work with adolescents in foster care is an adjunct service for specific common problems, such as depression. For the alleviation of depressive reaction, Lee and Park advocate the following process [64]:

> relating to depressive feelings
>
> dealing with anger and feelings of worthlessness
>
> encouraging coping
>
> promoting a climate conducive to mutual aid

The underlying process is as follows:

> As depression is dealt with, coping abilities are freed.
>
> As coping is more effective, depression is further dispelled.

## V.  INTERACTION BETWEEN FAMILIES

### A.  Introduction

Separation of children from their families or from significant relationships is a crucial issue in foster care. When children are placed in foster care or returned to their family, they are unavoidably wrenched from a relationship.

No matter how benign the family that the child moves to, both the child and the previous family react to and profoundly experience the rupture of their mutual family ties. After children are placed in foster care their ties to family are often fragmented, ruptured, or even severed.

Colón [7] notes that the psychological response by persons who have experienced permanent severing of family ties is very similar to the mourning reactions of people whose loved ones have died. Empirical evidence for this hypothesis is not yet well documented, but there is some support in the work of Weiss [35], Wallerstein and Kelly [34], Hetherington et al. [16] on divorce, and the adoption work of Trisiliotis [33].

During the past ten years there has been increased attention given to the relation between family ties and the placement of children. Kadushin [19] has summarized the extensive literature on the topic. However, this issue has not been systematically addressed across child welfare areas such as foster care and adoptive care.

The interconnectedness among the nuclear and extended family systems has been well described by Bowen [3, 4]. It is increasingly clear that when children are separated from their family system there is a deep sense of personal loss for all involved. Weiss [35] and Roman [26] relate this to children and parents in divorce situations; McAdams [21] considers the experience of children and parents when foster care placement is instituted, while Benet [2] and Trisiliotis [33] examine this loss as it applies to the adoptive placement experience.

Reasons why contact with families has not been foremost in child placement practices have been outlined by Steinhauer [32], Palmer [23], and Colón [7]. These include: (1) an incomplete understanding of the mourning process and its manifestations in children of different ages; (2) a failure to recognize symptoms of aborted or pathological mourning, partly because of the masking effect of the child's defences; (3) the worker's inability to tolerate feelings stirred up in the worker by the child's pain—resulting in selective inattention, if not an active discouragement, of the child's using the worker to work through the mourning process; and (4) societal forces that operate towards the loosening and breaking down of family ties.

Laird [20] states: "While children are in substitute care, whether temporary or permanent, the issues of biological family identity and maintenance of family ties can be crucial to the emotional growth of the child. However, we are usually more protective of the foster parents' feelings and privacy than of their natural parents' rights, feelings and concerns about their children, or of the child's right to family contacts and her need to 'belong' ".

## B.    Effects of Interaction

In the past it was assumed that children's continued contact with their family would interfere with their adjustment to the new foster home and thereby cause loyalty conflicts. But if children can maintain ties with both family systems, then their loyalty can be encouraged in both directions, thus reducing scapegoating and manipulating. It has been found that the well-being of the child is influenced by parental visits and visits are the best variable as a predictor of discharge from care [12].

The practice of involving the family with their children in care could have far-reaching positive effects if carried out consistently and sensitively. It could help foster families view the child's family (and vice versa) realistically, without distorted fantasies. It would provide children with more stability, continuity, predictability, and a subsequent sense of security. It would enable them to develop strong realistic ties to both sets of parents and to resolve loyalty conflicts. The reality of the family situation would be more readily assimilated and realistically appraised by children so that their guilt could be worked out more easily. Ideally, children would return to their family and because of continued contact between both families the return would be considerably less problematic.

## C.     Traditional Foster Care Roles

Based on traditional practice, foster parents have been limited almost exclusively to child care and have been relatively uninvolved in other aspects of the foster care service system. Interaction between foster parents and parents tends to be restricted or allowed only under certain structured conditions. This is influenced by the traditional role of the worker, which is to protect the foster family; such interaction has much potential for conflict. Since the primary focus has been on serving children and rescuing them from damaging influences, there has been a tendency for foster parents to react with hostility to persons who had previously neglected or mistreated the child. The parents, in turn, react with a sense of guilt which is projected onto foster parents as defensiveness, rejection, hostility, or suspiciousness (particularly since foster parents symbolize success in the parenting areas in which they have been found wanting). Agencies have tended to restrict visitation or to carefully control and limit it, thereby protecting the foster family from potential upset and protecting the child from loyalty conflicts and from possible emotional upset. In this instance, avoidance is utilized to master the separation and conflict. Unfortunately this practice decreases the opportunity for effecting a reunion of the foster child and parents [12].

## D.     The Developing Role of Fostering

Historically there has been debate regarding the conceptualization of the foster parent role. Research dealing with workers' perceptions of the foster parent's role indicates that they and foster parents view their respective roles quite differently. Therefore, workers and foster parents should together receive a basic orientation about their respective roles and responsibilities so that their philosophical orientation will be more congruent.

There have been two approaches to the conceptualization of roles. The more traditional approach views foster parents as working under the direction of agency workers while doing the day-to-day child management. Workers are seen as the major decision-makers with regard to the foster child and the ones who work directly with the child to resolve problems. Workers tend to move with the child because it is presumed that bonding and identification are with workers. This view promotes the treatment of foster parents as clients. However, Rosenblum's [27] research shows that this approach is generally disliked by foster parents.

The other approach views foster parents as the primary helpers who represent more stability and continuity to the child. The workers' role is one of consultation and support. They generally work with the foster family and foster child as a group. This approach is one of collegiality.

Whichever approach is used, there is one common element based on traditional practice. Foster parents are limited almost exclusively to the role of caring for the child on a daily basis and are relatively uninvolved or restricted in other aspects of the foster care system.

According to Seaberg [30] and Davies and Bland [11] the foster parent role is undergoing a state of transition. The role is now recognized to have the following characteristics:

> It is a unique child rearing role.
>
> It requires normal parenting skills.
>
> It requires skills related to the complexity of the foster care system.

This conceptualization has implications for all aspects of the foster care system.

The Halton Region Children's Aid Society (Ontario), as part of the Rosenblum project, assumed a process of collegiality with foster parents. In the Halton Model foster parents were given responsibility for having the primary relationship with the child and social workers were assigned to foster homes, and therefore did not move with the child. Foster parents were given responsibility according to how adequately they were prepared for involvement. One result of this approach was that children were re-placed less often than in other societies in Ontario.

Several factors have contributed to the changes now occurring in the foster parenting role:

> major problems with the foster care system as it has historically been conceptualized and implemented [61]
>
> new emphasis on work with parents and families as one aspect of permanency planning [17, 18, 24]
>
> concern over the current drift of foster children into long-term care
>
> the growing influence of foster parent associations, which stress recognition of foster parents' contributions and their capacity for a wider role
>
> interest within the human services regarding the development of roles for paraprofessionals and lay counsellors [14, 15, 29]
>
> growing concern over abused and neglected children and the need for their parents to learn more adequate parenting skills

## E.    Alternate Roles

Seaberg [30] proposes that foster parents should be asked to act as parent aides and models for selected parents in order to help them make the adjustments that would allow reunion with their children. He proposes that this could be effected by:

1. selecting foster parents capable of the new role
2. providing training programs for foster parents
3. selecting parents who could benefit from this type of service
4. implementing and supervising the program
5. evaluating the program

The influence of parent aides in almost all reported experiences is based on the strength of the relationship between parents and foster parents. This relationship is facilitated by an open, accepting attitude on the foster parents' part, their availability in times of crisis, and the careful selection of parents who might be responsive to having a parent aide.

Foster parents are in an excellent position to work with parents since they have first-hand knowledge of the child's needs and have experiences in dealing with the child. Ryan [28] suggests that foster families might further extend their role and provide valuable service by seeking out occasions during which to emphasize to the child's family *their* importance to the child, and to encourage the family's involvement by inviting them to birthday and holiday celebrations, by seeking their opinion on clothing purchases, and requesting their presence at school conferences. Foster parents can work with members of the professional team to assess specific needs of the family, they can be a source of emotional support for the family, be a source of parenting expertise, and provide knowledge of community resources.

In the literature there is a divergence of opinion as to which parents would benefit from having foster parents as aides or role models. Seaberg [30] rules out parents who display extreme individual psychopathology, marital problems, and alcohol or drug addiction. Others, however, would involve parents with multi-problem families including those classified as character-disordered, borderline, or schizophrenic [11].

In the work of Simmons et al. [31], parents with severe problems were included; however, they used child care workers in a group-home setting. Some aspects of this project may be transferable to the foster home situation. Parents were encouraged to share in the responsibility for their children's care and to contact and visit their children at their convenience. They were included in the intake and placement processes, medicals, decisions on the purchase of toys and clothing, and both parents and children took part in group and individual treatment methods.

When foster parents act as parent aides, or role models, they:

> are part of a professional team
>
> maintain logs and records
>
> attend regular conferences
>
> partake in training opportunities
>
> assist parents (are not substitutes for parents)
>
> complement parents (do not compete with parents)
>
> communicate with parents, relay parenting skill information, and demonstrate parenting skills

## F.   Developmental Stages in Role Modelling

Davies and Bland [11] outline the stages that usually occur as foster parents role model for parents and as their relationship develops. It is important to be aware of these stages so that all participants can anticipate and understand normal reactions.

> Stage I   Parents teach foster parents about their child.
>
> Initially, parents usually feel threatened by the foster parents' ability to

parent and therefore often attack them, trying to find fault. Foster parents naturally react with anger and/or hurt feelings. At this point workers should help the families share their feelings with each other. Parents are encouraged to take the role of teacher in helping foster parents understand their child and her or his daily routines and experiences. Foster parents are trained to ask about the child's likes, dislikes, and so forth, and thereby model listening and acceptance.

Stage II     Workers facilitate a shift in roles whereby foster parents take over the role of teacher.

Workers use individual therapy with parents to help them understand their feelings (e.g., anger), and foster parents role model and teach child management skills.

Stage III     Workers become less actively involved, thus allowing the rapport that has developed between parents and foster parents to grow.

This stage usually begins 2 to 3 months into placement when workers, as facilitators, encourage foster parents to become primary role models. Workers continue weekly therapy with parents. Meetings occur at the foster home without workers, but they retain responsibility for control should problems occur.

Stage IV     Workers help foster parents and parents to separate.

During the last few months of the year of placement, workers meet more frequently with foster parents and parents. Parents often test limits by trying to effect early termination or prolong the termination. Workers prepare parents for the child's testing and prepare foster parents for the parents' and the child's testing. Foster parents are to model separation without rejection. Workers help all involved deal with their feelings about separation.

The previous approach may work most successfully under the following practice conditions:

Family would comprise carefully chosen parents whose primary problem is lack of parenting skills and knowledge, and who would be interested in learning from a foster parent.

A written contract would be drawn up among the foster parents, parents, and agency caseworker as a way of committing everyone involved to plan for placement, treatment, and the return home of the child. This contract would specify:

    1. agreement on establishing a permanent plan within a specified time

    2. clearly defined responsibilities and roles of all involved

    3. explicit child management skills needed

    4. time-limits and frequency of visits

    5. parents' and child's regular therapy appointments

    6. parents' and foster parents' regular meetings with worker

The caseworker would continue as case manager, with emphasis on permanency planning, negotiating the service contract, and monitoring the contract. The worker must have an open and positive attitude towards the use of foster parents as parent aides.

The agency must provide ongoing training and consultation for foster parents, particularly if the mode of teaching parents involves modelling and behavioural rehearsal techniques (as opposed to an intuitive approach). Consultants might be psychiatrists, psychologists, and/or a foster care support group.

Selection of foster parents as parent aides should be based on their [6]:

> personal qualifications rather than their education or work experience
>
> having a sense of personal worth
>
> feeling comfortably successful as foster parents
>
> having adequate support systems
>
> positive attitudes towards parents
>
> empathic qualities
>
> appropriate perspective about whose child the foster child is
>
> understanding of child development needs
>
> understanding of the foster child's specific needs

## VI.  SUMMARY

This chapter has touched on the more sensitive issues associated with post-placement services for foster parents and children. Perhaps most noteworthy is the transformation of foster parent roles and the concomitant changes in modes of relating between the child's family and her or his foster family. Such changes in parental power positions and task definitions will inevitably lead to new ways of experiencing foster care by children who are separated from their family for established periods of time. For foster care workers, too, new challenges will be at hand.

### REFERENCES

1. Aldridge, M. and Cautley, P. "The Importance of Worker Availability in the Functioning of New Foster Homes", Child Welfare, Vol LIV, June 1975, pp. 444–453.

2. Benet, M. K. *The Politics of Adoption.* New York: The Free Press, 1976.

3. Bowen, M. "Toward the Differentiation of Self in One's Family of Origin," in Andres, F. D. and Lorio, J. (eds.), Georgetown Family Symposia: A Collection of Special Papers, Vol. 1. Family Section, Department of Psychiatry, Georgetown University Medical Center, Washington D.C., 1971–1972, 1974.

4. _____. "The Use of Family Theory in Clinical Practice", Comprehensive Psychiatry, 1966.

5. Cautley, P. and Aldridge M. "Predicting Success for New Foster Parents", Social Work, Vol. 20, January 1975, pp. 48–53.

6. Carrol, Nancy A. and Reich, John W. "Issues in the Implementation of the Parent Aide Concept", Social Casework, Vol. 59, March 1978, pp. 152–160.

7. Colón, F., "Family Ties and Child Placement", Family Process, Vol. 17, September 1978, pp. 289–312.

8. Province of Ontario Ministry of Community and Social Services. Foster Care: A Discussion Paper, Sept. 1979.

9. Davids, Leo. "The Foster Father Role." Dissertation. New York University, 1968.

10. _____. "Foster Fatherhood: The Untapped Resource", Child Welfare, Vol. LII, February 1973, pp. 100–108.

11. Davies, L. and Bland, D. "The Use of Foster Parents as Role Models for Parents", Child Welfare, Vol. LVII, June 1978, pp. 380–386.

12. Fanshel, D. and Shinn, E. "Overview and Prospects", Children in Foster Care: A Longitudinal Investigation. New York: Columbia University Press, 1978.

13. _____. Foster Parenthood: A Role Analysis. Minneapolis: University of Minnesota Press, 1966.

14. Gartner, A. Paraprofessionals and Their Performance. New York: Praeger, 1971.

15. Grosser, C., Henry, W., and Kelly, J. (eds.) Non-Professionals in the Human Services. San Francisco: Jossey-Bass, 1969.

16. Hetherington, E. M., Cox, M., and Cox, R. "Divorced Fathers", The Family Coordinator, 25 October 1976, pp. 417–428.

17. Jones, M. "Reducing Foster Care through Services to Families", Children Today, Vol. 5, November–December 1976, pp. 6–10.

18. _____, Neuman, R. and Shyne, A. "A Second Chance for Families: Evaluation of a Program to Reduce Foster Care", New York: Child Welfare League of America, 1976.

19. Kadushin, A. Child Welfare Services (2nd. ed.). New York: MacMillan Publishing Co., Inc., 1974.

20. Laird, J. "An Ecological Approach to Child Welfare: Issues of Family Identity and Continuity", in Germain, C. (ed.) Social Work Practice: People and Environment. New York: Columbia University Press, 1979, pp. 174–209.

21. McAdams, P. J. "The Parent in the Shadows", Child Welfare, Vol. LI, January 1972, pp. 51–55.

22. McKuen, R. Finding My Father: One Man's Search for Identity. New York: Coward Publishing, 1976.

23. Palmer, S. "Children in Long-Term Care—The Worker's Contribution", Ontario Association of Children's Aid Societies Journal, Vol. 17, April 1974, pp. 1–14.

24. Pike, V. et al. Permanent Planning for Children in Foster Care: A Handbook for Social Workers. Washington, D.C.: Children's Bureau, DHEW, 1977, pp. 35–62.

25. Reistroffer, M. "Participation of Foster Parents in Decision Making: The Concept of Collegiality", Child Welfare, Vol. LI, Jan. 1972, pp. 25–29.

26. Roman, M. "The Disposable Parent", paper read at the Association of Family Conciliation Courts, Minneapolis, Minnesota, May 11–14, 1977.

27. Rosenblum, B. "Foster Homes and Adolescents: A Research Report", Hamilton & Wentworth CAS, 1977.

28. Ryan, P., McFadden, E. J., and Warren, B. "Foster Families: A Resource for Helping Parents", in Maluccio, A. and Sinanoglu, P. (eds.), The Challenge of Partnership: Working With Parents of Children in Foster Care. New York: Child Welfare League of America, 1981, pp. 189–199.

29. Seaberg, J. R. "Lay Counselling: The Basis of Prevention in Mental Health", Journal of Sociology and Social Welfare, Vol. 6, No. 4, June 1979.

30. _____. "Foster Parents as Aides to Parents" in Maluccio, A. and Sinanoglu, P. (eds.) The Challenge of Partnership: Working With Parents of Children in Foster Care. New York: Child Welfare League of America, 1981, pp. 209–220.

31. Simmons, G., Gumpert, F., and Rothman, B. "Natural Parents as Partner in Child Care Placement", Social Casework, Vol. 54, April 1973, pp. 224–232.

32. Steinhauer, P. "How to Succeed in the Business of Creating Psychopaths without Even Trying," Paper delivered to the Ontario Association of Children's Aid Societies, Toronto, April, 1974.

33. Trisiliotis, J. *In Search of Origins—The Experiences of Adopted People*. London and Boston: Routledge and Kegan Paul, 1973.

34. Wallerstein, J. and Kelly J. "The Effects of Parental Divorce: Experiences of the Pre-School Child", Journal of American Academy of Child Psychiatry, Vol. 14, 1975, pp. 600–616.

35. Weiss, R. *Marital Separation*. New York: Basic Books, 1975.

36. Adler, J. "Separation: A Crucial Issue in Foster Care," Paper based on study in preparation. N.Y. State Welfare Conference, 1968.

37. Aust, P. "Using the Life Story Book in Treatment of Children in Placement", Child Welfare, Vol. LX, No. 8, September/October 1981, pp. 535–560.

38. Beste, H. and Richardson, R. "Developing a Life Story Book Program for Foster Children," Child Welfare, Vol. LX, No. 8, September/October 1981, pp. 529–534.

39. Ontario Ministry of Community and Social Services. "Foster Care: Proposed Standard and Guidelines for Agencies Placing Children", October 1981.

40. Cull, W. "Working with the Family", Ministry of Community and Social Services Training Program, Vol. 6, 1982.

41. Edelstein, S. "When Foster Children Leave: Helping Foster Parents to Grieve". Child Welfare, Vol. LX, No. 7, July–August 1981, pp. 467–474.

42. Semas, B. G. *A Time to Grieve: Loss as an Unusual Experience*. New York: Family Service Association of America, 1979.

43. Hancock, M. R. "While I Cry: Some Thoughts on Handling Grief," Ontario Association of Children's Aid Societies Journal, Vol. 11, April 1968, pp. 1–4.

44. Spitz, R. A. and Wolf, K. "Anaclitic Depression", Psychoanalytic Study of the Child, 1949.

45. Yarrow L. "Separation from Parents During Childhood", in Hoffman, M. L. and Hoffman, L. W. (Eds.), *Review of Child Development Research*, Vol. I, New York: Russell Sage, 1964.

46. Barker, P., Buffe, C., and Zaretsky, R. "Providing a Family Alternative for the Disturbed Child", Child Welfare, Vol. LVII, No. 6, June 1978.

47. Bauer, J. and Heinke, W. "Treatment Family Care Homes for Disturbed Children (Wisconsin, Fond du Lac)", Child Welfare, Vol. LV, July/August 1976, and *Treatment Home Program Manual*, Green Bay, Wis.: 1972.

48. Johnston, E. and Gabor, P. "Parent Counselors: A Foster Care Program with New Roles for Major Participants", in Maluccio, A. and Sinanoglu, P. (eds.), *The Challenge of Partnership: Working with Parents of Children in Foster Care*. New York: Child Welfare League of America, 1981, pp. 200–208.

49. Larson, G., Allison, J., and Johnston, E. "Alberta Parent Counsellors: A Community Treatment Program for Disturbed Youths", Child Welfare, Vol. LVII, January 1978, pp. 47–52.

50. Levin, S., Rubenstein, J., and Streiner, D. "The Parent Therapist Program: An Innovative Approach to Treating Emotionally Disturbed Children", Hospital and Community Psychiatry, Vol. 27 No. 6, June 1976.

51. Loewe, B., and Hanrahan, T. E. "Five Day Foster Care", Child Welfare, Vol. LIV, January 1975, pp. 7–18.

52. Martin, H. P. and Beezley, P. "Foster Placement: Therapy or Trauma", in Martin, H. P. (ed.) *The Abused Child: A Multidisciplinary Approach to Developmental Issues and Treatment*. Cambridge, Mass.: Ballinger Publishing Co., 1976, pp. 189–199.

53. Nayman, Louis and Witkin, Stanley. "Parent/Child Foster Placement: An Alternative Approach in Child Abuse and Neglect", Child Welfare, Vol. LVII, April 1978, pp. 249–258.

54. Williams, J. M., "Children Who Break Down in Foster Homes: A Psychological Study of Patterns of Personality Growth in Grossly Deprived Children", Journal of Child Psychiatry, 1961.

55. Silin, M. W. "Why Many Placed Children Have Learning Difficulties", Child Welfare, Vol. LVII, No. 4, April 1978.

56. Winter, A., "Only People Cry", Women's Day Magazine, n.d.

57. Lahti, J. and Dvorak, J. "Coming Home from Foster Care", in Maluccio, A. and Sinanoglu, P. (eds.), *The Challenge of Partnership Working with Parents of Children in Foster Care*, New York: Child Welfare League of America, 1981.

58. Stein, T., Gambrill, E. D., and Wiltse, K. T. "Dividing Case Management in Foster Family Cases", Child Welfare, Vol. LVI, May 1977, pp. 321–331.

59. Orlin, M. "Conflict Resolution in Foster Family Care", Child Welfare, Vol. LVI, January 1977, pp. 769–775.

60. Wilkes, J. "The Stresses of Fostering, Part I: On the Fostering Parents; Part II: On the Fostering Children", Ontario Association of Children's Aid Societies Journal, Vol. 22, Nos. 9 and 10, November and December 1979, pp. 1–5, 8; pp. 7–12.

61. Stone, Helen, D. (ed.), *Foster Care in Question: A National Reassessment by Twenty-one Experts.* New York: Child Welfare League of America, 1970.

62. Schutz, W. C., *FIRO: A Three-Dimensional Theory of Interpersonal Behavior.* New York: Holt, Rinehart and Winston, 1958.

63. Jurick, A., "Coping with Moral Problems of Adolescence in Foster Care," Child Welfare, Vol. LVIII, March 1979, pp. 187–195.

64. Lee, J. and Park, N. "A Group Approach to the Depressed Adolescent Girl in Foster Care," American Journal of Orthopsychiatry, Vol. 48, July 1978, pp. 516–527.

# 9
# Residential Child Care

JOSEPH PIPITONE, FRANK MAIDMAN

| | | |
|---|---|---|
| I. | INTRODUCTION | 264 |
| | A. Impediments to the Use of Milieu Therapy | 264 |
| | B. Practice Challenges for Residential Treatment Centres | 265 |
| | C. Goals of Residential Care | 265 |
| II. | RESIDENTIAL CARE AS AN OPTION | 265 |
| | A. Pros and Cons | 265 |
| | B. Who Gets Treated | 266 |
| III. | ASSESSING COMPETENCE IN RESIDENTIAL SETTINGS | 266 |
| | A. Intrapersonal Competence | 267 |
| | B. Interpersonal Competence | 268 |
| | C. Environmental Competence | 269 |
| IV. | TREATMENT OPTIONS IN RESIDENTIAL SETTINGS | 270 |
| V. | RESIDENCE AS A CONTROLLED ENVIRONMENT | 272 |
| | A. Physical Environment | 272 |
| | B. Routines | 273 |
| | C. Rules | 273 |
| | D. Limits | 275 |
| VI. | DEVELOPING POSITIVE RELATIONSHIPS | 276 |
| | A. Advantages of Positive Relationships | 276 |
| | B. Meeting Residents' Needs | 277 |
| | C. Stages of Relationship Building | 277 |
| VII. | THERAPEUTIC USE OF PHYSICAL RESTRAINT | 278 |
| VIII. | RESIDENTIAL GROUP WORK | 280 |
| | A. Purpose of Groups | 280 |
| | B. Types of Residential Groups | 280 |
| | C. Departures from Traditional Group Therapy | 281 |
| | D. Producing Changes | 282 |
| | E. Areas Appropriate for Group Teaching | 282 |
| IX. | OCCUPATIONAL HAZARDS IN RESIDENTIAL WORK | 283 |
| | A. Sources of Stress | 283 |
| | B. Effects on Workers' Performance | 284 |
| | C. Minimizing Occupational Hazards | 285 |
| X. | SUMMARY | 286 |
| | REFERENCES | 286 |

## I.     INTRODUCTION

Much of current residential child care work is rooted in concepts and principles of milieu therapy, a therapy which manipulates the environment with the goal of
creating behavioural changes in the client. The "total milieu" (i.e., environment,
surroundings) concept was first applied to work with children, and its emergence was
based on several factors. For example, there was an awareness that children are
vulnerable to parental influence and pathology and, in cases of abuse or neglect, need
relief and protection. Children as developing organisms can learn to adapt to changes
in the environment and benefit from interventions so as to achieve appropriate levels
of development. Furthermore, a prevailing social orientation which provides special
services for children with mental or physical handicaps, similarly endorses removing
children with emotional problems from their parents and placing them in special
public facilities for remediation. Coupled with this is an awareness that the traditional
therapy hour is inadequate in meeting all the emotional needs necessary to effect
desired changes. Finally, there is a conviction that a total milieu concept is appropriate for severely disturbed children, because it provides a specially controlled setting
outside of the child's home.

## A.     Impediments to the Use of Milieu Therapy

Although these factors remain prevalent as reasons to support the residential
treatment concept, and although milieu therapy concepts have survived and are used
in most residential care facilities, the total milieu approach has not become widespread. It is rare to find "pure" milieu therapy being practised today, due in part to
the following factors:

*Economic:* Enormous expenditures of time and money are required to
create significant behavioural changes.

*Social:* There is an increasing trend to maintain individuals in society
rather than to isolate them from it.

*Mental Health:* Scientific advances that have led to better diagnosis,
clarification, and treatment methods, permit outpatient (home-management,
re-education, medication, and other forms of treatment) rather than long-
term residential treatment.

*Familial:* There is recognition that long-term milieu therapy has disruptive effects on the child's and family's natural development.

*Research:* There is lack of sufficient evidence to support the claims of the
total milieu concept when compared to less expansive and disruptive approaches.

*Organizational:* Enormous implementation difficulties are evident when
lines of communication, authority, worker resources, and so forth, are organized in an attempt to form a uniform treatment strategy as part of the
therapeutic milieu.

Despite these impediments to widespread implementation of milieu therapy, its fundamental concepts serve as a guide for workers in conceptualizing, organizing, and implementing other treatment approaches used in residence.

## B.    Practice Challenges for Residential Treatment Centres

Workers in residential treatment centres have in common many issues and challenges with persons implementing milieu therapy. Both accept an integrated team approach which necessitates a unity of purpose and a clarity in goals, roles, patterns of authority, and operationalized theories of child dynamics, development, family and group processes.

Other challenges include learning how to best prepare the child and family for coming into care, how to provide treatment in a group setting which speaks to individual, family, and group needs, and how to utilize and coordinate potentially supportive services (e.g., family, school, community) to the child's best advantage.

Finally, there are continued efforts to create aftercare support services designed to minimize relapses and to assist the child in reintegrating into the family and community.

## C.    Goals of Residential Care

Goals of residential treatment are fairly straightforward; they include the encouraging of both behavioural and attitudinal changes in the context of a supportive environment. More specifically, residents are encouraged to learn and to display age-appropriate behaviours, cognitive and interpersonal skills for functioning in society, and appropriate interactions with workers and co-residents.

Further goals include the development of independence, individuality, increased self-esteem, a sense of security, and a more sensitive moral/ethical value system.

## II.    RESIDENTIAL CARE AS AN OPTION

## A.    Pros and Cons

Uprooting children and adolescents from their family and community ties is a serious step that requires careful consideration by those involved in the decision-making process. Recommendations to place a child in residential treatment are usually predicated on the need to protect the child's development, to provide protection and relief from severe or potentially damaging experiences, and to thereby prevent future disabilities (physical and emotional) which are likely to result from abuse or neglect.

Unfortunately, there are critical disadvantages and complications which can result from coming into care. These include:

the impact on the family system resulting from such a separation (e.g., parental denial and guilt; confused and distorted perceptions of other siblings; scapegoating)

the disruption of community relationships, (e.g., removal from the educational system, friends, neighbours, clubs)

the stigma of being placed in a residential setting with strangers and other youngsters with problems

the possibility of attachment and dependency in the situation

the possibility of generalizing and learning other inappropriate behaviours from more disturbed residents

the problem of re-integrating into society, which is likely to be less tolerant and responsive to individual needs and emotions

the potential inability to "fit" back into the original family structure

Each of these factors must be carefully weighed before taking the decision to place a child in a residential treatment centre.

## B.    Who Gets Treated

The decision to place a child in residential treatment is based in part on very pragmatic factors such as the availability of physical resources (space, appropriate location of residence, funding) and human resources (workers, support services). In addition, the number, sex, age range, and problems of existing residents affect the placement decision. Also, the types of therapeutic modalities available in residence are examined with an eye to their appropriateness for a particular client under consideration.

Some institutions, such as receiving and assessment centres, may not be able to select on the basis of philosophy or age, sex, and so on; because of their mandate they must adapt to client needs as best they can. In fact, current trends in treatment centres are towards adapting to client needs rather than selecting clients on the basis of ability, or appropriateness to the centres' structure and philosophy. This has led to increased utilization of the multimodal approach to treatment, which encourages experimentation, innovation, combinations of treatment philosophies and techniques, and more individualized programming. These and other factors such as the children's rights movement, changing social attitudes, funding, and government regulations have had a major impact on milieu management and specific treatment methods. It is critical that workers become aware of and learn to deal with internal and external shifts in philosophy, pressures, demands, and expectations in the delivery of services.

## III.    ASSESSING COMPETENCE IN RESIDENTIAL SETTINGS

In this section indicators and guidelines are presented for assessing competence problems in troubled children and for selecting appropriate treatment methods.

These ideas draw heavily from recent writings on therapeutic milieux by Whittaker and his colleagues [27, 30]. The ideas are based on the assumption that many children coming into residential care lack "competence" on one or more of the following levels of functioning: intrapersonal, interpersonal, and environmental. The following abbreviated description of these problems, and sub-types, may be used as a basis for an assessment instrument.

## A.    Intrapersonal Competence

Intrapersonal competence refers to the ability to deal appropriately with the "inner environment" of impulses and emotions. The assumption is that competence rests on appropriately identifying feelings, and linking them with thoughts and behaviour. Difficulties on this level are as follows:

*1.    Poorly developed impulse control*

low frustration tolerance and limited ability to postpone gratification

disruptive outbursts at home and school

frustration, strain, or anxiety dealt with by lashing out at other persons, objects, or self

inability to screen out peripheral stimuli; easily affected by the misbehaviour of other children; especially prone to group excitement

*2.    Low self-image*

child sees/describes self in such terms as "bad", "evil", "stupid", "troublemaker"

conveys a fatalistic view of potential for change

low self-esteem may be reflected in dress, gait, posture, and demeanor, sometimes masked with bravado or indifference

drawings or written narratives may reflect inner emptiness

*3.    Poorly developed modulation of emotion*

lacks skills in dealing effectively with anger, fear, elation, and sadness (e.g., anger expressed with extreme force)

shows difficulty in sorting out mixed emotions (e.g., mingling of anger and sadness)

emotional flatness

sometimes follows angry outburst with a quick return to previous emotional state, or mild depression

**B.        Interpersonal Competence**

Interpersonal competence summarizes those skills necessary for adaptive and rewarding involvement with others. Such competence may involve sharing positive feelings about others, enlisting cooperation in work or play, handling unpleasant behaviour directed towards oneself, avoiding undeserved blame, and so on. Children with problems in their interpersonal relations show one or more of the following characteristics:

1. *avoidance of eye contact*

2. *stereotypical reaction to male and female authority figures:* Male staff is seen as physically threatening, for example.

3. *few friends*

4. *manipulation:*
Plays one individual off against another.
Uses provocative information to "set up" others.
Provides "right answers" in therapy (adolescents).

5. *intimidation:* Uses physical size or force to dominate others and establish control over possessions, physical space, and privileges.

6. *bizarre behaviour:*
Uses physical and mental abnormality to frighten and repulse others.
Uses psychotic symptoms to keep peers at distance.

7. *overdependence:*
Makes excessive demands on the time and emotional resources of staff.
Constantly seeks approval and nurturance.
Checks every decision with adult.
Associates with other children only when adults are present.
Fears being alone with other children.
Constantly informs adults about what other children are doing.

8. *isolation:*
Has superficial peer relations.
Spends considerable time in private activity: daydreaming, reading.
Adult relationships are pleasant, but superficial.
Stays out of limelight and out of trouble.

9. *scapegoat:*
Is unable to deal with aggression.
Often puts self in injurious situations.
Denies seeking of persecution.
Insists situation is out of control and hopeless.
Scapegoating may be evoked by confused sexual identity, need for inclusion, being easily provoked, or having cultural or physical differences.

10. *lack of social skills:*
Has difficulty making small talk.
Has inability to join a game in progress.
Is unable to say 'I like you'.

When describing a child's interpersonal style, it is important to separate characteristics brought to the setting or displayed across all situations from behavior which is a response to the social milieu of the residence. To accomplish this, it is useful to observe or otherwise gather information on the child in different types of physical settings and social relationships (e.g., different size groups, different activities, different norms and requirements of individuals). For further verification, it may help to draw upon the experiences of those who know the child in different environments (e.g., teachers, parents, family doctor).

Observing the child in his or her family situation will provide insight into the interdependence between the child's behavior, family dynamics, and family problems. For example, the child's behavior may be a survival tactic in an unfortunate family situation, one which is learned and used in relationships with people outside of the family. The withdrawing child from a physically abusive family is a case in point. On the other hand, family patterns may have evolved in response to the child's behaviour, which may have a neurobiological base. Whatever their role in the child's behaviour, parents should not be quickly ruled out as sources of information about, or help for, the child in residence [30]. For other family and child assessment frameworks, see Appendix B. Also, the family factors affecting child neglect and abuse are reviewed in Chapters 4, 5 and 6. Adolescent problems and family life are reviewed in Chapter 10.

## C.    Environmental Competence

Whittaker's third category, environmental competence, refers to those capacities which may be primarily affected by the child's physical and physiological make-up (e.g., physical competence, academic competence). Difficulties in these areas are indicated by:

> 1. *limited play skills, as reflected in:*
> involvement in a narrow range of activities
> inability to follow rules in group play, enter a game in progress, or make use of private time
> avoidance of novel play situations
>
> 2. *learning problems:*
> hyperactivity
> rapid emotional changes
> impulsivity
> distractibility
> perseveration: extreme continuation of something (e.g., talk, activity)
> perceptual difficulties

It is important to note that the foregoing *may* indicate a learning problem requiring psychological, psychiatric, or medical consultation.

## IV.    TREATMENT OPTIONS IN RESIDENTIAL SETTINGS

Residential settings have the potential for offering troubled children broad-based programs for total growth. Selecting a particular program or therapeutic resource should follow the general principles for selecting any appropriate service. For a checklist of decision-making criteria, which can be adapted for the residential setting, see Appendix A, III.

Quite specific treatment options for use in residential settings can be considered, particularly if the setting is organized according to the therapeutic milieu philosophy. Whittaker's list of "teaching formats" [30], which follows, is accompanied by cross-references to other sections in this book, as well as additional readings:

1. *Rules:* "The formal and informal 'do's and don'ts' of the helping culture which tend to define what is important and what is not" [30]. See V, C of this chapter for an introduction to the therapeutic importance of rules.

2. *Routines:* Waking up; mealtimes; going to bed—all the basic activities in which all children participate (see V, B).

3. *Program Activities:* Arts, crafts, games, sports and the whole array of informal individual and group activities. See Whittaker [30] and VI.

4. *Group Sessions:* Cottage group meetings; group therapy; special interest groups. General guidelines for designing educational groups are provided in Chapter 4 of this book; see also VIII of this chapter.

5. *Individual Psychotherapy:* An important adjunctive therapy for children who can develop and act on the basis of insight. For readings on the use of individual treatment in residential settings, see Whittaker [27, 30].

6. *Life-Space Interviews:* A type of interview designed for use by child care workers to help a child deal with particular upsets or chronic patterns of behaviour. For readings on this technique, see Whittaker [27] and Long and associates [31].

7. *Incentive System:* "The contingent use of generalized reinforcers (tokens) throughout a total system—cottage, ward or classroom—for the purpose of teaching alternative prosocial behavior" [30].

8. *Special Education:* On-campus or community school program.

9. *Conjoint Family Treatment:* Intervention with the whole family as the unit of intervention. For a general outline of the family perspective, practice principles, and suggested readings, see Chapter 2, IV of this book. Selected readings on working with families in residential settings are available in Whittaker and Trieshman [27].

10. *Parent Education Groups:* Teaching groups on effective parenting. An introduction to designing parent education groups is provided in Chapter 4, Part 2, "Practice Guidelines", IV. Groups for high-risk parents are discussed in Chapter 4, Part 2, "Practice Guidelines", VI.

11. *Parent Involvement in Life Space:* "Use of parents as participants in life space intervention" [30]. For a discussion of how to involve parents in the child's residential life space, see Whittaker [30].

12. *Individual Behaviour Modification:* The use of behavioural approaches with a given child.

In the selection of a treatment modality, the most important consideration is the child's need, that is, the necessary changes for improved functioning. The following table, adapted from Whittaker, provides a quick guide to matching children's learning needs to various modalities.

| Teaching formats | Poor impulse control | Low self-image | Poorly developed modulation of emotion | Relationship deficits | Family pain and strain | Special learning disability | Limited play skills |
|---|---|---|---|---|---|---|---|
| Rules | // | X | / | X | X | X | / |
| Routines | // | / | X | / | X | X | / |
| Program activities | // | // | // | // | X | X | // |
| Group sessions | // | // | // | // | X | X | X |
| Individual psychotherapy | // | // | // | / | / | X | X |
| Life-space interviews | // | // | // | // | X | X | / |
| Incentive system | // | // | X | X | X | // | / |
| Special education | // | // | X | X | X | // | X |
| Conjoint family treatment | // | // | // | // | // | X | X |
| Parent education groups | / | // | X | X | // | X | / |
| Parent involvement in life space | // | // | / | / | // | X | // |
| Individual behaviour modification | // | // | // | / | / | X | / |

// Highly applicable     / Moderately applicable     X Minimally applicable

Reprinted, by permission of the publisher, from James K. Whittaker, *Caring for Troubled Children* (San Francisco: Jossey-Bass, 1979), pp. 40.

Assessing a child's needs and selecting an appropriate treatment approach does not assure successful intervention. Implementing the treatment, particularly in a complex institutional environment, requires systematic consideration of what human, material, and organizational elements are necessary to support specific change efforts with the child. For a general checklist which can be adapted to residential work, see Appendix A, IV.

Finally, troubled children from backgrounds of physical or sexual abuse, or general neglect, are likely to show very specific behavioural characteristics. To review these, the reader should refer to Chapters 2, III; 4, Part I, "The Cause and Consequences of Child Neglect", VI; 5, II; and 6, VI. Adolescent presenting behavioural characteristics are outlined in Chapter 10, III. For additional material on assessment, see Chapter 2, III; Appendices A, III; and B.

## V.    RESIDENCE AS A CONTROLLED ENVIRONMENT

Each centre organizes itself around its goals by organizing residents, workers, structures, activities, and the total environment to achieve its goals. Basic concerns include organization of the physical environment, rules, routines, limits, shifts, treatment strategies, and so on. Knowledge gained from milieu therapy experiences has provided useful information to consider in the operation of a residential treatment centre.

### A.    Physical Environment

Messages communicated non-verbally through the physical environment can be more important to a successful outcome in treatment than messages expressed verbally or behaviourally. The appropriate physical environment can reduce tension; define expectations; convey respect, thoughtful concern, trust, and respect for privacy; and is suggestive of fun and a playful atmosphere. It can establish an orientation towards interactions. Generally the aim is to provide a comfortable setting that is closely related to the resident's cultural and economic background in order to maintain continuity, familiarity, and a sense of self-identity. Factors that enhance this include:

> clean, comfortable, and lived-in atmosphere
> opportunity for privacy and withdrawal
> recreational and creative areas
> orientation objects (clock, mirrors, calendars)
> entertainment area (T.V., stereo)
> personal spaces (bedrooms, drawers, lockers, closets)
> safety areas (medications, records, fire prevention)
> food preparation and eating areas
> meeting areas (living room, common room, quiet room)

Such a design should create a secure and inviting ambiance that encourages self-control, responsible social and environmental interactions, independence, and healthy dependence on others.

## B. Routines

Residential routines reflect both the organizational and treatment needs of the resident. Work needs to be organized in order to achieve necessary daily tasks such as wake-up, mealtimes, school, play, therapy, and bedtimes. A clear and easily understood daily routine assists both the worker and the child.

For the child, a predictable schedule of events helps to reduce anxiety by promoting familiarity, consistency, and stability. The routine makes evident the community expectations for each child to either muster up energy or relax, depending on the demands of the routine. Furthermore, it serves as an orientation experience in which the child learns to judge time, progress, strengths, and weaknesses.

Routines are valuable for workers too. They provide guidelines in the planning, organizing, and coordinating of treatment plans, and in the allocating of staff time and resources. Furthermore, workers are provided with a structure in which to diagnose a child's adaptive ability, progress, and difficulties in response to certain routines. Finally, to the extent that routines provide feedback concerning specific needs of workers and residents, this may result in improved treatment strategies, planning, supervision, and staff development. Routines have a major impact on ways in which an organization functions and delivers its service; as such, they can induce unnecessary stress or promote growth. Routines represent compromises between reality and resources for the therapeutic needs of the child. Their effective use requires sound judgement, planning, and participation by those involved, and frequent modifications to meet the dynamic changes that occur over time.

Some suggestions for improving the use of routines include:

observing residents' responses to routines (e.g., are the routines producing unnecessary conflict?)

observing workers' responses to routines (e.g., are they having difficulty because a routine is too stressful for residents, or too rigid for inexperienced workers to enforce?)

inviting on-going participation of workers and residents in the establishment and modification of routines

presenting routines in a clear, brief, and easily understood manner and posting them in high-traffic areas for all to see

## C. Rules

Rules are similar to routines in that they represent compromises among reality, resources, and therapeutic needs. Rules attempt to shape behaviour in order that it conform with some social norm, law, or agreed-on form of conduct in a given situation. They are created in a residence to promote conformity to social norms, or sometimes for teaching purposes with a specific group or individual according to their treatment plan.

Certain rules which apply to all workers and residents are in the form of regulations or policies (e.g., the use of illegal drugs, dangerous weapons, alcohol, physical destruction, stealing). Conformity tends to increase if there are awareness and understanding of the rules, the purposes they serve, and the consequences attached to rule breaking. Participation in formulating rules and their consequences tends to further conformity and maintenance.

It is important to explain relevant agency rules (e.g., fire regulations, non-smoking areas) to each resident so that there is an understanding of why some rules exist. This can be handled as part of an overall therapeutic strategy in order to convey expectations, information, and a message that one must respect and care about the well-being of all residents.

As a therapeutic tool, rules can be used to:

establish expectations of appropriate behaviours

convey a sense of security through the vehicle of controls and responsibilities

reinforce internal controls through external structures

provide a vehicle for discussion of unexpressed feelings for workers and residents

teach appropriate social interactions and awareness in group settings

teach affective and negotiation skills

involve members in their own well-being and the control of their own and others' behaviour for enhancing group living and achievement

assist in defining self-identity, self-regulation, self-esteem, and responsibility for corrective action

Rules can be structured in terms of individual or group consequences, which can be either negotiable or non-negotiable. In each case, participation in the original rule-setting will improve the understanding and acceptance of the rule. Where consequences can be negotiated, the process can serve to develop problem-solving, negotiation, and interaction skills, thereby achieving many of the original treatment objectives. Non-negotiable rules with consequences often include dangerous or destructive behaviours that threaten everyone's safety or severely limit the ability of workers to do effective work. In addition to communicating the need for safety and protection, rules that have a consequence of discharge may signal a way out of the treatment arrangement for the resident who will not, or cannot, function within certain rules. It is important for workers to attach consequences which they can enforce fully, otherwise the intent and impact of these rules lose their value. Similarly, negotiable consequences should be practical, achievable, and in line with therapeutic and organizational objectives.

A common problem is the worker's often real or perceived need to respond immediately to rule-breaking. This can be problematic when the worker is unclear about individual, group, or organizational limits, or about enforcing certain consequences. The worker may be vulnerable to manipulation or may fear attack by the group or individuals. In addition, a resident's request may sound reasonable and yet run counter to the beliefs of other workers.

When confronted with these situations the worker must use her or his best judgement at the time while clearly stating the need for further consultation with fellow team members before making a final decision. Articulating the issue in this way can:

> satisfy the immediate problem by giving a tentative solution

> convey the stated belief that no worker can act separately without considering and respecting the opinions of fellow workers who share in the residents' care and planning

> minimize fragmentation of workers by the residents

> prevent individual workers from feeling compelled to make final judgements in uncertain situations

## D.    Limits

Limits on individual expression and gratification of desires are usually at least somewhat necessary for effective group living. Limits function as parameters, or boundaries for acceptable and non-acceptable behaviours. Effective limits can signal a clear and understandable warning that certain behaviours are nearing unacceptable levels, can suggest ways of controlling the behaviours, and can provide the external controls if the behaviour goes unchecked.

Difficulty with limits can occur when a resident is unable to recognize internal and external signals that her or his behaviour is becoming unacceptable, or has trouble knowing or accepting what to do when the behaviour is out of control, or finally, has difficulty in accepting or believing that external controls are imminent, fair, consistent, or effective in bringing the behaviour under control.

Limits in residences attempt to address all three levels of an individual's difficulty with them. Workers mobilize their energy to meet the individual at her or his greatest level of need. For example, with all delinquents, consistency of external control and consequences may be emphasized, while for the "unsocialized" resident, methods of self-control may be emphasized. Specific groups may require special limits in order for group teaching and development to be effective.

For limits to be useful they must be internalized so that they operate without supervised external control. Initially, limits need to be consistently applied over time and are used as opportunities to recognize and teach acceptable behaviours. Eventually they become internalized and operate as a self-guidance system. If the individual feels better, avoids repeating conflictive situations, learns to control her or his behaviour and respects others, then that individual has presumably learned to value limits as guides for daily functioning.

In their therapeutic function, limits must be applied as part of the total treatment program, based on the individual's ability to benefit from them immediately or within a reasonable period of time. Limits should be applied consistently and uniformly by all workers and should be realistically enforceable and understandable to both residents and workers. Some key points to consider in establishing limits are:

restrictions and opinions available in setting limits within the organization

limits appropriate for specific behaviours and residents

final objectives of each limit and alternative available methods for reaching the objective in addition to limits

follow-up consequences for each limit, and their enforceability

team support and ability to set and carry out limits consistently

methods for involving participation in limit-setting by workers and residents

periodic review of the effectiveness of limits

Implementation of effective limits is dependent on:

*Purpose:* clarity and understanding of the purpose that limits serve for each individual or group

*Knowledge:* recognizing when a behaviour is likely to go out of control

*Timing:* communicating verbally and non-verbally to the individual or group in ways that invite internal controls, when they are still possible

*Skill:* methods of control that are shown to be necessary and effective for each individual or group

*Enforceability:* security in knowing that a limit can be enforced if it becomes necessary

The question of enforceability of limits is dependent on the extent of powers granted to workers. For example, physical restraint, drugs, or discharge may or may not be options in certain residences. In each case it will be critical to know the extent of one's powers and abilities in order to authoritatively communicate one's intention. Otherwise, ineffective and unrealistic limit-setting will lose its value and lead to more anxiety and feelings of helplessness in both residents and workers.

## VI.   DEVELOPING POSITIVE RELATIONSHIPS

### A.   Advantages of Positive Relationships

All forms of treatment rely heavily on the formation of a positive relationship in order to exert influence on the client. Humans learn through experience, imitation, identification, modelling, trial and error, reward and punishment, and so on. Creation of a strong positive climate within a trusting relationship is central to influencing others' behaviour, thinking, feelings, and attitudes. A strong relationship between a worker and resident improves trust and communication, creates a desire to initiate and identify with the worker's attitudes and behaviours, and creates a climate that fosters behavioural experimentation and risk taking.

## B.    Meeting Residents' Needs

Central to forming a positive relationship is the worker's conveyance of genuine interest in each resident. One way in which to demonstrate interest is to meet the wide range of needs presented by the child. These include:

*Basic needs:* Food, shelter, clothing, and safety are important vehicles for conveying care and concern; the notion of the right to exist is conveyed forcefully and continuously to the child through the provision of good food, clean environment, emergency procedures, limits, rules, routines, and so on.

*Emotional needs:* Attending to crises and other emotional needs with sensitivity and caring can form the basis of trust and thereby open the doors to communication and problem solving of residents' difficulties.

*Social needs:* Helping children to get along with, and to enjoy, other human beings can have profound effects on their future self-image, learning, and relationships.

*Recreational needs:* Having fun, playing, and enjoying life are basic to mental health and provide a context in which to show affection, liking, and interest.

*Educational needs:* Acquiring skills enhances feelings of usefulness, self-sufficiency, and satisfaction while serving to improve self-image.

## C.    Stages of Relationship Building

The treatment process evolves through characteristic stages, the success of which is greatly facilitated by a strong relationship between residents and workers.

The building of a relationship begins with the development of trust and of a common base of communication through which information exchanges can occur. Open discussions provide opportunities to correct or alter distortions in thinking and behaviour patterns. Such alterations can result in anxieties and uncertainties as a new view of life unfolds; these anxieties can be handled in the context of a trusting, therapeutic relationship. Finally, the resident learns new adaptive skills to deal with old problems and to face new ones.

The skilled worker can engineer and seize opportunities to enhance the formation of trust and relationship building in countless situations that occur daily in the context of residential living. The use of play, food, rules, routines, limits, conversations, crises, and school can all serve to build a strong resident-worker bond with which to proceed through the stages of treatment.

A positive relationship is fostered by workers who can:

understand the needs of each resident realistically

listen effectively and suspend judgement in non-emergency situations

model what they expect others to learn

separate their needs from others' needs, in a working situation assume a friendly, caring, professional role rather than a parental, authoritarian, or friend role

respect themselves and others and have a genuine interest in people's welfare

remain objective, without over-identifying with their clients, in order to be effective catalysts, encouragers, and problem-solvers

recognize and deal with power struggles without the need to overpower others or experience a devastating loss of control and low self-esteem in no-win or lose situations

recognize and use the health or strong aspects of a client or group as the basis for positive interactions

trust others to assist them when they need help

For information on establishing relationships with difficult clients, see Chapter 2, V.

## VII.  THERAPEUTIC USE OF PHYSICAL RESTRAINT

Child care workers in residential settings inevitably encounter aggressive children who have lost control of their behaviour. Such children will:

Hit, bite, kick, throw anything within their reach, spit, scream, swear and accompany all this by disjointed and meaningless movement or lashing out at things or people 'without apparent reason' [29]

The physical restraint of children is a highly contentious issue in child care work, so much so that some agencies prohibit its use. Some workers are ambivalent about using such methods because they are interpreted as physical punishment or perhaps professional incompetence. If used thoughtfully and carefully, however, physical restraint techniques can be used for both safety and therapeutic purposes. Specifically, the professional goals of physical restraint are [29]:

to *assure the safety* of the out-of-control child, other children, and staff

to *prevent* or *end property destruction*

to *assist the removal* of a disruptive child from a group setting in which the child is losing control and causing others to lose control

to establish and reinforce *norms of order and safety* in the residence

to help the child *therapeutically* by (a) establishing *trust* in adult ability to limit out-of-control behaviour, (b) demonstrating that adults *care*, (c) allowing the *release of tension* in a safe environment, and (d) assisting the child to develop *inner controls*

Four general principles can guide the worker's effective use of physical restraint. First and foremost, restraint should never be used as a punishment or retaliation against the child. Secondly, it should be used when other measures (e.g., the invocation of rules and routines, relationship) have failed. Thirdly, physical restraint methods should be used within the context of an on-going relationship with the child.

Finally, such methods should be used flexibly, and should be gradually stopped as the child shows signs of gaining control.

In addition to these general principles, a number of specific guidelines will assist the worker who must physically restrain a child [29]:

1. During physical restraint, give directions loudly, clearly, and repetitively.

2. Hold the child no more firmly than is required for control; squeezing the child out of anger should be avoided, even though his or her physical movements may increase as restraint is used.

3. Safe physical objects may be used to assist the worker's efforts. For example, a blanket may be used as a shield against thrown objects or to confine the legs of a kicking child.

4. Workers are advised to reach for those parts of the body which will provide control but which are not easily injured (e.g., upperarm, forearm, calf, thigh). Avoid pulling hands, wrists, forearms; or grasping hair, neck, or ears.

5. Experiment and role play with methods for restraining the child in different postures. For example, a small child may be restrained in a sitting position on a worker's lap. The adult crosses her or his legs over the child's, while the latter's arms are crossed in front; to avoid head-butting, the worker's head is placed against the child's shoulder blades. For concrete descriptions of other methods, see Aichorn [2]. Also, many agencies have developed detailed outlines of holding techniques.

6. Avoid moving the out-of-control child, unless she or he is in a dangerous location. If movement is necessary, take a firm grip and avoid dragging the child. Children who are beginning to regain control can be guided from place to place.

7. Physical restraint techniques should be accompanied with verbal communication. A worker's calm, clear, and simple assurance that she or he intends to control and not hurt the child is particularly valuable. In addition, the child should be encouraged to show self-control.

8. Physical restraints should be relaxed as soon as the child begins to show signs of self-control. Such signs include bodily relaxation, emotional calming, the return of productive speech, and quiet sobbing. A gradual release (e.g., releasing one arm first) will help the worker ascertain whether the child is truly self-controlled.

9. In cases where a child uses an outburst as a tactic to manipulate or gain a worker's attention, physical restraint should still be used as a safety measure. However, in such instances, workers should take the opportunity to teach more suitable, less risky ways of gaining attention.

10. Carefully record all instances of physical restraint, including such

information as date, time, circumstances requiring restraint, method of restraint, duration, and so forth. Some agencies have specific policies concerning physical restraint practices, including a requirement to complete detailed
reports of physical restraint.

## VIII.   RESIDENTIAL GROUP WORK

### A.    Purpose of Groups

Groups in residential settings are a natural part of the total milieu. Group
forces can be utilized to promote types of learning and growth which might not occur
in individual therapy. As well, groups can be used to facilitate the child's return to the
community.

In group work, individuals learn to handle rivalries and resolve differences.
Through team-building, the group can be utilized for bolstering the child's accomplishment, but without losing a sense of individuality. Self-growing skills are developed which alter unwanted behaviour patterns such as explosiveness, over-
dependency, and so on. Sexual feelings that may develop between residents or between a child and a worker can be worked out and understood, thereby enhancing the
growth of sexual identity and appropriate sexual behavior. In addition, leadership
skills can be learned through planning and implementing activities and projects.

### B.    Types of Residential Groups

In a recent book on residential care, Whittaker discusses the objectives,
composition, and activities of four different groups which are appropriate for residential settings: daily management groups, problem-oriented groups, activity groups,
and transition groups. The following is a summary of that discussion [30].

### 1.    *The Daily Management Group*

The general objective of the daily management group is to assist children and
staff to live, play, and work with one another within the physical and social context of
the residence. Working through the problems of living in such a setting on a regular
basis (e.g., sharing resources, taking responsibility for daily tasks), allows the children
to learn through living. Such groups meet on a regular basis for about 30 to 40
minutes to discuss common concerns around residential tasks and routines. The
general functions are to (a) provide information (e.g., special events, staff changes),
(b) act as an arena for resolving disputes and grievances, for sharing disputes, and for
sharing positive feedback, and (c) provide an opportunity for scheduling chores and
activities.

The membership of daily management groups can include all staff and children from particular living units, as well as others who have particular agenda items.
Depending on the level of group development and individual maturity, group leadership either can be rotated among children or taken by staff [30].

2.    *Problem-Oriented Discussion Groups*

Problem-oriented discussion groups are treatment groups designed to address individual member problems or ones facing the whole group. In the course of problem-solving, feelings are explored, alternative behaviours are developed, support and encouragement are provided. As treatment groups dealing with private matters, membership is more selective than the daily management groups. Non-treatment residential staff and others are invited only with group agreement. Group leadership, whether single or co-leaders, requires knowledge of group dynamics and clinical methods. Leadership roles include facilitating the supportive activities of the group as a whole by encouraging positive feedback, modelling appropriate behaviour, offering support and encouragement [30].

3.    *Activity Groups*

Activity groups can be designed either for socializing, or for teaching basic physical and social skills through pleasurable activities. As well, they afford a break from established residence routines and permit the development of closer friendships with other children or special adults. Opportunities can be provided for special interest activities (e.g., photography, guitar playing, sports) or for special-needs clients. Membership in activity groups is self-selective, drawing on child care staff, other staff, and children with special interests and abilities. Staff members may take the initiative to invite interested parties to form a club or group [30].

4.    *Transition Groups*

One of the most challenging tasks for residential care programs is to help the client return to the community. Transition groups are designed to prepare for a return to community life by helping the child learn new routines, make new friends, master the new environment, including possibly a new family [30].

The membership of transition groups should include one or more children who are scheduled to leave the residence at approximately the same time. In addition, positive role models should be present, including past members of the program who are successfully involved in the community, and/or other neighbourhood peers.

Transition groups give the child an opportunity to learn about resources in the community. As such, community resource people and organizational representatives (e.g., Y.W.C.A. staff) are useful group participants. Such groups also help the child to separate from the residence through discussions of feelings about leaving and memories of pleasurable experiences. For more information on the topics of separation and client termination, see Chapter 8, III, and Appendix A, VI.

Finally, transition groups are particularly useful for adolescents who will be establishing independent living arrangements in the community. Those readers interested in pursuing the important subject of "building bridges to the community" should consult Whittaker [30; Chapters 5, 6 and 7].

## C.    Departures from Traditional Group Therapy

Residential settings do not share the same advantages as traditional group work because they do not have the opportunity to select candidates for optimum effectiveness. Also, several people are involved in working with the natural residential group rather than one consistent person who develops with the group.

By virtue of their intense living arrangement, residential groups develop more quickly and know each other faster than the workers can ever hope to understand. Since individual workers do not evolve with the group, as in group therapy, they are less able to understand and influence members to the extent that members can influence each other. Furthermore, residential groups have less time to be away from each other, thus increasing the amount of stress and reducing the amount of time for integration required for traditional group therapy.

These same conditions, however, can produce advantages over traditional group therapy. For example, continuous observation is possible, and follow-up on crises or conflicts can be pursued. The various workers who attempt to influence the group may create less threatening and defensive reactions than does a continuous group leader. Finally, the intensity of group living may accelerate learning, changing perceptions, and working through difficulties because it is hard to avoid confronting them in a residential setting.

## D.      Producing Changes

In encouraging group development and pro-social behaviour, residential workers must capitalize on existing group and individual needs. Group norms and structures can be altered by utilizing the following techniques:

Encourage the need to belong by allowing the expression of negative feelings, which are common to all individuals.

Use the positive abilities of the group and its members to promote constructive achievement, and group pressure to conform.

Provide for real opportunities to make decisions within reasonable limits.

Help the group achieve its goals through teaching better problem-solving skills.

Involve the group in setting expectations, rules, and consequences within the residence.

The residential group has a life of its own, where peer pressure and the need to belong to one's peer group are often more important in producing change than is the individual relationship with an adult. Workers provide opportunities for group satisfaction and achievement by granting adolescents some power to make decisions and influence the milieu.

## E.      Areas Appropriate for Group Teaching

Group teaching might involve enlisting residents for:

chairing regular residence meetings

> participating in menu and food selection and preparation
>
> deciding on activities they would enjoy doing as a group
>
> contributing to worker and program evaluations
>
> distributing a work schedule among members
>
> participating in the establishment of rules, routines, and consequences

Allowing group participation in the operation of the residence can initially result in poor or unrealistic decisions. It is important for workers to offer their advice, and equally important for the group to realize that some of their own decisions may be impractical (e.g., raising money for a new stereo by washing cars may not be within reason). However, the experience of trying may produce worthwhile benefits such as team spirit, fun, and the experience of organizing. Discussion of the partial failure can be utilized as encouragement to keep trying and as a vehicle for highlighting the positives. Workers can serve as models through the behaviour they display in disappointing situations and thereby help the group to stimulate alternative solutions to problems.

For additional material on group work with child welfare clients, see Chapters 4, Part 2, "Practice Guidelines", IV, VI; 5, IX, XI and XIII; and 12, VIII.


## IX.     OCCUPATIONAL HAZARDS IN RESIDENTIAL WORK


### A.     Sources of Stress

Those who work directly with children in residential work are well aware that there are very stressful, difficult, and hazardous aspects to their jobs which can affect their mental health and future career plans. Working with disturbed or aggressive children can be disturbing and threatening. It is helpful to understand why this occurs and what can be done to minimize the long-term impact on workers.

Stress can result in the following general areas:

> *Organizational:* The way in which a residence is organized can be a major source of stress and danger for both residents and workers.
>
> *Abilities:* Stress results when residents' demands exceed the experience, knowledge, readiness, and skill levels of workers.
>
> *Types and degrees of client problems:* Continued exposure to others with emotional difficulties activates often intense and stressful states in the helpers.

Working with emotionally disturbed individuals is upsetting because it activates intense feelings in the worker. With increased experience, knowledge, and skill, the intensity of emotions is brought under more control, resulting in lower levels of stress. Experienced workers develop a sense of when and where to seek help when they are in trouble, rather than trying to solve enormous problems on their own.

Some feelings are realistic and justified, while others which are not produce puzzling and unpredictable reactions for both the worker and client. These feelings and reactions may be elicited by (1) interactions that expose the worker to unresolved past or present personal experiences; (2) client transference of feelings to the worker as though the worker were someone else; (3) countertransference to the client as though the client were someone else; (4) exposure of the worker's weaknesses by skilled clients in order to keep the focus on the worker and thereby avoid pressure to change or to take responsibility for their own behaviour.

Other sources of stress include:

demands of shift-work and the withdrawal from normal social interactions with the community

being in a state of constant information-gathering, unpredictability, and decision-making involving complex levels of thinking

working with others (who have different orientations, abilities, and convictions) in a unified plan of action requiring confrontations, negotiation, and conformity

responsibility in planning and implementing decisions that affect a resident's future

threat of physical and verbal abuse and exposure to high levels of anxiety

organizational complexities resulting in feelings of alienation and confusion

spill-over of daily work tension, stress placed on others outside work, possibly affecting the worker's support system

## B.      Effects on Workers' Performance

The accumulated job and social stress can have a cyclical negative effect on the worker's performance. She or he might act out negative tension states through the child by either consciously or unconsciously encouraging poor behaviour (e.g., by being over-permissive; by defending the resident; by rationalizing the need to do certain things on therapeutic grounds; by not being where problems are likely to occur).
things on therapeutic grounds; by not being where problems are likely to occur).

A worker might act out stress with a resident. For example, a frustrated worker with no apparent outlet may set up a resident unknowingly. This can be accomplished by creating a situation that upsets the resident so that she or he misbehaves, which then allows the worker to ventilate angry feelings at the child's behaviour.

Sometimes workers avoid dealing with problems in order to avoid stress, or they simply change cases or jobs. Other symptoms of stress include:

talking too much or refusing to talk about the stress at home

treating clients as labels and not as persons

going by the book and losing flexibility, adaptability, creativity, and spontaneity

While the front-line worker is in the most vulnerable position, similar tactics to manage stress are often adopted by supervisors and administrators. All of these approaches tend to generate even more stress in that they do not deal directly with the sources, but rather delay, postpone, or perpetuate the cycle so that further tension is created. High levels of stress contribute to worker burn-out and inadequate levels of treatment, and can create explosive situations that threaten the welfare of all.

## C.    Minimizing Occupational Hazards

Suggested methods of reducing and managing stress among workers in residence include the following:

Develop sound eating, sleeping, and relaxation habits.

Organize your life away from work to enjoy friends, hobbies, interests that are non-work related.

If necessary, seek individual therapy or a support group for personal problems outside work as part of your own development.

At work, learn to use supervision more effectively and develop a broad base of support; no one person has all the skills you need.

Expand your professional network and skills outside your own agency to develop a sense of mastery, independence, and a gradually larger outlook on life and work.

Create learning opportunities at work to develop skills you are lacking and to better utilize skills you have.

Keep a balanced workload; if possible don't accept too many cases or cases that are similar, unrewarding, or extremely demanding in areas in which you are weak.

Develop self-defence skills (verbal and physical); it is difficult to be understanding and therapeutic when you are in a constant state of fear and feel vulnerable to physical attack.

A change of residence may be indicated after a reasonable time; no one is equipped to work with all types of problems at each stage of their career; learn to identify your strengths and limitations.

Learn to utilize the team you work with and share concerns and responsibilities.

Suggestions for ways in which supervisors might help reduce workers' stress are as follows:

Ensure an adequate rest period for workers on each shift.

Plan for appropriate distribution of workers and job assignments for each shift on the basis of their ability.

Facilitate group support and interdependence.

Provide feedback on performance in a balanced, realistic, and supportive way.

Provide relevant training as required for individuals and teams.

Develop career opportunities for workers and improve upward communication.

Follow the suggestions for workers to reduce stress and act as a model for staff.

## X.   SUMMARY

This chapter provides an overview of common problems encountered in residential work with emotionally disturbed and delinquent children and adolescents. Approaches to assessment, relationship building, limits, rules, routines, physical restraint, and group work are suggested. Special attention is given to the causes of occupational hazards for the worker and remedies for minimizing burn-out are outlined.

### REFERENCES

1. Cumming, J. and Cumming, E. *Ego and Milieu, The Theory and Practice of Environmental Therapy*. New York: Atherton Press, 1967.
2. Aichorn, A. *Wayward Youth*. New York: Viking Press, 1935.
3. Bettelheim, B. *Love is Not Enough*. New York: Eru Press, 1950.
4. Redl, F. *When We Deal With Children*. New York: The Free Press, 1967.
5. Treischman, A. E., Whittaker, J. K., and Bentro, L. K. *The Other 23 Hours; Child Care Work in a Therapeutic Milieu*. Chicago: Aldrich, 1968.
6. Klein, A. F., *The Professional Child Care Worker: A Guide to Skills, Knowledge, Techniques and Attitudes*. New York: Association Press, 1975.
7. Littner, N. "The Emotional Impact of the Emotionally Disturbed Child", paper presented to the Conference on Professional Practice, Toronto, 1968.
8. Fraiberg, S., "Some Aspects of Residential Casework with Children", Social Casework, Vol. XXXVII, April 1956, pp. 159–167.
9. Inglis, D. *Authority and Ability in Residential Treatment*. New York: Child Welfare League of America, 1954.
10. Konopka, G. "Implications of a Changing Residential Treatment Program", American Journal of Orthopsychiatry, Vol. XXXI, January 1961, pp. 17–39.
11. _____. "Institutional Treatment of Emotionally Disturbed Children", Crime and Delinquency, Vol. 8, No. 1, 1962.
12. McDermott, J. E., Fraiberg, S., and Harrison, S. I. "Residential Treatment of Children: The Utilization of Transference Behavior", Journal of the American Academy of Child Psychiatry, 1968, pp. 169–192.
13. Daley, M. R. "Preventing Worker Burnout in Child Welfare", Child Welfare, Vol LVIII, July/August 1979, pp. 443–450.
14. Child Welfare League of America. *From Chaos to Order: A Collective View of the Residential Treatment of Children*. New York: 1972.
15. Christ, A. E. and Wagner, N. N. "Iatrogenic Factors in Residential Treatment: A Problem in Staff Training", American Journal of Orthopsychiatry, Vol. XXXI, July 1966, pp. 725–729.
16. D'Amato, G. *Residential Treatment for Child Mental Health*. Springfield Ill.: Charles C Thomas, 1969.

17. Davids, A. "Personality and Attributes of Child Care Workers, Psychotherapist and Parents of Children in Residential Treatment", Child Psychiatry and Human Development, Vol. 1, No. 41, 1970.

18. Wallerstein, J. and Mandelbaum, A. "Countertransference in the Residential Treatment of Children", in Eissler, R. S. et al. (eds.), *The Psychoanalytic Study of the Child*, Vol. 14, New York: International University Press, 1959.

19. Bettelheim, B. and Sylvester, E., "A Therapeutic Milieu", American Journal of Orthopsychiatry, Vol. XVIII, April 1948, pp. 191–206.

20. Jones, M. *The Therapeutic Community*. New York: Basic Books, 1953.

21. McKrioch, D. and Stanton, A. H. "Milieu Therapy, Psychiatric Treatment", Proceedings of the Association for Research in Nervous and Mental Disease, Vol. XXI, Baltimore: Williams and Wilkins, 1953.

22. Alt, H. *Residential Treatment for the Disturbed Child*. New York: International University Press, 1972.

23. Foster, G. W. et al. *Child Care Work with Emotionally Disturbed Children*. Pittsburgh: University of Pittsburgh Press, 1972.

24. Carbonara, N. T. and Cohen, G. M. *Child Care with Emotionally Disturbed Children*. Pittsburgh: University of Pittsburgh Press, 1972.

25. Polsky, H. and Claster, D. S. *The Dynamics of Residential Treatment*. Chapel Hill: University of North Carolina Press, 1968.

26. Redl, I. and Wineman, D. *The Aggressive Child*. Glencoe Ill.: The Free Press, 1957.

27. Whittaker, J. and Trieshman, A. E. *Children Away from Home*. Chicago: Aldine Atherton, 1972.

28. Redl, F. "The Concept of a Therapeutic Milieu", American Journal of Orthopsychiatry, Vol. XXIX, October 1959, pp. 721–736.

29. _____ and Wineman, D. *Controls from Within*. New York: The Free Press, 1952.

30. Whittaker, J. K. *Caring for Troubled Children*. San Francisco: Jossey-Bass Publishers, 1979.

31. Long, N. J., Morse, W. C., and Newman, R. G. *Conflict in the Classroom* (2nd ed.). Belmont, Calif.: Wadsworth, 1971.

# 10
# Adolescent Problems: Dynamics and Practice

**SHARON KIRSH**

I. INTRODUCTION ....................................................... 290
   A.  Working Assumptions About Adolescent
      Development ...................................................... 290
   B.  Working Assumptions About Youth Work ............... 292
II. RESPONSES TO STRESS ........................................... 293
   A.  Family Crisis Theory ........................................ 293
   B.  Social Networks as Potential Supports ................. 294
   C.  Victim versus Bystander ................................... 295
III. THEORETICAL APPROACHES TO PRESENTING
PROBLEMS .............................................................. 295
IV. RUNNING AWAY ................................................... 298
   A.  Types of Runaways ......................................... 298
   B.  Factors Related to Running Away ....................... 299
   C.  Warning Signs ............................................... 302
   D.  Truancy as a Form of Running Away .................. 302
V. DELINQUENCY ...................................................... 305
   A.  Theoretical Approaches ................................... 306
   B.  Factors Related to Delinquency ......................... 306
VI. SELF-INJURIOUS BEHAVIOURS ............................... 308
   A.  Theoretical Approaches ................................... 310
   B.  Factors Related to Self-Injury ........................... 310
   C.  Warning Signs ............................................... 312
VII. WORKING WITH ADOLESCENTS .............................. 313
   A.  Three Orientations ......................................... 315
VIII. SUMMARY ......................................................... 318
     REFERENCES ................................................ 318

# I.    INTRODUCTION

Those who survive adolescence look back with a mixture of painful and pleasant memories. Some students of adolescent psychology maintain that "storm and stress" typify the experience of all teenagers, while others believe that cultural pressures and restrictions are the basis of adolescent tension and that not all adolescents are subjected to such forces. It can probably be said that most people between the ages of 11 and 20 undergo changes which are accompanied by a set of concerns, anxieties, and pleasures that are more common or intense during those years than during other phases of the life cycle.

Even adolescents who receive love and generally adequate parenting are forced to deal with the unfolding of a new physical and mental self which in and of itself can generate stress; adolescents whose lives are complicated by inadequate parenting, lack of affection and praise, economic pressures, and other contextual stressors, must deal with these additional burdens. When the pain is too much to handle, mechanisms (e.g., defense mechanisms; neurotic coping reactions) are brought into play to help deal with anxiety. Some adolescents run away from home or school, or escape into emotionally or physically self-injurious behaviors, and some choose that permanent problem-solving technique, suicide. Regardless of form, their intent is uniform—to remove themselves from, and perhaps to call attention to, a reality which they experience as painful and destructive.

This chapter aims to explore factors related to and treatment of the adolescent presenting problems which are most commonly handled by workers in the field of child welfare. They are problems which have repeatedly been linked with abuse and neglect; they are behavioural manifestations (for example, running away, truancy, delinquency, self-injurious behaviour) of family and environmental stresses, and they differ from those categories of behaviours which are commonly labelled "mental illness".

While the range of presenting problems handled by child welfare workers is vast, the scope of this chapter is highly focussed; it is the task of other chapters to deal with adolescent unmarried parents (Chapter 12), sexual abuse (Chapter 6), and with the practices of child care workers as these pertain to adolescents (Chapter 9). As a significant number of adolescent problems have been correlated with earlier child abuse, the reader is encouraged to review Chapter 5.

## A.    Working Assumptions About Adolescent Development

People whose job it is to protect and to support adolescents bump up against dilemmas and difficulties which derive, in part, from the developmental stage of their clients. While it seems a cliché to speak of adolescents in terms of changes in physical appearance, body image, cognitive abilities, social relationships with peers, and of mood and value swings (which the casual observer might mistake for severe disturbance), it nevertheless is the client's *stage* of adolescent development which will have an impact on the selection of therapeutic intervention.

Adolescence is divided conceptually into three phases: early, middle, and late. Not all young people fit each category chronologically, since people develop at different speeds and in different ways. Nevertheless, three stages can be delineated.

*Early Adolescence:* (for males, ages 12, 13, 14; for females, ages 11, 12, 13). The body experiences fast and consistent growth, sexual maturity moves towards its final stages, body appearance undergoes major changes; there is a tendency towards body consciousness and shyness which heighten mood fluctuation; much energy is expended in learning to deal with peers; this is a highly egocentric phase with difficulty in appreciating other's viewpoints; the sense of social justice is concrete, and thoughts are for the present, not the future; interest in sex is more social than physiological; home and family are the most significant socio-emotional factors, although the peer group competes; this is usually the least emotionally troublesome period of adolescence.

*Middle Adolescence:* (for males, ages 14, 15, 16; for females, ages 13, 14, 15, 16). Physical growth is less accelerated; height reaches adult level, skeleton assumes its adult form, strength and endurance increase, reproductive organs mature, secondary sexual traits appear, self-perception of being an adult rather than a child develops. There is an intellectual growth spurt in which thought becomes more abstract and less concrete, less egocentric, and more future-oriented. Awareness of the outside world and of the inner world of the personality increases, with more introspection and self-analysis (and self-doubt); moral outlook becomes more abstract, concerned with rightdoing versus wrongdoing; there is greater autonomy and interest in sexuality and more complicated relationships within the family unit; same sex groupings remain dominant; peers are vital for one's sense of achievement and accomplishment; conflict with parents in major areas tends to increase as leaving home or school become viable options; desire for sexual experiences and intimacy escalates.

*Late Adolescence:* (for both males and females, ages 16, 17, 18, 19). More self-directing, less influenced by peers, able to perceive others' uniqueness; they perceive the split between personal needs and society's interests (which can lead to cynicism and alienation). The body does not grow significantly, and the intellect begins to benefit from experiences; intimacy becomes more integrated with sexuality.

Teenagers have needs, some of which are specific to their developmental phases and others of which are appropriate to people of all ages. Adolescents tend to have a strong need for status and acceptance, for independence and self-assertion, for achievement and competence, and for role experimentation. They tend to want to contribute to important work, to analyze/synthesize their selves, to express themselves, and to make an impact on the world.

Priorities tend to vary according to the adolescent's developmental stage. For example, early adolescents are concerned about adjustment to their transforming bodies, about loss of self-control, newly emerging sexual feelings, and the fear of growing older and no longer being cared for as a child.

Middle adolescents are concerned with becoming emotionally independent of parents, with their maturing bodies (especially whether normal, attractive, and so forth), and with sexual adequacy.

Late adolescents tend to be concerned with their adequacy as women and men, with permanent relationships, with integrating sexuality and intimacy, and with establishing a personal identity.

North American adolescents occupy an ambiguous space: neither adult nor child, physically adult but economically dependent, politically powerless yet struggling to be recognized. These stressors can be further compounded by those parents who [73]:

> hold unrealistic expectations of their teenager
>
> impose their own values on their child rather than acknowledge peer behavioural norms
>
> emotionally neglect their child
>
> have difficulty separating from their child
>
> attempt to be contemporary friends of their child
>
> expect their child to achieve in ways which the parents have not accomplished as adults

As a response to developmental and environmental stressors, some adolescents may either act out or withdraw. Problems of adolescence which are of most concern to adults include:

> rebellious behaviour (at home/school/in the community)
>
> "immaturity" as a means of avoiding independence
>
> an inability to form "healthy", intimate peer relationships

To be sure, adolescence is the most difficult developmental stage for a parent.

## B.    Working Assumptions About Youth Work

Every social worker operates from her or his own set of premises about human behaviour, about the nature of change and growth, and about the parameters of a worker's tasks. Many of the difficulties in working with young people and their families are a consequence of the ambiguous status of adolescence.

Below is the beginning of what could easily be expanded into a very long list of working assumptions. Each worker could add her or his own premises to these:

> One major task of workers is to help the family recognize and utilize its own strengths, rather than to rescue the adolescent from the family.
>
> Responsibility for strengthening family dynamics must be put back on parents and adolescents; the worker's job is to facilitate this process (for example, by finding and focussing on positive aspects of the existing dynamic).
>
> Parents, especially those whose involvement with an agency is involuntary, may lack motivation to engage in interventions on behalf of their child; they may also lack skills necessary for supportive and instructive parenting; thus, generating parental and adolescent motivation, and teaching parenting skills are major tasks.
>
> Some parents do not recognize those behaviours which are widely

considered to be "normal" for adolescents and consequently treat their child as though she or he were "bad"; facilitating parental understanding of adolescent "normalcy" is a crucial task.

Adolescents who act out or who withdraw tend to have one cluster of characteristics in common: they have feelings of low self-worth, and believe either that they lack power and control over their lives, or that they have so much control and responsibility as to feel uncared for; thus, devising ways in which the adolescent can develop an appropriate balance between autonomy and dependence is a primary focus for workers.

Adolescents and/or their parents tend to first come into contact with an agency during times of crisis; workers often function under stressful time lines and must develop efficacious and efficient ways of handling problems.

Fair, consistent, and supportive counselling seems to work best regardless of the problem.

While youth work may at times seem to workers to be a fruitless and impossible task, there are, in fact, interventions which have been employed with successful outcomes.

At this point, it may be useful to review earlier chapters dealing with the ecology of child welfare problems (Chapter 1, II), the worker's ecology (Chapter 1, III), and the family perspective and practice principles (Chapter 2, IV).

## II.    RESPONSES TO STRESS

Workers in the field of child welfare are forced daily to confront the consequences of child abuse and neglect. While these may be viewed as a result of poverty and its correlates, or as a result of dysfunctional communication systems within the family, or as a result of parental mental illness or corruptness, or as a combination of any of the above, its consequences in terms of adolescent behavioural manifestations are well documented by child welfare workers and by other students of the problem. It is for this reason that we will look at some precipitators of family crisis, and as the chapter progresses, explore some of the direct and indirect consequences of such crises.

## A.    Family Crisis Theory

What leads to a family crisis, and what factors determine the way in which it is handled?

According to Hill's family crisis theory [44]:

A (the event) interacts with B (the family's crisis-meeting resources) which interacts with C (the definition the family makes of the event) to produce X (the crisis).

There are five different types of family events (A):

1. external (e.g., unemployment)
2. dismemberment only (e.g., death of spouse, separation due to hospitalization)
3. accession only (e.g., unwanted pregnancy, new stepparent in the home, adoption, adding a grandparent to the home)
4. demoralization only (e.g., incidents of alcoholism, drug addiction, delinquency)
5. combined events (e.g., illegitimacy, desertion, divorce, imprisonment of spouse, suicide, homicide)

Events can be chronic, unexpected stressors (e.g., unemployment, hospitalization), or immediate, acute (e.g., argument between spouses).

The family's vulnerability to the stressor event is dependent upon:

their definition of the seriousness of it
externalization (outward blame) for the event
time available to anticipate it
personal relationship among family members
their degree of family integration and adaptability

Their ability to recover from the disorganization produced by the stressor event depends upon several factors:

length of time disruption is experienced
degree to which family members share feelings and values
relative equity of power between spouses
spouses' marital adjustment
amount of help available from other sources

This final point, the amount of help available from other sources, is a crucial and yet much overlooked piece in the puzzle of family disintegration and deviance.

## B.   Social Networks as Potential Supports

Members of a family's network (kin, friends, neighbors, co-workers, physicians, clergy, institutions, agencies, and so on) [83] are social resources which can be called upon for aid.

Each member of a social network has the capacity to provide one or more of the following resources:

love, affection, intimacy, validation of personal worth, nurturance and dependency help with tasks

support in handling emotion/controlling impulses

guidance/information

Support systems are particularly important for families experiencing high degrees of stress. When there is a mismatch between the degree of stress and the availability/potency of support systems, the level of stress may become unmanageable. One response to unmanageable stress is child abuse. For further discussion of social networks, see community work (Chapter 3, III and IV).

One area of controversy is the "generational hypothesis", which holds that violence breeds violence, that the victim of child abuse will become an abusive parent. Although there is scant valid evidence to support this hypothesis, it is possible that if a relationship does exist, it is due as much to intergenerational transmission of social isolation as it is to transmission of violent child rearing practice [49].

Another area of debate is the relationship between child abuse and class; some researchers [47] claim that physical abuse is concentrated among poor and non-white minorities, while others [48] have found that child abusers can be of any class. It would seem that while there may be a positive correlation between material resource (class) and social resources (viable network), there is not a perfect correlation—affluent people can be "socially poor" and isolated.

## C.    Victim versus Bystander

Some children are direct victims of physical/emotional abuse, while others are bystanders to sibling abuse or wife-beating. It has been found that:

Bystanders tend to be less deviant than direct victims.

Abuse from mothers tends to demoralize children; abuse from fathers tends to anger them.

Effects of abuse are less disastrous when there are some positive aspects in the child's relationship with at least one parent.

Children who are behaviourally most deviant are (in descending order) first, those who suffer abuse from both parents, from mother only, from father only, those who are bystanders to wife abuse, and fifth, those who witness sibling abuse [83].

Children who are physically and/or emotionally abused and/or neglected often grow up to become troubled adolescents. The remainder of this chapter looks at behavioural consequences of abuse, neglect, and growing up.

## III.    THEORETICAL APPROACHES TO PRESENTING PROBLEMS

Every worker premises her or his approach to solving a behavioural problem on a set of assumptions related to causality. While the causes of human behaviour remain a matter of debate, there are at least three schools of thought around which assumptions of causality are organized. These theoretical orientations are:

> the social structural/environmental view
>
> the interactionist view
>
> the individual psychological view

These orientations are not mutually exclusive; a worker may pull from each perspective those pieces which make the most inherent sense and may reject whole chunks which are incompatible with her or his belief system and experience. There is no one panacea in the therapeutic field; thus it is in the best interests of all parties if workers are open to the exploration of a wide range of theoretical and practical possibilities.

It is critical to keep in mind that presenting problems (e.g., running away, delinquency, self-injury) are symptoms of painful situations—they relay to workers the message that something is happening in the youth's life which manifests itself in symptoms.

To illustrate the difference among theoretical orientations [73], the presenting problems of running away will be examined (see chart). Why do some adolescents run away from home?

## RUNNING AWAY: THREE VIEWS

| Social Structural-Environmental | Interactionist | Individual-Psychological |
|---|---|---|
| **Cause** | | |
| social conditions; social economic systems (e.g., economic deprivation, parental strains/stresses, alcoholism, child abuse, running) | dysfunctional interaction between the individual personality of the adolescent and her/his environment (e.g., relationship between adolescent and parents in which dynamic processes subvert the satisfaction of adolescent needs for love, security, affection) | faulty ego functioning (poor impulse control, neurosis, unresolved oedipal conflicts, severe narcissistic disorders, and/or low self-concept) |
| **Focus** | | |
| historical factors, social institutions, cultural | the parties involved in the interactional exchange | the individual adolescent |
| **Treatment/Intervention** | | |
| emphasis on modifying the social conditions which lead to neglect, abuse, rejections, etc., not on treating the individual; social/political organizing; interim measure is the provision of facilities for runaways (e.g., housing, medical care, crisis lines, etc.) | emphasis on modifying interrelationships, clarifying hidden expectations of parents, giving legitimacy to adolescent's criticisms of parents' behavior, lessening parental demands on adolescent misbehaviour and parental disapproval | emphasis on modifying the adolescent's behaviour to adapt to her/his situation/environment; adolescent is either sick (psychopathological) or bad (sociopathological) and should be either cured or punished |

## RUNNING AWAY: THREE VIEWS—*Continued*

| Social Structural-<br>Environmental | Interactionist | Individual-<br>Psychological |
|---|---|---|
| Critique of Treatment<br>  unrealistic—impossible to<br>  change the systems which<br>  create the social conditions | inadequate emphasis on social/<br>structural conditions which im-<br>pact on the family; inadequate<br>emphasis on the pathology of<br>the adolescent | (psychopathological):<br>unreasonable to impose indi-<br>vidual psychotherapy on an<br>adolescent who runs away to es-<br>cape a destructive family envi-<br>ronment or to assert<br>independence<br>(sociopathological):<br>unreasonable to involve the ju-<br>dicial system if running is a<br>*family* problem; isolating and<br>labelling the adolescent as delin-<br>quent/deviant reinforces low<br>self-esteem and loneliness |

The *social structural or sociological perspective* describes running adolescents as non-pathological, generally non-delinquent, and as products of the social/economic times in which they live. Each era is seen as bringing with it a set of reasons for the behaviour of its youth (for example, 1930s: economic hardship, high rate of alcoholism and child neglect and abuse, and a high rate of running away; 1940s: familial disruptions and hardships related to World War II and easy employment opportunities in far-off places; and so on for each era). This view turns to historical factors, social institutions, and cultural myths and attitudes for explanations of human behaviour [76].

The *interactionist or social-psychological perspective* describes running away as a coping strategy used as an escape from a destructive family situation; it may be a means of bringing to public attention the painful condition of the family. Developmentally, running can be part of a maturational process in which the adolescent seeks independence and separation from parents. Impatience to escape familial constraints may be due to the youth's rapid maturation and need for individuation, or to parental overcontrol and repression. This view emphasizes the interaction between people.

The *individual-psychological perspective* has two components: first, the psychopathological approach which describes runaways as "sick" and disordered, and second, the sociopathological/criminological approach which defines runaways as "bad"/criminal and therefore best handled (punished) by the juvenile justice system.

While there is no one "correct" explanation for running away, there may be several bits and pieces which individual workers will synthesize and thereafter employ as a guiding assumption when making decisions regarding treatment/interventions.

In this section we have differentiated among three perspectives on the causes of running away behavior. Virtually any behavior can be considered from these viewpoints.

## IV.    RUNNING AWAY

In the preceding section "Theoretical Approaches to Presenting Problems", we used as an example the behaviour of running away in order to better understand the orientation from which the problem can be explored. Because such a sizeable percentage of adolescent clients are those who have run away, or who have been thrown away, it is essential to look closely at the issue. In this section we will:

1. Examine the types of runaways described in the literature.

2. Explore the correlates reported in the literature, with special emphasis on the link between abuse and running away.

3. Note some of the warning signs of running behavior.

4. Comment on truancy as a form of running away (escape).


### A.    Types of Runaways

Runaways do not form a homogeneous group:

Twice as many females as males are reported to have run away from home (females may be more likely to be picked up by authorities or to be reported by parents for their own "protection" than males, whose acting-out, aggressive behavior is more condoned by virtue of their sex) [76].

Runaways come from a wide range of class backgrounds, although most reported cases are from lower income or lower-middle income families (under-reporting may be especially high in middle and upper-middle-class families) [76].

Runaways come from varied ethnic groups and from varied geographical locations (urban, suburban, rural) [76].

Runaways differ in their reasons for running.

Following are thumbnail sketches of various types of runaways [74]:


### TYPES OF RUNAWAYS

| Researchers | Labels | Reasons for Running |
|---|---|---|
| Homer, in Brennan et al., 1978 [73] | Running from<br>Running to | run because of family conflicts; run to seek adventure through experiences forbidden at home |
| English, 1973 [88] | Runaways | run from destructive family situation; run to call attention to the situation; run from fear of parental discovery of personal secret (e.;., pregnancy) |

## TYPES OF RUNAWAYS—*Continued*

| Researchers | Labels | Reasons for Running |
|---|---|---|
| | Floaters | tend to talk about running in order to relieve built-up tensions; usually return home within 48 hours |
| | Splitters | run because of minor frustrations; peer approval of running |
| | Hard Road Freaks | street people; severed family ties; nomad life style |
| Green and Esselstyn, in Brennan et al., 1978 [73] | Anxious Runaways | run from multi-problem family |
| | Rootless Runaways | pleasure seekers; quit school and jobs; drugtakers; sexually active; often reared with praise but no limits, they rebel and run |
| | Terrified Runaways | flee from father's sexual advances/abuse; guilt is high because they view themselves as perpetrators of the family's collapse |
| Brennan et al., 1978 [73] | Crisis Escapists | spontaneous escape from home problems |
| | Casual Hedonists | good-time seekers; return home on their own |
| | Crisis Escapists | planned, but sudden escape from home problems |
| | Pursued and Curtailed Escapists | planned and permanent split; usually leave problem family |
| | Deliberate, Independent Runaways | planned and permanent split; usually have happy episodes on the road |

## B.    Factors Related to Running Away

There is no proof that child abuse inevitably causes running behavior; however, it appears that the family dynamics in abusing families tend to be similar to those in families of runaways. In both cases:

Family members are probably highly involved in the family group, with strong affectional bonds among at least some of them.

There is considerable conflict among sub-groups; communications may be distorted.

There is likely to be task overload for one or more members (usually the mother).

Democratic decision-making is unlikely.

Adaptability to change is low.

There is a loose-knit social network, with a high value placed on independence and privacy [79].

When a crisis occurs, the network is often not notified and therefore cannot intervene; furthermore, the family's lack of flexibility makes it more vulnerable to stressor events; at this point, the family organizational problems may be brought to public attention through the behavior of a family member—for example, through running away by an adolescent.

For additional information on abusive families, see Chapters 4, 5, and 6.

The literature [73, 74] points to other aspects of family dynamics which are often associated with families of runaways. For example, in terms of discipline, parents of runaways when compared with parents of non-runaways:

> are more likely to control their child through withdrawal of love, deprivation of privileges, social isolation, and physical abuse
>
> are more likely to choose ineffective disciplining procedures, and these tend to be applied in haphazard ways
>
> are more likely to reject, use negative labelling, and show their dissatisfaction, all of which may undermine the adolescent's need for personal competence and recognition
>
> are less likely to nurture, show acceptance, satisfaction, or interest, or label positively

Parents of runaways, when compared with parents of non-runaways, are more likely:

> to be ambivalent towards conventional socialization, with a fairly high tolerance of deviance
>
> to have low self-esteem
>
> to have high social alienation
>
> to have lower demands for their child's academic achievement
>
> to be single parents

Runaway adolescents, when compared with their non-runaway counterparts:

> are more likely to have experienced transience and mobility, which creates stress through the loss of peers and supports, and through adjustment to new schools; these changes may lead to loneliness and isolation
>
> are more likely to perceive differential treatments between themselves and their siblings; this implies parental inconsistency in the application of discipline and other normative values; leads to anger, rebellion, depression, withdrawal, escape, and decreased self-esteem

are less likely to share affiliative and instrumental companionship with their parents

are less likely to have serious conflicts with parents pertaining to: choice of friends, absence from home, style of dress, smoking, drinking, drug-taking, school performance, family rules/values, and discipline

are more likely to feel that their parents do not listen to them, do not care about them

are more likely to experience stress in their lives in the form of: physical abuse, dealing with a parent's lover, being thrown out of a parental home, dealing with alcoholic and/or unemployed parent, school problems, parental conflict, separation or divorce, being placed in a children's shelter, and so on

are more likely to respond to stress by acting impulsively, having conflicts with parents, and by coping through the use of alcohol and other drugs rather than seeking advice/support from family or friends

are more likely to have lost respect for, and trust in, their parents, and therefore reject parental guidance

What emerges is a picture of pained youth. Runaways are described as feeling:

lonely, socially isolated

alienated

powerless, with lack of control over their lives

restless, bored

inadequate

unloved

These feelings often are handled in ways which exacerbate their isolation (for example, through excessive drinking and drug-taking, excessive television viewing, and chronic running away). These, in turn, may heighten feelings of depression and low self-worth.

With regard to school experiences, runaways (when compared with nonrunaways) [67] tend to experience greater conflict with teachers, to feel that teachers do not understand or like them, and are not interested in them. They feel more rejected, perceiving that failure roles are more available to them than are opportunities for occupational achievement. In addition:

They have lower marks, higher levels of truancy, more suspensions and expulsions, and a less positive attitude towards school.

They participate less in extramural school activities.

They are more often physically assaulted by other youths at school.

In terms of peer relationships, the literature [73, 74] describes runaways as:

spending proportionately more time with peers and less time with parents spending more time alone

experiencing stronger peer pressure towards antisocial attitudes/ behaviours

having friends who are more likely to have delinquent records and/or to be runaways

## C.      Warning Signs

Some investigators suggest that early warning signs can indicate the possibility of runaway behaviour. Adults who work with adolescents might pay special attention to the four strongest predictors [73]:

1. negative labelling by parents
2. absence of nurturance in parent-child relations
3. high levels of delinquent behaviour among peers (and heavily influenced by peer group)
4. negative attitudes towards school and teachers

Other possible indicators include [75]:

resentment of authority figures (parents, teachers)

resentment of over-protection and discipline

highly permissive parents

open conflicts with parents

general frustration

'antisocial attitudes'

heavy involvement with drugs

lack of self-confidence

negative self-labelling

In most cases, the decision to run is precipitated by stressful events and the adolescent is likely to feel uncertain as to her or his ability to deal with that stress. Many run from family turmoil and conflict.

## D.      Truancy as a Form of Running Away

To the extent that the truant student has absented herself or himself from school, she or he has run away from a setting and from a situation.

Three widely differing explanations for truancy are presented in the table below [86]:

## TRUANCY EXPLAINED

| Social Structural-Environmental | Interactionist | Individual-Psychological |
|---|---|---|
| **Cause:** | | |
| Both the educational and legal systems are operated by the contemporary State: what goes on in schools contributes to State control by teaching students to be "law-abiding citizens", to be punctual, uncritical, neat, and passive; the school makes legitimate only certain "kinds of knowledge" and information which reinforces the lessons of the State; students who do not conform to these stated and unstated rules are failed by the educational system; school failure affects commitments to the school and adolescent self-perceptions; thus, school *failure leads to* running away from school (truancy) rather than vice versa | A constellation of adverse features of family background lead to a constellation of anti-social behaviours which may begin as truancy at an early age, lead to delinquency, and to an anti-social adult life-style | Emphasis is on early learning experiences within the family; schooling is seen as a social "good" and an inability to accept this good is a result of a "cultural deficit" in the student and is symptomatic of a deep-seated disturbance |
| "Sub-cultural" theory: The educational system, not the student, is maladjusted to pupil needs (e.g., non-relevant curriculum, middle-class ethos, streaming, middle-class language codes); this may generate pupil deviance | | |
| "Symbolic interactionism": Schools have rules and students who break rules are *labelled* as deviant, which leads either to rebellion in the school or to retreat from the school (truancy); the school then punishes the truant: generates change in self-concept, change in behaviour (e.g., more truancy), further sanctions by school and other agencies | | |

inappropriate child rearing practices (cruel/harsh, passive/neglecting, or erratic discipline); parents showing little interest in child's education

parent unemployed; father has erratic job record

poor, crowded housing

poverty

Although there is a reported link between truancy and other forms of "delinquent" behavior, truancy does not cause delinquency; in fact, very little delinquency occurs during short-term truancy.

High-attendance schools have been compared with high-truancy schools:

### HIGH ATTENDANCE SCHOOL VERSUS HIGH TRUANCY SCHOOL

| High attendance school | High truancy school |
| --- | --- |
| small size | large size |
| lower institutional control | narrowly "custodial" in orientation |
| less rigorous enforcement of certain key rules (e.g., smoking, gum chewing) | harsh, strict rule enforcement |
| high co-option of student | isolation of the staff from potential sources of support among students and parents |
| closer parent-school relationships | |

There are many reasons why students stay away from school (other than alienation from school life and its values and peer pressure to be truant) [85]:

They are ill.

They fear school; fear leaving home to go to school.

They may need to get a job to help support the family, or may stay home to care for a sick sibling or parent, or to help with family-related chores.

Chronic non-attenders are likely to have one or more of the following key factors in their background [86]:

broken home for reasons other than death

marital disharmony

above-average number of children in the family (5 +)

one or both parents chronically ill

criminal parent or delinquent sibling

separation from parents before 10th birthday for reasons other than death or hospitalization

Truant students and their parents have also been dichotomized into:

1. Those students who:

> when absent from school are on the street versus those who stay at home

> have skills to find and hold a job versus those who are unlikely to succeed in the job market

2. Those parents who:

> support their child's nonattendance because they do not value education, or because the student fulfills a need or function for the family by staying home versus those who are as frustrated as the school with the student's refusal to "obey" [85]

Some researchers [83] have found that children who were physically abused were less likely than nonabused control groups to engage in aggressive crimes as adolescents (assault, armed robbery, and so forth), and were more likely to be arrested for escape acts (truancy, runaway). Physically abused children have a well-developed coping mechanism: escape. This is a highly functional response for the child who is being beaten, and escape may continue as a functional response to various forms of stress, including those associated with schooling.

## V.     DELINQUENCY

Adolescents served by child welfare agencies often appear as clients after they have been labelled either by the justice system, by parents, and/or by the school as "delinquent". This label implies that the youth has broken the law, is criminal, deviant, "bad."

It then becomes the task of the child welfare worker to "decriminalize" the delinquent, using therapeutic rather than punitive techniques. However, there is no coherent theory that explains why some young people steal cars, or break and enter, and so on, nor is there one theory that explains why some young people get caught while others do not. We do know from examining statistical data that:

> "Theft" is the juvenile crime most commonly charged; "break and enter," is the second most common; together they represent approximately 50% of juvenile charges in Canada.

> The vast majority of juveniles charged with offences (in all offence groups) are male.

> The age of first appearance in juvenile court is likely to be between 14 and 15 years for both males and females.

## A.    Theoretical Approaches

Why do some adolescents break the law and become delinquent? Each theoretical orientation offers its own set of explanations, some of which are set out in the following table.

### DELINQUENCY: THREE VIEWS

| Social Structural-Environmental | Interactionist | Individual-Psychological |
|---|---|---|
| a. Delinquency is a legal term for a social problem; delinquency is deviant behaviour only in so far as it is defined that way by those systems (e.g., legal and educational) which are operated by the ruling State. | a. Delinquent behaviour is a response to a dysfunctional interaction between the individual personality of the adolescent and her/his environment (particularly the parents); the adolescent's needs for love, security, and affection are not being met. | a. Delinquent behaviour is a pathological condition. |
| b. As with runaways, delinquents may be responding to abuse or neglect by parents: this abuse arises from stress created by prevailing social and/or economic conditions; the deviant behaviour is developed and maintained through the influence of peers, family, community and so on. | | b. Delinquency is passed on from one generation to another, or from one family member to another, through biological or constitutional factors ("bad seed"). |

Some researchers suggest that delinquency (in some form) is a universal phenomenon; the issue is not one of who is engaged in delinquent behavior, but rather who gets caught [83]. Some would suggest that middle-class adolescents commit as many crimes of comparable seriousness as do their poorer counterparts, but that they are not subjected to as harsh reprisals by the judicial and educational systems. There is evidence that in the case of both child abuse and delinquency, a relatively higher percentage of lower-class cases reach the judicial system; financial resources and the awareness of how to manipulate power systems result in frequent cover-ups of delinquency and of child abuse in higher social classes.

## B.    Factors Related to Delinquency

There is no proof that child abuse causes delinquent behaviour; however, there do exist indications of a connection between the two behaviours. The rate of delinquency among families in which abuse or neglect have occurred tends to be higher than among the general population. There appears to be a positive correlation between the severity of punishment experienced by children, and the aggressive, antisocial behaviour displayed by adolescents. Thus, while abuse does not cause delinquency, both are symptoms of deeper problems within the family environment and both have been viewed historically as criminal acts deserving of punishment [44, 83].

Abused children learn two things: (1) that abusive behavior is one way of child rearing; and (2) that violence is an effective and legitimate means of resolving conflicts. Abused children often feel very hostile towards their parents, and this anger is easily transferred to the rest of the world through delinquency in adolescence. As children, they have learned pro-violent norms and violent behaviours through daily interaction with their parents. Delinquent companions can also encourage delinquent behaviour; however, the adolescent's selection of peer group is (in part) a function of familial relationships—unpleasant or weak family bonds may increase the likelihood that the adolescent will be drawn to "unacceptable" peers.

Although delinquent adolescents often come from single-parent homes, they are just as likely to grow up in psychologically broken homes which were fraught with tension and which created in the child a sense of uncertainty and apprehension. Thus, a broken home is not by itself a significant component in delinquency, given that a single parent is not contributing to the strain which stems from a poor marital relationship [39].

Control problems are frequently occurring family and social problems. As a sub-category of delinquency, control problems include adolescent disobedience, and defiance of parental rules and wishes. Parents who describe their adolescents as uncontrollable may not be able to control their own lives—for example, parents with inadequate housing and income, with scant knowledge of child care skills, and with sparse and inadequate network links to family, friends, or social service resources [83].

Some parental correlates of adolescent "beyond control" behaviour include [38]:

> parents who are inconsistent in setting and enforcing rules
>
> parents who are not likely to encourage, verbally praise, or show much interest in their children's activities
>
> parents who are not likely to use reasoning and explanations in exercising discipline
>
> parents who provide inadequate supervision

Family dynamics related to juvenile criminal offenses (such as stealing) and to child neglect are strikingly similar [83]:

> Families have weak affectional bonds.
>
> There is a low task interdependence among family members.
>
> Meagre attempts are made to meet the emotional and physical needs of family members.
>
> There is a task overload for one or two members.
>
> Parents abdicate power; they are not authoritarian.
>
> Rational formal decision-making is rare.
>
> Communication is sparse and ineffective.

Social network is sparse and very loose-knit, except for the adolescent's peer group, which may meet needs unmet by the family.

The family tends to avoid outside interference by neighbors, agencies, and so on.

The one major and necessary (though not sufficient) condition for child abuse and for delinquency is isolation from powerful pro-social support systems. Additional correlates of delinquency include the following factors:

Delinquents tend to come from large families that have five or more children by the time the child reaches her or his early adolescence.

They tend to live in poor housing; their fathers tend to have erratic job records with periods of unemployment.

They are more likely than non-deviant adolescents to have criminal parents and delinquent siblings.

Their parents are reported to show poor child rearing behaviour (e.g., cruel, passive, or neglecting attitudes; erratic or harsh discipline).

Marital conflict is prevalent, as are families fragmented for reasons other than death.

They tend to come from the group of children who have been separated from their parents prior to the 10th birthday for reasons other than death or hospitalization.

In summary, adolescents who are labelled (i.e., "caught") as delinquent are likely to have one or more of the following key factors in their background:

one-parent family
above-average number of siblings
poor housing
parent(s) unemployed (or with erratic work history)


## VI.     SELF-INJURIOUS BEHAVIOURS


While workers in child welfare agencies may not be confronted with adolescent suicide attempts or gestures on a daily basis, they are likely to meet such behaviours on occasion, and it is those occasions which may be unusually anxiety-provoking for workers. Even one adolescent suicide can leave its devastating mark on a worker.

The number of adolescents who kill or maim themselves is on the rise [68]:

Suicide is the second leading cause of death (after accidents) in persons aged 10 to 20 years.

In the past 20 years the suicide rate of American youths 15 to 24 years old rose 300%.

There is an estimated ratio of 150:1 of adolescent suicide attempts or gestures to completed suicides; for adults the ratio is approximately 5:1.

Suicidal *gestures* are not attempts to kill oneself, but rather are means of communicating distress.

Adolescent gestures include making several slight cuts on the arms from wrists to elbows, or similar cuts across the chest.

Suicide *attempts* are usually intended to end in death.

The more planned the act or the more lethal the means, the more definite the intention to die.

Girls *far* outnumber boys in attempted suicides.

Boys outnumber girls in completed suicides.

Major modes of suicide are firearms, poisoning, and hanging.

Poisoning is the most common mode of suicide gesture in 15- to 24-year olds.

Self-destructive behaviour after age 6 is almost never accidental.

Accurate statistics in this field are difficult to obtain because:

1.  Many suicide deaths are reported as accidents in order to protect the family from public admission.
2.  Many car "accidents" may have been deliberate.
3.  Many drug overdoses may have been deliberate.
4.  Not all suicide attempts are reported to officials.

Self-injurious behaviours can be directly and immediately damaging to the body, as in [87]:

| | |
|---|---|
| abrading | hitting |
| biting | ingesting |
| burning | inhaling |
| cutting | inserting |
| constricting | severing |

Or self-injurious behaviors can be temporally more remote (i.e., the damage is not experienced immediately), as in [87]:

| | |
|---|---|
| alcohol abuse | obesity |
| drug abuse | refusing medical treatment |
| glue sniffing | smoking tobacco |

Workers may have few directly suicidal teenagers in their caseloads, but they are likely to spend a good part of every day dealing with adolescent behavior which, in its broadest sense, is self-injurious. For example, an adolescent who is depressed and who has been emotionally neglected for years may be detached, defiant, feeling a sense of emptiness, and involved in a variety of sensation-seeking behaviours (reckless driving, drug abuse, "promiscuity"). These behaviours may be a significant indication of deep depression and could be considered a type of suicidal or self-injurious behaviour.

## A.   Theoretical Approaches

As with most human behaviours, there is a huge array of explanations offered for self-injurious acts (including suicide), but there is a lack of coherent theory [57].

*Psychoanalytic theories* argue that suicide results from the strong assertion of an innate death urge (thanatos); that suicide is inverted murder which could not be expressed towards the other person because that person (usually a parent) is also a love object; that suicide is a means of retaliating abandonment, or of reuniting with a deceased loved one, or of confirming feelings of already being dead, or of punishing the self.

*Social-psychological theories* argue that the person who attempts suicide may perceive herself or himself to be in a hopeless environmental situation, often because of a series of losses, failures, unhappy relationships with the people she or he depends on; that suicidal acts are often genuine pleas for outside help or a way of dealing with an extremely difficult problem.

*Sociological theories* consider society (the environment) to be the main cause of suicide, in that society can create expectations, norms, pressures, alienation, loneliness, and ultimately a sense that life is not worth living.

## B.   Factors Related to Self-Injury

Factors associated with self-injury include those which are environmental and those which are individual [57].

Environmental factors include:

> social isolation
>
> stress
>
> loss
>
> abuse or neglect by parents

*Social isolation* refers to any factor which reduces or impedes the adolescent's interaction with the immediate community (e.g., frequent residential shifts; disorganized home). Many youths who kill themselves were considered "loners"; suicide rates vary inversely with the stability and durability of social relationships within a society.

Precipitating *stress* often is associated with "the five P's": parents, peers, privation, punctured romance, and pregnancy. A frequent source of long-standing stress is family disorganization, which is related to both delinquency and suicide. Delinquency and suicide indicate a desire to change or to end the social environment;

in fact, there seems to be an interrelatedness among family disorganization, delinquency, and suicide.

*Loss* is a recurrent theme associated with adolescent suicide:

> Suicide rates double in the second generation if the parent of the adolescent has committed or attempted suicide.

> In many cases there is a death or loss under tragic circumstances of a person close to the adolescent—in most cases that death/loss takes place before the youth has completed adolescence.

> One form of loss occurs when a parent leaves the family and does not maintain contact.

> In many cases, the adolescent had multiple separations from parents during the first three years of life.

The result of loss is a decrease in self-worth because loss (especially through death) is perceived by a young person as abandonment. Parental loss implies a disruption in the relationship, deprivation of the former emotional connection, and in some cases, a fear of the loss of love from the other parent due to the structural change in the family.

Loss may lead the young person to hate the love object (usually a parent) whom she or he perceives as having betrayed her or him. In order to absolve the parent, the youth assumes the burden of guilt for the loss. When the anger aimed at the parent, combined with feelings of guilt, is turned inward, the result may be self-destruction. Sometimes loss may cause identification with the deceased, and in an effort to rejoin the deceased the youth may attempt suicide.

*Abuse or neglect by parents* and marital disharmony are also often correlated with self-injury.

> Many mothers of suicidal adolescents are ambivalent about their children and have "hinted" at their negative feelings.

> Many fathers of suicidal adolescents have not supplied affection either to their children or to their wives.

> Rejection may be manifested by hypercritical discipline or by absence of parenting, which can lead to adolescent misbehaviour, more parental anger/rejection, and finally a desire to end the cycle.

> Arguments centering around separation or divorce occur more frequently in families of potential suicidal youth than nonsuicidal youth; early parent loss or the threat of parent loss through divorce seem to be a significant factor contributing to self-destructive behaviour in adolescents.

> The highest completed and attempted suicide rates tend to be among families with single, divorced, or widowed parents, whereas the lowest rates tend to be associated with strong family life.

> Self-injurious adolescents tend to experience a pattern of parental control which is characterized by either indifference, low expectations, and sporadic control, or by excessive expectations and all-pervasive control.

Extremes of parental control are highly associated with parental alcoholism, suggesting that the self-destructive behaviours of both the adolescent and the parent may be a self-perpetuating continuum.

There does not appear to be a correlation between suicidal tendencies and race, religion, or class.

Some correlates of self-injury which are related to individual characteristics include developmental stage and depression/aggression.

A general constitutional characteristic is the adolescent's *developmental stage:*

There is a sharp increase of reported suicide at the age of puberty, which may suggest that a newly awakened sex drive with attendant physical and social change can cause adjustment problems that are overwhelming.

The adolescent has a sense of personal immortality regardless of her or his stated concepts, because during adolescence one's death is so remote in time.

*Depression* is not uncommon among teenagers. It is often seen as aggression turned inward, resulting in a sense of hopelessness and poor self-esteem:

Feelings of helplessness appear to be a major factor in precipitating suicide.

Feelings of depression may not be readily apparent, since they may manifest themselves in boredom, restlessness, and preoccupation with trivia, or be acted out through delinquency, drug abuse, and so on.

The adolescent almost always keeps these feelings of depression to herself or himself.

For the adolescent who is too frightened to directly physically harm herself or himself, other forms of self-aggression may be substituted as "suicidal equivalents" (these include depression, accident-proneness, antisocial acts, neurotic physical complaints).

## C.    Warning Signs

Observable manifestations of suicidal thoughts and actions include:

a history of compulsiveness

frequent accidents

a family history of suicides or attempts

lack of planning and goal orientation

a positive response when one asks about suicidal thoughts

However, thoughts of suicide can be easily hidden. According to The American Association of Suicidology, there are four warning signs [68]:

1. A previous attempt at suicide (80% of those successful have attempted it before).

2. A suicide threat; threats can range from subtle to blatant—for example, from giving away possessions to stating: "You won't have to be bothered by me much longer."

3. Significant behavioural changes—for example, a "happy teenager" becomes morose.

4. Mental depression; physical manifestations include sleeplessness, headaches, loss of appetite, weight loss; psychological symptoms include lethargy, crying, apathy, an inability to concentrate, insistent isolation from family and peers.

Other significant risk factors are:

a pattern of drug abuse that shows a total disregard for one's physical safety

a strong identification with someone who has successfully killed herself or himself

a depression combined with an intense anger

a lack of potentially positive social supports

Unsuccessful suicide attempts may vary from the near fatal with obvious lethal intent, to a low-lethality plea for help, to very minor gestures with clearly manipulative intent. All attempts are a statement that something is very wrong in the adolescent's life which she or he feels powerless to change. Every "cry for help", no matter how remote, should be respected by adults because threats and attempts may be aspects of a continuum of suicidal behaviour which could end in death.

The most important preventive approach to self-injurious behaviour is the extension of reassurance, concern, and loving control by the worker.

(A book which deals sensitively and vividly with the treatment of self-injurious adolescent girls in care is *Self-Mutilation*, by Robert Ross and Hugh McKay, Boston: D.C. Heath and Company, 1979, 179 pages.)

## VII.   WORKING WITH ADOLESCENTS

Doing therapy is no mean feat. To begin with, there are the issues of where to direct the therapeutic emphasis and of which techniques to use. According to Smith and Glass [89], who studied the results of 400 controlled evaluations of psychotherapy, there is no significant difference, in terms of outcome, among the various types of psychotherapies. However, on the positive side, they did find that the typical therapy client was better off after treatment than 75% of the untreated individuals studied. It has been suggested that the subtleties in therapists' individual styles and techniques during the course of treatment have far greater significance than any particular theory of personality or technique to which the worker may adhere. Of importance, too, is the match of personalities between adolescent (and family) and worker, and between the adolescent's style and the worker's favoured therapeutic technique. The mass production approach in which clients are randomly assigned to whomever is available may be, in some cases, unproductive.

While many child welfare workers focus entirely on crisis intervention techniques because of lack of time to devote to longer-term therapies, most workers synthesize bits and pieces of various therapeutic procedures (e.g., TA, Reality Therapy, and so on). In fact, the list of approaches from which to select a morsel here or a bit of theory there is staggeringly long. The following list taken from Malmquist [72], categorizes numerous approaches. However, readers are encouraged to review the discussion on problem-solving in child welfare in Appendix A, and particularly those sections dealing with goals for intervention and the search for solutions.

## THERAPEUTIC PROCEDURES USED WITH ADOLESCENTS

I.   Individually Oriented Treatment
    A.   Direct Involvment with the Adolescent
        1.  Primary relationship therapy
        2.  Directive approach
            a.  Persuasion
            b.  Guidance
            c.  Attitude modification
            d.  Suggestive approaches
            e.  Rational therapy
            f.  Reality therapy
            g.  Existential therapy
            h.  Logotherapy
        3.  Abreactive approaches
            a.  Ventilation
            b.  Drug-induced catharsis
            c.  Hypnosis
            d.  Release therapy
            e.  Activity therapies
            f.  Sensitivity groups
            g.  EST
        4.  Drama types of treatment
        5.  Conditioning therapies
        6.  Ego-oriented therapies
            a.  Sector therapy
            b.  Adaptional therapy (reparative psychotherapy)
            c.  Crisis interventions (situational, developmental)
            d.  Transactional therapies
        7.  "Working-through therapies"
            a.  Psychoanalytically oriented therapies
            b.  Classic psychoanalytic approaches
            c.  Nonclassical psychoanalytic approaches

      B.   Environmental Treatments
         1.  Hospitals
           a.  Daycare
           b.  Evening units
           c.  Mental hospitals—adolescent units
         2.  Residential treatment centres
         3.  Correctional treatment centres
         4.  Group-living arrangements
         5.  Foster homes
         6.  Treatment in Schools
           a.  Special Classes
           b.  Counselling in school settings
           c.  Boarding schools
         7.  Camps
         8.  Therapeutic camps
         9.  Milieu approaches
      C.   Organic Treatments
         1.  Tranquilizers/anti-depressants
         2.  Sedatives
         3.  Stimulants
         4.  Megavitamin therapies (orthomolecular psychiatry)
  II.  Treatment Aimed at Larger Units
      A.   Collaborative therapy
      B.   Conjoint family treatment
      C.   Family-centred treatment combinations
      D.   Group therapies
      E.   Parent education training
      F.   Socio-cultural approaches
      G.   Variations of religious cults (western, eastern, altered conscious-ness, occult, and so forth)

## A.    Three Orientations

In the earlier sections of this chapter, the reader was directed towards three prevalent orientations found in the philosophical and practice literature pertaining to human behaviour. These are the social structural-environmental view, the interactionist view, and the individual-psychological view. Each worker will have approached her or his work throughout the years from one of these perspectives or from a combination thereof. The perspective adopted will necessarily have affected the worker's selection of treatment (e.g., a worker with a firm belief that "adolescent deviance" results from psychopathology (intrapsychic view) is unlikely to work towards the eradication of deviance by organizing within the community in order to bring about large-scale and fundamental changes in adolescents' living conditions).

In this section practice is divided into the three orientations and similarities and differences are examined.

*1.      Social Structural-Environmental Approach*

Workers whose values and interests lead them to assume that most presenting problems result primarily from a social structure grounded in fierce competition for allegedly scarce resources, in violence rather than cooperative effort, in mistrust, sexism, and racism, will likely be moved to attempt change in the structural foundations rather than in the individual. In Chapter 3, on community work, the critical issue of how to translate the environmental perspective into community action is addressed.

*2.      Interactionist Approach*

Perhaps most representative of this approach are family systems therapy and family-centred therapy [2, 4]:

> *Family systems therapy* treats the family as a human transactional system in distress; the adolescent manifests, through her or his symptoms, the symbolic distress of the family; the family is thus the unit of therapeutic attention; this approach maximizes any support and nurturance existing within the family; autonomy, growth, and the ability to be supportive/nurturant are difficult for the adolescent unless the family supports these processes.
>
> *Family-centred therapy* treats each member separately or in pairs, but not as family unit; this approach maximizes the separateness of the adolescent from the family and tends to weaken the support/nurturance aspects; when there is almost no support/nurturance present, this approach may be more advantageous than family systems therapy.

Goal of Family Therapy:

To help the separation of the adolescent from primary relationships within the family and to readjust her or his relationships outside the family; to see who is able to let go of whom within the family while maintaining/creating a positively supportive familial relationship; and at the same time to allow growth and autonomy without withdrawing support.

For further discussion of the family perspective and practice principles, refer back to Chapter 2, IV.

A weak parent-child bond increases tne probability of adolescent delinquent behaviour; one technique designed to help parents regain some parental control is that of behaviour contracting [14].

Goal of Behaviour Contracting:

The contract deals directly with issues of consistency, clarity of expectation, and a change in the family system from an emphasis on punishment to the use of rewards to improve behaviour.

For a general discussion of contracting, refer to Chapter 2, V, D).

Behaviorist techniques are sometimes used in modifying the behaviour of the individual, without much concern given to the family dynamic. One technique which, once learned, can be self-administered is that of self-relaxation [15].

Goal of Self-Relaxation:

To reduce emotional and somatic symptoms caused by stress, through the use of self-relaxation.

Another technique which is based on behaviourist learning theory is rational behaviour therapy, designed to change the client's habits of thinking that cause their painful emotions and to thereby eliminate their secondary acting-out behaviour; the fundamental hypothesis of RBT is that it is not facts or events that are upsetting, but the view that people take of them.

Often in residential settings the environment is geared to modify the behaviour of those who live within it. This environmental application of a behavioural model is milieu therapy, commonly implemented in hospital settings and in residential treatment centres [16].

Goal of Milieu Therapy:

To help residents through environmental manipulation (e.g., peer pressure) unlearn those behaviours learned in childhood which are no longer appropriate and to learn new behaviours appropriate to adulthood.

Goal of Mixed Transactional Model [24]:

To learn through discussion and activities to overcome relationship difficulties; since people learn through a variety of mediums (words, facial/body expressions, touch, shared experiences), these transactions cannot be dichotomized into "talking" and "doing". The task of the group worker is to identify these transactions and to see how they can be used to meet common needs.

Goal of Family Life Education Approach [37] (in the context of working with stepparents):

To prevent a repetition of family dissolution; to provide time for the couple to work on their relationship within the format of an educational experience; to help couples reassess their expectations concerning their stepfamilies; to help participants identify and cope with some of the pressures inherent in stepfamily situations; to help cut through the stepfamily's isolation; to share issues of common concern.

(For additional information on reconstituted families, see Chapter 5, X).

*3.      Individual-Psychological Approach*

Insight therapies are premised on the belief that alleviation of mental disorders and minor personality and adjustment problems is dependent upon achieving insight into the causes of present behaviour. The worker's task is to uncover basic sources of conflict.

Goal of Intrapsychic Therapy [19, 67]:

To help "patients" (medical model) understand the reasons for their present difficulties; if a "cure" can be achieved, it will be predicated on insight.


## VIII.   SUMMARY

In discussing just a few presenting problems child welfare agencies deal with, it becomes apparent that many behaviours defined by the helping profession as destructive or self-destructive (e.g., running, self-injury, and so on), are in fact behaviours of escape from a difficult life situation. Adolescence is a time when people begin to understand the meaning of their entrapment in an unhappy situation; it is also a time when people are not closely supervised and can thus act autonomously. However, adolescents do not have social or economic power, and are therefore largely dependent on adults for survival. At the same time they need, and often want, adult attention and affection.

Adults and adolescents constantly struggle to achieve a comfortable balance between their own needs for autonomy/power and protection/encouragement. For adults working with young people whose experiences have created in them extreme confusion and pain, there is the need to provide patient and loving care and, in the final analysis, to provide the client with what she or he needs.

## REFERENCES

1.  Andrews, E. "Family Therapy", Brandes, N. and Gardner M. (eds.), New York: Jason Aronson, Inc., 1973, pp. 83–100.

2.  Chase, A. et al. "Treating the Throwaway Child: A Model for Adolescent Service", Social Casework, Vol. 60, No. 9, November 1979, pp. 538–546.

3.  Friedman, A. "The Rationale and the Plan of the Treatment Method", in Friedman, A. S. (ed.), *Therapy with Families of Sexually Acting-Out Girls*. New York: Springer Publishing Co., Inc., 1971, pp. 21–36.

4.  Haley, J. *Leaving Home: The Therapy of Disturbed Young People*. New York: McGraw-Hill, 1980.

5.  Jenkins, R. "Family Therapy: Systems Approaches", in Sholever, G. P., (ed.), *Emotional Disorders in Children and Adolescents*. New York: Spectrum Publications, 1980, pp. 159–179.

6.  Johnson, J., "A Truancy Program: The Child Welfare Agency and the School", Child Welfare, Vol. LV, September–October 1976, pp. 573–580.

7.  Norlin, J. and Ho, M., "A Co-Worker Approach to Working with Families", Clinical Social Work Journal, Vol. 2, 1974, pp. 127–134.

8.  Orcutt, B. "Family Treatment of Poverty Level Families," Social Casework, Vol. 58, February 1977, pp. 92–100.

9.  Sonne, J. "Do's and Don'ts of Family Therapy", in A. S. Friedman (ed.) *Therapy with Families of Sexually Acting-Out Girls*. New York: Springer Publishing Co., Inc., 1971, pp. 66–69.

10.  Speck, R. "Some Techniques Useful with Acting-Out Families", in Friedman, A. S. (ed.) *Therapy with Families of Sexually Acting-Out Girls*. New York: Springer Publishing Co., Inc., 1971, pp. 118–123.

11. Visher, E. and Fisher, J. *Step-Families: A Guide to Working with Stepparents and Stepchildren*. New York: Brunner/Mazel Publishers, 1979.

12. Wodarski, J. and Ammons, P. "Comprehensive Treatment of Runaway Children and Their Parents", Family Therapy: The Bulletin of Synergy, 1980.

13. Burgess, A. and Baldwin, B. *Crisis Intervention Theory and Practice: A Clinical Handbook*. Englewood Cliffs, N.J.: Prentice-Hall, Inc., 1981.

14. Douds, A. et al. "Behaviour Contracting with Youthful Offenders and their Parents", Child Welfare, Vol. LVI, June 1977, pp. 409–417.

15. Elitzur, B. "Self-Relaxation Program for Acting-Out Adolescents", Adolescence, Vol. XI, Winter 1976, pp. 569–572.

16. Maultsby, M. "Rational Behaviour Therapy for Acting-Out Adolescents", Social Casework, Vol. 56, January 1975, pp. 24–38.

17. Millman, H., Schaefer, C., and Cohen, J. *Therapies for School Behaviour Problems*. San Francisco: Jossey-Bass, 1980.

18. Stuart, R. "Behaviour Contracting Within the Families of Delinquents", in Stedman, J., Patton, W., and Walton, K. (eds.), *Clinical Studies in Behaviour Therapy with Children, Adolescents and Their Families*. Springfield, Ill.: Charles C Thomas Publisher, 1973.

19. Copeland, A. "Aspects of Psychotherapeutic Technique" in *Textbook of Adolescent Psychopathology and Treatment*. Springfield, Ill.: Charles C Thomas Publisher, 1974, pp. 104–122.

20. Evangelakis, M. "Day Treatment", in Sholevar, G. P. (ed.) *Emotional Disorders in Children and Adolescents: Medical and Psychological Approaches to Treatment*. New York: Spectrum Publication, 1980, pp. 235–258.

21. Schneiderman, G. and Evans, H. "An Approach to Families of Acting-Out Adolescents—A Case Study", Adolescence, Vol. X, Winter 1975, pp. 495–498.

22. Arnold, T. and Simpson, R. "The Effects of a TA Group on Emotionally Disturbed School-Aged Boys", Transactional Analysis Journal, Vol. 5, July 1975, pp. 238–241.

23. Washington, K. "Success Counselling: A Model Workshop Approach to Self-Concept Building", Adolescence, Vol. XII, Fall 1977, pp. 405–410.

24. Waterhouse, J. "Group Work in Intermediate Treatment", British Journal of Social Work, Vol. 8, Summer 1978, pp. 127–144.

25. Adams, D. "Adolescent Residential Treatment: An Alternative to Institutionalization", Adolescence, Vol. XV, Fall 1980, pp. 521–527.

26. Carson, W. "A Canadian Therapeutic Community for Disruptive Youths". International Journal of Offender Therapy and Comparative Criminology, Vol. 17, 1973, pp. 268–284.

27. Jenkins, R. "Running Away and the Treatment of the Runaway Reaction", in Sholevar, G. P. (ed.), *Emotional Disorders in Children and Adolescents*, New York: Spectrum Publications, 1980, pp. 607–613.

28. Leher, P. and Kris, A., "Combined Use of Behavioural and Psychoanalytic Approaches in the Treatment of Severely Disturbed Adolescents", Seminars in Psychiatry, Vol. 4, May 1972, pp. 167–170.

29. Lewis, M. "The Undoing of Residential Treatment: A Follow-up Study of 51 Adolescents", Journal of Child Psychiatry, Vol. 19, Winter 1980, pp. 160–171.

30. Maloney, D. et al. "BIABH: Regional Adaptation of the Teaching-Family Model Group Home for Adolescents", Child Welfare, Vol. LVI, January 1977, pp. 787–796.

31. Neill, R. B. "Gestalt Therapy in a Social Psychiatric Setting: The 'Oil and Water' Solution", Adolescence, Vol. XIV, Winter 1979, pp. 775–796.

32. Phillips, E. "Achievement Place: Token Reinforcement Procedures in a Home-Style Rehabilitation Setting for 'Pre-Delinquent' Boys", in Stedman, J., et al. (eds.), *Clinical Studies in Behavior Therapy with Children, Adolescents and Their Families*. Springfield, Ill: Charles C. Thomas Publisher, 1973, pp. 226–243.

33. Taylor, J. et al. *A Group Home for Adolescent Girls: Practice and Research*. New York: Child Welfare League of America, Inc., 1976.

34. Tuss, C. and Greenspan, B. "The Transmission and Acquisition of Values in the Residential Treatment of Emotionally Disturbed Adolescents", Adolescence, Vol. XIV, Fall 1979, pp. 471–480.

35. Zaslaw, G. "Intensive Secure Treatment for Children and Adolescents", Child Welfare, Vol. LVI, September/October 1977, pp. 529–536.

36. Anderson, G. "Enhancing Listening Skills for Work with Abusing Parents", Social Casework, Vol. 60, December 1979, pp. 602–608.

37. Pill, C. "A Family Life Education Group for Working with Stepparents", Social Casework, Vol. 62, March 1981, pp. 159–166.

38. Robinson, P. A. "Parents of 'Beyond Control' Adolescents", Adolescence, Vol. XIII, Spring 1978, pp. 109–120.

39. Maskin, M. and Brookins E. "The Effects of Parental Composition on Recidivism Rates in Delinquent Girls", Journal of Clinical Psychology, Vol. XXX, July 1974, pp. 341–342.

40. Sack, W. H. "Children of Imprisoned Fathers", Psychiatry, 40, May 1977.

41. Campbell, M. and Cooper, K. "Parents' Perception of Adolescent Behaviour Problems", Journal of Youth and Adolescence, Vol. 4, December 1975, pp. 309–320.

42. Gutierres, S. and Reich, J. "A Developmental Perspective on Runaway Behaviour: Its Relationship to Child Abuse", Child Welfare, Vol. LX, February 1981, pp. 89–94.

43. Rutter, M. The Qualities of Mothering: Maternal Deprivation Reassessed. New York: Jason Aronson, 1972.

44. Lystad, M. H., "Violence at Home: A Review of the Literature", American Journal of Orthopsychiatry, Vol. 45, April 1975, pp. 328–345.

45. Ackley, D. C. "A Brief Overview of Child Abuse", Social Casework, Vol. 58, January 1977, pp. 21–24.

46. Kadushin, A. Child Welfare Services. New York: MacMillan Publishing Co., 1974.

47. Gil, D. Violence Against Children. Cambridge, Mass.: Harvard University Press, 1970.

48. Laskin, D. M., "The Battered Child Syndrome", Journal of Oral Surgery, Vol. 31, Dec. 1973.

49. Justice, B. and Duncan, D. "Life Crisis as a Precursor to Child Abuse", Public Health Reports, Vol. 91, 1976.

50. Maurer, A. "Corporal Punishment", American Psychologist, Vol. 29, August 1974, pp. 614–626.

51. Shamsie, S. J. (ed.) Youth: Problems and Approaches. Philadelphia: Lea and Febiger, 1972.

52. Kent, M. O. "Remarriage: A Family Systems Perspective", Social Casework, Vol. 61, March 1980, pp. 146–153.

53. Schulman G. L. "Myths That Intrude on the Adaptation of the Stepfamily", Social Casework, Vol. 53, March 1972, pp. 131–139.

54. Goldmeier, J. "Intervention in the Continuum From Divorce to Family Reconstitution", Social Casework, Vol. 61, January 1980, pp. 39–47.

55. Smith L. "A Review of Crisis Intervention Theory", Social Casework, Vol. 59, July 1978, pp. 396–405.

56. Duncan, J. W. "The Immediate Management of Suicide Attempts in Children and Adolescents: Psychologic Aspects", The Journal of Family Practice, Vol. 4, No. 1, 1977.

57. Miller, J. P. "Suicide and Adolescence", Adolescence, Vol. X, Spring 1975, pp. 11–24.

58. Schlachter, R. "Home Counseling of Adolescents and Parents", Social Work, Vol. 20, November 1975, pp. 427–428, 481.

59. Larson, C. and Talley L. "Family Resistance to Therapy: A Model for Services and Therapists' Roles", Child Welfare Vol. LVI, February 1977, pp. 121–126.

60. Smith, J. "The Early History of West Indian Immigrant Boys", British Journal of Social Work, Vol. 1, 1971, pp. 73–84.

61. Peck, D. "Adolescent Self-Esteem, Emotional Learning Disabilities, and Significant Others", Adolescence, Vol. XVI, Summer 1981, pp. 443–452.

62. Carp, J. "Youth's Need for Social Competence and Power: The Community Building Model," Adolescence, Vol. XVI, Winter 1981, pp. 935–952.

63. Gourse, J. and Cheschier, M. "Authority Issues in Treating Resistant Families", Social Casework, Vol. 62, February 1981, pp. 67–73.

64. Tolson, R. and Brown, L. B. "Client Dropout Rate and Students' Practice Skills in Task-Centered Casework", Social Casework, Vol. 62, May 1981, pp. 305–313.

65. Fiedler, P. et al. "Effects of Assertive Training on Hospitalized Adolescents and Young Adults", Adolescence, Vol. XIV, Fall 1979, pp. 523–528.

66. Saxon, W. "Behavioral Contracting: Theory and Design", Child Welfare, Vol. LVIII (8), September/October 1979.

67. Lamb, D. Psychotherapy With Adolescent Girls. San Francisco: Jossey-Bass, 1978.

68. DenHouter, K. "To Silence One's Self: A Brief Analysis of the Literature on Adolescent Suicide", Child Welfare, Vol. LX, January 1981, pp. 2–10.

69. Lourie, I. et al. "Adolescent Abuse and Neglect: The Role of Runaway Youth Programs", Children Today, Vol. 8, November–December 1979, pp. 27–29, 40.

70. Michaels, K. and Green, R. "A Child Welfare Agency Project: Therapy for Families of Status Offenders", Child Welfare, Vol. LVIII, March 1979, pp. 216–220.

71. Margolin, M. "Styles of Service for Runaways", Child Welfare, Vol. LV, March 1976, pp. 205–215.

72. Malmquist, C. Handbook of Adolescence. New York: Jason Aronson, Inc., 1978.

73. Brennan, T. et al. The Social Psychology of Runaways. Lexington Mass.: Lexington Books, 1978.

74. Roberts, A. "Crisis Concepts Applied to Adolescent Runaways and Nonrunaways", Ph.D. Thesis, Microfilms International, Michigan University, 1979.

75. Cull, J. and Hardy R. (eds.) Problems of Runaway Youth. Springfield, Ill.: Charles C Thomas Publisher, 1976.

76. Kosof, A. Runaways. New York: Franklin Watts Publisher, 1977.

77. Derrick, D. Bibliography of Youth, Youth Work and Provisions for Youth. National Youth Bureau, England, 1976.

78. Miller, D. et al. Runaways—Illegal Aliens In Their Own Land: Implications for Service. New York: Praeger Publisher, 1980.

79. D'Angelo, R. Dialogues on Key Issues Relevant to Runaway Youth Programs and Policies. Columbus, Ohio: Ohio State University, School of Social Work, 1974.

80. Van Houten, T., "Life Stress: A Predictor of Adolescent Running Away", Ph.D. Thesis, Michigan University: Microfilms International, 1979.

81. Lipsitz, J. Growing Up Forgotten. Lexington Mass.: Lexington Books, 1980.

82. Sugar, M., (ed.), Responding to Adolescent Needs. New York: SP Medical & Scientific Books, 1980.

83. Hunner, R. and Walker, Y. E. (eds.). Exploring the Relationship between Child Abuse and Delinquency. Montclair, New Jersey: Allanheld, Osmun and Co, Publisher, 1981.

84. McIntire, M. and Angle, C. (eds.) Suicide Attempts in Children and Youth. New York: Harper & Row, 1980.

85. White, R. Absent With Cause. London: Routledge & Kegan Paul, 1980.

86. Herson, L. and Berg, I. (eds.) Out of School: Modern Perspectives in Truancy and School Refusal. New York: John Wiley & Sons, 1980.

87. Ross, R. and McKay, H. Self-Mutilation. Boston: D. C. Heath and Company, 1979.

88. English, A. and Bock, R., Got Me On the Run: A Study of Runaways. Boston: Beacon Press, 1973.

89. Smith, M. L. and Glass, G. V. "Meta-analysis of Psychotherapy Outcome Studies", American Psychologist, Vol. 32, 1977, pp. 752–760.

# 11

# Adoption: Problems and Related Practices

**GREG CONCHELOS**

I. INTRODUCTION                                                    324
II. RECRUITMENT AND ORIENTATION                                   326
III. ASSESSMENT                                                    328
    A.  Criteria                                               328
    B.  The Rejected Client                                   330
IV. MATCHING ADOPTIVE FAMILIES WITH CHILDREN                      331
    A.  Characteristics of Families                           331
    B.  Characteristics of Adopted Children                   335
V. EXPANDED OPTIONS FOR PLACEMENT                                 338
VI. POST-PLACEMENT SUPPORT                                        343
    A.  The Need                                               343
    B.  Selected Dynamics in Post-Placement: The Romance
        Fantasy                                          344
    C.  Telling                                               344
VII. POST-ADOPTION                                                346
VIII. TRENDS IN ADOPTION                                          347
    A.  Drop in Availability of Babies                        347
    B.  Increased Role of Biological Parents                  347
    C.  Use of Groups                                         348
    D.  Independent Adoptions and Private Agencies            348
    E.  Rise of Lay Organizations                             349
    F.  Scientific Developments                               349
    G.  Adoption by Single Persons                            350
    H.  Elective Adoptions                                    351
    I.   Open Adoption                                        351
IX. SUMMARY                                                       351
    REFERENCES                                               351

## I.    INTRODUCTION

This chapter summarizes prevalent concepts and issues in adoption, with the goal of providing a comprehensive picture of adoption processes. It is organized around the major stages of adoption and practice. These stages are presented in terms of two themes—ecology and permanency. Adoption practice is affected by many personal, organizational, and societal factors. Each contributes to the likelihood of permanency for a child who has been separated from her or his parents.

The first section briefly discusses the organizing ideas. Subsequently, each of seven stages in adoption is discussed: recruitment, orientation, assessment, matching, placement, post-placement support, and post-adoption. Of these, considerable attention has been given to matching and placement. The chapter concludes with a discussion of the major trends now influencing the development of adoption. It may be useful to review the two earlier chapters on foster care (Chapters 7 and 8), particularly those sections dealing with permanency planning, when placement is appropriate (7, II), potential stressors (7, III), recruitment (7, IV), education and training (7, VI) and the separation process (8, III).

Adoption as an agency service can be divided into seven somewhat overlapping stages. Recruitment and orientation are the first two. In order for an agency to attract prospective parents it must alert the public to the needs of children and provide ways of allowing interested parties to make initial contact. Usually, general information is provided.

Orientation involves work with those who have expressed further interest. Through printed material, audio-visual media, and meetings, an agency educates applicants about the adoption process.

Perhaps the most challenging stages for agency and applicants alike are those of assessment and matching. Assessment of applicants attempts to determine their basic suitability, using a range of criteria from health to attitudes and values. Assessment presupposes that the agency has developed clarity and relative priority of such criteria—a difficult task.

Closely related to assessment is matching. Children available for adoption are assessed when they come into care, and the relative needs and strengths of child and applicants are compared. (In this chapter the importance of these stages is reflected in the extensive attention given to characteristics of adopting families and of adoptees.)

Placement is the result of such matching. It involves making the practical arrangements for the child's transition to the new family. It is more than a technical task since it involves acute sensitivity to the social, emotional, and other kinds of changes family and child begin to undergo. The next stage, post-placement support, is gaining attention. For a matter of months, or even years, the agency (and other sources) can provide both supervision and nurturance to family and child as adjustments are made. Among other things, this can involve identification of resources needed for support, monitoring of change objectives, and liaison by agency personnel as resource brokers.

Post-placement support involves a legal aspect: after a stipulated period an adoption is finalized legally; however, support can continue well into the post-finalization period.

Another salient aspect of adoption is the interest adoptees and natural parents have in learning about each other. This has been called post-adoption. Some agencies provide help to interested persons by giving basic legal and social information about contact with each other. In addition, the agency or other organizations may develop practical procedures by which adoptees or natural parents can explore the possibilities of learning more about each other or of meeting in a non-threatening way.

While both agency organization and research on adoption tend to treat these stages as somewhat separate and self-contained, they are very much inter-dependent and mutually contributory to a permanent placement. From the ecological point of view of child development, all stages are components of a broader environment which either helps or hinders the child's search for a satisfactory replacement family.

The present chapter proposes a particular viewpoint on adoption. This view, referred to as permanency, or permanency planning, is an attempt to respond to serious pitfalls in current adoption practice.

Permanency planning refers to the placement of a child with a family in the most direct manner and with the greatest chance of a permanent union.

Permanency can be seen as having three aspects: direction, momentum, and speed. At all points, from the time of leaving her or his natural parents, the agency must make decisions on the child's behalf which help move the child toward a permanent, adopting home. Permanency may not always be achieved. For example, for either accidental or deliberate reasons, a child may be "rotated" through several institutions: perhaps there is a long stay in a hospital for a medical condition; perhaps review procedures are not carried out quickly or according to law.

All of these aspects of adoption programs may turn the "straight" path from natural family to adopting family into a circular, or delayed, or even dead-end path. It is conceivable that a child may never reach an adopting home while still a minor. In such a case, permanency is not achieved, largely due to intended or accidental practices which were not viewed in terms of permanency.

This notion of "linear direction" is the essence of permanency. Two other aspects are momentum and speed. Where a direct, continuous "critical path" has been maintained in a given casework situation, it is desirable to keep the process continuous, with few needless, prolonged interruptions. Similarly, the process should be as speedy as possible, while still considering the child's needs.

While most of this appears to be common sense, the reality of day-to-day casework may obscure whether a given practice, at a given stage of the adoption process, is really contributing to or hindering permanency. Viewing practice in terms of permanency helps workers to remain critical of both how a particular step in the adoption process is being understood or construed and how choices in practice are being made.

In this chapter, the focus is upon how specific practices may or may not contribute to adoption permanency. However, the idea of permanency is not specific to adoption. In order to create a lasting family situation for a child, a worker has to draw upon resources outside of those normally associated with adoption. For example, a child may have been in one or more foster homes before placement. The choice of parents, frequency of review, and other factors influence whether a child's capacity for permanent adoption is increased or weakened. Without this view, even a well-designed adoption service will be limited in its effectiveness.

Any one stage of adoption contributes to the overall effectiveness of the adoption process. Consequently, the effectiveness of one stage influences the effectiveness of subsequent ones. For instance, recruiting families on the basis of their accessibility rather than their parenting experience may result in more applicants, but perhaps fewer well-qualified ones. This "pool" of parenting resources will surely influence criteria for assessment and other subsequent developments in adoption, such as increased rates of adoption breakdown in the post-placement stage.

A given stage in adoption consists of several factors, the nature of which will determine the likelihood of permanency. For example, recruitment outcomes are shaped by applicants' demographic characteristics, agency's financial situation, legal aspects of adoption, administration of a recruitment program, and the characteristics of various media used in recruitment campaigns. There may be others.

The condition or quality of these elements may help or hinder workers in the successful recruitment of appropriate adoption applicants. For instance, the intensity and frequency of the media messages to which the public is exposed may have a positive effect. Prospective families may have anxieties about the legal aspects of adoption which must be broached during the recruitment stage. If an agency does not respond to enquiries quickly, then public interest drops off.

The idea of permanency can be applied to the two tasks which confront adoption workers—understanding the nature of the particular adoption stage or situation at hand, and selecting and carrying out practices suited to it. This chapter discusses what is known about the major stages of adoption for the purpose of understanding what may or may not contribute to permanency.

## II.    RECRUITMENT AND ORIENTATION

Finding prospective adopting parents and helping them to learn about adoption are critical and challenging tasks. The current view is that virtually all children available can be adopted. Recruitment and orientation involve finding a family that will meet the specific needs of a particular child. There seems to be very little value in the notion of "general types" of families or children.

Elements of permanency enter at this stage. Recruiting a broad range of parents with high commitment results not only in more placements, but in fewer adoption breakdowns.

Effective recruitment and orientation require a close matching between the agency and the public. For instance, parents themselves have special needs or styles; a rigid or even too-uniform public relations approach may result in either missing or discouraging appropriate applicants. In one study it was found that black parents were recruited in proportionately smaller numbers than white parents [10]. This was attributed to the ways in which contact was made with the black community. Success in recruiting black parents may be related to whether or not the agency has a "black" image to offer [29, 30].

With regard to orientation, similar challenges exist with particular target applicants. For instance, even when recruited, there is a tendency for ethnic minorities to withdraw from the orientation or application process in proportionately greater numbers [10]. Again, the hindsight practical impression is that an agency must incorporate community habits or values into this stage of adoption: Are people more comfortable with an "ethnic" worker? Do they prefer or need after-hours meetings? How much does the approval or disapproval of friends in networks or neigh-bourhoods affect applicants' interest in adoption? These and other questions indicate the detailed attention which an agency can and must pay to "courting" even one community segment. Such attention can yield greater numbers in recruitments and more successful orientations.

For instance, community-oriented recruitment in Northern Ontario involved visits to Native Indian reserves. While the staff represented the agency, strong em-phasis was placed on visits to homes, the Band Council, teachers, and other groups. A number of prospective adopting parents became interested in adoption, presumably because the recruitment style closely matched community preferences.

The use of media can be a major step in this direction since it can be economical, concrete, direct, and tailored to market segments. "Today's Child" and other newspaper and video approaches show marked success in finding parents for children with special needs.

Recruitment means day-to-day adjustments of strategies as responses fluc-tuate [28]. Do people prefer to dwell on a child's face, or accompanying text (as in a newspaper)? Is repeated exposure important to viewer schedules (daily cable-TV announcements)? How quickly does an agency follow up an enquiry (days or weeks)? Are enquiries handled in person or via taped answering service?

Potential adopting families do a great deal of exploring even in the early stages of adoption, such as during recruitment. Legal responsibilities and uncertainty about the financial costs of adoption are examples of the kinds of concerns they have [60]. While it may appear more appropriate to discuss these concerns with them later in the adopting process, treating them in the publicity stages of recruitment could be useful.

Tailoring of recruitment and orientation to public needs requires time and money. For instance, budgets enlarge enormously in decentralized storefront opera-tions, TV spots are expensive, and the agency may need a media liaison. Some events need not be expensive, however. Adoption parties have now been successfully used to orient applicants to the children who are available. In one case, 14 children and 30 couples attended; there were games and food. Couples and children could interact without feeling self-conscious. In some cases, the event allowed couples to think through and change their preferences in children.

If the rationale of increased permanency through better recruitment and orientation is realized, some of these approaches may be worthwhile. It is important to identify the aspects of this stage of adoption which contribute to increasing adop-tion permanency.

Perhaps recruitment and orientation provide the most obvious examples of the ecological aspects of permanency. In the context of the broader community, the adoption agency is a social organism alongside other parties and forces. It cannot gain community interest and educate entirely on its own terms. Its strategies must incor-porate cultural, ideological, economic, and other kinds of factors. The broader the focus, the greater the chances for permanency.

In the following discussion of assessment and matching, many examples relate particularly to "special needs adoptions". These cases are particularly challeng-ing to assessment and matching processes, and for this reason are good for illustrative purposes. Agencies with few special need cases may not experience nearly the same assessment and matching difficulties.

## III.    ASSESSMENT

Assessment of parents and child, and subsequent matching of the two, are perhaps the most complex tasks in adoption. Workers and parents are being asked to imagine how this potential chemistry might work.

It is important to keep in mind that a major assessment (or reassessment) may have taken place before the adoption assessment begins. That is, the child may have been assessed during several stages since leaving the biological family.

There may be many qualified persons available who can offer assessment advice pertinent to matching. Beyond the professional realm, these may include birth parents, foster parents, and perhaps even former adopting parents. Whose opinions **are** accepted in the assessment/matching process is critical; this fact emphasizes the highly collaborative nature of arranging adoptions.

### A.    Criteria

A number of issues have arisen regarding the assessment of prospective adoptive parents. On an administrative level, practical issues such as fees, a waiting period, and fertility tests (now falling into disfavour) have been cited as assessment criteria. Families may be needlessly turned away from adoption by such things, whether or not the agency is conscious of their use in this manner [45]. Infertility as an assessment criterion has been particularly contentious for two reasons. First, it can be an emotionally trying experience if workers persist in dwelling on it. Secondly, there is a growing trend toward elective adoptions by fertile couples, who adopt for reasons other than biological ones [45].

Until recently there was emphasis upon objective criteria for assessment, such as:

> age of applicants
>
> religion
>
> race
>
> employment status of mother
>
> residency [28]

In addition, other factors such as capacity to pay fees were involved, depending on the agency's own needs.

These criteria have limitations. First, they are "rough cut", touching on only the most obvious characteristics of applicants [28]. Secondly, the applicants' highly specific qualities may be more important in relation to a child's needs.

Few studies indicate which criteria are really useful in assessment and matching. Findings permit only very general conclusions, such as "good parenting characteristics cannot be predicted", or "only a few factors of bad parenting have been identified" [79]. Some believe that professionals assess for prolonged periods and to needless depths.

In the actual matching process, agencies must necessarily depart from their ideal standards of applicant characteristics [50]. Usually this begins by dropping certain non-functional criteria (e.g., religion), in order to enhance the likelihood of placement [45, 50].

In short, institutional factors such as availability of applicants may limit the use of assessment criteria regardless of how well they might predict permanency in adoption [50]. This is not to deny the value of a continuing search for good assessment procedures, but rather to acknowledge both their current primitive state and the forces acting upon them.

There has been some discussion about the function of assessment. Historically, an adoption worker has taken on an evaluative role, attempting to pass judgment on the suitability of applicants. More recently, however, there is interest in using the assessment stage as an educational opportunity as well. The worker acts as an educator, helping applicants to learn more about themselves and about what adoption will entail [35, 99], particularly when adopting older children. While there are no clear indications of the success of this new thrust, it did grow out of the response to the one-sided, intellectualized styles of assessment which have characterized many agencies. Agencies are increasingly coming to respect the decision-making abilities of their applicants.

A paradox results when the key parties in adoption seem structurally locked out of the placement process. "Work with the child" and "selection of the families" are seen as separate activities. Coordination of the two activities is traditionally weak in most agencies which favour the traditional match-maker concept. One writer expresses the paradox:

> The potential partners in a life-time commitment are expected to remain on
> the periphery, without any communication, until the decision-makers and
> negotiators have made their selection [5].

Methods have been developed by which to make applicants comfortable in the early stages of assessment. Clients are more cooperative if time is taken to clarify the way in which things will proceed.

In one instance, a meeting was held and only applicants high on the waiting list were invited in order to avoid false expectations. Numbers were limited to eight couples. A social worker was employed at intake so as to ensure good screening. The 1½-hour meeting focused upon alleviating discomfort, the common concerns of agency and clients, and clarifying assessment criteria. There was emphasis upon the need for considerable self-examination as part of the assessment process; the leader tried to draw upon the experiences within the group as much as possible. There was clarity about what could not be handled in the group, and advice was given when an issue indicated a need for counselling outside of the group.

There is at least one comprehensive assessment approach which takes the broader context into consideration [104]. Emphasis is upon intensive self-assessment by applicants, using structured experiences. The approach focuses upon ecology (the relationship of people to their environment) and family systems theory (the family as a dynamic balance of interacting relationships). For a fuller discussion of the ecological perspective, see Chapters 1 and 2 and Appendix A, II. Also, Chapter 2, IV discusses the family perspective and family assessment protocols.

Basically, the first step involves engaging or contracting, in which worker and clients develop a congruence of expectations about the process. The next step is to construct an ecological map; this is a detailed diagram of the applicant's social world: church, recreation, school, health care, and so on. These indicate strong, tenuous, or stressful relationships. Areas where the client's energy flows out or in are also indicated. These are interpreted in terms of adoption planning.

Another device is the genogram, which shows the development of the family over time (e.g., the influence of family members). It is discussed in a way similar to the ecological map discussion.

A third stage is family systems analysis. Adoption is viewed as an event during which the family will be temporarily unbalanced. Certain questions are asked: What is the nature of the boundary around the family? What is the structure of family relationships? How do family members communicate? What are the family rules and roles?

These are discussed in order to make applicants concretely aware of the implications of the adoption.

## B.    The Rejected Client

A special area of concern in assessment is the rejection of applicants. They may be turned down as early as the recruitment stage, or as late as the assessment stage. While rejected clients are unlikely to have further involvement in the adoption process, two considerations are important:

> On an ethical level, there is debate about the quality of explanation owed to them [45]; even the application stage is a crucial personal investment, and agency response can be needlessly abrupt.

> On a practical level, the agency's public image can be improved by having the rejected clients leave on amicable terms and well-educated to agency policy. They may be chief resources for others seeking adoption.

A number of reasons for rejecting an applicant have been identified. These include:

> advanced medical or physical disease
>
> interest in the prestige or "differentness" which an adoption may bring
>
> the wish to replace a child if one's own has been lost
>
> the potential that the adopted child will be used as an object for unresolved hostility
>
> the hope that adoptive parenting will improve one's mental health (e.g., cure loneliness; avoid depression through responsibility)
>
> compliance with well-meaning social pressure (competition with the Joneses who have adopted) [4]

While these reasons are much more sophisticated and penetrating than simplistic criteria, they only begin to illustrate the kind of motives which can be involved in seeking a child and which can be a cause for rejection.

There is growing support for the idea that rejection itself is a social process, and one which the agency should help clients to work through [53]. It can become an occasion for new changes and growth; groups have been found useful for this because applicants tend not to feel as isolated or self-punished when they can choose to share their feelings [61].

Three general considerations are worth noting when handling rejection. First, it is useful to let the person take an active part in working through rejection [4]. This is in some opposition to the natural reflex of agencies and workers, who want to retain control of the process in such tension-filled, somewhat negative situations.

Secondly, it is useful to be explicit as to why an applicant was rejected [53]. There is some debate about this, of course, but secrecy or surface explanations do not provide a service to the client who may be ready for change.

One change-oriented approach is to actually engage the client in learning to grow, even in the light of rejection. The worker limits the discussion only to that which is concretely known about the client, and avoids clinical inferences. Where possible, she or he refers to direct observations of how the parents interact with their children so that concrete ideas, rather than abstract ones, are discussed. This avoids abstract conflicts between the client and the worker. Separate interviews with each parent may be useful.

The result may be that such active, supportive rejection encourages clients to pursue resolution of their problems by other means (e.g., contact with other agencies).

A final point relates to the worker's ability to deal with applicants' rejection. If agency and worker are not candid with each other about the worker's tolerance for an unsuccessful attempt at one stage of adoption, then abrupt closure or overly clinical explanations may result.


## IV.    MATCHING ADOPTIVE FAMILIES WITH CHILDREN

The current trend in adoption is to assess prospective adoptive parents with a view to matching their particular strengths and weaknesses with those of the child. Similar traits are not necessarily assets; e.g., a socially active, outgoing family may have more to offer an insecure, inward-oriented child. In fact, matching has been described as the process of establishing reciprocal relationships. Close studies of adoption successes support this approach [58].


### A.    Characteristics of Families

Matching can be discussed in two broad sections: the characteristics of adoptive parents and those of the child. The adoptive relationship is a product of these two factors. As will be seen, these are not purely personal in nature, but indicate how broader forces in history and the environment come to influence permanency in adoption.

Failure in permanency has been labelled "adoption breakdown" which refers to the inability of family and child to maintain a relationship. Breakdown may happen relatively soon after placement, or many years later (the adolescence of the adoptee is a particularly critical time, and breakdown of "old" adoptions is prevalent at this stage). A term related to breakdown is "disruption." This has been applied to breakdown in the placement stage, before the adoption is legally finalized [89].

In adoption breakdown or disruption of placement, impressions are gathered about the characteristics of family and child. These incorporate a range of factors which are crucial to successful matching.

As with other demographic characteristics, age as a criterion for adoption is now given less weight in parental suitability than in the past. There are some indications that age does not affect adoptees' adjustment or achievement in school [41]. On the other hand, adoption failure has been linked with older parents or those who have been married longer [48]. The evidence is not comprehensive enough to indicate patterns.

There appears to be general agreement that higher-income families are more likely to adopt. There is less clarity as to how income levels affect adoption permanency. Higher material standards and good education standards appear to be a necessary but not a sufficient condition [65]. Of importance here are the subtleties of definitions of class. Since lower-middle class and blue-collar families constitute a major source of adoptive and foster care families, economic elements may require more distinctions than have been used in current adoption research and practice. For instance, it may be that ability to manage money and the steadiness of employment are more important factors than absolute level of income [33]. Much more needs to be done to adequately define the economic indicators of adopting families before relationships between these and permanency can be determined.

Adoption agencies are quick to gather and study evidence about applicants' skills if they are already parents. These data may be more reliable indicators of suitability than verbal reports or personal references, which tend to be more remote than actual day-to-day dealing with natural children.

Applicants may have:

> no children
>
> one or more natural children
>
> one or more adopted children

Having children may or may not be an asset. Although there is some evidence of a higher incidence of adoption breakdown in cases of childless couples [45], one recent Canadian study found no difference [19].

A tendency has been identified within some agencies to favour parents who have already adopted [10]. At work here is the assumption that adoptive parental experience is an even more desirable requisite than that of natural parental experience.

Other agencies may take a less pragmatic view. Limited sources of certain children (e.g., white babies) may prompt agencies to give lower priority to applicants who already have natural or adopted children in order to make them available to those with none [10, 45]. Arguments raised against this have been twofold: (1) applicants with children are simply more experienced, having had their own; and (2) placing a child with a childless couple may be too isolating [45].

The structure and function of the large family have been viewed in terms of what it may offer adopted children. Certain characteristics of large families have been identified:

There is less "personal" parental interaction with each child.

There is more tolerance for deviant behaviour.

There is a greater variance of values held between parent and child.

Parents have high satisfaction in their parental roles.

One or both parents tend to see parenting as a full-time role.

There is less emphasis upon material wealth [94].

In short, large families may provide a rare mix: an opportunity for intense interaction of siblings, but within a protected social group—a sort of "surrogate society".

Some adoption professionals may ignore the strengths of large families because of the tendency to associate large families with lower-middle class status, and possibly more limited child rearing capacities [94].

Large families have been suggested for children who:

are cautious in forming emotional attachments

have experienced frequent moves

need social orientation, training, and discipline

need environmental stimulation and language development [94]

They are not recommended for children who:

are close in ages

are acting out

have some strengths which might lead to competition among siblings

have serious behaviour problems [94]

There are several dimensions to parental status and it forms a critical area in matching. Closely related to general family characteristics are those of the siblings.

The presence of siblings has been construed as an important determinant of adoption outcome. However, findings are mixed: in some cases the presence of siblings is less of an influence upon adoption permanency than is parental attitude [65]. Siblings arriving after the adoptee may make no difference [44]; those arriving earlier may have a positive influence [44]; the presence of *any* siblings may have a positive influence [44], or a negative influence [48]. In one case, jealousy by natural siblings, present before the adoption, contributed to breakdown [91]. It may be that the more siblings, adopted or natural, the greater the risk of breakdown. Whatever the situation, workers should think in terms of adopting families rather than adopting parents.

Infertility has been a primary reason for couples to seek adoption. This is less true now that elective adoptions have increased [27]. Still, childless couples bring to adoption feelings about their inability to have children, and this may influence the choices for permanent adoption.

In North America, it is estimated that 10% to 15% of all married couples cannot conceive. Another 10% to 15% have experienced repeated spontaneous abortion. About 50% of cases of infertility are attributed to the man, 30% to the woman, and 20% to a combination of conditions in both [56].

Infertility has several effects on marital life:

a possible decision to remain childless

anxiety about medical investigation of the problem

crisis in one's sexual identity (e.g., loss of masculine or feminine self-image)

anger toward those who can conceive; a feeling of injustice

use of the issue to focus upon unrelated emotional hurts

a process of mourning which may be long-term

fear of divorce

difficulties with pressure from relatives and community values; a sense of isolation from those who have children [56]

While infertility tends to be a reason for seeking adoption rather than an influence on adoption outcome, professionals are concerned about indirect effects (e.g., resolution of feelings about infertility may colour one's view of one's adopted child). However, more systematic investigations are needed.

Another aspect of childless adopting parents is their relationship with their *own* parents. Among a group of 80 infertile couples attending a clinic, those most likely to find adoption acceptable were the ones who perceived their own parents to have been happily married [42].

In a study of 395 adoptive couples, four areas of child rearing were explored with regard to negative childhood experiences. Those who had severe childhood deprivation problems did not differ significantly from those who did not. The four areas were:

1. The degree of inconsistency in discipline.

2. The process of telling the adopted child about adoption.

3. The experience of stress when helping the child in developmental tasks (e.g., school work).

4. The use of counselling services for family problems [88].

It appears that parents with deprived backgrounds are as resilient in coping with adoption stress as are those who are not deprived.

Some researchers would suggest that parental attitudes are more salient than age, income, education, or class in promoting permanency.

Acceptance of one's parental role, as well as positive satisfaction in it, have been considered as key factors [58]. More specific aspects include the need for a parent to be warm and affectionate towards the child [58], and ability to provide both emotional security and discipline [65]. Parents' ability to relate well in a variety of situations may be important [86]; other aspects of such a stance of flexibility include adopting parents' attitudes towards each other, childlessness, and towards the natural mother [39]. An open attitude towards illegitimacy has been noted as helpful [65], as well as an absence of parental demands for gratitude [65].

One source indicates that adopting parents are generally no more punitive than natural parents. Adopting families have been found not to differ significantly from non-adoptive families in attitudes towards authority [22].

There is a highly complex interaction of attitudes found within the pre-adoptive family system; attitudes appropriate to adoption are likely to occur in:

> Families (adults and children) who have demonstrated an ability to tolerate stress within their family system.

> Marital couples who have been able to make a commitment within the bonds of a relationship.

> Families (adults and children) who have exhibited some ability to tolerate differences in terms of behaviour and/or depth of relationship [19].

Several parental characteristics have been associated with adoption failure. While not defined, basic incompatibility, especially between mother and child, has been suggested as a decisive factor [43]. A large sample of adoptive families indicated that the adopting parents' inability to accept the child in general terms was a major reason for the breakdown [91]. Rigid religious views have been noted as a danger in one long-term study, although these views may not have actually caused failure [65].

A number of indicators do not directly involve the adopted child. For instance, illness of the adopting mother, general marital problems, and the inability of the extended family to accept the child [91] have been cited as reasons. Negative factors such as these, however, may have only limited influence.

Negative characteristics may simply be the lack of positive characteristics, or they may represent a mismatching in which family needs are not being met (e.g., parents want physical closeness from a child who has been abused and who does not want it) [19].

Particular causes of impermanency demand more study.

## B.    Characteristics of Adopted Children

Permanency in adoption results from the successful combination of two factors: (1) available resources of adopting families, and (2) the needs of adopted children. Although children tend to be characterized in terms of their needs, there are many factors which contribute to the "chemistry" created between them and their adoptive parents.

As contributing factors are reviewed, an ecological perspective should be maintained. Some factors are local or particular to the child, such as physical illness. Others relate to the history of that child's development. Examples of these are the number of pre-placement moves, or the mental health of the natural parents. Even larger-scale factors, such as race or culture, should be recognized.

The chances of an adoption remaining intact must be seen as a composite result of combined small and large-scale factors. Everyday adoption practice may treat only one factor, or a few at a time, but planning for permanency would appear to be a collaborative, agency-wide, even community-wide process which tries to deal with all levels: personal characteristics, family background, and societal attitudes.

There seems to be no age-related pattern. One comprehensive view concludes that: "Placement of an adoptive child should be undertaken as early as possible though there is still disagreement as to whether this means during the third and fourth weeks of life rather than during the first or even second year" [9]. Others support age two years as a critical point, where adoption problems greatly increase [48, 65]. Still others argue that at present no clear relationship between age at time of placement and permanency has been established [44].

Two studies [44, 49] of large samples of adoptees in adulthood indicate no relative difference in general adjustment—during or after adopted family life—based on age and number of moves. It may be that healthy feelings of identity were established through experience in relating to many people through multiple moves [59]. Therefore, an important factor in good adjustment may be the child's stage of development at the time of adoption.

It could be that age is only a surface factor. Older children are likely to have been abused more, put through more moves, and so on. In such cases, age may merely reflect the presence of these more direct influences upon permanency.

Sex, like age at time of placement, may be more of a surface factor to which culture and family dynamics have tied fundamental psycho-social pressures. Limited information prevents a clear picture at this point.

There is some indication that adopted boys are at a greater disadvantage than girls. This has been manifested in problems with peers, defiance, aggression, and in other ways. It may be that adopting parents tend to have a better attitude towards girls [9, 44].

Adopted boys have been found to be more vulnerable to emotional problems. Explanations have pointed to:

> the degree to which they perceive parental anxieties about them
>
> their ability to cope with rejection by natural parents
>
> their ability to deal with the need to know their origins

Medical conditions are among the chief reasons for non-placement, given the prevalent preference for healthy children. In addition, medical conditions may greatly influence the outcomes of adoption. As with any children with special needs, parents need special kinds of support [40, 55], including links to lay organizations, medical services, and others. Early placement [32, 5] and a detailed knowledge of the child's medical history may be crucial [40].

The medical condition itself, however, may not be a central factor in parents' satisfaction with adoption [32]. One possible reason for this may be the tendency to focus upon the child's intrinsic worth [32] rather than upon societal or family-imposed values or aspirations.

There is mixed evidence about the relationship of adoption to a child's emotional difficulties [100]. In some studies, adopted children have been found over-represented in clinical populations (e.g., seeing psychiatrists) [89]. In other studies, they have been labelled as more aggressive or anti-social [76].

Adopting parents may tend to see differences in an adoptee, and to attribute these to her or his being adopted [44]. This perception is somewhat related to a persistent difficulty which adopted families encounter with outsiders; that is, the adopted child is "pointed out" by friends or neighbours. This pattern can add to difficulties about "differentness". It can be even more serious if the family tends to foster differentness within its own confines.

Another dimension is discipline styles. Some believe that choice of styles is not an indifferent element in emotional development; one claim is that psychological discipline improves development of conscience and that this may relate to emotional development [58].

Adoption has been viewed as a way to halt maltreatment of the child and as a way of providing a limited substitute for the birth family. Adopting parents are usually cautioned that there may be limits to the extent to which their efforts can undo the effects of maltreatment. However, some evidence indicates that more can be accomplished than had been previously believed. Several explanations have been offered for reversibility. One has been the therapeutic character of the adopting family. Another has been the simple fact of removal from deprived circumstances [49]. For a review of considerations pertinent to the adoption of physically or sexually abused children, see Chapter 7, VI.

The third explanation relates to the child's characteristics, rather than those of the adopting family. Kadushin has described this as the child's general "constitution", as assessed immediately after birth. This includes "activity, adaptability, distractibility, persistence, mood, intensity of reaction to stimuli, and threshold of responsiveness". Evidence is offered which shows that this and the parental or family characteristics mentioned above account for surprising gains and adjustments even following massive deprivation. This indicates that constitution, if reliably assessed, may be a key characteristic by which to match and place children. One theorist has devised a typology of three kinds of children, divided by sex, each having specific characteristics in infancy. These are:

*Difficult males:* irregular biological functioning; negative and violent reactions to new situations; fussy, sensitive to environment

*Slow-to-warm-up males:* response to new situations is with initial mild negative reaction; eventual acceptance; no temper tantrums

*Easy males:* easy to be with; not overactive; easy in reactions to new situations, or to changes in environment

*Difficult females:* not as many indicators as for males; difficult temperament—frequent temper tantrums; difficult reactions to changes in environment, e.g., to hunger; unlike males, do not show fussy behaviour, but more overactivity and distractibility

*Slow-to-warm-up females:* timid in pre-school, not hyperactive; fearful in infancy

*Easy females:* none of the negative traits mentioned; even-tempered, accept new food easily [101]

One firm conclusion was offered: "Membership in the 'difficult' group predicted later childhood behaviour disorder in both sexes" [64].

Others also argue that some estimate of pathology is possible as early as 6 months of age. However, normalcy was not easily predictable [83].

Ascertaining types of constitutions needs to be distinguished from its use in assessment, and much development is necessary in each area.

These aspects of the child's background can be handled using specific methods for matching strengths and weaknesses of applicants and child. Giving the child's history is a critical process. History-giving is intended to improve the decision to place and to eventually provide the child with knowledge about the natural family.

Considerations that make the history-giving process more effective are the following:

> *Careful choice of material to be presented:* Avoid vagueness, similarity or difference with adopting parents, physical appearance.

> *Ways of presenting material:* Avoid focussing upon the child, rather than the background material; new issues may be raised (e.g., applicants' unresolved feelings about illegitimacy; need to keep worker's own values clear and distinct).

> *Participation:* Adopting parents may or may not want to use the history-giving as a time to disclose more about themselves.

> *Hereditary pathology:* There is danger of overplaying a minor pathology; worker needs to clarify own feelings about heredity; needs to focus on what is truly known—hard scientific data—or to point out the present lack of it.

> *Child's wish to know her or his background:* Also important are adoptive parents' feelings about child's wish to know it.

## V.    EXPANDED OPTIONS FOR PLACEMENT

The primary goal of child welfare agencies is the provision of resources by which family breakdown is either prevented or remedied. The principal thrust, then, is to help families either remain intact, or to re-build. The second line of defence is the use of foster or institutional homes as interim solutions until this can happen. When re-building the natural family is no longer possible, only then is adoption considered [45].

There is now a growing view that permanency must not be perceived as an either/or condition. One response has been to develop intermediate care situations which have the potential to become totally permanent. Several are discussed below.

One issue to keep in mind when discussing placement is its comparability to the natural family setting which it tries to replace. One position emphasizes the differences: an adopting family can never be a truly natural family to the adopted child [82, 102]; there is no adoptive "parental instinct"; social networks such as neighbours cannot supply the same education to them which they do to natural families, for adoptive parents require entirely new education about their roles [82].

Another position emphasizes the positive aspects of adoption. While the adoptive family may be different from the natural one, it is inaccurate to judge it in terms of its likeness to it. Rather, an effective adoptive family may be so *because* it is different, even superior in certain respects [45]. This relates to the idea of reciprocal matching, in which families have to compensate for certain greater-than-normal needs of the adopted child.

Debate continues as to the value of comparing adopting families with other families. There appears to be value in viewing both the differences and the similarities.

*Group care* (as opposed to family-based care such as foster homes) is a floating resource into which a child may pass both prior to and after adoption (breakdown). Since large numbers of children may return to it, it is still a necessary feature of the adoption process. Group care is likely to remain prominent in the process, especially for older children. It supports and feeds other placement practices which are more directly related to permanency.

In earlier periods, when adoption was not as common (or at least was not a formal social service), infants were the chief population. Now the majority are those who are handicapped, are members of ethnic or racial minorities, or simply older. Debate continues as to whether group care has a positive use. While it has a clear role as a fall-back service when it is not possible to restore the child to the family, some argue that it should be used as a deliberately planned stage before restoration, and especially adoption [68]. Others disagree [77]. For a fuller discussion of residential child care, see Chapter 9.

Foster family care has been the predominant alternative to restoring the child's own family; if there is hope of restoration, foster care is seen as the preferred interim solution. This places adoption as the third choice, to be resorted to only when restoration has been deemed impossible.

Foster family care has been defined as "boarding out with a view to adoption" [90]. It has become a main conduit or source for adoptable children. In the United States, for example, of 500,000 children in foster family care, 300,000 have been considered adoptable [45]. Foster family care, especially if it has been repeated or long-term, is both a major part of a child's history and a valuable resource for ideas pertaining to matching and placement. It has also been proposed that the recruitment and orientation of foster parents and adoptive parents be done together [45]. This view challenges the "pigeon-holing" of services which some agencies, struggling with time pressures, tend to foster. In an effort to respond to clients' needs and capacities, agencies have attempted to create new forms of care. One example of this is preadoptive foster family care.

Pre-adoptive foster family care is an arrangement in which foster parents actively consider the possibility of adoption from the beginning of the placement [62]. It is a way of allowing families to concretely explore adoption by removing two blocks: (1) concern over finances; and (2) concern over legal responsibility. The process of making a legal and financial commitment to the child, as their adopted child, becomes a longer-term, more gradual process [1, 96, 98].

Other characteristics of pre-adoption have been noted:

> It can be used when there is impermanancy, but where there is a chance of permanency (that is, the child may still not be legally freed from natural parents but it is likely that this will happen).

> It minimizes the number of moves to which the child is subjected.

Courts may be more prone to free a child for adoption if something more than normal foster care is in the offing:

There have been indications that stronger bonding between foster parents and child develops when adoption is a possibility [45].

However, there may be disadvantages to pre-adoption foster care:

There is a chance that the child may not be freed, putting both parents and child in an emotional bind in a situation of extreme uncertainty.

Presently, foster parents are not selected in the same way as are prospective adoptive parents—if anything, foster parents are selected with a view to imminent separation; however, a few agencies have begun to select foster parents who will accept the risk of pre-adoptive status.

If a child is adopted, payments for foster care may stop; such payments can be a major aid and incentive to child maintenance [45].

One proposed solution is to make pre-adoptive status time-bound: it is dropped if permanency cannot be resolved by legally freeing the child for adoption [45].

Pre-adoptive foster care is a particularly good example of creating "hybrid" child welfare services. By being more sensitive to certain ecological factors (e.g., economics, culture), it increases chances for permanency. A fuller discussion of foster care is provided in Chapters 7 and 8.

There are certain social forces such as race and culture which are related to social class in North America. The success of adoption practices depends upon how effectively these are taken into consideration by adoption agencies. The welfare of minority group children is determined by several influences, some possibly antagonistic (e.g., between agency and community values).

Children of certain racial and ethnic minorities constitute the majority of children who are waiting to be placed [52]. Many wind up in foster family and group care entrapped in a circle of impermanency. One response to this has been to de-emphasize racial and cultural matching in placements [51]. In the late 1960s, this resulted in an increase in agency efforts in transracial and transcultural adoptions [36, 45].

On the other hand, some groups prefer to adopt directly through relatives and friends rather than through agencies [18]. For some, adoption by grandparents is a regular practice. Adoption statistics for minority groups may be misleadingly low because informal adoptions are not reported. Adoption agencies must address not only their own needs and those of their clients, but also those of the community. For example, with the growth of transracial adoptions in the early 1970s, black social service professionals took a strong stand against what was for them another case of class domination by whites. They believed that the black community should be the chief advocate of the black child; they rejected the white model of such advocacy, namely, the predominant role of the adoption agency [18, 45]. This is an example of arguing for a cultural alternative to the traditional institutional form of child welfare.

According to some activists, transracial and transcultural adoptions are no less dangerous than impermanency, such as prolonged foster family or group care. For minority activists, such adoptions result in:

> loss of one's cultural identity
>
> loss of the survival skills one needs as a member of a minority
>
> loss of cultural and linguistic abilities needed in order to live in one's minority community [47]

The overall charge is that transracial and transcultural adoption leads to genocide through assimilation.

Critics of the militant black position have raised three points:

> Assimilation is a fact in North America; genocide is too strong a word given its normal historical use.
>
> A position advocating racially or culturally matched adoptions will deprive thousands of children of adoption permanency, in this case those who may need it most.
>
> Survival skills needed either in the broader society or one's own community group cannot be guaranteed by racially or culturally matched adoption [18].

In Canada, Native Indians have been particularly vocal in expressing potential dangers to their culture from transracial adoption. Native control of child welfare services has been strongly advocated and is about to begin in Northern Ontario.

The concern for permanency has meant that there is a great deal of support among professionals who see transracial and transcultural adoption as a way to achieve it [38]. They also argue that many intermediate solutions—group homes, foster family care, and quasi-adoption—are ultimately damaging. Many activists disagree.

This debate is far from over. Perhaps it is useful to avoid fixation upon ideology from either side, since the welfare of minority children is not a matter of opinion but rather of historical, class, economic, and social forces, in addition to the more obvious forces of agency policy and parental preferences. The agency can address this issue only if it sees itself within the context of its broader environment.

Debate aside, it is possible to present some impressions about those who attempt adoptions of children from minority groups. White couples who have adopted black or mixed-race children:

> are in the higher socio-economic levels (e.g., professionals) [70]
>
> have religious or humanitarian motives for adoption
>
> tend to be more isolated from their families
>
> tend to be more detached from their communities (i.e., are more self-contained as a family unit)
>
> tend to be less ethnocentric than the population average
>
> had parents with liberal child rearing attitudes [33]

As in the case of pre-adoptive foster care, the economic element of adoption is important. Through subsidies, agencies have attempted to respond to the economic environment of adopting parents in several ways [96]. Two main motives of permanency are at work here. First, at the recruitment stage, subsidies may remove a major obstacle to increasing the pool of prospective parents, particularly from lower socioeconomic levels [31, 34]. Second, in the post-placement stages, subsidies increase the family's general capacity for practical support of the child (food, clothing).

There are several kinds of subsidies, including combinations of them:

They can be short- or long-term (from several months or until the child reaches majority) [2].

Adoption fees can be waived.

The child's board can be paid partially or in full.

Medical, clothing, or other allowance payments can be involved [98].

Possible support services, such as casework, can be provided [57].

While subsidies have been used for a long time and are still strongly favoured [38, 45], there is some debate as to whether this is better than long-term foster care. Advantages of subsidized adoption, on one hand, have been articulated:

The adopting family takes on a full commitment for better or for worse, thereby eliminating the possibility of re-placement.

The biological family cannot re-enter the child's life, with consequent confusion.

The agency can reduce its caseload in that its relationship ends.

A child is relieved of being constantly reminded of her or his foster care status by a succession of staff personnel and is offered permanent belonging to a family whose name the child takes.

Relationships become more clearly defined among agency, family, and child.

Adoptive parents benefit from concrete evidence of the agency's confidence in them.

A subsidy can relieve adoptive parents of some budgeting strain, thereby facilitating family life [2].

On the other hand, there are advantages of long-term foster care:

The teamwork relationship between foster parents and staff may keep many more services "on line" for a longer period, thus augmenting adjustment and growth of parent and child.

More general ego-support is available for the foster parents.

The child can entertain a number of choices about the name she or he uses, acquiring knowledge about the past, learning the reason for foster care placement, and so on.

A child can retain personal bonds with others in the biological family. [2]

Some sources indicate that subsidies are less costly than foster care [72, 87]. Others have noted that a major advantage of increased subsidies is success in placing minority children or ones with medical problems [87].

Some feel that the debate is still open and, while subsidies are promising, more systematic investigation is needed [80].

Quasi-adoptions are very similar to pre-adoptive foster care and subsidized adoptions, but with less emphasis upon the certainty and formality of the adoptive process [87]. Some define quasi-adoptions as foster care with specific supports from an agency, depending upon the particular needs of the family [45, 63]. There have been general indications of success [1, 2].

The quasi-adoption strategy is also directed towards addressing economic and social ecological factors in the recruitment and post-placement stages.

Permanency has been enhanced by aiding prospective adoptive parents who, under traditional assessment criteria, would be considered marginal in eligibility.

There is the following information about the kinds of children placed in quasi-adoption:

They have had more foster-home placements than other children in care.

They have had longer stays in foster care institutions in their infancy.

They have had more abuse or neglect in their history.

In their family placement settings, however, they did not significantly differ in other ways from children who were normally adopted [63].

Some have argued that applicants who are of marginal eligibility tend to settle for children who are harder to place. This has been of great concern in the adoption field.


## VI.    POST-PLACEMENT SUPPORT


Agencies have taken an increasing role in providing help for parents during the post-placement period by linking them with various community services and groups (e.g., adopting parents groups, medical services, and others).


### A.    The Need

Some people involved in adoption believe that agencies give parents too little help in resolving post-placement conflicts. This is a critical issue because, until finalization, the post-placement stage puts liability upon the agency. Clearly, agency involvement in post-placement is important, particularly in the first few months [79].

Assistance may take many forms, but a key aid is giving parents an opportunity to talk out their initial difficulties in adjustment. Another consideration is that, while agencies may believe that much of their work is completed and that post-placement is mainly a monitoring stage, parents may highly value very frequent visits by a worker [35]. Both the worker's probation and helping roles are useful here [35]. In the post-placement stage, parents may come to view the agency as a therapeutic symbolic parent, that is, as a parent to them [59].

In many ways, post-placement is similar to the recruitment stage although they fall at opposite ends of the adoption process. In post-placement the agency is confronted with opportunities, and often demands, to be more involved in the community. It can initiate lay-support groups, influence policy in other helping services, and legitimize the adoption experience to the broader community on behalf of adopting parents. The agency then is a broker or co-ordinator of services.

For a discussion of post-placement needs and services in foster care, see Chapter 8.

## B.      Selected Dynamics in Post-Placement: The Romance Fantasy

In addition to the characteristics of family and child, there are processes or events in the adoptive relationship which determine the likelihood of permanence. Three of these are briefly discussed here.

The family romance fantasy refers to a child's dreaming about real or imagined "other parents" who would treat her or him better than do the adoptive ones. This is a dynamic which occurs both in natural and adoptive families. There has been some concern that, because an adopted child actually has two sets of parents, the never-present-but-real natural parents make it less easy for the child to let go of this fantasy once conflicting feelings about the adoptive parents are resolved. (Central to resolution, or discarding of the fantasy, is the child's increased identification with the present parents.)

While the fantasy is seen as a stage, something naturally-occurring during identification with parents, there is the possibility that parental behaviour can complicate it by threats (e.g., return to agency or natural parents [84]). Such threats may cause a fixation at a stage which would work itself out if it were not especially highlighted.

## C.      Telling

Telling the child that she or he is adopted has been described as the "most difficult, most troublesome, unique aspect of adoption". Some reasons for this are that [102]:

It forces parents (if they were childless) to acknowledge their infertility and their status as adoptive parents.

It threatens the exclusiveness of the relationship between the adoptive parents and the child.

It raises the question of sexuality, with which some parents may be uncomfortable.

It raises questions concerning which other publics should be told.

As an aid to workers who counsel adoptive parents about telling, Kadushin presents the following "principles of telling" [102]:

1. The child's receptivity to the fact of adoptive status is best assured if the parents themselves accept it and are convinced of the importance of telling.

2. The child needs be told at one time only as much as he or she can understand, so that telling is a gradual process.

3. There will be many opportunities to tell the child, and repetition in different contexts is useful. Everyday use of the word, when appropriate, helps make it comfortably acceptable.

4. Overemphasis, like avoidance, has some dangers. Telling children they were chosen may burden them with the need to live up to excessive expectations.

5. The parent must take the initiative in offering information about adoption.

6. Sharing of such information is not likely to threaten the relationship between adoptive parents and children if the relationship is an essentially positive one.

For additional readings on "telling", see McWhinnie [65] and Ansfield [3].

Adolescence may be complicated by adoption. Four areas of trouble have been identified:

the "family romance" fantasy

resolving the oedipal struggle

resolving identity crises

learning control of one's impulses [89]

As mentioned earlier, adolescence is a time when the likelihood of adoption breakdown may increase. It has been attributed to the need to define one's identity more clearly at this stage, both in personal terms and in terms of societal expectations of adulthood. The breakdown may not be the result of adoption factors, but rather other elements, including the normal course of adolescence.

This illustrates the need to find ways by which to distinguish dynamics which are germane to adoption from those which are not.

Older children may need particular help in the post-adoption stage. An approach has been to apply crisis intervention practice to this situation. One objective is to help the family view itself as a dynamic system (drawing upon family systems theory). Another is to emphasize and build upon family strengths in times of crisis.

If a child is adopted during the adolescent phase, then the family's desire to incorporate her or him as part of the family may conflict with the adolescent's developmental need to be a person in her or his own right.

Several strategies are used:

Help the family to become aware that the arrival of an older child will disrupt the family's balance for a while, and that this is normal.

Help the family to assess its current strengths and weaknesses.

Always deal with the whole family, not individuals.

Two techniques are used:

The family systems approach, in which the family is asked to discuss the adoption's impact in detail (e.g., who will lose their accustomed places in the family?); the family is helped to modify its previously healthy functioning in order to accommodate the adoptee.

Crisis intervention, in which accommodation is developed during an intensive, short period (4 to 6 weeks); focus is on family's definition of the crisis; the family does the major decision making; weekly contacts are made and the telephone is used for support; other adopting families are used as support groups.

A fuller discussion of the dynamics and problems associated with adolescence is presented in Chapter 10.

## VII.    POST-ADOPTION

Most stages in adoption are seen as necessary, and taken as a sequence, lead to or "add up" to permanency.

In some cases, a person who has lived happily in an adoptive family may still feel a sense of incompleteness. The adoption experience has failed to complete her or his identity. Consequently, there may be a search for one's natural parents.

Debate continues as to whether agencies should offer assistance in this process [45]. As the stages of adoption are seen as more closely interrelated, post-adoption, old adoptions, or re-unions are also seen as part of a lifelong adoption process [97].

With growing support for the right to know about natural parents and offspring [65, 67] debate has also centred around the degrees of confidentiality allowable among agency, adoptee, and natural parents. (Post-adoption searches may be initiated by natural parents as well, although it is much less frequent.)

Re-union with a parent is not necessarily the goal of searches. An adoptee may desire only more information, not personal contact.

There is evidence that during post-adoption many adoptees may need to talk about their natural parents. In terms of searching, there is some evidence that:

Good or bad adoption experiences are not connected with the motive to search.

Those persons with good adoption experiences have less weighty goals (e.g., to satisfy curiosity, or to fill in missing information).

Those with poor experiences may seek personal contact or more of a relationship with the natural parents [92, 97].

The post-adoption stage is a significant part of the adoptive process, and not simply a catch-all of after-effects. It is clear that it can involve the true completion of the adoption process, and may involve many segments of the community.

## VIII.   TRENDS IN ADOPTION

Just as adopting parents and child move through stages of agency services in adoption, the agency finds itself moving through stages and changes. Demographic changes, the rise of lay organizations, and other trends constitute new aspects of the environment in which adoption services must begin to operate. As a result, agencies may cease being the central "home base" for adoption. A few major trends are noted below.

### A.    Drop in Availability of Babies

Far fewer babies (i.e., children aged 18 months or less) are now available for adoption. Several factors have contributed to this:

Contraception and abortion are more widely available [15, 45].

Mothers are more likely to keep, rather than surrender their infants [15, 45].

There is an increase in adoption by relatives [18].

There is an increase in private adoption agencies.

However, this drop in availability has not meant a decrease in the numbers of hard-to-place children; these have increased [45]. The result is that agencies are confronted with a much more difficult task than even a decade ago—the task of continually educating the public.

### B.    Increased Role of Biological Parents

Some parents are demanding and being given increased recognition and roles in adoption, while others wish to remain removed from the process. One source notes that unwed mothers may view prolonged contact with agencies as a punishment rather than as a support in the relinquishment process [71]. Some mothers may strongly want to meet the adopting parents, although at present the percentage tends to be small [78].

Until recently fathers have largely been ignored in adoption, although changes are being made. In one program, agency policy insisted on the father's involvement prior to the adoption; the result was more effective matching [13].

While the issue of natural parents' rights is a crucial one, it is also critical to be aware of those processes which slow down or prevent freeing of the child for adoption, and are thus at odds with permanency planning [45]. To date, parents have been kept on the periphery of most of the adoption procedures. However, family service workers are developing creative new ways in which they can be more involved. A discussion of the interaction between natural and foster families is provided in Chapter 8, Section V.

## C.    Use of Groups

In adoption work, the prevalent use of the one-on-one casework counselling approach has been significantly tempered during the 1970s. Agencies are now using group settings in all stages of the process [6, 7]. A number of largely positive aspects of group work have been uncovered [73]. If well implemented, groups can be useful in aiding the main functions of adoption practice, including the provision of support to adoptive parents.

First, workers have found that groups allow applicants a greater role in their own selection as adoptive parents. This has meant that it is easier for both workers and applicants to allow those who are ineligible to withdraw with dignity [37, 69]. Others have found that groups reduce applicant anxiety mainly because people feel less alone when they can check out the "normalcy" of their concerns [37]. Encouraging applicants' mutual aid has been mentioned as another aspect of this [7].

In addition, sometimes cultural issues or issues related to hard-to-place children [81] can be better handled in groups [73, 74]. Finally, groups improve the content of home studies by enhancing discussion and/or through using experienced adopting parents [25, 99].

Groups seem to work best when there is one central problem being discussed rather than a broad, diffused agenda, and where participants are more similar than different (in income, education, and so forth) [66]. They seem not to work well when a person is dealing with a severe problem [66]; in such cases they are used in conjunction with casework counselling.

Although groups do not necessarily save staff time, they can be useful because they draw upon resources and dynamics modelled on society; as such, they replicate an ecological layer similar to personal networks; in addition, they show the potential for overlap between and among practice approaches. Detailed discussions of group work in other child welfare contexts are provided in Chapters 4, Part 2, "Practice Guidelines", IV; 5, IX, XI, XIII; and 9, VIII.

## D.    Independent Options and Private Agencies

Although reports conflict, there may be an increase in the initiative which applicants take in adoption. Agencies are finding that independent adoptions are on the rise. In such cases, interested parties are seeking out children on their own through doctors, lawyers, and informal networks. Related to independent adoptions is the increase in the number of private agencies. While these are likely to charge higher fees, they have become attractive too. One reason for this is that public agencies are perceived as too slow or even obstructive in the adoption process [8]. (Bureaucratic procedures and technical conditions, such as religious eligibility requirements, have been given as examples). A shift in the kinds of children available has made it difficult for agencies to balance "supply and demand", especially for those wanting white young children [14]. At present, public agencies need a wider group of parents from which to draw in order to provide permanent homes for those children who are not young and white.

These trends demand a final note regarding ethics, standards, and child protection. While independent adoptions and private agencies increasingly supplement the services of public agencies for certain segments of the "adopting public", public agencies still bear much responsibility regarding the quality of these adoptions. One example is the need to ensure that post-adoption support is available in adoptions "brokered" by independent professionals. This remains an area in which public agencies will need to develop new policy responses.

## E.      Rise of Lay Organizations

There has been increased self-organization by the adopting public; for example, in Ontario, Parents Concerned with Adoption staged its own conference in 1982. There are now specialist groups for single adopting parents [45], and foster parents organizations.

Lay organizations are educating their members about adoption and are creating their own policies, opinions, and wisdom. They have made adoption clientele increasingly skilled in such areas as initiating appeals on eligibility, the use of media, and the use of research, in order to take issue with "rules of convention" in agencies [95].

These lay organizations are demanding an increasing voice in agency policy and operations. Their demands serve to emphasize the wider and more complex social environment in which adoption takes place; there is almost a civil rights tone to many aspects of adoption today. The legal system has come to reflect various levels of interest groups within adoption; these include natural parents' rights, adoptees' search for parents, and childrens' rights [45]. Agencies may find themselves in increasing conflict with legal institutions.

## F.      Scientific Developments

A very recent trend is the involvement of a third party in the production of a baby; a woman consents to carry a child for a couple. This may involve the need for "parents" to formally adopt the child from the surrogate mother, as happened in Ontario in 1982. Science is providing new ways by which to define natural parenthood and adoption, and for the first time in history the lines between the two are becoming blurred.

Technologies such as test-tube births and sperm and egg banks may have

profound implications for post-adoption processes, re-unions, and the adoptee's identity. Biological links become very tenuous indeed with such innovations.

These trends exemplify the challenges placed before agencies in the 1980s
and 1990s, and show the increased involvement of other parties as part of the overall
pattern.

## G.    Adoption by Single Persons

Permanency has generally signified a permanent two-parent family, but
adoption theorists and practitioners are being asked whether it is possible to find
permanency in other family forms. Single and separated or divorced persons, many
with no children, are requesting adoption. Agencies are not totally resistant to this
new clientele (depending on the supply of applicants at the time), and especially since
such applicants will consider children with special needs [19, 38].

One major source of such one-parent families is single women. One study
found that single women seeking adoption:

> were not usually previously married
>
> may or may not have had other children
>
> were well above the average in income
>
> were well above the average in education
>
> were generally older than married adopting women

(average age 35) [24, 25]

Several reasons were given for their interest in adoption:

> Being pregnant and single is complicated socially.
>
> There is no willing or preferred man to father a child.
>
> There is a need to share one's life with a child.
>
> One has surplus resources (money, time) which make adoption

feasible [25].

Personal issues in adjustment tended to include:

> a greater strain on income
>
> feeling exhausted (a 24-hour responsibility)
>
> experiencing one's own temper and the need to control it

Social issues included:

> more restriction on dating
>
> finding out that, to professional friends, the child is out of place at

social events [25]

Of final consideration are the kinds of post-placement supports desired. Several needs are prevalent:

> establishing or finding groups for single parents
> finding ways to expose the child to male influences
> getting counselling on maternal issues
> getting counselling on the child's behaviour or concerns
> arranging daycare
> getting subsidies [25]

## H.       Elective Adoptions

There is a trend away from infertility as a central issue. Some people are now choosing to adopt because they have chosen not to have their own children, and the reasons for this are increasing as life-styles change [27]. For example, agencies are beginning to accept homosexual parents as adoptive parent possibilities; in the Province of Quebec several of these adoptions have taken place.

## I.       Open Adoption

In the U.S.A., there is at least theoretical acceptance of, and in some cases actual experimentation with, "open adoption". Such cases would involve contact between adopted older children and their biological parents and/or siblings. Also, open adoption may include contacts between children and former foster families, where established relationships existed.

These alternatives make it clear that the forms of adoption are rapidly increasing, reflecting societal changes in general.

## IX.       SUMMARY

This chapter described the major issues involved in the several stages of the adoption process. Of special importance were (a) the inter-relatedness among these stages, and (b) the fact that these stages involve the total community in addition to parents, children, and agency. As such, an ecological, or environmentally-oriented view of adoption is justified. The ability of agencies to provide permanency for children through adoption may be determined by how successfully theory and practice continue to take into account these increasingly inter-dependent relationships.

### REFERENCES

1. Andrews, R. "Permanent Placement of Negro Children Through Quasi-Adoption," Child Welfare, Vol. XLVII, December 1968, pp. 583–586, 613.

2. —— "When Is Subsidized Adoption Preferable to Long-Term Foster Care?", Social Service News, Vol. 1, No. 10, pp. 3–7; also Child Welfare, Vol. L, April 1971, pp. 194–200.

3. Ansfield, J. *The Adopted Child*. Springfield, Ill.: Charles C Thomas, 1971.

4. Aronson, H. "The Problem of Rejection of Adoptive Applicants", Child Welfare, Vol. XXXIX, October 1960, pp. 21–24.

5. Bass, C. "Matchmaker—Matchmaker, Older-Child Adoption Failures", Child Welfare, Vol. LIV, July 1975, pp. 505–512.

6. Biskind, S. E. "Helping Adoptive Families Meet the Issues in Adoption", Child Welfare, Vol. XLV, March 1966, pp. 145–150.

7. Biskind, S. E., Finger, S., Sacks, G. G., and Schwartz, W. "The Group Method with Clients, Foster Families, and Adoptive Families", Child Welfare, Vol. XLV, December 1966, pp. 561–575.

8. Bluth, H. "Factors in the Decision to Adopt Independently", Child Welfare, Vol. XLVI, November 1967, pp. 504–513.

9. Bohman, M. *Adopted Children and Their Families*. Stockholm: Propius, 1970.

10. Bradley, T. "An Exploration of Caseworkers' Perceptions of Adoptive Applicants", Final Report, project no. R-4, U.S. Children's Bureau, New York (no date).

11. Bratfos, O., Eitinger, L., and Tau, T. "Mental Illness and Crime in Adopted Children and Adoptive Parents", Acta Psychiatrica Scandinavica, Vol. 44, No. 4, 1968, pp. 376–384.

12. Ibid.

13. Burgess, L. "The Unmarried Father in Adoption Planning", Children, Vol. 15, March–April 1968, pp. 71–74.

14. Anonymous. "Adoption at the Crossroads", Child Adoption, Vol. 54, 1968.

15. Anonymous. "Adoption in Surrey", Child Adoption, Vol. 59, 1970.

16. Anonymous. "Adoption in New Zealand", Child Adoption, Vol. 60, No. 2, 1970.

17. Anonymous. "Children in the Journals Feature", Child Adoption, May–June, 1971.

18. Chimezie, A. "Transracial Adoption for Black Children", Social Work, Vol. 20, July 1975, pp. 296–301.

19. Cohen, J. *Adoption Breakdown with Older Children*, University of Toronto, Faculty of Social Work, Monograph Series, 109, 1981.

20. Costin, L. "Adoption of Children by Single Parents", Child Adoption, Vol. 59, No. 1, 1970.

21. Crellin, E. et al. *Born Illegitimate: Social and Education Implication*. Windsor, England: National Foundation for Education Research in England and Wales, 1971.

22. Cunningham, J. "A Comparison of Adopted and Non-adopted Emotionally Disturbed Adolescents and Their Parents", Dissertation Abstracts International, Vol. 30 (1-B), 1969.

23. Depp, C. "After Reunion: Perceptions of Adult Adoptees, Adoptive Parents, and Birth Parents", Child Welfare, Vol. LXI, February 1982, pp. 115–120.

24. Dillow, L. "The Group Process in Adoptive Home-Finding", Children, Vol. 15, July–August 1968, pp. 153–157.

25. Doughery, S. "Single Adoptive Mothers and Their Children", Social Work, Vol. 23, July 1978, pp. 311–314.

26. Edgar, M. "The Group Approach in Canada", Child Adoption, Vol. 65, No. 3, 1971.

27. Feigelman, W. and Silverman, A. "Preferential Adoption: a New Mode of Family Formation", Social Casework, Vol. 60, May 1979, pp. 296–305.

28. Felkner, I. "Recruiting Adoptive Applicants", Social Work, Vol. 13, January 1968, pp. 92–100.

29. Festinger, T. "Unwed Mothers and Their Decisions to Keep or Surrender Children", Child Welfare, Vol. L, May 1971, pp. 253–263.

30. Fischer, C. "Gallagher: The Black Experience" (letter), Children, Vol. 18, May–June 1971, p. 119.

31. Fowler, I. "The Urban Middle Class Negro and Adoption", Child Welfare, Vol. XLV, November 1966, pp. 522–525.

32. Franklin, D. S. and Massarik, F. "The Adoption of Children with Medical Conditions Part I—

Process and Outcome; Part II—The Families Today," Child Welfare, Vol. XLVIII, October 1969 and November 1969, pp. 459–467, 533–539.

33. Gallagher, U "Adoption Resources For Black Children", Children, Vol. 18, March–April 1971, pp. 49–53.

34. Gentile, A. "Subsidized Adoption in New York: How the Law Works—and Some Problems", Child Welfare, Vol. XLIX, December 1970, pp. 576–580.

35. Gochros, H. "A Study of the Caseworker–Adoptive Parent Relationship in Postplacement Services", Child Welfare, Vol. XLVI, February 1967, pp. 317–325.

36. Griffin, B. P. and Affa, M. S. "Recruiting Adoptive Homes for Minority Children: One Approach", Child Welfare, Vol. XLIX, February 1970, pp. 105–107.

37. Hartley, P., "Group Education to Assist in Adoption Assessment", Child Adoption, Vol. 60, No. 2, 1970.

38. Herzog, E., Sudia, Cecelia E., and Harwood, J. "Some Opinions on Finding Families for Black Children", Children, Vol. 18, July–August 1971, pp. 143–148.

39. Hewlett, J. "Approaches to the Selection of Adopters", Accord, Vol. 12, No. 1, 1967.

40. Hockey, A. "Evaluation of Adoption of the Intellectually Handicapped: A Retrospective Analysis of 137 Cases", Journal of Mental Deficiency Research, Vol. 24, Part 3, September 1980, pp. 187–202.

41. Hoopes, J. et al. A Follow-up Study of Adoptions, Vol. II, Post-Placement Functioning of Adopted Children", New York: Child Welfare League of America, 1970.

42. Humphrey, M. The Hostage Seekers—A Study of Childless and Adopting Couples. London: The National Bureau for Co-operation in Child Care, 1969.

43. Jackson, L. "Unsuccessful Adoptions; A Study of 40 Cases", British Journal of Medical Psychology, Vol 41 (Part 4) 1968, pp. 389–398.

44. Jaffee, B. and Fanshel, D. How They Fared in Adoption: A Follow-up Study. New York: Columbia University Press, 1970.

45. Joe, B. Public Policies Toward Adoption. Washington, D.C.: The Urban Institute, 1979.

46. Johns, R. "Non-Institutional Accommodation for Mother and Baby", Child Adoption, Vol. 61, No. 3, 1970.

47. Jones, C. and Else, J. "Racial and Cultural Issues in Adoption", Child Welfare, Vol LVIII, June 1979, pp. 373–382.

48. Kadushin, A. and Seidl, F. "Adoption Failure—A Social Work Post-Mortem," Social Work, Vol. 16, July 1971, pp. 32–38.

49. Kadushin, A. "Reversibility of Trauma: A Follow-up Study of Children Adopted When Older", Social Work, Vol. 12, October 1967, pp. 22–33.

50. _____ "A Study of Adoptive Parents of Hard to Place Children", Social Casework, Vol. XLIII, May 1962, pp. 227–233.

51. Kahn, R. "Black and White" (letter), Children, Vol. 18, July/August 1971, pp. 160.

52. Karah, D. Adoption and The Coloured Child, Epworth Press, 1970.

53. Kasprowicz, A. "Interpreting Rejection to Adoptive Applicants", Social Work, Vol. 9, January 1964, pp. 98–108.

54. Pringle, M. C. K. Adoption—Facts and Fallacies. London: Longmans, in Association with the National Bureau for Co-operation in Child Care, 1967.

55. Knight, I. "Placing the Handicapped Child for Adoption", Child Adoption, Vol. 62, 1970.

56. Kraft, A. et al., "The Psychological Dimensions of Infertility", American Journal of Ortho-psychiatry, Vol. 50, October 1980, pp. 618–628.

57. Lansberry, C. "A Major Question in Subsidized Adoption" (letter), Child Welfare, Vol. XLVIII, October 1969, pp. 499–500.

58. Lawder, E. A Follow-up Study of Adoptions: Post-Placement Functioning of Adoption Families. New York: Child Welfare League of America, 1969.

59. _____ "Postadoption Counseling: A Professional Obligation", Child Welfare, Vol. XLIX, October 1970, pp. 435–442.

60. ———— et al. *A Study of Black Adoption Families: A Comparison of a Traditional and a Quasi-Adoption Program*. New York: Child Welfare League of America, 1971.

61. Leeding, A. E. "Group Meeting with Prospective Adopters, A County Council Experiment", Child Adoption, Vol. 59, No. 1, 1970.

62. Madison, B. and Schapiro, M. "Long Term Foster Family Care: What Is Its Potential for Minority Group Children?", Public Welfare, Vol. XXVIII, No. 2, 1969.

63. ———— and ———— "Black Adoption—Issues and Policies: Review of the Literature", Social Service Review, Vol. 47, 1973.

64. Maurer, R. Cadoret, R., and Cain C. "Cluster Analysis of Childhood Temperament Data on Adoptees", American Journal of Orthopsychiatry, Vol. 50, July 1980, pp. 522–534.

65. McWhinnie, A. *Adopted Children; How They Grew Up: A Study of Their Adjustment as Adults*. London: Routledge and Kegan Paul, 1967.

66. ———— "Group Counselling With 78 Adoptive Families" (2 parts), Case Conference, Vol. 14, No. 11, 1968.

67. ———— "Who Am I?", Child Adoption, Vol. 62, 1970.

68. Anonymous. "National Children's Home: Residential Nurseries and Adoption Practices", Child Adoption, Vol. 54, 1968.

69. Parfit, J. *Spotlight on Group Work With Parents in Special Circumstances*, London: National Children's Bureau, 1971.

70. Pepper, G. "Interracial Adoptions: Family Profile, Motivation, and Coping Methods", International Dissertation Abstracts, Vol. 27, (8-A), 1967.

71. Platts, H. K. "Facts Against Impressions: Mothers Seeking to Relinquish Children for Adoption", Children, Vol. 17, January–February 1970, pp. 27–30.

72. Polk, M. "Maryland's Programme of Subsidized Adoptions", Child Welfare, Vol. XLIX, December 1970, pp. 581–583.

73. Rathbun, C. and Kolodny, R. "A Group Work Approach in Cross-Cultural Adoptions", Children, Vol. 14, May–June 1967, pp. 117–121.

74. Raynor, L. *Adoption of Non-White Children: The Experience of the British Adoption Project*. London: Allen and Unwin, 1971.

75. Raynirm, K. *Giving Up a Baby for Adoption*. London: Association of British Adoption Agencies, 1971.

76. Reece, S. and Levin, B. "Psychiatric Disturbances in Adopted Children: A Descriptive Study", Social Work, Vol. 13, January 1968, pp. 101–111.

77. Reid, B. and Hooker, J. "Residential Nurseries and Adoption Practice", Child Adoption, Vol. 55, 1968.

78. Richards, K. "When Biological Mothers Meet Adopter", Child Adoption, Vol. 60, No. 2, 1970.

79. Ripple, L. "A Follow-up Study of Adopted Children", Social Service Review, Vol. 42, December 1968, pp. 479–499.

80. Ross, S. "A Slighted Resource" (letter), Children, Vol. 18, May–June 1970, pp. 119–120.

81. Rowe, J. *Parents, Children and Adoption Workers*. London: Routledge and Kegan Paul, 1966.

82. ———— "The Realities of Adoptive Parenthood", Child Adoption, Vol 59, 1970.

83. Rutter, M. "Psychological Development—Predictions of Infancy", Journal of Child Psychology and Psychiatry, Vol. 11, No. 1, 1970.

84. Schwartz, E. "The Family Romance Fantasy in Children Adopted In Infancy", Child Welfare, Vol. XLIX, July 1970, pp. 386–391.

85. Seglow, J., Pringle, M. K., and Wedge, P. *Growing up Adopted—A Long-term National Study of Adopted Children and Their Families*. Windsor, England: National Foundation for Educational Research in England and Wales, 1972.

86. Senzel, Barbara and Yeakel, Margaret. "Relationship Capacity and Acknowledgment of Difference in Adoptive Parenthood", Smith College Studies in Social Work, Vol. XL, February 1970, pp. 155–163.

87. Anonymous. "Expanding Adoption Resources", Social Service Review, Vol. 42, June 1968, pp. 269–270.

88. Starr, P., Taylor, D., and Taft, R. "Early Life Experiences and Adoptive Parenting", Social Casework, Vol. 51, October 1970, pp. 491–500.

89. Tec, L. and Gordon, S. "The Adopted Child's Adaptation to Adolescence", American Journal of Orthopsychiatry, 1967.

90. Thomas, M. "A Contribution on the Work of Voluntary Societies in Adoption", Social Service News, Vol. 1, No. 8, 1971.

91. Thomas, M. "Foster/Adoptive Home Breakdowns", Child Adoption, Vol. 66, No. 4, 1971.

92. Thompson, J. "Adoption Today?, Viable or Vulnerable?", Ontario Association of Children's Aid Societies Journal, Vol. 22, April 1979, pp. 5–8.

93. Tizard, B. and Joseph, A. "Today's Foundlings", New Society, No. 418, 1970.

94. Ward, M. "Large Adoptive Families: A Special Resource", Social Casework, Vol. 59, July 1978, pp. 411–418.

95. _____ Exploring Adoption: A Guide for Prospective Parents, mimeo, available from the author, October 1979.

96. Watson, K. "Subsidized Adoption—A Crucial Investment", Social Service News, Vol. 2, No. 11, 1972.

97. Webber, J. et al. Adoption Reunion: A Struggle in Uncharted Relationship. Monograph. Toronto: Children's Aid Metropolitan Toronto (no date).

98. Wheeler, K. B. "The Use of Adoptive Subsidies", Child Welfare, Vol. XLVIII, November 1969, pp. 557–559.

99. Wiehe, V. "The Group Adoptive Study", Child Welfare, Vol LI, December 1972, pp. 645–649.

100. Kirk, H. D., Jonassohn, K., and Fish, A. "Are Adopted Children Especially Vulnerable to Stress? A Critique of Some Recent Assumptions", Archives of General Psychiatry, 14 March, 1966, pp. 281–298.

101. Maurer, R., Cadoret, R. J., and Cain, C. "Cluster Analysis of Childhood Temperament Data on Adoptees", American Journal of Orthopsychiatry, Vol. 50, July 1980, pp. 522–534.

102. Kadushin, A. Child Welfare Services (3rd ed.). New York: Macmillan Publishing Co. Inc., 1980.

103. Schwartz, E. M. "A Comparative Study of Some Personality Characteristics of Adopted and Non-Adopted Boys", International Dissertation Abstracts, Vol. 27, 7-B.

104. Hartman, A. Finding Families: An Ecological Approach to Family Assessment in Adoption. Beverly Hills, Calif./London: Sage Publications, 1979.

# 12
# Working with Unmarried Parents

SHARON KIRSH

| | |
|---|---:|
| I. INTRODUCTION | 358 |
| II. CAUSES OF TEENAGE PREGNANCY | 359 |
|    A. Theoretical Perspectives | 359 |
|    B. Developmental Tasks and Teen Pregnancy | 361 |
|    C. Who's Likely to "Get Caught"? | 362 |
|    D. Reasons for Not Using Contraception | 363 |
| III. CONSEQUENCES OF TEEN PREGNANCY AND CHILDBEARING | 365 |
|    A. Medical Consequences | 366 |
|    B. Educational Consequences | 367 |
|    C. Economic Consequences | 367 |
|    D. Marital Consequences | 367 |
|    E. Fertility Consequences | 368 |
|    F. Familial Support Consequences | 368 |
|    G. Child Rearing Consequences | 369 |
| IV. TEENAGE FATHERS: FORGOTTEN LINK | 371 |
|    A. Contraceptive Responsibility | 371 |
|    B. Consequences of Pregnancy and Child Rearing for the Father | 372 |
|    C. What Agencies Can Do | 372 |
| V. DECIDING: TO BE OR NOT TO BE A PARENT | 373 |
|    A. Abortion versus Carrying to Term | 373 |
|    B. Keeping versus Adoption | 373 |
|    C. Some Clinical Considerations | 374 |
|    D. Mourning Reactions | 375 |
| VI. SERVICE DELIVERY BY SOCIAL WORKERS | 376 |
|    A. An Ounce of Prevention | 378 |
|    B. Programs During Pregnancy | 379 |
|    C. Postnatal Programs | 379 |
| VII. PRACTICE APPROACHES | 380 |
|    A. Establishing Trust | 380 |

    B.  Providing the Necessities    380
    C.  Offering Emotional Growth    381
    D.  Groups    381
    E.  Family Therapy    382
    F.  Individual Therapy    383
VIII.  SUMMARY    384
      REFERENCES    385

## I.    INTRODUCTION

This chapter reviews work with unwed pregnant women and unwed mothers and fathers, with primary emphasis on those in their adolescent years. It examines proposed causes of teen pregnancy, its consequences for the young mother, father, and child, the factors associated with aborting versus keeping versus surrendering, the social work implications based on the data, and finally, the nature of child welfare practice with unmarried parents.

In dealing with UP (unmarried parent) clients, workers must consider the confounding effects of the individual's developmental level (e.g., stage of adolescence or adulthood) and class, race, ethnicity, religion, and region of residence, on early (and unwed) childbearing and child rearing. Researchers have tended to situate the problems within the individual teenager rather than acknowledging societal factors that make life difficult for her (e.g., lack of adequate prenatal medical care, affordable housing, daycare, jobs, training programs, and so on) [34].

While many teens expect to feel grown-up and well cared for while pregnant, they are soon confronted with endless decisions and tasks which may be compounded by their age and stage in their family's life cycle. One common theme is the teen's conflict regarding being a mother versus being mothered. At first, being a mother may be idealized, but when supports are not forthcoming, then a lonely, frightened, angry, and perhaps poor, young woman may want to once again be mothered [15].

It may be useful to review the discussion of the dynamics and problems related to adolescence, presented in Chapter 10.

Some pregnant young women choose to abort, others carry to term and then surrender their child for adoption, others keep their child during infancy and then relinquish her or him to foster care or adoption, while other young mothers raise their offspring. Some unwed, teenage women have more than one pregnancy.

That child welfare practice in this field is labelled "UP work" (unmarried parent) may speak to the assumption that if one is unmarried then one is likely to be in greater need of agency support. In fact, variables of class, ethnicity, race, and age may be more salient than marital status in terms of access to resources required to make successful pregnancy-outcome decisions and to parent adequately. Emphasis on marital status may become an outmoded issue as societal norms evolve towards an acceptance of single parenthood, unmarried serial relationships, divorce, and women's and society's need for economic independence for all adults.

At present, UP work is focussed primarily on females, most of whom are adolescents, although the mandate of child welfare agencies does not restrict them to a teenaged caseload. Any woman may be a UP client who is not presently married, who is pregnant, and who does not have another child under the protection of a child welfare agency. UP clients are voluntary; approximately three months after the baby's birth, the case is either closed or, if the worker determines that the child is "at risk", then the mother may become an involuntary client.

Several factors contribute to the incidence of teen pregnancy in our society, a society which has the technology for preventing unwanted pregnancies, but which fails to encourage members to employ it. Our society harbours several contradictions: while there is an adult focus on sexuality, especially on exploitative forms found in the media, there is at the same time a silence surrounding sexuality when teens seek information, especially from parents and teachers; there is a failure to provide easily accessible early pregnancy detection services and abortion or special support services to teens with repeat pregnancies. It is not surprising that many adolescents carry with them mixed messages pertaining to sexuality, pregnancy, and parenthood.

Planned Parenthood of Toronto reported in 1979 that in Canada there was a 1-in-10 chance of pregnancy among teenage females; however, while the number of teen pregnancies is increasing, this trend seems to hold primarily for females under age 16 [75].

Statistics pertaining to fertility are sexist in their unilateral concern with women—the underlying assumption is that pregnancy and parenting are female issues alone. In fact, teen pregnancies touch not only the mother, but also the father, parents of both the mother and father, siblings, other kin, friends, classmates, co-workers, and other members of social networks, both female and male. Just as sexuality is not confined to males (as it once was thought to be), contraceptive responsibilities, pregnancy, and parenting are not the sole domain of females.

## II.     CAUSES OF TEENAGE PREGNANCY

> Probably any teenager could tell us that out-of-marriage births are caused
> by intercourse together with insufficient contraceptive protection, lack of
> abortion, and failure to marry. [74]

### A.     Theoretical Perspectives

The thorny question of why some teens get pregnant while others do not remains unanswered. Various schools of thought have proposed reasons for this phenomenon, and it is the worker's task to select and/or to develop theoretical explanations that make inherent sense.

Teen pregnancy is both a personal and a public issue; it probably cannot be explained by a unitary theory [11]. The following brings together a collection of explanations offered in the literature, some of which will seem more valid than others to the worker [11, 15, 28].

*1.*     *Psychological explanations*

Psychological explanations tend to be posited for white, middle-class pregnant teens, while socio-cultural explanations (e.g., "moral laxity") tend to be put forward for black and poor pregnant teens.

Pregnancy is a synthetic substitute for love, resulting from defective mothering which has prevented the teen mom from learning self-protective restraint; it is a means of resolving a sense of deprivation or dependency, and is unconsciously motivated; weak ego strength results in sexual acting-out.

Pregnancy is a means of recouping a recent emotional loss; it is a means of "capturing" a particular male.

Pregnancy stems from familial conflict, especially with the mother; the pregnant teenager wants to punish her mother, or to compete with her, or to give her no-longer-fertile mother another baby; motherhood may be an escape from an unhappy family life.

Pregnancy is a source of self-esteem, especially to those who feel that there are few other options available (girls or women who do not know and accept themselves are less able to use and plan for contraception); assuming an adult role can lead to feelings of independence.

Certain family dynamics are related to teen pregnancy:

> closeness to father, not close to mother, and generally unstable relationships

> father absence and strong bond with mother accompanied by resentment of mother

> father absence, because he was too busy, or frightened by daughter's sexuality, or physically absent; the teen daughter may crave the love and attention of a male

There are common characteristics of teens who become pregnant. They:

> have an unconscious desire to be pregnant

> are highly dependent

> have a great need for affection and to please others

> feel rootless

> feel that their own lives are beyond their control; feel helpless

> have low self-concept and sense of worthlessness

> have a high need for immediate gratification in order to decrease anxiety/depression

*2.*     *Sociological explanations*

The definition of illegitimacy is indicative of society's sexual values (i.e., that intercourse and procreation are legitimate only in marriage).

"Illicit" sexual behaviour is learned through identification with others who accept that behaviour (e.g., peer pressure).

Pregnancy can result from accident/failure of contraception, or from lack of access to effective forms of contraception.

Pregnancy can be a result of rape or incest or coercion.

Continued pregnancies can result from a lack of money to pay for an abortion (in situations where abortion is not covered by medical insurance).

*3.     Economic explanations*

Analysis of family allowance programs in Canada (and other countries) does not lend support to the notion that levels or changes in family allowances are associated with levels or changes in illegitimacy rates—the hypothesis that a "welfare state mentality" causes high illegitimacy rates is not supported (for further discussion, see P. Cutwright, Family Planning Perspectives, Vol. 3, No. 1, Jan. 1971).

*4.     Physiological explanations*

A prolonged period of adolescence due to early menarche and later marriages results in more teen pregnancies (menstruation begins earlier than it did several decades ago because of improved living conditions, nutrition, and health care).

Improved overall health results in a higher incidence of teen pregnancy.

*5.     Cognitive explanations*

Pregnancy results from lack of understanding of the connection between intercourse and pregnancy (not cognitively mature enough to understand possible outcomes of their behaviour, or, because of communication difficulties between adolescents and adults, they are not taught the connection).

Maturity is necessary in order to exercise self-control, to foresee consequences of behaviour, to believe that one can become pregnant, and to acknowledge one's sexuality to oneself, or to a doctor.

Most teens do not have high levels of cognitive moral sophistication.

## B.     Developmental Tasks and Teen Pregnancy

What is it about adolescence as a developmental phase that lends itself to pregnancy?

a search for identity (involves looking to others for a definition of self and therefore a vulnerability to others' influence)

integration and formation of values which at times seem contradictory and confusing awareness of both dependency needs and need for independence, which can be frightening

immediate gratification desired in order to reduce insecurities and to achieve a sense of self-confidence

desire for responsibility/control mixed with a yearning to forfeit responsibility

Most adolescents are too busy growing up to spend time contemplating the vicissitudes of parenting. However, pregnant teenagers must handle a host of responsibilities (e.g., ensuring a healthy pregnancy or delivery, making psychological room for a child, learning how to be a parent, and so on), none of which has the appeal of dancing and romancing. For those who are poor and very young, these tasks may seem especially insurmountable and help from outside sources may be required for survival.

## C.    Who's Likely to "Get Caught"?

A high percentage of female adolescents have sexual relations, but not everyone becomes pregnant. Many students of the subject have suggested ways in which impregnated teens vary from those who avoid conception; some have suggested that the only difference is luck; while others have found no unique profile common to all pregnant females [15]—there appears to be no adolescent pregnancy "type" [35].

Low self-esteem appears to be a common element among pregnant adolescents and one factor that helping professionals can deal with through intervention. Maintenance of self-esteem levels is a universal adolescent problem, not restricted by class boundaries.

When life histories of economically poor pregnant and nonpregnant teens are compared, the following factors emerge:

minimal parental discipline within families of pregnant teens

extraordinary freedom to make decisions at an early age among pregnant teens

minimal exposure to church teachings or traditional morals and values concerning sexual behaviour among pregnant teens

a shift of the adolescent's identity and influence from parents to peers in early adolescence

strong identification with peers, to correspond with alienation from adults

Alienation from adults is an element of this group: it has an impact upon the teen's reaction to help being offered by adults (e.g., social workers).

All factors considered, there is no unique family or social relationship, no unique differences in "pathology", and no single personality pattern which leads directly to teen pregnancy.

In terms of class, ethnic, and racial factors, teen pregnancy is *not* the exclusive domain of nonwhite lower-income groups; unwanted teen pregnancies occur in all economic, ethnic, and racial groups; however, the impact and visibility of pregnancy are likely to be affected by class and other factors.

## D.    Reasons for Not Using Contraception

Perhaps the most frustrating unsolved mystery is why some females who claim to not want pregnancy in fact do become pregnant. The "blame" for such an occurrence has been placed on the girl/woman, the boy/man, the contraceptive device, parents, schools, media, a patriarchal (sexist) social structure, a racist and generally oppressive structure, and any combination of these factors.

Many teens become pregnant because they do not use contraceptives; when asked why they do not use contraceptives regularly, the most common reasons given are: "it-won't-happen-to-me", and "nice girls don't plan to have intercourse". Additional reasons popularly suggested are: an inability to obtain contraception, a frustration with public health facilities, a frustration with the methods themselves, and their partner objects to their using contraception [15].

"It-won't-happen-to-me" is a pervasive attitude among adolescents who generally do believe that they can come to no harm; many teens are simply unaware of the facts (e.g., widespread belief that one cannot become impregnated from having intercourse just once, or that the "safe" part of the menstrual cycle is in the middle). In fact, not all females who have reached puberty are biologically capable of conception—it may be a matter of a few years before they become completely capable of childbearing—and meanwhile unprotected intercourse without conceiving creates a false sense of security. This attitude is common among any group of young women who have not yet conceived, regardless of their biological readiness.

In a society which uses photographs and films of pubescent females to sell movies, cosmetics, jeans, cars, and any number of consumer goods and services, it is ironic that the morality of earlier eras continues to pervade our value systems and many of our institutions. Teenage females are bombarded by their seductive counterparts through the media, and yet the overriding message of parents, teachers, clergy, legal systems, welfare systems, and so on, is that nice girls do not intentionally engage in sex. In order to maintain a self-concept of righteousness/niceness, an adolescent female must explain her actions as unpremeditated. Thus, she finds herself in a double-bind: to acknowledge her sexuality (and thereby take contraceptive precautions) is an admission of evil; to have unprotected sex is to risk pregnancy and an admission of evil.

Some researchers have suggested that the adolescent must come to terms with her own sexuality and sexual identity before the use of contraception becomes an option; she must let go of the fantasy that all sex must be spontaneous and accept that sexual activity can be planned [49].

Young women who seek medical contraceptives reach this point through a stage-by-stage process [49]. First, the belief in the spontaneity of sex is slowly replaced by casually seeking information about contraception from friends. Next, the casual approach is slowly replaced by seeking information from a knowledgeable source as the commitment to contraception strengthens. The movement from acceptance of contraceptive use by peers to effective contraceptive use by the individual adolescent is critical in allowing the progression to contraceptive practice within the adolescent group.

Workers must acknowledge the emotional barriers to contraceptive utilization (e.g., being seen as "promiscuous") and realize that what is perceived as a remote risk of pregnancy is not as great as the immediate risk of the loss of reputation or self-esteem.

One motivator for contraceptive use is a stable relationship in which sex may be regarded as "more under control" and in which the power position of the woman tends to be enhanced [49].

Adolescent males, on the other hand, tend to be looked upon benignly for their sexual activities. A deep-rooted mythology has grown up around male sexual initiation rites and sexual competition and prowess. The bottom line in terms of contraception is that males cannot get pregnant and therefore tend to shirk responsibility for their part in contraception and conception.

Studies of factors associated with the non-use of contraception have pointed to the variables mentioned in the following table [15, 34]. It should be noted that these clusters of factors do not represent a profile of the "typical" UP client; rather, the factors are those which tend to be present among adolescents who do *not* use contraception, conversely, not all factors apply to all teens who are non-users).

## FACTORS AFFECTING FEMALE ADOLESCENT NON-USE OF CONTRACEPTIVES:

1. *Access to information and resources*
   unaware of pregnancy risks/misinformation
   unaware of family planning services
   lack of access to family planning service that does not insist upon parental consent
   contraceptives not available at the "right" moment
   lack of communication with parent(s) about contraception
   physicians reluctant to counsel young girls on effective usage or to prescribe oral contraceptives (in part, laws have discouraged this)

2. *Demographic factors*
   below age 18
   not married
   minority group member
   lower-class/poor
   never pregnant
   non-attendance at college

3. *Social factors*
   not in an on-going relationship
   has intercourse sporadically and spontaneously
   discouraged by partner from using contraceptives
   fear of contraceptive side effects
   relative lack of societal stigma associated with teen pregnancy

4. *Psychological factors*
   wants a pregnancy
   feels powerless, fatalistic
   feels alienated and incompetent
   traditional attitudes towards women's role (passive, dependent)
   high level of anxiety
   denial of one's sexuality; believes intercourse will not occur
   risk-taking attitude; impulsive
   pleasure-oriented

In a 1976 Canadian national survey (the Badgley Report), it was found that among sexually active females aged 15, non-use of contraception was 33% compared with 17% for those aged 16–17. Among sexually active males the incidence of non-use in those age categories was 66% and 28%, respectively. Two Toronto studies (Cowell, 1971 and Guyatt, 1972) found that among pregnant adolescents 50% had never used contraception [46].

In the United States between 1968 and 1974, approximately 50% of sexually active female high school students used contraceptives at their first intercourse. During the 1970s, studies show a marked increase in the use of the pill and reduction in the use of condoms and withdrawal (male methods) [35].

The following factors should be kept in mind:

Young teens who are recent recruits to intercourse are especially unlikely to use contraception [35].

It is common for teenage females to be sexually active for at least one year before seeking contraceptives [35].

Contraception is much more likely to be practiced by partners who have a stable relationship and emotional commitment [15].

Those who seek contraceptive counselling are more accepting of their sexuality and of their sexual activities than those who are unprotected [15].

Those who consistently use contraception tend to hold feminist attitudes and to be assertive about their needs and desires; they tend to share power with their partners [15].

Those who consistently use contraception tend to be effective communicators (express themselves with sensitivity, empathy, clarity, directness); pregnant teens tend to idealize interpersonal relations and to avoid expressing hostility [15].

Poverty can lead to a sense of personal incompetence, hopelessness, powerlessness, alienation, and fatalism, all of which are associated with non-use of contraception [34].

Contraceptive usage involves an acknowledgement of sexuality, thereby increasing the possibility of public exposure.

If parent(s) openly discuss birth control with their teens this serves to allow adolescents to acknowledge their sexuality and to understand sex as an activity that can be discussed, regulated, and planned.

## III.   CONSEQUENCES OF TEEN PREGNANCY AND CHILDBEARING

I almost had a breakdown. I got real upset. I took a bunch of pills and started acting crazy. After I took the pills, I started beating on the kids, starting with the oldest one. I just picked up a belt and started whipping them. I couldn't cope. Then my girlfriend came over and stopped me. She called my mother and she came and took the kids. She suggested I go

somewhere and get some help, like a psychiatrist, and after a while, I started
going to ——— Centre.

The lady there really tried to help me. Sometimes I got stuck on
words and she helped me with that. She helped me see that it was hard to
raise kids alone. Things have been easier since I went there. What I really
want is to find someone who will help out with raising my kids. [16: p.18]

Many of the supposed consequences of teen childbearing and child rearing
would be experienced by some teenagers whether or not they became adolescent
parents [35]. For young people who have lived with poverty, racism, unhappy family
relationships, school failure, and so on, becoming parents may simply add another
layer of complications/problems. While all of their problems would not be eradicated
if they were not parents, they probably would stand a better chance of completing
school, gaining employment, limiting family size, and creating satisfying family lives
[35].

## A.    Medical Consequences

The list of medical complications associated with teen pregnancy and childbirth is indeed long [15]:

> infections (including those from self-induced abortion attempts)
>
> anemia (weakness due to insufficient red blood corpuscles)
>
> toxemia (blood poisoning)
>
> urinary tract infections
>
> complications from long labour
>
> prematurity
>
> high rates of fetal perinatal (28 weeks to gestation to first week of life),
> neonatal (first 28 days of life), postnatal (28 days to end of first year) mortality
>
> low birth weight
>
> serious physical or intellectual impairment of the children of mothers
> age 15 or younger

Two critical points must be remembered [15]: (1) that it is not age per se that
leads to complications, but rather the factors associated with teenage childbearing
(e.g., the quality of prenatal care and nutrition); and (2) that these factors are associated with social class. Class is a more valid predictor of pregnancy/delivery complications than is age. Those teens older than age 15 who receive good prenatal care
and who eat a proper diet while pregnant are not at risk obstetrically [15]. In other
words, the adverse effects of early childbearing on the mother's health tend to disappear when high-quality medical care is made available; thus, the commonly-occurring
negative consequences are caused by lack of access to adequate obstetrical care, and it
can be assumed that if economic and social conditions do not change for this group of
women, they will experience the same types of problems at a later age of delivery, too
[15].

Dangers are multiplied at age 16 or younger, especially when pregnancy occurs within two years of the onset of menstruation. A biologically immature mother is two to three times as likely to deliver a premature baby.

## B.    Educational Consequences

Pregnancy remains the most common reason for school leaving among females. Although pregnant teens are no longer forced to leave school as they once were, it is not always possible for young women to stay; before delivery they may be physically unable to sit through classes, and once the baby arrives, a lack of infant daycare might make a return to school impossible [15].

Pregnant teens who marry are more likely to drop out of school than those who do not marry, and since young marriages tend to be short-lived (nearly half of all teen marriages break up within five years), and teen marriages resulting from pregnancy are three times more likely to dissolve, failure to complete school could affect a young mother's wage-earning capacities as a sole-support parent. Furthermore, most high school leavers never return to school. However, the availability of child care, especially by family members, is an important aid in school-return [15].

## C.    Economic Consequences

Young women who choose to keep their babies may find that their lack of skill-training and their community's lack of affordable daycare prohibit them from finding suitable employment; and the jobs which they do find are usually low-paying, non-unionized, and dead-end. The alternatives to such employment include family support, support by the child's father, or public assistance.

Adolescent single mothers are more likely than their married counterparts to be dependent on public assistance when they are very young, but this dependency tends to be short-lived (on average, two years); furthermore, dependency is more apt for very young mothers [34]. It is important to calculate the costs that result from pervasive poverty and to understand that public assistance to teen mothers is, by comparison, insignificant [11].

Poverty:

> intensifies a young mother's isolation/depression
>
> makes living in decent housing impossible
>
> prevents the obtaining of affordable, high-quality daycare
>
> complicates attempts to complete schooling/training
>
> heightens marital problems

## D.    Marital Consequences

The majority of teen mothers marry within a few years of their first child's birth. These early marriages are more likely to dissolve than are later marriages regardless of the timing of when the child was born. Early marriage is the key factor [34].

The economic situation of the male is an important determinant in the young woman's decision to wed and in the timing of marriage; marriage is more apt to occur during the prenatal period if the father has a full-time job. However, many young fathers have a low earning potential, especially if they have not completed high school, and perhaps the most important link between unplanned pregnancy and marital failure is the father's economic/employment situation. Finally, young mothers who marry are more likely to leave school, those with education or occupational aims tend to be reluctant to marry, and thereby become housebound and thwarted in their professional aims [49].

## E.      Fertility Consequences

The younger the woman at the time of her first pregnancy, the more children she is likely to have, the closer spaced they will be, and the more likely they will be unwanted at time of conception; these findings remain constant when education, religion, race, and marital status at the time of first birth are controlled [15].

Repeat pregnancies are common (50% of teens are pregnant again within three years). Some researchers suggest that teen mothers reconceive because:

> They want additional children (for a variety of reasons).
>
> They lack resources for controlling unwanted pregnancies [49].

When asked, teen mothers tend to give the following reasons for terminating contraceptive use:

> specific problems arose (e.g., physical side effects; fear of adverse side effects)
>
> religious/moral reservations
>
> no sexual activity

When a young mother loses her job and needs support, or has difficulties with her contraceptive, or when she becomes emotionally involved with a new man, then she may become more vulnerable to pregnancy. Whatever the reason for reconception, her problems are likely to be compounded by it [49].

The incidence of repeat pregnancies is greatly reduced when teen mothers return to school immediately following delivery, although even in these cases contraceptive usage is discontinued at a substantial rate by three years after delivery [49].

## F.      Familial Support Consequences

Fortunately there are grandmothers, because it is they who are a major source of support (child care, information, and so on) [15]. Daycare is costly and not

readily available; thus, whether a teen mother can seek employment is highly dependent on the supportiveness of her kinship network. Kin can provide food, clothing,
shelter, child care, advice, support, and companionship, all of which may enable the
young mother to pursue schooling/training/employment; however, kin are less likely
to continue providing supportive resources when she marries, thereby making marriage a less attractive option.

Likelihood of remaining with kin is influenced by [49]:

> the degree of affection between the young mother and her kin
>
> the economic position of the family
>
> the degree of dependency on parent(s)

Those mothers who do remain with their kin are more likely to return to
school, to graduate from high school, and to be employed. It may be that families who
support their daughters' educational goals are more likely to assist financially and with
the provision of child care as long as the young woman remains in school; however, if
she leaves school then there is less incentive for kin support [49].

Young mothers may become isolated from former friends, and experience
difficulty in creating new social networks; with few people with whom to share
problems, exchange child care services, and be sociable, a teen mother can easily
become depressed, suicidal, unhappy with her marriage if she is married, abusive or
neglectful with her children, and unmotivated to leave her home. Family members
and agency-formed groups are potential sources of emotional and material supports
[49].

## G.    Child Rearing Consequences

Are teen mothers more likely than older mothers to abuse or neglect their
children? As with most issues in social science, research results point to yes, no, and
maybe, and the majority of studies are not rigorous, valid investigations.

Those who do connect early parenting with abuse suggest the following:

> Teen parents tend to have been abused or neglected when they were
> children, which generated unresolved dependency needs, leading in turn to
> overdependence on their own child, combined with unrealistic expectations
> of the child; when this need is added to an ignorance of child development
> and of child care techniques, a low frustration tolerance, isolation from for-
> mer peers and social support systems, and low self-esteem, the result is a
> perception of the child as either the source or the solution of the parent's
> problems [19, 20].

When one examines child-abusing families, one is likely to find a higher
proportion of mothers who gave birth as teens than in the general population;
while this suggests a link between teen pregnancy and later child abuse, it
should be remembered that reported cases of teen births and reported cases

of abuse/neglect are more common among poor families; poverty may be the important factor, serving as a source of frustration and anger [19, 20].

Social histories of teen parents and of parents who abuse tend to have several features in common:

> They come from one-parent families.
>
> There is a family history of alcohol abuse.
>
> Parent suffered from depression.
>
> Parent was rejecting.
>
> Infants were premature.

However, while the level of social disorganization predicts maltreatment, the *age* of the mother at first birth does not significantly predict maltreatment [49].

Teen mothers compared with older mothers tend to be less involved with their children: that is, they do not talk to their babies as much, do not look at them as much, are less close emotionally, provide less intellectual encouragement, know less about infants and parenting, are inexperienced and highly stressed; as a result, children of teen mothers are more likely than children of older mothers to have behavioural problems [15].

On the other hand, some researchers refute all of the arguments and data presented. They [15] have found that the majority of teen mothers are as competent and caring as older mothers (race and class held constant). They have found no significant differences between teen and older mothers in terms of the number of accidents occurring to their children, maternal perception of infant's temperament, child rearing attitudes, warmth, and physical interaction; however, teen mothers tend to be lower on verbal interaction.

When the children of teen and older mothers are compared on measures of cognitive development, socio-emotional adjustment, and personal characteristics, the significantly lower scores for children of teen mothers tend to be eliminated when appropriate controls are employed for the adverse effects of poverty, racism, and the stresses associated with single-parenthood [34]. Even when these effects are controlled, children of teen mothers are slightly more likely to repeat the parental pattern of early childbearing and/or marriage and to have larger families.

If, in fact, teen mothers are more apt than older mothers to abuse or neglect their children, this is somewhat understandable given their insufficient incomes, high rate of subsequent fertility and therefore continuous childcare responsibilities, and lack of societal supports to ease their burdens. Interventions intended to eradicate poverty and social isolation/powerlessness would likely reduce many (alleged) negative consequences of teen parenting.

One might conclude that early parenting per se has few, if any, uniquely negative effects on the mother or child, but that early parenting imposes strains on adolescents who are already highly vulnerable socially, economically, and developmentally [15].

## IV.    TEENAGE FATHERS: FORGOTTEN LINK

Fathers of children born out-of-wedlock are labelled "putative" (reputed) [21]. It is true that some fathers do not want to be identified, and even when they are identified it is not always possible to ensure that they are both the biological and social father; however, many young men who are presently overlooked by agencies are in fact wanting to be considered. Sometimes fathers do not live with the mother and child because regulations governing public assistance punish co-habitation. Also, living together may take place after some period of time rather than within a few months of child delivery. Finally, living apart does not necessarily imply that the father is disinterested in the child or in the mother, or that he will not play a positive, important role in their lives [21].

### A.    Contraceptive Responsibility

While many theories have been proposed to explain why teenage females become pregnant, not much thought has been given to why teenage males impregnate their partners. In fact, most people would claim that teen males think only of the sexual act itself and do not stop to contemplate the possible consequences.

Some teen males disregard the risk of pregnancy because they perceive that *females* must pay the consequences of unprotected intercourse. In an American study of 1,017 males ages 15–19 (1977) two-thirds agreed that it is acceptable to say 'I love you' as a way of persuading a female to have intercourse, while three-fourths of this sample were anti-abortion [15].

Peers tend to provide support and a value system for sexuality; however, if peers are influenced by sexist, stereotypical messages and incomplete factual information, they become a source of misunderstanding [67]. Friends play the largest role in influencing teen males' sexual activities and contraception; boys/men who are highly involved with their families tend to be less active sexually, although parents are almost never relied upon for either information or advice [15].

Fifty percent of sexually active teens do not always use contraception, and 50% of those who do, depend on methods employed by males (withdrawal and condoms), which is somewhat surprising given the devaluation of the male role in family planning decisions [6]. It has been suggested that the rate of male use of contraception is as high as it is because [6]:

> The unplanned and sporadic nature of teen intercourse lends itself to condoms and withdrawal.
>
> Condoms are easily accessible, relatively inexpensive, and convenient to carry around; they may provide a degree of status to young males simply by being carried (even if they are never used); finally, condoms may make sex more attractive to females who are concerned about pregnancy or venereal disease.

At present, males tend not to be encouraged to share responsibility for preventing pregnancy. Because most young people do not talk about contraception with their partners, it remains an area of mystery and embarrassment. However, if non-exploitative sexual relationships are to occur between males and females, then males must be encouraged to help prevent pregnancy.

## B.    Consequences of Pregnancy and Child Rearing for the Father

Pregnancy has a range of possible effects on the father:

> It may confirm his "virility"; enhance self-esteem.
>
> He may leave school in order to support the child.
>
> He may disclaim responsibility for the pregnancy.
>
> He may continue his relationship with the mother and serve as a single father to the child.
>
> If pregnancy is terminated, he may feel the loss.

Approximately half of the teen fathers maintain some contact with the mother and infant during the first and second postnatal years, but this figure decreases rapidly with the passage of time after age two [21]. On the other hand, marriage is a factor that encourages a rapid second and subsequent pregnancies among teen mothers [21].

## C.    What Agencies Can Do

Some pregnant young women who seek assistance from social service agencies want to forget the identity of their child's father; others report to the agency that their relationship with the father has been ended in order to guard against what they perceive as interference by the agency; other clients and fathers wish to handle the pregnancy as partners in the fullest sense.

One researcher, after investigating agencies which do actively include fathers, has suggested the following clinical benefits of engaging the teen father in the pregnancy experience [21]:

> Counselling can be oriented towards stress reduction for the young parents; it can also begin to involve the father in caretaking decisions about the infant.
>
> Participation in prenatal visits and discussions regarding child development and child rearing can psychologically prepare him for fatherhood.
>
> Participation in discussions regarding pregnancy prevention can increase the likelihood that he will use effective contraception in the future.
>
> Providing supportive services may prevent school failure and accumulation of economic disadvantage (agency could ensure that fathers and mothers receive vocational guidance and access to alternative schools at the

appropriate grade levels if regular schools are not prepared to meet their needs).

Providing community support may have a profound (positive) effect on the kind of parenting the child receives [3].

Some researchers have speculated that one major risk in involving the father is the chance that the couple will feel covertly encouraged to stay together; however, the possibility of a second pregnancy can be reduced if the agency's intervention includes contraceptive information, counselling, and long-term follow-up [21].

## V. DECIDING: TO BE OR NOT TO BE A PARENT

### A. Abortion versus Carrying to Term

Approximately one-third of teens who become pregnant abort [15]. Data which compare young women who abort with those who carry to term may be misleading because abortion (that is, legally sanctioned abortion) has historically been more available to those who could afford it or who had the power to convince decision makers (e.g., a hospital board) that their case was legitimate; furthermore, abortion has never been considered a legitimate form of birth control in our society, in part because of moral considerations.

Studies comparing aborters with those who carry to term have turned up mixed findings [15]: for example, non-aborters have less supportive families versus aborters, who have more supportive families; or aborters who are from intact families versus no family differences between aborters and non-aborters. It has been suggested that abortion clients, as compared with term clients, are more likely to have a role model (especially a sister) who has had an abortion, are more likely to have educational and occupational aspirations (which holds even when groups are matched on class), and are more likely to have alternatives for recognition/status other than through motherhood.

### B. Keeping versus Adoption

Women who carry to term either keep or surrender the child (usually to an adoption agency). Until the 1970s when keeping became more normative than surrendering, those who kept were considered less stable and more emotionally needy than those who surrendered. Those who kept were considered to be social deviants. What has happened in the past decade? [8]

There has been a questioning of the need for marriage as the context in which to have children.

There has been a shift away from adoption as the only solution to an out-of-wedlock birth—it is no longer deviant for a pregnant teen to keep her baby.

There is a more relaxed attitude towards sex.

There is more social support provided by society for unwed mothers than in the past; women who receive benefits can choose to keep their baby without marrying.

Women are becoming conscious of their strengths and power and are realizing that they do not need men in order to survive economically or to help raise children.

According to Ontario Vital Statistics, in 1968, 30% of unwed mothers (all ages) kept their children, compared to 88% in 1977. There is now pressure on UP clients to keep their babies as a result of this trend; workers need to make apparent that not keeping is a viable option too.

When teens who keep are compared with those who surrender their child; once again there are mixed findings. However, it would appear that women who keep their child are less likely to be students, more likely to be from single-parent homes, and are more likely to have known the child's father for a longer time than women who surrender their child.

## C.     Some Clinical Considerations

Bracken et al. [76] have articulated four cognitive-affective stages in pregnancy resolution. Each step is a precondition for succeeding ones and thereby determines the subsequent step; each decision attempts to reduce cognitive dissonance and to maximize benefits. The four steps are:

1. Acknowledgement of the pregnancy with accompanying happiness or unhappiness about it

2. Consideration of the relative merits of the available options (abortion, adoption, motherhood) and an easy or difficult decision-making process

3. Formulation of alternative outcomes and acceptance or rejection of each

4. Commitment to the chosen outcome and accompanying gladness or sadness about the ultimate decision

All things considered, one of the major influences on pregnancy outcome is the psychological milieu in which the pregnancy occurs (e.g., relationship to the child's father and to the mother's family) [76].

Certain conditions should be in place before helping an adolescent consider surrendering her baby for adoption. These are:

improved self-esteem

sense of control over, and responsibility for, her own life

sense of self as person who has something to contribute to society

a goal for the future with which to identify (other than the care of her children)

realization that people can care for her, without having to take care of her

identification of her own needs as important; then, the ability to identify what her child's needs might be

acknowledgement of her love for the child, the grief she will feel if she surrenders, and the need for support to help her deal with others' reactions

support from people who acknowledge that it was a difficult decision and that she is capable of making and following through with a difficult decision

Three widely accepted factors which may influence the mother's decision to keep her child are:

a social milieu which does not stigmatize those who keep

her deep need for a primary relationship to fulfill unresolved dependency needs

her desire to demonstrate love for the child's father, or to demonstrate her child rearing capacities

## D.   Mourning Reactions

In working with pregnant adolescents, workers must consider not only birth and development but also death, loss, and separation. Some researchers suggest that second pregnancies may come about as a response to unresolved feelings of loss due to a previous abortion (induced or spontaneous), to a recent death of a parent, or to a separation from a significant other.

Response to loss depends on one's past experience with separation and loss, on cultural and family norms of appropriate response, and on the individual's psychic structure and level of development.

Adolescents must separate from parents and they may in fact experience a type of mourning in which they feel angry, depressed, and vulnerable. They may recover from this sense of loss by becoming intimately (perhaps sexually) involved with a new person. Expressing sadness for a loss may threaten an adolescent's attempt to be independent and "cool". Pregnant teens may have to deal, in addition, with a separation from their infant (through adoption or death), or in the case of those who keep, with the separation from the freedom of adolescence, with the "loss" of youth through the acceptance of adult responsibilities.

Adaptive mourning of an infant or fetal loss during adolescence tends to follow a sequence which, on the average, takes from 6 to 8 months to complete [73]:

shock and denial of the loss

fantasizing about the baby

expressing a need to investigate the possibility of reconceiving

feeling guilty about her role in the loss

feeling angry towards hospital personnel, family, baby's father

having physical reactions

feeling despair or apathy about herself and her future

separating and reorganizing: thinking about her future

Nonadaptive responses are exaggerations of, or the persistence of, mourning reactions; for example, there may be an absence of mourning and an inability to discuss the loss; or extreme, long-lasting anger, guilt, depression; or new forms of self-destructive acting-out.

Adolescents, by virtue of their stage, may not express their feelings for fear of being overwhelmed, crying, and appearing "childish". They are sensitive about their physical and sexual development, and spontaneous abortion or stillbirth may create anxiety about their ability to carry to term. When counselling, the worker might begin by exploring the client's understanding of the cause of the loss, and the implications this has for her physical and emotional self-concept. At all times, workers should acknowledge the client's pain associated with the decision taken and with the mourning process.

Before commencing the next section readers are encouraged to review the discussion of problem solving in child welfare, in Appendix A, and particularly those sections dealing with assessment and the search for solutions.


## VI.    SERVICE DELIVERY BY SOCIAL WORKERS

The goal of the adolescent pregnancy treatment program must remain the guidance of the adolescent toward functional acquisition of independent living skills in a variety of life areas. The identification of and guidance toward the acquisition of these skills may not be as exciting as attempting to unravel complex dynamics of each situation, yet they are more useful. Building skills will do more to serve the immediate task of helping the adolescent work toward a successful life experience. [19: p. 108]

Before looking at the specific intervention modalities discussed in the next section, this piece will first present a general overview of the types of programs presently available to pregnant/parenting adolescents, and will then point to suggested programs that do *not* exist.

### MINIMUM SERVICE ARRAY FOR ADOLESCENT
### PREGNANCY-PARENTING CASE MANAGEMENT [49]

Medical services
     contraceptive information and availability
     early pregnancy detection services

Reprinted, by permission of the author, from F. G. Bolton, Jr., *The Pregnant Adolescent: Problems of Premature Parenthood* (Beverly Hills, CA: Sage Publications, 1980), pp. 188.

maternal care
1. prepregnancy services
2. prenatal services
3. perinatal services
4. dental care
child care
maternal child care; well-baby services

Nutrition services
food and food supplement provision
nutritional education
consumer services and consumer training
cooking instruction

Housing and transportation
crisis shelter
caretaker services
parent aide services
short-term housing
long-term housing
homemaker services
subsidized public transportation

Child care services
parenting training
child management instruction
child development instruction
disciplinary alternatives
alternative child care for pre-daycare
daycare services selection and utilization

Independent living skills provision
homemaker training
decision-making skills instruction
assertiveness training
money management skill training
conflict resolution skill training
consumer skills training
recreational education

Education and training
cooperative school programming—pre/postnatal
occupational training and vocational education
participation
career awareness and selection
on-the-job training programs
vocational rehabilitation programs

Employment skills services
job services assessment
aptitude testing
career counselling and placement services

Financial support services
eligibility determination
subsidy services
loan availability
job search and placement assistance

## A.        An Ounce of Prevention

Cross-cultural studies of teen motherhood have unearthed six preventive measures that societies have tried since illegitimacy first became labelled as a problem [11]:

| | |
|---|---|
| 1.  penalizing the parents | Numbers 1 to 3 have had |
| 2.  forced marriages | little effect in curbing |
| 3.  early marriages | illegitimacy rates. |
| | |
| 4.  legalized abortion | Numbers 4 to 6 have |
| 5.  birth control | never really been |
| 6.  sex education | sanctioned or tried. |

Some researchers [61] would argue that failure to use contraception has little to do with a woman's ignorance about reproduction or contraception, or her unconscious desire to bear children out of wedlock; rather, the problem is that young unmarried women, especially minors, are denied access to effective medically prescribed contraceptive methods (in descending order of effectiveness: the pill, I.U.D., diaphragm, condom, withdrawal, rhythm, and foam). Access is difficult for young women of all classes—the stigma of premarital sexuality remains. Evidence [61] suggests that school-based educational programs, as they are presently designed, will not decrease the teen pregnancy rate; that public policies cannot reduce teen sexual activity; that there is no new "miracle" contraceptive about to be produced; that increased contraceptive use among males seems unlikely; that merely reforming abortion laws will not affect illegitimacy rates; and that economic change (e.g., increased employment) cannot be relied upon to drastically reduce illegitimacy rates.

The problem may be solved, however, through the widespread development of public and private fertility planning programs offering contraception on request for people of all ages. At present, family planners do not reach out to teen populations in order to provide young men with contraceptive counselling and to encourage them to take more responsibility.

Although data are not conclusive, some researchers [15] suggest that sex education courses in the early teen years are a useful preventive measure (50% of premarital teen pregnancies occur within six months of the young woman's sexual initiation, with 20% happening in the first month). However, presenting the facts is not enough; small group rap-sessions may be more effective. Sex education should also deal with child development, basic life maintenance skills, and parenting. It should also provide opportunities for students to care for young children and to speak with teen parents about their experiences. The school is a potential site for pregnancy testing, counselling, and referral programs; public television may be appropriate for disseminating information; special training for physicians might help them to improve their communication skills and service delivery to adolescents [49].

Being pregnant brings attention/affection to a young woman who might feel that there is little else from which she can derive status and other rewards; perhaps the fundamental means of discouraging early pregnancy is to provide adolescents with attractive options (e.g., enjoyable, useful jobs; relevant training) [49].


## B.    Programs During Pregnancy

Programs are required to serve young women once they have become pregnant and have ruled out abortion as an option. Most programs are crisis-oriented, designed to address emergency issues relevant to the prenatal and early postpartum periods. The assumption appears to be that early parenthood is a crisis from which one "recovers" in time, and therefore most programs stop offering services just when the weightiest problems arise for the young parent [49].

Services tend to be compartmentalized, which provides the basis for the argument that assistance programs should reach out to clients, or at least provide transportation to the program. At present, educational programs, medical clinics, family planning clinics, career counselling, daycare, job placement services, personal counselling, and recreation facilities tend to be scattered throughout a geographic region, thereby creating one more source of discouragement for the potential client [66].


## C.    Postnatal Programs

Most postnatal programs are of brief duration (e.g., 6 weeks; 3 months). Very few supports exist for the adolescent who relinquishes her baby, or for the young mother or father who chooses to keep. At present, the teenager who surrenders her infant has little say in the selection of the adoptive family, and usually has no group of peers whose common experience of mourning could be shared through group exchanges.

For young women who keep their infants, there is a lack of infant daycare; job placement or training programs; affordable housing units which accept children; adequate public assistance benefits; outreach programs to help them prevent unwanted repeat pregnancies; attempts at establishing informal support networks within the community (e.g., drop-in centres, support groups, volunteer visitor/helpers, and phone-in services to reduce isolation); supervised, post-delivery residences which could help the young mother to adjust to parenthood, build interpersonal skills, reduce isolation, and plan or implement a productive future; parenting courses and supportive services for fathers and grandparents; and foster homes for mother and infant together.

At present, service providers tend to not coordinate efforts; certain forms of public assistance are provided only if there is no male living with mother, which tends to be punitive and self-defeating; and no financial encouragement is provided to family members who are willing to support the teen mother and her child. Some researchers have suggested that agencies should provide a minimum of three-year follow-up if they sincerely wish to assist young unwed parents and their children.

No services are possible without government spending. Interest groups must lobby vigorously for such funding.

For a discussion of community approaches to provide support services, see Chapter 3, IV, V.

## VII.  PRACTICE APPROACHES

UP workers do more than provide direct service—they also act as case managers, arranging for the wide array of services required by pregnant teens and young parents. While these client groups may voluntarily seek help, they will reject this help if it does not provide effective, concrete services during the initial phases of agency-client relationship [70, 49].

### A.  Establishing Trust

According to Bedger [70], the adolescent client is apt to be frightened, feeling hopeless about the future, suspicious, and burdened by inertia. It is suggested that the social worker adopt a helping style which is congruent with the client's remoteness and inertia by being pragmatic, concrete, and personal, and by dealing with problems in basic life maintenance (food, clothing, shelter).

Ensuring the basics is a frustrating and time-consuming casework task, but one which is necessary before other interventions can be started. In assisting with the recruitment of resources, the worker is reducing the effects of the crisis and perhaps is paving the way for better relations between the mother and her child. The client is more likely to agree to examine emotional/social problems once the worker has proven her sincerity by coming through with the basics.

In their need to rebel and to seek independence, adolescents tend to perceive adults who are in official capacities as lacking in sincerity and a genuine desire to be helpful; even in the face of this, workers must maintain a caring and consistent position in order to allay such suspicions. Once a trusting relationship has been established with the worker, the client is more likely to utilize other services. It has been suggested that the personal relationship between worker and client be established in such a way as to imply that the condition of pregnancy or motherhood is incidental to the relationship, and that the client is a unique person rather than a "case type". Through the establishing of such a bond, the client is likely to acknowledge her self-worth, and to stop testing the limits of the worker and ignoring her advice. It appears that patience combined with the provision of concrete services will create a basis for a trusting relationship [70].

### B.  Providing the Necessities

In focussing on the provision of concrete fundamentals, the worker is acknowledging that crisis events (e.g., child maltreatment) are as likely to arise from a paucity of material resources (e.g., money to pay for rent, food, and clothing) as they are to result from the psychodynamic elements of the situation.

The worker and client may have definitions of "basics" that are at odds; the teen's priorities may include items/services which the worker perceives as frivolous, not unlike the common dynamic between parent and teen (she wants to spend her money on new records, her parent(s) perceive this as a wasteful choice). Some clients lack motivation to avail themselves of necessary services; they may act in ways which prove harmful to themselves or to their unborn/infant child. The worker's task is to remain supportive and encouraging. This might mean discussing the issues and then supporting the client in a graduated acceptance of responsibility for her child, rather than overloading her with a number of tasks that will only discourage her. With each successful task completion, the client's self-esteem and confidence rises, and eventually emphasis on concrete services and instructions in dealing with day-to-day tasks can be replaced by other supports [70].

## C.    Offering Emotional Growth

Establishing rapport with an untrusting adolescent requires considerable skill and sensitivity. Several points should be kept in mind [70]:

The worker can easily become overwhelmed by the number and magnitude of problems that each adolescent brings to him or her; for this reason, workers must have a strong support system to aid them in the challenge they have accepted in dealing with adolescents, and in particular, with pregnant adolescents.

Cues for each session should (ideally) emanate from the client rather than from the worker; the client can set the tone and decide on a focus, thereby increasing the likelihood of client motivation.

The client is likely to display both adult and child behaviours in the treatment setting, and the worker must accept that the client is part adult, part child.

The client may present a "flat affect", especially if she has been coerced into seeking help; also, she may lack the vocabulary to describe her feelings and may lack experience in disclosing feelings, especially to adults.

The worker must teach the client that their relationship is a safe one; this can be accomplished in part by being readily available, by being understanding even when being rejected, and by avoiding judgemental statements/non-verbal expressions; the worker must prove trustworthiness and prove ability to provide useful concrete help before the client is likely to express her deepest feelings.

Educational services, particularly through groups, can help bridge the gap between provision of concrete services and the pathway to emotional growth.

## D.    Groups

Peer group therapy is the most frequently suggested milieu for the emotional/

social care of the pregnant/parenting adolescent. There are several reported merits of groups: (1) they provide the opportunity to make friends with others who share common experiences; (2) independent living skills can be taught, rehearsed, and reinforced within the group; (3) the social worker can observe and surmise as to which group members would benefit from more in-depth explorations; (4) groups rely on peers rather than on a lone, adult social worker for social rewards and recognition:

> When the hostility of the normally developing adolescent, including a rebelliousness toward authority figures, is heightened by the anger and anxiety of unintended pregnancy-parenting, it is erroneous to limit therapeutic relationships to those which would force the adolescent to interact with the adult authority figure only. Not only are such limited interactions not a good idea, but they are often doomed to failure. [49: p. 194]

(5) the group setting is an educational tool where teens can learn by doing— an approach generally favoured by young people, especially if they select topics and tone; (6) mutual support can create a group identity and a sense of belonging.

As valuable as groups have been shown to be, using peer group therapy to the exclusion of all other approaches is not necessarily suggested. However, much of the UP practice literature does focus on groups [17, 44].

### Overall Goal of Groups

To enhance the process of self-realization; to serve as a place in which adolescents can retreat from expectations of the adult world, and where they can test values and weigh choices in an atmosphere of support

## E.     Family Therapy

The pregnant/parenting teen exists not in isolation, but in a network within which she interacts with individuals and groups; she affects their lives, they affect hers. Perhaps the most influential group or individual is the family or the parent (where the client has only one parent and no siblings) [7, 26].

Families are intended to function in contemporary society as mediators of stress; however, not all family units function in this supportive capacity. Research suggests that when major conflict arises within a dysfunctional family at the time of pregnancy, this is only the tip of the iceberg—usually when family problems result in extensive dysfunction this reflects a long-term, well-established response pattern. While work with such families is a lengthy and difficult process, it may produce many benefits for the adolescent who might otherwise receive scant support from other sources. A supportive family can provide a sense of self-esteem, satisfy a wide array of needs, and encourage development and growth. A non-supportive family may have anticipated that the client would "mess up", get pregnant, and bring added burdens to the family; the client may have become pregnant as part of a self-fulfilling prophecy— and the worker must strive to break this negative self-image.

Some families initially agree to support the client and in fact behave that way, except for subtle remarks/actions which signal to the client that her family is angry or disgusted with her for having become pregnant. The client tries to win her family's favor by behaving in a responsible manner, and although the social worker rewards this behaviour, the family only appears to be supportive—therefore the worker must intervene or the client will lose any motivation to please her family.

The following guidelines should be kept in mind [70]:

The worker's role is to assist the family in its attempts to cope with the responsibility of providing support to the client.

It is essential to bring the family to a healthy balance in order to avoid future scapegoating of the pregnant/parenting teen.

The goal of family therapy is to determine where the systemic dysfunction lies; all members of the system are the worker's responsibility.

When entry to the system has been gained (with caution), then goals must be established and each member's role identified: family members are to be partners, not saviors, and they must treat the client with dignity, which can be built into the therapy process.

One major objective is to increase effective communication within the system and within the individual (this can often be taught through role-playing, role-rehearsal, modelling); the worker's task is to interpret, enforce rules, and to model during practice sessions; increased effectiveness in communication builds on the concept of cooperation and expands each member's view of self and others.

Another objective is to teach a sense of mastery of the environment, with a concomitant sense of self-esteem; the worker teaches the family that the environment is somewhat predictable (and therefore manageable); that the family can have some impact upon their environment because they are not helpless victims (once again, modelling and role-playing can be used to demonstrate revised modes of interaction with the environment).

A third objective is to educate the family regarding the client's condition and to explain ways in which they can enhance the experience for her.

Throughout therapy there may be an underlying fear on the part of her family that the client will become pregnant again in the future; this is not an irrational position, given the high proportion of teen repeat pregnancies; however, the worker should focus on the adolescent's strengths rather than on her vulnerabilities.

## F.    Individual Therapy

Counselling pregnant/parenting teens [10, 39, 45] differs from work with other adolescents in a few specific ways: first, client's low self-esteem and lack of trust are exacerbated; second, the worker must be more actively involved with the pregnant/parenting client; third, a greater dependency between worker and client is allowed to build.

Lack of trust will get handled only if the worker survives the "tests" presented by the client (e.g., missed appointments; endless demands), and if the worker maintains a nonjudgemental stance (within reason).

In preparing for parenthood, the young woman must learn to deal with individuals with whom she might not otherwise have come into contact. Skills required for accomplishing daily living tasks might include: assertiveness training, relaxation training, rational thinking, and behaviour modification.

Once worker-client trust has been established, emphasis must shift to the client as an individual person. Although the worker may be the first stable model the client has ever experienced, the young woman can begin to appreciate the value of being close to, *and* of being separate from, others. Learning to avoid involvement in self-defeating relationships, to plan realistically for the future, to establish achievable goals, and to own up to one's feelings about pregnancy and parenting are crucial tasks [70].

It hurts to relinquish an infant, but if the young mother is allowed to care for her baby while in hospital, then she will have proven to herself and to others that she is capable of loving; this may help to eliminate some pain associated with surrendering. The worker can help her to distinguish between her needs as an adolescent and her capabilities as a parent.

Denial of future sexuality is a common theme: 'I'll never have sex again'. The worker would be irresponsible to ignore the contraceptive issue; however, if the client wishes to ignore contraceptive information then the worker can suggest that she call in the future if she wishes, or can provide her with information about family planning services. In addition, if parents can be helped to accept their daughter's sexuality, then this may allow her to acknowledge it and to plan for sexual encounters.

The young woman should always feel that her worker will be available should she need advice, support, or help. The most effective relationships are those which take the client from rehabilitation to prevention and which continue service provision for as long as the teen parent may need it [70].

## VIII.    SUMMARY

Many critical decisions must be made by young women when they discover that they are pregnant; will they continue the pregnancy, abort, surrender the child for adoption, rear the child as a single-parent, form a family unit with the child's father or with another person, and so on? Will they continue in school, in their job? Where will they live? How will they financially support the child? Where will they learn to physically care for a child? These are only a handful of the myriad questions that UP workers examine with their clients. This chapter has examined some of the tasks of UP workers, and has explored: why young women who claim not to want pregnancy do in fact become pregnant; ways in which society shirks responsibility for young people's sexuality, and its consequences; the issue of male responsibility for birth control and for decision-making during and after pregnancy. Many philosophical, medical, and political questions remain to be asked and answered.

## REFERENCES

1. Child Welfare League of America. "Early Childbearing and Young Parenthood Loan Packet", Child Welfare Informational Resource Services, 1981.

2. Kaplow, E. and Terzieff, N. "An Experiment in Group Service to Unmarried Parents", Project of the Unmarried Parents Department, Children's Aid Society of Metropolitan Toronto, 1971.

3. Hendricks, L. "Unwed Adolescent Fathers: Problems They Face and Their Sources of Social Support", Adolescence, Vol. XV, Winter 1980, pp. 861–870.

4. Bemis, J., Diers, E., and Sharpe, E. et al. "The Teen-age Single Mother", Child Welfare, Vol. LV, May 1976, pp. 309–318.

5. Furstenberg, F., Jr. and Crawford, A. "Family Support: Helping Teenage Mothers to Cope", Family Planning Perspectives, Vol. 10, No. 6, Nov.–Dec. 1978, pp. 322–333.

6. Scales, P. "The Context of Sex Education and the Reduction of Teenage Pregnancy", Child Welfare, Vol. LVIII, April 1979, pp. 263–273.

7. Palmer, E. "A Community-Based Comprehensive Approach to Serving Adolescent Parents", Child Welfare, Vol. LX, March 1981, pp. 191–197.

8. Grow, L., "Today's Unmarried Mothers: The Choices Have Changed", Child Welfare, Vol. LVIII, June 1979, pp. 363–371.

9. Enos, R. and Hisanaga, M. "Goal Setting with Pregnant Teen-Agers", Child Welfare, Vol. LVIII, September/October 1979, pp. 541–552.

10. Cartoof, V. "Post-partum Services for Adolescent Mothers: Part 2", Child Welfare, Vol. LVIII, December 1979, pp. 673–680.

11. Plionis, B. M. "Adolescent Pregnancy: Review of the Literature", Social Work, Vol. 20, July 1975, pp. 302–307.

12. Sung, K. and Rothrock, D. "An Alternative School for Pregnant Teen-agers and Teen-age Mothers", Child Welfare, Vol. LIX, July/August 1980, pp. 427–436.

13. Johnson, C. Trends in Services For the Pregnant Adolescent. Athens, Georgia: Dept. of Child and Family Development, University of Georgia, (no date).

14. Miller, S. Children as Parents: A Progress Report on a Study of Childbearing and Childrearing Among 12–15 Year Olds. New York: Research Center, Child Welfare League of America, 1981.

15. Phipps-Yonas, S. "Teenage Pregnancy and Motherhood: A Review of the Literature", American Journal of Orthopsychiatry, Vol. 50, July 1980, pp. 403–431.

16. Moore, K., Hofferth, S. and Wertheimer, R. II. "Teenage Motherhood: Its Social and Economic Costs", Children Today, September–October 1979, pp. 12–16.

17. Middleman, R. "A Service Pattern for Helping Unmarried Pregnant Teenagers", Children, Vol. 17 May–June, 1970, pp. 108–112.

18. Hodson, N., Armour, M., and Touliatos, J. "Project Uplift: A Coordinated Youth Services System", The Family Coordinator, Vol. 25, July 1976, pp. 255–260.

19. Bolton, F. G., Jr., Laner, R., and Kane, S. "Child Maltreatment Risk Among Adolescent Mothers: A Study of Reported Cases", American Journal of Orthopsychiatry, Vol. 50, July 1980, pp. 481–488.

20. Kinard, E. M. and Klerman, L. "Teenage Parenting and Child Abuse: Are they Related?", American Journal of Orthopsychiatry, Vol. 50, July 1980, pp. 469–480.

21. Earls, F. and Siegel B. "Precocious Fathers", American Journal of Orthopsychiatry Vol. 50, No. 3, July 1980.

22. Wise, S. and Grosman, F. "Adolescent Mothers and Their Infants: Psychological Factors in Early Attachment and Interaction", American Journal of Orthopsychiatry Vol. 50, July 1980, pp. 454–668.

23. Lewis C. "A Comparison of Minors' and Adults' Pregnancy Decisions", American Journal of Orthopsychiatry, Vol. 50, July 1980, pp. 446–453.

24. Olson, L. "Social and Psychological Correlates of Pregnancy Resolution Among Adolescent Women: A Review", American Journal of Orthopsychiatry, Vol. 50, (3) 1980, pp. 432–445.

25. Gill, D., *Illegitimacy, Sexuality and the Status of Women*. Oxford: Basil Blackwell, 1979.

26. Benas, E. "Residential Care of the Child-Mother and Her Infant: An Extended Family Concept", Child Welfare, Vol. LIV, April 1975, pp. 290–294.

27. Wright, M. "Comprehensive Services for Adolescent Unwed Mothers", Children, Vol. 13, September–October 1966, pp. 170–176.

28. McKenry, P., Henley, L., and Johnson, C. "Adolescent Pregnancy: A Review of the Literature", The Family Coordinator, Vol. 28, January 1979, pp. 17–28.

29. Hansson, R., Jones, W., and Chernovetz, M. "Contraceptive Knowledge: Antecedents and Implications", The Family Coordinator, Vol. 28, January 1979, pp. 29–34.

30. Kane, F. J. and Lachenbruch, P. "Adolescent Pregnancy: A Study of Aborters and Non-Aborters", American Journal of Orthopsychiatry, Vol. 43, October 1973, pp. 796–803.

31. Fischman, S. "Delivery or Abortion in Inner-City Adolescents", American Journal of Orthopsychiatry, Vol. 47, January 1977, pp. 127–133.

32. Campbell, B. and Barnlund, D. "Communication Patterns and Problems of Pregnancy", American Journal of Orthopsychiatry, Vol. 47, January 1977, pp. 134–139.

33. Kreech, F. "The Current Role and Services of Agencies for Unwed Parents and Their Children", Child Welfare, Vol. LIII, May 1974, pp. 323–328.

34. Chilman, C. "Social and Psychological Research Concerning Adolescent Childbearing: 1970–1980", Journal of Marriage and The Family, Vol. 42, November 1980, pp. 793–806.

35. ———. "Teenage Pregnancy: A Research Review", Social Work, Vol. 24, November 1979, pp. 492–498.

36. Johnson, C. "Adolescent Pregnancy: Intervention Into the Poverty Cycle", Adolescence, Vol. IX, Fall 1974, pp. 391–406.

37. Schinke, S., Gilchrist, L., and Small, R. "Preventing Unwanted Adolescent Pregnancy: A Cognitive-Behavioral Approach", American Journal of Orthopsychiatry, Vol. 49, January 1979, pp. 81–88.

38. Williams, T. "Childrearing Practices of Young Mothers: What We Know, How It Matters, Why It's So Little", American Journal of Orthopsychiatry, Vol. 44, January 1974, pp. 70–75.

39. Levenson, P. et al. "Serving Teenage Mothers and Their High-Risk Infants", Children Today, July–August 1978, pp. 11–15, 36.

40. Litton-Fox G. "The Family's Influence on Adolescent Sexual Behaviour", Children Today, Vol. 8, May–June 1979, pp. 21–25, 36.

41. Bogue, D. "A Long-Term Solution to the AFDC Problem: Prevention of Unwanted Pregnancy", Social Service Review, Vol. 49, December 1975, pp. 539–552.

42. Festinger, T. "Unwed Mothers and Their Decisions to Keep or Surrender Children", Child Welfare, Vol. L, May 1971, pp. 253–263.

43. Schinke, S. "Teenage Pregnancy: The Need for Multiple Casework Services", Social Casework, Vol. 59, July 1978, pp. 406–410.

44. Kolodny, R. and Riley, L. "Group Work With Today's Unmarried Mother", Social Casework, Vol. 53, December 1972, pp. 613–622.

45. Schloessinger, J. and Davis, S. "Problem Pregnancy and Abortion Counseling with Teenagers", Social Casework, Vol. 61, March 1980, pp. 173–179.

46. Guyatt, D. "Adolescent Pregnancy: A Study of Pregnant Teenagers In A Suburban Community In Ontario", Ph.D. thesis—University of Toronto, 1976.

47. Furstenberg, F., Jr. *Unplanned Parenthood: The Social Consequences of Teenage Childbearing*. New York: The Free Press, 1976.

48. Baizerman, M. et al. *Pregnant Adolescents: A Review of Literature With Abstracts, 1960–1970*. Washington, D.C.: Consortium on Early Childbearing and Childrearing, 1971.

49. Bolton, C., Jr. *The Pregnant Adolescent: Problems of Premature Parenthood*. Beverly Hills, Calif.: Sage Publications, 1980.

50. Oettinger, K. *Not My Daughter: Facing Up to Adolescent Pregnancy*. Englewood Cliffs, N.J.: Prentice-Hall, Inc., 1979.

51. Alan Guttmacher Institute. *Eleven Million Teenagers: What Can Be Done About the Epidemic of Adolescent Pregnancies in the United States.* New York: 1976.

52. MacIntyre, S. *Single and Pregnant.* London: Croom Helm, 1977.

53. Card, J. and Wise, L. "Teenage Mothers and Teenage Fathers: The Impact of Early Childbearing on the Parents' Personal and Professional Lives", Family Planning Perspectives, Vol. 10, July–August 1978, pp. 199–204.

54. Baldwin, W. and Cain, V. "The Children of Teenage Parents", Family Planning Perspectives, Vol. 12, January–February 1980, pp. 34–39, 42–43.

55. Furstenberg, F., Jr. "How Can Family Planning Programs Delay Repeat Teenage Pregnancies?", Family Planning Perspectives, Vol. 4, No. 3, July 1972.

56. Menken, J., "The Health and Social Consequences of Teenage Childbearing", Family Planning Perspectives, Vol. 4, No. 3, July 1972.

57. Torres, A. "Does Your Mother Know. . . ?" Family Planning Perspectives, Vol. 10, September–October 1978, pp. 280–285.

58. Ambrose, L. "Misinforming Pregnant Teenagers", Family Planning Perspectives, Vol. 10, January–February 1978, pp. 51–57.

59. Trussell, J. and Menken, J. "Early Childbearing and Subsequent Fertility", Family Planning Perspectives, Vol. 10, July–August 1978, pp. 209–218.

60. Moore, K. "Teenage Childbirth and Welfare Dependency", Family Planning Perspectives, Vol. 10, July–August 1978, pp. 233–235.

61. Cutright, P. "Illegitimacy: Myths, Causes and Cures", Family Planning Perspectives, Vol. 3, No. 1, January 1971.

62. Torres A., Forrest, J., and Eisman, S. "Telling Parents: Clinic Policies and Adolescents' Use of Family Planning and Abortion Services", Family Planning Perspectives, Vol. 12, November–December 1980, pp. 284–292.

63. Moore, K. and Caldwell, S. "The Effect of Government Policies On Out-Of-Wedlock Sex", Family Planning Perspectives, Vol. 9, July–August 1977, pp. 164–169.

64. Furstenberg, F., Jr., "The Social Consequences of Teenage Parenthood", Family Planning Perspectives, Vol. 8, July–August 1976, pp. 148–164.

65. Edwards, L. et al. "Adolescent Pregnancy Prevention Services In High School Clinics", Family Planning Perspectives, Vol. 12, January–February 1980, pp. 6–14.

66. Family Day Care Services, Toronto. "To Parent Is a Verb: A Discussion on Adolescent Parenting", 1980.

67. Shapiro, C. "Sexual Learning: The Short-changed Adolescent Male", Social Work, Vol. 25, November 1980, pp. 489–494.

68. Lindsay, J. *Pregnant Too Soon: Adoption Is An Option.* EMC Publishing, 1980.

69. Cheetham, J. *Unwanted Pregnancy and Counselling.* London: Routledge and Kegan Paul, 1977.

70. Bedger, J. *Teenage Pregnancy: Research Related to Clients and Services.* Springfield, Ill.: Charles C Thomas Publishers, 1980.

71. Schlesinger, B. "Children Having Children: Some Notes for Discussion", for Child Welfare League of America, April 24, 1981, Toronto.

72. Rosen, R. "Adolescent Pregnancy Decision-Making: Are Parents Important?", Adolescence, Vol. XV, Spring 1970.

73. Horowitz, N. "Adolescent Mourning Reaction to Infant and Fetal Loss", Social Casework, Vol. 59, November 1978, pp. 551–559.

74. Chilman, C., "Possible Factors Associated with High Rates of Out-of-Marriage Births among Adolescents", paper presented at the American Psychological Association, Washington, D.C., 1976.

75. Baum, J. *Teenage Pregnancy: A Handbook for Teachers, Parents, Counselors, and Kids.* Ontario: General Publishing Co., 1980.

76. Bracken, M. B., Klerman, L. V., and Bracken, M. "Coping with Pregnancy Resolution Among Never-Married Women", American Journal of Orthopsychiatry, Vol. 49, 1978, pp. 320–334.

# Appendices

A.      A PROBLEM-SOLVING APPROACH TO CHILD WELFARE
PRACTICE      391

B.      ASSESSMENT FRAMEWORKS      423

C.      STAFF PRACTICE STATEMENTS      437

# A
# A Problem-Solving Approach to Child Welfare Practice

FRANK MAIDMAN

I. INTRODUCTION: A CASE FOR PROBLEM-SOLVING        392
   A. The Case of Bill        392
   B. What Are the Problem-Solving Issues in This Case?        393
   C. What Is a Problem?        395
   D. What Is Problem-Solving?        395
   E. Knowledge and Problem-Solving        396
   F. How Can Bill Be Helped? A Brief Review of
      Problem-Solving Steps        396

II. UNDERSTANDING BILL'S PROBLEMS: TOWARDS A
GOOD ASSESSMENT        398
   A. What Are the Nature and Purpose of Assessment?        398
   B. Describing the Problem        399
   C. The Importance of Linking Private Troubles to
      Public Issues        400
   D. An Assessment Outline        401
   E. Formulation: Guidelines for Identifying the Central
      Factors in a Problem        405
   F. Establishing Goals for Intervention        407
   G. Understanding the Problem: A Summary        410

III. The Search for Solutions: What Is the Best Service
Plan for Bill?        410
   A. Criteria for Service Selection        410
   B. Selecting a Solution: A Summary        412

IV. IMPLEMENTING THE SOLUTION: MAKING THE
SERVICE PLAN WORK        412
   A. Planning the Implementation: Perspectives and
      Checklist        413
   B. Putting the Solution into Practice        413
   C. Implementing the Service Plan: A Summary        414

V. EVALUATING SOLUTIONS        414
   A. What Is Individual Professional Evaluation?        415

|   | B. | Evaluating Outcome | 415 |
|---|---|---|---|
|   | C. | Evaluating Process | 415 |
|   | D. | Useful Information for Evaluation Purposes | 416 |
|   | E. | Evaluating Solutions: A Summary | 416 |
| VI. | | TERMINATING THE INTERVENTION | 417 |
|   | A. | Deciding to Terminate an Intervention | 417 |
|   | B. | Preparing the Client for Termination | 418 |
|   | C. | Helping the Client Stabilize Changes Outside of the Problem-Solving Relationship | 419 |
|   | D. | Terminating the Relationship: A Summary | 420 |
| VII. | | REFLECTING ABOUT ONE'S PROBLEM-SOLVING | 420 |
| VIII. | | CHILD WELFARE PRACTICE AS PROBLEM-SOLVING: A GENERAL SUMMARY | 421 |
|   | | REFERENCES | 421 |

## I.    INTRODUCTION: A CASE FOR PROBLEM-SOLVING

Child welfare work has been described as the most challenging of the helping professions. Superimposed on the difficulty in changing undesirable human behaviour, is the burden of working with legally prohibited behaviour. Child welfare work is problem-solving work of the most complex kind, requiring a serious problem-solving approach.

This appendix presents a general framework for considering practice as a problem-solving activity. Like the previous chapters, it is theoretical in its level of discussion. For this reason it is not recommended as a quick reference resource. Rather, the appendix is best used as (a) a guide for worker reflection about practice either privately or in supervision; (b) a training resource; and (c) a guide to assessing a client's problem-solving techniques.

To appreciate the difficulties associated with child welfare problem-solving, consider the following hypothetical case:

### A.    The Case of Bill

Bill first came to a child welfare agency at 13 years of age because of truancy. Since beginning school, he has had a history of underachievement and unacceptable behaviour in class. Despite the efforts of teachers and the special services department, Bill's behaviour continued. With increased school absence and suspected parental neglect, the court finally charged him with truancy.

Initially, Bill was placed in an assessment home, but was returned to his

392

parents soon after on an order of supervision. Parental lack of cooperation made the order of supervision difficult; however, after committing vandalism, Bill was placed in the care of the child welfare agency by the court. Subsequent to his return to care, Bill spent time at an admission and assessment home, a detention home (after a row in which police were called in), another admission and assessment home, and, finally, a group home. Throughout this process, a number of assessments were made by psychiatrists, child care workers, and family service workers, although a lack of cooperation from Bill often made assessments difficult.

During his stay at the various homes, a number of observations concerning his behaviour were made by staff. The initial period was usually quite good, with Bill presenting as a reasonably cooperative, amiable, even charming fellow. As time progressed, however, his behaviour changed. Sometimes without apparent reason he would throw a tantrum, striking out physically and verbally against peers and staff. Many of his outbursts followed staff efforts to have him recognize rules and regulations. In addition, Bill was known to engage in bizarre behaviour, such as watching and talking to a blank television set for hours on end. He was also a frequent runner, often staying at his parents' home without any apparent encouragement to return.

Bill's family background and current family life are important factors in this case. He comes from a very large family, with older brothers and sisters presenting considerable problems in the community. An older sister had problems in school and problems described as sexual promiscuity. Efforts at family counselling through a community agency did not change the girl's or the family's problems.

Bill's natural parents divorced ten years ago. His mother, a Canadian, remarried a European and gave birth to another child. The stepfather's childrearing approach differed from the mother's. His attempts to take control of Bill with physical punishment contrasted with the mother's only intermittent efforts at physical control. Bill's relationship with his mother remains constantly on the verge of violence, and she often feels helpless and frightened. He frequently visits his natural father and sometimes his grandparents; these are usually enjoyable visits. The family has financial as well as family problems.

Despite an acknowledgement of her own difficulties as a parent, Bill's mother is opposed to seeking or receiving outside help. In particular, she resists the agency's involvement and appears to dread Court or Society Wardship. From the outset she has remained uncooperative in efforts to provide help. Bill's feeling about changing his life swings from a strong desire to change to a wish to be left alone.

The agency has had a difficult time with this case. Many different approaches have been tried to change Bill's behaviour and to enlist parental cooperation. However, except on an intermittent basis, none has been successful. The agency is now seeking an appropriate long-term placement.

## B.    What Are the Problem-Solving Issues in This Case?

Different people may isolate different elements in this case, elements which indirectly or directly affect efforts to solve Bill's problem behaviour. In general, factors affecting a child welfare practitioner's work with Bill and his family may be summarized as follows:

*Resources:* What professional knowledge and techniques might aid in understanding and alleviating Bill's problems? What material and staff resources are available? What community resources? Specialized resources in agency?

*Values:* Problem definitions are usually affected by people's ideas about what constitutes a desirable society, high quality of life, and personal behaviour. Initially, Bill's problems were manifested in his inability to meet school expectations for achievement and behaviour.

*Roles:* A practitioner's problem-solving efforts are enhanced or limited by her or his expected roles within the agency. Also, they depend on the reciprocal behaviour of others. Bill's reluctance during assessment sessions inhibited the acquisition of good information. Explaining and doing something about this reluctance is a necessary part of problem-solving.

*Goals:* What should the worker strive to change in Bill's situation? His truancy? Behaviour with peers? Reactions to authority? Family relations? Are some changes necessary before others can happen? Are some easier to accomplish than others?

*Social and cultural organization:* Efforts to understand Bill's behaviour and to do something about it have not proceeded randomly, although it may seem so. While not reported in the case, four different organizations or organizational departments have been involved in the process of gathering assessment information in order to understand the problem. Few have been successful in gathering full information, although copious data are available on file. Information-gathering has not been successful in this case, yet the worker needs it for problem-solving.

*Social policy:* The types of client problems faced by the worker are partially defined by legal and social policy. Bill's absence from school and suspicion of parental neglect initially caused school authorities to take legal action. In addition, this policy affecting initial contact with Bill and his parents introduces a legal element into the helping process. Is it possible to "help" under these circumstances?

*Societal conditions:* Bill's family is struggling with economic bad times. Both parents are working long hours to make ends meet. Have these conditions contributed to neglect and unwillingness to help in problem-solving? Also, economic conditions may limit the available services for Bill and his family.

These elements are not the only factors affecting the problem-solving process. For example, nothing has been said about worker skills and family dynamics. Nevertheless, in child welfare practice, these issues point the way to a problem-solving approach:

What information does staff need in order to understand why this child and the family behave as they do?

Which information is the most valuable in deciding what to do in this case?

How does staff decide what to change when there are so many evident difficulties in these clients' lives?

Of the various possible interventions, which is the best?

Given the difficulty in changing problem behaviour, what steps can be taken to assure that the service choice has a good chance of working?

How can it be determined whether or not the intervention is working?

How can a good termination of the case be assured?

How can a worker generally improve as a solver of problems?

For purposes of this Source Book, these questions are taken as the core of the problem-solving process. As this discussion proceeds, we will return to Bill's case for illustration of problem-solving steps.

A fully developed problem-solving model would provide guidelines for dealing with all features of the practitioner's environment which inhibit problem-solving (e.g., how to work with limited resources; how to resolve value conflicts; how to deal with the emotional elements in the case). For brevity, concentration will be on the practitioner's thinking and use of information.

As workers solve problems, they take into account other kinds of information, work with other scarce resources, and negotiate with persons and institutions other than clients.


## C.    What Is a Problem?

In colloquial terms, a problem is regarded as a source of perplexity, distress, or vexation. In child welfare practice, problems may refer to a child's problem, a client's family life and childrearing, the immediate work situations of the worker, the community, and so on. This manual concentrates on *client* problems. However, the problem-solving principles are adaptable to all situations.


## D.    What Is Problem-Solving?

Problem-solving is defined as those planned steps in thought and action which help to overcome a troublesome situation. This section will outline those steps and present guidelines for thinking about or monitoring one's own problem-solving. The professional dilemmas on previous pages are equivalent to the following stages of problem-solving:

1. Orienting to the problem
2. Defining the problem
3. Selecting a solution
4. Implementing the solution
5. Evaluating the solution
6. Terminating the problem-solving effort
7. Reflecting about problem-solving

Stages and guidelines are designed to aid specific problem-solving efforts and to enhance growth in problem-solving as a generalized skill.

**E.        Knowledge and Problem-Solving**

In the case of Bill and his family, child welfare workers require a variety of information: historical information about the problems, current facts, professional knowledge about problem families, information about possible solutions, professional assessment information, service experience with Bill and his family, and so forth.

The guidelines in this Source Book rest on the following general principle:

Problem-solving is enhanced by the expansion of information brought to bear on a particular problem, particularly when that information is systematically organized and applied to the problem.

Sources of information for successful problem-solving include:

> self (personal, practice wisdom, creativity, and intuition)
>
> colleagues (practice wisdom)
>
> published research and practice literature
>
> policy and program guidelines

A simple proliferation of information does not enhance problem-solving; it leads to "information overload" and confusion. Some means of organizing is necessary.

*Will we ever have enough information to help Bill?* Despite a considerable amount of information, practitioners may not have enough. For example, Bill's non-cooperation in assessment interviews and his mother's negative attitudes towards the agency prevented staff from gathering full information. Further, the professional literature may not provide research facts and theories which are suitable for understanding such seemingly unique circumstances.

Problem-solvers may never have enough information to fully understand a problem, to select among all possible service plans, to anticipate all possible impediments to these solutions, and to decide if, indeed, their solutions work. Therefore, child welfare workers must be prepared to take creative risks.

*What is creative risk-taking?* Risk-taking in problem-solving behaviour is a willingness:

> to live with a certain understanding of a problem when there is doubt
>
> to make selections among solutions when one is not sure of all the bases for making a selection (particularly whether or not the solution will work!)
>
> to begin implementing a solution when one is not certain as to whether all possible impediments have been taken into account
>
> to decide that the solution worked when one is not sure that the best indicators for measuring success have been used

**F.        How Can Bill Be Helped? A Brief Review of Problem-Solving Steps**

Bill's case is quite difficult, with no easy solution immediately apparent. However, perhaps the right solution can be found if an appropriate process is followed. Questions reflecting a simple problem-solving process are as follows:

What are the various possible explanations for Bill's behaviour? For example, is he brain-damaged or is he still responding to his natural parents' separation? Does he have a learning problem? Do we look into Bill's past, or are current events adequate to understand his behaviour? Do we focus on his school behaviour? His behaviour towards staff and peers in residence? Or towards his parents? Or all of these? What are we trying to explain?

Having settled on a description of the key patterns in his problem behaviour (e.g., difficulty with adult authority figures and rejection of peers), what are the various interventions that might help? At this point, it is best to suspend judgment about the most useful possibility. We are developing a pool of possibilities.

Now a choice among possible service solutions is necessary. How do we make such a choice? Choice-making should not be whimsical; it should be based on specific criteria, systematically applied to all possibilities. Obviously, such a choice of intervention should make a change in those factors. This will be reviewed later. Some of these have nothing to do with Bill's problems! Whatever the criteria for deciding among service plans or treatment approaches, it may be useful to assign weights to the criteria. In Bill's case, for example, access to the family may be an important criterion in deciding among options.

Having made a service choice for Bill, it is now useful to think through those factors which may either help or hinder the successful implementation of this plan. Bill's placement at a youth residence was constantly hampered by his running. His parents were uncooperative in aiding his return, and the efforts of staff were undermined. Could this, and other impediments to the service plan have been anticipated? If Bill's running had been avoided, would the residence placement have worked? (A systematic approach to service implementation is reviewed in section IV of this appendix).

How can one evaluate this attempted solution in Bill's case? An ongoing evaluation of efforts to help him has immediate and long-term use. If there is an apparent lack of success with current arrangements, plans for Bill may need modification. Evaluation may also aid in planning for other similar cases.

How can thinking about Bill's case be used to improve one's problem-solving skills in general? Was it the process of considering several different explanations for his behaviour? Or was it thinking through in the implementation of service plans? Where were the risks in this case, and how did they work out? Whatever the answers, such reflection about problem-solving is a useful way to consolidate one's skills.

To summarize: the difficult work of child welfare practice requires a systematic approach to problem-solving. Although many factors in a practitioner's environment can enhance or inhibit efforts to solve a client's problems, good information is an important resource. Because information is usually limited, some risk-taking is necessary. Suggested phases of problem-solving are:

consideration of alternative ways of understanding a problem generation of alternative solutions

development of criteria for systematically comparing solutions

weighing selection criteria according to degrees of importance

prior assessment of the impediments to implementing a solution, and to monitoring the implementation

verification or evaluation of one's attempted solutions

reflection about one's problem-solving efforts, both specific and general

use of creativity and risk-taking in problem-solving

This section continues with working through these problem-solving stages with reference to Bill's case.

## II.    UNDERSTANDING BILL'S PROBLEMS: TOWARDS A GOOD ASSESSMENT

Successful solutions require a sound understanding or definition of the problem. In complex cases it is easy to become mired in facts, possible explanations, and pessimism about doing anything helpful. Also, it is tempting and sometimes necessary to think about solutions before all the facts are in. In social casework and child **care** work, understanding client problems typically starts at the assessment phase. In cases such as Bill's, previous school records may suggest certain explanations (e.g., acting out, low self-esteem, inadequate social skills) without adequate descriptions of the behaviour which generates such labels. These "explanations" should be taken as suggestions, but should not substitute for comprehensive descriptions of the problem. This is the work of assessment.

### A.    What Are the Nature and Purpose of Assessment?

Problem assessment should aid the worker in understanding the situation. Specifically, assessment is used to aid the worker to make decisions about:

which aspects of the situation should be dealt with

the possible goals of the change or problem-solving effort

the means to be adopted for achieving these goals

Assessment is a process. As such it:

involves making assumptions and developing hunches about what is wrong in a given situation

involves gathering information to test out these hunches

requires keeping in mind alternative assumptions and hunches about the problem involves, if necessary, making revisions in one's initial tentative assessment

## B.    Describing the Problem

The three main practice objectives of assessment are: description, formulation, and goal-setting. Each of these will be defined briefly, with illustrations from our case study.

*Description* of the problem involves a specification of facts. These facts may be objective as in Bill's charge of truancy, the divorce of his parents, and the previous problems of an older sister. Also included in a description are subjective experiences, such as Bill's mother's fear of physical violence. Where possible, distinctions should be made between subjective and objective facts. Thus, Bill's behaviour is viewed by residence staff as "bizarre", and not "Bill is bizarre". This allows one to determine *who* judges *what* behaviour in *what circumstances.*

*Formulation* of the problem is the identification of significant factors in the development and maintenance of the problem. Among all the possible facts of a situation, one must highlight certain ones for a parsimonious understanding of the problem. This aids later decision-making about solutions. For example, Bill's parents' divorce, the family's financial and other crises, the absence of supervision and guidance, current inter-ethnic marriage, mixed parenting styles, enduring conflict between natural parents, and mother's resistance to help, may be the central components in explaining Bill's previous and current behaviour.

When formulating the problem, distinctions must be made between observed patterns or events (e.g., parents' divorce, Bill's constant running away) and hypothetical explanations (e.g., an assumed anger towards mother for the divorce). In this way one can test out one's hunches, and revise them if necessary. In addition, this helps to avoid placing a label on Bill, a label that properly belongs in one's assessment scheme and not on the client.

*Goal-setting* identifies those aspects of the client's situation which are targeted for change through intervention. This is an important part of problem-solving, because the selection of a service plan and resources is focussed on the change goal. Changing a conflictual relationship between Bill and his mother requires a different service solution than one which is designed to promote the development of peer group skills.

Having briefly defined three important elements of assessment, we turn to an elaboration of practices and decisions involved in each.

### What Kind of Information Should Be Included in a Good Assessment?

As indicated above, an essential part of the initial work in problem-solving entails providing sufficient and good quality information about the problem and possible contributing factors. The most important benchmark for doing an assessment is whether the information helps workers make appropriate decisions about what to do. In Bill's case study, available information describes several different types of phenomena, including the individual's inner states (e.g., mother's fear of Bill; hostility towards the agency), individual behaviour (e.g., Bill's tantrums), relationships (e.g., verbal and physical aggressiveness towards staff and peers), family characteristics (e.g., crisis states, economic hardships), legal judgements (e.g., judge rules in favour of residential placement; order of supervision) and, by inference, school-related law.

Recent social and behavioural science knowledge tells us that the kinds of problems facing child welfare workers can be traced to a number of different factors—biological, psychological, interactional, group, and societal. This means that assessment should be sensitive to a variety of factors.

The ecological approach to child welfare may provide the most useful guidelines for gathering assessment information. This approach has influenced recent thinking in social work, and is endorsed as a useful approach to children's services by Ontario's Ministry of Community and Social Services. For a description of the ecological approach, see Chapters 1 and 4.

## C.       The Importance of Linking Private Troubles to Public Issues

Bill's problems may have been indirectly affected by certain broad sociological and structural characteristics of society and of the child welfare system (e.g., economic conditions, long-term intervention possibility, multiple placements and assessments).

Socio-economic conditions, the legal context of child welfare, and the social organization of courts, hospitals, and child welfare institutions, all constitute the public issues touching Bill's life.

Understanding problems involves *making the link between private troubles and public issues.*

*Private troubles are:*

> within the individual and immediate relationship with others
>
> undesirable facts of life affecting self, and those limited areas of social life of which the individual is directly aware

Understanding and resolving private troubles usually involves a focus on an individual's immediate and experienced social milieus.

*Public issues involve:*

> matters that relate to societies or communities and which threaten the values of the public or certain publics
>
> matters that affect some people's private troubles

Other examples of private troubles and related public issues are the following:

> A young woman's unwanted pregnancy is due to inadequately distributed birth-control information.
>
> A father's sudden physical abuse of a young child is traced to the stress of being out of work and without proper accommodation.
>
> Inadequate development and dissemination of birth control knowledge to all people through social institutions.

Unemployment and inadequate housing, possibly attributed to government policies.

Child welfare workers work primarily with people's private troubles. However, they are in positions to know how public issues affect people's lives. Although not always in positions to take action on public issues, they can systematically provide information to those who can. This Source Book encourages, as part of assessment, the identification or speculation about the relevant public issues behind private troubles [4, 6].

## D.    An Assessment Outline

In the following pages a general outline for assessment is presented. This framework can be used to guide the development of specific assessment protocols in the various areas and programs.

An ecological framework broadens the scope of assessment information. Although specific formats differ according to the situation, one suggested general outline is as follows [5]:

| Section | Contents |
|---|---|
| 1. *Identifying data:*<br>This is the client. | Name, age, address, legal status (natural child, adopted, fostered, wardship) school, grade, occupational status |
| 2. *Referral Source:*<br>This is how the client was brought or came for help. | names of those persons involved in referral process |
| 3. *Presenting Problems:*<br>This is why the client came or was referred. | A list of issues of primary concern—usually behavioural description without evaluation |
| 4. *History of Current Difficulties:*<br>This is what has been happening in the child's life recently and has led to the referral. | *Description of Problems:*<br>How were they noticed?<br>For whom did they create difficulties? Who evaluated the behaviour as a problem?<br>What precipitates them? When? What makes them better or worse?<br>How are the causes of the problem explained? By the client? By family members? By other significant persons (e.g., teacher)?<br>What attempts have been made to help, and with what positive and negative effects?<br>What are everyone's goals? |
| 5. *History of Previous Difficulties:*<br>These are the problems which the child or the family members have experienced in the past. | A review of earlier problems of the client and the family or its members derived both from interviews and any reports from other services. |

Reprinted with the permission of the Ontario Ministry of Community and Social Services.

## GENERAL ECOLOGICAL FRAMEWORK—*Continued*

| *Section* | *Contents* |
|---|---|
| 6. *Family Development*<br>This is how the client's family began and how it evolved. | |
| Parents' early life experience | brief review of composition and style of family of origin |
| | quality of family relationships; management of discipline and conflict; sharing of affection and feelings |
| | attitudes to school, work, sex, money, the law, school and work achievements |
| Courtship and marriage | how the couple met and what attracted them |
| | what they expected in the marriage |
| | significant factors in early adjustment—sexual, social, and economic |
| Arrival of children | planning for children |
| | pregnancies, births, effects of child's arrival and reactions of parents and siblings |
| | personalities and achievements of children |
| | data about adoptions, fostering, placements |
| Current marital and family functioning | style of marriage, ability to cope with responsibilities and developmental changes in children |
| | sexual relationship, employment, economic factors, living conditions, cultural and ethnic factors, legal issues, antisocial problems |
| | significant illnesses, deaths, losses, changes, separations, divorce, and their consequences |
| | relationship to extended family, community, schools, church, courts, police, child welfare agencies and other services |
| 7. *Personal Development*<br>This is how the child has coped with normal biological, psychological, and social tasks from birth to the present. | |
| Data about the child: | pregnancy, delivery, neonatal period (including mother's reaction) |
| | early physical and temperamental style, developmental milestones |
| | establishment of feedings, sleeping, toilet routines |
| | quality of early relationships, bonding and attachment (to whom) |
| | potentially damaging experiences, both physical (illness and injury) and emotional (stresses and separations) |
| | pre-school development and personality in socialization, and play patterns in learning skills |

## GENERAL ECOLOGICAL FRAMEWORK—*Continued*

| Section | Contents |
| --- | --- |
| | school history: academic progress, behaviour relationships with teachers and classmates, adult models, friendships, hobbies, interests, sports, chores, job history |
| | age of maturation (first menstrual period, breast development, establishment of puberty, growth spurt) and reaction to it; interest in sexual matters, sexual relationships, sexual identity, masturbation, degree of adolescent individuation from family, involvement with peer groups |
| | individual relationship to community, agencies, police; development of conscience and morality |
| 8. *Observations of the Child*<br>This is (a) what the worker sees in the child; (b) what the worker hears from the child himself or herself, family and other aspects of life; and (c) how the worker feels about and consequently behaves towards him or her. | Data and inferences are drawn from direct examination, with all aspects being compared with developmental norms. |
| Appearance and relationship to examiner | physical appearance, dress, grooming, social manner, posture, gait, tension, mannerisms, voice and manner of speech, facial expressions, and eye contact |
| | examiner's reaction, nature of the reaction, nature of the relationship formed and working alliance |
| Behaviour and activity | energy and activity level, goal-direction and persistence, impulsiveness, aimlessness |
| | effectiveness, talents, skills, coordination |
| | compulsiveness and organization versus messiness |
| | behavioural patterns |
| Sensory and perceptual skills | orientation for time, place, and person |
| | memory for remote, recent, and immediate events |
| | attention span, concentration, and alertness |
| | responsiveness to stimuli |
| | auditory, visual, and recognition skills |
| | accuracy of perception |
| *Thinking process* | content: main themes, general knowledge, fantasies, day dreams, obsessions, delusions, suicidal thoughts |
| | functions: organization and coherence, abstraction and use of symbolism, understanding, estimate of intelligence, defense mechanisms, disturbances in flow of thought |
| | language: comprehension, expression, fluency, specific disorders |
| | insight and judgement: consequences, objectivity, and realistic thinking |

## GENERAL ECOLOGICAL FRAMEWORK—*Continued*

| Section | Contents |
|---|---|
| *Emotional tone and behaviour* | type of emotion in interview, variation, intensity, appropriateness, awareness and control of feelings |
| *Attitude to self and others* | ability to see self as individual; predominant models and ideals; aspirations, goals, ethical standards, responsibility, self-control, conscience, sense of guilt, self-esteem, feelings of belonging and being loved |
| | major relationships, number and depth, style of relating, degree of closeness and trust |

9. *Observations of the Family:*
This is what the family is like, how it feels to be among them, how they approach the child's needs, how they view the worker and other outsiders. This is how they share or do not share concerns and problem-solving. What are their mutual strengths and difficulties? This is what the client(s) and worker were able to achieve together.

| | |
|---|---|
| Structure and organization | power hierarchy |
| | degree of individuality |
| | special alliances |
| | enmeshment |
| | rigidity or flexibility of system |
| | clarity of generational boundaries |
| | closeness/distance |
| | clarity of roles and functions |
| Communication | content, themes, preoccupations, avoidances |
| | unspoken rules |
| | quantity, clarity, directness |
| | non-verbal expression and congruence with spoken word |
| Emotional tone and expression | mood |
| | openness/concealment |
| | intensity |
| | variation |
| | responsiveness |
| Control and decision-making | leadership style—flexibility, consistency, type and efficacy of reinforcement |
| | conflict resolutions |
| | attitudes to feedback and help |
| | cooperation and resistance |
| Development aspects | age-appropriateness of expectations, roles, and so forth |
| | management of autonomy and individuation |
| | parental and marital development |
| | intergenerational issues |
| | extended family—dependency, intrusiveness, support |

## GENERAL ECOLOGICAL FRAMEWORK—*Continued*

| *Section* | *Contents* |
|---|---|
| 10. *Public Issues*<br>These are some of the public issues and social conditions affecting this case:<br>community conditions: | lack of daycare facilities, recreational/housing inadequacies, discriminatory attitudes |
| policy considerations<br>elements of social structure: | inequality between sexes, different standards of child care, children's rights, childhood |
| 11. *Specialized Observations*<br>This is how some experts understand certain aspects of the child, family, and situation | tests, evaluations, reports, and earlier assessments (e.g., educational, psychological, medical, legal, child care observations) |

## E.    Formulation: Guidelines for Identifying the Central Factors in a Problem

A full ecological description of Bill's situation is a useful part of assessment. However, descriptive richness does not assure the understanding necessary for taking action. Understanding requires a narrowing of observations to a succinct formulation of the problem.

Formulation requires the selection and synthesis of significant information in order that working hypotheses can be developed. From these hypotheses, specific change goals can be identified.

Formulations "aim to combine facts, observations and knowledge . . ." [5]. The following simplified formulation of Bill's problems illustrates certain features of this phase of assessment.

During his younger years, Bill's large family experienced economic difficulties, and problems with other children. These conditions promoted a neglect of Bill and his needs through extensive parental absence, older siblings who were unwilling to babysit, stress within the family, and marital conflict. Parenting was inconsistent, autocratic, and abusive. Bill developed neither inner controls nor a trust of adults. Competition with siblings for parental attention and other family resources did not promote peer group skills within the family. Nor were such skills developed at school, where Bill was an academic failure and a social outcast. School had no attraction and a pattern of truancy, unchecked by parental controls, ensued. Bill's "problem identity" and low self-esteem developed at school and at home. The dissolution of his parents' marriage left him insecure, angry, and ambivalent towards his mother; conflict between the parents undermined Bill's attachment to them, and continued to hamper his growth. The addition of a stepfather into his already-troubled life further alienated him from adult authority figures, particularly when the stepfather's ways were different. This estrangement from his new father was increased by the parental disagreements over who should parent Bill. His bad reputation at school increased his punishment at home, which, in turn, further alienated him from school. An escalating cycle of school and family alienation was the context for the truancy charge. The mother's resistance to agency involvement in their lives is a key dynamic in Bill's residence behaviour. By not supporting staff efforts to keep him from running, she and her husband may also weaken Bill's respect for staff authority.

The formulation of problems should attempt to (a) classify the *significant factors* in major areas of functioning, (b) establish the *interdependence* of these factors and (c) identify their *sequential* relationship [5]. The following grid is an assessment tool for organizing elements according to certain factors:

## ASSESSMENT TOOL FOR PROBLEMS

| Factors | Biological | Familial | Socio-cultural | Psychological |
|---|---|---|---|---|
| Predisposing | Learning difficulties, including history | Large family History of problems Parents' divorce | Economic hard times History of difficulties with case in agency | Learning difficulties Low self-esteem Lack of peer skills |
| Precipitating | | Difficulty in making ends meet, and stress Parental absence at work Different standards | | Truancy |
| Perpetuating | | Resistance to help | Lack of organizational unity around assessments | Resistance to authority |
| Protecting | | Bond with grandparents Mother acknowledges difficulties as parent | | Pleasant nature, amiable at times Bill's intermittent desire to change |

*Predisposing factors:* those whose early or recent presence help set the stage for difficulties

*Precipitating factors:* events or changes within and outside the child which can be linked closely to the difficulties

*Perpetuating factors:* those which tend to block resolution of the problems, including responses to the problem which maintain a vicious circle

*Protecting factors:* strengths which have compensated for and prevented even greater difficulties

The grid illustrates a formulation using information from the case study.

It is important to remember that any classification system used in assessments is a tool for understanding and for action. All classifications are limited in some way, capturing only *some* elements of the problem at a certain point in time. In truth, assessment classifications represent the product of (a) an observer, who (b) organizes observations and inferences, (c) about others' behaviour, in (d) certain situations. To lose sight of this, and to assume that assessment results represent *all* of the *client's attributes* is dehumanizing.

Formulation, therefore, requires a tentative working understanding of the problem; this typically contains concepts, or mental tools, which summarize events and patterns, and their interrelationships. Formulation of the problem is of utmost importance because it *bridges* the phases of defining the problem and selecting a solution.

Therefore, many of the concepts used in one's framework for formulating the problem must be well connected to events in real life. The following checklist represents a beginning set of criteria for selecting concepts for problem formulation. Each of these criteria helps to make a link between knowledge and practice:

Do the concepts directly or indirectly refer to *identifiable events* in the real world? The concept "lack of peer skills", with adequate definition, can be linked to specific aspects of Bill's observed behaviour.

Are these events directly or indirectly *accessible* to the practitioner? Behaviour reflecting Bill's lack of respect for authority (e.g., disobedience of rules) can be noted and responded to by staff while his fantasy life is less accessible.

Can the events be *manipulated* (controlled, changed) by the practitioner? The marital conflict of Bill's natural parents is historical and cannot be changed, while parenting disagreements with Bill's stepfather are (all things being equal) changeable.

Which ideas are most *powerful* in explaining the problematic behaviour under consideration? Bill's low self-esteem may partially explain his running away from residences, while his mother's hostile attitudes and uncooperative behaviour may be more powerful explanations.

Do the events referred to *exist in the client's world* outside of the intervention situation? Bill's short attention span during attempted assessment interviews may not be generalized to all situations.

What is the *ethical suitability* of working with some events in a client's life, as suggested by certain formulations of the problem? A formulation giving emphasis to Bill's parents' marital sexual incompatibility may raise more ethical concerns than, say, their inadequate childrearing practices.

Can the formulation be linked directly or indirectly to the client's own definition of the problem? Bill's experience that everybody is telling him what to do can be linked to the concept "nonacceptance of authority".


## F.     Establishing Goals for Intervention

Having described and formulated the problem, the last phase of assessment establishes goals for intervention.

Too often the service plan or treatment is recommended without a clear indication of the changes that are required. Consider the typical recommendation on one of Bill's reports: Bill needs an environment which will provide him structure, clear expectations, and firm rules. Such a statement needs to be accompanied by clear criteria to assess goal-attainment.

*1.      The unit of intervention*

The first decision in establishing one's change goals is the unit of intervention; for instance, will the change effort be directed at the individual, a relationship, a whole family or (as in the case of community work), the neighbourhood? By focussing on Bill's behaviour (e.g., reduction of tantrums, changing physical abuse towards peers), the service plan clearly chose the individual as the unit. Another option may have included the relationship between Bill and his mother; however, Bill's mother resisted involvement in the service plan. A clear indication of the unit of intervention helps in the selection of an appropriate type of intervention.

The unit(s) of intervention may change as one works towards problem solution. In most cases there are several possible units of intervention. In Bill's case, this may be directed towards his mother's self-esteem and parenting skills (individual unit of intervention), or the parents' communications (dyad). Thus, several areas may receive concurrent attention.

*2.      Why is it important to specify goals?*

Having formulated an understanding of Bill's problems, and having made the decision to work directly on his behaviour, it is now necessary to specify exactly what should be changed. Why is this so important? Knowing what she or he wants to accomplish:

> helps the worker to be more specific when selecting the ways and means of making changes

> aids in monitoring progress and making decisions about staying on track, changing strategies, or changing goals

> sometimes gives the client a better feeling of being involved in a worthwhile activity with a competent person

> helps to avoid unnecessary activities which may not be useful in problem-solving

> helps to give direction to the worker's consultation with the literature, colleagues, and to previous professional experience

Bill's case suggests two other factors to keep in mind when setting goals. First, there are many possible change goals (e.g., helping to change Bill's responses to authority; changing his self-esteem and trust; helping Bill to further his education). This multiplicity of change goals suggests that priorities are necessary, since it usually is not possible to work simultaneously on multiple goals. How does one go about setting priorities for change goals?

*3.      Goal-setting: a checklist*

The worker might ask herself or himself the following set of checklist questions as she or he narrows the pool of possible change goals for Bill. Implicit in these questions are criteria for making decisions about goals. In reviewing them, readers might ask themselves whether different or additional criteria should affect this particular decision-making. Also, should some of these questions be given more importance than others?

Let us assume that the worker has developed the following pool of possible change goals for Bill:

| | |
|---|---|
| increase self-esteem | improve peer group skills |
| increase ability to trust adult | improve education opportunities |
| eliminate physical and verbal aggression | ventilate anger over parent separation |
| improve school performance | learn appropriate ways of asking for help |
| improve relationship with mother | improve functioning in community |

In order to establish priorities, consider the following questions:

Can the goals be directly or indirectly related to the *mandated goals* specified for child welfare agencies by the Child Welfare Act (e.g., reduction of risk of neglect and abuse; prevention of same)?

Can the goals be directly or indirectly related to the *goals* implied in the *policies of the agency?*

Do the goals directly or indirectly relate to the key patterns discussed in *the formulation* of the problem?

Are the goals *operational?* That is, can the goals be described in sufficient detail, and in terms of the *client's behaviour*, so that the worker:

can know the difference between the current "bad" situation and anticipated new "improved" situation?

can develop leads to specific ways and means for improving the situation?

Do the goals directly or indirectly address the *presenting problem?*

Do the goals relate to conditions and values seen as undesirable and desirable from a *client's perspective?*

Are the goals *feasible* in terms of a *preliminary judgement* concerning necessary human and material resources?

Are the goals *feasible* in terms of the *resistance* provided by *other* people's behaviour, attitudes, relationships? For example, will some goals require the cooperation of Bill's parents? How feasible are educational goals, given Bill's removal from the school system?

Will the goals aid in the *reduction of client stress? Bill's main source of stress* is his relationship with his mother and the anxiety about being removed from his home.

Will the goals aid in meeting *the client's basic needs* (e.g., food, housing, medical care)?

## G.    Understanding the Problem: A Summary

This section has provided important considerations for understanding client problems. A good assessment requires gathering and organizing information for problem-solving. There are three phases: (1) describing the problem involves gathering and summarizing data on the individual, interactional, family, and broader environmental aspects of the problem, including relevant public issues; (2) formulating the problem requires the selection of essential patterns or events in the client's situation which, along with theoretical assumptions, help explain the development and maintenance of the problem; (3) goal-setting is the process of identifying those aspects of the client's behaviour or existence which must be changed.

A solution-oriented formulation of the problem requires ideas (concepts) which can be easily translated into practice. A number of criteria for developing such ideas are presented, including the degree to which ideas point to accessible and changeable events in the client's life. Change goals are the key elements mediating the understanding of a problem and selecting a solution. For this reason, goals must be operational, linked to essential elements in the formulation, and potentially address the client's stress and experiences.

Taken together, guidelines accompanying these elements of assessment help the worker successfully bridge the worlds of knowledge and practice.

For additional material on assessments, see Chapters 2, III, IV; 9, III, and Appendix B.

## III    THE SEARCH FOR SOLUTIONS:
## WHAT IS THE BEST SERVICE PLAN FOR BILL?

## A.    Criteria for Service Selection

An adequate understanding of Bill's problem and a tentative identification of change goals do not guarantee change. The next major decision concerns the type of service or treatment.

In child welfare work, particularly protection cases, a major initial decision is whether or not the child should be removed from her or his natural environment. Although the judge has the ultimate authority to make this decision, social workers can aid the process by providing information about potential risk if the child were to remain at home. For example:

Are the parents absent?

Are the parents physically or mentally unable to provide adequate child care?

Despite clear evidence, do the parents deny the existence of abuse or neglect?

Do the parents seem clearly unmotivated to change the quality of their child care?

Assuming that the worker is in a position to decide the type of treatment or service plan, or to influence that decision, what guidelines should be followed?

The selection-of-a-solution process begins when the problem-solver makes a commitment to a particular change goal. After that, it is a matter of generating ideas about what can be done to assist the client to move towards the change goal. Detailed thought must be given to selecting the most appropriate intervention. The following checklist suggests criteria for judging service options. Elements from Bill's case are used for illustration:

What interventions might directly or indirectly aid the client in working towards *the change goals* identified by worker and client? Would Bill's changes in self-esteem, ability to trust adults, education, and so forth, best be accomplished by one-to-one counselling, family therapy, structured peer group therapy, milieu therapy?

What is the *scope of impact* of each intervention, that is, how many relevant factors in the formulation of the problem (e.g., attitudes, behaviours, skills, hostility) might be changed by each alternative?

What *general roles and/or role relationships are required* by the workers in these situations: Bill's need to trust requires consistency of adult response to unpredictable, sometimes abusive, behaviour; peer group socialization requires skilled group facilitation. Bill's complex home situation with a mother who is basically hostile to treatment requires mediation roles between service and home life.

What professional, agency, or community resources are needed to support these roles and intervention? For instance, Bill's needs require a service plan which bridges the world of peers, school, and family. Can the service organization successfully integrate these forces in different aspects of Bill's life? His running behaviour may be symptomatic of unsuccessful bridging.

What *professional knowledge* might assist service to Bill? His previous and present circumstances and behaviour suggest a number of potentially useful bodies of knowledge: scapegoating among peers, the bases of trust, running behaviour, dynamics of reconstituted families, and so on; the scope of influences on Bill's problem behaviour suggests broad-based knowledge.

What are the *known results of using these interventions* and what are the recommended cautions, limitations, and approaches, for example, of assuming family support or full family involvement?

If more than one intervention is required, are they *compatible?*

What *behaviours* will the interventions require *from the client?* Talk? Participation in groups? Independent action? Community involvement? Keeping appointments?

What *client attitudes, skills, and values* are necessary to support participation in the intervention? As a European, how much does Bill's stepfather support the involvement of others in family problems?

What *other changes* might the intervention promote in the client's situation? Is Bill's problem behaviour a source of equilibrium in his family? Who else might be vulnerable?

What is the *usual way that the client learns* or changes? Which previous change efforts with the client have been successful or unsuccessful? what can be learned from a previous unsuccessful attempt at family counselling with this family?

What *client strengths* will support the intervention? where are the closest relationships in this family? How can Bill's strong relationships with his grandparents and natural father be used as a leverage for change?

In addition to the above, for what *types of clients* (e.g., age, cultural background, developmental stage, demographic characteristics) are the interventions *particularly appropriate?*

## B.      Selecting a Solution: A Summary

Deciding upon a treatment or service solution does not flow automatically from the assessment of the problem. It requires a pooling of possible interventions that are thought to be potentially useful. Each of these is then evaluated according to a set of criteria. Although the potential for realizing the change goals may be the most important criterion, other important considerations are the scope of possible impact, necessary staff roles, skills and knowledge, resources, limitations of the interventions for some clients, the compatibility among parts of the service plan, necessary client support characteristics, possible unanticipated changes in the client's situation, and the client's most appropriate learning style.

In short, a *matching system* between client, treatment, and other resources has been described. However, this system recognizes that treatments and clients are parts of larger wholes, and that these conditions have an inevitable impact on the treatment process.

## IV.     IMPLEMENTING THE SOLUTION: MAKING THE SERVICE PLAN WORK

Once the worker and the client have decided upon the main change goals and a particular course of action, the next broad phase involves *putting the solution into practice*. For example, the decision was reached that Bill's needs could be best met through placement in a youth residence. However, the appropriateness of this decision is not guaranteed by the correctness of the initial thinking. Good decisions need to be translated into actions. Whether a social worker is actually doing treatment or monitoring the service plan, several practice functions are recommended to assist successful implementation of the service decision: (a) planning the implementation; (b) putting the plan into practice; (c) evaluation; and (d) problem-solving. Evaluation will be discussed separately in the next section.

## A.    Planning the Implementation: Perspectives and Checklist

Once the worker has decided upon a solution, she or he must plan how to implement it. It is the viewpoint of this book that thorough planning requires thinking through conditions which may either help (facilitators) or hinder (barriers) efforts.

Anticipating implementation problems can be open-ended or structured. In a structured approach the worker might follow a systematic checklist to identify problems, such as the following:

What people should be involved and what roles are required to make this intervention work? How can these be assured? How should the various participants contribute, and at what stages in the change process?

What knowledge and skills are required to make the intervention work is a question that applies to both clients and staff members. Do clients know the legalities of an order of supervision? Do foster parents know that close observation of children is necessary to assist the monitoring function of the children's service worker?

What client/staff values and attitudes would support the service plan? What if these were not compatible?

What are the proper organizational supports for this intervention? What is the organization's policy for involving parents in the treatment process, particularly in cases where parents are hostile? What procedures are taken in treatment problems (e.g., runaways)?

Bill's treatment plan broke down at a number of places: an order of supervision was difficult to fulfill; during residence placement, Bill ran home frequently without parental encouragement to return. Obviously, parental factors played a significant role, yet parental hostility was known from the beginning. What pre-service planning could have avoided these problems? Would a systematic approach to service implementation have involved the natural father and grandparents in the treatment process?

## B.    Putting the Solution into Practice

Section A above provides a series of concepts and checklist questions designed to aid in the process of implementing the service plan, after the solution has been decided upon. Ideally, the worker should have a good understanding of those individual and environmental factors which might aid or inhibit the process. However, despite the value of such planning, there is no guarantee of success. It remains necessary to create better conditions for implementing the solution. It is beyond the scope of this phase of the *Source Book* to elaborate upon all such activities, for now the following inventory of practice skills is presented:

> entry skills
> negotiating
> forming action systems
> networking
> exercising influence
> problem-solving
> evaluating results

This list of practice elements forms a scheme for categorizing activities which set the appropriate conditions for treatment (problem solution). Or, in our terms, they aid in the implementation of the solution.

Problem-solving activities are important in the implementation of interventions. Despite meticulous planning and negotiation of the appropriate conditions for carrying out plans, events occur which block the steps towards attaining change goals. In such instances, a problem-solving process *within* a problem-solving process goes into operation. The same problem-solving phases discussed in this appendix provide guidelines for working with implementation problems. Systematic attention to problem-solving helps to avoid premature out-of-context "blaming" of individuals. As with parents' or children's problems, professional practice difficulties are often "symptomatic" of larger problems.

## C.      Implementing the Service Plan: A Summary

A service plan may go awry because it was not successfully implemented. Planning the implementation aims to "translate" the service decision into specific behaviours that assure change in the client problems. Such planning requires a clear specification of what will be done, by whom, at what point in time. Thinking through the contributing activities of the client and client's family is important. Finally, a service plan is supported by specific knowledge, skills, and organizational arrangements. Barriers to a successful service plan can be pinpointed on any of the above dimensions.

A successful service implementation process is more likely to occur if an ongoing case evaluation is built into the process. We now turn to the evaluation function.

## V.      EVALUATING SOLUTIONS

"Doing social work without systematic evaluation throughout the entire process is like driving a car with your eyes closed—you are going places but you don't know for certain where you are or what you did that got you there, to say nothing of being a hazard while you're in motion" [7].

The next phase of problem-solving urges an ongoing verification of the effectiveness and efficiency of one's individual professional efforts. This should be distinguished from performance appraisal, program evaluation, and system evaluation. Individual evaluation is a case-by-case examination by the practitioner of the usefulness of her or his intervention in the client's problem.

## A.      What Is Individual Professional Evaluation?

Although ideals are always difficult to realize in a practical world, professionals can work towards ideal solutions through a process of reflection on a case-by-case basis. Technical procedures, such as evaluation guidelines and journal-keeping, assist this reflective process. Although evaluation requires specific training, the following guidelines constitute some introductory principles for professional evaluation.

A distinction should be drawn between the evaluation of *outcome* versus *process*. In outcome evaluation, the worker is primarily interested in accomplishments: Did Bill's peer group skills change over the course of treatment? How do his current skills compare with change goals? In process evaluation, the worker examines the technical steps by which she or he achieved prescribed goals (techniques, methods, strategies) in addition to examining efforts to implement the solution: Did Bill benefit from one-to-one counselling within a residence, or peer group recreational activities?

## B.      Evaluating Outcome

The following points should be kept in mind in evaluating outcome:

Establish a clear *specification of change goals* in such a way that *measurement* is possible: what specific behaviour changes would demonstrate a change in Bill's self-esteem and peer skills? (e.g., Bill makes positive comments about himself, asks for permission from friends to borrow things).

Obtain a clear *description of the client situation prior to the intervention*: Bill's frequent verbal and physical attacks during early phases of residence placement should be compared systematically with later stages.

Ideally, also obtain *information* sometime *after the intervention* so that the assessment of the lasting effects of intervention can be made: What reports on Bill's post-residence behaviour might indicate a lasting change?

When noting the changes in the problem situation, look at both positive and negative, anticipated and unanticipated changes; an image of the *net balance of changes* is useful for an overall assessment of intervention.

## C.      Evaluating Process

When evaluating the process of intervention, it is useful to keep in mind the distinction between effectiveness and efficiency. Effectiveness asks whether the problem-solver's actions actually promoted change: How did such actions lead to change? What helped and hindered the process? Efficiency analysis raises questions about cost, whether calculated in terms of money, time, psychological stress, relational problems, reduced status, the loss of alternative actions, and so on.

When evaluating process it is useful to examine those *actions* which were *not directly related* to the problem-solving methods, but which were instrumental in making it work. Sometimes, "accidental" events seem to contribute to changes in client behaviour; their contribution should be understood.

When evaluating process, it is necessary to have a clear picture of the *model of intervention*. In Bill's case, what specific aspects of residence—policy, staff, behaviours, peer interaction—were presumed to promote change in which aspects of Bill's behaviour? Through what intermediary processes do these cause change? For example, if peer and staff interaction is designed to enhance peer skills, who or what is the source (model) of appropriate behaviour? By being sufficiently specific about the intervention model, the worker can identify (a) factors that may have inhibited the change process (e.g., did Bill's role as peer scapegoat lead to anxiety and disorganization, thus inhibiting the learning of new skills?), and (b) factors unrelated to the planned change efforts that may have promoted change; thinking through how unplanned events have caused change aids in the modification of strategies for future intervention.

### D.    Useful Information for Evaluation Purposes

Several kinds of data may be gathered to evaluate the process and outcomes of intervention. Some information comes from: (1) *observations* of the worker, the client, or other parties; (2) *reported experience* of change (e.g., a client reports feeling better about being a parent); (3) *sources* not requiring new information, such as changes in school grades or other kinds of administrative records. A good rule of thumb for deciding about types of measurement is to use multiple sources of information. For example, if a change goal requires increasing a parent's use of positive rewards in parenting, a worker may use the following sources of information: his or her own observations of the parent's behaviour with the child, a child care worker's reports of several home visits, both parents' qualitative reports, and the mother's systematic record-keeping of her use of positive rewards during a given time period. By *combining these multiple data*, the worker gains confidence in the validity of any conclusions drawn concerning the intervention's effectiveness.

It is useful to gather information throughout the problem-solving process. This provides greater flexibility in problem-solving approaches because seemingly successful or unsuccessful methods can be identified early in the process.

### E.    Evaluating Solutions: A Summary

Case evaluation is an adjunct to successful practice, aiding both successful service implementation and professional growth. Outcome evaluation focuses on the achievement of change goals; process evaluation concentrates on the ways and means of realizing these goals. Process evaluation allows early detection of weakness in the service plan. Evaluation information is best gathered from several sources.

## VI.    TERMINATING THE INTERVENTION

In child welfare work, problem-solving typically sets up new and complex relationships with people. Termination of the planned change requires serious attention to:

> psychological reactions to termination
>
> the changed relationship between the worker and the client
>
> steps required to sustain the changes established in the problem-solving process

The goals and tasks required for termination should be regarded as an integral part of the change process. Planning and actions for termination actually begin early in the problem-solving process.

### A.    Deciding to Terminate an Intervention

Helping professionals are sometimes criticized for retaining relationships with clients for an excessive period of time. That many clients receive service for lengthy time periods is probably due to several factors, including the complexity of problems, the client's reality situation, inadequate service technology, unclear agency policy, and so on. Among these factors is probably a lack of clear criteria for deciding termination. The following is a tentative checklist for helping to make this decision:

> What are external requirements for termination of this case? (e.g., court prescriptions)?
>
> What is agency policy, if any?
>
> Have the change goals for the case been attained, without any new problems?
>
> If change goals have not been fully attained, does the client show a gradual change away from the problem pattern and towards the change goal?
>
> If the change goals have not been attained, are there changes in the client's natural situation (e.g., development of problem-solving capacities, linkage with natural resources such as kin, friends, job status, attitudes) which suggest a potential for change?
>
> If the change goals have not been attained, what are the probabilities of linking the client to alternative sources of help both within and outside the agency?

What recommendations for length of service, if any, does the literature recommend?

What are the client's feelings about continuation, or non-continuation of service? What understandings were developed in the original contract?

Decision making about termination is frequently complicated by a worker's sense of futility concerning a particular case. If workers have considered all their options, then ending the treatment relationship may be the best available strategy. Extreme complexities of many child welfare problems, plus the undeveloped state of the art in helping services, often make child welfare problems insurmountable.

## B.      Preparing the Client for Termination

Ending a service relationship may mean different things to different clients (e.g., relief, loss of a friend, end of a punishment, anxiety about independence). These unique sentiments are inevitable and must be checked out by the worker as termination approaches. However, the worker has helped to shape the meaning of termination by the way it is handled in the contract and throughout the intervention process. The worker can help create and sustain a neutral attitude towards termination by:

setting time-limits to the change efforts at the beginning of the problem-solving relationship

throughout the process, reinforcing in the client's mind the notion of time-limits and termination

keeping "time" as an important constraining factor in any renegotiations of service contracts or understandings

involving clients in periodic evaluations

Despite the worker's best efforts, many clients will show diverse reactions as termination approaches. Research on groups reveals the following types of responses:

*Denial:* Clients forget they have been told about termination, act surprised, and ask about the next group.

*Return to previous patterns:* Clients backslide in coping with interpersonal and organizational tasks; return to previous levels of functioning; eruption of previous disagreements; demands for dependence on leader; outburst of anger.

*Expression of need:* Clients display problem behaviour as a demonstration that service is still needed.

*Recapitulation:* There is revival and discussion of earlier experiences in groups.

*Evaluation:* Client evaluates the worth and meaning of earlier experiences.

*Flight:* This is either a destructive reaction (denial of positive meaning of the intervention experience, attacking worker for terminating the group) or positive (constructive disengagement from the group—finding new contacts, friends, interests from the group)[9].

Other researchers and clinicians have noted phases of *bargaining* and *despair*.

The worker must remember that the termination phases of service elicit various types of behaviours in clients. Care must be taken not to let such behaviour extend service or make the worker feel bad about the quality of intervention. Having an informal social get-together prior to termination may help to neutralize negative feelings and end the relationship on a happy note.

In many cases, termination marks *a transition phase* to the involvement of a new worker or a new agency. Such transitions can be less problematic if the previous worker participates with the new staff for a short period. Assuming that the previous relationship was a good one, the former worker can aid the transition by:

> helping to assure consistency between the two situations
>
> assisting in the resolution of crisis situations growing out of the transition
>
> helping to build a bond between the new worker and the client
>
> helping in the development of those bases of influence (liking, trust, respect of expertise, acknowledgement of authority) through which the new worker can help the client

In all cases of termination, a new relationship will exist between the worker and the client which may involve no contacts, limited contacts (e.g., special meetings, follow-up, crisis resolution), or even extensive open relationships (e.g., telephone call whenever wanted). Whatever the case, the worker must help the client understand the nature of the new relationship. In many ways this is a renegotiation of the previous service contract. One certain element of the new relationship is an increased independence of the client from the worker.

## C. Helping the Client Stabilize Changes Outside of the Problem-Solving Relationship

One of the most challenging aspects of problem-solving is ensuring that the changes induced by one's efforts continue after the intervention process. This concern should not be raised at the termination phase only; in fact, it should be an issue throughout the problem-solving process. Workers can aid the generalization and stabilization of change in the client's life in the following ways:

> Initial and on-going assessment of the client's problem situation should take into account the role of factors in the client's life external to the intervention situation; the intervention should try to address such factors.
>
> Help the client anticipate possible termination problems and imagine or practice various solutions.

Provide the client with problem-solving skills which can be used in other problem situations.

Analyze the functions provided by the worker or agency to the client's life during the intervention process (e.g., friendship, feedback about parenting, crisis resolution) and assure that these will be provided for in other ways through formal or informal support systems.

Assure that the client actually maintains a link with alternative support systems subsequent to termination.

Obtain quick measures of the stabilization of change as part of a post-termination evaluation process.

### D.    Terminating the Relationship: A Summary

Terminating the intervention process with the client is as important as selecting the appropriate treatment or service plan. The timing of termination is key, and may be determined by a host of factors. Preparing a client for termination should begin early in the treatment process. Despite detailed preparation, a number of client reactions may occur as termination approaches, reactions which should not discourage or sidetrack workers. Finally, a number of steps can be taken to help the client stabilize and consolidate changes. These, too, should start early in the service process.

## VII.    REFLECTING ABOUT ONE'S PROBLEM-SOLVING

The final phase of problem-solving helps the worker to consolidate any gains in her or his problem-solving abilities. This involves a comparison between one's typical approach to problem-solving as described in phase one, and the approach used following these guidelines. To aid this comparison the following questions can be raised:

1. How did this approach compare to my previous problem-solving approaches in terms of:

> understanding the problem?
>
> setting change goals?
>
> considering and selecting alternative solutions?
>
> implementing the solution?
>
> evaluating the solution?
>
> terminating the change process?

2. What is my overall assessment of the value of the foregoing differences in problem-solving?

3. Can I see myself using the new approach?

4. What factors in myself, my work situation, or the *Source Book* might inhibit the use of a problem-solving process as described in the section? How can these be overcome?

## VIII.   CHILD WELFARE PRACTICE AS PROBLEM SOLVING: A GENERAL SUMMARY

This appendix urges a systematic problem-solving approach through which difficulties associated with child welfare practice can be reduced. Although the scheme is not designed to cope with every element of service, the following phases were described: understanding the problem, searching for solutions, implementing solutions, evaluating solutions, terminating the intervention, and reflecting about problem-solving. To simplify matters, this discussion was guided by the following general principles:

Problems and solutions occur in broad ecological contexts.

Understanding problems is most likely when information about the problem and its context is maximized.

The best solution is likely to occur from the generation of a wide pool of alternatives which are systematically compared according to a set of criteria.

Problem-solving is enhanced by an ongoing process of reflection about one's problem-solving approach, potential problems in implementing one's solutions, and the effectiveness of solutions.

### REFERENCES

1. Germain, C. B. (ed.) *Social Work Practice: People and Environment.* New York: Columbia University Press, 1979.
2. Germain, C. B. and Gitterman, A. *The Life Model of Social Work Practice.* New York: Columbia University Press, 1979.
3. Mayer, C. *Social Work Practice, The Changing Landscape.* New York: The Free Press, 1976.
4. Pincus, A. and Minahan, A. *Social Work Practice: Model and Method.* Itasca, Ill.: F. E. Peacock Publishers, Inc., 1973.
5. Ontario Ministry of Community and Social Services, Children's Services Division, "Clinical Assessment in Children's Services," April 1979.
6. Schwartz, W. *Private Troubles and Public Issues: One Social Work Job or Two.* The Social Welfare Forum, New York: Columbia University Press, 1969.
7. Bloom, M. *The Parodox of Helping: Introduction to the Philosophy of Scientific Practice.* New York: John Wiley & Sons, 1975.
8. Thomas, E. J. "Selecting Knowledge from Behavioral Science", in Thomas, E. J. (ed.) *Behavioural Science for Social Workers.* New York: The Free Press, 1967.
9. Garland, J., Jones H., and Kolodry, R. "A Model for Stages of Development in Social Work Groups", in Saul Bernstein (ed.), *Explorations in Group Work.* Boston: Boston School of Social Work, Boston University Press, 1965.

# B
# Assessment Frameworks

FRANK MAIDMAN

I. INTRODUCTION                                                423
II. ECOLOGICAL APPROACH TO ASSESSING
CHILDREN'S DIFFICULTIES IN PSYCHOSOCIAL
FUNCTIONING                                                   424
III. MCMASTER MODEL OF FAMILY FUNCTIONING:
SUMMARY OF DIMENSION CONCEPTS                                 428
IV. LIST OF INDICATORS OF ABUSE AND NEGLECT
AND OPERATIONAL DEFINITIONS                                   431
   REFERENCES                                                 436

## I.      INTRODUCTION

Upon meeting their clients, child welfare workers typically encounter a potentially complicated picture, one which must be immediately simplified for decision-making purposes. Chapter 2 emphasized the importance of *assessment frameworks* in developing a simplified understanding of problems, client needs, and intervention. An assessment framework is a conceptual framework, sometimes with specific guidelines for the work, containing a number of core dimensions for classifying client functioning. Such a framework is typically informed by some image, based on theory, research, or clinical observation, of the elements defining or affecting the client's problem. By describing the client in these terms the worker is better able to *formulate* the essential nature of the problem and thereby determine a good plan of action.

Appendix A outlined an abstract assessment framework based on an ecological/development perspective, one requiring more development before being sufficiently operational for direct worker practice. This appendix provides three more

423

examples of assessment frameworks, only one of which has operational guidelines for direct application. The recently published Hess and Howard framework continues in the ecological tradition. It requires initially a description of the child's crisis state or ecological transition, defined as "the experience of disequilibrium created by a reaction to a change in setting, role, or physical status (including both developmental stages and health)"[1]. Beyond this, the child's functioning is described in her or his many immediate and distant environments (components 2–5). As well, the interaction between the environments are assessed (component 6).

The assessment of family functioning is an important part of child welfare practice, as reflected in component 4 of the Hess and Howard framework. The McMaster Model of Family Functioning [2] has evolved from extensive research on problem families, and is included for its elaboration of important internal dimensions of functioning.

Finally, the instrument for assessing abuse and neglect (IV) is the most elaborate scheme found during the research for the *Source Book*. Although included here as an example of a diagnostic tool, it can also be used as an aid to program evaluation and supervision. Readers are urged to consult the original sources [3] for a discussion of the development and uses of this instrument, as well as its limitations.

## II.  ECOLOGICAL APPROACH TO ASSESSING CHILDREN'S DIFFICULTIES IN PSYCHOSOCIAL FUNCTIONING [1]

I.  Crisis/Ecological Transition (Component 1)

1.  Person(s) experiencing setting- , biological- , or role-related crises or eco-transitions (may be child or significant other), for example, hospitalization, birth of sibling, sudden death of family member, serious illness

2.  Specific nature of crisis/transition, including whether anticipated or non-anticipated

3.  Vulnerable state (subjective reaction of person, affect, level of copying)

4.  Precipitating factor (may be transition designated in no. 2 above or a second transition, or a series that combines with other events or changes to prompt vulnerable state)

5.  Phase in reaction to transition (point in series of reactions, as phase in grief process)

6.  Methods for collecting information: interviews/conversations with the child, family members, and others with whom child has close relationships; focus on crisis as experienced by child

Adapted from Peg Hess and Tina Howard, "An Ecological Model for Assessing Psychosocial Difficulties in Children", *Child Welfare*, Vol. LX, September/October 1981, pp. 512–516, by permission of the Child Welfare League of America, Inc.

  II.  Child's Broader/Remote Environment (Component 2)

    1.  Delineate all systems, *excluding* family (to be included elsewhere) in which child is directly involved. Examples: classrooms, peer groups, class at Y.M./W.C.A., agency providing foster care.

    2.  Examine each system in terms of:

      A.  Child's current psychosocial functioning in that environment

      B.  Social climate of environment, as to:

         i.  Relationship dimensions (e.g., involvement of individuals in the environment and extent to which they support and help one another)

        ii.  Personal development dimensions (directions along which personal growth and self-enhancement tend to occur in the particular environment, including autonomy, task orientation, competition, cultural orientation, other)

        iii.  System maintenance and system change dimensions, including processes of order and organization, clarity of expectation, and control

      C.  Processes and nature of linkage between this system and other systems

      D.  Flexibility of system boundaries

      E.  Knowledge within this system concerning child and child's other environments

      F.  Personal nature, ease, and extent of communication between this system and others in child's environment

  III.  Child's Broader/Remote Environment (Component 3)

    1.  Delineate all systems known currently to indirectly impact on child as related to psychosocial functioning (e.g., policy-making systems, service systems).

    2.  Examine each in terms of:

      A.  Exact nature and relationship between broader environment and child's psychosocial functioning

      B.  Nature and extent of communication between this system and spokespersons or representative for child

      C.  Knowledge within this system concerning needs of children

      D.  Knowledge within this system concerning impact of this system upon children's psychosocial functioning

      E.  Boundaries of system: flexibility, process for entering system, and so on

    3.  If these categories above are not relevant (such as in examining culture or impact of sex roles or racism), examine in terms of:

      A.  Exact nature of relationship between broader system and child's psychosocial functioning

        B.   Potential for child's environment to influence or compensate for broader or remote environment

IV   Family Functioning, Physical Home Environment (Component 4)

1. Designate child's family of residency (birth, foster, adoptive, other)
2. Designate other families of attachment (foster care, birth family)
3. Document families' compositions
4. Document frequency and nature of contact with extended family
5. Examine each family (of residency and attachment) where possible and indicated in terms of:

    A.   Social climate

        i.  Relationship dimensions (cohesion, expressiveness, conflict)

       ii.  Personal development dimensions (orientation toward independence, achievement, intellectual-cultural, recreational, and moral-religious emphases)

      iii.  System maintenance and system change (emphasis on neatness, structuring family activities, financial planning, punctuality, extent to which the family controls by relatively strict rules or procedures)

    B.   Interactions

        i.  Nature (process, frequency, and topics forbidden and allowed)

          a.  Whole family

          b.  Marital pair

          c.  Subsystems

          d.  With extrafamilial systems

       ii.  Problem-solving and decision-making processes

      iii.  Permitted affective expression and process

    C.   Family developmental phase/tasks

        i.  Current developmental phase/tasks

       ii.  Current nature of developmental task mastery

      iii.  Family goals with relation to developmental tasks

    D.   Structural-functional aspects

        i.  Family roles

          a.  Age appropriateness

          b.  Role flexibility

          c.  Cognitive awareness of role structure

          d.  Personal growth allowed within role

          e.  Successful filling of all necessary family roles

      ii.  Family patterns of behaviour with relation to crisis and problem-solving

     iii.  Level of successful family task accomplishment

        a.  Material provision

        b.  Predictable meeting of needs (mealtimes, children's bedtimes)

        c.  Affective caretaking (support, expressed fondness, and inclusion)

        d.  Stimulation sufficient for personal growth (books, conversation)

        e.  Organizational planning (coordination of schedules, allocation of financial resources, balancing individual family member's needs)

        f.  Child socialization and supervision

        g.  Creation of family support systems

     iv.  Boundaries—flexibility, permeability

        a.  Willingness to incorporate newcomers

        b.  Willingness to share information with other systems regarding family

        c.  Methods of boundary protection

  E.  Home environment examined in terms of:

      i.  Adequacy of space for accommodating the number of persons living within it

     ii.  Adequacy of space for allowing individual privacy

     iii.  Adequacy of space for allowing accomplishment of family tasks

     iv.  Adequacy of space for maintaining intergenerational boundaries (e.g., parent-child)

     v.  Adequacy of space for common family-oriented areas

     vi.  Similarity of environment to family interaction patterns.

     vii.  Adequacy of space for facilitating interaction between families and other systems (e.g., easily identified entrance spaces for conversations with friends, teachers; space for entertaining

     viii.  Space allows for privacy but friendly interaction with neighbours

V.  Child-Centered Characteristics (Component 5)

  1.  Age, sex, racial/ethnic background

  2.  Life-history as pertinent

  3.  Physical health and characteristics

    4. Primary dyadic attachments

    5. Primary family attachment

    6. Age-appropriate development stage

    7. Observed functional development stage

    8. Child's perception of problem

    9. Nature of self-concept

    10. Existence of handicapping conditions (intellectual, emotional, physical)

    11. Overall coping capacity, skills, and typical reactions to stress

    12. Defenses utilized

    13. Overall cognitive, social, and emotional capacity, and performance

    14. Social relationships

VI. Interactions Between Components (Component 6)

    1. Nature of interaction

    2. Frequency

    3. Strength

## III.    McMaster Model of Family Functioning: Summary of Dimension Concepts [2]

### McMASTER MODEL OF FAMILY FUNCTIONING: SUMMARY OF DIMENSION CONCEPTS

| Dimensions | Key Concepts |
| --- | --- |
| (1) Problem-Solving | Affective and Instrumental Problems<br>Seven stages to the *Process:*<br>1. Identification of the problem<br>2. Communication of the problem to the appropriate resource(s)<br>3. Development of action alternatives<br>4. Decision on one alternative<br>5. Action<br>6. Monitor that action is taken<br>7. Evaluation of success<br><br>*Postulated:*<br><br>Most effective—carry out all 7 stages<br>Least effective—when cannot identify (stop before stage #1) |

Reprinted, by permission of the publisher, from N. B. Epstein, D. Bishop, and L. Baldwin, "McMaster Model of Family Functioning: A View of the Normal Family", in Froma Walsh (ed.), *Normal Family Processes* (New York: Guilford Press, 1982), pp. 120–121.

## McMASTER MODEL OF FAMILY FUNCTIONING: SUMMARY OF DIMENSION CONCEPTS—*Continued*

| *Dimensions* | *Key Concepts* |
|---|---|
| (2) Communication | Affective and Instrumental Areas<br>two independent *dimensions:*<br>1. Clear vs. Masked<br>2. Direct vs. Indirect<br>Above two dimensions to yield four *patterns of communication*, as follows:<br>1. Clear and Direct<br>2. Clear and Indirect<br>3. Masked and Direct<br>4. Masked and Indirect<br><br>*Postulated:*<br><br>Most effective—Clear and Direct<br>Least effective—Masked and Indirect |
| (3) Roles | Two function types—Necessary<br>                    —Other<br>Functions also broken into Affective and Instrumental areas<br>Necessary function groupings are:<br>1. Provision of resources<br>2. Nurturance and support<br>3. Adult sexual gratification<br>4. Personal development<br>5. Systems maintenance and management<br>Role functioning is assessed by considering how the family *allocates* responsibilities and handles *accountability* for them.<br><br>*Postulated:*<br><br>Most effective—all necessary functions have clear allocation to reasonable individual(s) and accountability built in.<br>Least effective—necessary functions are not addressed and/or allocation and accountability not maintained. |
| (4) Affective Responsiveness | Two groupings—Welfare emotions<br>                   —Emergency emotions<br><br>*Postulated:*<br><br>Most effective—full range of responses appropriate to amount and quality of stimulus.<br>Least effective—very narrow range (one or two affects only) and/or amount and quality distorted, given the context. |

## McMASTER MODEL OF FAMILY FUNCTIONING: SUMMARY OF DIMENSION CONCEPTS—*Continued*

| *Dimensions* | *Key Concepts* |
|---|---|
| (5) Affective Involvement | A spectrum of involvement with six *styles* identified:<br>1. Lack of involvement<br>2. Involvement devoid of feelings<br>3. Narcissistic involvement<br>4. Empathetic involvement<br>5. Over-involvement<br>6. Symbiotic involvement<br><br>*Postulated:*<br><br>Most effective—Empathetic involvement<br>Least effective—Symbiotic involvement and Lack of involvement |
| (6) Autonomy<br>(7) Behaviour Control | Applies to three *situations:*<br>1. Dangerous situations<br>2. Meeting and expressing of psycho-biological needs and drives (eating, drinking, sleeping, eliminating, sex, and aggression)<br>3. Interpersonal socializing processes inside and outside the family<br>*Style* is determined by the standard and latitude of what is acceptable in each of the above. Four styles are defined:<br>1. Rigid behaviour control<br>2. Flexible behaviour control<br>3. Laissez-faire behaviour control<br>4. Chaotic behaviour control<br>To maintain the Style, various techniques are used and implemented under Role functions (systems maintenance and management)<br><br>*Postulated:*<br><br>Most effective—Flexible<br>Least effective—Chaotic |

## IV. LIST OF INDICATORS OF ABUSE AND NEGLECT AND OPERATIONAL DEFINITIONS [3]

| Indicators | Operational Definitions |
|---|---|
| *Medically Diagnosed Injuries*—Verified by a Physician or Nurse | Indicators 1 through 14 are checked as present *only* if these were diagnosed or verified by a physician or nurse. |

*Medically Diagnosed Injuries*—Verified by a Physician or Nurse

1. Skin Damage
2. Bone Fracture(s) (Not Skull)
3. Skull Fracture
4. Previous Fracture
5. Internal Injury
6. Healing Injury
7. Old Scars
8. Sprains or Dislocation
9. Dismemberment
10. Brain Damage
11. Subdural Hemorrhage or Hematoma
12. Malnutrition
13. Failure to Thrive
14. Hospitalization Required

*Observable External Injuries*—Seen by Worker or Reliable Collateral

15. Burns
16. Welts
17. Wounds
18. Bruises
19. Malnutrition or Underdeveloped for Age Group
20. Injuries Located in More Than One Place on the Body

*Lack of Medical Care*

21. Untreated Cuts or Sores
22. Untreated Illness
23. No Preventive Medical Care
24. No Immunizations

*Poor Hygiene of Child*

25. Dirty Child, Clothes
26. Parasites on Child
27. Animal Bites

*Punishment*

28. Excessive Punishment — Overbeating a child with a hand or belt strap so that bruises are left. The mode of punishment would have been acceptable had parent not overdone it.

Reprinted, by permission of the publisher, from P. Combes, M. McCormack, M. H.Chipday, B. Archer, and J. C. Norman, *Manual for Using Abuse and Neglect Indicators* (Austin, TX: Resource Center on Child Abuse and Neglect, School of Social Work, the University of Texas at Austin, 1978).

**IV.   LIST OF INDICATORS OF ABUSE AND NEGLECT AND
        OPERATIONAL DEFINITIONS [3]—*Continued***

| *Indicators* | *Operational Definitions* |
|---|---|
| 29.  Inappropriate Punishment | Child punished in a "non-traditional" manner. Examples: beaten with an electric cord, locked in a closet for prolonged periods, beaten with a club, hit with an iron. |
| 30.  Bizarre Punishment | Sadistic torture of child called "punishment" by parent. Examples; pouring boiling water on child, bamboo under fingernails. |
| 31.  Other Physically Abused Siblings in Family | |
| *Lack of Supervision* | |
| 32.  Child Regularly Unsupervised for Short Periods of Time | |
| 33.  Child Unsupervised for One Extended Period of Time | |
| 34.  Child Unsupervised for Many Extended Periods of Time | |
| 35.  Child in Presence of Obvious Physical Hazards | Child in presence of obvious physical hazards such as exposed gas heater, or windows open on the second floor. |
| 36.  Child Locked In or Out of House | |
| *Desertion* | |
| 37.  Whereabouts of Caretaker Unknown | |
| 38.  Caretaker Expressed the Intention Not to Return for Child | |
| 39.  Inadequate Plans for Extended Care | |
| *Runaway* | |
| 40.  1st or 2nd Runaway | |
| 41.  Runaway 3 or More Times | |
| *Lack of Physical Necessities* | |
| 42.  Low-Income Family | Family income below the poverty level. |
| 43.  Lack of Appropriate Food | Child may receive food but it is not nutritious. For example: the child eats only soda and potato chips. |
| 44.  Lack of Appropriate Clothing | The child does not have appropriate clothing for his or her age, sex, or the weather. For example: child may not have a coat for the winter or may be wearing diapers at age 5. |
| 45.  Lack of Utilities | The child's home does not have light and/or heat and/or water and/or indoor plumbing. |
| 46.  Dirty Home | The home exhibits poor housekeeping. It is dirty but not a health hazard. |
| 47.  Filthy Home | The home is an immediate hazard to health. Examples: insects everywhere, excrement on the floor, huge piles of dirty dishes and clothes, no furniture. |

# IV.   LIST OF INDICATORS OF ABUSE AND NEGLECT AND OPERATIONAL DEFINITIONS [3]—*Continued*

| *Indicators* | *Operational Definitions* |
|---|---|
| *Sexual Abuse* | |
| 48.  Child Is Seductive | The child is inappropriately flirtatious. |
| 49.  Child Acts out Sexually | The child initiates sexual acts with anyone. |
| 50.  Perpetrator Habitually Forces Child Into Inappropriate Social Roles | The perpetrator of the sexual abuse forces the child into social roles inappropriate to age and/or familial relationship. Examples: a mother treats a 12-year-old son as if he were her husband or a neighbour treats a 10-year-old girl as a mature girlfriend. |
| 51.  Parent Inappropriately Restricts Child's Social Contacts | A parent inappropriately limits the social contacts of the child with the opposite sex. Examples: a father won't let a 16-year-old daughter date or is jealous of her boyfriends. |
| 52.  Perpetrator Initiates Verbal Sexual Overtures | |
| 53.  Perpetrator Initiates Sexual Petting/Fondling | |
| 54.  Perpetrator Initiates Sexual Intercourse | |
| 55.  Other Instances of Sexual Abuse in Family | |
| *Exploitative Victimization* | |
| 56.  Child Forced to Beg or Steal | |
| *Parental Behaviour Towards Child* | |
| 57.  Name-Calling/Derision | |
| 58.  Parent Ignores Child | |
| 59.  Unrealistic Expectations for Developmental Stage | The parents expect more from the child than age and developmental stage will allow. Examples: parents expect a 6-month-old to be toilet trained or a 2-year-old to dress and feed self. |
| 60.  Parent Shows No Affection | |
| 61.  Parent Holds Child Responsible for Family Problems | |
| 62.  Parent Perceives Child as Undesirably Different | |
| 63.  Parent Too Restrictive of Normal Childhood Behaviour | The parent places severe restrictions on the child for his age group. Example: an 8-year-old is not allowed to play with other children after school. |
| 64.  Parent Creates Severe Double Bind for Child | The child is damned if he does, damned if he doesn't do what the parent asks. Example: if he eats food, he's a hog; if he doesn't, then he doesn't appreciate mama's cooking. |
| 65.  Parent Cannot Explain Why Child Is Injured | |
| 66.  Parent Believes Child Got What Was Deserved | |
| 67.  Parent Feels No Guilt for Physical or Emotional Injury to Child | |

**IV.    LIST OF INDICATORS OF ABUSE AND NEGLECT AND OPERATIONAL DEFINITIONS [3]—*Continued***

| Indicators | Operational Definitions |
|---|---|
| 68. Parent Does Not Accept Responsibility for Child | Parent does not want the responsibility for the child. The school, the police, someone else should take care of the child. |
| 69. Parent Unable to Control Child | Parent cannot control the child's behaviour. |
| 70. Parent Does Not Recognize Child's Needs | Parent does not recognize the physical and emotional needs of a child. Example: parent does not recognize the child's need for balanced, regular meals or the child's need for affection. |
| 71. Spouse (Passively) Consents to Abusive Parent | Spouse does not protect child from perpetrator's abuse. |
| 72. Parent Uses Child as Vehicle for Marital Fighting | Parent involves the child in arguments with husband/wife. |
| 73. Parent Won't Change Behaviour Toward the Child | The parent won't stop abusing or neglecting the child. |

*General Parental Behaviour*

| | |
|---|---|
| 74. Parent Acts Impulsively or Irresponsibly. | |
| 75. Parent Would Not Accept Help | Parent would not accept the help of the agency or others referred. |
| 76. Parent Is Hostile | |
| 77. Parent Displays Lack of Consistent Behaviour | Parent seems incapable of planning and carrying out decisions. Example: Parent cannot plan family finances or meals or housekeeping. |
| 78. Parent Disassociates | Parent doesn't follow any train of thought, makes seemingly unrelated statements. |
| 79. Parent Unable to Meet Eyes While Talking | |
| 80. Parent Manipulative | |
| 81. Parent Not Interacting with People | |
| 82. Parent Does Not Accept Severity of Family Problem | Examples: Parent explains kids are tough, those bruises will go away, or, It will make him strong. |
| 83. Parent Gives Poor Explanation of Situation to Worker | The parent cannot explain the causes of a child's abuse or neglect. The parent either does not give any explanation or gives one that is patently false. Example: 2-year-old Johnny lifted the iron to his own body and gave himself repeated burn marks. |

*Parent Economic/Social Problems*

84. Abused or Neglected as a Child
85. Parent Abuses Drugs
86. Parent Abuses Alcohol
87. Parent Mentally Retarded
88. Parent Mentally Ill
89. Parent Physically Ill
90. Parent Incarcerated
91. Serious or Repeated Conflict with Law
92. Parent Has Chronic Marital Problems

## IV.    LIST OF INDICATORS OF ABUSE AND NEGLECT AND OPERATIONAL DEFINITIONS [3]—*Continued*

| Indicators | Operational Definitions |
|---|---|
| 93.  Parent Separated or Divorced | |
| 94.  Parent Frequently Changes Sexual Partners | |
| 95.  Unstable Family Composition | The composition of the family changed from month to month. Lovers, friends or relatives drift in and out of the family. |
| 96.  Breadwinner Without Income | Whatever person(s) is taking care of the child is unemployed. The child doesn't have a supporter. |
| 97.  Dysfunctional Employment Patterns | Parent changes jobs frequently, has erratic job attendance, or loses job because doesn't bother to go to work. |
| 98.  Family Socially Isolated | The family has few or no contacts outside school or work. There are few friends or supportive relatives. The mother who is a housewife may be especially isolated with no regular contacts outside her children and husband (if he is in the home). |
| 99.  Parent Has No Routine in Home | Example: breakfast can be at 10 one morning, 6 the next. |
| 100.  Parent Provides Unstable Home Environment | The family moves frequently and the parent(s) make no effort to provide a permanent home. |
| 101.  Inadequate Effort to Obtain Funds | The parent(s) do not really attempt to find a job, earn more money or apply for aid. |

*Child's Behaviour*

| Indicators | Operational Definitions |
|---|---|
| 102.  Child Withdrawn | |
| 103.  Child Displays Inappropriate Affect | The child has inappropriate reactions to surrounding and events. Examples: the child laughs at sad things, cries at happy things. |
| 104.  Child Extremely Fearful | |
| 105.  Child Fears Adults | |
| 106.  Child Extremely Dependent | |
| 107.  Child Is Sadistic | |
| 108.  Child Is Extremely Provoking | The child is a 'Dennis the Menace'. Anybody would beat this child. |
| 109.  Child Avoids Eye Contact | |
| 110.  Child Refuses to Discuss Family Situation | The child will not discuss allegations of abuse or neglect. |
| 111.  Child Makes Inappropriate References to Family Problems | Examples: the child makes a joke about parents' drinking, or filthy house. |
| 112.  Child Is Manipulative | |
| 113.  Child Wets Bed | |
| 114.  Inappropriate Behaviour for Age or Role of Child | This depends on the age of the child. Example: a 10-year-old who is not retarded acts like a baby. |
| 115.  Child Hides Injury | |
| 116.  Child Is Self-Destructive | Child tries to physically injure himself or herself. |
| 117.  Child Is Hostile/Aggressive | |
| 118.  Child Is Ashamed | |

## IV.    LIST OF INDICATORS OF ABUSE AND NEGLECT AND OPERATIONAL DEFINITIONS [3]—*Continued*

| Indicators | Operational Definitions |
|---|---|
| 119.   Child Away from Home at Inappropriate Times | This depends on the age of the child. Example: a 10-year-old child who is out at 2 a.m. |
| *Child's Economic, Social Problems* | |
| 120.   Child Abuses Alcohol | |
| 121.   Child Abuses Drugs | |
| 122.   Child Mentally Retarded | |
| 123.   Child Mentally Ill | |
| 124.   Child Physically Ill | |
| 125.   Lacks Interactive Skills | Child does not know how to communicate with adults or peers. |
| 126.   Lacks Fundamental Social Skills | Examples: child does not know how to use a knife and fork, eats with hands; or child does not know how to use a handkerchief, uses fingers. |
| 127.   Child Intellectually, Emotionally Immature | |
| 128.   Child Truant 3 or More Times | |
| 129.   Low Academic Achievement | |
| 130.   Discipline Problems in School | |
| 131.   Child Predelinquent | |
| 132.   Child "Arrested" by Police | Child is detained by law enforcement officials for an offense for which he or she would be arrested if he or she were older. |
| 133.   Child Is Pregnant | |
| 134.   Is There Any Indication of Abuse/Neglect by Substitute Care Personnel? | |

## REFERENCES

1. Hess, P. and Howard, T. "An Ecological Model for Assessing Psychosocial Difficulties in Children," Child Welfare, Vol. LX, No. 8, Sept.–Oct., 1981.

2. Epstein, N. B., Bishop, D., and Baldwin, L. "McMaster Model of Family Functioning: A View of the Normal Family," in Walsh, Froma (ed.) *Normal Family Processes.* New York, NY: Gilford Books, 1982.

3. Combes, P., McCormack, M., Chipday, M. H., Archer, B., and Norman, J. C. *Manual for Using Abuse and Neglect Indicators and Index.* Austin, Texas: Resource Center on Child Abuse and Neglect, School of Social Work, The University of Texas at Austin, 1978.

# C
# |Staff Practice Statements

Introduction    437

Group Work with Unmarried Parents    437
Pat Convery

Do We Serve the Best Interests of the Infant? An
Unmarried Parents Worker's Dilemma    441
Lyn Ferguson

Working with West Indian Adolescent Mothers    445
Betty Kashima, Debra Feldman, Christine Lowry

## INTRODUCTION

In the course of researching and writing this *Source Book*, research staff became aware of a dearth of literature on concrete practice activities in the child welfare field. Further, there is a suspicion that a sophisticated level of professional wisdom informs the everyday work of practitioners across North America, but is rarely available to professional colleagues through existing journals. As a way of encouraging the codification and sharing of such knowledge, three samples of practice statements are included in Appendix C. Two statements were written by staff members of the Metropolitan Toronto Children's Aid Society. The third, "Working with West Indian Adolescent Mothers," was written by a member of the project staff (Sharon Kirsh) after interviewing the agency staff. It is written as an abstract in a style and format that may make practice knowledge more accessible to practitioners than the usual prose form.

## GROUP WORK WITH UNMARRIED PARENTS

**Pat Convery,** *Unmarried Parent Coordinator, Children's Aid Society of Metropolitan Toronto*

Groups have always been viewed as an interesting and innovative way of dealing with the unmarried parent. For many reasons, groups have not been orga-

437

**nized** or run for any period of time. The purpose of this section is to look more closely at the mechanics of running groups for the young parent.

### Why Use the Group Format

The majority of girls who come to us as young, single parents are adolescents. Much study and practical experience in the area of adolescence have shown that adolescents work well in groups, and this is even more true for the adolescent parent.

For the adolescent, peer group is extremely important. They more readily accept guidance and explore alternatives from peers than from any other source, particularly persons seen as having an authoritarian role. The group serves as a special force in altering attitudes and behaviours.

As a worker dealing with adolescent parents it is difficult to realize their level of maturity and ability to separate their adolescent needs from the needs of their child for parenting. A group provides a setting through which a worker can observe and assess more accurately the individual girl's level of functioning.

An important task of the teenage parent is to work through the developmental stages of adolescence. These needs, such as social identity and peer support, must be met adequately in order to allow the mother to devote energy to her role as a parent.

Through the group, the teenager can achieve the developmental tasks of adolescence, as well as those of pregnancy and parenthood. The teen must develop a new identity as a mother, for which she needs a peer group with which to identify. As well, the teens must learn to make responsible decisions for themselves and their babies, independent of their families, sooner than the normal flow of adolescent development would demand. Problem-solving in a group promotes this happening in a positive, supportive way.

Once in a group, adolescents tend to feel more comfortable than in individual sessions. They become more open about their feelings, and issues can be discussed with a greater ease. This allows the worker to devote more energy to the tasks of assessment, guidance, and teaching.

A further advantage of group work is the flexibility it allows the worker in using her many skills selectively for various purposes. While the focus of the group may be problem-solving or socialization, she has the opportunity to introduce topics, teach directly, encourage discussions, give opinions, clarify misconceptions, and generally promote good communication and resolution of problems.

Groups are cost-effective. With the use of volunteers for daycare and transportation when possible, most groups for the adolescent parent can be run with minimal costs. Through a successful group, more clients are seen more regularly, with less worker time being used. The quality and quantity of contacts offsets the time needed for preparing for the group, outreach, and follow-up.

A good group experience gives the adolescent parent a good base for seeking and accepting assistance for future problems. She will see the helping professions in a more favourable light, be less threatened by demands made on her to discuss problems, and be more willing to take some responsibility for acting on problems. Experience has shown clearly that, as a result of a positive prenatal or postnatal group experience, mothers are more likely to seek assistance for problems *before* they reach crisis proportions.

*Planning Guidelines*

In the initial planning of any group program there are some factors that must be considered to ensure that the group (a) complements the overall service plan of the agency, and (b) does not unrealistically add to the worker's or agency's workload. This is particularly important in a child welfare agency where caseloads are already demanding, where there is little hope for much increase in funding or staffing, and staff turnover is high. A well-planned group must be extremely cost-effective, productive, and must become an integrated part of our service delivery system.

The result of a poorly planned group is that the worker feels isolated, overworked, and frustrated. The group or program terminates prematurely and there is little change in the social situation of the client group. The following are guidelines that may help prevent these problems.

The mandate of a child welfare agency is to provide service for the unmarried parent and her child. Clearly, the purpose of this mandate is preventative in terms of their future together or apart and problems they may encounter. Theory suggests and practice demonstrates that by adequately meeting the needs of the pregnant teenager or adolescent parent, we can either prevent future problems or pave the way for their accepting assistance at times of crisis in the future. This cannot be done in isolation. The programs we run *must* fit into a total community picture. Ideally, a group should run in conjunction with other agencies—as preparation for a community program that is perhaps more sophisticated or comprehensive, or to meet a clearly defined gap in service that inhibits these parents from adequately meeting the needs of their children. In other words, while we can identify the need for many programs, we must assess if we, as a child welfare agency, should run the group or play an advocacy or community development role. As well, because the unmarried parent is often a voluntary client and a part of the community at large, part of the program should directly or indirectly prepare her for working with other community agencies and resources available to her.

Having assessed the need for a particular group program, the next step is to plan for its becoming an integral part of the overall service delivery. Since a short-term group, albeit successful, is necessarily limited in the social needs it can meet, planning must be done to ensure the longevity of a program, if it continues to be successful in meeting a particular need, in spite of staff changes and limited initial funding sources.

The first question is how will the worker who is to run the group be relieved of some casework responsibilities to allow time to run the group properly. This question can be rephrased: how can the team, department, or branch as a whole incorporate the task into its workload? Without the support of co-workers, supervisors, and administrators, a group becomes little more than a source of frustration that contributes to worker burnout.

A group need not mean more work for a department, but rather a different allocating of caseload demands. Even when a computer dictates worker caseloads, cases can be assigned to allow time for a well-run program. A reduction in workload can be achieved by being relieved of some responsibilities (e.g., intake), or possibly by planning allocation of cases for a period of time (e.g., no cases that will require evening work, or no cases that can be serviced through regular sessions). Open communication between workers about group progress and caseload numbers on an ongoing basis will enhance the functioning of all services.

The onus is on the group leader to ensure that he or she does not work in isolation and become alienated from colleagues. Ongoing verbal reports to other workers about happenings in the group, feedback about clients in the group, and requesting of referrals are important jobs of the group leader in a casework agency. This is particularly important when the group is not run in the office but occupies a community facility.

### Steps in Planning a Group for the Unmarried Parent

1. Type of Group

The type of group should meet the need presented by current caseloads and identified gaps in service within the total community. Initial focus should be stated in the group title. Some very obvious examples of groups for the teen mom are prenatal, postnatal, infant stimulation, and adjustment to parenting.

2. Who Will Attend

It is important to decide initially how flexible or rigid the intake process will be in terms of age, stage of pregnancy, or age of children. An open-ended group may encompass wide variations among members; however, a clearly stated common focus is imperative.

3. Length of Group

A group may be short-term or long-term. A short-term group must have a very clear, resolvable focus, that is, prenatal, teaching parenting, life skills, and so on. Prior to the group's beginning, plans should be made for setting up a support system for the members after the group terminates. This may consist of referrals to appropriate programs in the community or planning individual support systems. Ideally, a short-term group will be run as a series with plans for another to start when one ends, in order to accommodate new referrals.

A long-term group for the unmarried parent is ideally flexible in terms of membership, allowing for new members to begin as they become in need of or ready for a group experience. As individuals prepare to leave the group, plans should be made for continued assistance to them as needed. The worker must constantly re-focus the group in terms of the goals and focus of sessions.

### Intake Process

Referrals should be elicited from all sources deemed appropriate. While it is not necessary to have a complete history about the prospective member, it is important to decide initially how much information is desirable. All prospective members should be interviewed prior to attendance in the group. The purpose of the interview is threefold: (1) to discuss with them their desire to come to the group; (2) to assess their obvious strengths, weaknesses, and suitability for the group; (3) (but not lastly) to lessen their anxiety about attending the group by their getting to know you as a person. As well, it is important to discuss the mechanics of their attendance in terms of transportation, daycare, re-scheduling conflicts, and so on. New young mothers tend to need a lot of outreach in postnatal programs. This is because of their nervousness about and/or inability to venture out with a young baby. Much encouragement and concrete support (phone calls, transportation) are often needed to help them make it to the first meeting.

*Setting up the Group*

1. Location
The location of the group is a major consideration. It is important that the place be easily accessible, which generally means no more than one bus ride if transportation is not provided. Unless babies are staying with the mothers, two rooms will be needed. The room for the children should ideally be located near a washroom and have adequate heat control and ventilation. This room will need to be equipped with age-appropriate toys and baby equipment such as diapers, bottle warmers, trainer cups, Arrowroot cookies, Kleenex, a few blankets, and wash cloths.

Teen moms seem to be able to make themselves comfortable in most rooms. Juice, coffee, tea, and biscuits are best provided throughout the group. Pamphlets and resource books are useful to have in the room for early arrivers to read.

2. Time
Most group sessions run for two hours. This is usually the maximum length of time the children can be entertained. The worker should allow at least an hour before the meeting to set up the rooms and greet people, and at least an hour after the group to clean up, confer with baby-sitters and/or co-leader, and to deal with any crisis that could not be dealt with during the group time. A few hours between groups should be set aside for collateral contacts, planning, outreach, and follow-up.

Thus, 4 to 6 hours a week are needed to run a group properly. This amount of time is minimal compared with the number of client contacts achieved through the group. Approximately 10 clients would be involved in the program and, for many, the group could be the only service offered.

## DO WE SERVE THE BEST INTERESTS OF THE INFANT? AN UNMARRIED PARENTS WORKER'S DILEMMA

**Lyn Ferguson,** *Children's Aid Society of Metropolitan Toronto*

Few would argue that the best interests of an infant are met by a permanent placement as soon as possible in her or his young life. Yet the child welfare system in many ways militates against meeting this fundamental goal. Operating within this paradoxical situation is one of the major dilemmas of the unmarried parent worker.

The frustrations inherent in working with legislation that carefully safeguards parental rights, too often at the expense of the child's rights, are not new to the field. The UP worker must deal with this fact as it pertains to infants and face dilemmas within the legislation, the legal process in and out of court, and in the bureaucratic process of the Children's Aid Society itself.

It is the purpose of this article to explore this dilemma and to raise pertinent issues for those of us working within the child welfare system.

In several ways, the Ontario Child Welfare Act of 1978 specifically supports strong parental rights in regard to infants. Any natural parent presenting a plan for her or his child must be allowed the opportunity to parent the infant. Evidence needed to deny this right must be very weighty and *usually cannot include evidence related to parenting other children* or to prenatal behaviour. Only recently have inroads been made in this area with several court decisions made in Ontario and British Columbia. In 1981 an Ontario Judge in Kenora questioned the rights of an alcoholic mother who gave birth to a baby with fetal alcohol syndrome. In April 1982, Madam Justice Patricia Proudfoot of the British Columbia Supreme Court overturned a ruling of a family court judge and argued that anticipating abuse or neglect is the proper concern for social workers and child welfare. She argued that the B.C. Family and Child Service Act in that case placed the child's welfare above parental rights. Such court decisions are only very recent and certainly not binding in Canadian courts of law. However, that they are occurring at all is a reflection of the concern for infants within this present balance of parental versus child's rights.

If a parent should choose to relinquish her or his rights to an infant, the Ontario Child Welfare Act allows considerable protection to this parent. Whether this is done outside of Family Court through signing "Consents to Adoption", or through the Court process itself, no decision can be made until eight days after birth at the earliest, and after that there is either a 21-day appeal period after consents, or a 30-day appeal period after Crown Wardship. For purposes of comparison, Manitoba's Child Welfare Act allows the parent seven days before signing consents and allows no appeal period once that child has been placed. The *Globe and Mail*, June 6, 1981, reported on a Supreme Court of Canada decision regarding a 19-year-old Manitoba woman who relinquished her child and changed her mind the following day. The Manitoba Court of Appeal ruled that the hasty placement of the child had made a mockery of the provision allowing a change of mind, and ordered the infant returned to the mother. However, the Supreme Court of Canada reversed that decision and ruled that the mother had forfeited her rights once she relinquished the child. As the *Globe* editorial stated: "This is a thorny issue, affecting the welfare of the child, the mother and the adoptive parents". However, the editorial continues by stating the Globe's position on the matter: "At the very least, the law should include a provision which holds off the placing of an infant until a week or so after the papers have been signed. To rush the child into the adoptive family's arms before the ink is even dry on the contract serves nobody".

This is certainly a defensible position and those of us who work with relinquishing parents can appreciate it fully. At the same time, however, when we verbalize an equally strong commitment to "bonding" and the best interests of the child, the controversial aspects of the issue become clear.

The role of the man named as the father of the child (putative father) is a dilemma that is becoming an increasingly frequent one for UP workers. The intent of the changes in the 1978 Act was to more fully protect the rights of the putative father. In a world where equality between men and women is increasingly accepted as the social norm, this position is neither surprising nor indefensible. However, the implications of these changes further underscore the strength of parental rights and add a whole set of processes that can delay the permanent placement of the child. A mother may not wish to name the putative father, which can propel a case into court to dispense with his consent; or a putative father may accept paternity but refuse to plan, again often sending a case through the court process; or a woman may have lived common-law with the father, thus invoking the assumptions of the Children's Law Reform Act and forcing his involvement; or the father may choose to plan and the mother may oppose this.

The court system should be, and often is, the ultimate protector of a child's rights. The C.A.S. of Metropolitan Toronto manual states clearly that although Consents to Adoption may often be the "preferred method" to the court process, consents should not be considered in the following circumstances: a history of parental disturbance, mental health or retardation, where the mother is under 16 (the father is not mentioned), where a child appears to be in need of protection, where the mother refuses to name the father and swear an affidavit to that effect, where the circumstances of the child's best interests would recommend transfer of guardianship, *or in any case of an unusual nature not covered above where the child may be at great risk unless an application for guardianship is made.*

Consents to Adoption are considered the preferred method for several reasons. The court process can be an anxiety-producing experience for the parent(s) and worker alike. No matter how much "preparation" is done for the client, it is rarely a comfortable experience for them. For even an experienced UP worker, the Court experience is time consuming, both in preparation of documents and waiting time outside the court. It is also an expensive process, utilizing expensive Judge and Legal Counsel's time. However, the most serious implication from the standpoint of this UP worker's position is the greater likelihood of further delays for the child.

If a matter is straightforward and "on consent", the very court process itself almost always excludes the possibility of a hospital adoption placement for the child. As a child stays in hospital for a period of 10 days, the most intensive period of work is between the eighth and tenth day. Within these three days the parent(s) must relinquish the child, the adoptive family must be chosen and contacted, the child must be "shown" to the prospective adoptive parents, and finally the child can be discharged to them. This requires careful organization and planning on the part of the UP worker, the adoption worker, the hospital, and the parents themselves. It can be done, particularly if the UP or Family worker can free time on short notice and has the preparatory social history information completed ahead of time. However, the added involvement of the court process would make this very difficult at best, and probably impossible, given the realities of the processes involved, worker's caseloads, and court waiting time.

Few would argue that a hospital placement is "best" for the child and the adoptive parents from the perspective of "bonding". It is also frequently requested by our relinquishing parents, especially if they appreciate the concept of bonding.

Once a matter is before the court and the matter is not straightforward for any reason, the chances for delay increase markedly. Adjournments are very common, especially in matters where there is confusion or dissension between the parties. New court dates are chosen at the convenience of legal counsel, the judge, the workers, and the family members (probably in that order of importance). Weeks and months in a child's life can disappear in a few short minutes. A party who is attempting to prevent the plan of another may have an already understood goal to delay proceedings as long as possible. Even the choice of appointing legal counsel to represent the infant can in reality go against the best interests of the child by creating further delays, either by requesting further information and assessments or by adding an additional professional to be considered when scheduling further court hearings. Such dilemmas are commonly stated in regard to children and Child Welfare Court. The O.A.P.S.W. is sufficiently concerned that they have set up a task force to look at the implications of increased litigation for the field of child welfare. The implications for infants are very serious.

A UP worker must also deal with the frustrations inherent in dealing with an infant within the structure of a large bureaucratic structure. Once the child is taken into C.A.S. care she or he runs the risk of further delays. The agency, at present, has no firm guidelines as to the length of time a natural parent may remain ambivalent. Workers may use their own discretion as to the length of time they will give a client to resolve ambivalence. Once consents are signed or Crown Wardship is obtained, appeal periods must be waited and then the child will await her or his turn for conferencing for the choice of the adoptive family. Children's Service workers are responsible for juggling the various needs of 30 infants and children's service, family service, and adoption workers must all be free to attend the conference. To plan adoption, documentation must be prepared ahead of time and the infant must be medically stable. Further delays can result from problems in any one of these areas.

If the child welfare system is going to live up to its stated goal of meeting the best interests of the child, it must further address the issue of time in the infant's life and plan priorities. Certain constraints will remain inherent within the system as it stands. Parental rights will be paramount within our child welfare system and parents will continue to remain ambivalent. The court system will remain a slow and cumbersome institution, child welfare workers will continue to be overworked and bureaucracies will continue to create delays by their very structure.

However, given the above constraints, a child welfare system cognizant of the importance of *time* in an infant's life can strive to value this factor more highly.

The agency can set guidelines establishing time limits for ambivalent parents. Workers can aim, as much as possible, to resolve issues of ambivalence prior to a child's birth and can relay to the relinquishing parents the importance of placement as soon as possible. Putative fathers can be contacted, social histories obtained, and differences in custody plans thoroughly discussed prior to the birth.

Hospital placements can be facilitated by increased flexibility on the part of both UP, family service workers, and adoption workers. The adoption department is recently showing greater flexibility in accepting less formalized social history information, more broadly interpreting children's birth histories, providing alternative methods of choosing adoptive families, providing placements with adoptive applicants prior to consents being signed, and stressing to adoptive applicants the importance of "taking the risk".

The importance of specialized workers delivering UP services must be appreciated. Hospital placements are difficult enough for a worker familiar with the process and with the freedom to hasten the UP service. A generalized family service worker has other priorities to address and has less familiarity with the process. In addition, a UP specialist can develop professional contacts with hospitals, legal, and adoption workers that can greatly facilitate a hospital placement.

The child welfare system and the workers within it can also strive to make the court system as sensitive as possible to the needs of the infant. Priorities for infants could be considered in establishing court dates. When working with legal counsel, the issue of time can be raised and reinforced by social workers as *the* crucial issue.

Within the child welfare system itself, first priority should be given to moving infants to permanent placements as soon as possible. Guidelines can be established to speed up completion of relevant documentation, and the earliest possible choice of an adoptive family. The age of a child can be an important factor in guiding a worker's establishment of priorities within his or her own caseload. Special consideration should be given to Children's Service workers with a high turnover of young infants. Caseload requirements should be protected so that workers are not forced to hold up infants' placements because of workload.

Changes are occuring throughout the child welfare system and courts are questioning traditional views of child/parental rights, particularly as they pertain to infants. Recent publications such as *The Unborn Child*, by Dr. Thomas Verny, and the court decisions regarding children "in utero" are challenging us to consider the needs of the infant prior to birth. Implications for child welfare authorities are far-reaching.

Front-line child welfare workers will have no choice but to live with the frustrating and paradoxical position of attempting to meet children's needs in our present system. However, one can hope that there will continue to be a slow but steady move to further honour our commitment to "serve the best interests of the child".

## WORKING WITH WEST INDIAN ADOLESCENT MOTHERS

### Betty Kashima, Debra Feldman, Christine Lowry

*[Betty Kashima is a C.A.S. Family Service Supervisor (North York, Toronto); Debra Feldman and Christine Lowry are C.A.S. Family Service Workers (North York, Toronto) whose caseloads are made up of both UP work (33%) and other family service casework (67%).]*

*1.    Statement of Problem*

Children born to adolescents tend to form a high-risk population. Because it is the task of child welfare workers to serve teenage mothers, it is important that practitioners be aware of varying treatment approaches that are sensitive to cultural differences among clients. The present study uses the West Indian culture as one example.

Statistics show that teen mothers are tending towards keeping their babies. Included in this group is a significant number of West Indian adolescents whose distinct culture and system of values must be considered in developing a treatment plan and approach.

2.      *Subjects or Recipients of Intervention*

Recipients are likely to be:
between age 14–19 years
West Indian-born Canadian immigrants
pregnant and unmarried
living with their family or extended family or friends of the family (many clients have never lived with their biological mother)
economically dependent on the people with whom they live, not necessarily the State
students at the time of pregnancy
either no longer associated with the putative father, or involved in a relationship which is unstable (the putative father is unlikely to provide either financial or emotional support)

3.      *Milieu of Intervention*

Outreach is an important aspect of service; worker/client meetings tend to be carried out either: (1) in the community (e.g., in a restaurant), especially if the client's family is unaware of the pregnancy or of the agency contact or if the client is not mobile or motivated enough to come to the office; or (2) in the client's home in order to allow the worker to see where the prospective baby will live and with whom and under what physical/social conditions. When the client begins to feel comfortable with the worker, she may then be asked to make her way to the agency office if she is mobile enough to do so.

4.      *Theoretical Base of Intervention/Practice/Treatment*

eclectic theoretical base is:

reality based
task-oriented (problem-solving orientation)
behaviouristic in its use of positive reinforcement for appropriate behaviours

5.      *Previous and Current Research Influencing Intervention*

Research on the children of teen parents indicates that they are at risk physically and emotionally.

Teen mothers tend to be a hard-to-serve population because while they assume an adult role they are in fact adolescents and therefore cannot be treated in casework with approaches appropriate to mature adult clients.

6.      *Objectives of Intervention*

To ensure that the client obtains the material and emotional supports which are necessary in order for her to keep her baby and to adequately care for the child in her role as the primary parent.

To find a support person for the client when one does not exist, and to facilitate that relationship.

To ascertain the existence of a primary relationship in the client's life (usually mother, grandmother, aunt, friend) and to look at the strengths this relationship has in supporting the client.

To reunite the client and her primary support when they are separated by shame, anger, and other negative feelings brought about by the pregnancy.

7. *Strategies and Procedures*

This approach is based on the knowledge that the client has decided to keep her baby; she is unlikely to be ambivalent about keeping the baby.

The client may first present herself to the agency when she is in the advanced stages of pregnancy (months 7–9), thereby limiting the amount of relationship-building that can be done, because of time limitations.

The initial phase of intervention is pragmatic, with a task-focus. By helping the client with personal, life-sustaining concerns (e.g., obtaining prenatal medical care), the client comes to see the worker as a caring, helpful, and competent person. Simultaneously, the worker can assess the client's skills by having her take on the responsibility of performing certain tasks on her own.

This treatment approach consists of three levels of intervention:

1. one-to-one counselling with the client

2. counselling the client within her family (or surrogate family)

3. linking the client with community supports (e.g., classes, material supports, welfare, public health nurse home visits, OHIP coverage)

*Client assessment:* During this ongoing assessment of the client, the worker examines:

1. potential sources of support for the client (e.g., family, friends)

2. potential strengths and weaknesses of the client as a parent (e.g., how she handles anger and frustration; the degree of responsibility she demonstrates; her knowledge of infant care; her past experience with infant caretaking (e.g., with a sibling)

3. client's stage of adolescent development (e.g., how much does she know about herself; is she goal-oriented; does she have verbal skills; is she able to assert herself; is she aware of, and responsible for, her baby's needs; does she perceive a baby to be a 'toy' or a responsibility)

4. client's decision-making ability (e.g., on what did she base her decision to keep the baby)

5. client's appropriateness of affect

During this ongoing client assessment the worker encourages her to talk about her childhood, helping her to acknowledge and to work through separation issues (e.g., separation from her mother during early childhood).

The client may need to work through grief in separating from the putative father or in dealing with inconsistencies in that relationship.

Often the client requires a boost to her self-esteem (the worker may deal with this by unconditionally accepting her as a person, by being consistent in the relationship to her, and by providing her with age- and stage-appropriate tasks which she can easily perform successfully and for which she can then be positively reinforced (e.g., asking her to telephone her welfare worker).

The client may use denial as a defense mechanism—she may subtly deny that she is pregnant. The worker approaches her in a confronting, but support-ive manner. For example, the worker might label for her what she is possibly feeling: (I guess it's so scary to be pregnant that you've put the whole thing out of your mind), or she may use a modelling approach to tasks associated with preparing for the baby. The worker acknowledges the denial to the client and by her presence in the client's life makes denial more difficult to maintain.

The client may deny that she will have sexual needs in the future. In order to deal with the issue of birth control, the worker may need to make the rational connections for the client between having a boyfriend and wanting sexual intimacy with him, and between sexual intimacy and the possibility of preg-nancy.

*Assessment and recruitment of personal supports:* the worker explores with the client the nature of her personal support system: is her primary support her mother, grandmother, aunt, friend; will this person continue to be supportive after childbirth, and if so, what types of support is she likely to provide—room and board, clothing, money, child care, emotional support. If there is no primary support at present is there a possibility of finding an appropriate person. How does the primary person feel about the pregnancy, and so on.

If the baby will be living with the client in the family's/friend's home, then the worker insists on meeting the involved parties in their home in order to ensure that suitable material resources are available, that the physical environment is suitable for an infant (e.g., adequate space), that the baby will not be at risk in that home environment, and to ensure that the plan has been approved by the residents (e.g., a surrogate parent might state that she in fact does not want the baby living in her home).

If the client is hesitant to tell her primary person(s) about the pregnancy, then the worker may help her to tell them.

If the client's primary person is not supportive initially, then the worker may spend some time dealing with the issues related to this resistance. Most clients live with a woman who had gone through an early pregnancy when she was younger. In the case of mothers (or mother substitutes), often there is a sense of remorse regarding the client's pregnancy because the mother had hoped for a life-script for her daughter which would differ from her own. When the daughter begins to repeat history the mother may experience a resurfacing of old feelings which can be manifested in anger/

disappointment towards the client. Often the client and her mother had been separated throughout much of the client's childhood (e.g., the mother was in Canada while her daughter was in the West Indies), and the process of reuniting had been difficult. The daughter's pregnancy serves to compound the readjustment.

The worker may meet with the mother alone if there is anger between mother and daughter; however, when possible, the mother and daughter meet together with the worker (the worker tries to have the client invite her mother to join them—if not, then the worker gets the client's permission to telephone the mother). The mother is encouraged to ventilate her feelings, to explore her social history, to assess her feelings about her daughter, to gain insight into past-present connections, and to build on her positive feelings towards her daughter.

*Recruitment of community supports:* The worker helps the client to activate community supports such as prenatal and postnatal classes, nutrition classes, housing, public assistance, OHIP, public health nurse visits, and so forth; if the worker is concerned about the client's health or about her diligence in attending doctor's appointments, then she may call the client's physician so that they can directly exchange information about the client's health—the client's permission to do so would be necessary, however.

8.    *Results*

Most clients successfully return home from the hospital with their babies and manage to provide adequate parental care. Postnatal follow-up with UP clients continues for a 3-month period, and in some cases clients wish to continue their relationship with the worker even though the worker has no protection concerns.

In the majority of cases, the worker is ultimately perceived by the client to be a helping person upon whom one can rely.

9.    *Conclusions*

Some possible limitations of this approach:

The worker's value system must be flexible enough to incorporate and to understand the value system of another cultural group.

This is a short-term approach to the issue of teenage motherhood and it does not address needs and concerns associated with the long-term effects of early parenting.

The worker must be ever vigilant of the tendency to stereotype human behaviour.

Some resources which would enhance this approach:

the availability of prenatal and childcare classes associated with regular school programs

educational opportunities for non-West Indian workers regarding those aspects of West Indian culture which are likely to have an impact upon the worker's understanding of, and solution to, their clients' problems or concerns

the availability of prenatal and postnatal groups both for peers only and for teens and their families (or substitute families)

*10.    Assumptions*

Motherhood is highly valued within the West Indian community.

The teenage mother will not be isolated with her child; she will receive support from her personal network and will not, at least initially, be solely responsible for the baby.

Babies are perceived to be the responsibility of females, especially as pertains to their caretaking.

There is pride of paternity both among the putative fathers and the teenage mothers; many fathers insist on registering their child's birth and to give the child their surname.

West Indian clients differ from other clients in that:

West Indian clients are likely to be less ambivalent about keeping rather than relinquishing the baby.

The putative father is more likely to support the mother's desire to keep the baby.

They are more likely to get support from their personal networks (family and friends).

They may be less knowledgeable about CAS role and therefore more cautious in engaging in counselling with their social worker; hence, a more task-oriented, concrete approach is more effective.

# Index

Adolescence
  Residential placement, and the establishment
    of independent community living
    through transition groups, 281
  and foster care, 251
  and development, 290
  presenting problems, theoretical approaches,
    295
  and running away, 298
  and delinquency, 305
  and self-injurious behaviours, 308
  and suicide, 312
  treatment approaches for adolescent prob-
    lems, 313
  and adoption, 345
  and Canadian statistics on pregnancies, 359
  developmental tasks and pregnancy, 361
  working with West Indian adolescent
    mothers, 445
Adoption
  stages of practice, 324
  permancy planning, 325
  community-oriented recruitment, 326
  the media and recruitment for adoption, 327
  assessment of adoption applicants, 328
  contentious issues in assessment, 328
  functions of assessment of adoption appli-
    cants, 329
  an ecological approach to adoption assess-
    ment, 329
  working with the rejected adoption applicant,
    330
  matching adoptive families with children, 331
  factors associated with adoption permanency
    and breakdown, 331
  history-giving and adoption, 338
  and group care, 339
  and foster family care, 339
  pre-adoptive foster family care, 339
  transracial and transcultural adoption, 340
  subsidized adoption, 342
  quasi-adoptions, 343
  post-placement support for adoptive families,
    343

  and the family romance fantasy, 344
  and telling, 344
  and adolescence, 345
  post-adoption, 346
  trends in adoption, 347
  availability of young children for, 347
  biological parents and the adoption process,
    347
  use of groups in adoption practice, 348
  independent adoptions, 348
  lay organizations concerned with adoption,
    349
  scientific developments and, 349
  by single persons, 350
  by homosexuals, 351
  open adoption, 351
Anxiety
  Working with client anxiety, 46
Apprehension
  guidelines for immediate apprehension, 31
  temporary removal, 20
Assessments
  definition of, 23
  general standards for, 23
  and problem-solving, 24, 423
  assessment frameworks, 24, 423
  assessing high risk of abuse and neglect, 25
  information and conclusions, 25
  methods of gathering information for, 30
  assessing child competence in residential set-
    tings, 266
  assessment of adoption applicants, 328
Authority
  and the therapeutic relationship, 56
  as a basis for influence, 39

Behaviour Therapy
  and child abuse, 171
  and adolescence, 316
Bureaucracy
  and the helping process, 58
  combining administration and helpfulness, 59

Child Abuse

definition, 137
characteristics of victims, 138
behavioural indications, 139
characteristics of abusing parents, 139
theoretical approaches, 140, 152
societal conditions, 144
family characteristics, 145
social isolation, 148
family interaction, 149
role of child, 150
consequences of, 152
guidelines for engaging child abusers, 36, 155
crisis intervention as an approach, 157
resocialization of parents, 161
individual psychotherapy, 167, 170
group psychotherapy, 167
transactional analysis, 168
behaviour therapy, 169
foster care of the abused child, 171, 227
marital therapy, 172
family therapy, 173
multiple intervention methods, 173, 174
and adolescent running, 299
Child Care
child care standards and practice, 38
Child Neglect
definition of, 92
indicators of, 94, 423
theoretical approaches to, 94
socioeconomic and cultural factors and, 95
neighbourhoods and, 98
family resources and, 98
family composition and, 99
isolation, support and, 100
treatment of, 113
Child Welfare Work
roles, activities, and functions, 16
Clients
involuntary, 36
factors affecting client-worker relationships, 36
attitudes towards help, 44
feelings of inadequacy, 47
anger, 47
client-staff relationships in residence, 276
Communication
literature on communication and the helping relationship, 45
Community Work
and child welfare, definition and objectives, 66
history of, 66
activities and approaches, 68
and the ecological framework, 69
and casework, 69
resource exchange and, 70
and social networks, 72

and neighbourhoods, 73
Contraception
and teenage pregnancies, 362
and teenage fathers, 371
Contracting
definition and objectives, 48
as a relationship, 48
factors inhibiting successful contracting and how to deal with them, 49
and rewards, 50
Court
preparing for, 51
factors contributing to frustrations in, 52
and the helping process, 52
preparing the child for, 53
participation in, 54
Crisis Intervention
general guidelines, 157
and sexual abuse, 198, 204
Daycare
definitions and types of, 78
difficulties in accessing, 81
debates about, 81
and community work practice, 83
models of, 83

Delinquency
and child welfare, 305
theoretical approaches, 306
factors related to, 306
Documents
as a source of assessment information, 31

Ecology
and the child welfare worker, 11
and child welfare problems, 4
implications for practice, 3
and child neglect, 98
and child abuse, 152

Family
perspective for assessment, 32
problem families, 33
family practice guidelines, 34
influence on client resistance, 44
problem-solving, 116
advocacy, 128
unmodifiable families, working with, 130
interaction, 102
family characteristics and physical child abuse, 140
family characteristics and child neglect, 98
family characteristics and sexual abuse, 189, 190, 191, 192, 194, 196, 197
Family Life Education
in groups, 122
for high-risk parents, 130

in mother-child groups, 130
in multiple method programs, 174
Family Therapy, 173, 315
  with unmarried parents, 382
Foster Care
  guidelines for placement, 214
  and stress, 215, 240
  recruitment of foster homes, 217
  selection of foster parents, 218, 222
  education and training of foster parents, 223
  matching, 227
  fostering the abused child, 171, 227
  planning for placement, 230, 238
  permancy planning, 230
  foster fathers, 237
  placement difficulties, 239
  helping the resolution of conflicts, 242
  and the separation process, 243
  foster parent separation, 248, 250
  and adolescents, 251
  foster parent and biological parent interac-
    tions, 253
  facilitating foster parent and biological parent
    interactions, 253
  and adoption, 339
  disadvantages to pre-adoption foster care, 340

Group Work
  in residences, 280
  parent groups, 119
  with child abusers, 167
  with child neglectors, 122
  with sexual abusers, 206
  with sexual abuse victims, 206
  and adoption practice, 348
  with unmarried parents, 381
Guilt
  and child welfare clients, 47

High Risk
  assessing high risk, 126
  indicators of high risk of physical abuse and
    neglect, 26
  indicators of high risk of sexual abuse, 28
  working with high-risk parents, 125
  individual councelling with high-risk parents,
    130

Interviewing Clients
  interviewing the child for assessment, 30
  interviewing the non-verbal client, 112
  interviewing the sexual abuse victim, 202
  interviewing mothers of sexual abuse victims,
    202
  interviewing the perpetrator of sexual abuse,
    203
Influence

basis of worker influence over the client, 39
  mutual influence attempts by worker and
    client, 42
Investigations
  purpose of, 20
  worker attitudes and, 22

Matching
  foster parents and children, 227
  adoptive parents and children, 331
Milieu Therapy
  and residential care, 264
  and adolescent problems, 317

Neighbourhoods
  types of, 75
  factors in child welfare problems, 73
  and community work, 74
  and problem-solving, 74
Networks
  social networks as parental support, 72

Observations
  for assessment purposes, 30

Parent Education Groups
  for high risk parents, 127
  mother-child groups, 128
Parents Resources, 119
Parenting Skills
  teaching parenting skills, 114
  teaching skills for coping and independence,
    123
Physical Restraint
  in residential settings, 278
Problem-Solving
  and child welfare practice, 391
  and verbal accessibility, 112
  factors affecting problem-solving in child wel-
    fare practice, 423
  stages of, 395, 396
  knowledge and, 396
  and risk-taking, 396
  assessment as a stage of, 398
  and establishing intervention goals, 407
  and the search for solutions, 410
  implementing the problem solution, 412
  and the evaluation of solutions, 414

Reconstituted Families, 164
Relationship-Building
  and the involuntary client, 36
  with parents, 115
Removal of the Child
  conditions for temporary removal, 20
Reports
  types of, 19

Residential Care
and the therapeutic milieu, 264
and general goals, 265
pros and cons of, 265
and the physical environment, 272
and routines, 273
and rules, 273
and limits, 275
and staff-client relationships, 276
physical restraint of child, 278
and treatment options, 270
and group methods, 280
and assessment, 266
and staff stress, 283
Resistance
client resistance to help, 36
Running Away
types of runaways, 298
factors related to, 299
and child abuse, 299

Self-Injurious Behaviour
types of, 309
suicide, 308
theoretical approaches to, 310
factors related to, 310
Separation
and fostering, 243
assisting the separation process, 245
Sexual Abuse
definition, 184
prevalence, 185
incidence, 185
societal context, 188
and the incest taboo, 190
and the breakdown of social control, 191
fear of abandonment, 193
denial of, 196
victim characteristics, 197
consequences for victim, 199
general practice guidelines, 201
interviewing the victim, 202
interviewing the mother, 202
interviewing the perpetrator, 203
and crisis intervention, 204
and family therapy, 205
and group methods, 206
multiple programmes, 208
and the humanistic treatment approach, 208
Stress
and ecological development, 11
and foster care, 215
and residential child care work, 283
Suicide
and adolescence, 308

factors associated with adolescent suicide, 310
warning signs in adolescent suicide, 312

Teenage Parents
and agency services for, 376
postnatal programs for, 379
practice guidelines for working with, 380
Teenage Pregnancies
causes of, 359
theoretical explanations of, 359
and adolescent developmental tasks, 361
and use of contraception, 362
and medical consequences, 366
and educational consequences, 367
and economic consequences, 367
and marital consequences, 367
and fertility, 368
and family support, 368
and child abuse, 369
teenage fathers and contraceptive responsibility, 371
agency series for teenage fathers, 372
and the decision to give birth, 372
and agency services, 372
prevention of, 378
Termination
through residential transition groups, 281
Transactional Analysis, 168
Transference, 47
Truancy
and running away, 302
explanations of, 303

Unmarried Parents
(see also Teenage Pregnancies, Teenage Parents)
family therapy with unmarried teenagers and their families, 382
individual therapy with parenting teenagers, 383
group work with, 381
programs and service guidelines, 376
and the best interests of the child, 441

Verbal Inaccessibility
interviewing, 112
assessment of, 112
enhancement of, 113
family problem-solving and, 113
Volunteers
use of, in child welfare work, 60

Workers
Worker-client differences, and practice, 36

Youth Work
working assumptions, 290